MW01004651

ISBN 0-933546-45-9

9 780933 546455 >

Hard Back

ISBN 0-933546-46-7

9 780933 546462 >

Perfect Bound

KHANIQAHI-NIMATULLAHI
(CENTERS OF THE NIMATULLAHI SUFI ORDER)

306 West 11th Street
New York, New York 10014
Tel: 212-924-7739

4021 19th Avenue
San Francisco,
California 94132
Tel: 415-586-1313

4931 MacArthur Blvd. NW
Washington, D.C. 20007
Tel: 202-338-4757

84 Pembroke Street
Boston,
Massachusetts 02118
Tel: 617-536-0076

310 NE 57th Street
Seattle, Washington 98105
Tel: 206-527-5018

11019 Arleta Avenue
Mission Hills,
Los Angeles,
California 91345
Tel: 818-365-2226

4642 North Hermitage
Chicago, Illinois 60640
Tel: 312-561-1616

405 Greg Avenue
Santa Fe, New Mexico 87501
Tel: 505-983-8500

219 Chace Street
Santa Cruz, California 95060
Tel: 408-425-8454

95 Old Lansdowne Road
West Didsbury, Manchester
M20 8N2,
United Kingdom
Tel: 061-434-8857

Kölnerstrasse 176
5000 Köln 90 (Porz)
Federal Republic of Germany
Tel: 49-2203-15390

Van Blankenburgstraat 66b
2517 XS's-Gravenhage,
The Netherlands
Tel: 070-450251

50 Rue du 4em Zouaves
Rosny-sous-Bois
Paris 93110
France
Tel: 48552809

63 Boulevard Latrille
BP 1224 Abidjan,
CIDEX 1
Côte d'Ivoire
Tel. 225-410510

The Old Windmill
Sulgrave, Banbury,
Oxfordshire OX17 2SH
United Kingdom
Tel: 0295-760361

41 Chepstow Place
London W2 4TS
United Kingdom
Tel: 071-229-0769
Fax: 071-221-7025

THE LEGACY OF MEDIÆVAL PERSIAN SUFISM

Edited by Leonard Lewisohn

Foreword by Dr. Javad Nurbakhsh

Introduction by S.H. Nasr

KHANIQAHI NIMATULLAHI PUBLICATIONS
LONDON NEW YORK

Khaniqahi Nimatullahi Publications
LONDON
in association with
the SOAS Centre of Near and Middle Eastern Studies
University of London

British Library Cataloguing in Publication Data

Legacy of Mediæval Persian Sufism
I. Lewisohn, Leonard
297

Hardback: ISBN 0-933546-45-9
Paperback: ISBN 0-933546-47-5

Printed in Great Britain
First British edition published 1992 by KNP
41 Chepstow Place London W2 4TS
Tel.: 071 229 7025
FAX: 071 221 7025

CONTENTS

IV. METAPHYSICS & ONTOLOGY

V. SUFI PRACTICES & METHODOLOGY

VI. COMPARATIVE RELIGION & SYMBOLISM

ILLUSTRATIONS

CONTRIBUTORS

R.J. W. AUSTIN, Lecturer in Arabic and Islamic Studies, University of Durham Durham, England

JOHANN CHRISTOPH BÜRGEL, Professor, Head of Islamic Department, Bern University, Switzerland

J.T.P. DE BRUIJN, Professor of Persian and Iranian Cultural History, Leiden University, Leiden, The Netherlands

WILLIAM C.CHITTICK, Professor of Religious Studies, State University of New York, Stony Brook, New York

MICHEL CHODKIEWICZ, Professor, École des Hautes Études en Sciences Sociales, University of Paris, Paris, France

DEWIN DeWEESE, Assistant Professor, Department of Uralic & Altaic Studies, Indiana University, Bloomington, Indiana

JEAN DURING, Lecturer in Music, University of Strasbourg, Strasbourg, France

CARL W. ERNST, Assistant Professor, Dept. of Religion at Pomona College, Claremont, California

TERRY GRAHAM, Editor, Persian Translation Series, Khaniqahi Nimatullahi Publications, London, England

JO-ANN GROSS, Assistant Professor, Department of History at Trenton, State College, Trenton, New Jersey

JOHAN TER HAAR, Lecturer, Department of Languages and Cultures of the Middle East,University of Leiden, The Netherlands

VICTORIA HOLBROOK, Assistant Professor, Department of Judaic & Near Eastern Languages & Literatures, Ohio State University, Columbus, Ohio

HOMA KATOOZIAN, Former Professor of Economics, Kent University, England

B. TODD LAWSON, Assistant Professor, Department of Middle East & Islamic Studies,University of Toronto, Toronto, Canada

LEONARD LEWISOHN, Nimatullahi Research Centre, London, England

SACHIKO MURATA, Lecturer in Islam and Oriental Studies, State University of New York, Stony Brook, New York

SEYYED HOSSEIN NASR, University Professor of Islamic Studies, The George Washington University, Washington, D.C.

IAN RICHARD NETTON, Head of the Department of Arabic & Islamic Studies, University of Exeter, Exeter, England

H.T. NORRIS, Former Professor of Arabic and Islamic Studies, School of Oriental & African Studies, University of London, London, England

JAVAD NURBAKHSH, Professor Emeritus, University of Tehran; Master of the

Nimatullahi Sufi Order
ANNEMARIE SCHIMMEL, Professor of Indo-Muslim Culture, Harvard University, Cambridge, Massachusetts
MOHAMMAD ISA WALEY, Curator of Persian and Turkish Manuscripts, British Library, London, England
RODERIC VASSIE, Librarian, Oriental Collection Department at British Library, London, England
JOHN WALBRIDGE, Assistant Editor, *Encyclopædia Iranica*, New York, New York

System of Transliteration

CONSONANTS

ء	'	ظ	ẓ
ب	b	ع	'
پ	p	غ	gh
ت	t	ف	f
ث	th	ق	q
ج	j	ك	k
چ	ch	گ	g
ح	ḥ	ل	l
خ	kh	م	m
د	d	ن	n
ذ	dh	ه	h
ر	r	و	w
ز	z	ى	y
ژ	zh	ة	-a (-*at* in construct state)
س	s		
ش	sh		
ص	ṣ		
ض	ḍ		
ط	ṭ		

VOWELS

Long:	آ	ā
	أو	ū
	اِى	ī
Doubled:	ـِيّ	iyy
	ـُوّ	uww
Diphthongs:	أو	aw
	أى	ay
Short:	ـَ	a
	ـُ	u
	ـِ	i

PREFACE

The purpose of the present volume is to examine the roots of the artistic, literary, and cultural renaissance in the three centuries immediately preceding the Safavid period (1500-1720), which was accompanied by the great expansion of various Persian-speaking Sufi orders, and caused the blossoming of an entire literature of Sufism. In many respects, this focus on the religious topography of the Persian society of the mediæval period which was predominantly 'Sufi' in orientation, is unique, for the spiritual and cultural renaissance in these three centuries (1200-1500) has never before been the subject of a monograph – much less of a volume of essays by some of the foremost authorities in the field.

Although the division of this book into six chapters represent many of the dominant themes and issues in the Sufi tradition, they cannot hope to provide a final or even a comprehensive coverage of all the mystical contexts which they discuss. They are rather intended to serve as a surveyor's map of the vast uncharted territory still to be explored. There are still many areas deserving of further attention: the organizational development of mediæval *khānaqāh* life, the politics and mysticism of chivalry *(futuwwat)*, *malāmatī* spirituality, etc., which are omitted from this volume as deciderratum for future research.

Following Dr. Nurbakhsh's reflections on the limitations of a purely academic approach to the principle of the Unity of Being and the necessity to realize and not merely to audit the teachings of the Sufis, S. H. Nasr's introduction provides an admirable summary of the main aims of this volume. Nasr also comments on the transmission of Persian Sufi literature beyond the frontiers of Iran proper, indeed, to the vast segment of the world embraced by the Atlantic coast of Africa—from Morocco to Senegal on the west—to the Pacific isles of Southeast Asia; from the Malay archipelago through Indonesia to the southern Philippines on the east and from the Indian Ocean to the south to the sub-Arctic steppes of Central Asia to the north. This is followed by Leonard Lewisohn's overview of recent research on mediæval Sufism, elucidating the concept of 'Iranian Islam' within its particular historical, religious and academic context, and discussing the political causes and the cultural background of the renaissance of Persianate Sufism in the twelfth and thirteenth centuries.

Chapter two, devoted to 'Poetics and Imagery', begins with Annemarie Schimmel's evocative essay on the imagery associated with Joseph in Rumi's poetry, followed by J. C. Bürgel's analysis of the process of thematic repetition in Islam, as reflected and paralleled in Rumi's lyrical poetry, this repetition being a feature of the chanting of *awrād*, or 'litanies', in the Sufi *samā'*, as a 'controlled' manner of arriving at 'ecstasy'. The chapter concludes with J.T. P. de Bruijn's reflections on the origin and character of Islamic Sufi antinominism, with particular reference to Sanā'i's *Qalandariyyāt*.

The interdependence which exists 'Between History and Hagiography' is the general theme of chapter three. It begins with H.T. Norris's broad discussion (the analytical scope of which embraces the fields of Arabic culture and Western folklore) of the legacy of the founder of the Hurūfī movement, Faḍlullāh Astarābadī, whose influence affected proto-Sufi movements from Azerbaijan to Albania. Next Victoria Holbrook's long essay presents us with previously untranslated material on the literary history of the post-Rumi Mevlevi Order with particular reference to antinominian attitudes in the spiritual life of its masters. Devin DeWeese discusses two important hagiographies of Sayyid 'Alī Hamadānī and their relevance to the evolution of the latter-day Kubrawī *ṭarīqa* in Central Asia and Iran, while Jo-Ann Gross's essay explores the function and role of *karāmat* in the hagiographies of the Naqshbandī master Khwāja Aḥrār. Terry Graham examines the biography, religion and political life of the founder of the Ni'matullāhī Sufi Order, Shāh Ni'matullāh Walī, followed by Homa Katouzian's presentation of Sa'dī's view of Sufism.

Chapter four is devoted to philosophical themes, beginning with a study by W.C. Chittick on the ontology of Sa'īd al-Dīn Farghānī, an author singularly neglected both in the East and the West, and a follower of Ibn 'Arabi. Prof. Chittick raises the question of the dichotomy between 'Unity' *(waḥdat)* and 'multiplicity' *(kathrat)* which is found in the philosophical writings of Farghānī, who contrasted the Akbarian doctrine of the 'Unity of Being' with its polar opposite, namely, the 'multiplicity of knowledge'—noting that this distinction is scarcely mentioned by the Ibn 'Arabī's follower and Farghanī's teacher, the renowned Ṣadr al-Din Qūnawī. Also faithful to the school of the Magister Maximus, M. Chodkiéwicz charts a skillful course through the labyrinth of enigmas in the *Futūḥāt al-Makkiyya,* citing the remarkable correlations between the chapter sequences of the *Futūḥāt* and the structure of the Koran, demonstrating that the former's structure was precisely modelled upon the latter. This is followed by R. J. W. Austin's essay on the love-devotional aspect of Sufism: what he terms the 'Sophianic Feminine' in the writings of Ibn 'Arabi and Rumi, tracing the archetype of the Eternal Feminine as beheld through the eyes of these two giants of mystical Islam. I.R. Netton discusses the Neoplatonic substratum of Suhrawardī's *Ḥikmat al-ishrāq* while B.Todd Lawson focuses on a fundamentally philosophical thinker, Rajab Bursī, a Shi'ite mystic who was influenced by the Sufi perspective and author of the *Mashāriq anwār al-yaqin fī asrār Amīr al-mu'minīn*, .

The fifth chapter examines the practical 'applied' aspects of Sufism and features five essays: on *samā'*, the role of the spiritual master, the methodologies of two different Sufi manuals and lastly, a discussion of Sufi perspectives on marriage and sexuality. Prof. During focuses on the aesthetic features of Islamic mystical music in order to define the parameters of Sufi music as a specific genre. M. I. Waley's essay provides an overview of the contents of an important but neglected manual of Sufism: the *Fuṣūṣ al-ādāb* by a lesser known Kubrawī Sufi, Abū'l-Mafākhir Yaḥyā

Bākharzī. Johan ter Haar discusses of the rules and manners of the master-disciple relationship in the Naqshbandiyya tradition. John Walbridge's contribution examines the biography of Quṭb al-Dīn Shīrāzī, the famous philosopher, astronomer, mathematician, musicologist and mystic, focusing on the final chapter of his philosophical encyclopedia, the *Durrat al-tāj,* which explains the sage's views on marriage, travel, work, spiritual discipline and etiquette. Sachiko Murata completes this chapter with a summary and detailed examination of an unpublished mediæval Sufi treatise on the mysticism of marriage and sexuality.

The final chapter brings the focus of the book back from the intellectual to the ecstatic, being devoted to comparative religion and symbolism. It begins with Carl Ernst's essay on the fantastic symbolism of flight in Rūzbihān Baqlī's writings, in which the symbol functions as a "locus of encounter between the Divine and the human." It is translucent and must not be taken as an object in itself, so that it does not conceal the Divine from the inward eye. Roderic Vassie deals with 'Abd al-Raḥmān Chishtī's application of the Sufi theory of the 'unity of religions' to the study of the Hindu scripture, the Bhagavad Gita, in his Persian translation of this work, with reflections on those Hindu doctrines from Rammanuja and Sankaracarya relating to Sufism, namely, *bhakti,* or love-devotion, and *advaita Vedanta,* or non-dualistic Hindu philosophy. Leonard Lewisohn in the final essay concentrates on the 'unity of religions' and the doctrine of 'esoteric idolatry' found in the the writings of Maḥmūd Shabistarī; his study emphasizes that it was not the mediæval scholastic theologians nor the jurisprudents who sucessfully maintained the inter-faith dialogue with other religions, but rather the Sufis, who endeavoured to integrate, within the framework of the Koranic doctrine of transcendent divine Unity (and hence, to tolerate), divergent doctrines deriving from sources as far afield as Hinduism and Neo-Platonism.

Throughout the preparation of this volume, the editor has had much help from many people and institutions. First and foremost, I must acknowledge my deepest gratitude to Prof. H.T. Norris, Dean of Undergraduate Studies and Professor of Arabic and Islamic Studies in the School of Oriental and African Studies, London, and to Dr. Muhammad Isa Waley, curator of Persian and Turkish Manuscripts at the British Library. The homegeniety, intellectual direction and academic quality of the essays in this volume is much indebted to their input, both in terms of their own written contributions as well as excellent editorial advice. I am also deeply grateful to John Cooper, Lecturer in Persian at Cambridge University, and to Prof. Carl Ernst of Pomona College, California for their constructive comments and reading of the overview. I would also like to thank Mr. Terry Graham of the Nimatullahi Research Centre for his editorial work on the various essays in the volume.

Initial drafts of many of the essays in this book were written as contributions to a conference on "The Legacy of Mediæval Persian Sufism" organized in December, 1990 at SOAS by H.T. Norris and the editor, which furnished a local habitation and place for the imaginal concept. In this regard, our thanks extends to Dr. R. Tapper, Director of SOAS's Centre of Near and Middle Eastern Studies (CNMES) for his initial support and supervision of the conference project. We are also beholden unto Prof. John Wansbrough, Pro-Director, SOAS, along with other members of SOAS's Research Committee for their propitious underwriting of some of the costs of the conference and to the CNMES for it support of the present publication. We would also like to thank all the staff of the CNMES—in particular, Prof. J.A. Allan, Series Publication Editor, Diana Gur, Centre Publication Editor, and Pauline Rose, Centre Organizer—for their sustained professional services in the preparation and editing of the present volume.

Most of all, however, we must express our profound gratitude to Dr. Javad Nurbakhsh, Master of the Nimatullahi Sufi Order, for publishing this volume with KNP.

Leonard Lewisohn

FOREWORD

Two Approaches to the Principle of the Unity of Being

Dr. Javad Nurbakhsh

It is an honor to contribute a foreword to this volume of essays on the Legacy of Mediæval Persian Sufism which covers the three centuries preceding the Safavid period, namely, the period stretching from the beginning of the thirteenth century to the end of the fifteenth century. I am also delighted to see that Khanaqahi Nimatullahi Publications [KNP] has undertaken to publish this collection of essays written by some of the world's foremost scholars in the field. This collaboration of the publisher and the contributors is very appropriate, for the Nimatullāhi Order under the direction of Shāh Ni'matullāh Walī was established and formally recognized in the Islamic world during this period.

In this brief space, I would like to offer a few observations about two completely different approaches to the principle of the Unity of Being *(waḥdat-i wujūd)*. The first is an intellectual one, while the second is founded on love. The reason for presenting this topic by way of foreword to this collection of essays is that I feel that the slant of the book is based fundamentally on an intellectual approach to various aspects of Sufism, while for me Sufism is and always has been primarily a practical and experiential school. In order to illustrate the main characteristics of this principle as simply and concisely as possible a few analogies may be useful.

I. THE UNITY OF BEING: SOME ANALOGIES

The reader is no doubt aware that Sufism is principally a school of the Unity of Being *(waḥdat-i wujūd)*. The basic tenet of this school can be summarized in the following way: There is only One Being and whatever exists is a manifestation or realization of that Being. In the words of Hātif Iṣfāhānī:

There is only One and nothing but Him,
He is the only One and there is no one but Him.

From the Sufis' point of view, God is Absolute Being, and whatever exists is a determination or manifestation of Him. The Sufis maintain that all existence exists through God's being and is a manifestation of that being, without which there would be nothing. In Rumi's words:

We are non-existence, displaying the illusion of existence;
You are Absolute Being and our only existence.

Here one may recall the words of the Koran, "All things perish but His face,"

(XXVIII: 88)—with the understanding that there is nothing but Him in the abode of existence.

The Sufis do not separate the realm of Existence from that of God's Existence. Thus, while the Koranic verse, "God is the light of the heavens and the earth"' (XXIV: 35), has been interpreted by the exoteric Islamic clergy to mean that God is the source of all illumination for the heavens and the earth, the Sufis, on the other hand, take this verse to mean that God is the very Being, the Reality of the heavens and the earth.

The insight that there is only one Absolute Being in the whole Universe and that whatever exists does so through His existence has been called 'the philosophy of the Unity of Being.' We, however, do not consider this a 'philosophy.' A philosophy is something invented by the mind and, hence, subject to change. The awareness of the Unity of Being, though, is a perception of the heart, so that it is everlasting and unchanging. Philosophy pertains to the mind and discourse, whereas perception of the Unity of Being pertains to love, revelation, and vision. Therefore, in our view, it is better to refer to it as the principle, rather than the philosophy, of the Unity of Being. The following analogies may serve to illustrate the principle as the Sufis understand it:

If we liken Absolute Being to an ocean, then the waves of this ocean can be thought of as individual beings, the true reality of which is water. The transitory form of each being is the individual wave, which lasts for but a moment and is then obliterated, whereas the reality of the wave—that is, the water—is everlasting. Until each individual is aware of his waveform, he can know nothing of the water. When the conception of the ocean as transitory waves disappears, one will then realize that there is in reality nothing but the water. Hence, the great Sufis have annihilated their wave-selves in the water of Absolute Being, crying from the depths of their souls expressions like "I am the Truth," "Glory be to My sublime station," and "There is nothing under this garment but God," expressions that leave other people astounded and dumbfounded. In the words of Shāh Ni'matullāh:

Wave sea and bubble—all three are one;
Though there appear to be many and few,
in truth, there is but One.

According to another analogy, Absolute Being can be compared to light and individual beings to shadows. As long as the shadow remains a shadow, it can know nothing of the light. If the light moves away from the shadow, the shadow will always follow it. Thus, if one attempts to pursue the Truth under one's own power—that is, as a shadow—one will never attain it. Such an action in fact indicates that the Truth is actually moving away from one. Only when the light moves towards the shadow, thereby relieving it of its 'shadow-ness,' will the shadow become the light. As Maghribī has said:

No one can journey toward God on his own feet;
To arrive at God's district, one must go with God's feet.

To strike a final analogy, if Absolute Being is conceived of as a point, then individual beings may be compared to lines or patterns, springing into existence from a single point. Whatever form is displayed outwardly is, in fact, merely transitory.

Whatever form we see is, in truth, no more than a point. In the *Gulshan-i rāz*, Shabistari has written:

> *All these forms of 'other-ness' are,*
> *in reality, only illusions from you,*
> *What makes the point appear a circle*
> *is simply the speed with which it moves.*

As it says in the Koran, "Everything passes away; and there remains the face of your Lord, of Majesty and Honor" (LV, 26-27).

In conclusion, from the Sufis' point of view, the realm of individual existence, which is one of the levels of being, is imaginary—and imagination is one of the levels of Being—while at the same time, in truth, it is Real. It is imaginary from the perspective of 'shadow-ness,' yet it is the foundation of Being from the perspective of Reality (that is, light).

II. TWO APPROACHES TO THE UNITY OF BEING

Having summarized the essential tenets of this principle, the first question that should be raised with respect to *waḥdat-i wujūd* is whether the human intellect is capable of comprehending such a principle and ascertaining its truth. In other words, is an intellectual grasp of *waḥdat-i wujūd* possible? Modern man's only approach to understanding the world is scientific and his only means are his own intellect and sensory perceptions. The intellect can comprehend only a realm which is based on sensory perceptions, so that the world becomes intelligible to modern man only when his sensory experience is subjected by his intellectual powers to the process of differentiation and categorization. In order to make the world intelligible to himself, modern man constantly distinguishes certain elements from others by noting their different causal properties and associates other elements by noting their similar properties and lumping them together under one category. For example, he differentiates water from fire by citing their different causal properties, and puts ocean, river and rain under a single category by identifying the element that all these seemingly different things have in common, namely water. This process of categorization and differentiation has also been extended to encompass more abstract concepts, such as 'beauty', 'justice', 'democracy', 'truth' and so forth. Man distinguishes, for example, the concept of beauty from that of justice, by contrasting the properties that one has and the other lacks, and he carries on such differentiation and categorization by scrutinizing the attributes of what he takes to be just and beautiful in the actual world. This is how modern man makes the world intelligible to himself, and this is the only way the intellect knows how to understand something. It is an analytic approach, a rational approach, rather than the holistic, or intuitive method, preferred by the Sufis.

Now the principle of the Unity of Being implies that whatever the human senses observe or the intellect comprehends, whether subjective or objective, is a manifestation of only One Being. How are we going to understand this? How can you and I together, along with this room and everything in it, as well as all that one can imagine or perceive, be a manifestation of only One Being? The intellect cannot see the Oneness in all creation. Why not? Because, as we mentioned, the intellect perceives things as one and the same only insofar as they have certain perceptible properties in common. For example, the intellect can ascertain the oneness of water in the various forms of river, ocean and a drop of rain, by analyzing water and discerning the one chemical substance which is shared by all the various forms of water, namely, H_2O. Yet, one cannot comprehend the principle of Unity of Being in this manner. There is nothing perceptibly common to everything in the universe which the intellect can bring to bear in order to arrive at the principle of Unity of Being. This is where, I believe, a purely intellectual approach to the principle of the Unity of Being may lead us to skepticism and ultimately the denial of the very principle itself.

Although an intellectual and analytical approach to what the Sufis have said or written about Sufism may have historical and anthropological significance, it cannot and should not be the ultimate approach to Sufism on the part of the reader. To understand Sufism in its entirety one has to embark on the Sufi Path and be a Sufi. No one has ever comprehended *waḥdat-i wujūd* and no one has ever become a Sufi by concentrating on what the Sufis or the scholars of Sufism have said about Sufism. When Shah Ne'matullāh says:

Wave, ocean and bubble, all three are one;
There is nothing but One, no more and no less,

he is not describing an intellectual discovery about *waḥdat-i wujūd*. Rather, he is expressing his heart-findings in metaphorical terms and in poetic language. By the heart here, of course, as you all know, the Sufis do not refer to one's 'feelings,' which are usually controlled by either the passions or material reason. Rather, for Sufis, the heart refers to an organ of spiritual perception which is a gift of God's grace and by means of which they perceive this Unity of Being.

So, what about the non-intellectual or practical approach to Sufism? First of all, let me say at the outset that without God's grace and attention no one can embark on the Sufi Path. Only when God plants His love and the state of seeking *(ṭalab)* in one, can one become a seeker who, with the help of the master of the Path, may travel the Sufi Path and ultimately experience the Unity of Being within oneself.

Traveling the Path can be both easy and difficult. There have been many who have spent a lifetime struggling with the first step on the Path, while others have completed the journey to God in a single night. The step which can be difficult for some, yet easy for others, is the annihilation of one's self, where one's 'commanding soul' *(nafs-i ammāra)* is transformed into the 'soul-at-peace' *(nafs-i muṭma'inna)*. Those people who have been blessed by Divine grace to undertake such a step can truly comprehend the principle of the Unity of Being through direct experience and vision of the Divine. A Sufi is one who takes this step with the foot of love and loving-kindness and under the guidance of a master who has already taken such a step. Ultimately, he leaves his self behind, transcends his ego and reaches God. We live in a period where taking such a step is harder than ever before. Modern man is more than ever attached to his ego. He is constantly trying to become something, to possess and consume, without questioning the forces that desperately drive him towards self-glorification and self-satisfaction.

I am very sure that the efforts of the scholars contributing to this volume have produced something which is worthwhile and beneficial to everyone, leading us to a better understanding of the historical and theoretical aspects of Sufism, but I would also hope that the reader might also direct his or her attention to the source of all this literature: the heart. This is a path that should be traveled and experienced. Although reading the travelogues of the prominent Sufis who have actually traveled the Path may be beneficial, it cannot take one to the ultimate goal.

In conclusion, on behalf of the Center of Near and Middle Eastern Studies of London University and the Khaniqahi Nimatullahi Publications, I would like to warmly thank all the contributors to this volume for providing us with a better understanding of the theoretical and historical aspects of classical Persian Sufism.

Persian Sufi Literature: Its Spiritual and Cultural Significance

I

Seyyed Hossein Nasr

It is proper that a volume of essays on Persian Sufism should begin with a Sufi poem, and so I begin with one that is perhaps the most famous of all for such occasions, a verse from the *Gulshan-i rāz* by Shaykh Maḥmud Shabistarī:

> *In the Name of He who taught the soul how to meditate;*
> *And illuminated the heart with the light of the Spirit.*

The compilers of this volume have given me the task of providing a general panorama of the spiritual significance of Persian Sufi literature of the period in question in order to set the background for this rich collection of essays by many of the outstanding scholars in the field of Persian Sufi literature, ranging from the *doyenne* in this field, Prof. Annemarie Schimmel, to the youngest scholars who are now just beginning their work. I hope that the few comments that I shall be making here will set the stage for the more detailed studies which feature in this 'intellectual and spiritual feast' contained in the coming pages.

First of all it should be stated that Persian Sufi literature occupies a unique position not only in the history of Persia but in the whole of Islamic civilization. It is like what one would call a miracle of sacred art in its literary form which, for that very reason, broke out of the boundaries of the traditional Persian world where the Persian language was spoken as the mother tongue and reached far beyond the borders of Persia, becoming, in a sense, the 'language of the heart' (and also of the intellect, if 'intellect' is understood in its original sense) for a vast area of Asia. There is no other phenomenon of this kind in Islamic civilization. Besides Arabic which, being the language of the Koran, was and is used of course by all Muslims, Persian is the only language of the Islamic peoples which, thanks to Sufism, was able to spread beyond its borders and create a literature which even today is shared in one way or another by the vast population living from Iraq through present-day Iran and all the way to the walls of China.

Now, this literature is at once the supreme expression of what is most universal and profound in the Persian soul, as well as a prime crystallization of what is most universal in Islamic spirituality. These two realities cannot be separated in this case. It was in fact, *Islamic* spirituality which caused the poetic dimension of the Persian soul to flower as never before. For this reason Persia was not known especially as a land of great poets before the rise of Islam. There were, of course, poets; the Gathas of Zoroaster, for example, are very beautiful and powerful poetic expressions. Yet the poetry produced in the history of Persia during the Islamic period cannot at all be matched by the works of pre-Islamic Persian history, a period which created notable masterpieces of art in the field of architecture, the plastic arts and also music.

For this reason, the understanding of Persian Sufi literature necessarily demands a comprehension of the effect that the inner meaning of the Koran and the spirituality of the Prophet had upon the soul of the Persians. The Sufi masters who actualized the possibilities of spiritual realization within the souls of their disciples emulated the mastership of the Prophet, the supreme exemplar of the spiritual life in Islam. And the heart of these masters, which is the ultimate source of Persian Sufi literature, is the heart which had become illuminated by the inner dimension of the Koranic Message. For this reason this literature represents at once what is most universal in Persian culture and what is most universal in Islam.

It is not accidental that when the rise of interest in the Orient took place in the modern West during the nineteenth century, it was through Persian Sufi literature. It was the universal spiritual appeal of this literature which first caught the eye of some of the outstanding Orientalists of the 1820's and 30's at the beginning of contact between the Romantic movement in Europe and the culture of the Islamic world.

Now, as is well-known, Persian Sufi literature written in the Persian language (putting aside works written by Persian Sufis in Arabic) began in the 4th/10th and 5th/11th centuries with the simple quatrains by Bābā Ṭāhir and Abū Sa'īd Abī'l-Khayr (or purported to be by them and, in any case, known under their names for over a thousand years) and was soon followed by the outwardly unexpected and peculiar phenomenon of Ḥanbalī Persian Sufism. This type of Sufism was associated with the name of Khwāja 'Abdullāh Anṣārī, patron saint of Herat, and author of some of the earliest classics of Persian Sufi literature which have found a permanent place in the minds and hearts of the Persian people to this day. There are also other figures belonging to this school whose names are only now just beginning to be resuscitated, such as Abū Manṣūr Iṣfahānī. And finally, with the great Aḥmad Ghazzālī, not known in the West as well as his brother, the Persian language becomes in a sense a kind of 'sacred language' for spirituality. It was he, more than any other author, who transformed Persian Sufi literature and especially Persian Sufi prose into a perfect vehicle for the expression of the most delicate ideas and concepts of Sufism.

Needless to say, this is the immediate background of the period that is especially under discussion in this volume, namely the full flowering of Persian Sufi literature in the works of poets such as Sanā'ī, 'Aṭṭār and Rumi. Sanā'ī was not very much appreciated by E.G. Browne when he first studied Persian poetry and Persian literature. Therefore, Sanā'ī did not receive the kind of reception which was due to him in the West. His *Ḥadīqa* is often underrated as being a kind of prosaic and staid work, whereas, in fact, it is a very important model for the later elaborations of the two great poets of Divine Love, 'Aṭṭār and Mawlānā Jalāl al-Dīn Rumi.

One would think that by this time, after the appearance of figures such as Rumi, the possibilities of Persian Sufi literature would have become exhausted. In fact one sees a new literary flowering in the 8th/14th and 9th/15th centuries with figures such as Sa'dī. Many consider Sa'dī to be simply a moralist, but, of course, he was both a Sufi of the Suhrawardiyya Order and also an author in whom Sufism was reflected in a very deep manner, as can be seen in certain sections of both the *Gulistān* and the *Būstān*. One must also include among these later Sufi poets, the divine Ḥāfiẓ, Maḥmūd Shabistarī, Shāh Ni'matullāh Walī and Jāmī, the last of the classical poets – many of whom are discussed in this volume.

Now, this vast literature which was produced during the 4th/10th to the 9th/15th centuries—during a period of four to five hundred years, and especially the three centuries which constitute the period under consideration in this book—is a literature which deals with what the Sufis call both *qāl* and *ḥāl*. It is not only a literature of *qāl*. For those not acquainted with this expression, it must be mentioned that *qāl* is derived from the Arabic word *qāla* which means "he said," in reference to those discursive sciences in which there exists a discourse and dialogue expressed in the form "he said," "you say" and "I say." Following this discursive method, the mind tries to approach the understanding of a particular subject. The Sufis contrast *qāl* (hearsay) with *ḥāl* (direct spiritual experience and realization) which is the fruit of spiritual practice or a gift from heaven. The literature of Sufism is composed not only of indirect 'report', hearsay or *qāl* (although there are many outstanding contributors to this volume who might spend the next fifty years engaged in the activity of *qāl*, that is, discoursing about this literature), it is also, and above all, the literature of *ḥāl*. It is a literature which reflects of the deepest longings and yearnings of the human soul for God and communicates the ecstasy of union with the Beloved and nostalgia of separation from that Reality which is the source of all that is beautiful and all that can be loved.

* * *

If one were to ask what is the content of Persian Sufi literature or, in fact, Sufi literature in general—as it has developed also in Arabic as well as in other major Islamic languages—for the sake of simplifying a complex subject we might answer this query by dividing it into five major categories:

First of all, Persian Sufi literature is associated with the Spiritual Path *(al-ṭarīqa ilā'Llāh* in Arabic, or, as they say in Persian: *ṭarīq-i sū-yi Ḥaqq),* and all that is involved therein. That is why most of Sufi literature, even its poetry, seems to deal with ethics, not so much with what to do and what not to do, but with an ethics which is internalized, that is to say, concerned with the transformation of man's entire being – for without becoming a new being one cannot see things in a new way. And of course, Sufism exists to enable us to become what we should really be, what we are already *'ind Allāh,* that is, 'in God', to become ourselves. To become ourselves is to become that archetype or essence which is our very 'self' and inner reality. Here we are referring to what the Sufis call the *'ayn* (plu.: *a'yān*), or the divine prototypes of all created forms which exist in the Divine Intellect or Divine Knowledge prior to our descent into the realm of creation.

Most Sufi literature, therefore, concerns itself with the Spiritual Path and deals with such issues as how to follow this Path, the conditions of the Path, the significance of the spiritual master, and the role of the disciple. It also deals with what the

Sufis usually call the mystical states and spiritual stations of the path (the *aḥwāl* and *maqāmāt)*, discussing the various states and the stations which the soul is able to attain and also the methods for their attainment.

Now Sufism, in comparison to other major spiritual traditions, has been somewhat silent on the subject of method, explicitly speaking, which is usually passed down only orally. Sufi literature deals with this subject mostly in allusions *(ishārāt)* although there are many allusions to it in both poetry and prose. To present just one famous example, the well-known Persian verse,

> *Invoke until your invocation leads to meditation,*
> *And meditation becomes the cause of a thousand virginal ideas.*

This one verse contains the whole program of the Sufi Path, but in a hidden fashion – such that it is not possible to explicitly formulate from it a method such as you would find, say, in the treatises on Yoga in Hinduism or in certain other traditions. (It is interesting to note that where there have been more explicit discussions of the methods of Sufism, they have been more often in Arabic rather than in Persian, as one can see in the works of Ibn 'Aṭā' Allāh al-Iskandarī).

The second important category of the content of this Sufi literature is doctrine, that is to say, Metaphysics, Cosmology, Eschatology, Psychology and Philosophy as these terms are understood in their traditional context. One could say that this literature contains, albeit not necessarily in a systematic way, the complete doctrine concerning the nature of reality.

This more doctrinally oriented literature, with which several of the chapters of this book are concerned, became formulated and crystallized at the moment when the need for exposition of such doctrine became more felt in the Islamic community. This type of Sufi literature begins with 'Ayn al-Quḍāt Hamadānī, Aḥmad Ghazzālī and his brother Abū Ḥāmid Muḥammad Ghazzālī, and then flowers fully outside the Persian-speaking world with Ibn 'Arabī, whose teachings, in turn, spread so rapidly in the Persian-speaking world.

It is one of the great mysteries of Islamic thought as a whole that a single person from Murcia in Spain could have such tremendous impact on the far-away Persian world – more than perhaps upon any other part of the Islamic world including North Africa (the Maghrib) itself – although this statement must be made cautiously since the study of the Akbarian tradition in the Maghrib has not as yet been fully carried out. Yet, if one tries to remember the names of the famous Arab poets of the Maghrib, or even the Eastern part of the Arab world influenced by Ibn 'Arabī, and the names of the famous Persian poets influenced by him, at the end of the account, one will certainly find a larger number on the Persian side. As to why this happened, there is no definitive answer as yet. The spread of the School of Ibn 'Arabī must be studied further along the lines already pursued by a number of scholars such as W. Chittick in order for the full picture of this important spiritual and intellectual tradition to become clear.

But whatever the dynamics of this phenomenon might have been, the result is that later Persian Sufi poetry and prose, from the 7th/13th century onwards, reflect the full flowering of the doctrinal exposition of Sufism. The vast Sufi literature of this period in fact complements, in many ways, the philosophical works which appear at this time in Persia.

Thirdly, this literature deals with what one might call the 'esoteric sciences', by which we do not mean what has come to be known as 'occult science' in English with its limited current meaning, but such sciences as the inner meaning of the sacred text, the symbolism of the letters of the alphabet, of certain myths and symbols which are expressed in the *ḥadīth* or the Koran themselves, and of certain sounds (what has come to be known today as 'mantra' in the English language, adopted from the Sanskrit), that is, the science of sound. There are many other sciences which have never been part and parcel of the curriculum of the *Madrasa* system in the Islamic world, having been taught only orally in private circles, but which gradually became reflected in the writings of Sufi authors during the three centuries under discussion here. Earlier Persian Sufi literature is not as rich in this field as was this later literature, which was also confined to certain sects such as the Ḥurūfīs.

Fourthly, Persian Sufi literature is a vehicle for accounts of sacred history and also the history of Sufism. Certain works belonging to this literature depict the sacred history of Islam from the time of Adam up to the particular figure with whom the author was concerned during the Islamic period itself. In the famous works of Sulamī, 'Aṭṭār, Jāmī and many others there are also important accounts of the history of Sufism, the history of famous masters and their disciples, as well as records of works written concerning Sufism. But what is particularly interesting is that this body of literature represents perhaps our most important source for the understanding of the inner meaning of the sacred history of mankind as seen through the eyes of Islam. Thus, what we have called Islamic 'sacred history' stretches far beyond the life of the Prophet to the beginning of humanity itself.

Finally, Persian Sufi literature contains what one could call the depiction of paradise, that is, it creates a kind of celestial atmosphere for the soul to breathe in. When Persian Sufi poetry is read, its didactic elements become to some extent eclipsed by the presence of an atmosphere of celestial quality. This atmosphere has been of utmost importance not only for Persian culture and the nourishment of the Persian soul, but has also had a profound effect on those outside of Persia proper. The reputed effect of this literature, especially the poetry more than the prose—and we could call its therapeutic effect—has to do with this kind of atmosphere into which the soul enters through the recitation of this poetry.

As a matter of fact, in older days much of this poetry was memorized when children were young. Following the routine memorization of the Koran, Persian children used to memorize much of the poetry of Sa'dī, Ḥāfiẓ, Rumi and others. To this day there is hardly anyone in Persia, even among the most so-called illiterate people, who does not remember a number of verses of this poetry. This mystical poetry has created a kind of world into which the human soul can withdraw for nourishment and protection, and a kind of complement to the external world. It is this phenomenon that many modernists and especially leftists in Iran used to criticize, claiming that this kind of poetry prevented Iranians from progressing and turning their attention to the world. This claim is based on total misunderstanding and the only reason that we mention it now is that two generations ago in Iran much of the scholarship carried out by modernists and especially leftists was directed against

Persian Sufi poetry. Their idea was that poetry protects the soul artificially, makes it lazy and prevents it from going out and achieving practical ends in the world. One could comment in reverse that, in the present situation, it would be wonderful if people in America and Western Europe could do nothing for the next ten years but read Ḥāfiẓ and Rumi and so allow the natural environment to improve and the air to become a bit less polluted so that they can breathe more easily. Their kind of interpretation is, of course, not true at all. Sufi poetry is not simply an opium for its readers and even it be opium for some people, it is much less harmful to the body and soul than the drugs being used so extensively in the modern world today.

The depiction of this paradisal world has a profound and positive significance in that it makes possible access to a world of objective reality other than the physical one, complementing in a way the Persian miniature whose space is also the space of the celestial abode. This world cannot be sensed externally but remains accessible to one who can appreciate this literature through which the soul enters into what one could call a 'heavenly atmosphere'. The full significance of this aspect of Persian Sufi poetry is far from being negligible. On the contrary, it is of great importance from both the spiritual and psychological points of view. It is this dimension of Sufi poetry which attracted a large number of Persians, as well as non-Persians in other parts of the Islamic world, especially in the subcontinent of India, as well as among the Turks, to Sufism.

Usually the traditional aspirant who became a Sufi was one whose father, uncle or some friend or relative happened to know a Sufi Shaykh and introduced the aspirant to him through personal contact. Since there were only a few people who were philosophically minded enough to ask themselves the questions for which they could only find answers in Sufi texts, the vast majority of those who came to know of Sufism were attracted to it in the first place through poetry which then led them to the presence of the Sufi master. Thus poetry became in a way the main bridge which provided for those qualified among the general public access to Sufi teachings themselves.

However, it must be added here that Sufi poetry must not be confused with Sufism itself. As the English proverb states, "Where there is smoke there is a fire," but there are many fires which do not emit smoke. The fact that some masters were not great poets does not mean that they were not masters. Nor does the fact that there are periods of history without Sufi literary masterpieces nullify the spiritual significance of that period. This is true in many parts of the Islamic world and even in Persia itself. For example, we do not have as many well-known Balūchī poets as we have Shīrāzī ones, but only God knows whether there have been greater saints in Shīrāz than in Balūchīstān. We cannot decide on that matter; it is for Him to decide, but we cannot certainly exclude the possibility of the presence of great Sufi masters in such out-lying regions even if these climes did not produce a Rūzbihān or Ḥāfiẓ. It is important, therefore, not to confuse this incredible theophanic beauty, which is Persian Sufi poetry, with Sufism itself, which is really quite something else. The two are closely related, but the latter does not necessitate the existence of the former.

* * *

The vast literature of Persian Sufism did not die out or exhaust all its possibilities with Jāmī. It continued to produce notable figures within Persia through the Qajar period and, in fact, up to the present day, while its influence spread to an even greater degree beyond the confines of its original homeland. Its influence in nearly all the languages used by Muslims in Eastern Islamic lands is an incredible fact and a notable phenomenon within Islamic civilization. The other universal language and literature of Islam, which is Arabic, had a tremendous impact upon the development of the various languages and literatures of Africa, including Swahili, Hausa, and Berber, but Arabic had less influence than Persian upon the development of Sufi literature. It exercised influence, of course, through the Koran, but the literary genres of Arabic poetry did not have all that much influence.

Needless to say the Koran, and through it the Arabic language, spread throughout the Islamic world, but it has actually Persian Sufi literature—Persian being the only other non-vernacular language in the Islamic world along with Arabic—which exercised a decisive influence upon the Turkish people and the Turkic languages all the way from Aḥmad Yasawī (d. 1167) to Yunus Emre (d. ca. 1321). Persian also had a tremendous impact upon all the great Muslim poets in the subcontinent of India, whose vast literature has now been studied in the West – thanks most of all to the pioneering work of Annemarie Schimmel and some of her students. Even the rise of Malay literature as an Islamic literature in Malaysia and Indonesia, which in fact made possible the spread of Islam in that land, was not possible without the influence of Persian poets such as Jāmī. Among the Muslims in China, whose the Sufi literature is only now beginning to be studied, one can also discern strong Persian influences.

Not only this vast area of the eastern Islamic world but also the Christian West was influenced to some degree by the body of literature being discussed in this volume. It is remarkable that four of the greatest literary figures of the West, that is Dante, St. John of the Cross, Goethe and, indirectly, William Blake have been influenced in one way or another by some aspect of Persian Sufi poetry (not to speak of Ezra Pound and many modern poets who were very much interested in Persian poetry). Here it is sufficient to recall that when St. John of the Cross migrated to Granada in the early 16th century, there was much influence of Persian Sufi poetry in Andalusia. He actually met a number of Moriscos, some of whom were most likely of Persian origin and there he learned something about Persian poetry. Some of the latest research in this subject has shown that certain poems of St. John of the Cross reflect not only the influence of Arabic poetry but of Persian Sufi poetry as well. One can therefore say that the influence and impact of this poetry is vast indeed and cannot be in any way delimited by the immediate world in which it arose.

* * *

Something should also be said here about the form and content of Persian Sufi poetry. There is an elaborate theory, or rather more than theory, in a sense, doctrine, which has been propounded concerning the poetry of Rumi and which constitutes the foundation of his work from the metaphysical perspective. This is the relationship between form *(ṣūrat)* and meaning *(ma'nā)*. In the language of Sufism, the word *ṣūrat* (not to be confused with the Aristotelian meaning of *ṣūrat* which is juxtaposed to matter) corresponds to the external form and *ma'nā* to the inner essence. According to the Sufis, the *ma'nā* reflects itself in the *ṣūrat* or external form. This form can only be the vehicle for the expression of the inner meaning provided that it is already in accordance with the nature of that inner meaning. Therefore, while the inner meaning 'rides,' in a sense, upon the vehicle of the external form, as Rumi would say, the vehicle is already conducive for the inner meaning 'to ride' upon it. Therefore, there exists a delicate wedding between form and meaning which characterizes the greatest Persian Sufi literature.

The form is there not only for itself but in order to express the inner meaning. That is why one can always tell second-rate poets who simply emulate the forms of Sufi poetry from those Sufi poets who have actually experienced the reality of Sufism. In the case of the latter, the form of their poetry is inbreathed with the archetypal meaning *(ma'nā)* which in Persian also means the 'spiritual' aspect of things. In Persian, the word 'spirituality' corresponds to *ma'nawiyya* rather than to *rūḥāniyya*, which is derived from the term 'spirit' *(rūḥ)* more commonly used in Arabic. In Persian, the two terms are interrelated, so that 'meaning' can be said to be 'spirituality'. God is meaning in the deepest sense of the word. Therefore, it is the inner meaning which creates, in a sense, the poetry itself and moulds the outer form—and this is exactly what happened historically. The reason why Persian Sufi literature is so rich is that its language was moulded at a time when it was fluid and malleable. It did not have to start with extremely strict forms and laws of prosody which pre-Islamic Arabic poetry already possessed. This very malleability of the Persian poetic medium provided Sufism with the possibility to develop its forms with great variety and perfection, which still characterizes Persian Sufi poetry to this very day.

Needless to say, the language of Sufi poetry is eminently symbolic – 'symbolic' not in the modern and psychological sense of the word, but in the traditional sense of the term. Symbolism relates a particular lower level of reality to a higher one. This poetry, being symbolic, is able to carry us to the far shore of existence precisely because it issues from that shore, precisely because its language is never what it appears to be in its literal and external aspect. One penetrates into the language to be carried by it to the inner meaning, from the *ṣūrat* to the *ma'nā*. It is precisely for this reason that this poetry is ultimately concerned with ecstasy and leads to the world of ecstasy which is none other than the world of *ma'nā*. In this regard, it is important to note the interdependent and symmetrical relationship between Sufi poetry and music—a phenomenon analyzed by Jean During in his essay on Sufi music in this volume.

For those who are alien to the subject of Sufism it needs to be mentioned that most of the great Persian Sufi poetry has either been created in, or has been related to, the inner harmony and rhythm created by Sufi music in the Sufi gatherings or seances (*majālis*) and within the individual soul of the poet. This nexus is to be seen even to the present day in the Islamic world, despite the decadence that has taken place in certain popular practices. The relationship between Sufi poetry and music is not an accidental but an essential one. And the reason for it is that there is something within this poetry which is concerned with ecstasy, and both this poetry and music are related to that universal harmony which pervades all things and causes the soul of the lovers of God to resonate in ecstasy in the recollection and proximity of the Beloved.

Of course, Sufi poetry does deal with doctrine, the conditions of the Path, spiritual instructions, and other related aspects, but these constitute only one pole of it. The other pole of this poetry is its transforming alchemy which enables one to go beyond oneself. It is able to accomplish this task both through its allusions and symbolic imagery referring to the states of the soul which the hearer already possesses within himself or herself, and by its rhythm and music – as anyone who has heard the traditional recitation of the *Mathnawī* or a *qawwalī* performance in India or Pakistan will bear out. This poetry, which is so often combined with music, is designed to shatter the barrier within the soul of the hearer that separates the ego from God. Ecstasy arises from the lifting of the veils and transcendence of the limitations of our ordinary consciousness. We live in a world in which our consciousness is limited by the confinements of our ego, which usually defines who we are. Once this veil is lifted, the person experiences—even if it be for a short while—that Infinite Reality from which ecstasy issues. Since all mystical paths are concerned with that Ultimate Reality which is at once absolute and infinite, they are therefore concerned with ecstasy, although not only with ecstasy. They are also concerned with discipline and the control of ecstasy, elements characteristic of as certain types of Sufi poetry, such as that of Rumi, as J.C. Bürgel points out in his essay in this volume. Without that discipline the soul simply frets away an opportunity to elevate and transcend itself.

Nevertheless, the element of ecstasy is present and is closely related to the great beauty of this poetry. The Sufis have continued to repeat over the ages the famous *ḥadīth* of the Prophet that "God is beautiful and He loves beauty," a *ḥadīth* that in a sense defines the religion of love and beauty to which the Sufis adhere. Beauty and love are complementary realities; there is no beauty without love and no love without beauty, a truth which we experience that in our everyday human life. On the exalted level of Sufism, however, beauty is seen as that which melts the hardness of the soul and the heart. The soul of the person qualified to follow Sufism cannot resist beauty and the person who is not sensitive or open to beauty (of either an outward or inward nature) is not qualified to pursue the Sufi Path and will probably not be attracted more than superficially to Sufi poetry. There has to be something within the soul which attracts it to beauty and, furthermore, the virtue of the soul itself is none other than its 'beauty', as the Arabic and Persian word *ḥusn,* meaning at once 'virtue' and 'beauty', testifies. The virtue of the soul consists in its beauty, and thanks to that virtue the soul is attracted to all levels of beauty, ranging from that of outward forms to the ultimate beauty which belongs to God. From the Sufi point of view, beauty is able to attract the soul and to enable it to break this hardness which prevents it from reaching the heart. This is precisely the function of beauty in Persian Sufi poetry: it is there to complement and aid in the process of reaching, through spiritual discipline and practice, the heart, which is the center of our being. Herein lies the highest function of the beauty of this poetry, which is thereby able to help man in the process of spiritual realization whose end is union and ecstasy.

So let us conclude with a verse by the greatest of all Persian Sufi poets as far as the power of beauty and the presence of ecstasy in poetry in concerned, that is, Ḥāfiẓ

What wonder if from the word of Ḥāfiẓ in Heaven,
The music of Venus brings Christ into an ecstatic dance.

OVERVIEW: IRANIAN ISLAM AND PERSIANATE SUFISM

Leonard Lewisohn

I. RECENT RESEARCH ON PERSIAN SUFISM IN HISTORICAL CONTEXT

While the conspicuous entry of 'fundamentalist Islam'[1] onto the contemporary political scene has underlined the need for the deeper study of mediæval Islam and its culture and literature[2]—the accelerated pace of present-day political events in Iran has tended to eclipse historical and literary studies of Persian culture. Major research work done on mediæval Persian culture over the past thirty years has largely been overlooked by non-specialists, and consequently, the role of Sufism in the formation of the intellectual life of mediæval Iran, found in all its diverse contexts—from ethics to political science, from philosophy to the visual arts, from cosmology to theology, from psychology to poetry—remains comparatively neglected.

When in 1956, A.J. Arberry likened classical Persian literature[3] as a wilderness yet to be signposted and surveyed, some two hundred and fifty years of orientalist scholarship stood behind him as testimony both to his predecessors' efforts to establish the prominent landmarks and to the dearth of real and intimate recognition of the Persian literary masters by its students. Now, at the end of the twentieth century, despite passage of decades, Persian literature, especially that of the late mediæval period—from the 13th to the 15th centuries, which is the focus of the present book—remains an enigma both to those generally familiar with world literature in translation and, on occasion, to scholars deeply engaged in its study as well.

One reason for this is an evident unfamiliarity with the mystical side of Islam, or Sufism. Yet it is upon the very principles and practices of Sufism that a great deal of Persian poetry, from the twelfth century onwards, was based. One of the most distinguished scholars of Persian Sufi literature, 'Abd al-Ḥusayn Zarrīnkūb, has

1. Among the vast and growing literature on the subject, the following works are especially relevant to our discussion here: A.K.S. Lambton, 'The Clash of Civilizations: Authority, Legitimacy, & Perfectibility' in R.M. Burrell (ed.) *Islamic Fundamentalism* (London: Royal Asiatic Society 1989), pp. 33-47, and B.B. Lawrence, 'Fundamentalists in Pursuit of an Islamic State' in his *Defenders of God: The Fundamentalist Revolt Against the Modern Age* (London: I.B. Tauris 1990), pp. 189-226.
2. In part, herein lies the motive for researches into the historical background of Islamic fundamentalism by sociologists such as Said Amir Arjomand; e.g. his *The Shadow of God and the Hidden Imam: Religion, Political Order, and Societal Change in Shi'ite Iran from the Beginning to 1890* (University of Chicago Press 1984).
3. *Classical Persian Literature* (London: Allen & Unwin 1956), p. 303.

gone so far as to say that, "Persian poetry of classical times was so extensively influenced by Sufi philosophy that almost every great lyric poet of that period was a Sufi, as nearly every great Sufi of the time was a poet."[1] In examining the historical background of Persian Sufism it is apt to bear this important observation in mind, which attests to the importance of Sufism in formulating the Persian models of literature, both classical and vernacular, which evolved during the mediaeval period – still used and elaborated upon today throughout Central Asia, Northern India, Iran, Turkey, Bangladesh, Malaysia, Pakistan, and Indonesia.[2]

Sufism is, in fact, the central facet of traditional Islam and as Victor Danner observes in *The Islamic Tradition,* constitutes its very essence. Danner notes that "when al-Ghazzālī (d.1111) turned to Sufism to save his soul, the world of Islam had already been worked over by these numerous popular expressions of Sufism: the Sufi saints and their charismatic deeds were well known and loved by the people and even by some of the doctors of the Law." He goes on to comment that Sufism flowed into the molds of Islamic civilization established in the eighth century with relative ease, mainly because "The ground of Islam had been well churned over by Sufism and had yielded considerable spiritual fruit everywhere. Sufism was not, in other words, a tangential or exotic element in the Islamic world, as the term 'mysticism' in the pejorative meaning it has today, might lead us to believe. It was, instead, an all-pervasive reality that touched everyone, even the scoffer and critic of the Path."[3]

In the second volume of his monumental study of Islamic cultural history, *The Venture of Islam,* Marshall G.S.Hodgson also emphasizes "the pre-eminent place in Persian letters'[4] enjoyed by mystical poetry since the eleventh Islamic century, and underlines the fact that "from the twelfth century on, increasingly Sufism was the inspiration of more and more of the important poets....It was a recognized part of religious life and even of religious *'ilm* knowledge. Thus gradually Sufism, from being one form of piety among others, and by no means the most accepted one either officially or popularly, came to dominate religious life not only within the Jamā'ī-Sunnī fold, but to a lesser extent even among Shī'īs."[5] Hodgson also stresses the predominance of Sufi attitudes and aspirations in eleventh-century Islamic

---

1. 'Persian Sufism in its Historical Perspective', *Iranian Studies,* vol. 3, nos. 3 &4 (1970), pp. 139-40. Cf. J.C. Bürgel's remark (made in reference to Sanā'ī, Niẓāmī, and Rumi): "There can be no doubt that without the miracle wrought by Islamic mysticism, Islamic poetry would not have developed as it did." *The Feather of Simurgh:The Licit Magic of the Arts in Medieval Islam* (New York University Press 1988), p. 84. Many of the observations made by H. Moayyad, in 'Lyric Poetry' in (ed.) E. Yarshater, *Persian Literature* (New York 1988), especially in his section on 'The Influence of Sufism', pp. 132-37, are also highly relevant in this context.
2. A. Schimmel, *Mystical Dimensions of Islam* (N. Carolina: Chapel Hill 1975), pp. 327-402; *As Through a Veil: Mystical Poetry in Islam* (New York 1982), Chap. 4.
3. V. Danner, *The Islamic Tradition* (New York 1988) p. 95.
4. M.G.S. Hodgson, *The Venture of Islam,* vol. 2: *The Expansion of Islam in the Middle Periods* (University of Chicago Press 1977 rpt.), p. 295. The theme of poetry as the 'monumental art' of Persia also has been admirably expounded by Ehsan Yarshater ('Some Common Characteristics of Persian Art and Poetry' in *Studia Islamica,* 16, 1962) and its pre-eminent importance in Persian literature noted by Muḥammad Dabir Sayāqī (See the introduction, p. 12, to his edition to the *Kulliyyāt-i Shāh Dā'ī Shīrāzī* [Tehran 1339 AHsh]).
5. *The Venture of Islam,* II, p. 203.

poetry and aesthetics.[1]

During the Mongol and Timurid domination of Persia three fundamental social institutions underpinned Muslim civic life: Islamic 'canon' law *(Sharī'a);* the charitable *(waqf)* foundations; and the Sufi Orders *(ṭarīqa)*, the creditability of the last two depending upon the observance of *Sharī'a* norms.

> Accordingly, in addition to the ordinary mosque, each Muslim community now had its *khāniqāh* (Arabic, *zāwiyah),* where the Sufi *pīrs* lived. There they instructed and housed their disciples, held regular *dhikr* sessions (often for a fairly wide congregation), and offered hospitality to wandering Sufis, especially those of the same *ṭarīqah.*[2] Even when endowed by an *amīr,* they retained this air...the *khāniqāhs* became the foci of the more private, personal side of worship.[3]

The political substructure and social fulcrum of the Sufi Orders lay in the establishment and diffusion of these centres, so understanding their traditional status in mediæval Persian society is necessary to grasp the historical situation of Sufism. In the 7th/13th century the *khānaqāh* institution became greatly diffused throughout all Islamic lands touched by Persianate culture, reaching the apex of its social and political influence. Aḥmad Rajā'ī, describing this growth of institutional Sufism, notes that in the 6th/12th and 7th/13th century:

> *Khānaqāhs* were not reserved exclusively for the Sufis but were also open to all travelers, functioning as hotels where room and board were provided. This social aspect of the *khānaqāh* greatly increased its appeal, especially since all classes of people were allowed to participate in the Sufi assemblies, listen to their sermons, public teachings and musical concerts....In fact, so widespread did the social influence of the *khānaqāh* institution during this period become, that the State authorities began to 'credit' the institution officially—giving the director *(pīr)* of the *khānaqāh* the title of *Shaykh al-shiyukh,* ('Master of masters') which, like the rank of *Qaḍī al-Quḍāt* ('Attorney-general'), became an official position.[4]

According to Qāsim Ghanī, the *khānaqāh* institution during this period had both a private and a public aspect. The public, social dimension of the *khānaqāh* involved the giving of spiritual counsel to non-initiates, delivery of public homilies on various moral themes as well as general proselytizing of Sufi teachings. The private, individual dimension addressed contemplative disciplines such as fasting, meditation, prayer and retreat. The atmosphere of the *khānaqāh* was especially enlivened by the presence of *Samā'* ceremonies, which tended to dissolve class differences.[5] Such a bold 'mixing of classes' was quite uncharacteristic any other institution in mediæval Europe of the same period. "Perhaps more than their peers in any other major cultural environment," observed Marshall Hodgson (describing Persian *ṭarīqa* Sufism), "the Sufis succeeded in combining a spiritual elitism with

---

1. *Ibid,* II, pp. 304-05.
2. Cf. V. Danner's comments on 'The Early Development of Sufism' in S.H. Nasr, (ed.) *Islamic Spirituality: Foundations,* vol. 1 (New York: Crossroad 1987), p. 263.
3. *The Venture of Islam,* II, pp. 211- 214.
4. *Farhang-i ash'ār-i Ḥāfiẓ* (Tehran 1985, 2nd ed.), p. 456; these reflections are also echoed by Q. Ghanī, *Baḥth dar āthār wa afkār wa aḥwāl-i Ḥāfiẓ* (Tehran 1967, 3rd. ed.), p. 500.
5. Q. Ghanī, *op. cit.*, p. 501.

a social populism."[1]

By the fifth/eleventh century *khānaqāhs* or similar houses of retreat for mystics existed in all the major towns in Khurasan and Persian Central Asia. In the following century, the construction of *khānaqāhs* continued apace. It is known, for example, that Shaykh Aḥmad Jām (d. 536/1142) constructed some ten *khānaqāhs* during his lifetime throughout this region. In the seventh/thirteenth century the Bākhārzī family, to give but one example out of a myriad, constructed and endowed the most impressive *khānaqāh* in Fatḥābād, a suburb of Bukharā which contained a *madrasa* attached to it. Abū'l-Mafākhir Bākhārzī (d. 736/1336)[2] constructed a hospice for travellers, stables and a public bath in the 8th/14th century annexed onto the original edifice there.[3] Throughout the rest of Persia intensive activity in the construction of *khānaqāhs* continued during this period. In the seventh/twelfth and eighth/thirteenth centuries in the province of Yazd (southern Persia) alone, according to the mediæval histories (such as the *Tarīkh-i Yazd* and the *Tarīkh-i jadīd-i Yazd*) some forty-five *khānaqāhs* are recorded as having been constructed and charitably endowed.[4]

Although it is pure hyperbole to declare (as does J.S. Trimingham) that from their very inception the *khānaqāhs* "had been defined and regulated by the state – the price they paid for official recognition and patronage,"[5] it is true that the Sufis often enjoyed close relations with local authorities and dignitaries, who in turn greatly respected the mystics' rites conducted within their cloisters. According to Hodgson (who here strongly disagrees with Trimingham), the *khānaqāhs* were basically designed to house wandering Sufis, especially those of the same order. The *khānaqāhs* were so widespread that they could found in every Muslim community which contained a mosque. Often, the *khānaqāhs* were financed by laymen and partially connected with an order whose primary affiliation was to a guild and so provided financing for its upkeep. They "had some of the same functions as a European monastery," being "basic centers of social integration" for both men and women. It was the mosque rather than the *khānaqāh* which was the particular protégé of the State:

> The worship at the mosque never ceased to be associated in some degree with political authority; it was a state function. The *khānaqāhs* were eminently private from the very beginning. Even when endowed by an *amīr*, they retained this air. When the *khānaqāhs* became the foci of the more private, personal side of worship, they reinforced the fragmentation of Muslim societies in apolitical social forms (and at the same time gave these forms legitimacy and spiritual support.[6]

The *khānaqāh* institution was thus relatively apolitical,emphasizing the individual's relation to God, rather than his condition as a social or political entity. Albeit, the socio-political dimension of the institution became stronger in the late fifteenth

---

1. *The Venture of Islam*, II, pp. 217-18.
2. See the essay on his mystical rule and writings by M. Waley in the present volume.
3. *Tārīkh-i khānaqāh dar Irān* (Tehran: Kitābkhāna Ṭahūrī, 1369 A.Hsh./1990), pp. 192-95.
4. Īrāj Afshār, 'Khānaqāh-hā-yi Yazd' in *Sufi: Faṣl-nāma-yi Khānaqāh-i Ni'matullāhī*, no. 8 (Fall 1369 A.Hsh.), p. 11.
5. *The Sufi Orders in Islam* (Oxford University Press 1973), p. 69.
6. *The Venture of Islam*, II, pp. 213-14.

century and came to the fore in the Naqshbandī order, as, for instance, Jo-Ann Gross's study of Khwāja 'Ubaydullāh Aḥrār (d. 895/1490) in this volume (chap. 3), illustrates.

Hodgson notes that from 692 to 945 A.D. (his so-called 'High Caliphal Period') the religious topography of Persia was totally pervaded and dominated by the forms of Sufi piety, that furnished "a pervasive set of spiritual presuppositions and sanctions which the undergirded the whole pattern"[1] of Islamic spirituality. Thus, it was largely the Sufi Orders which, from the twelfth century onwards, set the tone of Islamic spirituality – Sufism becoming from the twelfth to fifteenth centuries (as is still the case in many Muslim countries of West Africa such as Senegal) "an institutionalized mass religion."[2]

> Sufism... became the framework within which all popular Muslim piety flowed together... Guilds commonly came to have Sufi affiliations. Men's clubs [i.e the *futuwwah* institution] claimed the patronage of Sufi saints... It is probable that without the subtle leaven of the Sufi orders, giving to Islam an inward personal thrust and to the Muslim community a sense of participation in a common spiritual venture quite apart from anyone's outward power, the mechanical arrangements of the *Shari'ah* would not have maintained the loyalty essential to their effectiveness.[3]

Writing in the 1950's, the same decade as Hodgson, G.E. von Grunebaum, also described twelfth-century Sufism as "the repository of the religious psychology of Islam;...its analysis of the religious life the timeless enrichment of human self-interpretation and the most delicate crystallization of the Muslim's spiritual aspirations," noting, as does Danner, that after Ghazzālī secured "Sufism its place within orthodoxy, the emotive life of Sunnite Islam came to be concentrated in the Sufi orders."[4]

Such testimony by two of the foremost Western orientalists (many others having made similar observations) concerning the pre-eminent role played by Sufism in the formation of the intellectual life of mediæval Persianate Islam, is also echoed by many prominent Iranian literary historians of this century. A good example is Qāsim Ghanī's survey of the life of Ḥāfiẓ, *Baḥth dar āthār wa afkār wa aḥwāl-i Ḥāfiẓ*[5] *(Studies in the Life, Works, and Thought of Ḥāfiẓ* – and subtitled *A History of Sufism from its Origin until the Age of Ḥāfiẓ*. Ghanī stresses the importance of Sufism to the formation of Persian poetry and civilization:

> Sufis recited poetry both in their circles of remembrance of God and in public preaching assemblies, believing discourse to be ineffective without the proper poetic

1. *Ibid*, II,125.
2. See 'Sufism as institutionalized mass religion: the techniques of *dhikr*', *ibid.*, II, pp. 210-14.
3. *Ibid.* Also cf. J.S. Trimingham, *The Sufi Orders in Islam*, p. 9ff.; A.J. Arberry, *Aspects of Islamic Civilization* (University of Michigan 1990 rpt.), p. 16.
4. G.E. von Grunebaum, *Islam: Essays in the Nature and Growth of a Cultural Tradition* (London: RKP 1961 2nd ed.), p. 28. However, von Grunebaum was biased in his other views about Sufism, equating the focus of the Sufis on contemplative disciplines with political quietism and perceiving mysticism as a direct cause of cultural decay and social decline.
5. This work, though owing much to the historical researches of E.G. Browne's four-volume *A Literary History of Persia*, displays greater comprehension of the importance of Sufism to the Persian psyche than Browne's.

> devices to adorn it. Because of the illustrative brilliance of their verse, Sufi poetry came to be widely diffused and popular, in turn giving great social impact to Sufism. Although in the Sāmānid and Ghaznavid epochs, Persian poetry was broadly patronized by aristocrats and princes... its imaginative reach and range of ideas was strictly limited by its panegyric orientation. Sufism gave poetry a new and independent lease on life, broadening its conceptual scope and imaginative power, effectively transforming it into a public art-form.[1]

Both Hodgson and Ghanī in the late fifties and early sixties had perception enough to voice such insights about the fundamental importance of Sufism in the cultural history of Islam. Both had to overcome preconceptions: on the one hand, the anti-mystical, rationalist bias of a secular academic milieu,[2] and on the other, the fundamentalist prejudices inherited from an exoteric Islamic conservatism which repudiates mysticism.[3] Nevertheless, they were ahead of their times, for the dominant view of Persianists remained that Sufism's esoteric nature made it a 'tangential' and 'exotic' phenomenon (in Danner's words) and hence, outside mainstream Islamic culture and piety![4]

In fact, up until the early sixties and the following decade which heralded the advent of the pioneering researches *"En Islam iranian"* by Henry Corbin,[5] accompanied by the penetrating historical scholarship of S.H. Nasr, H. Landolt, A. Schimmel, and several others—the role of Sufism in guiding mediæval Persian literary history remained largely unrecognized. The voices of individual scholars like L. Massignon, R.A. Nicholson, Laurence Binyon[6] and G.M. Wickens,[7] who earlier in this century had accorded some positive cultural or sociological signifi-

---

1. *Baḥth dar āthār...Ḥāfiẓ*, II, p. 555.
2. On the conflict between the secular and sacred visions of religion see S.H. Nasr, 'The Rediscovery of the Sacred' and 'Knowledge and its Descralization' in *Knowledge and the Sacred* (Albany: SUNY 1989), pp. 1-64, 93-129; and the same author's 'Islam and the Encounter of Religions' in *Sufi Essays* (London: Allen & Unwin 1972), pp. 123-51.
3. Fundamentalism, as S.H. Nasr has observed in *Traditional Islam in the Modern World* (London: KPI 1987), is, along with modernism, one of the chief enemies of both traditional Islam and Sufism. "The attitude of traditional Islam to Sufism reflects that which was current during the centuries prior to the advent of puritanical and modernist movements in the 12th/18th centuries... considering it as the inner dimension or heart of the Islamic revelation." (p. 15)
4. Western anti-religious secularism and Islamic puritanism are both, for altogether different reasons, opposed to Sufism. The radical Iranian modernist, Aḥmad Kasravi (d. 1940), for instance, held mysticism to be an opiate infused into the Eastern soul by Western imperialism to prevent its awakening. See Kasravi's *On Islam and Shi'ism*, translated by M.R. Ghanoonparvar (Washington, D.C.: Mazda 1990). The Shi'ite *'ulamā'* also have had a historical antagonism to Sufism; see J.R.I. Cole, 'The Battle with Sufism' and 'Uṣūlī-Sufi Polemics', *Roots of North Indian Shī'ism in Iran and Iraq* (University of California Press 1988), pp. 146-155; M. Bayat, *Mysticism and Dissent: Socioreligious Thought in Qajar Iran* (Syracuse University Press 1982), pp. 26-27.
5. *En Islam iranien (Aspects spirituels et philosophiques)*, 4 vols. (Paris: Éditions Gallimard 1971).
6. See L. Binyon's comments on the close association between Persian painting and Sufi poetry in 'Art in Persia', in *The Spirit of Man in Asian Art* (Harvard University Press 1935), pp. 123, 132; and in the introduction to his edition of illustrations by Persian miniaturists to *The Poems of Nizami* (London 1928, p. 134) in a 16th-century MS. in the British Library.
7. Who, on the role of Persian Sufism in Islamic history, commented: "In Sufism we have what is generally regarded, and not without much justice, as the supreme manifestation of the Persian mind in the religious sphere." 'Religion' in A.J. Arberry (ed.) *The Legacy of Persia* (Oxford University Press 1963 reprt.), pp. 158-59.

cance to Sufism's role in Persian history, were all but drowned in the rising tide of Western secular humanism, branding mysticism as anathema.

In Iran the situation was slightly more hopeful, thanks to a generation of scholars raised in the 1940s and the 1950s such as 'Alī Aṣghar Ḥikmat,[1] Badī' al-Zamān Furūzānfar,[2] Irāj Afshār,[3] Ehsan Yarshater,[4] and Qāsim Ghanī[5] had produced works which showed the centrality of Sufism in mediæval Perso-Islamic literary culture. In 1970, 'Abd al-Ḥusayn Zarrīnkūb contributed a lengthy article to *Iranian Studies* (vol. 3, nos. 3 & 4), on 'Persian Sufism in its Historical Perspective'. This overview of the main theosophical doctrines of Sufism was followed by a weighty tome with a more historical focus: *Justujū'-i dar taṣawwuf-i Irān*.[6] Here Zarrīnkūb devotes an entire chapter to 'The Sufi Masters of Khurasan', concluding an instructive review of the subject with a convincing argument that Khurasan was the "cradle of Islamic Sufism."[7]

Also in the 1970s Western scholars made similar observations about the dominance of Khurasan as the centre of intellectual ferment in classical Islamic culture and Sufism. Richard Frye's studies, for example, brought him to conclude that "the manpower, or brainpower, for the 'Abbasid flowering came from Khurasan, and not from western Iran, Arabia, Syria or elsewhere." He also emphasized "the immense contribution of the Iranian peoples to the culture of Islam, so much so that one might be entitled to designate the Islam which came into being in the tenth and eleventh centuries as Iranian Islam using the Arabic language."[8] The views of Western Persianists such as Frye and Schimmel, and of Iranian scholars such as Zarrīnkūb and Ghanī, have been confirmed by the researches of A. Bausani and H. Corbin as well.

Perhaps one of the main reasons for this lack of recognition of classical Persian Sufism lies in the effective political eradication of the *khānaqāh*s and the cultural

1. Cf. his Persian translation of the third volume of E.G. Browne's *Literary History of Persia*, entitled *Az Sa'dī tā Jāmī* (Tehran 1960).
2. Cf. his articles, 'Fārābī va taṣawwuf', 'Abū 'Alī Sīnā wa taṣawwuf', Khwāja 'Abdullāh Anṣārī wa Mawlānā Jalāl al-Dīn', in *Majmū'ah-yi maqālāt wa ash'ār Badī' al-Zamān Furūzānfar* (Tehran: Kitābfurūshī Dihkhudā 1351 A.Hsh.)
3. I. Afshār has published several critical editions of classical Sufi texts and is the compiler of a 3-volume *Index Iranicus: Répertoire Méthodique des Articles Persans concernant les Études Iranologiques, publiés dans les Périodiques et Publications Collectives* (Tehran 1910-1989).
4. Cf. his *Shi'r-i fārsī dar 'ahd-i Shāh Rukh* (Tehran University Press 1955).
5. *Op. cit.*
6. *Researches in Iranian Sufism* (Tehran: Amir Kabir 1978).
7. *Justujū-yi dar taṣawwuf-i Irān*, pp. 81-83. Although Zarrīnkūb's observations were partially derived from the researches of S. Nafīsī's *Sar-chishma-yi taṣawwuf*, recent Iranian scholarship, such as M. Kiyānī's *Tārīkh-i khānaqāh dar Irān* (e.g. p. 182), confirms their accuracy.
8. 'Iranian Contributions to Islamic Culture' in *The Golden Age of Persia* (London: Weidenfeld & Nicholson 1975), p. 165.

obliteration of the activity of the Sufi Orders under the Safavids.[1] The Safavid's "totalitarian state" as Roger Savory termed it,[2] was based on a politicalization of the master-disciple relationship, focusing upon an idolatrous cult of personality built around the ruler as both 'perfect master' *(murshid-i kāmil)* and absolute monarch.[3] Shāh Ismā'īl became apotheosized by his followers as a divine incarnation: they alternated between lauding him as Mahdī and God.[4] Here he followed the extremist cult of personality instituted by the previous Safavid masters Junayd (1447-1460) and Ḥaydar (1460-1488) who had transformed the peaceful Safavid Order into "a militant *ghāzī* movement,"[5] thus beginning what was to become—with the possible exception of the Tijāniyya *jihād* conducted in West Africa in the late nineteenth century by Ḥājj 'Umar[6]—the darkest chapter in the entire history of Islamic Sufism.

Of course, Sufism did not 'vanish' under the Safavids. The sun of Gnosis, says Rumi, does not ever set, for the Orient of its dawning lies forever in the human heart and intellect.[7] But its outer rites did suffer an eclipse. Writing in 975/1567 of a certain *khānaqāh* in Tabriz deserted by Sufis but still standing, Ibn Karbalā'ī laments the lack of dervishes in Persia, declaring, "This age is under the aegis of the divine Name 'the Inward' *(al-Bāṭin)*. Outwardly there are no mystics in the world but inwardly they exist, because the world could not last an instant without this class

---

1. According to Ḥāfiẓ Ḥusayn Ibn Karbalā'ī, Shāh Ismā'īl I (reg. 1501-1524) "eradicated, destroyed and extirpated most of the initiatic lineages [*silāsil*= Sufi Orders] of the Sayyids and Shaykhs" in Persia (*Rawḍāt al-janān wa jannāt al-jinān*, ed. Ja'far Sulṭān al-Qurrā'ī [Tabriz, B.T.N.K., 1344 A.H.sh./1965], vol. II, pp. 159). In 909/1503 he drove the followers of the Kāzirūnī out of Fars after a massacre of 4,000 persons and the desecration of the tombs of the Sufi Shaykhs of that region (Arjomand, *The Shadow of God*, p. 112). As for the Nasqhbandiyya, all trace of this Order "was extirpated from Western and Central Iran by the Safavids, for whom the slaughter of Sunni scholars and shaykhs was an essential part of establishing Shi'i supremacy." (H. Algar, "The Naqshbandī Order': A Preliminary Survey of its History and Significance', *Studia Islamica* 44, 1976, p. 139) When Ismā'īl I conquered Herat in 1510, he desecrated Jāmī's tomb. (Arjomand, *ibid.*) The Khalwatī Order fled the Shi'ified Safavid regime for the more congenial Ottoman domains and the Nūrbakhshī branch of the Kubrawī Order also declined sharply – the great grandson of Sayyid Muḥammad Nūrbakhsh, Qawām al-Dīn was exectued by Shāh Tahmāsp (reg. 1524-1576). (Arjomand, *ibid.* p. 115) During Tahmāsp's reign Sufi practices were abandoned as politically inexpedient and with the succession of his son, Ismā'īl II, further efforts to eradicate Sufism from Persia (e.g. the massacre of the Sufis in Qazwin) were made. 'Abbas the Great (1587-1629) continued this anti-Sufi policy with the massacre in 1023/1614 of his Safavid Sufi followers in Qarajadājh who were accused of collaboration with the Ottomans. (Arjomand, *ibid.*, p. 110)
2. 'Some Reflections on Totalitarian Tendencies in the Safavid State', *Der Islam*, 52 (1976), pp. 226-41.
3. S.A. Arjomand, 'Religious Extremism *(Ghuluww)*, Sufism and Sunnism in Safavid Iran (1501-1722)', *Journal of Asian Studies*, 15, no. 1 (1981), pp. 4-5; R. Savory, 'The Consolidation of Power in Safavid Persia', *Der Islam* (1976), p. 91; R. Canfield, 'Theological "extremism" and social movements in Turko-Persia' in R. Canfield (ed.) *Turko-Persia in Historical Perspective* (Cambridge University Press 1991), pp. 132-60.
4. R. Savory, *Iran Under the Safavids* (Cambridge University Press 1980), p. 17.
5. Arjomand, *op. cit.*, p. 79.
6. See Jamil M. Abun-Nasr, *The Tijaniyya: A Sufi Order in the Modern World* (Oxford University Press 1965), pp. 108-28.
7. *Mathnawī-yi ma'nawī* (ed.) R.A. Nicholson (Gibb Memorial Series, n.s. 4, London 1925-40), *Daftar* II 43.

of people [the Sufis]."[1] One notable form in which Sufi teachings did continue to flourish in the Safavid period was in the remarkable elaboration of the philosophical *'irfānī* tradition, which brought together Kalām, Peripatetic and illuminationist philosophy and the theosophy of Ibn 'Arabī. The outstanding figure in this endeavour was Mullā Ṣadrā,[2] who, following on the writings of the Pre-Safavid Ḥaydar Āmulī, effectively integrated Ibn 'Arabī into the new Shi'ite-Persian religious world.

Aside from the above-cited historical factors, the survival of institutional Sufism in any society depends upon public opinion, which is susceptible to the vagaries of changing relations between the ruling authorities and the *'ulamā'* with the mystics. The terrorist policies of the Safavid sovereigns combined with a bitter propaganda campaign carried out by the Shi'ite clerics against Sufism effectively signified the social obliteration of the *ṭarīqa*s and their traditions from the frontiers of Persia.[3]

Although the beginning of the destruction of institutionalized Sufism was largely a political act by the early Safavid Shāhs aimed at eradicating any opposition from the same poular Shi'ite-*ghāzī* background, their initiative was largely supported by the Shi'ite clerics from Iraq, Lebanon and Syria who were welcomed when the Safavid state turned to consolidating Shi'ism as the official religion. The background to the historically long-founded antipathy between the clerics and both organized and unorganized Sufism is examined in the next section.

II. SUFIS AND MULLAS

> God created no one more onerous and troublesome for the Folk of Allah than the exoteric scholars (*'ulamā' al-rasūm*)....In relation to the folk of Allah the exoteric scholars are like the pharoahs in relation to God's messengers.
>
> – Ibn 'Arabī[4]

The history of Islam testifies to the continuous use of the metaphysical categories of the esoteric and exoteric within polemical debate, and to the development of religious and social dichotomies which these terms came to represent, In particular, any history of Persian Sufism must give some account of the demonstrable antagonism between the clerical perspective and the Sufi outlook, which was largely seen by both sides in terms of the esoteric/exoteric polarity. W. Chittick devotes several pages of his study of Farghānī to discussing what he terms the "creative tension" between these two groups and an analysis of this dichotomy is also fundamental to Jo-Ann Gross's essay in this volume.

Opposition to dogmatic clericalism appeared in Iranian Islam quite early in Bāyazid Bisṭāmī's (d. 261/875) bold characterization of the transmitters of prophetic traditions as "dead people narrating from the dead."[5] Bāyazid also

1. *Rawḍāt al-janān*, II, p. 75.
2. See S.H. Nasr, *Sadr al-Din Shirazi and His Transcendent Theosophy* (Tehran: Iranian Academy of Philosophy 1978).
3. Muḥsin Kiyānī, *op. cit.*, p. 500.
4. *Futūḥāt al-makkiyya*, vol. I, p. 279, cited by W. Chittick, *The Sufi Path of Knowledge: Ibn 'Arabī's Metaphysics of the Imagination* (Albany: SUNY 1989), p. 247.
5. *The Sufi Path of Knowledge*, p. 249.

claimed to have visited the Almighty's court and to have found it empty of all members of the clergy *('ulamā')* and devoid of any jurisprudents *(fuqahā')*.[1] Expression of such opinions (along with other provocative behavior) caused him to be exiled seven times from his native city to Gorgan. Similar opinions led to Sahl Tustarī's (d. 283/896) exile to Basra from Ahwaz and Ḥakīm Tirmidhī (d. 295/908) being driven out of Tirmidh.[2] With Ḥallāj's (d. 309/922) espousal of Islam as a 'religion of love', Sufism was transported, in Louis Massignon's words, "to the political plane as a social force, for he had given it an original theological and philosophical superstructure; but this also had made it vulnerable, exposed to theological charges of *takfīr*, and even threatened by effective legal penalties."[3] Thus, by the fifth/eleventh century, historians of Sufism such as Sulamī (d. 412/1021) would begin to formulate lists of *miḥan al-ṣūfiyya* (inquisitions conducted by legalists against Sufis).[4] Summarizing the historical origins of the exoteric/esoteric controversy, Danner observes:

> Sufism arose to denote the esoteric Path precisely at the time the different schools of exoteric Law arose...The exoteric aspect of Islam soon grew into a body of teachings, practices, and moral legislation, all under the watchful control of the *'ulamā'*. The rise of Islamic exotericism in an institutionalized fashion provoked the rise of Sufi esotericism, with its own Shaykhs, its own practices, and eventually its own institutions. From that period on down to our time, we will find the two levels of authority in operation throughout the Muslim world, the Sufi Shaykhs and the *'ulamā'*.[5]

The veneration which the founders of the fundamental schools of Islamic jurisprudence, Shāfi'i and Aḥmad ibn Ḥanbal, had for Sufi teachings, considering them an integral element of Koranic studies, if not actually its basis, demonstrated the high respect which Muslim mysticism enjoyed among the intelligentsia during the High Caliphal Period. But this union of jurisprudence and Sufism was unfortunately short-lived – fanatical exotericism being a better ideology for blood-thirsty empire-builders than tolerant mysticism of an anti-sectarian and ecumenical nature. A good summary of the early relations of Sufism with legalism is given by Muhsin Mahdi, who notes that in the seventh and eighth Christian centuries:

> Sufism meant the effort to follow all the demands of the divine law as fully as possible....As understood by the Lawgiver, his companions, and the generation that followed them, these demands consisted of external acts of worship, customary practices, and ways of life, and internal acts promoting the good attributes or virtues of the heart. These internal acts were considered more important than the external acts and the source that feeds and controls them and determines their efficacy. For early Muslims, "faith" *(īmān)* meant primarily these internal acts of the heart; good intention (*niyya*) was the principle, the "soul," of all actions; and the discordance between external and internal acts was "hypocrisy" (*nifāq*) and tantamount to a return

1. Zarrīnkūb, *Justujū*, p. 44.
2. Muḥsin Kiyānī, *op. cit.*, p. 513.
3. *The Passion of al-Ḥallāj: Mystic and Martyr of Islam*, translated by H. Mason, Bollingen Series 97 (Princeton University Press 1982), vol. I, pp. 379-80.
4. See *ibid.*, I, pp. 384 for lists of some early inquisitions conducted against the Muslim mystics.
5. *The Islamic Tradition*, pp. 91-92.

to *shirk,* to associating someone other than God with him as the object of one's worship and devotion.[1]

Early Sufism began as an attempt to observe the 'rule of the heart' in accordance with the spirit of the *ḥadīth:* "Seek the decree of the heart, even if the judges decree otherwise,"[2] – for as Ibn 'Arabī was to comment, "The name *faqīh* is much more appropriate for the Tribe [i.e. the Sufis] than for the exoteric scholar, for... it is he [the Sufi] who calls to God 'upon insight',[3] just as the Messenger of God calls upon insight." The Sufi speaks from vision, not from ratiocinative reason. "He does not call on the basis of the 'predominance of surmise' *(ghalabat al-ẓann),* as does the exoteric scholar. When a person is upon insight from God and 'upon a clear sign form his Lord' (11:17) when he calls to Him, his giving pronouncements and speaking are totally different from those of the one who gives pronouncements in the religion of God by the predominance of his surmise."[4]

Mahdi also observes that true understanding of what such esoteric *tafaqquh* (striving in religion) implied, gradually became eclipsed with the spread of Islam as a political power, so that "the majority of Muslims... concentrated instead on the external acts. The few who continued to engage in the battle for piety and salvation in the world to come and who preserved the original emphasis on the acts of the heart stood out as a distinct group and were given such names as 'ascetics', 'worshipers', and finally 'Sufis'."[5] Hence arose the differentiation between the internal demands of the divine Law, the piety of the heart before God *(fiqh al-bāṭin),* and the external demands of the divine law *(fiqh al-ẓāhir).* Mahdi reflected that

> Out of fear of the loss and complete forgetfulness of the more important part of the divine law, the early Sufis elaborated on the other hand the demands of the divine law regarding the acts of the heart into the knowledge of the internal demands of the divine law *(fiqh al-bāṭin),* which is contained in al-Muḥāsibī's "Devotion," *(al-Ri'āya)* the writings of Ibn 'Atā al-Adamī (d. 311/928), and al-Ghazzālī's "Revival."
>
> The separation of the jurist's inquiry into the divine law from that of the Sufi is, nevertheless, accidental as far as the true Muslim is concerned; for the two inquiries deal with two complementary aspects of his religious life and two complementary aspects of the divine law.[6]

By the twelfth century, however, this "accident" had developed into a "substance," and the struggle between the partisans of the jurisprudents of the heart (the Sufis) and the dogmatic jurists of the letter of the Law (the Mullas)—the eternal conflict between *Eros* and *Nomos*[7]—had become *the* vendetta of mediæval Islamic history.[8] "Wherever the *'ulamā'* became unusually strong, the life of the high

1. See Muhsin Mahdi, 'The Book and the Master as Poles of Cultural Change in Islam' in (ed.) S. Vyronis, Jr.) *Islam and Cultural Change in the Middle Ages* (Wiesbaden 1975), pp. 9-10.
2. See Abū Naṣr Sarrāj's *Kitāb al-luma' fī l-taṣawwuf,* ed. R.A. Nicholson, Gibb Memorial Series No. 22 (Leiden and London 1914), p. 16.
3. From the *Futūḥāt,* chap. 54, cited by W. Chittick, *op. cit.,* p. 249.
4. Ibid.
5. 'The Book and the Master' *loc. cit.*
6. Ibid.
7. Cf. A. Nygren, (trans. P.S. Watson) *Agape and Eros: A Study of the Christian Idea of Love* (London SPCK 1982), pp. 334-48.
8. Muḥsin Kiyānī, *Tārīkh-i Khānaqāh dar Irān,* p. 498.

Islamicate culture was put in doubt," stated Hodgson, noting that between the exoteric Mullas – "the *Sharī'ah*-minded guardians of the single Godly moralistic community," – and the Sufis, whom he characterizes as "the sophisticated culture of Islamdom... a frustrated tension which they could successfully condemn but not effectively destroy," was maintained.[1]

Quṭb al-Dīn Shīrāzī's mystical rule, as analysed by J.T. Walbridge (below, chap. 5) clearly exemplifies this "sophisicated culture" of mediæval Sufism, showing the highly refined ethical conception of *fiqh al-bāṭin* held by the mystics. B.T. Lawson's discussion in this volume (chap. 4) of the persecution endured by Rajab Bursī (d. 843/1440) at the hands of the jurisprudents (characterized by this Shi'ite Sufi as "those whose belief is corrupt") not only illustrates the Sufi background of Shi'ite mysticism of this period, but also demonstrates the general antipathy of most Muslim esotericists—whatever *madhhab* they adhered to—for the exoteric jurisprudents. The tension and hostility between the two opposing camps also appears vividly in H. Norris's study of the Sufi origins of Ḥurūfism in this book (chap. 3), in what he deems the founder of the Ḥurūfī movement, Faḍlullāh Astarābādī's (martyred 1394) "theodicy of suffering." It is highly instructive to see how the greatest sixteenth-century historian of Persian Sufism, Ḥāfiẓ Ḥusayn Ibn Karbālā'ī, describes in his *Rawḍāt al-janān* how during Jahānshāh Qarā-quyūnlū's reign (ca. 850/1447—872/1467) "some five hundred adherents of Ḥurūfism and many other Ḥurūfī-sympathizers...were slain and burnt" in Tabriz in accordance with the *fatwā* of a bigoted jurisprudent. Ibn Karbālā'ī concludes his account of the massacre with typical Sufi tolerance, however, remarking, "But the most extreme accusation that one can level at Faḍhallāh, is that his disciples did not understand his esoteric knowledge *(ma'rifat-i way rā mu'taqidānash nafahmīda-ānd)* and so fell into heresy and apostasy."[2] – a tale which encapsulates the tragedy of the esoteric/exoteric schism in mediæval Persian society.

The polarization of the Sufis and Mullas into two opposing camps was also due to the fact that the mediæval Persian clerics were salaried servants of the State, as Aḥmad 'Alī Rajā'ī notes:

> Since most of the jurisprudents and *'ulamā'* [in the 12/13th centuries] were on the payroll of the State treasury and received regular stipends from the government, naturally their legal pronouncements were usually unfair, tending to abuse and prosecute the public sector instead of questioning the activities of the local authorities. If people had any respect for these clerics, it was simply because they were forced by social circumstances to comply with and pay them lip-service and external obeisance. The jurisprudents' position as official state prosecutors made it natural that the people should turn towards the Sufi masters, famed for their unworldliness and indifference to social status and political power. The Sufis were also renowned for their highly ethical natures, and usually did not forgo any opportunity to admonish and upbraid the *amīrs* and princes of their epoch to behave with justice and beneficence to their subjects.[3]

1. *The Venture of Islam*, II, p. 200.
2. *Rawḍāt al-janān wa jannāt al-jinān*, I, pp. 480-81.
3. *Op. cit.*, pp. 456-57.

Anti-clericalism was as much a topos among the mediæval Persian Sufi poets as anti-sectarianism, and as J.T.P. de Bruijn's essay (chap. 2) demonstrates, anti-clericalism particularly typifies those poets who composed verses in the *qalandariyyāt* genre. Following the 'Greatest Master', the Persian poets of Ibn 'Arabī's school who flourished during this period such as Fakhr al-Dīn 'Irāqī (610/1213-688/1289), Awḥad al-Dīn Kirmānī (d. 635/1238), Muḥammad Shīrīn Maghribī (d. 810/1408), Maḥmūd Shabistarī (687/1288-737/1337), and 'Abd al-Raḥmān Jāmī (b. 817/1414-d. 898/1492) often gave vent to their ill-opinion of the mediæval Mullas. Shabistarī, to cite one example from a myriad, concludes his 6000-line *mathnawī* poem, the *Sa'ādatnāma* by virulently deriding the jurisprudents:

> Although the Mulla takes sixty kilograms of water to make his ablutions to pray, his head seems hollower than a calabash in Koranic recitation. Like the Devil performing the act of ritual prayer, he will reveal to you worlds of scruples and irresolution. The Mulla's flesh and blood receives all of its nourishment from the kitchen of the local *amīr:* Look, he wipes his arse with his own sweat. They are all enslaved by property and possessions – don't call them 'jurisprudents' because they are lords... Through them the world becomes an idiot's kingdom, so 'donkey-head' is a proper epithet for a jurisprudent. By them all artists are discomposed, for they all wear scowls on their faces.[1]

The Sufi poet Qāsim-i Anwār (d. 837/1433-34) composed much poetry upon the same lines. The following verses, for example, reflecting his own personal distaste for this class as well as the general schism in mediæval Persian society between the two camps:

> *Go ask His Reverence, His Worship, the learned municipal judge,*
> *"What use is your prattle, when your heart is dead?"*
> *Snow showers down from the clouds of the realm of imitative learning* (taqlīd) –
> *That is why the speech of ascetics is so frozen.*

* * *

> *Will Qāsim tolerate the society of the imitative jurisprudent?*
> *We'll recite an incantation to avert such a calamity!*[2]

This unfortunate controversy between Mullas and Sufis continued to rage on through the centuries following the Safavid takeover in Iran. Two hundred years later, the ecumenical Sufi Dārā Shikuh,[3] in the introduction to the first Persian translation of the Upanishads, would refer to the jurisprudents as "brigands on the path of God."

A thorough analysis of this profound dichotomy in Iranian Islam, however, would require a monograph in itself and thus far excels the scope of the present essay. Mention of this schism is given below: in section VI where the divergences

1. *Majmū'ah-yi āthār-i Shaykh Maḥmūd Shabistarī*, ed. Ṣamad Muwaḥḥid (Tehran: Ṭahūrī 1365 A.Hsh), *Sa'ādatnāma*, vv. 1535ff.
2. *Kulliyyāt-i Qāsim-i Anwār*, ed. S. Nafisī (Tehran 1958), pp. 727, 729, 467.
3. See Daryush Shayegan, 'Muḥammad Dārā Shikūh: Bānī-yi 'irfān-i taṭbīqī', *Iran Nameh*, vol. 8, no. 2 (1990).

between exoteric and esoteric Islam, and the ascendancy of the latter during the late mediæval period in Persia, are discussed in its socio-cultural context, and in two other sections (IV and V) where the political background and renaissance of twelfth and thirteenth-century Sufism during the Mongol and Timurid periods in Iran are analysed. The following section is devoted to an exploration of the notion and characteristics of Iranian Islam.

III. IRANIAN ISLAM AND PERSIANATE SUFISM

The term 'Persian' usually denotes the rich and widespread cultural heritage of a Persian-speaking peoples and races which predated Islam.[1] From the fourth/tenth century onwards, as Hodgson observed,

> in an increasingly large part of Islamdom, [Persian was] the language of polite culture; it even invaded the realm of scholarship with increasing effect. It was to form the chief model for the rise of still other languages to the literary level... Most of the more local languages of high culture that later emerged among Muslims likewise depended on Persian wholly or in part for their prime literary inspiration. We may call these cultural traditions, carried in Persian or reflecting Persian inspiration, 'Persianate' by extension.[2]

It is this Persian or 'Persianate'—as Hodgson terms it—element which is the 'eternal' spirit and abiding 'genius' which has survived through the dismal centuries of ruthless autocratic dynasties. As A.J. Arberry notes, the value of Persian literature lies less in its form but in "the spirit which inhabited that form....In her writings, as in her art, the soul of Persia lives; compared with this abiding triumph, the ruin of her politics matters very little."[3] Whether the Sufi or *darwīshī* element is to be considered as a part of a distinctly Iranian ethos, as do many anthropologists,[4] or the Persian predilection for mysticism as an innate trait of the Iranian 'national character''[5] or one element among many in an Iranian 'belief sys-

1. Cf. Ehsan Yarshater's observation: "To educated people everywhere the name 'Persia' is associated with a number of pleasing notions that in the main emphasize the country's cultural heritage. One speaks of Persian art, Persian literature, Persian carpets, Persian miniatures, Persian mosques, and Persian gardens, all of which attest to a general refinement of taste and culture. It is true that 'Persia' also brings to the Western mind the Persian wars with Greece, and the home of an absolute monarchy that is often contrasted to Greek democracy; but even then 'Persia' does not evoke the image of a weak or backward country, but rather of a robust and mighty empire... 'Iran', on the other hand, possesses none of these associations. It is a barren word in languages other than Persian, denoting a country without a past or a distinctive culture." – 'Communication' in *Iranian Studies,* vol. 22, no. 1 (1989), p. 63.
2. *The Venture of Islam,* II, p. 293.
3. 'Persian Literature' in *The Legacy of Persia,* p. 228.
4. See M.C. Bateson, J.W. Clinton, J.B.M. Kassarijan, H. Safavi, M. Soraya *'Ṣafā-yi Bāṭin:* A Study of the Interrelations of a Set of Iranian Ideal Character Types' in (ed.) N. Brown & N. Itzkowitz, *Psychological Dimensions of Near Eastern Studies* (Princeton 1977), pp. 267-71.
5. Cf. D. Lerner, *The Passing of Traditional Society: Modernizing the Middle East* (New York: Free Press 1958); and Roy Mottahedeh's observation, *The Mantle of the Prophet: Religion and Politics in Iran* (London 1987, p. 144): "Mysticism, the ambiguity of poetry, belief in the many-faced subtlety of evil, and the never fully resolved choice between the roles of hedonistic cynic and selfless devotee have created the great interior spaces in which the Iranian soul has breathed and survived over at least half a millennium."

tem' as understood by the sociologists[1]—is not the focus of our discussion here.

In the present context our purpose is to define the parameters of Iranian Islam and to sketch a portrait of Persianate Sufism as it existed during a certain historical period. In the present volume our purview is confined to the 13th through the 15th centuries, beginning as the great Sufi orders are experiencing their first expansion and ending with the suppression of most of the outward forms of Sufism in Safavid Iran. Although some scholars[2] have maintained that the term 'mediæval' (coined, as it was, by Petrarch in 1341 to refer to a period of darkness from the time of the adoption of Christianity by the Roman emperors to his own time), is inappropriate with reference to Islamic civilization, this negative view overlooks its convenience as a chronological term.

The 13th through the 15th centuries saw the appearance of major Sufi Orders, and of great intellectual figures among the Sufis. These include 'Aṭṭār, Najm al-Dīn Rāzī, 'Umar Suhrawardī, Rumi, Shabistarī, Ḥāfiẓ, 'Abd al-Karīm al-Jīlī, 'Ala' al-Dawla Simnānī, Ibn al-Fariḍ, and Ibn 'Arabī, all of whom, excluding the last two, were of Persian background and origin. There were, of course, a host of others who, had they been Westerners, would surely today be world-renowned, and who, to quote W.C. Chittick, "would have been looked upon as landmarks in the spiritual and intellectual geography of Islam, had lived at any other time and place."[3]

This volume explores the legacy of the Persianate (including Ottoman Turkish, Timurid and Mongol) culture of Sufism from what Victor Danner has called the "thirteenth century revival of Sufism"[4] down to the beginnings of the Safavid era (1501-1722). More precisely, it focuses on the literary and philosophical renaissance which began with the flourishing of the Kubrawiyya, Suhrawardiyya, and Mawlawiyya Orders in the 13th century and ended with the suppression and exile from Iran of the Ni'matullāhiyya and Nūrbakhshiyya *ṭariqas* in the late sixteenth century.

Discussing the cosmopolitan nature of the composite high-cultural tradition of this period, Hodgson observes that many of the "basic forms and institutions" of Islamic culture "can be first traced to Khurāsān: the *madrasah* college, the *ṭariqah* form of Sufi organization, the acceptance of kalām as integral to Islam."[5] Hodgson furthermore commented how the greater part of the Fertile Crescent, the Iranian highlands, and the Syr-Oxus basin, "has been more or less Iranian in ethnic colour – a point that emerges the more strongly if one includes the Syr-Oxus basin along with the Iranian highlands proper. Only the Fertile Crescent has been predominantly Semitic. Scholars used to debate about the extent to which the flowering of Islamic culture was due to some disproportionate 'Persian' (or even 'Aryan') genius; as if the most ordinary Muslims were Semitic, but had yielded to the cultural leadership of a Persian minority."[6]

1. See R. Loeffler, *Islam in Practice: Religious Beliefs in a Persian Village* (New York: SUNY 1988), introduction.
2. Cf. R.M. Rehder, 'Persian Poets and Modern Critics', *Edebiyat*, vol. 2, No. 1 (1977), p. 111-12.
3. See his article in the present volume, s.v. 'The School of Qūnawī'.'
4. *The Islamic Tradition*, pp. 99-100.
5. *The Venture of Islam*, II, pp. 69-70.
6. Ibid.

This is, in fact, a gross misconception for any serious student of Islamic history; we "must learn to revisualize our material," Hodgson stresses, "and deliberately choose sounder categories; recognizing that the majority of the main cited areas from Nile to Oxus used one or another Iranian tongue (among which, Persian, was, of course, merely the most prominent)."[1]

As noted above, Hodgson was not the first historian to perceive this all-pervasive influence of the 'Persianate genius' on Islamic culture.[2] Alessandro Bausani, in attempting to define the concept and reality of 'Iranian Islam,' singled out the 'Persianate element' as the essential catalyst in the alchemy of Islamdom and asserted that Persian civilization expressed a "perfect balance" between a primitive and undeveloped Islam and the rich archaic culture of ancient Mazdean Iran. Only the addition of the Persianate element to Islam, he speculated, was capable of producing a "universal culture":

> At the end of the Sassanian Empire both Islam and Iranism were nourished, in different ways, by the syncretic soil formed by the dissolution of the great archaic civilizations during Hellenistic time, so that late Sassanian Iran is not an essentially "pure" Iranism (which perhaps never existed as such) and Islam, too, was not that "monolithic" pure monotheism...From this mutual fecundation is born Iranian Islam. It is a universal culture, whose dynamic extremes are the purity of the monistic faith of Abraham on one side and the ever present archaic-mythical symbolism on the other. Between these two poles Irano-Islamic culture at its best created expressions of perfect balance.[3]

Another Italian Islamicist, Francesco Gabrieli, had expressed nearly identical views, stating that:

> The Persian genius alone gave to Muslim mysticism the glory of a luxuriant poetic bloom in which the innate aptitude of the Iranians for narration and the sentence combined with the energy of a highly stimulated emotionality and with the audacity of the most unbridled esoteric speculations.... All the great minds of the West, from Goethe to Hegel, who sought to approach this aspect of Muslim spirituality, actually took as their guides not the Arabic ascetics or doctors but the great Persian poets we have just named.[4]

Outlining the legacy of Persian culture to Islam in general and to Sufism in particular, other scholars, such as G. M. Wickens (whose knowledge and love of Persian poetry was expressed in his numerous translations and studies of Sa'dī and Ḥāfiẓ),[5] likewise affirmed that "in Sufism we have what is generally regarded, and not without much justice, as the supreme manifestation of the Persian mind in the religious

---

1. *Ibid.*
2. On Hodgson's terms 'Islamdom' and 'Islamicate', see *The Venture of Islam*, I, p. 58.
3. A. Bausani, 'Muhammad or Darius? The Elements and Basis of Iranian Culture' in (ed.) S. Vryonis Jr., *Islam and Cultural Change in the Middle Ages* (Wiesbaden: Otto Harrassowitz 1975), pp. 47-48.
4. 'Literary Tendencies' in (ed.) G.E. von Grunebaum, *Unity and Variety in Muslim Civilization* (University of Chicago Press 1955), p. 100.
5. 'The Persian Conception of Artistic Unity in Poetry and its Implications in Other Fields' in *BSOAS*, vol. 14, part 3 (1952), pp. 239-43; 'An Analysis of Primary and Secondary Significations in the Third Ghazal of Ḥāfiẓ' in *BSOAS*, vol. 14, part 3 (1952), pp. 627-38); (trans.) *Morals Pointed and Tales Adorned (The Bustan of Sa'di)*, (Toronto, London and Buffalo 1974).

sphere."[1]

The purpose of adducing such quotations is not to revive the so-called 'Aryan-reaction' theory popularized by a few German scholars at the end of the 19th century such as I. Goldziher,[2] that Sufism is essentially a product of the Persian mind – a theory refuted in 1912 by R.A. Nicholson.[3] Spirituality transcends nationality. Prophecy is the grace of God, not the stock-in-trade of Arabs or Persians, as Rumi says:

> *Whether they hail from Baghdad,*
> *come of Ray – or from Herat,*
> *the Sufis are all the Prophet's kin*
> *beyond their bodies.*
> *A rose is still a rose*
> *no matter where it grows;*
> *The vat of wine only ferments wine*
> *– wherever the vat is put it boils fine.*
> *If the sun should raise its head*
> *from the West*
> *it's just the sun*
> *—naught else.*[4]

Yet few will dispute the fact that the cultural development of Islamic spirituality owes much both to Iranian Islam and to Persianate Sufism. This is especially true during the period under consideration.

The principal language of both the Mongol and Timurid courts was Persian. In India, "more Persian works than Iran proper" were produced. "India was the home of poets writing in Persian as early as the eleventh century. ...In the thirteenth and fourteenth centuries mystical and mystically inclined poets like Amir Khosrau and Ḥasan Dihlavi created a highly refined lyrical poetry... The literature of the Sufi urban orders was generally composed in Persian, the standard language of literature and, from the late fifteenth century, of administration."[5] Many of the Timurid princes were not only familiar with Persian *belles-lettres;* some actually composed poetry in Persian,[6] in which regard the Divans of Sulṭān Aḥmad Jalāyir[7] (1382-1410) and Jahān-shāh Qara-quyunlu (d. 872/1467), as well as the Persian

1. G. M. Wickens, 'Religion' in A.J. Arberry (ed.) *The Legacy of Persia* (Oxford University Press 1963 reprint), pp. 172, 151, 158.
2. 'The Influence of Parsism on Islam', trans. G.K. Nariman, in (ed.) C.P. Tiele, *The Religion of the Iranian Peoples* (Bombay: Parsi Publishing Co. 1912).
3. 'A Historical Enquiry concerning the Origin and Development of Sufism, with a list of definitions of the terms *ṣūfī* and *taṣawwuf*, arranged chronologically', *Journal of the Royal Asiatic Society* (1906), pp. 303-53. Nicholson's reflections on Sufism's origins have been considerably updated by later scholars, in particular H. Corbin, V. Danner and Martin Lings.
4. *Mathnawī-yi ma'nawī*, edited by R.A. Nicholson, *Daftar* VI: 187-189.
5. A. Schimmel, *As Through A Veil* (Columbia University Press 1982), p. 55 and N. Aḥmad, 'The Influence of Persian and Persian Culture in India', *Indo-Iranica*, vol. 38, nos. 1-4 (1984), pp. 1-30.
6. See E. Yarshater, *Shi'r-i fārsī dar 'ahd-i Shāh Rukh*, p. 5, 49.
7. See F.R. Martin, *Miniatures from the Period of Timur in a Ms. of the Poems of Sultan Aḥmad Jalair* (Vienna 1936); D. E. Klimburg-Salter, 'A Sufi Theme in Persian Painting: the Divan of Sultan Ahmad Galair in the Freer Galery of Art, Washington, D.C.', *Kunst des Orients*, vol. 11, nos. 1-2 (1976-77), pp. 43-84.

correspondence carried on in verse between Jahān-shāh Qara-quyunlu and his son Pīr-Būdāq, comes to mind.[1] Even in non-Persian-speaking lands, Persian literary models were widely preferred, as E. Yarshater noted:

> In the vast territory stretching from Asia Minor to Turkestan and to Bengal, poetry employed the same outlook, literary conventions, forms, metres, rhyming patterns, and above all the same imagery. The choice of language was an accident of birth, habitat, patronage, or predilection, but the models for it were and continued to be Persian.[2]

Elsewhere, Prof. Yarshater points out that "Sufism developed in all Muslim lands, but its literary expression reached its zenith in the countries located within the sphere of Persian cultural influence."[3] On both the contemplative disciplines and the literary forms of Sufism, as A. Schimmel has noted, Persian also had an overwhelming influence.[4] The main spiritual themes of languages such as Kurdish, Baluchi, Simnani, as S.H. Nasr and J. Matini have shown, "remains close to the themes found in Persian Sufi literatures."[5]

In respect to Turko-Persian culture, Victoria Holbrook in this volume (chap. 3) emphasizes that Persian remained the sacred language of the Mevlevi order, that an Ottoman literary Persian was developed and a Mevlevi spoken Persian even survived into the twentieth century. (The first Turkish translation of the *Mathnawī* was not produced until the eighteenth century.) Although in the sphere of Sufi philosophy, the school of the Andalusian sage, Ibn 'Arabī, prevailed over that of the Persian, Suhrawardī, the Master of Illuminative Wisdom, the majority of the well-known commentators on Ibn 'Arabī's works, especially his *Fuṣūṣ al-ḥikam*, were Persians.[6]

To summarize then, Iranian Islam and Persianate Sufism might best be viewed as separate yet inextricably linked tableaux of a single cultural mural. The 'New Persian' language that developed under the Persian Sāmānid dynasty (reg. 262/875-388/998), which contained a composite vocabulary of Middle Persian or Pahlavi, and Arabic, and after a few decades, became the main administrative and literary language of Central Asia and Transoxiana, soon rivalled Arabic in importance, and subsequently became the lingua franca of all Middle Eastern high culture. The simultaneous rise of Iranian Islam and Persianate Sufism in the fourth/tenth centuries and their socio-political co-development over the succeeding centuries is the most salient (if not the most important) historical feature in Islamic cultural history.

---

1. See Dawlatshāh's *Tadhkirat al-shu'arā*, ed. M. 'Abbāsī (Tehran: Kitābfurūshī Bārānī 1337 A.Hsh.), pp. 518-523; also cf. V. Minorsky, 'Jihān-shāh Qara-qoyunlu and His Poetry' in *Medieval Iran and its Neighbours* (Variorum Reprints, no. xii; London 1982), pp. 271-97.
2. E. Yarshater, 'Persian Poetry in the Timurid and Safavid Periods' in *The Cambridge History of Iran* (Cambridge University Press 1986), vol. 6, p. 979.
3. 'The Development of Iranian Literatures', in (ed.) E. Yarshater, *Persian Literature* (New York: Persian Heritage Foundation 1988), p. 23.
4. See her 'Mystical Poetry in the Vernacular' in *As Through a Veil*, pp. 135-69.
5. See S.H. Nasr & J. Matini, 'Persian Literature' in *Islamic Spirituality II* (New York: Crossroads 1991), p. 347.
6. See Muḥsin Jahāngīrī, *Muḥyī al-Dīn ibn 'Arabī: Chihra-yi barjasta-yi 'irfān-i islāmī* (Tehran 1980), p. 422 and S.H. Nasr's 'Introduction' above.

In the following section, the spiritual background of Mongol and Timurid politics is examined, followed by a study (section V) of the twelfth and thirteenth-century renaissance of Sufism in Persia. The final section, devoted to Sufism as the common ground of Iranian Islam, elaborates and brings to a close our discussion begun above.

IV. THE POLITICS OF PERSIANATE SUFI CULTURE IN THE IL-KHANID AND TIMURID PERIODS

If the formulation of Sufi metaphysics in Persian began in the twelfth century with the writings of 'Ayn al-Quḍāt Hamadānī (executed 525/1131) and Shihab al-Dīn Yaḥyā Suhrawardī (executed 587/1191)[1] this development owes a great deal to the patronage of a branch of the Saljuqs of Asia Minor (470/1077-707/1307), who actively supported Persian culture and *adab* and introduced Persian as the literary and administrative language in Anatolia.[2] Yet the actual reasons for the rise and ascendancy of the Persian over the Arabic language are hard to ascertain. There are the linguistic explanations advanced by Hodgson, that "Persian poetry is more varied in content than Arabic"[3] and hence easier to translate and more susceptible to cultural transference; and by Frye: that, as the English language which is rich in vocabulary because it has a double source for words (Latin, French and a German basis), so "the New Persian langauge...draws on Arabic as well as its own Iranian base....Arabic provided the catalyst to make a world literature in New Persian...-whereas the Persians gave their energies to many facets of culture, the Arabs concentrated on the spoken word."[4] There are also more historical reasons adduced by Ibn Khaldun (d. 808/1406), the founder of Islamic sociology and himself of Sufi affiliation,[5] who (basing his view on a saying ascribed to the Prophet: "If wisdom were to be found in the Pleiades, the Persians would find it there") remarks how the vast majority the great scholars of *ḥadith,* jurists, Koranic exegetes, speculative theologians, philosophers, and natural historians in the history of Islam were, from its first generation, of Persian descent.[6]

Hodgson describes the florescence of Persian literary culture in the twelfth century as representing "a new overall cultural orientation within Islamdom," transcending the realm of mere literary influences. While "Arabic held its own as the primary language of the religious disciplines and even, largely, of natural science and philosophy,

> Persian became, in an increasingly large part of Islamdom, the language of polite culture; it even invaded the realm of scholarship with increasing effect. While Arabic remained the language of science and religious scholarship... Persian became in

1. See S.H. Nasr & J. Matini, 'Persian Literature' in *Islamic Spirituality II*, p. 336.
2. Ehsan Yarshater, *Cambridge History of Iran,* vol. 6, p. 978.
3. *Op.cit.*, II, pp. 296.
4. Frye, *op. cit.*, p. 168.
5. See Stephen Casewit, 'The Mystical Side of the *Muqaddimah:* Ibn Khaldun's View of Sufism', *Islamic Quarterly*, vol. 29, no. 3 (1985), pp. 183.
6. F. Rosenthal (trans.), Ibn Khaldun, *The Muqaddimah* (New York 1958), III, pp. 311-15. Cf. Frye, *op. cit.*, p. 150.

> wide areas the language of polite intercourse and poetry... Arabic during this period continued to be a major literary tongue, but it was increasingly restricted as to the area where cultivated circles used it for *belles-lettres;* even in the Fertile Crescent some rulers, notably in Iraq, eventually preferred Persian.[1]

Sufism in its Persianate form was to develop into a culture unto itself; from its inception it exerted a civilizing and "democratizing"[2] influence upon both the fanatics and the bloodthirsty tyrants of its times. It was ultimately through the cultivation of Sufism that the Persian soul managed to survive the Mongol holocaust. "It was the wide vogue of mysticism, far more than formal theology, that enabled Islam to survive this appalling catastrophe," pronounced A.J. Arberry. The spiritual disciplines developed by the Sufi mystics and

> the hope and realization of experiencing the love of God, sustained the men's hearts and souls through the senseless butchery and insane devastations of the terrible thirteenth century. By then the political device which had contrived, though in decreasing effectiveness, the unity of Islam, the Baghdad caliphate, vanished in the holocaust; it was replaced by a less spectacular but in the end more enduring bond, the worldwide network of the Sufi brotherhoods.[3]

The Sufis—the Kubrāwiyya in particular—generally considered the Mongol invasion of Khwārazm in the years 615/1218-620/1223, ultimately resulting in ninety years of rule by non-Muslim 'infidels', as due in part to the misbehaviour shown by previous Muslim rulers towards the 'Friends of God'. In line with the Sufis' conception of the sovereignty *(dawlat)* of the worldly ruler as being subject to the spiritual authority *(wilāyat)* of the saints,[4] Nūr al-Dīn Isfarāyinī (639/1242—717/1317) believed, for instance, that the execution of Majd al-Dīn Baghdādī (d. 616/1219) at the hands of the Shāh of Khwārazm, Muḥammad ibn Tikish, was the true cause of the Mongol holocaust. He interpreted the destruction of the kingdom of Khwārazm, as a "summons issued from the court of Divine Grandeur to the *Simurgh* of Kingship *(salṭānat)* to fly from the blessed branch of Islam and to alight on the cursed tree of Infidelity *(kufr)*."[5] This opinion held by many Sufis, that temporal powers make secret obeisance to the spiritual hierarchy, and that the true imperial court was in fact, the *khānaqāh,* was also buttressed by scriptural references which lent their outlook credence.[6] This mystical point of (over-) view

---

1. Hodgson, *op. cit.*, II, pp. 293-94, 307.
2. The term is used here by Y.E. Bertels (*Taṣawwuf u adabiyāt-i taṣawwuf;* translated into Persian by S. Izadi [Tehran 1976], p. 46), in reference to mediæval Persian Sufism.
3. A.J. Arberry, *Aspects of Islamic Civilization* (Ann Arbor: University of Michigan Press 1967), p. 16.
4. According to Simon Digby, "The territorial *wilāyat* of the Sufi shaykh was considered as having a direct influence on the political events and material destiny of the realm over which it was exercised....The corollary of the belief that an offence against a Sufi shaykh will lead to the downfall of a ruler, is the belief that such shaykhs also have had the power to bestow kingship upon individuals whom they encountered, or to foresee the attainment of a throne by such men." – 'The Sufi Shaykh and the Sultan: A Conflict of Claims to Authority in Medieval India' in *Iran: Journal of the British Institute of Persian Studies,* vol. 28 (1990), pp. 71, 75.
5. Cited by H. Landolt, *Nuruddin Isfarayini: Le Revelateur des Mysteries* (Paris: Verdier 1986), French introduction, p. 34.
6. E.g."There is no power beyond God's power" and "The hand of God is above their hands" [Koran XLVIII 10].

was reiterated in Rumi's *Mathnawī,*[1] while verses such as the following by Ḥāfiẓ are often interpreted in the same sense by the Sufis:

bar dar-i maykada rindān-i qalandar bāshand
kay sitānand u dahand afsar-i shāhanshāhī[2]

Around the tavern door
the wild, the vigilant swarm
They withdraw and they bestow
the diadems of Empire.

***

qadam mana ba kharābāt juz ba sharṭ-i adab
ki sākanān-i darash maḥramān-i pādishahand.[3]

Without manners never attempt to step
within the tavern of ruin,
for the residents of its court
are confidants of kings.

However, such explanations offer small consolation before the utter horror and terror of the Mongol conquests, which brought genocide and a scorched earth policy; recent scholars have confirmed the possibility of a ninety-percent extermination rate among the Persian populace of Khurasan.[4] Chingiz Khān's catastrophic invasion of northern Iran, for instance, was accompanied by the systematic extermination of the civilian population of all its major towns (Balkh, Marv, Nishapur, Herat, Tus, Ray, Qazwin, Hamadan, Ardabil, etc.).[5] These ravages by both Mongol and later, Timurid, tyrants, whose capricious wills wreaked havoc with the feudal economy of mediaeval Iran, transforming it into a slave economy[6]—brought lasting destruction. A constant state of insecurity, violence, internal warfare, banditry on the highways and the pillaging of private property by state officials, prevailed in the thirteenth and fourteenth centuries.[7] The Mongol tax collectors produced unprecedented economic distress, previously free peasants—now serfs and slaves—being forced to keep their dwellings in deliberate dilapidation lest they risk a visit from a Mongol dignitary whose very presence entailed a tax *(nūzūl).*[8] In the words of a contemporary Iranian scholar, ʻAli Rajāʻi Bokhārā'i, (penned by way of exposition of the political backdrop of the mystical ambience sustaining the poetry of Ḥāfiẓ during this period in Persia):

1. *Mathnawī-yi maʻnawī,* (ed.) R.A. Nicholson, V: 2341.
2. *Diwān-i Ḥāfiẓ,* edited by P. Nātil-Khānlarī (Tehran 1359 A.Hsh.), p. 974.
3. *Diwān-i Ḥāfiẓ,* edited Nātil-Khānlarī, p. 408.
4. I. P. Petrushevsky ('The Consequences of the Mongol Invasion' in *The Cambridge History of Iran*, vol. 5, pp. 484-88) discusses the Mongol massacres in Tabaristan (Mazandaran) and Khurasan in great detail.
5. *Ibid.*
6. A. Bausani, *The Persians: From the Earliest Days to the Twentieth century,* translated by J. Donne (London 1971), p. 116; Ghanī, *op. cit.*, pp. 497-99.
7. See Anjawī Shirāzī (ed.), *Divān-i Shams al-Dīn Muḥammad Ḥāfiẓ* (Shiraz 1982), introduction, p. 85ff.
8. Bausani, *The Persians,* p. 115.

> The Persian writer of the twelfth and especially the thirteenth century has witnessed his house burned down, his city destroyed, his beloved relatives murdered and his independence eradicated. Foreigners control his possessions, his property, his very being. In such circumstances, how can one sing songs of joy or compose rhapsodies, how should the world be thought a happy abode or life seem sweet? Thus the poetry of this period and the following century [eighth Islamic/fourteenth Christian century]—composed, as it was, by writers subjected to savage marauding Mongols and plundering Turks—is little more than an attempt to offer condolences to the reader.[1]

Nonetheless, Sufism paradoxically survived during this gloomy period – in fact, not only survived, but blossomed, becoming

> the sole force capable of saving the soul of the Iranian populace, casting a ray of hope and courage into the traumatized hearts of the inhabitants of mediæval Persia. For the Sufi masters promised the populace—in the safety of Sufism—liberation from the aggravation of their corrupt contemporaries, offering as companions individuals of refined and sensitive feelings, instead of blackguards and tyrants. They allowed their followers to pass their days without trouble in their *khānaqāhs*, engaged in musical concerts and dance, states of rapture and spiritual feelings.[2]

Thus, in spite of anxiety, despair, apathy, political corruption and psychological terror, the Mongol rule of Persia did have compensations. In terms of the arts, Persian miniature painting flourished in the ateliers of Shiraz, Baghdad, and Tabriz almost without any break of style,[3] while in Iraq and Azerbaijan under the patronage of the Jalāyirid Mongol princes (1336-1410) Persian miniature painting entered its formative period. In calligraphy, the *ta'liq* style which had been developed by the Tabrizi master, Mīr 'Alī (d. 1420), in the fourteenth century was transformed into the *nasta'līq* script under later Timurid patronage in Herat,[4] while Persian Sufi poetry, in particular in its *mathnawī* and *ghazal* form, realized its greatest perfection in the poetry of Sa'dī and Ḥāfiẓ.[5]

If terrorism was the norm in political life during the thirteenth century, in the realm of ideas there was a "greater freedom of speech and thought than in Seljuq times while open expression of ideas and divergent religious beliefs prevailed."[6] Insofar as the Mongols espoused Buddhism and made it the official creed in the lands they ruled (at least from 1221-1295), Muslims were forced to tolerate differences of religious belief, leading among other factors, to the rise in the popularity of Sufism—to which tolerance is second-nature.

---

1. *Farhang-i ash'ār-i Ḥāfiẓ*, pp. 454-55.
2. *Ibid.*
3. *Ibid.*, pp. 116-17. See also L. Binyon, J.V.S. Wilkinson & B. Gray, *Persian Miniature Painting* (New York: Dover Books reprt., 1971), p. 21. According to Sussan Babaie and M.L. Swietochowski (*Persian Drawings in the Metropolitan Museum of Art* [New York 1989], p. 3), "The earliest substantial number of Persian drawings on paper that have survived date from the second half of the fourteenth century, the period associated with Muzaffarid and Jalayrīd rule in Iran."
4. A. Schimmel, 'Poetry and Calligraphy: Some Thoughts about their Interrelation in Persian Culture', in R. Ettinghausen & E. Yarshater (eds.), *Highlights of Persian Art* (Colorado: Westview Press 1979), p. 196.
5. J. Rypka, 'Poets & Prose Writers of the Late Saljuq and Mongol Periods' in *The Cambridge History of Iran*, vol. 5, p. 555.
6. 'Azīz-i Nasafī, *Zubdat al-ḥaqā'iq*, edited by Ḥ. Nāsirī (Terhan 1985), introduction, p. 13.

One important aspect of the Mongol conquest is that for the first time Persia and other large areas of the Muslim world found themselves governed, at least from 1221 to 1295, that is to say for three generations, by non-Muslim rulers, pagan shamanists or Buddhists who ignored differences of religious belief among their subjects, who used Christian auxiliaries, and who employed Jewish ministers alongside administrators from the Far East.[1]

In the first volume of his *Tārīkh-i jahāngushā'i*, 'Aṭā Malik Juwaynī states that Chingiz Khān followed no particular religion, opposing all religious bias towards both paganism and monotheism.[2] This policy provided very favorable conditions for Sufi mysticism and an original 'Islamic transcendentalism' to emerge and blossom. For the above reasons, during most of the thirteenth century under Mongol rule, when Persia was administered by non-Muslims, the originality of Sufism as the quintessential Islamic expression transcending the sectarian distinctions of Sunnism and Shi'ism and demonstrating its capacity for inter-faith communication, became apparent. The Sufi concept of the Transcendent Unity of Religions (within the framework of Islamic *tawḥid)* permits, for example, understanding and toleration of the doctrines of Hindu Advaita Vedanta, Jewish Cabbalism, Christian mysticism and Zen Buddhism—providing greater possibilities for a universal expression than exists when exoteric Islam dominates.[3]

V. THE TWELFTH & THIRTEENTH-CENTURY REVIVAL OF SUFISM

"The twelfth century was a great age, probably the culminating age, of religious poetry." So wrote Charles Haskins, one of the foremost scholars of mediæval history concerning the revival of the Latin mystical tradition in the so-called European 'Dark Ages' in his study of *The Renaissance of the 12th Century*[4] – remarks which appear remarkably relevant to Islamic civilization during this period as well. William Chittick in this volume and Victor Danner, elsewhere, have described this religious revival as derivative in part from two of the many major prodigies among Sufi poets of this period, namely Ibn 'Arabī and Rumi:

> The philosohical mysticism of Ibn 'Arabī and the poetical mysticism of Rūmī are but two of the different genres used by thirteenth-century Sufism to effect a spiritual reanimation of Islam that would be the literary counterparts to the eruption of Sufi oreder all over the face of the Islamic world... In more ways than one, it is possible to speak of the Sufi literary and spiritual fruits of the thirteenth century as forming, in their ensemble, a veritable spiritual message that would govern the general outlook of Islamic civilization and affect all facets of society for centuries.
>
> For the Islamic faith, the definitive ascendancy of thirteenth-century Sufism, with its gnostic and devotional spirituality that included all aspirations, kept the door of spiritual realization open to its seekers for centuries, right into the twentieth century. It had no need to hide the Path under a thicket of dissimulative practices and teachings. The Caliphs, the sultans, the *amīrs*, and even many of the religious chiefs of the later States, often had their own Sufi teachers whom they consulted regularly. The

1. Bausani, *The Persians*, p. 117.
2. See Ḥ Nāṣirī, *op. cit.*, p. 14.
3. See S.H. Nasr, 'Islam and the Encounter of Religions' in *Sufi Essays* (London 1972), pp. 123-51.
4. (New York: World Publishing Company 1961), p. 166.

Path was everywhere in evidence; the many Sufi orders had millions of adherents coming from all ranks of society.[1]

These broad-based observations are further substantiated by the observations of other scholars, such as J.S. Trimingham, who describes the two-century period prior to the Safavid regime in Persia as

> a time of ferment, crucial for the future of Islam in the region. The immediate consequences of the Mongol conquests had been the displacement of Islam as the state religion throughout the region. Islam had now to prove itself and accommodate itself to non-Muslm rulers, shamanist, Buddhist, or crypto-Christian. It was a time pregnant with possibilities, and the outcome was the triumph of Islam as the dominant religion of Central Asia. Sufism's role was of considerable significance... It is significant that two of the first Mongol princes to adopt Islam, Berke of the Golden Horde and Ghāzān of Tabriz, sought out a Sufi rather than a Sunnī *'alīm* before whom to make their public declaration of adhesion to Islam.[2]

The conversion of the Mongol ruler Berke (reg. 1257-67) to Islam was officiated by the Kubrāwī master, Sayf al-Dīn Bākharzī;[3] that of Ghāzān Khān in 694/1295 was presided over by another Kubrāwī Shaykh, Ṣadr al-Dīn Ibrāhīm Ḥamūya. A recent study of the latter ceremony demonstrates than Ghāzān not only embraced Islam but was also initiated into Sufism on this occasion, demonstrating the "clear preference among the Mongols for Sufism rather than the more formal orthodox *madhhabs,* due in part to various areas of similarity between Shamanist and Sufi rituals and ideas."[4] This predilection of Mongol princes for Sufi rather than purely exoteric and legalistic religiosity has been established by H. Landolt's monograph on the Kubrāwī master Nūr al-Dīn Isfarāyinī.[5] Sufi affiliations of the Mongol Īl-Khān Öljeitü (reg. 1304-1316) appear in his reconstruction of the tomb of Bāyazīd Bisṭāmī[6] and his naming of three sons after this Sufi saint: Bisṭām, Bāyazīd, and Ṭayfur.

One may also see how deeply the Iranian culture of the period was steeped in mysticism by recalling the tale related by Sayyid 'Alī Hamadānī[7] about Isfarāyinī's illustrious disciple 'Alā' al-Dawla Simnānī (659/1261-736/1326) presiding over a convocation of four hundred scholars assembled by Öljeitü Khān. Here, and elsewhere in his biography Simnānī appears in the history of his day as the scholar who 'held the King's ear', the Sufi master most heeded by the Tartar state. According to

---

1. *The Islamic Tradition*, pp. 99-100.
2. *The Sufi Orders in Islam*, pp. 90-91.
3. See the article by M.I. Waley in the present volume on Bākharzī's grandson, Yaḥyā, in the present volume (chap. 5).
4. C. Melville, *'Pādishāh-i Islām:* the conversion of Sultan Maḥmūd Ghāzān Khān', in (ed.) C. Melville, *Pembroke Papers* (Persian & Islamic Studies in Honour of P.W. Avery), I (Cambridge 1990), p. 168. Melville furthermore notes that Ghāzān Khān was obliged to wear wool *(ṣūf)* during his conversion ceremony and that this "apparently confirms the Sufi affiliations of Ṣadr al-Dīn and suggests that Ghāzān was himself initiated as a Sufi."
5. See 'Le milieu baghdādien: politique et religion' in H. Landolt, *Nūruddīn Isfarāyinī: Le Révélateur des Mystères (Kāshif al-Asrār)* (Paris: Verdier 1986), 'Étude Préliminaire', pp. 31-36.
6. *Ibid.*
7. Recounted by M. Molé, 'Les Kubrawiya entre sunnisme et shiisme aux huitième et neuvième siècles de l'hégire', *Revue des études islamiques,* 29 (1961), pp. 112-13.

the *Ḥabīb al-siyar,* Öljeitü's successor to the Mongol throne, Sultan Abū Sa'īd, on visiting Simnānī, "after rising to pay his respects, sat the Shaykh beside him, and then knelt respectfully before him."[1] It is also interesting to note that the post of 'Shaykh al-Islām', archbishop or supreme authority in matters pertaining to the religious law, was held in Northern India from the thirteenth century down to Mughal times by the Sufi masters,[2] reflecting the general political position of the Sufi masters in their post of *Shaykh al-shiyukh* in mediæval Muslim Persia.[3]

Sufism's centrality in late mediaeval Persian culture is also reflected in the literary history of the period, as Ehsan Yarshater notes:

> What is clearly evident, however, is that mystical concepts, Sufi theoretical constructs and the theosophical doctrine of dervishhood *(mashrab-i darwīshī)* permeated the entire socio-cultural milieu, so that one rarely encounters a poet or scholar in the annals of the age who did not 'relish the taste of Sufi theosophy' or who had not traveled a few steps along the Sufi Path.[4]

For this reason Hodgson characterizes Sufism during this period as "the most important inward religious experience in the region from Nile to Oxus,"[5] while S.H. Nasr describes Sufism as "the most important spiritual force to be reckoned with in studying the background of the Safavid period."[6] During the later part of what Hodgson describes as the "Earlier Middle Period [945-1258]," the most significant period of activity in the development of Sufism occurred:

> The *'ulamā'* scholars, who had been wary of the early Sufism of an elite, were mostly persuaded by the early twelfth century to accept the new Sufism of the masses....Then with their acceptance, around the latter part of the twelfth century the reorganization of Sufism was completed with the establishment of formal Sufi brotherhoods or orders *(ṭarīqah)*....The distinctive marks of the new Sufism were two: its organization into these formal 'orders' and its concentration on a formal method of mystical worship, the *dhikr.*[7]

Thus, gradually, Sufism became the dominant cultural and intellectual current during the thirteenth to fifteenth centuries. By the end of the period, "the most important religious issues were no longer fought out, for the most part, between schools of *fiqh* or kalām but rather within and between differing *ṭarīqa* orders. Often it was the same perennial human issues that were being debated, only now cast in Sufi terms."[8] "It was reserved for the thirteenth century," notes Victor Danner, "to witness the explosive nature of Sufism in the century-long manifestations

1. See the introduction by Dhabīḥullāh Ṣafā to 'Abd al-Rafī' Ḥaqīqat (ed.) *Divān-i kāmil-i ash'ār-i fārsī wa 'arabī-yi 'Alā' al-Dawla Simnānī* (Tehran 1985), p. 15. On the Mongols' patronage of Sufism, see Aḥmad Rajā'ī's lengthy discussion (*Farhang-i ash'ār-i Ḥāfiẓ*, pp. 465-68) where he observes that "the strongest patrons of the eighth [fourteenth]-century Sufis were the Īl-Khānid Mongols."
2. See Aziz Ahmad, 'The Sufi and the Sultan in Pre-Mughal Muslim India', *Der Islam* (1963), pp. 142-43.
3. Cf. Ghanī, *op. cit.*, p. 500 and *Farhang-i ash'ār-i Ḥāfiẓ*, p. 456.
4. *Shi'r-i fārsī dar 'ahd-i Shāh Rukh*, p. 19.
5. Ibid.
6. *The Cambridge History of Iran*, vol. 6, p. 658.
7. *The Venture of Islam*, II, p. 211.
8. *Ibid.*, II, p. 455.

of its spiritual and intellectual vitality. From then on, the term *ṭarīqah* would refer simultaneously to the mystical Way in general and to the specific Sufi orders in particular."[1]

The historical rise of Sufism to a position of dominance in mediæval Persian religious culture during the twelfth century has also been otherwise documented by Marshall Hodgson who describes this renaissance as "a reorientation of the piety of Islam on the basis of Sufism."[2] The role of Abū Ḥamīd Muḥammad al-Ghazzālī (450/1058–505/1111) in this renaissance was central, insofar as he "combined a mastery of the teachings of the *'ulamā'* scholars on *Sharī'ah* and kalām with a respect for the independent wisdom of the Sufi mystics." Thus Ghazzālī's teachings

> helped to make Sufism acceptable to the *'ulamā'* themselves. By the twelfth century it was a recognized part of religious life and even of religious *'ilm* knowledge. Thus gradually Sufism, from being one form of piety among others, and by no means the most accepted one either officially or popularly, came to dominate religious life not only within the Jamā'ī-Sunnī fold, but to a lesser extent even among Shī'īs.
>
> From this point on, Islam presented persistently two faces: one, *Sharī'ah*-minded, concerned with outward, socially cognizable behavior; the other mystical-minded, concerned with the inward, personal life of the individual, accepted as their care by the Sufi *pīrs*. Often the same religious leader was at once *pīr* and *Shar'ī* scholar, or at least took both sides of Islam very seriously; just as most of the Muslim public respected and took guidance from both *pīrs* and *'ulamā'*.[3]

In the following section some of the socio-cultural and psychological factors which provoked this rise of Sufism are examined, and concluding reflections upon the relation, in both an essential and historical sense, of Persianate Sufism to Iranian Islam are provided.

VI. SUFISM: IRANIAN ISLAM'S COMMON GROUND

Sufism and the Persian Psyche

There are a number of reasons why in the twelfth and thirteenth centuries what appeared as the Persian fusion of Islam into Sufism, or, as Hodgson expressed it above, "the reorientation of the piety of Islam on the basis of Sufism," was accomplished: why Islam, in its Persianate milieu, came to be conceived of in primarily mystical terms. How Sufism, with its exotic symbolism, esoteric disciplines, its highly refined aesthetics and arcane philosophy – came to dominate the religious conscience and popular piety of the entire Islamic world is difficult (for modern man, at least) to understand. The mystical perspective is particularly alien to the present age – we equate science and knowledge with a dispassionate 'objective' analysis of particular 'facts', find our intellectual salvation in a bland business-like

---

1. The Islamic Tradition, p. 96.
2. *The Venture of Islam*, II, p. 203.
3. *Ibid.*

pursuit of secular 'truths', and are extremely uncomfortable in discovering the presence of an unquantifiable ecstasy or beauty in our psychologies.[1]

Yet the existence of certain *psychological* factors and causes underlying the predominance of mysticism in the religious piety of the period is possible to demonstrate. (Some of the diverse *socio-cultural* factors stimulating the rise of Sufism to the foreground of mediaeval Persian society—a society which bears many striking resemblances to Renaissance Italy during the same period[2]—are discussed below). However, the specifically psychological factors appear to be principally three:

1. The legalistic and moralistic values espoused by the *Sharī'a*-centered *'ulamā'* of the period tended to downgrade basic intellectual and academic freedoms, recovery of which was only possible in another religious guise. Sufism here filled the vacuum: since (in M. Hodgson's words) "mystical forms and language can sanction elements of religious life downgraded by a strongly kerygmatic approach."[3] Research by many modern Iranian writers, such as Sa'īdī Sīrjānī, into the history of this period, testifies to the validity of Hodgson's thesis.

2. Reliance on mystical experiences and metaphysical speculation for the purposes of science is forbidden only when human experience and self-knowledge is based on research into purely material phenomena. However, when the psycho-sociological mores of a society, such as those of the mediæval Islamic *umma,* are non-material—condoning religious sentiments as sources of information—a Sufi orientation easily becomes 'rational'. Hence, "Mystical experiences... however private they still remain, take on comprehensive implications [and] become conscious objects of cultivation. If such experiences carry authority and are found relevant to our ordinary course of living—the decisive criterion of mysticism from a historical viewpoint—then their consequences will be unpredictable and may invade any sphere of human activity. Once their validity is accepted, they must determine all of life."[4] Here then is the reason why philosophy in mediæval Persia became wedded irrevocably to Sufism:[5] rationality combining with visionary experience *(shuhūd)* both in the 'Oriental Theosophy' of Suhrawardī[6] and in the transcendental theomonism of Ibn 'Arabī.

3. However, the prime psychological cause of the efflorescence of Sufism during the mediæval period might be posited as what 'Abd al-Ḥusayn Zarrīnkūb describes as an innate predisposition to mysticism in the Persian psyche:[7] or what H. Corbin

---

1. Cf. Henry Corbin, 'The Configuration of the Temple of the Ka'bah', part 4: 'Potestas clavium' in *Temple and Contemplation,* trans. Phillip & Liadain Sherrard, (London: KPI 1986), pp. 253-62.
2. Cf. *The Venture of Islam,* II, p. 372.
3. *The Venture of Islam,* II, pp. 204-5.
4. *Ibid.* Cf .Qāsim Ghanī's observations, *Baḥth dar āthār...Ḥāfiẓ,* II, p. 501; as well as Zarrīnkūb's study of Al-Ghazzālī, *Farār az madrasa* (Tehran: Amīr Kabīr 1364 A.Hsh.), p. 96.
5. See the provocative discussion of the relationship between philosophy and Sufism in mediæval Persia by S.H. Nasr, 'Rābaṭa-yi bayn-i taṣawwuf wa falsafa dar farhang-i Irān', *Iran Nameh,* vol. 1, no. 1 (1982), pp. 46-56.
6. See H. Corbin (traduction et notes), *Shihāboddīn Yaḥya Sohravardī: Le Livre de la Sagesse Orientale (Kitāb Ḥikmat al-Ishrāq)* (Paris: Éditions Verdier 1986).
7. *Justujū-yi dar taṣawwuf-i Irān,* pp. 1-29.

has called "le génie iranien...la vocation imprescriptible de l'âme iranienne."[1] This thesis is not, I think, merely a few orientalists' subjective and personal sentiment, but represents the opinion of a wide spectrum of Islamicists, literary historians,[2] religionists[3] and historians.[4]

Socio-cultural Causes of the Mediæval Sufi Renaissance

Hodgson describes *ṭarīqa* Sufism as providing "a wide field of free development for the exceptional individual" and as "a vehicle for expressing every aspect of popular piety within Islam."[5] This popular outreach of Sufism, based on its tolerant blend of popular spirituality and "Sunni *Sharī'ah*-mindedness"[6] came to provide the moral support for the *madrasa* colleges and became, in Hodgson's words, "a mainstay of the international social order."[7] The first socio-cultural factor by means of which Sufism broadened its appeal to the masses, which was to be become, in fact, the hallmark of the *ṭarīqas*, was, in fact, tolerance.

1. Tolerance

'Tolerance' was a central characteristic of Persian mysticism during the 13th-15th centuries, as Hodgson observes:

> The Sufis tended to be as naturally tolerant of local differences as the *Shar'ī 'ulamā'* tended to be intolerant. The *'ulamā'* had to concentrate on matters of external conformity, as dictated by the *Sharī'ah*, in order to maintain the legal and institutional framework for social unity...For the Sufis, on the contrary, externals were secondary. For many of them, especially by the Earlier Middle Period, even the difference between Islam and other cultural traditions such as Christianity was of secondary importance in principle; of still less moment were the various differences in social custom within the community of Muḥammad. What mattered was the inner disposition of the heart to God.[8]

---

1. See *En Islam iranien*, I, p. x, where Corbin describes this genius as "Aptitude...à conjoindre la recherche philosophique et l'expérience mystique..."
2. Cf. A. Schimmel, 'Tiny Mirrors of Divine Beauty: Classical Persian Mystical Poetry', *As Through a Veil*, pp. 49-55. Cf. M. Ṭawḥīdīpūr's introduction to Jāmī's *Nafāḥāt al-uns* (Tehran 1964).
3. Cf. S.H. Nasr, 'Sacred Art in Persian Culture', *Islamic Art & Spirituality* (Suffolk: Golgonooza Press, 1987), pp. 64-83; A. Coomaraswamy, 'Note on the Philosophy of Persian Art', *Coomaraswamy: Selected Papers on Traditional Art and Symbolism*, vol. 1, Bolligen Series 89 (Princeton University Press 1977), pp. 260-65; Daryush Shayegan, *Henry Corbin: La topographie spirituelle de l'Islam iranien* (Paris: Éditions de la Différence 1991), p. 24.
4. Cf. R. Frye, *The Golden Age of Persia*, p. 234. Thus B.S. Amoretti argues (in reference to the politicalization of the *pīr/murīd* relationship) that during 9th/15th century "the particular kind of religious feeling permeating, with its longing for renewal, the conscience of the Iranian Islamic world at that time, had as its essential component a certain type of sufism." 'Religion in the Timurid and Safavid Periods', *Cambridge History of Iran*, vol. 6, p. 631.
5. *The Venture of Islam*, II, p. 218.
6. *Ibid.*
7. *Ibid.*, II, p. 220.
8. *Ibid.* However, A. Rajā'ī is of the opinion that the Sufi doctrine of religious tolerance had its social origins in the popular disgust felt by Persians for the both the Crusades and internal sectarian intracreedal fighting of Muslim theologians. *op.cit.*, p. 455.

The same scholar goes on to note that despite the fact that the "*Sharī'ah* Law afforded legitimatization on a universal basis, on the assumption that nothing mattered legally but relations between individuals, equal anywhere in the world," this theoretical egalitarianism was rarely put to practice since it was the local grouping (class-structures, guilds, etc.) which ultimately determined a Muslim's status. Sufism was thus a leaven which molded nobles and commoners together, providing the necessary ethical integrity for the Muslim community to survive. "Persian Sufism," states H. Landolt, "is animated essentially in its practice as well in its theory, by something which must be called its poetic spirit, a spiritual liberty whose corollary is the absence of all rigorous legalism."[1] Hodgson believed that it was the broad-mindedness and "the spiritual authority of the Sufi *pīr*s and the ethic they preached [which] proved able to relate the conscience of ordinary men to the institutions they needed." Furthermore, Sufism became a kind of mediæval 'counter-culture':

> The Sufi tie at once deepened the local moral resources and tied them in to a system of brotherhoods in some way as universal as the old caliphal bureaucracy had been, which had disappeared. The refusal of some Sufis to permit any association with the *amīr*'s court served to underline the alternative social outlook. It was as if the court were carefully quarantined so as to minimize its influence. Thus Sufism supplemented the *Sharī'ah* as a principle of unity and order, offering the Muslims a sense of spiritual unity which came to be stronger than that provided by the remnant of the caliphate. They developed a picture of the world which united the whole *Dār al-Islām* under a comprehensive spiritual hierarchy of *pīrs*.[2]

Prof. Holbrook's study in this volume of the spiritual genealogy and ideals of the successive leaders of the order founded by Rumi illuminates the unique role which 'Mevlevi tolerance' (which she defines as "a relaxed attitude marked by acceptance of diversity in points of view and a more specific disregard, even an aggressive challenging of exclusive norms of behavior characteristic of establishment Muslim sensibilities") played in mediæval Seljuk and later Ottoman Anatolia. The Sufis' doctrine of tolerance is also exemplified in the literary motif of the *qalandar*, which, as Prof. de Bruijn's essay on this topos in the present volume demonstrates, made its first appearance in the early eleventh century. The *qalandar* motif is, in fact, an ancient feature in Persian Sufism, associated with the figures of Abū Sa'īd ibn Abi'l-Khayr (357/967-440/1049) and Aḥmad Ghazzālī (d. 520/1126), denoting the type of mystic, who, in Einstein's words, finds "solitary virtue better than ostentatious piety" and who seeks to find truthfulness *(ṣidq)* before God in his devotions by subjecting himself to public censure *(malāmat)* by purposely dissimulated antinomian behavior.[3] In the early thirteenth century, according to Prof. de Bruijn,[4] special *qalandar* Sufi Orders made their appearance with extremely tolerant rules and rites set aside for extravagant manifestations of the spiritual life. In general, tolerance and social egalitarianism earmarked the subsequent history of Sufism in

1. 'Two Types of Mystical Thought in Muslim Iran: An Essay on Suhrawardī *Shaykh al-Ishrāq* and 'Aynulquẓāt-i Hamadānī', *Muslim World*, vol. 68 (1978), p. 192.
2. *The Venture of Islam*, II, pp. 221-22.
3. See Javad Nurbakhsh, *Farhang-i Nūrbakhsh* (London 1364 A.Hsh.), vol. 6, p. 167, s.v. *qalandar*.
4. See chap. 2 below.

Asia Minor and Persia:

> The sufi movements... were characterized by a progressive socialization, the first consequence of which was access to the 'mystic path', open to those social classes who, because they were poor, were ready to accept any authority having the seal of religious legality, as opposed to the political reality which was proving more and more disappointing. The shaykhs to whom they had recourse appear to have represented a court of appeals for complaints, even when the only solution they could suggest was a disdainful liberation from worldly needs pending the arrival of better times. [1]

The philosophical mainstay of this religious tolerance was the doctrine of the 'unity of religions', analyzed by L. Lewisohn and R. Vassie in this volume (chap. 6). According to this doctrine all true religions represent diverse manifestations of One Being, their divergent principles being but 'forms' of Archetypal Meanings *(ma'ānī)* attired in the vestments of multiplicity.

Hodgson contrasts the persuasive power of the Sufi preachers with the dogmatic homiletics of the exoteric clergy, remarking how "the comprehensive humanity from which a Sufi could preach gave the Sufi tradition an often spectacular advantage.[2] ...The Sufi piety, tolerant of human weakness, did not generally separate itself from common beliefs and from the sensibilities of the common people; unlike the Manicheans, the Sufis were willing to accept as valid at least externally whatever religious notions they found among them."[3] On the other hand, this tolerance espoused by the Sufis did not obscure or 'water-down' its essentially Islamic character, as Danner emphasizes:

> Even when the Sufis are eclectic, drawing now from Neoplatonic or now from Hindu formulations... this eclecticism is organic and compatible with the integrity, or let us say the *ṭawḥīd*, of the Islamic revelation... It is more than likely that when Islam sees *ṭawḥīd* as underlying the different revelations given to the world, so that Islam is merely a reconfirmation of what was previously revealed, it is really of that ultimate, non-anthropomorphic Divine Unity, that is speaks, not of God in personal nature as Lord of the Creation, possessed of anthropomorphic aspects. The abstract, nontheistic Divine Unity permits the integration of Buddhism into the perennial message of *ṭawḥīd*. But that is a proposition that ordinary, exoteric Islam cannot make.[4]

This 'Sufi tolerance' is central to many of the essays by contributors to the present volume, in particular: V. Holbrook, L. Lewisohn, and R. Vassie.

2. *Anti-sectarianism*

Although there were admittedly 'dark chapters' in mediæval Persian Sufism (the cases of the Mar'ashī Shi'ite Order, the dervish founders of the Sarbidār movement, and Shi'ite Sufi militancy of Shāh Ismā'il I in the early 16th century clearly exemplifying perversions of the ideal), due to politicization of the master-disciple relationship, the general attitude of the mystics of the period towards the four orthodox

---

1. B.S. Amoretti, *The Cambridge History of Iran,* VI, p. 613. Cf. *Farhang-i ash'ār-i Ḥāfiẓ,* p. 457.
2. *The Venture of Islam,* II, p. 209.
3. *The Venture of Islam,* II, p. 207.
4. *The Islamic Tradition,* pp. 103, 107.

legal Islamic legal schools was anti-sectarian. For example, describing the sensibility of the Sufi poet, Qāsim-i Anwār (d. 837/1434) towards religious creed *(madhhab)*, the great Iranian scholar Sa'īd Nafīsī remarked:

> The Sufis essentially believed their doctrine to transcend the confession of a certain Sunni or Shi'ite creed. From the Sufi perspective, both Sunnis and Shi'ites—nay, even Muslims and non-Muslims—are to be considered equally. Sufis have always upheld the Principles *(uṣūl)* of Religion, paying scant heed to the Derivatives *(furū')* of Faith. For this reason, one finds that in the works of Qāsim-i Anwār the orthodox Sunni caliphs as well as the Shi'ite Imams, such as 'Alī, Ḥusayn, Ja'far al-Ṣādiq, are mentioned. Moreover, it may generally asserted that this honour, veneration and impartial consideration which all Persian Sufis accorded to both Sunni caliphs and Shi'ite Imāms alike in their compositions, is something very evident. It must be definitely recognized that Sufism is something more universal, or better said – more transcendent – than this sort of dualistic sectarian vision.[1]

3. Direct Experience (taḥqīq) versus Dogmatic Imitation (taqlīd)

The intellectual foundation of this mystical vision of Islam, as noted above, was indebted to Muḥammad Ghazzālī's revalorization of Sufism in the late eleventh century. Ghazzālī recognized that sectarian dogma must necessarily be complemented by the inwardness and inspiration of the doctrines found in Sufism.[2] "...Thus the Sufis were assigned a crucial role in supporting the historical Muslim community as a body, as well as in guiding personal lives."[3]

One reason for this was the open-minded attitude of the Persian Sufis, and their respect for genuine spiritual research *(taḥqīq)*: a virtue the philosophers shared with them. The Sufis' conviction that the truths of mystical vision *(kashf)* equalled, or at least paralleled, the certainty found by following the 'revelation-theology' of the scholastic jurisprudents, was shared by Peripatetic philosophers such as Avicenna (d. 428/1037) whose 'Treatise on Love' provided a speculative basis for the love-mysticism of 'Aṭṭār and Sanā'ī. Thus Avicenna stimulated the development of both theoretical (speculative) and practical (ecstatic) Sufism.[4] It should be emphasized that all mediaeval *'ulamā'*, Sufi and *faqīh* alike, supported the mystical doctrine of 'unveiling' *(kashf)* as a proper means of scientific knowledge or *'ilm*. Even scholars such as Ibn Taymiyya, firmly believed in the authority of mystical unveiling as a alternate source of learning alongside the study of the Koran and the pursuit of the Prophetic Sunna.[5]

Ghazzālī's demonstration of the complementarity of esoteric and exoteric knowledge, so that the latter no longer appeared to be in competition with the former, but rather as its valid and acceptable complement, was central to the devel-

---

1. *Kulliyyāt-i Qāsim-i Anwār*, ed. S. Nafīsī (Tehran 1958), p. 90.
2. Cf. A.J. Arberry, *Aspects of Islamic Civilization*, p. 16; *The Venture of Islam*, II, p. 188.
3. *The Venture of Islam*, II, p. 188..
4. See J.N. Bell, 'Avicenna's Treatise on Love and the Nonphilosophical Muslim Tradition', *Der Islam* (Bond 63, 1986) pp. 73-89; Furūzānfar, 'Abū 'Alī Sīnā wa taṣawwuf' in *Majmū'a-yi maqālāt wa ash'ār Badī' al-Zamān Furūzānfar*, pp. 310-15.
5. See Muhsin Mahdi, 'The Book and the Master as Poles of Cultural Change in Islam', p. 13; J. Michell, 'Ibn Taymiyya's *Sharḥ* on the *Futūḥ al-Ghayb* of 'Abd al-Qādir Jilanī', *Hamdard Islamicus*, vol. 4, no. 2 (1981), pp. 8-9.

opment of Islamic esotericism.[1] The late twelfth century's intellectual renaissance was generated, in part, from the increased metaphysical speculations on the part of Sufis, since "Sufism, especially the new intellectualizing expression of it, served more than any other movement to draw together all strands of intellectual life."[2]

Henry Corbin has demonstrated that the sources of the Ishrāqī philosophy of Suhrawardī can ultimately be traced to notes that Avicenna wrote on the margin of the so-called 'Theology of Aristotle'.[3] In these notes, Avicenna referred to a certain *ḥikmat mashriqiyya* or Eastern/Aurorial/Illuminative Wisdom: the very term which Suhrawardī, (whom Corbin described as "an irregular Sufi of no formal affiliation")[4] was later to employ and elaborate his theosophy upon. Corbin observed that the term *ḥikmat ishrāqiyya,* which persisted down to the times of the later Iranian sages, Mulla Ṣadrā Shīrāzī (d. 1640) and Hādī Sabzawārī (d. 1878) derived from what he designates as "Avicenna's *'erfān*" and that no one belonging to the Persian Ishrāqī tradition "ever doubted that the author of the last section of the *Ishārāt...* was an *'ārif,* a mystic-gnostic. What has been doubted is the fidelity of these Orientals'to Islam, and it is this that distinguishes them from orthodox Sufism."[5]

Corbin also convincingly identified Suhrawardī's *ishrāq* with the "philosophy of *Xvarnah* of Zoroastrian Persia," giving this concept an Iranian geographical context and connotation.[6] Avicenna, according to Corbin (who bases his assertions on Muḥammad Mu'īn's edition of the *Dānish-nāma-yi 'Alā'ī)* was conscious of the dual geographical/metaphysical notion; in fact, the later development of Iranian Avicennism under Ishrāqī auspices amplifies and confirms this latent identity of 'Oriental Philosophy' with ancient Persian sources.[7] Again, the "esoteric tone" of Muslim philosophers such as Suhrawardī, stresses Hodgson, owed its vitality to "the persuasive importance of Sufism in Islamicate culture."[8] I.R. Netton in this volume (chap. 4) also demonstrates by semiotic analysis how "*falsafa* metamorphoses into *taṣawwuf* in Suhrawardī's thought, revealing the inseparability of Sufism and philosophy in the intellectual life of Islam."

Despite the very real presence of the *contra inanem philosophiam* motif (the famous 'theologians versus philosophers' dichotomy) in Islam,[9] many of the Sufis did respect certain aspects of Avicenna's teachings. In fact, in contradistinction to

1. *The Venture of Islam,* II, p. 195.
2. *Ibid.,* II, p. 230.
3. H. Corbin, *Avicenna and the Visionary Recital,* translated by W. Trask (Dallas: Spring Publications reprt. 1980), p. 39.
4. *En Islam iranien,* II, p. 340.
5. *Avicenna and the Visionary Recital,* p. 39.
6. *Avicenna and the Visionary Recital,* p. 40: "The philosophy of *Ishrāq* is in the last analysis a philosophy of the *Xvarnah,* of the celestial lambence of the sacral light of Zoroastrianism."
7. Cf. the correspondances between Avicenna's theory of Intelligences and Suhrawardī's Zorastrian-based angelology. *(Ibid.,* p. 120); also see the same author's notes on 'Visionary Geography,' *Spiritual Body and Celestial Earth: From Mazdean Iran to Shī'ite Iran* (London: I.B. Tauris, 1990), translated by N. Pearson, pp. 17-36; p. 110.
8. Hodgson, *op. cit.,* II, p. 198.
9. See Chittick, 'Mysticism Versus Philosophy in Earlier Islamic History: The Al-Ṭūsī, Al-Qūnawī Corrrespondence', *Religious Studies* 17 (1981), pp. 87-104.

the jurisprudents, they usually sided with the philosophers in the call for direct experience and research in all matters of the spirit and the psyche. Thus, 'Ayn al-Quḍāt Hamadānī praised the Koranic hermeneutics of Avicenna, and in his later compositions, such as the ***Tamhīdāt,*** followed his eschatological doctrines.[1] 'Azīz Nasafī made frequent praiseworthy references to his treatises, while Shabistarī observes with enlightened fairness that "Vanity is still vanity, although a 'saint' *(walī)* confess it /Truth is truth, although Avicenna profess it."[2] In psychology, "the Sufi study of the unconscious self eventually came to presuppose the terminology of Ibn Sina."[3]

4. Mystical Aesthetics & Beauty

Another by-product of the Sufis' receptiveness to direct experience, their tolerance and ecumenical vision which "transcended the Gods of Belief,"[4] was their practical patronage and support for the arts of music, painting, and poetry. In fact, without Sufism, iconoclastic tendencies in Muslim jurisprudence would have severely censored if not totally destroyed the imaginative arts.[5]

To summarize then, the 12th-13th-century revival of Sufism was chiefly due to a type of theological humanism (or even 'sacred humanism'),[6] the origins of which are evident quite early in the Persian ecstatic Bāyazid Bisṭāmī (d. 261/875) and Ḥallāj (d. 309/922), being subsequently reaffirmed in Ghazzālī's legitimatization and inclusion of esotericism into the curriculum of mediæval religious studies. Whether this reanimation, this 'revival of soul' of mediæval man by medium of Persian Sufism was due to Persian genius—as would Corbin, Bausani and Zarrīnkūb would have it—is secondary. More importantly, what permitted Sufism's revival—and probably its survival—were certain humanitarian values: tolerance, anti-sectarianism, the emphasis on direct experience in spiritual matters and love of beauty coupled with veneration for aesthetics. Such were the virtues which have endeared the Sufis to the hearts of Persians, both mediæval and modern.

---

1. *Tamhīdāt,* edited by Afif Osseiran (Tehran 1962), p. 289; and the editor's introduction, pp. 69-70.
2. Shabistarī, *Sa'ādatnāma,* in Ṣamad Muwaḥḥid (ed.) *Majmū'a-i āthār-i Shaykh Maḥmūd Shabistarī,* vv. 713.
3. Hodgson, *op. cit.*, II, 173-74.
4. See W. Chittick, *The Sufi Path of Knowledge,* Chap. 19: 'Transcending the Gods of Belief'.
5. "In orthodox Islam most of the fine arts—poetry, music, and in particular painting—were usually viewed with more or less objection or reprobation. Had they not been so cultivated by Islamic mysticism, these arts would have probably have dried up in Islamic culture sooner or later. Painting did, in fact, cease to flourish after the thirteenth century in large parts of the Sunnite world. Secular poetry lost its buoyancy, and music had to give ground time and again to the attacks of the orthodox." J.C. Bürgel, *The Feather of Simurgh*, p. 7.
6. The use of the term "humanism" and sacred humanism here is inspired by V. Holbrook's exposition in this volume of the "spiritual humanism represented in Mevlevi practice and literature" as well as by G. Makdisi's recent study of *The Rise of Humanism in Classical Islam and the Christian West* (Edinburgh University Press 1991; pp. 88-115). Makdisi, who constantly translates the word *adab* as "humanism" or "humanistic studies", observes that (p. 113) "The ties between *adab* studies and religious studies being as close as they were, it was almost a contradiction in terms to speak of secularist humanism. There was never a break between humanism and religion." The term 'sacred humanism' perhaps may serve to absolve any such secularist connotations which remain in the word today.

Yūsuf in Mawlānā Rumi's Poetry

II

Annemarie Schimmel

One of the first Urdu translations of Mawlānā Jalāl al-Dīn Rumi's *Mathnawī*, which appeared in Lucknow in 1889, was called *Pīrāhan-i Yūsuf*, 'Yūsuf's shirt,' alluding to the name of the translator, Muḥammad Yūsuf 'Alī Shāh, as well as to the tradition that the fragrance of Yūsuf's shirt restored his blind father's eyesight. Thus, the translator assumes, his attempt to convey something of Rumi's spiritual fragrance may open his readers' eyes. At the same time it sums also up the content of many allusions and references to Yūsuf, the paragon of beauty, in Mawlānā's work.

At the very beginning of the *Mathnawī*, Mawlānā conjures up the memory of Shams-i Tabrīzī.[1] When this spiritual sun is mentioned "the sun of the fourth heaven draws back her head:"

And this moment the Soul (i.e. Ḥusām al-Dīn) twisted my hem
—He had found the fragrance of Yūsuf's shirt.
(M I 125)

To remember the beloved is like inhaling a fragrance, a fragrance that reminds the lover of happy days and quickens the heart (D 17697). That is why Rumi closes a *ghazal* with the words:

The pre-eternal moon is his face, verse and ghazal are his scent—
Scent is the portion of him who is not intimate with the view.
(D 4976)

Scent brings refreshment to those who are deprived of the actual view, like Jacob, and Mawlānā's words heal the spiritually impaired. For the friend's fragrance is life-giving:

He said: "Did you not die?" I said: "Sure, but
When your fragrance came I jumped out of the grave."
(D 15309)

It is due to the fragrance that one recognizes the friend when he suddenly knocks at the heart's door (D 4618)[2] and the poet, who wonders whether it is ambergris,

1. Note on Abbreviations: The sources below quoted as "D" (with number of line) indicate the *Dīwān-i kabīr yā Kulliyyāt-i Shams*, ed. Badī' al-Zamān Furūzānfar, 10 vols. (Tehran: 1957) ff.; "M" (with number of the volume and line) refers to Mawlānā Jalāl al-Dīn Rumi's *Mathnāwī-i ma'nawī*, ed. Reynold Alleyne Nicholson, 8 vols. (London: 1925-40). Further references will be found in my forthcoming book based on the Bampton Lectures delivered in New York at Columbia University: *Yūsuf's Fragrant Shirt: Studies in Islamic Symbolism*.
2. Cf. D 134: Is it Yūsuf's shirt or Muḥammad's heart?

musk and aloes-wood or whether Yūsuf has arrived from the bazaar (D 6237) may ask:

> *I asked: "How did Yūsuf's scent travel to all cities?"*
> *God's fragrance from the world of Hū wafted: "Thus!"*
> *I asked: "How could Yūsuf's scent open the eye?"*
> *Your breeze gave light to my eyes - thus!*
>
> (D 19188-89)[1]

The story of Yūsuf, called in the Koran itself "the most beautiful story" was dear to poets from early days onward, probably even before Kisā'ī had elaborated it in his *Qiṣaṣ al-anbiyā*. They alluded to his beauty in which two-thirds of all created beauty was brought together; Zulaykhā's longing for him; to the healing scent of his shirt as well as to his suffering in the pit and in the Egyptian prison.

We may ask, then: is the frequent use of the Yūsuf-theme in Rumi's work just formulaic as it seems to be with many other poets, or does it reflect something more? Has his preference for the word *bū*, 'scent, smell', which is so central in his verse, something to do with the Yūsuf story? To be sure, Rumi's use of the Yūsuf-theme is protean, as is his use of most symbols and metaphors. Yūsuf is, of course, the beloved, but he can also be the symbol of the soul that is fallen in the dark pit of matter or smarts in fear and constraint until God rescues it to restore it to full glory; the poet appears now as Jacob who preferred Yūsuf to his brothers and thus incited their envy, or else he plays the role of Zulaykhā and the Egyptian women, madly in love with the paragon of beauty.

Stories connected with Yūsuf appear in the *Mathnawī* where allusions to his role as interpreter of dreams are more common than in the *Dīwān* although the other aspects of his career are also mentioned.[2] Most prominent is the story of the mirror which was presented to him (M I 3157ff) and the description of Zulaykhā's love (M VI 4023 ff.).

In the *Dīwān*, the beloved is alluded to hundreds of times as Yūsuf. Often, the descriptions and epithets are stereotyped. In different poems he is addressed with almost the same words, sometimes with a change of meter: *ay yār-i mā, dildār-i mā* (D 457) or *yār-i mā, dildār-i mā* (D 2666), *rawnaq-i bazār-i mā* occurs several times,[3] and even more often he is the *Yūsuf-i khūshnām-i mā*.[4]

Mawlānā follows the tradition of Persian rhetoric in combining the names of several prophets to achieve harmony of imagery—and after all the fate of all of them foreshadowed that of the Prophet of Islam who, like Yūsuf, suffered from "cunning brothers." (D 23553) The poet praises God who has miraculously provided for His messengers' rescue:

---

1. For further references to the scent of Yūsuf's shirt, see: M II 917; D 1503, 4550, 9598, 10530, 17697, 19916, 23529, 25062, 25599, 32640-41.
2. The most important references are M I 2787; M II 918, 1405, 1903, 2057; M III 397, 2333, 2338-40 (God's promise to Yūsuf), 2831, 3035 (scent of his bread); M V 1994 ff., 3300; M VI 1175-77, 3091 (illuminates the house where he passes), 4571-75.
3. See D 2666, 15412 for *rawnaq-i bazār-i mā.*
4. See D 50, 199, 25693, and often, *khūshnām-i mā.*

He made a cell for Yūnus in the fish's stomach
And drew Yūsuf out of the pit.
(D 36064)

Yūnus and Yūsuf belong together as both have survived in the darkness of the prison (D 19649, 28107) and are thus witnesses to God's unlimited power. Yūsuf in the pit is also comparable to Moses when he was still a shepherd: neither of them knew of his future glory (D 31656).

Both Yūsuf and Jesus can heal the blind (D 176), and as Yūsuf's scent is life-giving, so is Jesus's breath: these two are thus fitting symbols for the beloved whose kiss quickens the near-dead lover (D 7394, 24665). Jacob, on the other hand, is combined with Job, for both of them suffer and need the beloved as a physician; the grammatical form of their names—Ayyūb, Ya'qūb—facilitated such combinations.[1]

Almost all the ingredients of the Koranic story and its elaboration in the *Qiṣaṣ al-anbiyā* appear in Rumi's work although Yūsuf's role as an interpreter of dreams is rarely mentioned in the lyrics. (On the other hand, one may recall that the Realm of Imagination, as manifesting itself in Yūsuf's dreams and their interpretation, is the starting point for Ibn 'Arabi's chapter on the "Wisdom of Light in the Word of Yūsuf" in his *Fuṣūṣ al-ḥikam).* Yūsuf's brothers typify envy and ignorance and are thus similar to some people in Mawlānā's entourage, including his own family and in particular, his son 'Alā' al-Dīn, who were averse to his mystical beloved, Shams, and denied his spiritual beauty - and yet, Yūsuf prayed for them (D 9789-91).

On rare occasions Mawlānā compares himself to Benjamin, suspected of theft (D 20335) and asks the beloved Yūsuf to look kindly upon him (D 15065, 18041). Much more prominent, however, are allusions to the wolf who allegedly devoured young Yūsuf "because Yūsuf appeared to his envious brothers like a wolf."[2] (D 4852) Hypocritical people can therefore be called 'wolves in Yūsuf's shape' (D 3622), but Mawlānā thinks that a normal wolf could never have eaten Yūsuf for even the lion of the sky (the constellation Leo) would not dare to attack him (D 9288). He also reverses the image, describing Love as a wolf that tears to pieces every beautiful Yūsuf (D 9124). Of course, Rumi knows that all these manifestations are due only to a Divine miracle: for without the beloved, Yūsuf turns into a wolf (D 27035), while Love can transform the wolves into moon-faced beloveds (D 17152). Therefore he addresses Love:

You enter the ugly jinn and make him a Yūsuf,
You enter the wolf's character and make him a shepherd!
(D 31630)

This is the transformation of the *'anima bruta'* or *nafs ammāra* (D 16527, cf. 25926) into a 'soul at peace' *(nafs muṭma'inna).*[3]

---

1. See D 13515, 19646, cf. 18825. Sulaymān appears only once along with Yūsuf: D 27500.
2. Cf. D 11407, 19423, and also 27706. The brothers sold Yūsuf for little (D 8876). As long as the soul is wolfish it cannot see Yūsuf (M III 2831), but the wolves are overcome when Yūsuf arrives (D 9371).
3. For such a transformation, cf. D 951, 14529; for more wolves, see D 5455, 7008, 21721, 28210, 29293.

Yūsuf is indeed used as a soul principle both in Rumi's and in other poets' verse. He has to undergo trials and tribulations[1] but is consoled in the darkness of the pit by God's promise to bring him to a high rank (M III 2337ff., D 15395):

One should see wine in the sour grape and something in Nothing,
And Yūsuf in the pit should see his future rank as a ruler
(D 3548)[2]

The pun *chāh,* ('pit') and *jāh* ('high rank') is therefore frequently applied by Mawlānā.[3] Separation is necessary for union, suffering for joy:

Did not Yūsuf go away, weeping, from his father,
And did he not find fortune, kingdom, and victory by traveling?
(D 12114, cf. 2403)

Thus asks Rumi in his *ghazal* in praise of traveling, drawing a parallel between Yūsuf and the Prophet Muḥammad—who, by leaving his home town, became a ruler in Medina—and the rain drop which, leaving its home in the ocean, may be transformed into a precious pearl once it returns to the sea. He also sees in Yūsuf's fate an allusion to the pitcher that goes down empty and returns filled with water, or—as in Yūsuf's own case—with something infinitely more precious (D 16517). Why then worry about the soul's fate after death when a glorious spiritual resurrection lies before you? (D 9564)

The soul, in the pit of hopelessness or in the dark world of matter has to grasp the rope that comes from heaven. (It was not difficult to combine this rope with the *ḥabl matīn,* the firm rope):[4]

God twisted a rope from you and my sighs—
Yūsuf, the Soul, came from the pit, the body, and went to his nest.
(D 26306)

Sometimes the poet even sees himself as the bucket lowered into the well by travelers by means of which the lovely Yūsuf is rescued. (D 16517).[5] Similarly, in the pit 'World' the Yūsuf 'Beauty' is hidden and:

I wind myself on this wheel around him like a rope.
(D 17143)

However, Rumi is convinced that the pit or dark prison in the company of the friend is preferable to lovely meadows (D 14502); when Yūsuf is present, the deep, murky pit becomes radiant and joyful like the gardens of Iram (D 18533; cf. 1872,

---

1. He is admonished to go like sugar to the poison of overwhelming power: *qahr,* D 2006.
2. For related verses concerning this motif, see: D 1936 in a nice dancing song, 6577, 15195, 18515; Yūsuf in the pit: D 10575-76, 15724, *chāh-i tan* D 9349; rescue from the pit 2096 ('come into the dance'!), 5313, 5434, 13537-8, 13378, 15821, 16845, 25403, 25431, 29955, 32988. "Yūsuf is with you when you are a pit yourself" D 30955; "When do we come together: you, Yūsuf and I, the pit?" (D 27680). A combination that is frequently found in other poets, such as Ḥāfiẓ and his followers, that of the *chāh-i zinakhdān,* the 'pit' of the chin or *chāh-i dhaqan,* occurs very rarely in Rumi's verse. (D 27599, 24494-95).
3. D 5574, 5585, 14611.
4. On *ḥabl,* see D 6726, 28400, 28440.
5. On the pitcher or bucket, see D 6313, 24211, M VI 4571.

15161)—an idea repeated in *Fīhi mā fīhi,* and which can be found also in the works of numerous writers in Iran and elsewhere: Hell with the beloved would be preferable to a Paradise without him. Mawlānā sometimes complains that he has fallen in the pit of separation, but a rope has come from the king of Egypt (D 17415).

What is this rope? It is the *dhikr,* the remembrance of the friend's name that will bring the lover out of the pit of separation (D 19325). For to remember the beloved's name is the best way to overcome one's loneliness. The dream image of Yūsuf too can serve as a rope that draws him from the pit of this world to the highest heavens (D 2578). Rumi also inverts the image: he knows that the very reflection of Yūsuf's beauty makes the water in the well boil from love (D 24199), and even more, he sees

A strange Yūsuf like the moon, who is reflected in a hundred wells
So that the Jacobs are fallen into his snare and pit.
(D 683, also cf. 19139)

Otherwise, the importance of suffering in love is emphasized: pit and prison are necessary for the development of the Yūsuf 'Soul,' for:

Prison and suspicion are the part of the lover,
Throne and pulpit are the place of the scholar.
(D 16580-81)

This line reflects the never-ending tension between Love and Reason, between *'ishq* and *'ilm,* between rapture and law, which was usually expressed by the Persian Sufi poets from the days of Sanā'ī to contemporary literature, by the juxtaposition of gallows and pulpit *(minbar).*[1]

Rumi knew that although Yūsuf stayed in prison, yet: "this lovely rose never became bitter" (D 13658), rather, "his radiant cheek made the entire prison resemble a rosegarden" (D 29980)—the comparison of the rose with Yūsuf is commonplace in poetry as the rose "tears its shirt" and exudes sweet fragrance like Yūsuf.[2]

Tear your collar from joy like the red rose—
It's the time that the shirt comes to Jacob!
(D 21179)

That happens in spring: whereas the pit is the place where the soul prepares itself for greater glory, winter is the time when the trees and the earth, practicing "beautiful patience," prepare for spring:

You see the cheeks of Yūsufs who lift their heads from the pit -
You see the rose-cheeked ones that manifest themselves.
(D 30302, cf. 7375, 14145)

1. The theme begins with Sanā'ī and finds its classical expression in Mirzā Ghālib's (d. 1869 in Dehli) verse:

The secret that's in the heart is no sermon-
You can say it on the gallows but not on the pulpit.

Numerous contemporary poets in Indo-Pakistan and Turkey have repeated this combination which contains in a nutshell a major problem of the relation of mystical experience and legalism.

2. Cf. D 396, 17607, also 2442.

Just as life is hidden beneath the veils of the seemingly dead earth, so the longing lover knows that there are a hundred Yūsufs of Canaan in the veil of hiding (D 27319),[1] and the lover, asking where the 'Yūsuf of all Yūsufs' is, will turn his face to the yonder country (D 16278). In rare cases, the imagery is changed. Yūsuf 'with the beautiful name' is exhorted not to cut himself off from the Jacob 'Reason' and wander alone lest he fall in the pit (D 25693). And even more surprising is the following verse which praises the transforming power of fasting, which will lead to the realm of Divine Love provided the fasting person is patient and grateful:

Everyone who is patient in the pit 'Fasting'
Will grasp the kingdom of the Egypt 'Love' like Yūsuf.
(D 24805)

Of course, it is difficult to accept that the beautiful Yūsuf should have fallen in the hands of blind people or remained with lowly slave dealers to be sold in the bazaar.[2] Turning to the soul principle once more, Rumi admonishes the listener to become a Yūsuf, even though ignorance may have brought him to the slave dealer, and to become a rosegarden, not caring whether or not the thorns know him, (D 20645)—one has to know one's own worth. Otherwise one is an idol-worshiper, a worshiper of forms, and although one is a Yūsuf, one does not look into one's own self (D 30022).

The story of Yūsuf in the bazaar is mentioned rather frequently, sometimes elaborated into little anecdotes. When the lover weeps in separation from Yūsuf, God addresses him, asking what price he has paid in the auction. For he is so precious that even Egypt's kings become bankrupt by bidding for him (D 29548).

Of course, the glory of the Yūsuf of these latter days, thus thinks Mawlānā, is a hundred times greater than the beauty of which Zulaykhā had dreamt (D 27780).

He is superior to all Yūsufs[3]—a theme that is commonplace in poetry but which seems particularly important in Rumi's verse: is not the sun of the fourth heaven ashamed before the Sun of Tabriz? Thus, the friend ruins the bazaar of all Yūsufs and surpasses the shop of all the sugar merchants (D 25260). It behoves Zulaykhā to buy him,[4] and Rumi alludes to the story that the loving woman became blind like Jacob from weeping, but was then rejuvenated by Yūsuf, and "thus, the old world becomes young again thanks to this star" (D 32306), that is, the beloved. One is immediately reminded of the *maqṭa'* of a *ghazal* where Rumi relates how "Grief for him made me old, but when you mention Shams al-Dīn, my youth returns, for people a hundred years old have been rejuvenated thanks to such a Yūsuf." (D 27943)

1. For the term *tutuq*, see also D 26001, and s.v. D 11668.
2. For *bāzār*, see: D 14706-9, 31180-81, 29376, 32383.
3. Cf. D 1101, 1563-4, 1727, 5176ff., 28863, 29577, 29806; also related is D 29800. A beautiful variant is given in D 20239-40:

When the Yūsuf of Yūsufs sits on the throne, smiling
—the door that was always closed opens, smiling.

4. M V 1105 ff, the story of the attempt at seduction in the castle; M V 3873 warning against the ruses of women in this context. See D 6162, 6578, 7606.

Yūsuf, Mounted and Crowned, Encounters Zulaykhā in the Street. From Jāmī's *Yūsuf u Zulaykhā*. From a manuscript of the *Haft awrang*. MS. Elliott 149, fol. 182b (Courtesy of the Bodleian Library, Oxford).

Yūsuf Sold as a Slave. From a manuscript of ʻAṭṭār's *Manṭiq al-ṭayr*, dated 898/1493. MS. Elliott 246, fol. 96r (Courtesy of the Bodleian Library, Oxford).

Yūsuf did not know Zulaykhā's pain; he was as unaware of her suffering as is the snare of the suffering of the birds it has caught (D 732), for most beloveds in Persian poetry are cruel and do not care for their poor longing lover's pains. Rumi knows, however, that Zulaykhā's love, which has brought Yūsuf to prison (D 21305) is finally transformed into Divine Love, as 'the metaphor is the bridge to Reality', and he mentions the scene which was elaborated so skillfully by Jāmī, e.g. that in the end Yūsuf tried to grasp Zulaykhā's shirt and tore it as a talio for the shirt she once tore, but she reminds him:

Many such things are done
by the transforming power of Love for Divine glory ('ishq-i kibriyā).
(D 339-41)

As we shall see, Rumi has also invented the most moving version of Zulaykhā's longing in which, as it seems to me, he has completely identified himself with her (M VI 4021 ff.).

However, lovesick Zulaykhā is not as prominent in his verse as are the Egyptian ladies *(zanān,*[1] *khātūnān,*[2] *mastūragān*[3]*)* who cut their hands instead of the fruits when gazing at Yūsuf, and the reader is warned to watch his hands carefully as "our Yūsuf struts intoxicated out of that curtain." (D 2450) To look at the ravishing beauty of the beloved, to be submersed completely in the beatific vision makes the lover oblivious of all pain (D 20505). Rumi's lyrics abound in allusions to this, for:

We are not less than the Egyptian women—
You are the Yūsuf of beautiful countenance.
(D 26158)[4]

The lover does not complain when the beloved carries off all his belongings for it is fine that hands be cut in the presence of this lovely Yūsuf (D 4400). Rather, one should put away the healing salve (D 20054), for only Yūsuf's beauty is the lover's medicine—why run to physicians? (D 28157):

Look at the cupbearer, don't look at the intoxicated!
Look at Yūsuf, don't look at the hand!
(D 11000)

The same idea is adapted into an elegant Arabic verse (D 3053):

And we became confused by Yūsuf's beauty - then we came to ourselves,
and lo, there were goblets with wine like blood in our hands!

Once more, Rumi's beloved is infinitely superior to the historical Yūsuf for whose sake only a few people hurt their hands, while:

You have cut off from heart and reason a hundred Yūsufs of the soul.
(D 29945)

1. For *zanān,* see D 3600, 7854, 12015, 20505, 26648, 31026.
2. For *khātūnān,* see D 15868, 26444, 28474.
3. For *mastūragān,* see D 12741.
4. See D 1611, 29148, 31552, 32835; also D 405 (in a poem for Sulṭān Walad's wedding); D 590, where Yūsuf thinks of the one who has cut his hand; further allusions occur in D 7504-5, 12621, 15310, 15775, 17138, 17228, 17808, 20981, 22311, 30202.

In one verse Mawlānā even combines the lovers' pain with birthpangs:

Don't lament about your hand because of this dagger
for a jewel has come into your palm:
To be pregnant with the love of Yūsuf is worth thousands of birthpangs.
(D 26649)

Birth pangs are the condition for the appearance of the longed for result or else for a wonderful surprise: did not the dried-up date palm shed sweet fruits upon Mary who had grasped her during her labor? And—as the poet says in *Fīhi ma fīhi* (Chapter 5)—they are required for a 'Jesus' to be born in the soul.

Egypt, where Yūsuf found his noble rank, was known in the Middle Ages as a sugar-producing country, and what was easier than combining the Egyptian Yūsuf, the friend with sugar-lips, with Egyptian sugar?[1] He comes strutting with 200 ass-loads of sugar (D 8386) and even more: his beauty equals a hundred Egypts filled with sugar (D 16481). Did not numberless souls eat bitter poison like Jacob until the Yūsuf of the Soul brought them into the sugar garden (D 13258), until the manifestation of beauty recompensed them for their faithful waiting? Egypt and sugar should begin to dance the very moment Yūsuf entered that country (D 2089), for he is everything lovely and sweet. In a poem in alternating Persian and Arabic lines Rumi sees a hundred Egypts and a hundred places full of sugar and closes with the Arabic proverb (used also in the *Fīhī mā fīhī)* about the all-comprehensive presence of the Beloved:

All game, large or small, lies inside the wild onager.
(D 2956-58)

That is: one who has found the Friend has found everything.

Mawlānā often compares himself to Jacob, for this theme seems to correspond particularly well to his own situation.[2] It allows for lengthier elaborations of the experience of separation and the restoration of the eyesight thanks to the fragrance (D 15227) or the arrival (D 19880) of the beloved (D 6298). In his oft-quoted *ghazal* in quest of the ideal Man, he says:

Like Jacob I cry ' O woe!'...
My wish is the beautiful view of Yūsuf of Canaan.
(D 4633)

Rumi sits in the corner (D 17607, 22910) or in the 'house of sorrows' (D 15144) beseeching the beloved to make the ship 'Union' move from the ocean of darkness toward the "old man of Canaan" (D 27158)[3] and thus to transform the night into a luminous *laylat al-qadr,* to be the candle of his hut (D 22910) which has become pitchblack in separation (D 177)—verses which well translate his feelings after

1. Cf. M V 3302; D 10454:
The scent of our beloved does not come,
The parrot does not chew sugar here.
For further references, see D 1082, 6121, 6425, 11210, 13460.
2. See D 14797, 35552.
3. For further references, see D 177, 2552, 7356, 10915, 13241, 13668, 27136; with bū: D 5635, 13241, 30778.

Shams's disappearance. Only when hearing the murmuring of Yūsuf's voice does he begin to dance (D 6523) while Yūsuf stamps his feet because "the cupbearer 'Union' has poured out his divine wine." (D 30460)

It is Yūsuf's shirt that healed his blind father, and the shirt (which according to some interpreters was a heavenly robe sent by God to His messengers)[1] has a threefold connotation in the story: the bloodstained shirt which the treacherous brothers offered to Jacob to prove Yūsuf's death; the shirt torn by Zulaykhā in her vain attempt to seduce the innocent young prophet who was, however, protected by God, and finally the shirt whose scent opened Jacob's eye. These different aspects could be woven together:

> *My heart tears the collar from grief:*
> *How can I grasp the shirt of the one with a lovely name?*
> (D 15912)

And he asks:

> *What shall the lover do if he does not tear his shirt*
> *When the fragrance of that shirt arrives?*
> (D 8725)

To be sure, Rumi knows that union with the beloved Yūsuf would be better in the state of complete nudity; yet only *his* shirt helps open man's two eyes (D 21995), for the full manifestation of the Divine radiance cannot be experienced. One needs the veils which hide the Absolute Beauty but point to it and thus, along with the fragrance of remembrance, open man's sight to the light.[2]

> *You sent me Yūsuf's shirt as a gift*
> *So that the sun may tear its gold-embroidered shirt*
> (D 32060)

Thus sings Mawlānā and seems to allude covertly to *his* sun, Shams al-Dīn.

But what can one do when Yūsuf is not found any more?

> *Only his frock has remained, that is, expressions;*
> *But for the heart, Yūsuf's frock is like antimony.*
> (D 35692, cf. 22273)

To console the heart, blinded by grief, it is enough to mention the name of Yūsuf: words, like the scent of heavenly apple trees (M VI 84 ff.) can bring back the memory of the days of happiness.

To remember Yūsuf is a consolation, and as he is the manifestation of Divine Beauty, he is more than simply handsome: Rumi understands that during the seven years of famine in Egypt people survived as Yūsuf's beauty was their nourishment. (D 23646, 29731)[3]

---

1. A lengthy description of Yūsuf's shirt, which is mentioned in general in Kisā'ī's *Qiṣaṣ al-anbiyā*, is found in the fifth volume of Abū'l-Faḍl Rashīd al-Dīn al-Maybudī, *Kashf al-asrār wa 'uddat al-abrār*, ed. 'Alī Aṣghar Ḥikmat (Tehran 1339 ash/1960).
2. For further references, see: D 6298, 7142, 14797, 18184, 28090, 35552.

From what does the angel eat? From God's beauty.
The nourishment of moon and stars is from the sun of the world
The nourishment of people during that famine was Yūsuf's beauty
So that the people of Egypt were rescued from grief for bread.
(D 21945-46)

Yūsuf's beauty and radiance is so overwhelming that the poets, in particular Rumi, have wondered what the lover should bring as a present for him—for how could one come into the beloved's presence empty-handed? In the *Mathnawi,* Mawlānā tells the story of the visitor who brought a mirror so that the very friend could admire his own beauty, for such a modest gift is necessary for his knowledge of himself: "Lowliness is the mirror of Perfect Glory" (M I 3200 ff.). The story of the mirror is mentioned in *Fīhi mā fīhi*[1] and alluded to in the *Dīwān* several times:

For you, oh Egyptian Yūsuf, I have brought
Such a radiant mirror as a present.
(D 15880)

This mirror is the heart of the lover which, like a steel mirror, has been polished—polished by passion and suffering, "and thus I go into Yūsuf's presence with a gift." (D 17950)[2]

The lover's heart is in the hand of the wondrous mirror-holder where it both silent and speaking like a mirror—silent in itself but speaking to the friend's reflection (D 28604). It may also be that his heart, pure like water, is able to reflect the moonlike or sunlike beloved's countenance, and, having reached complete selflessness, he pours the blood from his cheeks to make them shining white like a mirror and thus becomes, in perfect union with Yūsuf, "the redness of the friend's face." (D 14664, final verse)[3]

Not only is the loving soul transformed into a mirror for Yūsuf, rather, heaven and earth reflect the beauty of his face (D 24203). Did not mystical Islam incessantly repeat that God was a hidden treasure who wanted to be known and loved and therefore created the universe as a mirror for His Beauty? However, one should not look at the highly decorated backside of the mirror but at its face wherein Yūsuf is reflected.(D 12884)

To become a mirror means purification and transfiguration. Therefore Rumi feels that the beloved has given him his true value, led him to his true goal.

I was a piece of iron without worth and value—
You have made me a mirror, polishing me.
(D 28457)

3. Cf. M III 3034:

Jacob was hungry for Yūsuf:
The scent of his bread came from afar.

1. *Fīhi mā fīhi,* Chapter 49. The story of the mirror has been transformed into a German poem by Friedrich Rückert in his *Morgenländische Sagen und Geschichten,* 1837.
2. Cf. D 13425: "I am a mirror."
3. Cf. also D 30652; and D 23677 in which the lover sees his own beauty in His Beauty.

Only by maturing in the hardships of love, separation, and longing, will one eventually reach one's proper destination, will become what one was intended to become: a mirror to receive the rays of the Divine Light. Yet, Rumi would not be honest if he did not admit that the form of the beloved's perfection cannot be contained by a mirror. The mirror shows things according to its own capacity (D 22986); it may even be crooked (D 24676) and thus distort the lovely picture, for human hearts can grasp only a tiny fragment of the Divine Beauty. As we saw, Yūsuf often stands for the human soul; hence Rumi remarks that this beautiful Yūsuf has fallen among the blind and that the mirror is held in the hand of negroes (D 27652); to understand one's own loveliness one should rather look at the mirror. (D 30115)

But in general, Yūsuf is the symbol of the beloved *par excellence*. However, while in *ghazal* poetry on the whole the beloved's name is not mentioned, Rumi's case is different. As often as he uses the name of Yūsuf as a general term for 'the friend,' there are a substantial number instances where the equation Yūsuf=Shams al-Dīn is evident, and since Ṣalāḥ al-Dīn and Ḥusām al-Dīn are, for him, mere reflections of the overwhelming light of the Sun of Tabriz, both of them can assume the character of Yūsuf as well. For the story of Yūsuf contained the same elements as Mawlānā's own experience: an infatuation that made him forget everything while looking at the beloved, loss of the beloved, suffering in the pit of his absence, and consolation by the fragrance of remembrance.

In an early *ghazal* where the name of Shams al-Dīn appears in the first line, he is said to be 'superior in coquetry to all Yūsufs' (D 20716), and if this still may be taken as a general remark, the situation changes after Shams had disappeared, 'gone into the pit like Yūsuf' (D 29701) and at his return he is greeted as comparable to Yūsuf who came to the bazaar of Purity: the *Ikhwān al-ṣafā,* the Brethren of Purity, should seek him there (D 12982). The lover is like Zulaykhā who tore Yūsuf's shirt, and; 'the shirt of every patience' is torn by Shams, the prince (D 6550). The friend's return is also celebrated in a poem with the beginning: "My sun *(shams)* and moon came... and that silver-breasted Yūsuf came suddenly to my breast" (D 6596).[1] In another early poem, with Shams' name in the middle, the listener is asked to proclaim ("to beat the drum about") his name because from Yūsuf's beauty the drum becomes new like a shirt (D 20914). In still another *ghazal* (where the sun: *āftāb* and *shams al-ḍuḥā* appear in the last verses) the beloved is addressed at the beginning as having become both Yūsuf of Canaan and the glory of Muṣṭafā's Light (D 297) (—the role of Shams al-Dīn as the one who is closest to the light of the Prophet is frequently expressed in the *Dīwān).*

The comparison of Shams with Yūsuf is then fully developed in a *ghazal* where Rumi states:

1. Cf. D 4897:
I am Yūsuf of Canaan, my moonlike face is my witness.
No one requests witness and document from the sun!

Jacob's eye opened from the fragrance of that rose...
Don't look with contempt at the breeze of our Yūsuf:
Who is the Yūsuf of the soul? Shāh Shams-i Tabrīzī...
(D 12240-41)

One can also sometimes find the words "You are our Yūsuf" instead of a proper *takhalluṣ* (viz. D 22055), and in Shams's beauty, hundreds of thousands of Yusuf's beauties lie hidden. (D 20506)

In the same manner that Shams seemed to reappear in a certain way in the person of Ṣalāḥ al-Dīn, the change is visible in the poems as well: a *ghazal* with Ṣalāḥ al-Dīn's name in the middle—composed, that is, at a time when this new love grew stronger—ends with a praise of Shams, the "Sultan of all beautiful ones," whose "equally beautiful companions" may be Yūsuf (D 8339).

Then, the motif is completely transferred to Ṣalāḥ al-Dīn (D 18687), and an interweaving of the topos of 'Yūsuf in the bazaar' with Ṣalāḥ al-Dīn Zarkūb appears when Mawlānā praises 'the bazaar of the goldsmiths' where the secrets of the Jacobs are located (D 26611). It has still to be studied whether the poet's tendency to compare himself to Jacob occurs more frequently in verses written under the spell of Ṣalāḥ al-Dīn *(vide* D 31358), who was his junior by some twelve years, than in other *ghazals*. References of this kind occur, for example, in the wedding poems for Rumi's son Ṣultān Walad, who married Ṣalāḥ al-Dīn's daughter (D 2662).

Finally Yūsuf also becomes a designation for his last friend, Ḥusām al-Dīn and it seems not too farfetched to see the transition in a poem where Rumi sings:

Like Zulaykhā I became old from grief;
Yūsuf prayed and made me young.
(D 10275)

As the rhyme contains the word *shamshīr* ('sword'), Rumi may have concealed here, as he did in other verses, an indication that actually Ḥusām, 'sword,' is meant. Perhaps one can also interpret D 20594 as pertaining to Ḥusām al-Dīn, where Mawlānā sings:

After so many years the beauty of Yūsuf returned.

But such a Yūsuf can be seen only by the lover's eye; only Jacob, and later Zulaykhā, knew of his eternal beauty while his brothers were not aware of it (M III 3030), for the eye of envy does not know Yūsuf, just as a deaf ear does not hear the sound of the harp (D 6968). The scent of congeniality is required to understand the secret of beauty, and Rumi himself had often smarted under the lack of understanding among his contemporaries. It seems to me, then, that the lines from the *Mathnawī* which we quoted in the beginning are much more than a mere poetical phrase. The scent of Yūsuf's shirt, which young Ḥusām al-Dīn feels, points, as Mawlānā explicitly says, to Shams, but in reply to the disciple's urging, he tells him:

It's better that the friend remain in veils—
You listen to the contents of the tales!
It's better that his mysteries be told
In other people's stories, tales of old.

From that very moment onward the name of Shams is no longer openly mentioned in the *Mathnawī* and—as far as we can judge—in the later *ghazals*, although all the stories point to him or to the "ray of his light": Ḍiyā' al-Ḥaqq, Ḥusām al-Dīn. But shortly before his death, at the end of the *Mathnawī,* Mawlānā once more turns to the lovesick Zulaykhā and reveals how she concealed Yūsuf's name in everything:

And when she said: The wax is melting softly!
That was to say: My friend was kind to me.
And when she said: Look, how the moon is rising
And when she said: The willow is now green!
And when she said: The leaves they are a-trembling
And when she said: How nicely burns the rue!
And when she said: The birds sang for the roses
And when she said: Beat firmly all my rugs!
And when she said: The bread is all unsalted!
And when she said: The spheres are going wrong...
She praised something–that meant "His sweet embracing;"
She blamed something–that meant: "He's far away!"
And when she piled up names and names and names all—
Her sole intention was but Yūsuf's name...

Whatever she saw, she discovered and concealed Yūsuf in it, so much so that his name became a fur coat for her in winter and was her food when she was hungry, for his beauty is nourishment for the soul.

With this scene Mawlānā takes up the thread of the dialogue in Book I: just as Zulaykhā meant Yūsuf with every word of hers, Rumi meant Shams with every tale, every word, every verse, and his name—the name of *Yūsuf-i khūshnām*—sustained him in times of spiritual dearth, in the long nights of suffering—Yūsuf's (that is Shams al-Dīn's) name was for him like a cloak in which he wrapped himself completely, so much so as to sing many of his most powerful poems in his name. He had become his mirror, reflecting his radiance through which the Divine Beauty was revealed to him. Thus, it seems not surprising that he felt his own poetry to be a reflection of Yūsuf's, that is, of Shams's, beauty:

After me this ghazal will be an evening talk
for another hundred years, just like Yūsuf's beauty.
(D 11640)

Ecstasy and Order

Two Structural Principles in the Ghazal Poetry of Jalāl al-Dīn Rumi

J.C. Bürgel

I shall divide my essay into seven parts:

1. Ecstasy and control as the structural pattern of religious and artistic experience in Islam.
2. The motif of mightiness.
3. Repetitive structures in the sacred texts of Islam.
4. Ecstasy and mightiness in Rumi's *ghazal* poetry.
5. Repetitive structures in Rumi's *ghazal*s.
6. The superimposing of systems as a literary device in Rumi's poetry.
7. Rumi's *ghazal* as dance.

1. ECSTASY AND CONTROL

The most intrinsic realm of ecstatic experience in Islam is, no doubt, the mystical practice of *dhikr* and *samā'*. However, ecstasy is not, as one might surmise, restricted to mystical experience. It is, I believe, a genuine part of religious experience in Sunni and Shi'ite Islam as well. We need only look at pictures, or read reports of the ceremonies of the pilgrimage, to become aware of the amount of joy, rapture or ecstasy involved. The same is certainly true for the feelings experienced by the warriors of Holy War, particularly in a victorious battle. Moments of ecstasy may flash in the hearts of believers also during prayer, particularly if the congregation is large, or in the month of fasting towards the end of a day, and even more so, when the period comes to its end, and the feast of breaking the fast is nigh.

All these rites, which do thus have a dimension of sacred joy and elevation, are at the same time controlled by strict rules, rules which give them a repetitive structure, and that in a double sense. For every execution of the rite forms part of its immense total existence in time and space, and the rite itself consists of movements, circumambulations, prostrations, throwing of pebbles, etc., that have to be repeated. It is this repetitive structure that greatly contributes to a rising feeling of joy often verging on or growing into ecstasy, yet it is also the prescribed number of repetitions which prevents this ecstasy from going out of control. Ecstasy and control condition each other, and this is the pattern-giving law not only of Islamic rites, but also of many phenomena of Islamic art, indeed, of sacred art in general.

This assertion is corroborated if we look at the dominant structures of poetry and music in Islam in which repetition not only plays the main role but is the structural means by which ecstasy is aroused in the hearer, as, in fact, it is up to the present day, particularly when poetry is being read, or music played for a group of people.

Repetition alone, however, would hardly suffice to create ecstasy. It is the reiteration of things, gestures, ideas, that move the soul, in other words, the intensification of a given motif by its repetition, which is capable of elevating, ravishing man's mind or soul to the degree of ecstasy. The things that are repeated are either holy, as in religious rites, or beautiful, as in art, or both, as in religious art.

2.THE MOTIF OF MIGHTINESS

This brings me to the notion of mightiness, which I have discussed at length elsewhere.[1] It hardly needs to be proven in detail, I think, that there exists power, or, as I call it, mightiness, in the arts. Personal experience apart, all of us have probably read stories about the power of poetry, its enormous political role, in ancient Arabia and in mediæval Islam.[2] The power of music was no less remarkable, for it could send people into ecstasy[3] and it could heal. Musicotherapy was widely practiced in medieval Islamic hospitals,[4] and according to a wide-spread belief, a certain musical mode could put the listener into a death-like sleep, a motif used by Niẓāmī in his *Iskandarnāma* and Amīr Khusraw Dihlavī in his *Hasht Bihisht.*[5] Similar stories exist about the power of pictures.[6] All this was due to the magic of the arts—the mightiness, which, I think, is the intrinsic reason for the restrictions imposed upon the fine arts by the religious law of Islam.

To a large extent, the history of the Islamic arts may be described as a process of sacralizing, and thereby legitimizing, the mightiness of the arts, a process by the way, that has its parallel in the history of the sciences in pre-modern Islam.[7] This is because in Islam legitimate power can only be derived from God's power. *Lā ḥawla wa lā quwwata illā billāh. (*There is no power except through God.) Time and again, it is emphasized in the Koran that there is no prophet or legitimate ruler without having been given *sulṭān* from God.[8] The unbelievers are those who venerate something on which God's power *(sulṭān)* has not descended.[9] Mightiness can only exist if delegated by the Almighty; the way to attain mightiness is submission. Islam means participation in sacred mightiness achieved through submission. This holds true for every kind of power, and thus also for the power, or mightiness, of the arts and the sciences.

---

1. J.C. Bürgel, *The Feather of Simurgh: The "Licit Magic" of the Arts in Medieval Islam* (New York University Press 1988)
2. Cf. e.g. Ibn Rashīq, *al-'Umda* I, 40: *bābu man rafa' ahu sh-shi'ru wa-man waḍa' uh.*
3. Cf. J. During, *Musique et extase, L'audition mystique dans la tradition soufie* (Paris: Albin Michel, 1988).
4. Cf. my *'Musicotherapy in the Islamic Middle Ages'*, in: *Studies in History of Medicine* (New Delhi 4/1980), pp. 23-28.
5. Cf. my 'The Romance' in. E. Yarshater (ed.) *Persian Literature* (New York: The Persian Heritage Foundation 1988), pp. 161-178, p. 172f.
6. Cf. my 'Der Wettstreit zwischen Plato und Aristoteles im Alexander-Epos des persischen Dichters Nizami', in: *Die Welt des Orients* 17/1986, pp. 95-109; *Persian Literature*, pp. 172-75.
7. On the Islamization of sciences, cf. my (forthcoming) book: *Allmacht und Mächtigkeit: Religion und Welt im Islam* (München: Beck 1991).
8. Cf. Koran, XXIII, 45; XL, 23.
9. Cf. Koran, III, 151.

3. REPETITIVE STRUCTURES IN ISLAMIC TEXTS

Repetition was one of the early means used in various arts to create mightiness. Important repetitive structures occur in the sacred texts of Islam, the Koran and the *ḥadīth,* as well as in prayers and in amulets. Some of these patterns are palpably linked with assertions of divine power. Thus, the Surah of the Koran in which the repetitive structure is most conspicuous, Surah 55, is a hymn to God's power, in which the question, *fa-bi' ayyi lā' i rabbikumā tukadhdhibān* (Which of the miracles of your Lord will you deny?), addressed to men and jinn, is repeated thirty-one times within a text of seventy-eight verses.[1] The frequency of the occurrences dramatically increases towards the end of the text; the structure is not only repetitive, but what we might call a stretto structure. This latter is a second system superimposed upon the text, a device, to which we shall return later in this paper.

Even more remarkable in this respect are certain *ḥadīths* in which the repetitive structure is a direct literary reflection either of *Heilsgeschichte*—sacred history structured by the appearance of prophets from Adam to Muḥammad—as in the *Ḥadīth al-Shafā' a,* or of the Koranic universe with its various spheres inhabited by prophets, as in the *Ḥadīth al-Mi' rāj.* [2] Both *ḥadīths* have, by the way, inspired many later literary works in which the basic repetitive structures reappear, sometimes in an enlarged and multiplied form. The *Ḥadīth al-Shafā' a* is at the bottom of 'Aṭṭār's *Muṣībatnāma,* as was shown by H. Ritter.[3] The *Ḥadīth al-Mi' rāj* is the nucleus of all the many short and long reports of Muḥammad's Ascension, as they appear in the prologues of Persian epics since Niẓāmī, and of the soul's journey as described in two of Ibn Sīnā's mystical treatises, as well as in Sanā'ī's *Sayr al-ibād,* 'Aṭṭār's *Manṭiq al-ṭayr* and so many later variations of the same motif.[4]

In all these cases the space structure of the universe imposes itself upon the time structure of the soul's life. This is most evident in the division of the life of Ḥayy ibn Yaqẓān, the hero of Ibn Ṭufayl's philosophical novel, into seven heptads.[5] The same structure of the universe, the Koranic and the Ptolemaic cosmologies meanwhile having merged into one concept, is also mirrored in Niẓāmī's *Haft Paykar.* The acquisition of mightiness through the building up of certain correspondences between one's life and the structures of the universe was one of the basic ideas of magic and astrology in antiquity and was continued in Islamicized forms.[6]

The soul's journey, divided either into heptads according to the seven spheres or into the forty stages of mystic's practical path, may also be understood as an image

---

1. Cf. A. Neuwirth, 'Symmetrie und Paarbildung in der koranischen Eschatologie,' Philologisch-Stilistisches u *Sūrat ar-Raḥman, in: Melanges de l'Université Saint-Joseph* 50/1984, pp. 445-80.
2. Cf. my 'Repetitive Structures in Early Arabic Prose', in (ed.) F. Malti-Douglas, *Critical Pilgrimages: Studies in the Arabic Tradition* (Literature East & West 25, Austin, TX, 1989), pp. 49-64.
3. H. Ritter, *Das Meer der Seele: Mensch, Welt und Gott in den Geschichten des Farīduddīn 'Aṭṭār.* Nachdruck mit Zusätzen und Verbesserungen, (Leiden 1978), p. 18f.
4. Cf. my 'Die Symbolik der Reise in der islamischen Geisteswelt', in: A. Zweig/M. Svilar (eds.) *Kosmos-Kunst-Symbol.* Akten des 3 Symposions der Gesellschaft fur Symbolforschung und Vortrage eines Zyklus des Collegium Generale der Universität Bern. (Schriften zur Symbolforschung 3, Bern, Lang 1986), pp. 113-38.
5. Cf. F. Zimmermann, in L. Conrad (ed.) *The World of Ibn Tufayl.* (Papers of a Symposium on Ibn Tufayl's Ḥayy Ibn Yaqẓān, forthcoming).
6. Cf. my (forthcoming) book: *Allmacht und Mächtigkeit.*

of its growing participation in divine power by increasing submission, until, in the moment of complete self-annihilation, it merges with the divine power. In earthly life, this divine mightiness of the mystics would often manifest itself by their miracles.[1]

Seven however, which as we know rules the repetitive rites of the pilgrimage, like forty, seems a modest number if compared with numbers dominating the phenomenon of repetition in popular piety. Think of the ninety-nine pearls or even the thousand pearls of the rosary, the endless repetitions of God's name in *dhikr*, and the huge numbers of pious formulas and mighty names reiterated in amulets.[2] As if the One God, who seems so fond of multiplication in his creation, could be impressed by such multiplied efforts!

However, there was also another way of charging oneself with divine mightiness. This method bordered on ecstasy, and consisted of the practice of mystical love, the veneration of a mystical friend.

4. MIGHTINESS & ECSTASY IN RUMI'S LYRICAL POETRY

Such is the case we are presented with in the life and poetry of Jalāl al-Dīn Rumi.[3] The verses in which Rumi derives mightiness from the reality, the presence or the promise of his mystical friend are countless. It is, as all of us know, a simple set of—ultimately Neoplatonic—ideas, which explain this being empowered through love. God is beautiful and His beauty manifests itself in earthly phenomena; by this beauty, the soul is inspired to love. Love thus becomes the life force of every motion, as Ibn Sīnā explained in his *Risāla fi' l-'ishq*.[4] Even the stars are moved by love, as Rumi stated in more than one of his verses

Through Love, the spheres are in harmony;
Without Love, the stars would be in eclipse...[5]

Usually, in Rumi's poetry, love appears personified in his mystical friend Shams-i Tabrīz who is invested with a supernatural and absolutely cosmic mightiness:

You are the river that moves the green wheel of the sky!
You are the face that amazes the moon and Venus!
You are the princely polo-stick that alone on the playground
of the mind sets all balls into motion![6]

1. Cf. R. Gramlich, *Die Wunder der Freunde Gottes. Theologien und Erscheinungsformen des islamischen Heiligenwunders; Freiburger Islamstudien 11*, (Wiesbaden: Steiner 1987).
2. Cf. R. Kriss & H. Kriss-Heinrich, *Volksglaube im Bereich des Islam* (Wiesbaden: Harrassowitz, 1960), II, pp. 53-57; 69-71; Kirfel, Der Rosenkranz (Beiträge zur Sprach und Kulturgeschichte des Orients, Heft 1, Walldorf 1949).
3. Cf. A. Schimmel, *The Triumphal Sun. A Study of the Works of Jalaloddin Rumi* (London: East-West Publications 1978).
4. A. Ates (ed.), *Rasā'il Ibn Sinā 3*: *'Risāla fi māhiyyat al-'ishq'* (Istanbul 1953).
5. *Kullīyyāt-i Shams yā diwān-i kabīr, (*ed.) Badi' al-Zamān Furūzānfar (Tehran, 1976, 2nd ed.) 2: 24 ('D' refers to the published book, the first number refers to the *ghazal* number in Furūzānfar's edition, the second to the verse, 'u' indicates the last verse).
6. D 729: 1-2

O light of the spheres and of the earth!
O lamp-like eye perceiving the invisible!
O thou before whom angels and kings
are one poorer than the other,
O you, the adored one of my soul—Shams al-Din![1]

In other poems, Rumi identifies or parallels the great prophets of monotheism from Adam to Muḥammad with Shams-i Tabrīz. This again may lead to repetitive structures like the following which appears in an Arabic *ghazal:*

Come, for you are Jesus, so revive our dead ones!
Come and ward off from us the Antichrist's fraud!
Come, for you are David, so take a coat of mail
To protect our life from the hitting of arrows!
Come, for you are Moses, and split the sea of perdition!
But drown the evil-doer Pharaoh!
Come, for you are Noah and we are in the deluge!
Is not the ark of Noah prepared against all dread?![2]

Very often Rumi's praise of the friend verges on deification, and he himself occasionally admits it, as for example, with these very plain words in an Arabic poem:

Your spirit is a sea of fidelity,
Your color the brilliance of purity,
By your life, but for piety,
I would exclaim: "O you, the Lord of Majesty!"[3]

At any rate, the Friend's presence, coming and image fill our poet's mind, heart and soul with immense joy, transforming a gloomy environment into a bright one, a negative reality into a positive one:

As long as the image of the friend is with us,
our whole life is full of vision.
Where there is union between the lovers,
By God, a confined room becomes an open plain.
When the reflected image of his beauty shines,
mountains and earth become silk and brocade.[4]

This is why to die before the Friend would be bliss.[5] In one of his love hymns Rumi confesses:

My love for you intoxicated me and made me dance,
I am intoxicated and in ecstasy (bīkhūdī), *what can I do?*
I will render the thanks of earth and Heaven,
for I was earth, He made me Heaven.[6]

---

1. D 1812
2. D 1369, 3-6; cf. also D 16.
3. *'umruka lawlā at-tuqā qultu ayā dhā' l-jalāl*, D 1368: 3.
4. D 364: 1,2,6.
5. *Khalqān zih marg andar ḥadhar, pīshash marā murdan shakar. D* 1791: 39; cf. also 26D 1639: 1 and the respective remarks in my 'Speech is a Ship and Meaning the Sea,' paper given during the Eleventh Levi Della Vida Conference on Islamic Studies, Los Angeles 1987 (forthcoming).
6. D 971: 1, 11b.

Ecstasy, ecstatic joy, enthusiasm and a feeling of cosmic mightiness are thus a predominant state of mind, a fundamental psychic condition in Rumi's poetry.

5. REPETITIVE STRUCTURES IN RUMI'S *GHAZALS*

How is this feeling expressed? Apart from the wording, which can no longer be dealt with in this paper, there are some structural elements which strike the reader as all-pervasive. These are structures of recurrence or repetition. Of course, the *ghazal* is by definition a repetitive structure. Its origin goes back to pre-Islamic times and thus can not be said to be sacred. The mono-rhyme and the monolithic structure cannot, tempting as the idea is, be called an original symbol of monotheism. Nevertheless, the clinging of Muslim poets to the *ghazal* and to the *qaṣīda* may well have to do with a feeling that this form was particularly apt for expressing ideas within a monotheistic culture. However this may be, the element of repetition appears amply enriched in Persian poetry, and particularly so in Rumi's *ghazals*. In addition to the repetitive structure of rhyme and rhythm, very often we encounter interior rhymes arranged after a rigid pattern so as to transform the *ghazal* almost into a strophic structure, as, for example, in the following line:

Makhdūm-i jānam Shams-i Dīn! az jāhat ay rūḥu'l-amīn
Tabrīz chūn 'arsh-i makīn, az masjid-i aqṣā biyā![1]

Adored one of my soul, Shams-i Dīn,
Through your glory, Oh trustworthy Spirit,
Tabriz is like the Heavenly Throne,
From the Remote Mosque, come!

—a clear identification of the friend with the Holy Spirit and with Muḥammad, if not with God himself.

Actually, there also exist some real strophic poems in Rumi's *Diwān* and the frequency of interior rhymes may also be even greater, as in the following line:

Ay nūr-i mā, ay sūr-i mā, ay dawlat-i manṣūr-i mā
jūshī binih dar shūr-i mā tā may shawad angūr-i mā[2]

O our light, our feast, O our victorious happiness,
Stir our ardour, so that our grapes become wine!

We find repetitions of words, as in the following quatrain:

Imrūz ṭawāfast u ṭawāfast u ṭawāf
Divānih mu'āfast u mu'āfāst u mu'āf
nay jang u maṣāfast u maṣāfast u maṣāf
waṣlast u zifāfāst u zifāfast u zifāf[3]

Today is round-walk, round-walk and round-walk!
The mad one is excused, excused and excused!
No war is it, nor battle, nor battle, battle!
It is union and wedding, wedding and wedding!

---

1. D 16: u.
2. D 4: 2.
3. D *rubā'ī* No. 1061.

Very often such word repetitions are used in vocatives and imperatives. Sometimes, similar structures stretch over a whole *ghazal*, as in the following poem, which begins with this line:

> Ay 'āshiqān, ay 'āshiqān, man khāk-rā gawhar kunam
> way muṭribān, ay muṭribān, daf-i shumā pur zar kunam
>
> *O lovers, O lovers! I turn the dust into jewels!*
> *O minstrels, O minstrels! I fill your tambourine with gold!*
> *O thirsty ones, O thirsty ones! Today I shall bring water*
> *and change this dry dust into a paradise, into a heavenly fountain!*[1]

—And so it continues throughout the poem, every line starting with a new doubled vocative followed by a mighty promise. One of the finest examples of repetitive structure is again a strophic poem, the opening poem of the letter *nūn,* in which every clause is repeated, obviously reflecting a musical structure:

> Biyā biyā, dildār-i man, dildār-i man, dar-ā dar-ā dar kār-i man, dar kār-i man
> tū-i tū-i gulzār-i man, gulzār-i man, bigū bigū asrār-i man, asrār-i man.[2]
>
> *Come, come, my beloved, my beloved—*
> *Be engaged, be engaged in my affairs, in my affairs;*
> *You, you are my rosegarden, my rosegarden—*
> *Tell me, tell me my secrets, my secrets.*

The most important repetitive structure in Rumi's *Diwān* is, however, a device called *radīf,* consisting of one or several words following the rhyme at the end of each line unchanged as an echo or a refrain. Space does not permit discussion of all the countless examples of repetition which Rumi's poetry contains, nor is it possible to give even a faint idea of the baffling variety of *radīf*s handled by him. Here are only a few examples: *'āshiqān* (lovers),[3] *khandih* (laughing),[4] *mīlarzī* (you tremble),[5] *bigirīstī* (he/it would weep),[6] *bīkhwīshī* (selflessness),[7] *bīkhūdī* (of self bereft),[8] *Iblīsī* (a Satan)[9] *Shams al-dīn,*[10] *sāqiyā* (O Saki),[11] *pūshīdih* (veiled),[12] *samā'* (concert),[13] *dīwānagī* (crazy),[14] etc.

Sometimes, the *radīf* is a whole phrase, resembling very much our refrains, consisting now in a religious formula like *Lā ilāha illā'Llāh* (There is no god but

1. D 1374
2. D 1785: 1.
3. D 1939; c.f. also *ay 'āshiqān in* D 1954.
4. D 2316; cf. also similar *radīf* like *Khandan* (1924), *mī-khand* (661) *mī-khandī* (2868) *khandīdan* (1989), *bi-khandīdī* (2525).
5. D 2877.
6. D 2893.
7. D 2504.
8. D 2775.
9. D 2879; 3250.
10. D 1859; 1960. Cf. also the elongated *radīf* of *"makhdūm-i jānam Shams-i Dīn"* in a strophic poem: D 1812.
11. D 149.
12. D 2420.
13. D 1295.
14. D 2895.

God),[1] *fi satr Allāh* (behind the veil divine)[2] or *al-ṣabru miftāḥu'l-faraj* (Patience is the key to delivery),[3] now in an address of mystical tinge like *ay māh tu kerā mānī* (O moon, whom do you resemble?)[4] or *chīzī bi-dih darvīsh-rā* (Give something to a dervish!)[5] now in an exclamation savouring rather of worldly than of mystical affairs: *tu chanīn shakar chirā'ī* (Why are you so sweet?)[6] or *āhistih kah sarmastam* (Go slow—because I am drunk).[7]

However, it is less difficult to annex a refrain than to integrate a word into the syntax of the verse. Very often, Rumi combines interior rhymes and *radīf*. Such combinations may be used for intensification so that the structure becomes tighter, as in a musical stretto. Thus, in a *ghazal* with the *radīf* of *biyā* (come!), we find the following line, in which, in addition to rhyme, radīf and interior rhymes, the poet repeats the word *jān* five times.

Ay jān tū jānhā chū tan, bījān chih arzad khūd badan
dil dādah'ām dīrast man, tā jān daham jānā biyā[8]

O thou the soul, before whom all other souls are but as bodies,
What use is a body without a soul?
I gave my heart away, it is late,
Come, O my soul, before I give my soul away!

The penultimate line of this *ghazal* introduces a new stretto by repeating the *radīf* already after the interior rhymes:

Ay Khusraw-i mahvash biyā, ay khūshtar az ṣad khūsh biyā
ay āb u ay ātash biyā, ay durr u ay daryā biyā[9]

O moon-like emperor, come!
O thou more beautiful than a hundred beauties, come!
O water and O fire, come!
O pearl and O sea, come!

In another *ghazal*, the friend has in fact come, and Rumi uses a *radīf*, interior rhymes and echo-like word repetitions, in order to express his joy. If one takes away the mass of repetitions, freeing the text of its redundant information, there remains less than half of the words. The poem is—one is tempted to say—an orgy of sound, or rather, for 'orgy' may sound blasphemous in our context, a gorgeous, neatly woven word-carpet, with all the ecstasy turned into ornament, as we know from Persian carpets. All these considerations may help us to read Rumi's mystical poetry with a new awareness of the structures he uses and their relatedness to a sparkling, many-faceted and yet, in the final analysis, surprisingly homogeneous religious and aesthetic context:

1. D 2407.
2. D 2418.
3. D 519.
4. D 3123 & 2604.
5. D 15.
6. D 2857.
7. D 1446 or 1448.
8. D 16: 7.
9. D 16: 12.

Spring-time has come, Spring-time has come,
Spring-time a-spreading musk has come!
The Friend has come, the Friend has come,
the Friend of patient grace has come!
The morning wine has come, the morning wine has come,
The morning wine for mirth and mind has come!
The moon-faced cupbearer with grace of gait
and gift of wine has come!
Clearness has come, clearness has come,
irradiating stone and sand;
Healing has come, healing has come,
healing of all the weak has come!
The beloved has come, the beloved has come,
drawn by the love of those who long!
The doctor has come, the doctor has come!
a doctor clear of mind has come!
The round-dance has come, the round-dance has come!
a round-dance without headache has come!
Spring-time has come, Spring-time has come,
an unheard-of Spring-time has come:
Sweet-scented basil, anemones
and fine-cheeked tulips now have come!
Somebody's come! Somebody's come!
turning into somebody a nobody!
A great one's come, a great one's come,
who has removed all the flying dust.
A heart has come! A heart has come!
A heart which makes laugh the hearts of all mankind;
A wine has come, a wine has come,
removing every hangover.
A foam has come, a foam has come,
through which the sea is full of pearls;
A king has come, a king has come:
who is the soul of every land.
How has he come, how has he come?
for he had never left this place.
It's just that the eyes are sometimes alert
and sometimes cease to look.
I close my eyes, saying: 'He's gone!'
I open them, saying: 'He's come!'
And he is—when I wake and when I sleep—
my cave's companion and my friend.
Now the speakers becomes mute,
Now the mute one begins to speak:
Give up the numbered letters
for letters beyond count have come.[1]

This structure, instead of—as one would surmise—hampering the poet's imagination to the degree of breaking its wings and turning the poetry into handicraft, can thus have the contrary effect, if the poet is a genius such as Mawlānā. Rumi made

1. D 569.

ample, even lavish use of this device, which evidently challenged his creative mind and mightiness and inspired his imagination. By mastering the imposed difficulties with apparent ease, he manifests his artistic skill over and over again. In other words, the *radīf* functions as a structure of increased mightiness.

6. SUPERIMPOSED SYSTEMS IN RUMI'S LYRICAL POETRY

The *radīf* is, in fact, a second system superimposed upon the traditional one of the *ghazal.* If we look for parallels in other forms of art, we may think of a musical structure in which a melody unfolds over a *basso continuo,* a device which actually occurs in the *samāʿ* ceremonies of the Niʿmatullāhī order in Iran, the Khalwatī-Jerrahi Sufi order in Turkey, and other mystical fraternities in the Muslim world.[1] Or we may think of a piece of calligraphy set upon a repetitive ornamental structure.[2] In all these cases, we have a contrast of change and continuity, and a dialectical or—to use a musical metaphor again—a contrapuntal relationship between these two systems, one static, the other dynamic. Actually, this relationship between the constantly repeated *radīf* and the contents—changing from verse to verse—can be very exciting and, in fact, create a continuum of varying nuances within the *radīf,* leading to a gradual transformation of its meaning. At any rate, both the element of ecstasy and that of control are intensified by this literary device, the poem is charged with a greater than normal creative power, its mightiness is enhanced.

One can imagine what amount of mightiness accrues to Shams-i Dīn in a poem of twenty-four lines, where his name functions as the *radīf,* with verses like the following:

There has not been before him nor will be after him
—I know for sure—
there has been no one similarly aware of the tablets of secrets
and as cognizant of them as Shams-i Din!

He himself, with his extraordinary qualities,
has nailed shut the door of potentiality,
so never again can come the like of Shams-i Din![3]

Another—seemingly inconspicuous—case, which, however, is a telling example of the above-mentioned dialectics, is found in a *ghazal* with the *radīf* of *khandīdan* (laughing).[4] The laughing 'because of' in the first few lines is gradually turned into a laughing 'in-spite-of;' the repetitive structure serves to express the transmutation of this laughter, its perseverance on another ontological level, its mightiness.

Another interesting example of the alchemical transformation of a meaning during the poem is a *ghazal* with the *radīf* of *ṭawāf,* or 'circumambulation', in which

1. See the discussion of music and *dhikr* in J. During's essay in this volume.
2. Cf. my 'Some General Features of Islamic Arts', paper given during a symposium on 'The Iconography of Islamic Art' at the University of Edinburgh, 26-27 October 1990.
3. D 1860: 17-18.
4. D 1989.

Shaykh Muḥammad Tabākānī (d. 1486) with Dervishes Dancing in *Samā'*. From a manuscript of the *Majālis al-'ushshāq*, dated 959/1552. MS. Ouseley Add. 24, f. 119r (Courtesy of the Bodleian Library, Oxford).

the word is totally divested of its exoteric ritualistic meaning and filled with mystical significations:

You are the Ka'ba of the souls: it is you whom I circumambulate!
I am no owl; not a ruin shall I circumambulate!

How many circumambulations does the clever pilgrim make?
Seven, seven! I am a frenzied pilgrim:
I don't count how often I circumambulate.

Love praised me, it made the circumambulation
around my dust every night like the moon on its face, on its head.
Love kneels like Heaven down before my clay,
and me, so drunk, like a goblet it circumambulates.[1]

With the repetitive pattern of the *radīf,* the poet thus disposes of various possibilities to create a tight or tightening structure, be it by simply phonetic or by semantic devices, or by both at the same time. Such structural tightness, in which we have discerned a manifestation of mightiness, has a certain affinity to the *horror vacui* in Islamic ornament and miniature. In an important article on the subject, Ettinghausen already expounded, although without pointing to parallels in poetry, that *horror vacui* often comes about by the superimposition of two or more systems of ornament.[2]

7. RUMI'S *GHAZAL* AS DANCE

We might, however, also draw another parallel, which seems to be nearer at hand in the case of Rumi. We might think of the whirling of the Mevlevi dervishes and call the *radīf* the axis, the pole, about which the poem turns or dances. Actually, Rumi not only speaks very often of the mystical round-dance, he has a number of poems in which this topic is pinned down in the *radīf* itself, either by a noun like *samāʿ* or by a verb like *gashtan,* 'to turn,' in various conjugated forms.

This brings us back to our initial point of departure: ecstasy and control. The whirling of the Mevlevis is certainly the most persuasive, most beautiful incarnation of the two polar principles of ecstasy and control. The rite is certainly performed with the aim of reaching ecstasy, mystical unity, or in other words, the repletion with divine mightiness. This is expressly stated in many of Rumi's verses dealing with the round-dance, as for example:

Come, come! Let us whirl about in the rose-garden!
Let us whirl like a compass around that point of divine grace!

We have sowed many seeds in the ground
and turned about the barren place.
Let us now whirl about the grain which no granary comprehends![3]

* * *

1. D 1305, 1, 7, 10, 11.
2. R. Ettinghausen, 'The Taming of the Horror Vacui in Islamic Art,' in *Proceedings of the American Philosophical Society* (123/1979), pp. 15-28.
3. D 1473: 1, 3.

As long as you are far from me, O soul, I am turning without soul.
Yet, since you set me whirling, I am turning around you!
I am as fragrant as the garden of union, I am like clear water in a brook,
Since favour is all around me, I will turn within this favour!

This last poem is again full of interior rhymes, as for example:

Kasī bāshad malūl ay jān kih u nabwad qabūl ay jān
manam āl-i rasūl ay jān pas-i sulṭān hamī gardam

One becomes sulky, O soul, who is not accepted, O soul!
I belong to the house of the Prophet, O soul,
I am turning behind the Sultan!

I am like a goblet in this circle of dancers,
turning from one hand to another with my story.[1]

The preceding *ghazal* also contained a similar structure:

Ṭawāf-i ḥājjiyān dāram bī-gird-i yār mīgardam
na akhlāq-i sagān dāram na bar murdār mīgardam

I shall make the circumambulation of the pilgrims around the friend,
I don't have the nature of dogs, that I should turn around a corpse!
I am not a moth that I should burn my wings in the fire,
I am the moth of the sultan, turning about a flood of light.
Come, O Shams, from Tabriz, for if you fade like the dawn,
I shall turn on your traces like dawn in these lands.[2]

As a final example let me quote a few lines from the great *ghazal* on the round-dance, based on the *radīf* of *samā'*, which shows the mightiness to be gained by this ceremony:

Come, come, o thou, who are the soul
of the soul of the soul of the round-dance!
Come thou, who are the walking cypress
in the garden of the round-dance.
Come thou, under whose feet is the fountain of light,
who hast a thousand Venuses in the heaven of the round-dance!
You leave the two worlds when you enter the round-dance!
Beyond the two worlds is this world of the round-dance!
The roof of the seventh sky is certainly high,
yet this roof does not reach where lies
the ladder of the round-dance.[3]

There are certainly other ghazals in which the aspect of mightiness is less conspicuous, or where the dynamics even tend in the opposite direction, with the poet emphasizing his weakness. But this is then exactly the other pole, the pole of control, and it usually carries the day at the end of the *ghazal*, when the poet withdraws into silence, having reached the point where the ineffable is reached, comparable to the moment when the Sufis of a convent have reached ecstasy and cease

1. D 1423, 1, 2, 5, u.
2. D 1422, 1, 16u.
3. D 1295: 1, 3-5.

dancing or singing. Rumi's lyrical poems thus oscillate, in fact, between the two poles of ecstasy and control, creating a potential of divine mightiness that can be tapped by every sensitive reader, like the *baraka* available at the shrine of a saint, yet on another level.

The fascination of Rumi's poetry cannot be completely explained by a structural analysis. Yet such an analysis can certainly show that form in Rumi's poetry is not accidental, but almost as important as the words; it is, in fact, part of the message. Rumi's poetry shows that tight repetitive structures represent the formal expression of ecstasy. Furthermore, it exemplifies the intrinsic Islamic principle of gaining mightiness through submission. By submitting to additional, self-imposed rules, Rumi executes, as it were, supererogatory works, but does he do this to gain mightiness, to realize ecstasy, or rather, because he is already so filled with might, so driven by ecstasy?

Finally, thus, his poetry incarnates by its very form man's whirling around himself, around his beloved, around the pole of the universe, around God, a whirling in harmony with the universe, because the whole universe—as we now know even better than Rumi—is full of dance, a "dance with God," as Rūzbihān Baqlī[1] put it,—and dance is controlled ecstasy.

1. A. Schimmel, *Mystical Dimensions of Islam* (Chapel Hill: University of North Carolina 1975), p. 182.

The *Qalandariyyāt* in Persian Mystical Poetry, From Sanā'ī Onwards

J.T.P. De Bruijn

I.

Already quite early in the history of Islamic mysticism it was realized that piety could easily become a great danger to spiritual life. The mental process which led to this insight could, for example, be the sudden awareness of an advanced mystic that his position as the leader and the revered model of a host of admiring followers is really a pitfall, because it tempts him to become convinced by his own holiness. The story of Shaykh San'ān, as it is told by Farīd al-Dīn 'Aṭṭār in the *Conference of the Birds (Manṭiq al-ṭayr),* is the classical illustration of this precarious situation. In a dream this great mystic is instructed to abandon his glorious role as a teacher of four-hundred adepts near the Ka'ba and to travel to the Byzantine lands where he falls in love with a Christian girl of superior beauty. The girl treats him very badly: she forces him to perform the most abject acts imaginable to the pious Sufi: to drink wine, to burn the Koran as well as his own Sufi cloak, to put on the Christian cincture *(zunnār)* and, in the end, even to become a swineherd. The descent of the Shaykh into utter humiliation is, however, a stage in the pursuit of his spiritual aims which cannot be avoided. It is a process of purification: there is no other way for him to overcome the formidable obstacle of his *riyā*—the 'self conceit' of the pious man.[1]

At the background of this parable stands the concept of *malāma,* 'blame'. From the late 3rd/9th century, onwards the attitude, designated in Sufi textbooks as *malāmatiyya,* is known to have been current especially in Khurasan where its first proponent would have been Ḥamdūn al-Qaṣṣār (died 271/884).[2] This tendency has found its reflection in several works on the theory of mysticism written in the subsequent centuries. The way out of the impasse into which piety almost inevitably leads is sought in the purifying force of criticism on the mystic's soul. Blame has, as Hujwīrī has put it, "a great effect in making love sincere"[3] The essence of the doctrine on blame is that the mystic should strive to become totally indifferent to the judgment of his behaviour by other people, either in a negative or in a positive

1. Cf. Farīd al-Dīn 'Aṭṭār, *Manṭiq al-ṭayr,* ed. Ṣādiq Gawharīn (Tehran 1348 sh.), pp. 67-88. In the text of this edition the name of the Shaykh is read Sam'ān on the basis of one of the oldest manuscripts of the poem.
2. On Ḥamdūn-i Qaṣṣār see 'Attār, *Tadhkirat al-Awliyā,* ed. R.A. Nicholson, vol. I (Leiden 1905), pp. 331-35.
3. *Kashf Al-Maḥjūb of Al-Hujwiri: The Oldest Persian Treatise on Sufism,* tr. R.A. Nicholson (London: Luzac & Co., 1976 New Edition; Gibb Memorial Series, vol. 17), p. 62.

sense. To reach this mental state of total detachment it is necessary to hide one's laudable deeds from the eyes of the people so as to avoid the damage their admiration might do to one's sincerity. One may also go further on this road and erect a facade of blameworthy behaviour which provokes the criticism of the respectable community. The fiercer the stings of the critics are, the more the mystic will be forced to detach himself from everything besides the object of his devotion. Blame, therefore, is often said to serve the same purpose as suffering does in a relationship of love.

However, this sophisticated attitude of the mystic has a pitfall of its own. The extreme practices based on the principle of blame could easily degenerate into an indulgence of antinomian behaviour for its own sake. Already Hujwīrī put his finger on this excess of blame, but a clear distinction between acceptable and unacceptable forms of *malāma* was made for the first time by Shihāb al-Dīn ʻUmar Suhrawardī (539/1144-632/1234) in a famous passage of his *ʻAwārif al-maʻārif*. Suhrawardī restricts the application of *malāmatiyya* to the former code of behaviour which he defines as the principle of *katm al-ʻibādāt,* the dissimulation of acts of obedience. The excessive consequences of this point of view, which were drawn by those whom Suhrawardī accuses of the 'destruction of conventions' *(takhrīb al-ādāt),* is called *qalandariyya*. There is no indication that Suhrawardī meant by this anything else but a tendency which began to manifest itself in the life of the Sufis in his age.[1]

This censure of antinomianism in the Sufi tradition did not prevent that, very soon, the type of the extreme *malāmatī* mystic manifested itself in practical life under the very name of the *'qalandar'*. Legend will have it that a group calling itself 'followers of the *qalandar* way' emerged about 620/1223 in Damascus, from whence they spread first to Dimyat in Egypt and then to many other countries. The founder is said to have been Sayyid Jamāl ad-Dīn from the Iranian city of Sāwa, who introduced the basic rules of the *qalandar*s: the complete shaving of hair on the head, the initiation through a four times repeated *takbīr* (symbolizing irrevocable divorce from all values of earthly existence), the wearing of sacks *(juwāliq)* and the prescription to lead the life of a wandering beggar. The hagiography of Jamāl ad-Dīn is contained in a *mathnawī* poem written in the foutteenth century which was published by Tahsin Yazici.[2] Whatever the historical value of this account may be, it is certain that, from about the early 7th/13th century, what became known as the way of the *qalandar* was inseparable from the spectrum of Sufi life in most countries of Islam. In spite of the bad reputation they usually had vis-à-vis the moderate mainstream of Sufism, the *qalandar* dervishes were not always outcasts: some of the great Sufi orders were tolerant enough to assign a special rite to these extravagant brothers apart from the rules set for the ordinary adherents.

Besides the two areas mentioned so far—mystical theory and the actual life of the Sufis—the *qalandar* has manifested himself in a third manner, namely as the

1. See the German translation of this passage by Ritter, 'Philologika XV: Farīduddīn ʻAṭṭār...Der Dīwān,' in *Oriens* 12 (1959), pp. 14-16, and further the German translation by R. Gramlich, *Die Gaben der Erkenntnisse des Umar as-Suhrawardi (ʻAwaref al-maʻaref)* (Wiesbaden 1978).
2. *Manākib-i Camāl al-Dīn-i Sāvī* (Ankara 1972).

principal character of a literary genre. Since mediæval times, he has wandered through the works of the Persian poets in the garb of provocative poetical motifs. Even in the present century the force of these motifs has not yet worn out, for they still play a conspicuous role in the work of one of the greatest Muslim poets of our age, Muḥammad Iqbal.[1]

II.

In spite of the ubiquity of *qalandar* motifs in Persian poetry, the subject has played only a minor role in modern literary scholarship. The first serious studies on *qalandarīyyāt* as a literary phenomenon only date from the 1950's and early 1960's when Hellmut Ritter published the results of his investigations into the works of Farīd al-Dīn 'Aṭṭār. Particularly important is his article of 1959 which appeared in the journal *Oriens,*[2] under the unpresuming title of *'Philologika XV'*. Instead of a survey of philological data concerning the Diwan of 'Aṭṭār which one would expect to find under this heading, the article actually contained a detailed analysis of *qalandar* motifs in the *ghazals* of this poet. Ritter also makes some comparisons with the older Sanā'ī and with the younger Ḥāfiẓ, but the emphasis is on portraying 'Aṭṭār as a *qalandarī* poet. The article reveals a rich flowering of *qalandarī* motifs in mystical poems dating from the first few decades of the 7th/13th century. It may not be a coincidence that they were written about the time when an influential Sufi Shaykh like Suhrawardī found it necessary to censure the *qalandar* attitude and when, to all probability, the first mystics using this name made their appearance. By this the question is raised what the connection between the three kinds of *qalandariyyāt* really was.

III.

The word *qalandar* can indeed be attested in earlier sources dating from the late 5th/ llth or 6th/12th century, the best known among them being a few quatrains connected with the names of famous mystics like Abū Sa'īd, Bābā Ṭāhir and Aḥmad-i Ghazzālī, often cited by modern writers on the *qalandariyyāt*. In 1976, Fritz Meier gave a comprehensive survey of this scattered data on *qalandariyyāt* in an Appendix to his monumental study on Abū Sa'īd.[3] It is important to note that, prior to the beginning of the 13th century, all instances of the use of the word *qalandar* which are on record belong to the realm of literature.

By far the most interesting of these early documents is a short prose text entitled *Qalandarnāma,* ascribed to the 11th century mystic 'Abdullāh Anṣārī Harawī (1005-89) together with a number of similar texts.[4] The *Qalandarnāma* contains

1. See J.C. Bürgel, 'The Pious Rogue: A Study in the Meaning of *qalandar* and *rend* in the Poetry of Muḥammad Iqbal', in *Edebiyat: A Journal of Middle Eastern Literatures,* Vol. 4, no. 1 (1979), pp. 43-64.
2. *Oriens,* Vol.12 (1959), pp. 1-88.
3. *Abū Sa'īd-i Abū'l-Ḫayr (357-440/967-1049): Wirklichkeit und Legende* (Acta Iranica 11, Tehran and Liège 1976), pp. 494-516
4. The *Qalandarnāma* was published by M.J. Sharī'at, *Sukhanān-i Pīr-i Harāt* (Tehran 1358 A.Hsh.). pp. 34-42.

the story of the sudden appearance of a *qalandar* in a *madrasa* where young boys (including the writer himself) are absorbed in their theological studies. The stranger blames the boys for their vain ambition to become great scholars. Instead, they should show their respect to the 'elders' (that is: the Sufi *shaykhs)* who attend to their spiritual needs. The students become fascinated by these words and throw their books away, following the *qalandar* to a place called 'the place of the chains' *(zanjīrgah),* by which a madhouse is presumably meant. There he goes on to preach to Anṣārī personally, both in prose and verse.

The attribution of the *Qalandarnāma to* Anṣārī is not beyond doubt, but it is extremely difficult to arrive at a firm conclusion one way or the other. Anṣārī is mentioned in the concluding lines of the poems where he is addressed as *'Anṣārīyā'* or *'yā pīr-i Anṣār.'* As far as their prosodical form is concerned, these poems are undoubtedly *ghazals*, but they do not contain any of the characteristics of the anacreontic genre. They are didactic poems and are, on that account, closely related to the surrounding prose text. It is quite evident that they are integrated parts of the latter and cannot be dismissed as later insertions. Although this is, of course, insufficient proof of the authorship of Anṣārī himself, it makes it at least very likely that the text was produced in an environment which kept his mystical tradition alive. As we know, the Sufi convent of Herat, founded by Anṣārī, was perpetuated by his descendants and his pupils well into the 6th/12th century. There is also evidence that the poet Sanā'ī was in contact was this circle in Herat at some time in the early decades of that same century.[1]

IV.

Rather surprisingly, Sanā'ī of Ghazna (d. 525/1131) has so far received no more than passing attention in the study of the literary *qalandariyyāt*. The reason for this must be that his work was overshadowed by the abundant growth of Persian mystical poetry in subsequent centuries. However, there can be no doubt that his name should be at the center of a study of this subject especially if such a study takes into account the development of the genre. Sanā'ī was indeed the first Persian poet who exploited the motif of the *qalandar* to the full.

Even the term *qalandariyyāt* itself was for the first time applied to a collection of poems in the textual tradition of Sanā'ī 's Divan. We find such collections in two of the earliest manuscripts: in a MS. in the Millī-yi Malik collection, formerly at Tehran but now kept at Mashhad, and a MS. in Kabul which was published in a facsimile edition in 1977.[2] Both manuscripts are undated but, to all likelihood, are to be attributed to the 8th/13th century. They use the term *'qalandariyyāt'* as the heading of a collection of about one hundred poems. A similar heading occurs in the *Mukhtārnāma, in* a collection of quatrains by Farīd al-Dīn 'Aṭṭār.[3]

It is certain that Sanā'ī did not himself select this group of poems from his works in order to distinguish it as a special collection. The selection must be due to the in-

1. See the present writer's *Of Piety and Poetry: The Interaction of Religion and Literature in the Life and Works of Ḥakīm Sanā'ī of Ghazna* (Leiden: E.J. Brill 1983), pp. 74-77.
2. *Kullīyyāt-i ash'ār-i Ḥakīm Sanā'ī Ghaznavī*, ed. 'A.A. Bashīr (Kabul 1356 A.Hsh.).
3. See H. Ritter, 'Philologika XVI...Muxtārnāme' in *Oriens* 13-14 (1961), pp. 219-222.

tervention of a later editor of the Diwan, who recognized the outlines of a specific genre in the many motifs related to *qalandarī* imagery used by Sanā'ī. Terms like '*qalandariyyāt*', which are based on the ending *-iyyāt,* were frequently coined in the traditional philology of the Arabs and the Persians to serve as names for diverse 'kinds' *(anwā')* of poetry.[1] In the same manuscripts similar headings are given to other thematic collections, such as *zuhdiyyāt* (poems on ascetic themes) and the *ghazaliyyāt.*

Sanā'ī's collection of *qalandariyyāt* appears on closer examination to be a very mixed group of poems, some of which show only a few traces of the typically *qalandarī* motifs. As far as the formal characteristics of the poems are concerned, it is not quite clear whether they should be regarded as *qaṣīdas* or *ghazals,* and modern editors of the Diwan have for that reason classified them alternatively in the former or in the latter category. Moreover, a fairly large number of his poems outside this collection—mostly *ghazaliyyāt* or *rubā'iyyāt,* but occasionally a *qaṣīda* or a *tarkīb-band* as well—should have been included as they also contain elements which unmistakably belong to the *qalandarī* genre.

V.

For the purpose of the present paper I have made the following rough classifications of the poems in Sanā'ī's Divan which contain *qalandarī* elements:

a. Poems in which the term *kharābāt* (literally meaning the ruins) plays a leading part, both as far as form and content are concerned.

b. Poems marked by the presence of a short narrative or sometimes no more than an anecdotal trait, based upon *qalandarī* motifs.

c. Poems in which *qalandarī* motifs are used as one of the many ingredients in an *andarz* poem, and as such, is mingled with motifs belonging to quite different genres (most of Sanā'ī's *qalandarī* poetry is of this type).

The *kharābāt* type is the most easily recognizable kind of the three, mainly because of a conspicuous prosodical feature found in these poems, which is that they nearly all have a rhyme on the Arabic feminine plural suffix: *'āt'*. The word *kharābāt,* which is always included among the rhyming words, is sometimes repeated in each line by way of an *iltizām.* There is a preference for words borrowed from religious terminology like *ṭāmmāt* (here used in the sense of the inspired speech of the Sufis), *libāsāt* (disguises, meaning hypocrisy), *ṭā'āt* (acts of obedience), *karāmāt* (miracles, as conspicuous tokens of holiness) and *munājāt* (pious prayers). The point of this kind of poem is to give such terms an ironic twist and thus to create a sharp contrast to the terms characteristic of the *qalandarī* way, of which the *kharābāt* is the most important motif.

The *kharābāt* (ruins), according to the traditional dictionaries, refers to 'a tavern, a gambling-house or a brothel' (Steingass).[2] Although this definition is already a figurative extension of the literal meaning, such definitions give a very incomplete

---

1. Cf. Gregor Schoeler, 'Die Einteilung der Dichtung bei den Arabern', in *ZDMG 123* (1973), pp. 9-55; the same, *Arabische Naturdichtun,* (Beirut 1974), pp. 1 ff.
2. The meaning of *kharābāt* in the social history of mediaeval Islam had been studied by 'Abd al-Ḥusayn Zarrīnkūb, in *Yaghmā* 7/5 (1344/1965), pp. 225-29.

picture of the wide range of figurative notions which were attached to the word in the course of its functioning as a *qalandarī* term.

In Persian literature, an early example of its use in a straightforward negative sense is given by Manūchihrī (died about 1040). One of his poems features a 'gathering of gentlemen' *(Majlis-i aḥrār*—wherein one enjoys drinks, listens to the music of the *rabāb* and eats *kabab)* contrasted to the disreputable *kharābāt-i kharāb* where the customers indulge in the game of backgammon.[1]

Almost a century later, Aḥmad Ghazālī mentioned the *kharābāt* in a quatrain inserted in the *Sawāniḥ* in which 'a beggar in the street of the ruins' who frequents these wicked places asking for the 'charity of wine' is introduced. Ghazālī uses the images of the beggar (*qalandar*) and the ruins to illustrate the state of the lover who has subjected himself entirely to the demands of his love. Both *qalandar* and *kharābāt* have, therefore, acquired positive values within this context. However, the connotation of disrespectability has been preserved because it is essential to the effect the author wanted to achieve through the choice of this imagery.[2]

At a further stage, *kharābāt* often became a mere allegorical item. This is, for instance, the case when Rūzbihān Baqlī (d. 606/1209) uses the expression *kharābāt-i maḥabbat* (the ruins of love)[3] or when Najm ad-Dīn Dāya Rāzī (618/1221) speaks of *kharābāt-i fanā* (ruins of effacement) and the *kharābāt-i arwāḥ* (the ruins of the spirits).[4] The final stage of the development toward allegorization was reached by Maḥmūd Shabistarī (d. 737/1337) who, in the section of the *Gulshan-i rāz* devoted to explaining the meaning of the *kharābātiyyān* (Tavern-haunters in Whinfield's translation) draws up a catalogue of the symbolic meanings of *kharābāt:*

> *To be a haunter of taverns is to be freed from self,*
> *Self-regard is paganism, even if it be righteousness.*
> *They have brought you news from the tavern*
> *That unification is shaking off relations.*
> *The tavern is of the world that has no similitude,*
> *It is the place of lovers that reck not.*
> *The tavern is the nest of the bird of the soul,*
> *The tavern is the sanctuary that has no place...*[5]

Going back to Sanā'ī the question should be raised how far this development had proceeded in his particular case. The short *mathnawī* poem, *Sayr al-'ibād ila'l-ma'ād* provides two interesting examples of the allegorical use of *kharābāt,* both of which have to do with the theme of love, although referring to one of its extremes. The first passage mentions *kharābāt* as symbolic of sensuous love: it is described as a desolate place where the planet Jupiter *(hurmuzd)* reigns over the forces of lust which are controlled by the animal soul. Another powerful emblem mentioned in this context is the 'sea-dragon of love' *(nahang-i 'ishq).* At a much later stage of the

1. Manūchihrī Dāmghānī, *Dīwān*, ed. M. Dabīr-Siyāqī (Tehran 1347 A.Hsh.), p. 7.
2. Aḥmad Ghazālī, *Savāniḥ*, ed. H. Ritter (Istanbul 1942), p. 15.
3. *Sharḥ-i shaṭhiyyāt*, ed. H. Corbin (Tehran 1981), p. 7.
4. *Mirṣād al-'ibād*, ed. M. Riyāḥī (Tehran 1972), pp. 219-20.
5. Sa'd al-Dīn Māḥmud Shabistarī, *Gulshan-i Raz: The Mystic Rose Garden*, ed. & translated by E.H. Whinfield, (London 1880), p.81.

soul's journey towards its perfection, is dealt with in the *Sayr al'ibād* there is another place called *kharābāt*. This is the stage to which the Koranic phrase *qāba qawsayn* (LIII: 9; "He approached to two bow-lengths") refers. Dervishes who have traveled that far are able to devote themselves to mystical love.

In the poems of the *kharābātī* type, on the other hand, the concreteness of the original imagery has been retained. Most poems take the form of a defiance of respectable piety through a declaration of adherence to life in the *kharābāt*. The following paraphrase of a typical specimen provides an impression of the recurrent motifs:

Why do you read the Koran like a pious Muslim?
Go and have a look at the ruins!
Sometimes I play backgammon with the tramps,
Sometimes I move my castle, sometimes I am checkmated.
Sometimes I moan like the mouthpiece of a flute.
Sometimes I raise my cup in the middle of my devotions,
Sometimes my cheek lies in the dust on the ground.
Sometimes I cry out towards the heavens.
Drunkenness has devastated me so much
That I cannot discern words from their meanings.
The minstrel is to me a muezzin;
I cannot tell deceit from a sincere prayer...[1]

Apart from this emphasis on a debauched life Moses *(Mūsā)* and Pharoah *(Fir'awn)* frequently appear as exemplary characters: the former provides an example of the uncompromising attitude of the customer of the *kharābāt;* the latter for the state of selfishness from which he wants to detach himself.

In one of these poems, which comes close already to the narrative type, the situation has been reversed: the poet's beloved is inside the ruins whereas the poet remains outside adopting an attitude which ironically is called *it'ikāf,* 'seclusion', as if he were a pious hermit:

Since the king of the ruins made his way into the ruins
I live in seclusion along the way that leads to the ruins.[2]

By chance, evidence has come to light which may be relevant to the origin of this type of poems. In an article published in 1948, Muḥammad Mu'īn has shown that one of the *kharābātī* poems of Sanā'ī is by and large identical to the *nasīb* of a *qaṣīda* of Burhānī, the court poet of Sultan Malikshāh. A very similar version of the same poem is contained in a poem by Burhānī's son Mu'izzī. The existence of these two specimens of secular court poetry makes it clear that the type cannot have been a personal invention of Sanā'ī. Mu'īn saw no other explanation for this than the suspicion that Sanā'ī just plagiarized Burhānī.[3] Even if were be correct, it would still provide an interesting example of the way in which Sanā'ī built up his repertoire of *qalandarī* poetry. Perhaps these strange poems about the ruins had their origin in a popular tradition. With their emphasis on sound effects and the repetition of

1. *Dīwān-i Sanā'ī*, ed. Mudarris Raḍavī (Tehran 1341 A.Hsh.), *Qaṣīda* no. 29, bb. 1-7
2. *Dīwān-i Sanā'ī, Qaṣīda* no. 28, b. 1.
3. Cf. Mu'īn's *ta'līqāt*

phrases, they make the impression of having been intended as songs. Unfortunately, we know next to nothing of the actual use that was made of the poems which have only reached us as isolated pieces of a literary tradition.

The *kharābātī* type has been remarkably successful in the tradition of mystical *ghazals*. Through its distinct features of form and content it lent itself easily to imitations. We find poems clearly derived from Sanā'ī's models in the works of all poets in the following centuries who, in some degree or another, were influenced by the *qalandarī* literary genre. Amongst them are, in the 13th century, 'Aṭṭār, Sa'dī, Rumi, Sulṭān Walad and 'Irāqī; in the 14th century, Ḥāfiẓ and Shāh Ni'matullāh Walī.

In Sanā'ī's *qalandariyyāt,* the narrative elements which are the distinctive feature of our second type are still rather simple. A common scene depicted in such poems is the sudden appearance of the poet's beloved as a *qalandar* from a tavern. The poet especially deals with the effect this event makes on the awaiting lovers.[1] Another important subject is the report of the experiences in a *qalandarī* environment during the previous night *(dūsh)*. In one instance, this is described as a journey to the heavens *(mi'rāj dar kharābāt)*.[2] An encounter with a 'spiritual leader' of the *qalandar* rite, the *pīr-i qalandar*, well-known from Ḥāfiẓ, was already a theme in Sanā'ī's poetry.[3]

The most elaborate specimen is a rather long poem about a meeting between the poet and a person described as 'a shining figure, an ornament of old age' whom Sanā'ī sees coming down towards him from the mountain when he leaves his house 'in all ignorance.' The old man invites him to accompany him to a party. Together they go to a house which is beautiful, pure and without any sign of decay. However, the people inside are a bunch of rascals *(qawmī hama qallāshān)* and *pīrān-i kharābātī* who indulge in all sorts of debaucheries. When the poet is shocked by this scene, the old guide withholds him from a condemnation: "Do not regard their doctrine as sinful, but keep their secrets hidden from the people."

Such anecdotes occur with more frequency among *qalandarī* poems of Farīd al-Dīn 'Aṭṭār who was undoubtedly a much greater story-teller than was Sanā'ī. No more than one example can be mentioned here. This *ghazal* is of particular importance because it shows how 'Aṭṭār amalgamated this type with the previous one: the characteristic rhyming words are there as well as the usual references to *Mūsā* and *Fir'awn*. The poem describes the visit of a pious Shaykh, "well-known as a miracle-worker," to a *kharābāt* in order to admonish the drunkards living there, but his effort has a reverse effect. When one of the *kharabātī*s lets him taste from the dregs of his wine it is in the end the Shaykh who becomes converted:

> *My brain stumbled, I left aside all idle talk* (khurāfāt).
> *Delivered from the Pharaoh of my existence*
> *I took my way like Moses to the Appointed Time* (mīqāt).

1. *Dīwān-i Sanā'ī, Qaṣīdas* nos. 42, 67, 77; cf. *ghazal* no. 302.
2. *Dīwān-i Sanā'ī, Qaṣīda* no. 93: *shab-i mi'rāj dar kharābāt.*
3. *Dīwān-i Sanā'ī, Qaṣīdas* nos. 43 and 294.

Fakhr al-Dīn ʿIrāqī and the *Qalandar*s on the Road to India. From a manuscript of the *Majālis al-ʿushshāq*, dated 959/1552. MS. Ouseley Add. 24, f. 79b (Courtesy of the Bodleian Library, Oxford).

Finally, when the converted Shaykh has regained enough self-consciousness to want to approach the goal of his desires, the *kharābātī* reminds him once more of the futility of such a wish:

> *You will see many games going on and forth*
> *But in the end you will always be checkmated* (shāhmāt).[1]

The poems of the third type really defy a proper classification. They deal, for instance, with the formulation of the intention to visit the *kharābāt* and the explanation for its 'reasons':[2] they provide a definition of what is meant by the expression *kār-i qallāshī*, 'the work of the rascals';[3] they discuss the meaning of wine-drinking as an element of the 'rule of the *qalandar*' *('āyīn-i qalandar)*,[4] or examine the association between love[5] and unbelief *(kufr)*[6] on the one hand and the theme of the *qalandariyyat* on the other hand.

Many of these poems are really religious *andarz* poems in which the *qalandarī* elements are only part of a variegated imagery serving as illustration to a point made in a continuing homily. One finds them, for instance, in hymns on the Prophet *(na't* poems),[7] in discussion on the theory of mystical love[8] or on the rejection of the world[9] and several other ascetic and religious themes, which could also be classified under the heading of the *zuhdiyyāt* genre.[10]

The combination of *qalandarī* motifs with those of other genres, which is characteristic of the last-mentioned group of poems, points to the importance of the terminology for the definition of the genre. Only a few remarks can be made here.

Next to *kharābāt,* which we discussed earlier, *qalandar* is a pivotal term. Many suggestions have been made as far as the origin of this word is concerned, but none of them is really convincing. Nevertheless, the question of its etymology remains of considerable importance because the correct answer could help us to solve another problem, namely that of the relationship between the earliest references to it in literature and the history of Sufism: was the term *qalandar* already used for antinomian mystics before it was adopted in literature, or was it by origin no more than an appellation for a begging tramp and an outcast of medieval Muslim society? A parallel term is *qallāsh* (rascal), which Sanā'ī uses even more frequently than *qalandar*. One of his *andarz* poems is entirely devoted to an exposition of the 'rite of the *qallāsh*' *(āyīn-i qallāshī)*. In this case there also exists an unsolved etymological problem. Although the word seems to be an Arabic *fa'āl* formation, it does not really go back to an Arabic root.

---

1. Farīd al-Dīn 'Aṭṭār, *Dīwān-i ghazaliyyāt va qaṣā'id,* ed. Taqī Tafaḍḍulī (Tehran 1341 A.Hsh.), no. 17.
2. *Dīwān-i Sanā'ī, Qaṣīdas* nos. 51, 92, 98, 108, 144.
3. *Dīwān-i Sanā'ī, Qaṣīdas* nos. 60, 145,166; see further: 225, 254, 259, 276, 213, 214, 262, 51.
4. *Dīwān-i Sanā'ī, Qaṣīdas* nos. 191, 222.
5. *Dīwān-i Sanā'ī, Qaṣīdas* nos. 138-156; cf. 48, 154, 137.
6. *Dīwān-i Sanā'ī, Qaṣīdas* nos. 196, 200, 221, 135, 182.
7. *Dīwān-i Sanā'ī, Qaṣīdas* nos. 3, 111.
8. *Dīwān-i Sanā'ī, Qaṣīdas* nos. 196, 200, 221, 135, 182.
9. *Dīwān-i Sanā'ī, Qaṣīdas* nos. 149, 188, 266.
10. *Dīwān-i Sanā'ī, Qaṣīdas* nos. 11, 35, 180, 187, 198, 206, 219, 262.

Particular to the *qalandar* genre are more terms which refer to gambling, games of chess and backgammon. The *qalandar* is described as a *kamzan:* a person who has put everything on one stake. He has run into checkmate *(shahmāt).* Since he is also a heavy drinker *(rind),* terms belonging to the genre of wine poetry are hard to distinguish from those of the *qalandariyyāt.* The same should be said about terms suggesting the *qalandarī*'s involvement in non-Islamic cults which were traditionally subsumed under the heading *'kufriyyāt'*. Mention is made in Sanā'ī's poetry of the 'rite of Zoroaster' *('āyīn-i Zardusht),* of taking on the girdle of the unbelievers *(zunnār bastan)* and of encounters with 'a young Christian' *(tarsābachcha)* or the 'Shaykh of the Magians' *(pīr-i mughān).* All these terms are familiar from the works of later Persian poets.

The inventory of these terms and their distinction from different sets of terms is one of the essential requirements of a further study of the *qalandariyyāt.* At least one general trait of this terminology can already be formulated: nearly always, a reversal is involved of the values originally attached to these terms. The change may work in two directions. The most central terms of the *qalandarī* vocabulary initially possessed a strongly negative connotation, which undoubtedly was the cause for their inclusion in this set of terms. Following the role played in the genre, they ended up having acquired a new and equally strong positive value. On the other hand, there are also terms derived from a religious vocabulary which in the course of their use as *qalandarīyyāt* terms were loaded with a distinctive negative charge.

In my book *Of Piety and Poetry*[1] I have proposed to call Sanā'ī a homiletic poet The choice of this particular qualification of his function as a religious poet was founded, on the one hand, on the evidence of his biography, which shows clearly that preachers played a large part in his career as a religious poet. The most important among these preachers was the chief-judge in the Khurasanian city of Sarakhs, Sayf al-Dīn Muḥammad ibn Manṣūr. To this influential protector Sanā'ī addressed himself in his most interesting work, the short *mathnawī* poem, *Sayr al-'ibād ila' l-ma'ād.* Another poem composed in honour of this patron is a *tarkīb-band* of which one stanza is a *qalandarī* poem of the *andarz* type.

On the other hand, many of his works can best be described as sermons in poetical form. This is true not only of his *mathnawī*s but also of numerous short poems in his Divan. The *qalandarī* genre which we have discussed appears to have become an integral part of Sanā'ī's homiletic discourse. The sensuality and coarseness of some of the poems, which Hellmut Ritter pointed out in making comparisons with the *qalandariyyāt* of 'Aṭṭār, is not in contradiction with their figurative intention. The shocking nature of such passages only served to enhance their effect on the public to whom these poetical sermons were addressed.

If these poems were, therefore, never intended as statements of plain libertinism, it is also likely that they are not direct reflections of an antinomian practice, although the legends which grew up around Sanā'ī have indeed tried to picture him as a real *qalandar.* The relationship with the milieu of his literary activities, notably with a distinguished Ḥanafī scholar like Muḥammad ibn Manṣūr, allows us to con-

1. J.T.P. De Bruijn, *Of Piety and Poetry: The Interaction of Religion and Literature in the Life and Works of Ḥakīm Sanā'ī of Ghazna.*

clude that Sanā'ī intended the *qalandar* and all that was connected with this character as a set of symbols for the preaching of a kind *malamātī* spirituality which remained within the boundaries of Islamic orthopraxis.

VI.

The three forms of the *qalandarī* tradition which we have mentioned at the outset—the theoretical, the practical and the literary—can best be studied separately, at least up to the point where sound documentary evidence for their interrelationship appears. As far as Persian literature is concerned, we have a substantial corpus of poems at hand for the study of the adoption of the *qalandariyyāt* into a homiletic tradition. The remarkable success of these terms and motifs owes much to the succession of prominent Sufi poets in the 13th and 14th centuries, but first of all to Sanā'ī who developed a varied imagery to be used in his own homiletic poetry.

Already in the case of Sanā'ī, a development can be noticed in the use of the *qalandarī* motifs. This development transformed what originally was but daring imagery, derived perhaps from secular poetry, into items of a set of symbolic allegories. In any case, it is perfectly clear that Sanā'ī always used the *qalandarī* motifs in a figurative sense. This leaves no room for speculations either about his personal life or his adherence to antinomian views.

The Ḥurūfī Legacy of Faḍlullāh of Astarābad

III

H. T. Norris

Brother Yves found a book by the head of the Old Man's bed, and in that book were written words that our Lord when on earth had said to St. Peter. And Brother Yves said to him: "Ah! for Gods sake, sire, read often in this book, for these are very good words." And the Old Man said he ofttimes did so. "Since our Lord St. Peter, " said he, "is very dear to me; for at the beginning of the world the soul of Abel, when he was killed, went into the body of Noah; and when Noah died it returned into the body of Abraham; and from the body of Abraham, when he died, it came into the body of St. Peter, at that time when God came on earth."

When Brother Yves heard this, he showed him that his creed was not sound, and taught him with many good words; but the Old Man would not listen to him. And these things Brother Yves told to the king, when he came back to us.

When the Old Man rode abroad, a crier went before him bearing a Danish axe, with a long haft all covered with silver, and many knives affixed to the haft; and the crier cried: "Turn aside from before him who bears in his hands the death of kings!"[1]

Thus wrote De Joinville in his *Memoirs of the Crusades of St. Louis*, in 1309, some thirty years before the birth (in 739-40/1339-40) of Shihāb al-Dīn ibn Bahā'l-Dīn Faḍlullāh of Astarābad, the founder of what has been variously described as the Ḥurūfī sect, religion, heresy and religious order.[2]

The Old Man of the Mountains was not a Ḥurūfī, in the sense that he adopted as his revelationary premise the interpretations that were set out in the *Jāwidān-i-kabīr* and those other works that are attributed to Faḍlullāh or to his successors. Yet the fact cannot be ignored that inasmuch as the Ḥurūfiyya are a genuine expression of Sufism at a particular point in its history; the movement is also Janus-faced and peculiar in its visage. I do not apologize therefore for beginning this essay with some comment upon the Ismā'īlī or *bāṭinī* tradition in the Ḥurūfiyya. I can but cite the close of the *Jāwidān* itself: "He (the Prophet), peace be upon him, said, 'Verily, the Koran has an outward (meaning), and an inward (meaning) and the inward an inward unto seven inwards'," recalling the revolutionary theory that the Koranic text possesses seven esoteric levels of meaning each of them corresponding to one of the subtle centers of light. Faḍlullāh was both an heir and a legator and it would be

1. De Joinville, in *Memoirs of the Crusades by Villehardouin and De Joinville*, translated by Sir Frank Marzials, Everyman Series, 1908, London and New York, pp. 250-1.
2. For most recent lists of sources referring to the principal articles and books on Faḍlullāh and the Ḥurūfiyya, see the article by H. Algar in *Encyclopedia Iranica*, vol. 2, pp. 841-4, s.v. 'Astarābādī' and A. Haas, *Die Bektaşi Riten und Mysterien eines Islamischen Ordens* (Berlin: Express Edition, 1987).

آمن است و بعد دست کلم؛ آلٰی که بآدم عالم آمد لجهة آن نٹش بارت وننش بآر
انذ که سرینی؛ که مست از نٹش جهة خالی نیست که سرجهتی ت وت دراز؛
ت وت کلم؛ آلٰی که اکر آن ست کلم وت کلم؛ آلٰی را از ایشان درکشٹی ایشان
خود موجود نباشند جون روشن شد که اکر میخوانی که از بآره، دستک که
از و بکل کلم؛ خدای ظاهر شو د نوآن کلم را بفرض و سم از و جداتوانی
کرد نمکن نیست و اکر برسبیل و سم وفرض اذ و جداکنی از ان سنک و متٰی که
او جداش باشند جیج جیز با فی نباشند نی ماند که اطلاق شیٹیة برو کنی
جیزی بماند با زنقل کلام کن نآ بٰی اسم اسم ضواهد داشت و او آبٰی بالغو

Folio from the *Jāvīdān-i kabīr*, MS. Ee.1.27. by permission of the Syndics of Cambridge University Library.

dishonest to pretend that the syncretism in his teaching did not exceed those bounds that were normally acceptable in the great spiritual movement that we call Sufism.

To what extent the transcendent *Shi'ite* movement that was set in motion by Faḍlullāh was unashamedly Ismā'īlī, or neo-Carmathian, is a question that has exercised the minds of those interested for centuries. Al-'Asqalānī, cited in the *Inbā' al-ghumr fī abnā' al-'umr by Ibn Ḥajar* (d. 852-3/1448-9) described Faḍlullāh as an ascetic and a heretic who claimed that the letters were metamorphoses of men, "together with many idle and baseless fancies." Isḥāq Efendi in his denunciation of the Bektāshiyya, which was to become the official Sufi depository of the Ḥurūfī classics, in his *Kāshifī al-asrār wa dāfi' al-ashrār,*[1] refers to the Ḥurūfī writings as heresies, the "blasphemies of the Jāwidāns." He perceives the Ḥurūfīs, Faḍlullāh especially, as the latest in a line that passes from the Ibāḥiyya (Mazdakites), through the Qarāmiṭa, through Faḍlullāh to his 'vicars' or *khalīfas,* especially to 'Alī al-A'lā who allegedly divulged and explained the 'immoral' and esoteric secrets of the *Jāwidān* to the inmates of the *tekke* of Ḥājjī Bektāsh.[2]

Some qualified views on these lines have shaped the thinking of Orientalists down to the present time. E. G. Browne was of the opinion that the Ḥurūfīs were without doubt within the Ismā'īlī tradition.[3] This view was echoed by F. W. Hasluck, though modified and carefully analyzed by E. K. Birge.[4] W. Ivanow in his *Ismaili Literature,* (Tehran 1963), devotes three pages to the Ḥurūfīs and to the Nuqṭawīs. He refers both to Faḍlullāh as a "philosopher" and to the *Jāwidān.* This work displays many contacts with Ismā'īlism, Alamut, even refers to "Sayyidna Ḥasan ibn al Ṣabbāḥ." Significant are the *Jāwidān* references, in passages in a West-Persian dialect akin to Bakhtiyārī and Kurdish, where there is a mention of former strongholds of the Assassins: Rūdbār-i-Astarābād, and the fortress of Gird-i-Kūh. To be fair to Ivanow, he also casts doubts on the alleged distortion of the Bektāshiyya by Ḥurūfī ideas. In the view of Riẓá Tevfiq,[5] the Ḥurūfīs are part of a "brotherhood" that includes the followers of Ḥasan-i-Ṣabbāḥ, the Nuṣayris and the Druze. "All these religions *(sic)* are founded upon the principle of the 'epiphany'...- The power that sustains the world is manifest in everything, but above all it manifests itself in Man who is the mirror of its perfection." Riẓá Tevfiq saw the self-deified Sufi Muḥammad ibn 'Alī al-Shalmaghānī, beheaded in Baghdad in 934, as Faḍlullāh's most obvious predecessor. Nikki Keddie links together the Ḥurūfīs, the

1. On Isḥāq Efendi's description of the Ḥurūfīs, see Browne's, *A History of Persian Literature under Tartar Dominion,* (AD 1265-1502), III (Cambridge University Press, 1920), pp. 450-2. A more recent study of the vilification of the Ḥurūfīs, is to be read in A. Gölpinarli, *'Hurûfîlik ve Mîr-l 'Alem Celâl Bîk'in Bîr Mektuba,'* Türkiyat Mecmuasi (1965), pp. 93-101.
2. An example of the traditional view (aside from Hasluck's writings) is to be found in J. Brown, *The Darvishes,* (Oxford/London 1927), pp. 223-4. J. Birge, in his *The Bektashi Order of Dervishes,* (London 1937), pp. 60-2, gives a sober assessment of the relationship between the Ḥurūfiyya and the Bektāshiyya.
3. For a statement of E. G. Browne's view, within the context of the *Jāwidān* itself, see his A *Catalogue of the Persian Manuscripts in the Library of the University of Cambridge,* (Cambridge, 1896), pp. 69-86. *The Jávidán-i-Kabír* (E.1.9.27).
4. See Birge, *op cit,* pp. 58-62.
5. In C. Huart, *Textes Persans Rèlatifs à la secte des Houroûfîs* (Leyden/London, 1909), pp. 307-11.

Nuṣayris, the Ahl-i-Ḥaqq and Kizilbas as popular groups within the ideology that fueled and sustained the Safavid movement.[1] Irène Mélikoff attributes these similarities to her notion of an original nomadism; the nomad to her is one who "lives to the rhythm of the seasons, with a conception of cyclic time and of the eternal return." Day succeeds night, spring follows winter and life follows death. These beliefs are, she says, at the base of all the sects that are called "extremist," be they Turk like the Ḳizilbas, Iranian or Kurdish—like the Ismaelians and Ahl-i-Ḥaqq—or Arab like the Druze or the Alawites.[2]

The Druze might be selected in order to illustrate certain similarities in the evolution of the doctrines though, of course, in an earlier age. They draw upon such Ismā'īlī notions as were expressed by the *dā'ī* Abū Ḥātim al-Rāzī (d. 322/934) in Ifrīqiyyā in his *Kitāb al-zīna fi'l-kalimāt al-islāmiyya al-'arabiyya.*[3] "We hold by tradition that (the *Imām)* Ja'far (al-Ṣādiq) ibn Muḥammad said: 'In the first place a thought surged in God, an intention, a will. The object of this thought, this intention of this will were the letters from which God made the principal of all things, the indices of everything perceptible, the criteria of everything difficult. It is from these letters that everything is known.'"

According to David Bryer, Ḥamza ibn 'Alī (b. 374-75/985-86), "like some juggler threw up the whole Isma'īlī system into the air." He reshaped what he needed to furnish the keystone of his beliefs, namely the divinity of al-Ḥākim and the falsity of all previous *sharī'as.*[4] In this religion of *tawḥīd* God is existence itself. All existent beings derive their existence from Him. Passages from the Gospels of Matthew, Mark and John, where relevant, make their appearance. This is also a feature in Ḥurūfī writings where Matthew and John are also quoted. Ḥamza, hailed as Messiah and "Universal Mind" by Bahā' al-Dīn (d. 422/1031), after whom "the door of the Unitarian religion was closed" was reinterpreted and expanded by the latter, in his *al-Juz' al-awwal.* Here there is a resort to Pythagorean subtleties, to the occult art of letter manipulation and the assignment of numerical values to letters. Seven is a sacred number; the Heavens, the Earth, the Climes, the Height of Man by his own span, the Prophets and the *Imāms* are also sacralized.

However, by the fifteenth century it is significant that these and other long-held or refashioned Druze beliefs are transformed in the many writings of the Amīr Sayyid Jamāl al-Dīn 'Abdullāh al-Tanūkhī (1417-1479). Especially in his treatises on the attributes of the Universal Intelligence, and on the conduct of the Elect, and in his fifth epistle, *al-Mīthāq,* in particular, al-Tanūkhī's writings are indebted to Sufism. Referring to his library of "500 volumes," Nejla M. Abu-Izzeddin remarks: "That the works of the Sufis figured among the contents of the library is to be

1. See N. Keddie's, *Scholars, Saints and Sufis, Muslim Religious Institutions in the Middle East Since 1500,* (University of California Press, 1972,) pp. 217-9.
2. Mélikoff, *'Un ordre de dervishes colonisateurs: Les Bektachis,' in Memorial Omer Lufti Barkan,* Bibliothèque de l'Institut Français d' Etudes Anatoliennes, XXVIII (Paris, 1980), pp. 149-57, 156 in particular.
3. See G. Vajda, *'Les lettres et les sons de la langue arabe d'après Abū Ḥātim al-Rāzī' Arabica, VIII,* (May 1961), pp. 113-30.
4. See David Bryer, 'The Origins of the Druze Religion,' *Der Islam, (*Berlin/New York, 1975-76), p. 47ff.

expected, for the Sayyid was a Sufi himself and often quoted Sufis in his writings and teachings."[1] This observation is significant. Not only has it a relevance for the late mediaeval age wherein Faḍlullāh was born, lived and died, but it illustrates a flexibility and a power to transform and to reshape in the Sufi-trained mind of a creative thinker a received legacy that had been viewed by others as alien or heretical.

That Sufism lies at the heart of Faḍlullāh's seeming Ismā'īlism is revealed in his biography in the *Encyclopedia Iranica*[2] provided by Ḥāmid Algar, who stresses that Faḍlullāh was strongly drawn to Sufism at an early age, when his mind was fired by words of Rumi about the Light of God as the essence of Eternity. He regularly attended the *dhikr*. After his second *ḥajj* he dreamt vivid dreams about Solomon, about the hoopoe, and about the raven, symbolic of God, the spirit and the soul. He dreamt of a star rising in the East. All of this appeared to herald a mission that would bring him to fame after meeting saints and visiting cities and eventually to martyrdom. His following in Isfahan included Sufis who are referred to as "*ḥalāl*-eating and truth-speaking dervishes." Even in Tabriz, after 775/1373, when Faḍlullāh gained an elite following in the Jalayerid court, including Sultān Uways ibn Ḥasan and where the descent of the essence of beings into "the luminous consciousness" of Faḍlullāh, the 'Lord of Time' *(Ṣāḥib al-zamān)* allegedly took place in 788/1386, and where the writing of the *Jāwidān* commenced, one is constantly aware of a continuous inspiration from main-stream Sufi tradition. Though failing to convert Tīmūr and executed in Shirwān by the latter's son, Mīrānshāh (d. 802-03/1400-01, the Anti-Christ of Ḥurūfī legend) in 1394, the theodicy of suffering which Faḍlullāh's execution (ordered by Tīmūr) inspired amongst his Ḥurūfī followers, draws upon a Ḥallājian inspiration, even if one suspects with Massignon,[3] that it is Nesīmī who achieves this identification to its fullest in his verse.[4]

Faḍlullāh's dilemma was not unlike that which was to be faced by certain of the Protestant reformers in Europe. A radical break with a medieval Orthodoxy posed problems as to how to interpret revealed scripture with the help of an alternative channel of revelation, or by some hitherto unknown 'hotline' direct to Divinity. This problem faced the revolutionary saint, a contemporary of Luther, Müntzer of Zwickau:

Müntzer had not been troubled like Luther as to how to get right with God, but as to whether there is any God to get right with. The Scripture as a mere written record did not reassure him because he observed that it is convincing only to the convinced. The Turks are acquainted with the Bible but remain completely alienated. The men who wrote the Bible had no Bible at the time when they wrote. Whence, then, did they derive their assurance? The only answer can be that God spoke to them directly, and so must he speak to us if we are so much as to understand the Bible. Müntzer held, with the Catholic Church, that the Bible is

1. Nejla Abu-Izzeddin, *The Druzes, A New Study of Their History, Faith and Society*, (Leiden 1984), pp. 96 and 174-7.
2. The Sufi activities of Faḍlullāh in his earlier years are brought out in the article by H.Algar, *op. cit.*
3. See Louis Massignon, 'Imād Nesīmī and the poets of the Janisseries' in *The Passion of al-Hallāj*, trans. H. Mason, (Princeton University Press 1982), II, pp. 249-56.
4. On Nesīmī, see in particular, E. J. W. Gibb, *A History of Ottoman Poetry*, vol. 1, (London 1958) pp. 343-68.

inadequate without a divinely inspired interpreter, but that interpreter is not the Church nor the pope but the prophet, the new Elijah, the new Daniel, to whom is given the key of David to open the book sealed with seven seals.[1]

To Faḍlullāh, the key to open the seven sealed book, the Koran, is a cabalistic system of letters that is expounded, by him, or by others, in the *Hidāyat-nāma,* the *Jāwidān,* and in the *Maḥram-nāma.* and elsewhere. The universe is eternal and moves by rotation. God's visage is imperishable and is manifest in Man, the best of forms—*zuhūr kibriyā*. Each atom is a manifestation of Deity (Koran XXVIII, 88). Faḍlullāh is the manifestation of God's force after Adam (to whom were revealed nine letters), Moses (to whom were revealed twenty-two letters) Jesus (to whom were revealed twenty-four letters) and Muḥammad (to whom were revealed twenty-eight letters). There is no fixed *wird,* no open *dhikr,* but rather a communal agape, a breaking of bread and a drinking of wine. The 28/32 letters are God's attributes. Adam's visage was the exact replica of the face of God and, as with the Druze, seven is a key number corresponding, as it does, to the parts of the face, the verses of the *fātiḥa* (the *bā* of which, in the *basmāla,* is the secret of the Koran itself since the dot in the *bā* is ʻAlī who is the secret through which the revelation to Muḥammad was made known), and likewise the verbal confession of faith. Man is a universe *(kawn jāmiʻ)* in whom all is resumed. He is the supreme copy *(nuskha kubrā)* and the key to the *Ḥaqīqa*. The location of this 'supreme copy,' according to Faḍlullāh, is to be found in the substance of the letters rather than in the Imām's person. As B.S. Amoretti has observed, Faḍlullāh's revelation is "a new type of Koranic *taʻwīl* related to what might be called the materials rather than the symbolic form in which the word as revealed was incorporated in the sacred text."[2]

A careful examination of the *Jāwidān* (in this instance the Cambridge University Library copy: E.1.9.27, entitled *Commentarius Persicus in Alcoranum dictus Jawidán Cabír,* a manuscript purchased in Istanbul in 1681) reveals this to be so. In this text appears an inflated, yet not disorganized, kind of *taʻwīl,* with extensive Arabic passages, even whole folios, where certain Surahs are repeatedly introduced (for example, *al-Baqara, al-Aʻrāf, Āl-ʻImrān)*, and with a concentrated comment on Islamic characters, beliefs and pillars of faith, that stem directly from holy writ (for example, Yūsuf, Hūd, the Messiah as both human and divine, the *Miʻrāj,* dreams and visions, ritual ablution, alms-giving and the Prophet himself, who is everywhere exalted). The Koran is nowhere superseded. However, it is, of necessity, explained. *Umm al-Qurʻān shifāʼ min kulli dāʻ*. An obsession with seven is to the fore and *Sūra* XV, 87 *(al-Ḥijr)* opens the entire massive work with *wa-laqad ātaynāka sabʻan min al-mathānī wa-l-Qurʻān al-ʻaẓīm,* a significant quote in view of its intended parallel to the *fātiḥa*. Adam is the prototype link betwixt God and man, furthermore he is, in his corporeal form, one with the Kaʻba and the divinely created *milieu,* or 'Gaia,' of which man himself is an integral part:

> *Khalaqa Allāha taʻalā raʼsa Ādama wa-jabhatahu min turbati-l-Kaʻba wa-ṣadrahu wa-ẓahrahu min Bayt il-Maqdis wa-fakhdhayhi min arḍ il-Yaman wa-sāqayhi min*

1. See Roland Bainton, *Here I Stand,* (Tring, 1978), pp. 260-1.
2. 'Religion in the Timurid and Safavid Periods' in *The Cambridge History of Iran,* vol. 6, pp. 623-5.

arḍi Miṣr wa-qadamayhi min arḍ il-Ḥijāz wa-yadahu-l-yumnā min arḍ il-Mashriq wa-yadahu'l-yusrā min arḍ il-Maghrib.

God, Almighty, created the head of Ādam, and his forehead, from the earth of the Ka'ba, his chest and his back from Jerusalem, his two thighs from the Yemen, his two legs from the land of Egypt, his two feet from the land of Hijāz, his right hand from the land of the Arabic East and his left hand from Morocco and the Maghrib.

Much of the substance of Faḍlullāh's cabalistic scheme, insofar as its complexities may be understood, was current in Sufi circles well over a century before his lifetime. Another prominent figure in the elaboration of such a system was Abraham Ben Samuel, Abū'l-'Āfiya (1240-1291), who besides being a cabbalist, composed in 1273 mystical essays and lived at Patras in Greece. There he wrote his Prophetic books signed with a pseudonym which was the numerical value of his name. According to Gershom Scholem, who has contributed to the article on Abraham Ben Samuel in the *Jewish Encyclopedia,* the latter "based his ecstatic mysticism on rational foundations." Scholem adds, furthermore, that "points of contact can be found between it and the doctrine of the Muslim Sufis at the height of its development."[1] Speculations and facts regarding the debt owed by Faḍlullāh and Ḥurūfīsm (and by Sufism in general) to this particular source have been aired for some time and have been commented upon afresh in Abdülkadir Haas's recent book *Die Bektaşi.*[2] That Faḍlullāh, his successor, 'Alī al-A'lā (d. 822/1419), and other members of their fraternity, were acquainted with a source of this kind would seem to be a reasonable assumption.

Diffused ideas of cabalism they were, far beyond the Ḥurūfiyya, and independent of Faḍlullāh's peculiar contribution. Annemarie Schimmel in her 'Letter Symbolism in Sufi literature'[3] has furnished a number of examples indicating how such ideas predated Faḍlullāh, and how they continued in unexpected corners long after he had written the *Jāwidān.* She herself remarks: "The idea that the face of the Beloved is like a marvelously written manuscript of the Koran is widely accepted even outside Ḥurūfī circles... Man is the perfect copy of the Well-preserved Tablet, in which all wisdom and beauty take shape."

Ḥurūfī-type speculations and fancies, lingered on in both courtly and plebeian, but especially artisan, circles in Mamlūk Egypt (centered around the *tekke* of Kaygusez Sulṭan). Nesīmī's poetic bouquets of Faḍlullāh's doctrines were admired by Sultan Qānṣawh al-Ghawrī (1500-16), who venerated the memory of both martyred Nesīmī and Ḥallāj. Among the most popular of the Mamlūk era's literary works, its recension of the *One Thousand and One Nights,* shows structural or symbolic traces of these *bāṭinī* sources, according to Ferial Jabouri Ghazoul who comments:

---

1. *Ibid,* pp. 150-1 and 154, and Haas, *Die Bektaşi, op. cit.,* pp. 150-67. See Gershom Scholem, *'Die Jüdische Mystik in ihren Haupstömungen,'* (Frankfurt, 1980), p. 145ff. A composer, such as Jacob Obrecht (1430-1505) was indebted to the speculations of Pico della Mirondela who, in Renaissance Italy, penetrated the Cabbalah. Numerical progressions and the symbolics of figures and of names are to be found in Obrecht's Masses.
2. *Ibid,* Haas, pp. 150-64.
3. *Mystical Dimensions of Islam,* (Chapel Hill: North Carolina Press, 1975), pp. 411-25.

> The one thousand and one can stand equally for the New Era. In Islamic civilization, the millenium has a particular appeal to the masses who feel that after the millenium the promised Mahdi comes and a new era of justice and benevolence begins. Shahrazad's condition is transformed on the night after the thousandth, ushering in a new regime and a new life. The significance of one thousand and one as leading to metamorphosis is exploited in some of the esoteric Islamic sects. The Truth worshippers *(Ahl al-Ḥaqq)* who are prevalent among the Kurds of Iran and Iraq, and of whom the first substantial account was given by Gobineau in *Trois ans en Asie*, possess a rigorous theological system based on the central belief of metepsychosis. Human beings supposedly pass through one thousand and one incarnations. Here are some quotations from their Shaykh, Nur Ali-Shah Elahi: "Each soul has a path to trace and this consists in donning one thousand and one 'corporeal habits'. Our souls, we who belong to the human species, once the one thousand and one vestments have been donned, no more appear in human guise."[1]

The number one thousand and one suggests a terminal transformation.

Ḥurūfī beliefs of an Ismā'īlī or a cabalistic origin were a very important element in Persian and Turkish poetry of the later Tīmūrid period. It is not certain that Qāsim-i al-Anwār (d 835/1432) was a wholehearted Ḥurūfī. His Sufism was catholic, his poetry akin to that of Maghribī (d. 810/1408). Browne, however, has translated verses by Qāsim that indicate both a taste for numerology, as well as a deep-rooted belief in the divinity in every atom.

> *"In six days" runs God's Word, while Seven*
> *Marks the divisions of the Heaven,*
> *Then at the last "He mounts His Throne,"*
> *Nay, Thrones, to which no limit's known.*
> *Each mote's a Throne, to put it plain,*
> *Where He in some new Name doth reign.*
> *Know this and so to Truth attain!*[2]

In his study of the poetry of Nesīmī of Baghdad, or Tabriz, (d. 820/1417-18 in Aleppo) Gibb pointed out that already by the 15th century cabbalism was subordinate to those features that united the Ḥurūfis with main-stream Sufism; particularly to the example of Ḥallāj and to the self-revelation of God in humanity framed within the physical form of man. He writes:

> It is therefore the Ḥurūfī element in his work that really gives Nesimi his unique position. Being a true poet, he selected and presents almost exclusively that aspect of Ḥurūfism which alone is capable of poetic treatment. Except for a stray line or two, chiefly in the quatrains, where the mystic import of the numbers 28 and 32 is suggested, the cabbalistic side of the doctrine is largely ignored. What took captive Nesimi's imagination, and what he lovingly dwells on in every poem in his book, is the conception embodied a little while ago. The root of this conception, the self-revelation of God in humanity, is a perfectly familiar Sufistic idea; but to the Sufi the fair human form is only a mirror in which is reflected the Divine Beauty, and so the love which such mirror inspires is merely the 'Typal Love' which is but the 'Bridge' to the 'Real Love,' that is, to the love of the Reality shadowed therein. To the Ḥurūfī, on the other hand, the fair human form is not simply a reflection, it is an incarnation

1. *The Arabian Nights: A Structural Analysis*, (Cairo: UNESCO, 1980), pp. 62-8.
2. See E. G. Browne, *A History of Persian Literature under Tartar Dominion*, III, pp. 474-81.

of the Deity; and the love which it inspires is not a mere 'Bridge' to something else, but is itself a goal.[1]

Rafi'ī, brought to the truths of the Ḥurūfiyya by his teacher, Nesīmī, expressed his thoughts in his *Bishārat-nāma* (812/1409), a work that provides a typically orthodox and authoritative account of all Ḥurūfī beliefs, giving equal emphasis to all the tenets of the sect, lauding Faḍlullāh himself, embracing his cabbalisms and accepting the *Jāwidān-nāma* as the uniquely divine revelation.[2] Farther on in his work, Rafi'ī composed a panegyric on Faḍlullāh, the founder of his sect. Whatever exists, he says, are but the Divine Names; but the Most Great Name is he, he who showed to us the true path. All that exists is the Word, but the Sultan of the Word is he, to wit, Faḍlullāh, the Grace of God, the Lord of the Worlds, he to whose *Jāvidān-nāma* the poet refers the reader for proofs of what he has just advanced.

Nesīmī's love of beauty and of Ḥallāj and of *muwashshaḥāt* on God's unity had other followers besides Rafi'ī, Timinnā'ī, Uṣūlī and Sārī 'Abdullāh Çelebi, Niyāzī, and Kanī. He inspired Azeri poets and popular poets of the Janisseries, poets such as Ḥabībī and Ruşeni.[3]

It is probably in the Balkans, above all, in the remote and majestic mountain terrain of Shqiperia and its borderlands, that the legacy of Faḍlullāh survived the longest, cherished, as it was within the bosom of the Bayrāmiyya-Hamzawiyya and especially in the literature and pictorial art of the Bektāshiyya. Degrand visited the stronghold of that Order (founded, circa 1700, by Bābā 'Alī Khurāsānī) at Kruja, once the capital of Skanderbeg, around 1900.[4] He learned that 'Fazil Yezdan' of Khurāsān was the 'master' of Hājjī Bektāsh. He was the author of the *Jāwidān* and he was a follower of Ḥallāj. His informants had added that the *Jāwidān* was the book of rules of their Order. Faḍlullāh had died before its completion. It was Ḥājjī Bektāsh or 'Alī al-A'la who had completed it.

How the Bektāshiyya became the principal depository of the Ḥurūfiyya is far from clear. Whether Bālim Sultān the reformer, was a Ḥurūfī is doubtful. What is known is briefly set out by Irène Mélikoff in her 'Ahmed Yesevi and Turkic Popular Islam,' where she writes:

1. E. J. W. Gibb, *op. cit.*, pp. 343-68.
2. *Ibid*, page 375.
3. In every respect the most recent major contribution to Ḥurūfī studies, especially the legacy of Ḥurūfism, and that of the poet, Nesīmī more especially, is the book by Kathleen R. F. Burrill, *The Quatrains of Nesimī: Fourteenth Century Turkic Hurufi, with annotated translations of the Turkic and Persian quatrains from the Hekimoğlu Ali Paşa Ms* (Mouton: The Hague/Paris, 1972).
In her fifth chapter, especially pp. 72-84, she surveys the varied poets, Sufis and men of letters who were influenced by Nesīmī, and through him by Ḥurūfī concepts, for example: Niyāzī (d. 1693), the founder of the Misriye branch of the Khalwatiyya, Muḥyī'l-Dīn Abdal, Gül Baba (Misali), Ibrahim Efendi (Oğlanlar Şeyhî), Kani, Refīī, Uṣuli, Ruhi, Virani, Halili of Diyarbekir, Sultan Sülayman, the Law-giver, Baki (1526-1600), poets of Khurasan and Transoxania, a number of Azeri poets, for example Habibi (1515-19), Hakîkî (d. 1467), Hatai (Ṣah Ismael d. 1594), Ruşenî (d 1486). The latter resided in Baku where he became a dervish under Şirvanli Seyit Yahya.
There is hardly a page in her study that does not illustrate the impact of Faḍlullāh's ideas through Nasīmī, within the Near and Middle East and beyond it.
4. *Souvenirs de Haute Albanie* (Paris, 1901) pp. 228-36.

In Anatolia and Rumelia the name of Ahmed Yesevi is connected with the Bektashis. Hadji Bektash was certainly a heterodox dervish; 'Ashiḳpashazāde is there to state it and he is well aware of the facts, being himself a descendant of Baba Ilyas-i Horasānī whom Hadji Bektash is said to have followed. But the heterodox elements of the Bektashis were still to be developed and amplified after the XVI th century, where the order acquired a syncretistic character through the addition of Hurufī doctrines and the incorporation of the Kizilbash belief in the divinity of 'Ali. To these elements must be added the belief in reincarnation and sometimes metempsychosis, but these creeds may have existed amongst the pre-Islamic Turks.[1]

When Birge followed in Degrand's steps he found the Ḥurūfī books listed and stacked side by side with the Bektāshiyya works in the library of Sulo Bey Çela of Tirana. The doctrines, he concluded were deemed distinct. A Bektāshī might find them edifying, inspiring, uplifting and helpful. There was however no obligation for him to follow the Ḥurūfī path. Faḍlullāh's revelation left its mark on those who studied in the libraries of the Albanian *tekkes*. The Ḥurūfiyya are especially notable in such poets as Hoxhe Dobi of Gjirokastra, where certain Sufi *tekkes* were founded, *circa* 1700, by 'Āṣim Baba. His verse is permeated by its doctrines with reference to 'Alī's presence in the *basmala,* to Adam's in the letter *Alif,* and, in its form clearly built on Ḥurūfī models. The great poet Naim of Frashër (the ash tree) (1846-1900) had, as a boy, attended the *tekke* (founded by Nasib Tāhir Baba) amidst the wildly beautiful terrain that was to fill his verses and to stir his patriotic heart. A master of Persian verse, lettered also in Turkish and Arabic, he absorbed the teachings of Faḍlullāh, just as he absorbed *mathnawīs* of Nesīmī, and verses of the earlier Albanian Bektāshī poets of Kosovo. In his *Flowers of Summer (Lulë e Vërëse)* published in Bucharest in 1890, Naim's couplets, in Mann's translation, re-expressed those same epiphanic concepts, with which we have been particulary concerned:

The road that leads to God's own mind
Is nothing more than of mankind.
If man holds man in high esteem,
He has revered his Maker's name.
Look in our hearts, and He is there;
Our hearts are homes with Him to share.
When God first sought to show His face
He made mankind His dwelling-place.
A man who knows his inward mind
Knows what God is. It is mankind.[2]

Man 'arafa nafsahu 'arafa rabbahu

---

1. See Irène Mélikoff's article in *Utrecht Papers on Central Asia,* (Utrecht Turkological Series, No 2, 1987), p. 90. The Ḥurūfī face of the Bektāshiyya among the Albanians, in essence was neither Sunnite nor Shi'ite. Ḥurūfī ideas penetrated the Balkans and Eastern Europe independent of that specific order which had adopted it. Traces of Ḥurūfī doctrine have been found in the ideas and beliefs of the tiny Polish Lithuanian Orthodox Tatar community and in other scattered Muslim communities in the Soviet Union.
2. See Stuart E. Mann, *Albanian Literature* (London, 1955) p. 41. As for the West (and here a detailed study of what elements in Baha'ism share some common ground with Faḍlullāh's doctrines has yet to be undertaken I suspect) it would be very hard indeed to find a direct or an indirect inspiration amongst the sundry translations of Oriental literature, Sufi poetry included, that had such an impact on Western literature during the last century.

1

1. *Continued from the previous page:*
Yet, in a way, the kernel of Faḍlullāh's non-cabalistic message is nowhere better expressed in English, though unwittingly, than in the writings of Thomas Carlyle, who, in a lecture delivered in May 1840, and published in his *Sartor Resartus, On Heroes and Hero Worship,* phrased his firmly held beliefs in words of a high artistry. That Carlyle had a passing acquaintance with Sufism is hardly surprising in view of his friendship with Edward Lane and his pioneer essay, advanced for its time, on the Prophet Muḥammad. However, Carlyle had no true sympathy for the Muslim's mystical quest. This is readily apparent from the following passage:

> "Religion," I said; "for, properly speaking, all true Work is Religion: and whatsoever Religion is not Work may go and dwell among the Brahmins, Antinomians, Spinning Dervishes, or where it will; with me it shall have no harbour. Admirable was that of the old Monks, *'Laborare est Orare,'* Work is Worship."

Only slightly more sympathetic is the following description of a "Whirling Dervish," both of these passages being quoted from *Past and Present,* ed. A. M. D. Hughes, (Oxford, 1858; 1918) pp. 181 & 232:

> Again, are not Spinning-Dervishes an eloquent emblem, significant of much? Hast thou noticed him, that solemn-visaged Turk, the eyes shut; dingy wool mantle circularly hiding his figure; —bell-shaped; like a dingy bell set spinning on the tongue of it? By centrifugal force the dingy wool mantle heaves itself; spreads more and more, like upturned cup widening into upturned saucer: thus spins he, to the praise of Allah and advantage of mankind.

Elsewhere *(Heroes and Hero Worship* [Dent: London 1940] pp. 247-8), however, Carlyle's sentiments undoubtedly come close to those of the Ḥurūfī's, though the conception of the idealistic vision that he espoused was not Faḍlullāh's and owed much to Novalis, to Fichte and to Goethe:

> But now if all things whatsoever that we look upon are emblems to us of the Highest God, I add that more so than any of them is man such an emblem. You have heard of St. Chrysostom's celebrated saying in reference to the Shekinah, or Ark of Testimony, visible Revelation of God, among the Hebrews: "The true Shekinah is Man!" Yes, it is even so: this is no vain phrase; it is veritably so. The essence of our being, the mystery in us that calls itself "I," — ah, what words have we for such things? —is a breadth of Heaven; the Highest Being reveals himself in man. This body, these faculties, this life of ours, is it not all as a vesture for that Unnamed? "There is but one Temple in the Universe," says the devout Novalis, "and that is the Body of Man. Nothing is holier than that high form. Bending before men is a reverence done to this Revelation in the Flesh. We touch Heaven when we lay our hand on a human body!" This sounds much like a mere flourish of rhetoric; but it is not so. If well-meditated, it will turn out to be a scientific fact; the expression, in such words as can be had, of the actual truth of the thing. We are the miracle of miracles, the great inscrutable mystery of God. We cannot understand it, we know not how to speak of it; but we may feel and know, if we like, that it is verily so.

On a link between Edward Cowell (d 1903), Professor of Sanskrit at the University of Cambridge, Edward Fitzgerald and Thomas Carlyle, see Peter Avery, 'Fitzgerald's Persian Teacher and Ḥāfeẓ' in *Sufi: A Journal of Sufism (*Issue 6, Summer, 1990), pp. 10-15.

P/S Recent thinking about the relationship between the Ismā'īlīs, the *bāṭiniyya* tradition, Persian Sufism and the beliefs of Faḍlullāh and his supporters and his successors in the Nuqṭawiyya (Ahl-i-Nuqta), may be read in Farhad Daftary's book, *The Ismā'īlis: Their History and Doctrines,* (Cambridge University Press 1990), pp. 455-457.

Diverse Tastes in the Spiritual Life: Textual Play in the Diffusion of Rumi's Order

Victoria Rowe Holbrook

The late Abdülbaki Gölpınarlı[1] observed that there has been more written and said about the *Mesnevî-i ma'nevî*[2] of Mevlânâ Jelâleddîn Rumi (d. 671/1273) than any other book save the sacred texts of the major religions (1983:147). Most of this has been written in Turkish, Persian, and Arabic, though Orientalist scholarship opened up another international sphere of reception for Rumi's six-volume masterwork. Excellent contributions have been made in many languages to translation of his poetry and analysis of his thought and practice. Less attention has been paid to the history and literature of the Mevlevî dervish Order. It is my purpose here to introduce to a wider audience Mevlevî texts of the first two centuries of the Order's diffusion, and my hope that those interested in the legacy of mediæval Persian Sufism may be encouraged thereby to examine them.

Few Mevlevî texts have been edited, and attention to these has focused primarily on personal biography. The writings of Sipahsâlâr and Aflâkî,[3] and to a lesser extent those, various in nature, of Rumi's son Veled (623/1226–712/1312), have been

1. Gölpınarlı, who passed away in 1982, wrote the only history of Rumi's Order from its origins through the twentieth century, *Mevlânâ'dan sonra Mevlevîlik* [Mevlevî-ism after Mevlânâ] (Istanbul: Inkılâp ve Aka 1983, 1st ed. 1953). The volume is the second of a pair, the first, *Mevlânâ Celâleddîn: hayatı, felsefesi, eserleri, eserlerinden seçmeler* (Istanbul: Inkılâp 1959), deals with Rumi's life, teachings, heritage, and works. Both were based on unique and extensive research in manuscripts located at various Turkish libraries. This article is based primarily upon Gölpınarlı's research, although I evaluate the material from a different point of orientation. Gölpınarlı's main concern was to delineate the social history of Rumi's Order; mine is to investigate its legacy in the development of Ottoman literary institutions and genres. Both of Gölpınarlı's volumes will be so often cited herein that I will indicate them throughout only by publication date followed by a colon and page number in parenthesis.
2. The Arabic word usually transliterated *mathnawī* passed through Persian into Turkish acquiring the spelling *mesnevî* as both the name of Mevlânâ Rumi's *Mathnawī-yi ma'navī* and the name of a genre of narrative verse in rhyming couplets. Turkish now shares our alphabet, and so cannot be transliterated into it. When I refer to usages in the Turkish context of words and names of Arabic or Persian derivation, I spell them according to current Turkish usage. I distinguish between the characters *hamza* (') and *ayn* ('), and indicate long vowels.
3. See Farīdūn ibn Aḥmad Sipahsâlâr, *Manâqib-i Haḍrat-i Mawlânâ Jalâl al-Dîn Rûmî,* trans. Tahsin Yazıcı as *Mevlânâ ve Etrafındakiler* [Mevlânâ and his Circle] (Istanbul: Tercüman 1977); and Shams al-Dîn Aḥmad al-Aflâkî al-Ârifî, *Manâqib al-Ârifîn* [Ways of the Gnostics], ed. Tahsin Yazıcı, 2 vols. (Ankara: Türk Tarih Kurumu 1959-1961); each book is a kind of communal biography told through anecdote. Yazıcı also translated into Turkish Aflâkî's work as *Ariflerin enkıbeleri* (Istanbul: Hürriyet 1973).

edited and incorporated into international scholarship concerning Rumi, his ancestors, family, and immediate followers. Less mention has been made of the writings of Rumi's grandson Ârif Çelebi (670/1272–720/1320), and those of Şâhidî (d. 957/1550), Dîvâne Mehmed Çelebi (d. after 952/1545),[1] and Yûsuf Sîneçâk (d. 1546/953), authors active in the Order's widest diffusion from Turkish Anatolia during the fourteenth and fifteenth centuries. Frequent reference in these writings to miracles performed has moved some modern writers to question their reliability as historical sources. Judged as hagiographies and devotional or celebratory literature, they may be discounted as historical sources, even while questions of genre, and their relation to representation of events and literary expectations of readers, remain to be considered. It is possible to examine the values presented—and not presented, through selection and omission of detail—by the texts, as such. These are matters I refer to as 'textual play.' Here I investigate values presented, whether straightforwardly or indirectly through articulation of genre, by the early generations of Mevlevî literature. My investigation of continuity and play in form and value is intended as a way of understanding the legacy of the spread of the Order in the development of Turkish literature.

It is well-known that the Mevlevî Order had an inestimably large effect upon Turkish literature and culture. Rumi's poetry was immensely popular both locally and abroad from the moment it was written down. New literary genres were developed in Anatolia in response to his work: *Mesnevî* parallel *(nazîre),* commentary *(şerh),* and selection-book or anthology *(müntahabât)*; biography *(menâkıb)* and autobiography of members of the Mevlevî Order; poetry and collections of poetry characteristically Mevlevî; and treatises on the Order's custom and rule.

Emerging first in Persian, these types of literature were, during the fourteenth century, articulated in a developing Anatolian literary Turkish and bilingual works of Turkish and Persian which played a decisive role in forming Ottoman literary style, offering patterns of style for various literatures of the Ottoman Empire, whether written by Muslims, Christians, or Jews. Many Ottoman poets now considered major were members of the Order. Similar patterns in the history of Ottoman music and visual arts can be observed; many of the more influential Ottoman musicians, composers, musical theorists, and calligraphers and other visual artists, traced their artistic genealogy through the Mevlevî Order. Persian remained a language sacred to the Order; members continued to read, write, and to an increasingly limited extent speak the language, developing an Ottoman literary Persian, and a Mevlevî spoken Persian (restricted to conversation on certain subjects) which has survived into the twentieth century.[2] Rumi's works continued to be read in Persian,

---

1. The exact date of Mehmed's death is not known. Gölpınarlı found the latest reliable date at which he was still alive to be 952/1545, when he bore witness to a *vakf* document. Mehmed signed his name "Muḥammed ibn Muḥammed al-Meşhûr Dîvâne Muḥammed Çelebi." His signature proves that the title 'Sultân-ı Dîvanî,' by which Mehmed was also known, is a later invention (1983:103).
2. I have observed this survival among descendants of the last Istanbul Mevlevî şeyhs holding office, before the Orders were outlawed during the Turkish Republican revolution.

and the first Turkish translation came only in the eighteenth century.[1]

The Mevlevî Order was formed in Konya at a time when the Seljuks of Rum[2] were disappearing as the major power on the Western edge of the Islamicate world. Mongol incursions, breaking that power, ceased almost as soon as its decimation was complete. The vacuum left by Seljuk demise and Īl-Khānid retreat was populated by local *beys* who insured their influence by appeal to the support of local spiritual leaders, themselves influencing the *beys* by virtue of the authority they had over the people. While these spiritual leaders were many, the most influential were *Horasânî*—a term meaning literally 'of Khurasan,' but associated with unconventional tastes in spiritual life—in ilk if not origin, as was Rumi.

Rumi was the most immediately influential of a circuit of personalities residing in Konya and connected to centers around the Seljuk domain and abroad, who were aware that a new world—a western Islamic world—was being born, and took a conscious, active part in its birth. The Mevlevî Order spread under conditions which offered little of an institutionally stable character attractive to the individual, and the modes of Persian Sufism which the Mevlevî, among many other Orders, propagated in Anatolia in heterogeneous forms had a permanent effect upon traditions emanating from the area. Konya passed into the hands of the strongest local Turkish dynasty, the Karamanids, who remained the more resistant of many rivals in Anatolia to the Ottomans as they rose swiftly to empire during the fourteenth century. Konya was only taken by the Ottomans in 1466, after their conquest of Constantinople in 1453. But from its beginnings the Ottoman state had incorporated intellectual traditions established by Seljuk policies, among others, and a kind of spiritual humanism represented in Mevlevî practice and literature.

The valuing of *semâ*—recitation and participation in performance of poetry, music, and the whirling dance—by Rumi and his followers is internationally known, having earned the Order the name of the 'Whirling Dervishes' abroad. But the contexts in which these values were assigned have been less often discussed. There was no Mevlevî Order as such during Rumi's lifetime. His friends and admirers gathered with him, and the characteristic activities at these gatherings, becoming emblems of association or affiliation with Mevlânâ Rumi, were practiced in gatherings held without him and came to be recognized as 'Mevlevî' activities. In these we can see the beginnings of what later became rituals and customs of the Order as they took shape during the fifteenth century in the definitive forms they

1. I refer to the Ottoman verse translation of the *Mesnavî* by Nahifî Süleyman (d. 1738). Nahifî enjoyed both a Mevlevî and Hamzavi affiliation, and had formerly been a Halvetî *şeyh*. His work was printed in the *talik* script by the Bulak press in Cairo in 1268/1851-1852. This printing included a Turkish translation of a 'seventh' volume written by Ferruh Efendi (d. 1840), in addition to Rumi's six (1983:145). The whole was reprinted by the Sönmez Press in Istanbul during the 1980s. The late date of this first translation—after some four centuries of oral and literary converse, of multiple forms, with the text—is itself evidence of the survival of the Persian language as a usage of the Mevlevî Order and of literate Ottomans in general.
2. *Rûm*, 'Rome,' was the Greek West for Muslims of that time, and the name 'Rumi' may be translated 'Westerner.' The Seljuks were a Turkish dynasty who carried many Persian traditions with them to Anatolia.

would retain through the twentieth.[1] Performance of music, dance, and poetry was assigned a positive value in contradistinction to the more conservative ideals and graver norms of behavior that Marshall Hodgson has termed "the Jamâ'î-Sunnî synthesis."[2] Without going into development of philosophical positions here, I use a very broad term, 'tolerance,' to refer to a range of behaviors, attitudes, and activities represented by the early texts as higher in value than their contrasting conservative ideals and norms.

By 'tolerance' I mean both that relaxed attitude marked by an acceptance of diversity in points of view which the word has in current English usage, and a more specific disregard, even an aggressive challenging, of exclusive norms of behavior characteristic of establishment Muslim sensibilities. Gölpınarlı remarked that Rumi would have been martyred had he not lived in a political climate rare for the time in its tolerance of his reform-minded clash with orthodox religiosity. In comparing the personality of Veled with that of his father Mevlânâ, Gölpınarlı emphasized Veled's prudent, rational accommodation to the exigencies of his time while organizing the Order upon principles introduced by his father (1983:35).

Rumi's prestige was such that after his death in 671/1273, his followers were able to justify Mevlevî tolerance by appeal to his precedent. Aflâkî related that on one occasion Çelebi Husâmeddîn (d. 1284/683)[3] was called to defend before a judge the playing of the *rebab*.[4] A group of the "very rich and very wicked" gathered there "out of envy and disbelief," and said such music was forbidden by religious law. The judge replied that this was what the religious authorities say, but asked the Çelebi his opinion. Husâmeddîn asked the judge in turn whether he regarded the staff of Moses as a stick or a serpent. Receiving no reply, he declared that the *rebab* had also been an ill-esteemed piece of wood until Mevlānā, at God's command, gazed upon it with favor, and in his hand it had become a serpent swallowing up the bonds of deceitful person's illusions.[5] Aflâkî related that on another occasion a cer-

1. Attribution of these formalizations to Rumi's son Veled is a traditional error; Gölpınarlı established that the custom and rule of the Order was defined during the time of Pîr Âdil Çelebi (d. 864/1460).
2. Marshall G. S. Hodgson, *The Venture of Islam: Conscience and History in a World Civilization*, vol. 2 (Chicago & London: University of Chicago 1974), p. 371.
3. Husâmeddîn was Rumi's third major representative (*halife*), after Shamseddîn Tabrîzî and Salaheddîn Zarkub. The central representative of the Mevlevî Order later came to be called "the Konya Çelebi." Gölpınarlı listed their death dates through the fifteenth century as follows (1983:152; he did not give *hijrî* dates):
Husâmeddîn (1283); Veled (1312); Ârif (Veled's son) (1320); Âbid (Veled's son) (1338);Vâcid (Veled's son) (1342); Âlim (Ârif's son) (1350); Âdil (Ârif's son) (1368); Âlim II (Âbid's son) (1395); (Pîr) Âdil II (Âlim's son) (1460); Cemâleddîn (Âdil II's son) (1509).
4. The *rebab* is like a violin, though constructed somewhat differently and played in the lap, bowed like a bass.
5. Aflâkî, *Manâqib al-Ârifîn*, 6/16.

tain Ahî Ahmed[1] objected on grounds of religious law to the singing of musical compositions at a certain funeral, though this was requested by the parents of the deceased. Veled grasped his arm firmly and said that a great man had approved of this custom, and only a greater man could forbid it. Ahmed had nothing to say to this.[2] In both accounts argument won the day. Oratory, and the ability to leave one's opponent reduced to silence thereby, was given a high value by the early texts. In the case of these two anecdotes, argument ended with rhetorical aggression. Husâmeddîn warned those petitioning the judge that it would be inauspicious to oppose such a serpent, and Veled asked Ahî Ahmed why he would impale himself upon the swords of saints. Aflâkî's accounts favored tolerance in fidelity to Rumi's precedent and ridiculed those who opposed it.

The early texts are evidence of a high value placed on writing, and on accurate recording of the Order's history and preservation of its favored texts; Aflâkî usually named the source of his account, often an eyewitness, and he himself was a participant in many of the events he described. He related that he wrote his book at the direction of Veled's son Ārif. Gölpınarlı found Veled's verse-narrative, the *Ibtidânâma* the soundest and first primary source for the events of Rumi's and his contemporaries' lives and the history of the Order.[3] Veled commemorated the building of Rumi's tomb with poems of praise to its benefactor, recorded in his Divan (collected lyrics). He likewise produced poems praising notables of Konya and the Mongol regime who benefited the emerging Mevlevî Order or favored calligraphic production of its texts.[4]

The son of one of Veled's representatives *(halîfes)* had a copy of Shamseddîn Tabrîzî's *Discourses (Maqâlât)* calligraphed. The copy of Rumi's *Mesnevî* consid-

1. 'Ahî' is a title; the *âhis*, variously equivalent in Anatolia at this time with the *ahl-i futuwwa* and *rindân*, were a fairly interdependent series of groups affiliated by mystical association and trade. They were of relatively lower social status and could function as urban militias; see Claude Cahen, *Pre-Ottoman Turkey: A General Survey of the Material and Spiritual Culture and History c. 1071-1330*, trans. from the French by J. Jones-Williams (New York: Taplinger 1968), pp. 195-200. Referring to an earlier occasion, Aflâkî described Ahmed as a "local tough" and "leader of *rindân* jailbirds" who challenged Rumi over Husâmeddîn's appointment as *şeyh* to the *tekke* of Ziyâeddîn Vazir in Konya, upon which a knife-fight ensued *(Manâqib*, 6/12). Thus the opponents in the *rebab* anecdote and this one at the funeral were characterized as being from opposite ends of the socio-economic sphere.
2. Aflâkî, *Manâqib*, 7/34.
3. The *Ibtidânâme* was composed c. 691/1291, and provided a source for Sipahsâlâr's book, its continuation by Sipahsâlâr's son, and for Aflâkî's work finished in 1353. It was edited by Jalāl Humā'ī and published under the title *Mathnawī-yi Valadī bi baḥr-i khafīf ma'rūf bi Valadnāma* (Tehran: Iqbal 1315). The Istanbul University manuscript Gölpınarlı consulted (F.Y. No. 1205) consists of a prologue and 9432 *Mesnevî* couplets written in Persian with some verses in Turkish (close to 100) and in Greek (1983:35, 47, 49, 61, and 1959:31-32).
4. The Divan published by M.N. Uzluk (Ankara: Uzluk 1941) contains *kaside, gazel, terci', kit'a* (11809 *beyts*), and *rübâ'î* (12719 *beyts*) in 29 meters, those verses in each meter arranged, as in Rumi's Divan, alphabetically. Veled composed poetry mostly in Persian, though his divan contains ten poems in Turkish and a number containing Turkish and Greek verses or words. The Turkish verses of Veled's Divan, *Ibtidânâme*, and *rabâbnāme* were collected by Veled İzbudak, edited by Kilisli Rifat, and published separately under the title *Dîvân-ı Türkî-i Sultan Veled* (Istanbul 1341/1925). Gölpınarlı noted that Veled, unlike his contemporary Yunus Emre, did not use the *hece* (syllabic-stress, as opposed to *'arûz)* meter at all (1983:267-268 and 1959:36-38, 46, 61).

ered by Gölpınarlı most reliable was calligraphed by a freed slave of Veled's, and a copy of Rumi's Divan, and one of Veled's Divan, by a calligrapher whom Gölpınarlı suggested might have been that freed slave's son (1983:44, 46, and 1959:30).[1] This attention to copying of manuscripts and recording of praise for patrons may indicate a value set on writing and its uses in constructing an institution. Wealth and position, when bestowed by the rich and powerful in recognition of spiritual influence, was assigned a positive value in the early texts, although self-sufficient independence in matters of material need was assumed as a spiritual requisite. Growth of the Order—increase in number of followers, who participated in the preservation of Rumi's practices, and recognizing the authority of his successors—was a positive value.

Gölpınarlı noted that the building of Rumi's tomb during the tenure of Husâmeddîn provided a center where Mevlânâ's followers gathered, and became the occasion for organization of a group supported by perpetual endowments *(vakf)* assigned to the tomb. In an account of Çelebi Husâmeddîn's death, Aflâkî related that the Çelebi had fulfilled his duties as Mevlânâ's representative to perfection. Among those which Aflâkî mentioned were distribution of revenue and gifts of money, and furnishings and clothes coming in, to each member of the group according to station. Husâmeddîn kept table ready for travellers, neighbors, and gatherings numbering in the several hundreds. Aflâkî remarked that wealth accruing to the tomb was sufficient to support a designated prayer-leader *(imâm)*, readers of the Koran *(ḥuffâz)*, caller to prayer *(mu'adhdhin)*, readers of the *Mesnevî (Mathnawî-khwân)*[2] story-tellers *(shayyâdân)*, singers *(guyandagân)*, and resident servants *(khuddâm-i ḥaḍrat)*. Husâmeddîn delivered special allowances to Veled and his intimates, and to Mevlânâ's widow, Kira Hâtûn, and daughter, Melike Hâtûn. Husâmeddîn preserved the custom of performing *semâ* after the Friday prayer, and reading of the *Mesnevî* following recitation of the Koran.[3] This selection of detail approved proudly of the attraction of wealth and its appropriate distribution to an extended community whose center was composed of Rumi's family and those serving the community by preserving practices associated with Rumi's precedent.

Gölpınarlı found it appropriate to emphasize that when Rumi died, Veled turned aside suggestions he should succeed his father, saying that nothing had changed; he and his father's followers should continue to look to Husâmeddîn as they had when Rumi was alive. But when the Husâmeddîn died in 683/1284 and Veled began to represent the nascent Order, he took a first step in what became a tradition of inherited leadership of the Order through Rumi's descendants, thereafter titled 'Çelebi.'[4] When Veled passed away in 1312 and his son Ârif took his place, the tra-

1. The freed slave was Abdullahoğlu Osman; he calligraphed the *Mesnevî* in 723/1323. The calligrapher of Rumi's Divan (Konya Müzesi K. No. 66) and Veled's Divan (see Uzluk's edition, p. 616) was Osmanoğlu Hasan.
2. This was a salaried office in Ottoman times, also forming a regular part of Friday services in Ottoman mosques.
3. Aflâkî, *Manâqib*, 6/25.
4. Husâmeddîn was not a descendent of Rumi; for him 'Çelebi' retains the meaning of its former usage as an honorific title preceding his name.

dition was established; it was then that Rumi's ancestry began to be traced through the maternal line to the Caliph Abu Bakr, and his son Veled became known as "Sultân" Veled (1983:22, 94-95). The organization of Aflâkî's work by sections, each bearing the name of a person about whom anecdotes were related, a majority of them family members of Rumi's, may confirm the value placed on his family by the third generation.

The early texts do not show much concern for documenting the course of the Order's spread through designated representatives *(halife)* and founding of Mevlevî dervish houses abroad,[1] and so tracing this requires painstaking reconstruction through other than literary sources.[2] Sipahsâlâr and Aflâkî did carefully record the passage of primary authority—the central leadership of the Order, residing in Konya—but not the designation of representatives who spread the Order abroad. Their accounts refer to Mevlevî representatives and existing Mevlevî houses by name, but rarely is there indication of precise relationships and dates; persons are often referred to in ways implying the reader's familiarity with them. Gölpınarlı suggested that Veled may have tried not to call attention to his relationship with Bektemüroğlu, fearing the tragic circumstances of the death of Shams might recur.[3]

The lack of attention to this particular range of detail may be evaluated as a function of the genres employed. The *menâkıb* genre, for the most part limited to quotation of oral accounts, perhaps could not easily be revised to allow for systematic description; neither perhaps could prevailing standards for verse, whether lyric or narrative. The authors certainly showed their concern to glorify the Order and emphasize its successful spread; in this case the textual play allowing them to describe it would be limited by rules of genre. A chart showing genealogical relationships among exponentially multiplying representatives, for example, would have been out of place, and the function of documentation of authority to represent

1. The term most broadly used for a dervish house is *tekke*. It was an establishment, whether of modest or grand size, where those affiliated with the Order gathered. In Ottoman times a *şeyh*, appointed with the approval of the *Şeyhülislâm* as director, would live at a Mevlevî house in quarters reserved for his family. Members who so chose could reside in small rooms there as bachelors; these members, as specifically appointed, oversaw and carried out house activities and looked after the daily needs of the establishment such as housecleaning, shopping, cooking, serving, sewing, and laundry. Such a member would move to a separate, privately-owned home upon marrying; some remained as bachelors, or retired there if single.

   Among the activities taking place at a Mevlevî *tekke* were rituals of the Order, including initiation, some of which were open to a viewing public; practice of and instruction in various arts, crafts, and sciences, available to the public; manufacture (and often invention) of instruments, tools, and costumes used in activities special to the house; social gatherings, often centered around an artistic performance, literary or philosophical discussion, or political concern; and rest and relaxation. Mevlevî *tekke*s were a significant site of libraries, both public and private. In later periods the grander Mevlevî houses, as institutions, may usefully be compared with that of the college or university.
2. See, for example, Gölpınarlı's tracing of the founding of a Mevlevî *zâviye*, hostel, in Kırşehir in 1297 by Veled's representative Süleyman Türkmânî; he noted that among the *vakf* conditions were that its *şeyh* must "be of the party of prayer, good-tempered, know Mevlevî terminology, and wear Mevlevî clothes." (1983:45).
3. It is generally believed that jealousy of his intimate relationship with Shams among Rumi's followers led some of them to murder Shams. Bektemüroğlu apparently served as spiritual advisor to Veled after Husâmeddîn's death (1983:31-34).

the Order and thus initiate others was fulfilled by certificate of designation *(hilâfetnâme)*. In any case, these authors apparently did not predict the future existence of an audience such as the present one. Treatises on the custom and rule of the Order also did not appear until much later, with the writings of Dîvâne Mehmed and Şahîdî. Rather, the early texts propagated the nascent Order by glorifying Rumi and those close to him, his precedent, and his poetry.

Gölpınarlı decided that the Divans (volumes of collected lyrics) of Veled and his son Ârif consist largely of parallels to poems by Rumi.[1] Works tracing these parallels—the genre of *nazîreler mecmuasi*—were produced.[2] Veled's verse narratives *Ibtidânâma,*[3] *Rebâbnâma,*[4] and *Intihânâma,*[5] and his prose *Discourses* or *Ma'ārif*[6] proclaimed his imitation of his father and continuation of projects begun by his father. As Gölpınarlı often observed, Veled's subsuming of his self unto his father's example is remarkable. Veled's humility may be interpreted to have served a number of functions, given the political instability at large during his leadership.

Veled wrote that he composed his first verse narrative, the *Ibtidânâma,* in imitation of his father: "My father distinguished me among my siblings, the disciples,

1. Ârif's Divan, of which the quatrains *(rübâîler)* have been published, is entirely in Persian; see Feridun Nâfiz Uzluk, *Ulu Arif Çelebi'nin Rübâîleri* (Istanbul: Kurtulmuş 1949). There is a manuscript of his Divan in the collection of Nâfiz Paşa now housed in the Süleymaniye library, and a selection from the Divan in the Fatih National Library in the collection of Pertev Paşa (Uzluk, pp. 4-5). Gölpınarlı's comments on Ârif's writings were based on his examination of the Fatih manuscript. This selection, calligraphed in 1610, consists of 82 *gazels*, one of which is an elegy *(mersiye)*, and 80 quatrains (1983: 47, 90-92).
2. Gölpınarlı mentioned a *Kitâb-i munâzara-i Mevlânâ bâ Sultan Veled* (Istanbul University K. F.Y. 1205) and other such parallel-collections noted by Uzluk, one written during Veled's lifetime (1983:47).
3. Gölpınarlı noted that this was the first *mesnevî* Veled composed, that in his preface Veled titled it *Masnavî-yi Veledî* and declared that while Rumi had called to mind the legends of spiritual heroes of former times in his works, he, Veled, wished to record his own and those of Seyyid Burhâneddîn, Shamseddîn [Tabrîzî], Salâheddîn [Zarkūb], and Çelebi Husâmeddîn; and that Veled said furthermore that some had not understood these men, adding: "I have clearly described these saints *[evliyâ]* in my book, making known their spiritual states and the events in which they participated when Mevlânâ was alive. At the same time the aspirant *[murîd]* must, in such matters concerning the *tarikat* as investment of robe, shaving, and whirling, conform to what those whose nature accords with God's nature say, following the *şeyh*'s path, in so-far-as his/her capacity allows (1983:47-48).
4. In Persian. Gölpınarlı noted that this was the second *mesnevî* Veled composed, and referred to a Persian manuscript, No. 1375 in the Istanbul University Library, calligraphed in 746/1345 and comprising 8091 *mesnevî* couplets plus a prologue. Veled metaphorized the *rebab* as his father had the ney; the work begins with the verse: *"Bishnavīd az nāla u bāng-i rebab / Nuktahā-yi 'ishq dar ṣad gūna bāb"* (1983:49-50).
5. In Persian; the third and final verse narrative Veled composed. Gölpınarlı referred to an Istanbul University library manuscript (F.Y. No. 10009) calligraphed in 1020/1611 in Aleppo by Gazanfer al-Mevlevî, containing 8313 couplets and 120 headings plus a preface. Veled explained that he had written of Mevlânâ, Shams, Salâheddîn and Husâmeddîn in his first *mesnevî;* that in his second, written in the same meter as Mevlânâ's *Mesnevî,* he began by mentioning the *rebab* and engaged in giving counsel; and that this third contains advice to travellers in truth, to the effect that they should not conform to the demands of the self and the devil (1983: 50-51).
6. Translated from the Persian into French by Eva de Vitray-Meyerovitch as *Maître et disciple* (Paris: Sindbad 1982). Gölpınarlı referred to an Istanbul University library manuscript (F.Y. No. 672) containing 56 sections, and a Turkish translation by Meliha Tarıkâhya (Ankara: Millî Eğitim, 1949), 19th in the Şark-Islam series (1983:51-52).

and scholars by saying I most resembled him in nature and temperament. I have tried to conform to the saying, 'He who resembles his father will do no evil;' I have tried to be like him. He composed poems and quatrains in various meters, and produced a Divan. I too, like him, produced a Divan. Then my friends said to me: 'You have conformed to Mevlânâ's practice and produced a Divan; you should also conform to him in producing verse narrative.' I took up this task in order to be like him...."[1] Veled declared that he composed the *Rebabnāma* when friends asked him to write a verse narrative in the same meter as his father's.[2] Gölpınarlı noted that in his *Ma'ārif* Veled adopted the style of the *Ma'ārif* of his grandfather, Rumi's father Sayyid Burhān al-Dīn. Veled likened his book to his grandfather's *Ma'ārif* and his father's *Fīhi mā fīhi,* and declared he wished to produce, like they had, a work of prose, and so had adopted the title of his grandfather's book (1983:51).

The life-style of Veled's son Ârif (d. 720/1320), however, exhibited a different spirit. Ârif's career seems to mark a sea-change in the character of the Order. He spread the Order more through his travels than his writings, and found new followers on a series of journeys he took, visiting Lârende, Beyşehir, Aksaray, Akşehir, Karahisar, Amasya, Niğde, Sivas, Tokat, Birgi, Denizli, Menteşe, Alâiye, Antakya, Bayburt, Erzurum, Iraq, Tabriz, Marand, and Sultâniyya (1983:69). He did not produce anything like the literary output of his father; his compositions were largely extemporaneous, many recorded only by Aflâkî, who travelled with him, Ârif being Aflâkî's *şeyh*; and there is no text extant produced by Ârif's immediate successors as central representatives of the Order—the 'Konya Çelebis.'

Some modern generalizing characterizations of the Mevlevî Order classify it as primarily urban and elitist or as catering to an elite. It has been recognized to a limited extent that this was not the Order's primary character during the period of its widest diffusion (late thirteenth through early sixteenth centuries), and recognized to a lesser extent that classification of Turkish culture of Ottoman times as elite vs. popular or 'high' vs. 'low' has been a function of turn-of the-century politics, and not always as accurate or productive as once was hoped. However, concentration on Rumi's highly sophisticated writing and thought without regard for its historical context, and with pious observation of his prestige with Seljuk administrations and his son Veled's efforts to preserve that prestige with subsequent rulers, has tended to support a misconception that the Mevlevî continuously represented 'high' culture. Research into the period under consideration belies that impression.

Aflâkî portrayed Ârif in action, demonstrating—often by means of shocking behavior punctuated by recitation of verse—rather than explaining or accommodating as did his father Veled. His victories by rhetoric, however, are a continuity in textual value. Life on the road in this politically fluid, at times chaotic, period seems to have been rough and ready; Ârif got into fights with fists and knives, and drank wine in public, regularly to excess (1983:69-82). Behavior startlingly in contrast to accepted canons was assigned a particular value within a perceived spiritual dynamic. If sincerity in the spiritual life can be measured by a willingness to sacrifice, then during a period whose circumstances were such that survival depended upon

1. Istanbul U. F.Y. No. 1380, 2-5 (1983: 48).
2. Istanbul U. F.Y. No. 1375, 1.b-2.a.; Gölpınarlı (1959:49). *Mevlānā'dan sonra,* p. 49.

maintaining favorable patron-client relations, sacrifice of reputation could be an ultimate sign of sincerity, proving one's willingness to give up everything for the sake of spiritual virtue.

This type of signifying behavior is termed *melâmet*—self-deprecation—which, as Gölpınarlı reiterated often in his *Mevlânâ'dan sonra Mevlevîlik,* was the mode of the Order dominant during its diffusion.[1] In such a climate, practice of those behaviors most contrary to convention would acquire the most positive value, and the use of intoxicants as portrayed in the Mevlevî texts may be intended as a sign both of the passionate sincerity of those who engaged in them (see Şâhidî's autobiography below), and of how much-disapproved these activities were. Ârif's life-style was harbinger of a new phase in the history of the Order, one which remained dominant through the early sixteenth century. The value of tolerance reached its limit in this period. It may also be observed that although Şâhidî (d. 1550), Sîneçâk (d. 1546), and Dîvâne Mehmed (d. after 1545) seem to have been the last of their flamboyant travelling breed, and the Mevlevî Order subsequently took on the graciously urbane tone for which it has been most generally known, its spiritual traditions as inherited by the Ottoman Empire were maximally inclusive, and wide-ranging alternatives offered by the various Ottoman dervish orders insured an extraordinary tolerance for diverse tastes in the spiritual life.

Ârif's style may be interpreted as suiting his time, for he was very successful, and his time was characterized by difficult conditions which might demand relaxation of public discipline; it seems that more Mevlevî houses were founded through his agency, and that of Dîvâne Mehmed, than any other.[2] One striking feature of Aflâkî's accounts of Ârif is their representation of Ârif's love affairs with women (1983:82-83). Although mention has been made, in the very limited literature on the subject, of Rumi's respectful associations with females and of leadership roles taken by women in the Order, male-male love had certainly been more generally praised in texts. Other significant features of Ârif's literary image were emphases on esotericism and miracle. Esoteric interpretation, whether of literary texts or events, had formerly been favored, often as a way of resolving apparent difference. The Islamicate West which evolved under Turkish rule accommodated new religious, ethnic, and linguistic groups in part by liberal interpretation. Gölpınarlı contrasted what he called Veled's 'mystical' tendencies with Rumi's 'realist' attitudes (1983: 39); but the degree of emphasis upon esotericism and miracle is greater in portrayals of Ârif.

The attention to writing and historical record noted earlier would wane for a time; though Ârif directed Aflâkî to write his work, the members of Ârif's family who first succeeded him as Konya Çelebi did not play a central role in development of literature. Konya was no longer, as it had been in Seljuk times, a city to attract intellectuals in residence. Centers of power had shifted as the Ottomans, active on

1. For an introduction to the history of *melâmet* in Ottoman times, see the writer's 'Ibn 'Arabi and Ottoman Dervish Traditions: The *Melâmî* Supra-Order,' *Journal of the Muhyiddin Ibn 'Arabi Society*, vol. IX (1991), pp. 18-35.
2. Gölpınarlı summarized what he was able to discover about the locations and founding dates of Mevlevî houses (1983:330-340).

the western edges of Anatolia, began to import near-eastern luminaries to populate their new institutions of knowledge. Their reliability as patrons would not be assured until the conquest of Constantinople in 1453; others to the east were offering opportunities at least equally attractive. Ârif was succeeded by two of his brothers, then two of his sons, a nephew and a grandson, the last dying in 1421; the first son, Âlim, was absent from Konya during the whole of his tenure.[1] There are no literary works extant by any of these men, and there was no subsequent Mevlevî chronicler having Aflaki's dedication to precision of record. Thus little is known of the Order during this period, and we are limited to later sources for explication of the subject at hand.

The next major historian of the Order would be Sakıb Mustafa Dede (d. 1735), *Şeyh* of the Kütahya Mevlevî house; there is a gap of some four centuries between Aflâkî and Sakıb. Gölpınarlı subjected Sakıb's *Sublime Vessel of the Mevlevîs*[2] to the historical critique modernist philology required of a work composed at such a degree of temporal distance and relying largely on oral sources. While the formal leadership of the Order remained special to the Konya Çelebis, active dissemination of Rumi's teachings was carried out by many others, Mevlevî or not. Among those who were, Şâhidî ('The Witness,' d. 957/1550), Yusûf Sîneçâk ('Rent-Breasted,' d. 953/1546), and Dîvâne ('Mad') Mehmed (d. after 952/1545) exemplified, in their lives and writings, something of Ârif's spirit. All were active in the fifteenth -century, though each died in the sixteenth.

Şâhidî was a disciple of Mad Mehmed, rather than of a Konya Çelebi. Gölpınarlı described nine works he composed; the volume and character of his compositions establishes the high value placed on the continuity of writing in the Mevlevî tradition, a revival—after a haitus of more than a century—by affiliates of the Order. Şâhidî dated his *Tuhfe,* a slim Persian-Turkish dictionary in verse, 921/ 1515.[3] At the beginning of the work he declared his father Hüdayi had taught him Persian (1983:138). Verse dictionaries became a standard Ottoman genre,[4] but Şâhidî's early *Tuhfe* seems to have been especially popular. Biographers of the poet and scholar Galib (d. 1213/1799), *Şeyh* of the Mevlevî house at Galata in Istanbul, boasted that his education consisted exclusively of studying this one book with his father. There may be here some indication of a tradition among the Mevlevî of

1. Seepage 102, note 3 for a genealogy of the Konya Çelebis. Gölpınarlı noted that no tomb of Âlim exists in Konya, and he thus must have died abroad; Gölpınarlı added that Âlim was the "Hüdâvandgârzâde" and "Şâhzâde" Aflâkî mentioned as having met with Âbid in Tabriz, who continued on to Turkestan when Âbid returned to Konya. It is not known why Âlim went to Turkestan or why he did not return (1983:98).
2. Composed in a highly Persianate Turkish; *Sefîne-yi nefîse-yi Mevlevîyân* (Cairo: Matba'a-i Vehbiye, 1283/1866-1867).
3. The dictionary was printed in 1858-1859/1275 at Tophane in Istanbul, by İstihkâm Alayları Litografya Basmahanesi, and other printed editions exist (1983:138). Printing became general in the Ottoman Empire late; calligraphic copying, not printing, was the primary mode of textual dissemination in Ottoman times. The first printed editions of many Ottoman texts date back only to the nineteenth century.
4. In a later work, *Gulshan-i asrâr,* discussed below in my text, Şâhidî wrote that his father took great care to educate him, and succeeded, for "I have produced dictionaries in verse." (1983, 138) This may indicate that verse dictionaries were a well-known genre at the time.

instruction in Persian by father to son, and/or the use of Şâhidî's dictionary as a text for instruction in Persian. Production of such dictionaries may date the progress of change in linguistic and literary practice in the area, by which knowledge of Persian among the literate gradually became a matter of book-learning, and book-learning became a Mevlevî value. These developments may also be connected with shifting patterns of orality and literacy.

Şâhidî's *Gulshan-i tawḥîd* (937/1529-1530), second of his works mentioned here, is an early example of the *Mesnevî* selection book *(müntahabât)* genre, which also became quite widespread, perhaps serving as a kind of handbook for dervishes. It consists of 600 verses selected from Rumi's *Mesnevî,* accompanied by 3000 verses of commentary (also in Persian, in the same meter). In his preface, Şâhidî wrote that he had made a selection of certain couplets from the *Mesnevî,* but when someone objected that there was no meaningful connection between them, he composed a five-couplet commentary for each verse, thus producing a connection between verses which made for a coherent whole.[1]

Gölpınarlı found Şâhidî influenced in this work by his contemporary Yusûf Sîneçâk's *Island in the Sea of the Masnavi (Cezîre-i Mesnevî),* a selection of 360 couplets from Rumi's work (60 from each of the six volumes, chosen so that they appear to be consecutive and form an independent text). Sîneçâk completed his *Mesnevî* selection book in 901/1495-1496 or 903/1497-1498,[2] some thirty years' prior to Şâhidî's *Gulshan-i tawḥîd.* Sîneçâk's *Island* was known and used among the Mevlevî from the time it was composed. Abdullāh of Bosna (d. 1644/1054), the famed Melâmî-Hamzavî commentator on Ibn ʻArabī's *Fuṣūṣ,* was among those who wrote later commentaries on Sîneçâk's book (1983:125-126).[3] There is a pattern among the commentators of Sîneçâk's *Cezire* of affiliation with the Mevlevî and Melâmî.[4] Gölpınarlı found Sîneçâk's works evidence of his extreme *Vahdet-i*

1. Istanbul University Library, F. Y. No. 1018, calligraphed in 1073/1661-1662 from a copy by Shahîdî's son, as can be understood from a one-couplet fragment at its end. Gölpınarlı noted that the chronogram in this fragment giving the year 996/1586-1587 refers to the date of the son's Mevlevî affiliation; Shahîdî dated his composition 937/1529-1530. The book was printed, in a version by Ahmed Niyazi, in Istanbul by the Tıbbiye publishing house in 1298/1880-1881 (1983:137).
2. Calculation of its date differs according to whether or not one takes into account the *hamza* of Sîneçâk's chronogram; see Abdülbaki Gölpınarlı, *Şeyh Galib: seçmeler ve Hüsn-ü Aşk,* Istanbul Kültür ve Sanat Vakfı Yayınları, No. 1 (Istanbul: Murat 1976), p. 30.
3. Istanbul University Library, Nafız Paşa Collection, No. 528.
4. Turkish commentaries upon it were composed in 979/1571 by Ilmî Dede (d. 1071-1072/1661) of Baghdad, *Şeyh* of the Damascus Mevlevî House, and by the aforementioned *Şeyh* Galib. Ilmi Dede's commentary is titled *Samahâtü Lamaʻât-i bahr il-maʻnevî bi şerh-i ceziret il-Mesnevî;* a MS. calligraphed in 1013/1604 may be found in the Istanbul University library (T.Y. No. 2334). A MS. of Galib's commentary, calligraphed one year after his death by his disciple Süvari Mukabele Kalemi Hulefası Abdülhalim, may be found in the same library, T.Y. No. 2222 (1983:126). Gölpınarlı also mentioned a selection by Cevrî (d. 1654-1655/1065) from Sîneçâk's *Cezire,* titled *Şerh-i İntihâb;* Cevri selected 40 couplets which he paralleled with five Turkish couplets apiece in the same meter, to form a commentary. Cevri's work was published in 1269/ 1852-1853 (Takvîm-hâne-i Amire) together with his *Hall-i tahkikat.* Cevri and Abdullah are known for their *Melâmî* affiliation, as is Galib's father, and it is possible that Galib also enjoyed this dual affiliation, but that his highly public status prevented its being announced after his death, as would have been customary among the *Melâmî.*

vücûdî, Hurûfî, and Alevî inclinations. The following verses from a letter which Sîneçâk wrote to the Konya Çelebi make his *melâmet*[1] tendencies obvious:

> *Those scorned by customers at this sad bazaar*
> *Have neither name nor shame at* melâmet*'s ball*
> *Rare heroes at the city of love, they wail*
> *Like nightingales in gardens of love's thrall*
> *Residing in the dervish house of* melâmet
> *Waiting the Shah of regret's beck and call.*[2]

After Sîneçâk's death, Sûrî, a student of his, and Günâhî, a follower of his, joined other Mevlevî affiliates to visit the Istanbul Ca'ferâbâd graveyard on the tenth of the month of Muharrem in 954/1547. There they cooked *aşûre* (a sweet dish composed of grains and dried fruits supposedly favored by Noah's family during their expedition on the ark), performed *semâ'*, shaved their heads and slashed their heads and breasts with a razor for love of Imam Huseyn, and composed verses to be engraved on Sîneçâk's tombstone (1983:125).[3] Şâhidî and Mad Mehmed shared these inclinations, exemplifying a Mevlevî type found throughout the history of the Order and forming its avant-garde wing, often in association with Melâmî affiliates.

Returning now to Şâhidî's works, there are three that Gölpınarlı mentioned but had not seen: a *Gülistan şerhi* (commentary on Sa'dī's Persian *Gulistān)*; a *Gulshan-i irfân;* and a treatise entitled *Sohbetnâme* which Sakıb Dede characterized as describing modes of behavior *(âdâb)* proper to the relationship between guide and aspirant—this last would be an early example of a treatise on Mevlevî custom and rule. Sakıb related that when the Ottoman prince residing in Manisa at the time heard of it, he invited Şâhidî to visit him. While in Manisa Şâhidî composed a verse announcing the prince's accession to the throne, and afterwards the new Padishah assigned a number of pious foundations *(vakf)* to the local Mevlevî house (1983:138-139).[4] The approval paid in this anecdote to attraction of patronage is familiar from the earliest Mevlevî texts; in this case patronage is paid in recognition of literary composition and miraculous prediction.

---

1. One distinguishes between the Ottoman *Melâmî* Order, with which Sîneçâk seems not to have been affiliated, and *melâmet* as a principle and range of attitudes and behaviors pre-dating and current in Ottoman times; see page 108, no. 1.
2. Quoted by Gölpınarlı from the *Tezkire* of Esrar Dede (1983:126). Sîneçâk was brother to the poet Hayretî. Before becoming affiliated with the Mevlevî he had a position in one of the learned professions and was affiliated with the Gülşenî Order. He was appointed *Şeyh* of the Edirne Mevlevî House, but upon the opposition of the governor, moved to Istanbul. There he resided in Sütlüce, a district on the north side of the Golden Horn across from Eyyub, until he died (1983:124). This writer has visited Sîneçâk's overgrown grave, finding it on the bend in that road winding uphill from the Golden Horn to the *Ca'ferâbâd* graveyard, directly across from the house where *Şeyh* Galib lived with his father.
3. According to Sakıb Dede (II/20-21), Sîneçâk travelled to Jerusalem, staying at the Mevlevî House there for a time, and later journeyed to Karbalā, visiting the tombs of the twelve Imams, including that of Imām Riḍā in Mashhad (1983:125).
4. Sakıb Dede, p. 17. Aşık and Hasan Çelebis mentioned the *Gülistan şerhi* in their *tezkires*. Esrar Dede, in the entry on Şühûdî in his *tezkîre*, called the *Gulshan-i irfân* "a rare work," and explained it was addressed to Şühudi (1983:138).

Gölpınarlı speculated that either Şâhidî never collected his poems into a Divan or that his Divan was lost, for the collections extant are slim.[1] He found Şâhidî's Persian verse "weak," saying it was all one could expect of a Persian acquired exclusively from book-learning (1983:139-140). This is a rare evaluation of late fifteenth/early sixteenth-century Ottoman Persian verse, and interesting for how it dates use of Persian by speakers whose primary language was Turkish.[2] However, it is clear that a tremendous volume of linguistically correct and graceful Arabic and Persian verse and prose was produced by Ottomans who acquired the languages through book-learning, and Gölpınarlı's judgement seems in this respect overly subjective.

Şâhidî's *Gülşen-i vahdet,* seventh of his works mentioned here, is a Turkish verse narrative of 448 couplets composed in the meter of Rumi's *Mesnevî,* dated 943/1536 with two Persian couplets. Its Turkish preface is followed by one in Persian of three and one half pages; therein Şâhidî explained that, just as 'Aṭṭār had assigned voices in his *Manṭiq al-ṭayr* to the *Sîmurgh* and other birds with the intention of explicating truth, he too assigned voices to the hair, face, beard, mole, eye, eyebrow, and mouth, intending by the human face the site where those who recognize God's unity congregate.

Şâhidî provided an allegorical reading of the story, declaring that by 'face' he intended the beloved who illuminates that gathering; by 'hair,' the lover, and by 'beard,' the ascetic, who attain to the mystery of unity and conceal its secrets; by 'mole,' the libertine *abdâl* and persons stripped of self who find the way from imitation to realization and, knowing the self, see the beloved; by 'eye,' one drunk with truth who sees nothing but unity; by 'eyebrow,' the most distinguished of the heroes of unity who rule the world, and by 'mouth,' the *kutub,* spiritual axis. Hair quarrels with Beard, Beard replies to Hair, Mole speaks of unity. Eye and Eyebrow join the fray, and all claims are settled by Mouth. Gölpınarlı quoted Mouth's statement at this point: "The chess pieces are six in number and twofold in color. They oppose one another, and support one another. But collectively they are called chess." He noted that while Şâhidî referred to 'Aṭṭār, his book also shows the influence of Maḥmūd Shabistarī's *Gulshan-i rāz* (1983:136).[3]

Şâhidî's *Mushâhadât-i Shâhidiyya* is known only through Sakıb Dede's reference. According to him, Şâhidî recommended at the close of this Arabic treatise that it not be copied, but be kept secret until 'spiritual permission' might be granted (1983:139). Gölpınarlı translated into Turkish one of four passages Sakıb quoted from the work:

1. The manuscript in the Konya Museum contains 32 poems (D.4.37). Gölpınarlı found three more in a collection in the private library of Osman Ergin, two more in Esrar Dede's *tezkire,* and seven more in a collection in his own possession. He noted that among them are some authored by another Şâhidî, of Edirne, praising the Ottoman prince Cem. Gölpınarlı printed four of Şâhidî's Turkish poems at the end of his *Mevlânâ'dan sonra Mevlevîlik,* two *gazels* in the *Mevlevî siirinden örnekler* section, one in the *arûz* meter and the other in *hece* (p. 500); a *müstezad,* on page 107, and another *gazel* on page 135.
2. Gölpınarlı said furthermore that, after reading Şâhidî's Persian, he strongly suspected that two works traditionally attributed to Rumi or his son Veled were written by Şâhidî: the verse narratives *'Ishqnāma* and *Tirāshnāma* (1983:140).
3. Gölpınarlı omitted an MS. citation for Şâhidî's *Gülşen-i vahdet.*

> My spiritual guide *(mürşid)* slit my throat and I died. I saw my body being washed on the funeral bench. I had emerged from my body as an egg emerges from its shell. I was very light, very pure, I flew like a bird. All at once I felt hatred for my body. My guide was watching me and paying attention to my condition. He forbade this hatred of mine, and at his command I fell in behind my body. Then I looked and saw that I had come to an amazing, unique realm whose delicacy cannot be described or praised. There were lofty mansions and exquisite domes. Rivers were flowing, flowers were blooming, everything shone brightly. My guide said: "This place is Mevlevî-Land in the World of Likeness *(misâl âlemindeki Mevlevî ili)*." We went to see the Shah of this land. When we reached his court, Mevlânâ's likeness *(misâlî sûreti)* appeared. He put a bright and beautiful Melevi crown on my head, blessed it *(tekbîr etti)*, and dressed me in a robe green and translucent as emerald. After that, we returned. I sneezed, opened my eyes, and fell down at my guide's feet.

The autobiographical use of the first person in this passage and its candid tone are worthy of remark, and the imperative of secrecy (and choice of Arabic for composition) may be in some way concomitant with these stylistic developments. Perhaps an increase in directness of personal voice required a greater privacy be insured by formal means.

Gölpınarlı gave particular emphasis to Şâhidî's Persian *Gulshan-i asrār,*[1] ninth and last of his works to be mentioned here, because the autobiographical section at its end has unique historical value. He speculated that manuscripts of this longest work of Şâhidî's are rare because it was banned—and so destroyed wherever it was found, probably in the 17th century—due to its references to the smoking of hashish by Mevlevî affiliates. Şâhidî wrote that he finished his *Gulshan-i asrār* in 1544 at age 76, and from the certainty of this date, rare for the period, other dates significant for Mevlevî literary and social history have been reconstructed. In the present investigation the emergence of self-reflective autobiography as a topic of Mevlevî literature at this time is significant as a literary-historical development, for it is generally assumed to be a genre special to modern times and modern notions of individuality. My following account of the autobiographical section is based on Gölpınarlı's summary and Turkish translation of selected passages (1983:104-107, 132-135).

Şâhidî recorded that his grandfather, of Muğla,[2] was a jurist, soldier, and *hafız* (someone who knows the Koran by heart). This combination of accomplishments is typical of figures prominent in this period. Şâhidî's grandfather participated in Ottoman campaigns in the Balkans, and, during a journey to an Arab country, eloped with a Christian girl and moved thence to Cairo. Şâhidî's father Hüdâyî Sâlih was born of this union. Hüdâyî lost his own father when only one and a half months

---

1. Composed in the meter: u- - - / u- - - / u- -. Gölpınarlı mentioned the manuscripts: Konya Müzesi 2194 A.6.56 and 2195 E. 4. 40; Halet Efendi K. (Ilâve) mecmua No. 74—but mis-recorded in the library index as *Gulshan-i rāz*, perhaps intentionally; this MS. was calligraphed in 1212/1797 by Derviş İbrahim Edhem, a disciple of Ali Nutkî (d. 1804), *Şeyh* at Yenikapï (1983:137). In his preface Şâhidî wrote that his *Gulshan-i tawḥīd* had been well-received, and a youth to whom he taught the book suggested he write another work and title it *Gulshan-i asrār*. Şâhidî likened his relationship with this disciple to that of Mevlânâ with Husâmeddîn, who asked Mevlânâ to write the *Mesnevî* (1983:138). Gölpınarlı found a connection between the book's title and its recounting of hashish-smoking (1983:137-138), *esrar* being a Turkish word for that drug.
2. Muğla is a town inland and west of Bodrum on the Aegean coast of Turkey.

old. He eventually migrated to his father's city Muğla, and became the disciple of Seyyid Kemâl there. Seyyid Kemâl sent him to Iran to study. When Hüdâyî Salih returned home, having completed his studies, he requested and was granted, through the auspices of Fatih Mehmed II's vizier Mahmud Paşa (d. 879/1474), the position of *Şeyh* at Kemal's *tekke*. Although Şâhidî wrote that his mother "loved Mevlânâ," and a *gazel* praising Mevlânâ has been attributed to his father, Şâhidî said nothing specifically about his parents' affiliation with the Mevlevî Order.

Şâhidî wrote that his father died of plague when he was ten (c. 1478);[1] three of his six siblings also died of plague one night. His father, on his deathbed, entrusted Şâhidî to the care of a friend, a "Sufi" and silk manufacturer. But Şâhidî was not interested in the silk trade and wanted to study. When he was old enough to grow a beard (c. 1480) his mother agreed to let him go to Istanbul, where he became a student *(softa)* at the recently founded Fâtih *medrese* college. Occasionally he travelled on lecture tours *(cerr)*. He described his student years with candor, admitting that he used to go out drinking in Galata and one night was so inebriated that he fell from off a caïque into the ocean. On that night he saw the *Şeyh* of his father Seyyid Kemal in a dream.

Şâhidî complained that his professors at Fatih were overly proud of their knowledge. He longed to become a dervish, but found the *şeyhs,* too, hypocrites. He wrote of a certain event which changed his life: while in Bursa reading the *Kanz al-rumûz* of Seyyid Husaynî (d. 718/1318) in the "heated room"[2] at the Yıldırım Han [named after Sultân Beyazid II], a fellow student asked him what the book was about. Şâhidî summarized its contents and explained that it recommended abandonment of worldly affairs. The student laughed derisively, saying, "So, after all the trouble I've taken [to study], I should reject the world! What I need is a position. I want property and children." The student's reaction much disturbed Şâhidî; then, the student no sooner returned to his room than he fell dead of plague.

After this Şâhidî abandoned his studies and returned to Muğla, telling his mother he wished to become a dervish. In Muğla at that time (presumably the late 1480's) there was a *Şeyh* at large, not possessed of directorship of any dervish house, who wore an old dervish robe *(hïrka)*, and slept little: *Şeyh* Hayreddîn. He was a *halife* of *Şeyh* Vefâ (d. 895-896/1490-1491), but had truck neither with *şeyh*-hood nor dervishood. On the other hand, there was a certain *Şeyh* Bedreddin, who had a *tekke* and disciples, held gatherings for *semâ'* and *tevhîd,* and enjoyed the patronage of princes and beys. Hayreddin ridiculed Bedreddin for his grand ways. Şâhidî was not much impressed with him either, but because Hayreddin was criticized for his *melamet* and called *'rind-i cihân,'* Şâhidî did not become his disciple; at his mother's protective direction, he affiliated himself with Bedreddin. Bedreddin wanted Şâhidî to read Rumi's *Mesnevî* with him, but Şâhidî's knowledge of Persian was more advanced than Bedreddin's. So, Şâhidî studied Arabic Koranic commentary *(tefsîr)* with him.

---

1. Since Şâhidî was 76 when he wrote *Gulshan-i asrār* in 1544, he should have been ten years old in 1478.
2. *Tâbhâne:* the room among those of an establishment especially heated in winter.

Şâhidî wrote that he was not satisfied with this affiliation, although he had come closer to the sort of life's path he desired. During one winter season he accompanied Bedreddin to Lazkiye.[1] They spent their time there at *semâ'* gatherings, where poetry was sung and the whirling dance performed, and one day Şâhidî was affected by the voice of a youth who sang a musical composition. He lost his senses and fell down in prostration to God, begging that he might become friends with this youth.

Şâhidî wrote that when he returned to Muğla his mother was engaged in efforts to marry off his younger brother, but lacked funds. So Şâhidî set out on a lecture tour to earn cash. Along the way he came to Kozluk,[2] and while making ablutions before the Friday prayer felt strange, and swooned. Someone there asked him whether he had looked at the sky while making his ablutions, saying that all the angels had gathered upon his head. Şâhidî was much affected by this. After the prayer, he mounted the pulpit *(minber)* to deliver the sermon. Among those listening in the congregation at the mosque was a Mevlevî *Şeyh* wearing robe and a crown with a green *istivâ*,[3] who sat in a corner staring at him.

After finishing his sermon Şâhidî said a prayer and descended from the pulpit, when suddenly all present gathered around him, anxious to kiss his hand. The Mevlevî *Şeyh* reached him first, asking why he, having such knowledge, was not wearing a Mevlevî crown. When Şâhidî replied that he would don the Mevlevî crown at once if only he could find a guide *(pîr)*, this man, whose pen-name was Fenâyî, said: "There is a descendant of Mevlânâ's in Lazkiye; come, let us go there together."[4]

Şâhidî wrote that he travelled with this Mevlevî *Şeyh* Fenâyî. After becoming a disciple of the descendant of Rumi whom Fenâyî had mentioned, Paşa Çelebi,[5] Şâhidî was employed as tutor to that youth whose voice had so affected him–as it turned out, this was Paşa Çelebi's son Emir Âdil. Gölpınarlı translated into Turkish Şâhidî's account of this journey and his meeting with Dîvâne Mehmed:

> When I was twenty-four years old [c. 1492][6] I met a Mevlevî named Fenâyî. At that time Mevlânâ's descendant Paşa Çelebi, who lived in Karahisar, had gone to Lazkiye. Wherever fine horses were found, they were brought to Paşa Çelebi for sale. He would sell them in turn for profit. Prince Alemşâh, son of Beyazit II, was in Lazkiye. The Çelebi brought horses to him for sale.
>
> We travelled to Lazkiye. Fânî Dede was *Şeyh* at the Lazkiye Mevlevî dervish house, and Şeydâyî was a young disciple serving him.[7] We all went to see Paşa

1. This Lazkiye seems to be the village near Konya; Suraiya Faroqhi mentions it in her 'Agricultural Crisis and the Art of Flute-Playing: The Worldly Affairs of the Mevlevî Dervishes,' *Turcica* XX (1988), p. 47. The present al-Lâdhiqîyah, north of Beirut on the Mediterranean coast opposite Cyprus, would require travel by boat and Şâhidî referred to his trips as if they were short.
2. Gölpınarlı noted that this village should be located near Lazkiye (1983:134, n. 162).
3. A strip of green cloth of two finger's width draped over the headgear from front to back, identifying the wearer as a Mevlevî *halife* (1983:429); for the Hurûfî signification of the term, see Gölpınarlı's same work, p. 312.
4. Fenâyî is included in the *tezkire* of Esrar Dede, who relied on this source (1983:104).
5. Not to be confused with any of the Konya Chelebis.
6. Since Şâhidî was 76 when he wrote *Gulshan-i asrār* in 1544, he should have been twenty-four years old in 1492.
7. Esrar Dede referred to Şeydâyî as Derviş Şeydâ, and noted that he was also called Şeydâyî (1983:104).

Çelebi together. I became affiliated with the Mevlevî then. At the time a few travellers arriving at Lazkiye spoke of Mehmed Çelebi. The Şehir Kethüdasi Geredeci Ali said that he transformed vats of wine into honey. Muarrifoğlu, author of a work entitled *Vahdetnâme,* told of how the moment Mehmed Çelebi was born, Fenâyî went to kiss his feet and declared that this verse referred to him:[1]

My beloved plays at joy and pleasure in these days
All within him is struggle, though he appears to play.

It was said that he wandered the plains of Konya. He had forty followers, wearing haircloth. One day in the depths of winter [Mehmed] came into Rumi's tomb, mounted his coffin, and put the *külah* [conical felt dervish crown] at the head of the coffin on his own head. He had a jug of wine in one hand and a glass in the other. While he drank he poured wine on the coffin and around the tomb. Those present said Mevlânâ's rage would destroy him, and he cried: "Do you not see Mevlânâ?" They looked and saw it was Mevlânâ himself mounted on the coffin. Dîvâne Mehmed left the tomb, went straight to a public bath, and walked into the stokehole; he was not burned or harmed in any way.

I met seven of those forty and heard many stories [about Mehmed] from them. I wanted to meet him, I had fallen in love with him with all my heart. He often appeared in my dreams, and sometimes I saw him in broad daylight. At that time I was tutor to Paşa Çelebi's son Emir Âdil, but I had to go home to Muğla to see my mother, and I left.

One night in Muğla I heard Mehmed Çelebi's voice loud and clear, saying "Get up Şâhidî, if you want to find me, if you love us, be a drunkard." I asked my mother for *rakı* and wine. She found some and brought it to me. I told her not to think badly of this, and began to drink. At winter's end I and a scholar who, like me, wanted to meet Dîvâne Mehmed Çelebi, and whom I called Baba Acem because he always spoke Persian, set out on the road.[2] We went to Bursa, and from there to Kütahya. Paşa Çelebi had been appointed *mütevelli* at Kütahya. Mehmed Çelebi had returned from Arabia, and was staying with Paşa Çelebi.[3] When we arrived, Emir Âdil [Paşa Çelebi's son] told his mother that his tutor had come, and she had a rug spread out for me to sit next to Mehmed Çelebi. When, standing at the door of the room, I saw Mehmed Çelebi, I fell into a rapture and began to weep. He said, "Come, look, they've spread out this rug for you." I was in ecstasy as I sat down beside him, I shut my eyes. Everyone welcomed me as a dear friend, but I could not speak, I was trembling. I wanted to be alone with him.

Mehmed Çelebi said to one of the *abdâls* [his followers]: "Musa Abdâl, do you have any hashish?" He said he did, and Mehmed Çelebi told him to bring it out. Musa Abdâl brought the water pipe and declared in a loud voice: "For dear friends, the feast of our path, the tonic of elegant wit." He passed the water-pipe round to everyone, and those who would smoke did, while those who didn't touched the bowl with a finger, bringing the hand to touch the head.

1. *Yār dar ākhar zamān kard ṭarab-sāzī / Bāṭin-i ū jidd-u jidd, ẓāhir-i ū bāzī.* Gölpınarlı also found this Persian verse recorded in a *mecmua* of Enis Dede (d. 1147/1734), *Şeyh* of the Mevlevî house at Edirne, with the following note: "Our *pîr* Ḥazret-i Mevlânâ spoke this couplet in regard to Divânî Efendi [a later version of Mehmed's title]" (1983:105).
2. It is worthy of note that the speaking of Persian in Anatolia in the 1490's was, at least to Şâhidî, unusual enough to warrant invention of a nickname.
3. Paşa Çelebi and Dîvâne Mehmed were cousins. Their fathers were brothers. Paşa Çelebi was a son of Emir Âdil Çelebi, and Dîvâne Mehmed of Bâlî Çelebi, all descended from Rumi through Veled's daughter Mutahhara (1983:104).

Mehmed Çelebi said to me: "Therefore, my dear *dede*."[1] My excitement reached a feverish pitch, and the Sultân [Mehmed] frothed up with emotion. All present bade good night one by one, and we were left alone.

He shouted, like a madman, a few words in Turkish: "Give halva to the regiments of the ancients, to their horseshoes, their broken horseshoes, give halva to their old metal, tin their pots, their copper pots." He bubbled over strangely with excitement, wept, and recited the (Turkish) verse:

He whose gaze does not falter from what it sees
Is a man of vision, and without match will be[2]

He had his hair, eyebrows, beard, and moustache shaved with a razor; he drank wine, appeared base and debauched, and in this way concealed himself from the common folk. He was an object of scorn, his reputation was in ruin, he always had a cup of wine in his hand. But it is impossible for me to tell the miracles I saw him perform. He made sweet drink of wine, the earth he touched turned to gold. At gatherings he'd take an empty jug, give it to the cupbearer, and the jug would be [miraculously] filled. At sea he'd dip an empty jug in ocean water, and it would come up filled with wine.

I followed him and had myself shaved like him. I was one of his *abdâls*. I dove into the sea of nothingness; I saw in him a lover, an object of scorn, and I too became an object of scorn, I imitated him. I ran barefoot before him. On the road he'd give me a horse with shoes tied to its reins, and order me to mount. Even if I mounted, I'd soon dismount and take off the shoes. He'd give my horse to an *abdâl*, saying he shouldn't allow anyone else to ride him, and the horse would be led as a spare. He never left me for a moment. He'd say, "Şâhidî, why do you torture me so, why do you go on foot, why are your feet bare? My heart is ill at ease, I pity you." And I'd say, "O Shah of sainthood, I can't set foot wearing shoes upon the ground you've trodden." And he'd say, "O Şâhidî, you've set my heart aflame."

In every city we visited he'd buy me a pair of shoes and tell me to wear them. I'd set them down on the road and walk by. He'd say: "The *abdâls*' feet are sore, they complain, even if they go barefoot they step gingerly. They rest as often as they can, but you never stop running from dawn till dusk." I took pleasure in feeling the stones pierce my feet. I had a camel-hair shirt, a sleeveless shirt, full of fleas, it was all I wore. He gave me fresh robes, but I always gave them away....

Gölpınarlı was of the opinion that after Mad Mehmed's death, Şâhidî adopted a more sober style of life and made a Mevlevî house of Seyyid Kemal's *tekke* at Muğla, residing there until he died. According to Sakıb Dede, Şâhidî made a yearly pilgrimage to Mehmed's grave at Karahisar, visiting his disciples, and staying forty days. Esrar added that Şâhidî brought his disciple Şühûdî along on his final visit. Staying twenty-one days, he designated Şühudi as his *halife,* sent him back to

1. *Andan dedeciğim.* (1983:106). The title *dede* was later conferred upon someone who had completed their initiation *(çile)* into the Mevlevî Order. I find this phrase too unspecific to translate confidently–it could mean a number of things, among them, "Thereafter, my dear *dede;*" it could also contain a typographical error, of which the printing of Gölpınarlı's book is chock-full. Or it could be the sort of statement whose meaning is clear when one is intoxicated, though elusive when sober.
2. Baktığı yerden ırmyan gözünü / Nazar ehli vü bî-nazîr oldı.

Muğla and, dying in Karahisar, was buried in Mehmed's tomb there (1983:135-136).[1]

Şâhidî is the most immediate source for Dîvâne Mehmed's biography, though Sakıb Dede included a lengthy entry on Mehmed in his book. As Sakıb's is a difficult text containing anachronisms, I record Gölpınarlı's summary and critique of it (1983:109-114) here.

Mehmed Çelebi was descended from Rumi through Veled's daughter Mutahhara.[2] In his youth he wandered mountain and plain, wearing a Mevlevî skirt and *Kalender* cloak, leaving his breast bare. Sometimes he wore a Mevlevî crown on his head, and sometimes a 'twelve turret' crown signifying allegiance to Shams. His hair was left tangled. Sometimes he'd shave fourfold—head, eyebrows, beard, and moustache—like a *Kalender*. His father gave Mehmed the pen-name Semâ'.

On a visit to Mevlânâ's tomb, Mehmed mounted Mevlânâ's coffin in a greatly excited state and took hold of the edge of the turban wound around the *külâh* at its head, as if taking hold of a horse's reins, which much shocked those looking on. Gölpınarlı noted that Sakıb did not mention Mehmed's drinking on this occasion, of which Şâhidî had heard, and speculated that Sakıb expurgated this aspect of the event.

In the time of Pîr Âdil Çelebi (824-864/1421-1460), Mehmed returned to Konya with 40 Mevlevî dervishes. Gölpınarlı noted that since Mehmed was still alive in 1545, this visit must have occurred later. They continued from there to the *tekke* of Haci Bektaş, taking the Karaman road. Joined there by forty Bektaşî *abdâl,* they set out for the Iraq. After visiting the tombs of the Imams in Najaf, Karbala, Baghdad, and Samarra, they journeyed to Mashhad to visit the tomb of 'Alī al-Riḍā.

Mehmed was welcomed in Mashhad with much ceremony. The Iranian *qalandar*s showed him much affection. He was presented with gifts of two flags from Imām Riḍā's tomb, and a huge caldron and some of the pots from its kitchen. When he departed, among the Mevlevî dervishes on his right a certain Derviş Mehmed carried one of the flags, and among the Bektaşi on his left one Ali Rûmî carried the other, and Dîvâne Mehmed pronounced these (Persian) verses:

The eye turned away from Riḍa's gate
Though it be the eye of the sun, has no light.
The soul, ear pierced by ring, committed to service
Is resurrected in the circle of pure beneficence.

---

1. To the right of İlyas Çelebi, in the same row as Abâpûş Velî, in front of Dîvâne Mehmed. According to Sakıb Dede, Şâhidî's tomb in Muğla is actually that of Şühudî (1983:136).
2. Sakıb related that Dîvâne Mehmed Çelebi was a descendent of Süleymanşâh of Germiyan, who married Veled's daughter Mutahhara; they had two sons, İlyas Paşa and Hızır Paşa. Hızır had a son named Bâlî, who was Dîvâne Mehmed's father. But Gölpınarlı noted that Hızır Paşa must have died well before 1320, and Mehmed was still living as late as 1545, when he bore witness to a *vakf* document. Gölpınarlı found a more convincing genealogy in the final pages of the Konya Museum MS of Aflâkî's *Manāqib* calligraphed in 1464/2158 (No. 2158). There a family tree records two descendents, Mehmed Paşa and Ahmed Paşa, between Hızır Paşa and Bâlî. It also names Dîvâne Mehmed Çelebi as *şeyh* of the Karahisar Mevlevî House, appointed by and succeeding his father Bali Çelebi (1983:101-103).

From Khurasan Mehmed returned to Baghdad, revisiting the tombs of the Imāms, and continued to Aleppo. There he stopped at the dervish house of Abu Bakr al-Wafâ'î; Mehmed had him shaved like a *Kalender* and appointed him *halife,* giving him permission to perform all rituals of the (Mevlevî) Order, save the whirling dance.

Mehmed continued on to Konya, leaving one of the Bektaşi dervishes, named Baba Bayram, behind in Aleppo. Mehmed revisited Mevlânâ's tomb, going also to the mosque of Şerefeddin, where he drank wine in the *mihrâb* and splashed wine on the walls of the mosque. Gölpınarlı noted the resemblance here to the event of Mehmed's visit to Rumi's tomb which Şâhidî had heard of.

Mehmed visited Cairo and arranged for the release of Ibrâhim Gülşenî (d. 838/1534) from prison. From Cairo Mehmed went to Damascus, visiting the grave of Ibn 'Arabī (d. 638/1240; his tomb had not yet been constructed). It was the season of the Hajj. Though many recommended he make the pilgrimage, Mehmed refused, and refused permission to those of his disciples who wished to go. Two went on the Hajj regardless, after hearing Mehmed pronounce the (Persian) verses:

Where are you going, O caravan of piety?
You have already reached the prayer-niche of necessity
For shame! Even the stars circumnambulate it
Yet you've these forty years roamed the desert of fantasy.

Sakıb recorded that in the time of Sultan Suleyman the Magnificent (926-927/1520-1566) Mehmed travelled to Istanbul, staying at İskender Paşa's mansion. İskender made a pious foundation *(vakf)* of the orchards of Kule at Galata and had a Mevlevî House built there in Mehmed's honor. But Gölpınarlı noted that İskender, a close associate of Sultan Mehmed II, conqueror of Istanbul, in fact founded the Mevlevî House in 897;/1491-1492; the Ottoman ruler at that time was Beyazid II. So it was probably at the end of the fifteenth century that Mehmed visited Istanbul. Sakıb had Mehmed travel to Bursa from Istanbul, continue on to Kütahya and return to Karahisar, where he died. He also noted that most of those who accompanied Mehmed on these journeys died during the trip between Iraq and Khurasan (1983:109-112).

The Galata Mevlevî house of all the Ottoman Mevlevî houses founded in Mehmed's honor, became perhaps the one most brilliant in reputation, and is presently the Museum of Divan Literature *(Divan Edebiyatı Müzesi).* Like Rumi's grandson Ârif, Mehmed travelled more than he wrote. Gölpınarlı was able to discover only a few poems by Mehmed extant in scattered collections.[1] One of the poems is a brief verse narrative explicating the whirling dance (1983:189-190, 473-476).[2] Gölpınarlı speculated that two treatises, variously attributed, might be

1. On the basis of these few poems, however, Gölpınarlı judged Mehmed one of the strongest Ottoman Turkish poets (1983:119); they are printed at the end of Gölpınarlı's 1983 *Mevlânâ'dan sonra Mevlevîlik,* pp. 473-493.
2. This was translated into French by Marijan Molé in 'La Danse Extatique en Islam,' *Sources Orientales. Les Danses Sacrées* (Paris: Editions du Seuil 1963), pp. 248-251. It appears in the English translation by Simone Fattal of Eva de Vitray-Meyerovitch's *Rûmî and Sufism* (Sausalito: Post-Apollo 1987), pp. 49-51.

Mehmed's. The first, titled *Isharât al-bishâra,* describes the whirling dance.[1] The second, three pages long, instructs the reader in the ways of the Spiritual Path.[2] Both would be early Mevlevî examples of their genre.

The Mevlevî texts composed during the first two centuries of the Order's widest diffusion evidence a continuity of certain values and a wide range of play in their scope. A high value placed on verbal skill, writing and recording survived throughout the history of composition in the Order, although dynamics of orality and literacy may partly account for variations in volume of literary production and generic articulation. Further research could specify these dynamics more satisfactorily.

The forms of *mesnevî,* verse-narrative in rhyming couplets; the more often extempore lyric *gazel;* and prose biography based on oral account, developed throughout the period. Perhaps their status eased innovation of new genres and linguistic transposition which could be subsumed under their rubrics. The narrative and lyric verse forms served increasingly diverse purposes of commentary, often in the form of selections from the *Mesnevî* accompanied by Turkish commentary; and prose, that of autobiography. Treatises only began to be written at the end of this period, and Arabic, Persian, or Turkish, verse or prose, were employed in this form.

Tolerance for diverse tastes in the spiritual life retained its value as a high priority. Sober Veled and ecstatic Ârif remained as textual images of the limits of play. The legacy of mediæval Persian Sufism, as received by the Mevlevî texts, encouraged inclusion, rather than exclusion, of differences in sensibility. Contributions to the spread of the Rumi's teachings were portrayed favorably throughout the period.

1. Sakîb translated this Arabic and Persian work into Turkish, in a form Gölpınarlı speculated was much revised, and provided a commentary on pp. 68-75 of his *Sefîne* (1983: 123, 384).
2. The Konya Museum MS. is titled *Ṭarîqat al-ma'ârifîn al-Sultân-i Dîn quddisa sirrah al-Mawlâ;* Gölpınarlı found the title a corruption of the more probable *"Ṭarîqat al-'ârifîn li-Sultân-i Dîvânî.* From his summary, it does not seem that Mehmed emphasized a Mevlevî path in particular, but the spiritual path in general (1983:190).

Sayyid 'Alī Hamadānī and Kubrawī Hagiographical Traditions

Devin DeWeese

INTRODUCTION

The study of the Kubrawī Sufi tradition has been plagued by a number of misinterpretations and erroneous assumptions rooted, I believe, in two related tendencies: first, a habit of interpreting Kubrawī history solely on the basis of developments in western Iran in the 13th to 15th centuries, without proper attention to the religious environment of the other Iranian world of that era, Central Asia, where in fact the decisive events that shaped the Kubrawiyya unfolded; and second, a tendency to seek in Kubrawī writings and personalities signs of the Shi'ite proclivities which came to dominate religious developments in western Iran during this period. The latter tendency has proven especially persistent; beginning with the seminal article by Marijan Molé which appeared nearly thirty years ago,[1] it has become virtually axiomatic that the Kubrawiyya was in some way parallel to or preparatory for, at least from a doctrinal perspective, the transition to militant Shī'ism experienced by another Iranian Sufi order of the same era, the Ṣafaviyya.

I cannot review here the issue of apparent Shi'ite tendencies in the works of Najm al-Dīn Kubrā, regarded as the founder of the Kubrawiyya, or of his successors Najm al-Dīn Rāzī, Sa'd al-Dīn Ḥammūyī, or 'Alā' al-Dawla Simnānī, as explored by Molé. Rather, my goal is to focus on Amīr Sayyid 'Alī ibn Shihāb al-Dīn Hamadānī, the Kubrawī figure in whose life and works Molé claimed to find some of the clearest indications of the propensity towards Shi'ism, but whose legacy and role in Kubrawī history have been especially obscured by a lack of attention to Central Asian materials. For while there is no question that Sayyid 'Alī Hamadānī and his immediate successors mark a crucial stage in the development of the Kubrawī *silsilas,* the nature of the transformation during that crucial stage, marked by the schism in the Kubrawī 'Order' which I have discussed elsewhere, [2]has not been fully appreciated, again largely as a result of the misplaced focus on the search for Shi'ite tendencies and the neglect of Central Asian developments.

Here I intend to concentrate not on a reconstruction of events in that period or a

1. M. Molé, 'Les Kubrawiya entre sunnisme et shiisme aux huitième et neuvième siècles de l'hégire,' *Revue des études islamiques,* 29 (1961), pp. 110-124.
2. In 'The Eclipse of the Kubravīyah in Central Asia,' *Iranian Studies,* 21 (1988) pp. 45-83; on pp. 54-61, I addressed the problems arising from the adoption by Western researchers in Kubrawī history of the perspective of later writers belonging to Shi'ified Kubrawī offshoots in Western Iran in interpreting the Khuttalānī-Nūrbakhsh affair and the Kubrawī schism.

review of Hamadānī's own life or writings, but on the indirect evidence concerning the nature of the Kubrawī transformation during the 14th and 15th centuries contained in the hagiographical accounts contemporary with that transformation. In particular, I would like to re-examine two hagiographies devoted to Sayyid 'Alī Hamadānī, not so much to directly counter the ascription of Shi'ite leanings to Hamadānī, or even to revise our understanding of his career, but to highlight the important developments in Kubrawī history which a comparison of these two works may illustrate. Such a comparison shows that, in focusing on supposed Shi'ite tendencies in Sayyid 'Alī Hamadānī, many earlier students of the Kubrawiyya have missed the *real* story about what was happening among the Kubrawī lineages; for, in the development of the hagiographical tradition surrounding Hamadānī, we may witness signs of an actual *ṭarīqa*-organization emerging out of the Kubrawī lineages active in Khurāsān and Central Asia.

SAYYID 'ALĪ HAMADĀNĪ AND HIS BIOGRAPHIES

Sayyid 'Alī Hamadānī's fame rests on a number of foundations which reflect the enormous range of his own interests and talents as well as the evident impact of his personality on his contemporaries. He was, of course, a Sufi Shaykh active in the training of his followers, and as such he was a major link in the *silsila* stemming from Najm al-Dīn Kubrā of Khwārazm (d. 618/1221). He was, as a prolific writer of Sufi treatises, an important interpreter of mystical doctrine whose works were known far beyond the confines of the Kubrawī order. He was active in the defense and spread of Islam, and his role in the establishment of Islam in Kashmir is perhaps his most significant legacy in popular memory. He is revered as a saint to this day, and more in Srinagar, with only a *khānaqāh* ascribed to him (the famous *Khānaqāh-i mu'allā)* than at the actual site of his tomb in Tadjikistan. And he was, finally, a figure of political importance, whether through his relationships with local rulers and his correspondence with contemporary Sultans, or through what is no doubt his most widely known literary composition, the ethico-political work, *Dhakhīrat al-mulūk,* or even through the dim recollection in later generations of his hostility toward the dominant political fact of his lifetime, the rise of Timur.

Because of his prominence, Hamadānī has been comparatively well-studied, and several surveys of his life and writings are available. The most useful remains J.K. Teufel's monograph devoted to the earliest biography of Hamadānī,[1] and a number of general works have made him one of the better known figures from the later

1. J.K. Teufel, *Eine Lebenbeschreibung des Scheichs Alī-i Hamadānī (gestorben 1385): Die Xulāṣat ul-manāqib des Maulānā Nūr ud-Dīn Ca'far-i Badaxšī* (Leiden: E. J. Brill 1962); Teufel's introduction surveys Hamadānī's life and writings, while the *Khulāṣat al-manāqib* is in part translated, in part paraphrased.

Kubrawī lineages.[1] Hamadānī's literary legacy has been outlined in several of the surveys,[2] and a number of his writings have been published;[3] particular elements of his doctrinal presentations have attracted occasional attention as well.[4]

For our purposes his place in the Kubrawī tradition is of particular importance. Hamadānī was a pivotal figure in the Kubrawī lineage stemming from Kubrā's disciple Raḍī al-Dīn 'Alī Lālā (d. 642/1244) through the famous 'Alā' al-Dawla Simnānī (d. 736/1336): virtually all Kubrawī lineages existing later than the 15th century trace their *silsilas* through him and his chief disciple, Khwāja Isḥāq Khuttalānī (d. 826/1423). The 'schism' in this Kubrawī lineage referred to above occurred in the early 15th century, as followers of two of Khuttalānī's disciples, Sayyid Muḥammad Nūrbakhsh (d. 869/1465) and Sayyid 'Abdullāh Barzishābādī,

---

1. Cf. Agha Hussain Shah Hamadānī, *The life and works of Sayyid Ali Hamadānī (A.D. 1314-1385)* (Islamabad: National Institute of Historical and Cultural Research 1984); G. Böwering, ' 'Alī b. Šehab-al-Dīn b. Moḥammad Hamadānī,' art. in *Encyclopaedia Iranica*, I [fasc. 8], pp. 862-864; 'Alī Aṣghar Ḥikmat, 'Az Hamadān tā Kashmīr,' *Yaghmā*, 4 (1330/1951-52), pp. 337-343; A.A. Ḥikmat, 'Les voyages d'un mystique persan de Hamadan au Kashmir,' *Journal asiatique*, 240 (1952), pp. 53-66; Muḥammad Riyāḍ Khān, 'Khadamāt-i Amīr-i Kabīr Mīr Sayyid 'Alī Hamadānī dar shabh-i qāra-i Pākistān wa Hind (qarn-i hashtum),' *Ma'ārif-i islāmī* [Tehran], No. 6 (1347/ 1968), pp. 95-99; Ṣābir Āfāqī, 'Ṣūfiyān-i Kashmīr va naqsh-i ānān dar nashr-i farhang wa adab-i fārsī,' *Hunar wa mardum*, n.s., Nos. 112-13 (Bahman-Isfandmāh, 1350/ February-March, 1972), pp. 66-87, esp. pp. 70-72 on Sayyid 'Alī Hamadānī; and of course Molé's treatment in 'Les Kubrawiya,' pp. 110-124. Hamadānī's role in Kashmir is discussed in several general historical surveys; cf. S.A.A. Rizvi, *History of Sufism in India*, I (New Delhi 1978), pp. 291-292; Abdul Qaiyum Rafiqi, *Sufism in Kashmir from the Fourteenth to the Sixteenth Century* (Varanasi: Bharatiya Publishing House 1972), pp. 31-85; R.K. Parmu, *A History of Muslim Rule in Kashmir 1320-1819* (Delhi: People's Publishing House 1969), pp. 101-114; Prithvi Nath Kaul Bamzai, *A History of Kashmir* (New Delhi: Metropolitan Book Company, 2nd ed. 1973), pp. 525-527. A work that has remained inaccessible to me is noted in *Absracta Iranica*, 9, p.180, No. 653: Muḥammad Riyāḍ, *Aḥwāl wa āthār va ash'ār-i Mīr Sayyid 'Alī Hamadānī, bā shish risāla az way* (Islamabad: Markaz-i taḥqīqāt-i Fārsī-i Īrān va Pākistān 1364/1985).
2. Still the best survey is that of Teufel, *Lebensbeschreibung*, pp. 43-60; see also Hamadānī, *The life and works*, pp.28-35, and Ḥikmat, 'Les voyages', as well as Storey, *Persian Literature; A Bio-bibliographical Survey*, I/2 (London 1953), [PL] I p. 947, n.4.
3. Cf M. Molé, 'Professions de foi de deux Kubrawīs: 'Alī-i Hamadānī et Muḥammad Nūrbakhsh", *Bulletin d'étude orientales* [Institute français de Damas] 17 (1961-62), pp. 133-204; M. Molé, 'Kubrawiyat II: 'Alī b. Şihābaddīn-i Hamadānī'nin Risāla-i futtwwatīya'si ' *Şarkiyat Mecmuası*, 4 (1961), pp. 33-72; M. Molé, 'La version persane du Traité de dix principes de Najm al-Dîn Kobrâ par 'Alî ibn Shihâb al-Din Hamadânî,' *Farhang-i Īrān-zamīn*, 6 (1958), pp. 38-66; Muḥammad Riyāḍ Khān, ed., 'Futuwwatnāma az Mīr Sayyid 'Alī Hamadānī,' *Ma'ārif-i islāmī*, No. 10 (1348/ 1969, No 11 (1349/1970), pp. 32-39; Muḥammad Khwājawi, ed., *Mashārib al-adhwāq, sharḥ-i Qaṣīda-i Khamrīya-i Ibn Fāriḍ Miṣrī dar bayān-i sharāb-i maḥabbat*, (Tehran: Mawlā 1362/ 1404/1984); Muḥammad Riyāż Khān, 'Matn-i maktūbāt-i Mīr Sayyid 'Alī Hamadānī', *Majalla-i dānishkada-i adabiyāt wa 'ulūm-i insānī* (Tehran 1353/1974-75), 21, pp. 33-66. One of his major works has been edited and published by Sayyid Maḥmūd Anwārī: *Dhakhīrat al-mulūk*, (Tabriz, Intishārāt-i Mu'assa-yi tārīkh va farhang-i Irān, n. 35, 1357 A.Hsh.) and is considered in 'Alī Aṣghar Ḥikmat, '*Dhakhīrat al-mulūk* az nafā'is-i āthār-i manthūr-i fārsī dar qarn-i hashtum' *Yaghmā*, 4 (1330/1951-52), pp. 241-249. See further G. Böwering's article in *Encyclopaedia Iranica* on published versions of Hamadānī's work.
4. Cf. Fritz Meier, 'Die Welt der Urbilder bei Ali Hamadānī (d. 1385)', *Eranos Jahrbuch*, 18 (1950), pp. 115-172; M. Sultanov, 'Ideinye istochniki form irovaniia mirovozzreniia Ali Khamadani ', *Izvestiia AN TadzhSSR*, (Otd. Obshch. Nauk 1982), No. 4, pp. 43-47; 'Voprosy samosovershenstvovaniia v uchenii Ali Khamadani', *Izvestiia AN TadzhSSR*, seriia: Filosofiia, èkonomika, pravovedenie, (1987), No. 1, pp.10-15.

whose lineage proceeded through two relatively obscure Shaykhs to Ḥājjī Muḥammad Khabūshānī and several of the latter's disciples, most notably Shaykh Ḥusayn Khwārazmī (d. 958/1551). As stressed below, the fact that the Central Asian Kubrawī branch remained virtually unknown to western researchers was a key factor shaping evaluations of the hagiographical tradition surrounding Hamadānī.

Hamadānī himself was born in 714/1314 in Hamadān, where his father served as a governor under the Mongol Īl-Khāns. The hagiographical tradition consistently reports his extensive travels and his companionship with a large number of Sufi Shaykhs throughout the Islamic world; his primary Shaykhs, however, were disciples of 'Alā' al-Dawla Simnānī, chief among them Sharaf al-Dīn Maḥmūd Mazdaqānī (d. 761/1359-60). The center of his career as a Sufi Shaykh was Khuttalān, and his disciples, to judge from their places of origin as indicated by their *nisbas*, were drawn largely from the eastern reaches of Khurasan and Mawarannahr. He made further journeys as a Shaykh, most notably to Kashmir; he died in 786/1385 while beginning the *ḥajj* from Kashmir, and was buried in the town of Khuttalān (now Kulab in southern Tadjikistan).

Sayyid 'Alī Hamadānī does not appear in any historical works until the first half of the sixteenth century, when he is mentioned briefly in Khwāndamīr's *Ḥabīb al-siyar*, the *Bāburnāma,* and the *Tārīkh-i Rashīdī*; he is, of course, a common fixture in later histories of Kashmir, where his activity in establishing Islam in the region became a standard feature of its 'sacred history.' For the most part, however, aside from his own numerous doctrinal and devotional works, our chief sources on Hamadānī's life and mystical career are hagiographical works, and a complete analysis of the hagiographical traditions surrounding Hamadānī requires identification of the works dealing with him and their sources. An extensive list of works of all types which include biographies of Hamadānī was compiled by Teufel,[1] but, as will be noted shortly, Teufel was evidently unfamiliar with nearly all of the hagiographical works produced in the very environment in which one would expect Hamadānī's memory to be preserved most jealously—that is, works produced by Hamadānī's successors within the Kubrawī order.

Within the hagiographical tradition surrounding Hamadānī, two works stand out as devoted exclusively to him. The earliest, completed within a few years of the Shaykh's death, is the *Khulāṣat al-manāqib* of Nūr ad-Dīn Ja'far Badakhshī, a direct disciple of Hamadānī; as noted, it has been presented in translation and paraphrase by Teufel as the most "reliable" account of Hamadānī's life. Molé knew of

1. Teufel, pp. 9-18.

five manuscripts of the work, including the Berlin,[1] Oxford,[2] and Lahore[3] copies noted by Storey,[4] as well as a late 16th-century copy in Tashkent[5] and the oldest known copy found by Molé in Istanbul.[6] Molé noted that he was preparing an edition of the text based on the Berlin, Oxford, and Istambul manuscripts, but this was evidently either not completed or never published; Teufel's version was based on only the Berlin and Oxford copies. In addition to the manuscripts known to Molé and Teufel, I found one fragment and one nearly complete copy in Srinagar,[7] and it appears that other copies exist in Pakistan.[8] So far as I have been able to trace, only one substantial work on the *Khulāṣat al-manāqib* has appeared since the studies of Molé and Teufel, namely a 1971 article by Sayyidah Ashraf Bukhārī.[9]

---

1. W. Pertsch, *Verzeichniss der persischen Handschriften der königlichen Bibliothek zu Berlin* (Berlin 1888), No. 6 (8); according to Teufel this copy had been moved to Tübingen since the war and was still there at the time Teufel wrote. In her article devoted to the *Khulāṣat* ('Mu'arrifī-i *Khulāṣat al-manāqib* ta'līf-i Nūr al-Dīn Ja'far Badakhshī dar sharḥ-i aḥwāl-i Sayyid 'Alī Hamadānī az 'urafā-yi Kashmīr', *Oriental College Magazine [Lahore]*, 46/4 and 47/1-2 [1971] pp. 175-206) Sayyidah Ashraf Bukhārī (who confusingly refers to this manuscript as belonging to the "Bodleian Library, Berlin"), says that this copy comprises 39ff. (90b-129b) of 28 lines and is "old"; but for its date she cites (apparently—or were footnotes printed in the wrong order?) the colophon from a treatise in the Istanbul MS discussed by Molé in "Kubrawīyāt II." p. 39.
2. E. Sachau, H. Ethé (eds.), *Catalogue of the Persian, Turkish, Hindûstanî and Pushtû Manuscripts in the Bodleian Library*, I (Oxford 1889) No. 1264 (Walker 93; 111 ff., undated).
3. In Punjab University Library; this copy was noted by Storey (see following note), but apparently was not inspected by Molé or Teufel. It is described more fully in Bukhārī's article; it comprises, she says (pp. 176-177), 93 folios of 21 lines, and was copied in 1229/1814.
4. C.A. Storey, *Persian Literature; A Bio-bibliographical Survey*, I/2 (London 1953), pp. 946-947.
5. Institute of Oriental Studies of the Academy of Sciences of the Uzbek SSR; cf. Sobranie vostochnykh rukopisei, III (Tashkent 1955), p. 255, No. 2391 (Inv. No. 2312/XXIV, ff. 304b-358b), copied "somewhat later" than the first half of the manuscript, dated 991/1583.
6. Şehit Ali Paşa No. 2794, ff. 678a-751a [thus in 'Les Kubrawiya,' p. 110, n.135; in 'Kubrawiyāt II,' p. 35, n. 7, ff. 678a-771a], copied 21 Ṣafar 901/10 November 1495, by 'Abd al-Laṭīf Qalandar ibn 'Abdullāh b. Khiḍr Sabzawārī, who evidently transcribed all the works of Hamadānī contained in this manuscript. Sayyidah Ashraf Bukhārī ('Mu'arrifī', pp. 178-179) for some reason refers to this manuscript as belonging to the "National Library" in Istanbul and numbers its folios 1b-75a, but does give the text of the colophon from the manuscript itself (Molé gives only the date without specifying that the copyist of the *Khulāṣat* is the same as that of the other works of Hamadānī); she needlessly confuses the issue, however, by misquoting either the manuscript itself or Molé's excerpt on the date of another treatise in the manuscript to read "799" instead of "899," and then arguing that the "799" date is an error.
7. At the Government Oriental Research Library, housed (in 1988) at the Iqbal Library of Kashmir University: No. 1983 (31ff., late) and No. 658 (113ff., lacks beginning, undated); No. 2442 in this collection is a rather poor photographic (or microfilm reader-printer) copy of ff. 89b-126a of some unidentified manuscript containing the *Khulāṣat*.
8. The "union catalogue" of Persian manuscripts in Pakistan (vol. III, p. 1436) lists the *Khulāṣat* in the section on *'irfān* with the note that the work will be dealt with in the section on biography (which, if published, has not been available to me yet). In addition, a brief fragment of the work, not cited by Molé or Teufel, is mentioned in Munzawī's survey of Persian manuscripts (where, curiously no other copies of the work are listed), namely an uncataloged manuscript in the Kitābkhāna-i Majlis, No. 3660, ff. 59-60, dated 917/ 1511-12 (Aḥmad Munzawī, *Fihrist-i nuskhahā-yi khaṭṭī-i fārsī*, II/1;Tehran 1349/1970, p. 1139, No. 10558). Finally, the register of the Andhra Pradesh Government Oriental Manuscript Library in Hyderabad lists as "Tadhkira No. 285" the *Khulāṣat al-manāqib* by Aflākī; either the title or the author is clearly an error, but I did not manage to check this to learn whether the manuscript is Ja'far Badakhshī's *Khulāṣat* or Aflākī's *Manāqib al-'ārifīn*.
9. Cited above in note 1.

We know few particulars of Ja'far Badakhshī's life beyond the extensive personal reminiscences in his chief work;[1] his birth and death dates are not known. From the *Khulāṣat* we know that he met Hamadānī in 774/1373, when the Shaykh was already 60 years old, and remained his disciple until Hamadānī's death. As noted below, the disciples of Hamadānī by whose authority he relates certain episodes in his work[2] by no means include all, or even the most important, of the Shaykh's followers. He began the *Khulāṣat* on the last Friday of Ṣafar 787/7 April 1385, in Khuttalān, but its date of completion is not specified, nor, apparently, do his other brief works bear dates.[3] No doubt on the basis of Hamadānī's association with Kashmir—which however is not mentioned in Ja'far Badakhshī's work—it has been assumed that the "Mawlānā Nūr ad-Dīn" mentioned in the histories of Timur by Niẓām al-Dīn Shāmi and Sharaf al-Dīn 'Alī Yazdī as an ambassador to Timur from the ruler of Kashmir, Sultan Sikandar, in 801/1398, is the same "Nūr ad-Dīn" Ja'far Badakhshī who wrote the *Khulāṣat,* but I have not found independent confirmation of this identification in early sources.

The second hagiography devoted to Hamadānī was produced less than a century later by one Ḥaydar Badakhshī, of whom virtually nothing is known beyond the meager data provided in his work. Entitled *Manqabat al-jawāhir,* this later work was known to Teufel and Molé through two manuscripts, one in the India Office[4] (incomplete at the beginning and thus called in the catalogue description simply *Mastūrāt*)[5] and another in the possession of the Dhahabī *khānaqāh* in Tehran (its beginning, containing the full title and author's name, is published in transcription in Teufel's introduction[6] with acknowledgments to Molé, who first reported this manuscript). Molé mentions[7] that he collated the two copies and refers to his "edition in preparation," but this work likewise was evidently never completed for publication. Both these manuscripts are apparently quite recent copies; Teufel judges the (undated) India Office copy to be quite late, although it is certainly older than

1. On his life and other works see Teufel, pp. 1-4.
2. Cf. Teufel, p. 5.
3. Teufel, pp. 3-4, discusses his other works; one not mentioned there has been published by Īraj Afshār, ed., *'Iṣṭilāḥāt al-ṣūfiyya,* athar-i Shaykh Nūr al-Dīn Ja'far Badakhshānī,' *Farhang-i Īrān-zamīn,* 16 (1348-49), pp. 326-333.
4. H. Ethé, ed., *Catalogue of the Persian Manuscripts in the Library of the India Office,* I (Oxford, 1903), No. 1850.
5. Molé's assertion ('Les Kubrawiya', p.110, n. 139) that the India Office manuscript contains neither the title nor the author's name is not quite accurate; the introduction in which both would be mentioned is of course missing, but the author calls himself Ḥaydar three times (ff. 437a, 438b, 439a) and in verse refers to his work as the *Manqabat* of Shāh-i Hamadān (f. 438a). Similarly, Molé implies that the India Office copy is complete at the end, but despite the appearance of the characteristic concluding formulae at the end of this manuscript, the text is incomplete, as is clear from the manuscript I found in Srinagar (see below); this copy contains the rest of the section which breaks off in the India Office copy, but the arrangement of the sections in the Srinagar manuscript does not agree with that of the India Office copy. It appears, in fact, that both these manuscripts were transcribed from incomplete copies of the work, but without access to all known manuscripts of the work a useful collation cannot be undertaken.
6. Teufel, pp. 9-10.
7. 'Les Kubrawiya,' p. 110-111, n.139, and p.112, n.150.

the Tehran copy, which is evidently dated 1309/1891-92.[1] In addition I found one partial copy and one evidently complete, though late, copy of the work in Srinagar[2] while what is probably the oldest manuscript of the work, apparently not known to Molé or Teufel, is preserved in the Kitābkhāna-i Millī in Tehran.[3]

Of Ḥaydar Badakhshī's life we know only that he was a disciple of Sayyid 'Abdullāh Barzishābādī, and, as noted below, that before his entry into the Kubrawī Order he had been affiliated with the Shaṭṭāriyya. From the absence of any of the formulae for posthumous blessings upon Barzishābādī we may assume that the *Manqabat* was written before his death in 872/1467-68. Khwāndamīr's *Ḥabīb al-siyar* names a "Mawlānā Badakhshī" as an eminent poet of Samarqand in the time of Ulugh Beg,[4] but there is no firm basis on which to suggest this figure's identification with the *Manqabat*'s author.

The *Manqabat al-jawāhir* has, I believe, been seriously undervalued by students of the Kubrawiyya, in particular by Molé and Teufel, who have used it most extensively. In part their evaluation of Ḥaydar Badakhshī's work is colored by the general unfamiliarity of most students of the Kubrawiyya with the lineage to which Ḥaydar Badakhshī belonged, namely that of 'Abdullāh Barzishābādī. Molé, for example, notes Ḥaydar Badakhshī's lack of direct acquaintance with Hamadānī and implicitly ascribes the tone of the *Manqabat* to Khwāja Isḥāq Khuttalānī, whom he calls one of those chiefly responsible for "the exaltation of the personality of Sayyid 'Alī Hamadānī."[5] Elsewhere[6] he identifies Ḥaydar Badakhshī as a disciple of Barzishābādī but concludes on this basis that the *Manqabat* was written in Kashmir (which Barzishābādī, who died in 872/1467-68, never visited) toward the middle of the 10th century A.H., later (in 'Les Kubrawiya') modifying this to merely "two generations" after Ja'far Badakhshī's work.

1. Affirmed by Munzawī, *Fihrist*, II/1, p. 1428; Molé does not mention the date of the manuscript, referring only to its purchase "some years ago" by Aḥmad Khūshnawīs in a Tehran *bazār* for the Dhahabī *khānaqāh*.
2. The partial copy is preserved in the Iqbal Library of Kashmir University but bears no accession or inventory number; a photocopy was supplied to me through the kind efforts of Dr. J.A. Wajid, University Librarian. The copy runs to 43ff., is undated but clearly recent, and comprises a little over one-third of the work, including episodes 17-30, 50-51, and 31-33, in that order, of the India Office manuscript. In the Government Oriental Research Library in Srinagar, No. 3269 is the *Manqabat*, and includes the beginning as given in the Tehran Dhahabī copy; it runs to 65ff. and is dated 26 Sha'bān 1336/6 June 1918, but efforts to obtain a microfilm of this copy have been unsuccessful.
3. Cf. Munzawī, *Fihrist*, II/1, p. 1428, No. 13688: MS. Millī No. 224/2, apparently dated 1103/1691-92; Munzawī lists here (No. 13689 [printed incorrectly as 13589]) the other Tehran manuscript, noting that microfilms of both copies are preserved in the University Library (Nos. 1891 and 1901, respectively, cf. Muḥammad Taqī Dānish-pizhūh, *Fihrist-i mīkrūfīlmhā-yi Kitābkhāna-i markazī-i Dānishgāh-i Tihrān* (Tehran 1348/1969), I, pp. 630-631), but does not refer to the India Office copy.
4. Ed. Jalāl al-Dīn Humā'ī (Tehran 1333/1959), IV, p. 38.
5. Molé, 'Les Kubrawiya,' p. 123.
6. 'Kubrawīyāt II,' p.35, n. 7.

For his part, Teufel labels Ḥaydar Badakhshī a Shi'ite,[1] without explanation (a view now unfortunately perpetuated in the recent article on Hamadānī in the *Encyclopaedia Iranica)*[2] indicating most probably that Teufel knew only of Barzishābādī's spiritual ancestry in the Shi'ite Dhahabī order (and not of his Sunnī Central Asian Kubrawī successors) and simply assumed that Ḥaydar Badakhshī must be a Shi'ite like the lot of them. More recently, Sayyidah Ashraf Bukhārī, whose interest in the *Khulāṣat al-manāqib* was simply as a straightforward source on Hamadānī's life, especially his career in Kashmir (as with Agha Hussain Shah Hamadānī, who simply refers to both hagiographies with no critical evaluation), compares the *Manqabat* unfavorably with the earlier work. She does not seem to have directly consulted manuscripts of the *Manqabat,* but, no doubt following Teufel, asserts that its author simply took most of his narratives from the *Khulāṣat.* She is unaware of who Ḥaydar Badakhshī was, however (she suggests that he may have been a *murīd* of "one of Hamadānī's *murīd*s named Isḥāq Khuttalānī.")[3] And although she acknowledges that Ḥaydar Badakhshī supplemented the material from the *Khulāṣat* with information from "another writer named Qivām ad-Dīn Badakhshī," she is evidently unaware of his identity as well, and states that no such work is known; she therefore concludes that Ja'far Badakhshī's work is the oldest and most important of Hamadānī's biographies.

None of the relatively few researchers to discuss the two works together has pursued, however, the details of the Kubrawī lineage to which Ḥaydar Badakhshī belonged. They appear to have been familiar with only the Dhahabī branch of Barzishābādī's line, and both Molé and Teufel in particular clearly adopt the 'Nūrbakhshī' version of Kubrawī history (and the Nūrbakhshī evaluation of the Barzishābādī lineages as well), the result strengthening their inclination to dismiss the *Manqabat al-jawāhir* as a less reliable source than the *Khulāṣat al-manāqib.* This unfamiliarity with Ḥaydar Badakhshī's religious environment and Sufi background must be kept in mind when considering the avowed justification for dismissing the *Manqabat al-jawāhir:* both Molé and Teufel compare the work of Ḥaydar Badakhshī unfavorably with that of Ja'far Badakhshī, citing the later work's 'legendary' and miraculous tone and its 'distortion' of accounts preserved in the *Khulāṣat al-manāqib.* Teufel did in fact use the *Manqabat* as a basis for occasional commentary on his primary text, but nevertheless illustrates his basic conclusion about the relative merits of the two works by presenting their respective versions of one narrative as evidence of the "additions" and elaboration of the later work.[4]

The *Manqabat al-jawāhir,* then has gained a poor reputation as an example of 'miracle-mongering' and fantastically embellished hagiography consistently judged to be inferior to the earlier and therefore presumably 'original' *Khulāṣat al-manāqib. Y*et while this reputation is itself undeserved, I believe, it seems clear that the unanimously disparaging comments about the *Manqabat* have been based more

1. Teufel, p. 10
2. G. Böwering, "Alī b. Šehāb-al-dīn b. Moḥammad Hamadānī', *Encyclopædia Iranica,* I [fasc. 8], pp. 862-864.
3. Bukhārī, 'Mu'arrifī-i *Khulāṣat al-manāqib,*' p. 204.
4. Teufel, pp. 10-11; for his translation of the *Khulāṣat's* account, pp. 69-70.

on a lack of awareness or consideration of its provenance than on any systematic evaluation of its style or content.

REHABILITATING THE *MANQABAT AL-JAWĀHIR*

A closer study of the *Manqabat* as a whole shows that the relationship between the two works is not as simple as Molé and Teufel assumed, and that *Manqabat al-jawāhir* ought not to be dismissed so lightly as a source on Kubrawī history. My contention is that whatever its 'tone'—and here I would suggest that the atmosphere of dreams and visions and miracles whose prevalence in Ḥaydar Badakhshī's work bothered Molé and Teufel is by no means absent in Ja'far Badakhshī's work—the *Manqabat al-jawāhir* must be taken seriously as a product of Kubrawī hagiography, for a number of reasons to which we may now turn.

1. The Authority of the Manqabat al-jawāhir

First, whether or not the narratives of the *Manqabat* are more offensively 'miraculous' in tone compared with those of the *Khulāṣat*, the fact is that Ḥaydar Badakhshī's sources for his narratives were every bit as authoritative as those of the earlier work. While it is undeniable that Ḥaydar Badakhshī did not know Hamadānī personally, but was instead a disciple of a Shaykh separated from Hamadānī by one 'spiritual generation,' it must be remembered that in compiling his work he utilized not only the earlier hagiography itself, but an extensive body of tradition—in part oral and in part written—passed down within the Kubrawī lineages stemming from Hamadānī. By comparison with the sources cited by Ja'far Badakhshī, the *Manqabat*'s author used a wider range of 'informants' in compiling narratives, drawing from several direct disciples of Hamadānī and from those of his chief disciple.

The figures named as transmitters of narratives given in the *Manqabat* include not only Ja'far Badakhshī (with the *Khulāṣat al-manāqib* mentioned by name three times) and most of his sources (such as Ja'far's brother Qivām al-Dīn Badakhshī, Shaykh Rukn al-Dīn 'Abdullāh Shīrāzī, and Shaykh Muḥammad Sarāy-asani [transcription uncertain]), but a wider range of figures as well. Thus, among other direct disciples of Hamadānī who are mentioned rarely or not at all in the *Khulāṣat*, Ḥaydar Badakhshī cites Shams al-Dīn Khuttalānī (not mentioned),[1] Sayyid Zayn al-'Ābidīn, known as *majdhūb* (not mentioned), Muḥammad Shāmī (who accompanied Hamadānī to Kashmir,[2] not mentioned), and Bahrām-shāh [al-Kishmī] al-Ḥūshī (transcription uncertain, who is *mentioned* in the *Khulāṣat*,[3] including at least once by Hamadānī, but is not cited as a source of a saying or narrative). More im-

1. He may be mentioned where "Shams al-Dīn" and "Isḥāq" are named together in an episode set in Khuttalān (cf. Teufel, p. 135); Teufel (probably erroneously) identifies this 'Shams al-Dīn' with Shams al-Dīn Mākhānī, and a later source (the *Riyāḍ al-awliyā*, on which see below) mentions both as separate figures, so it is not certain which Shams al-Dīn is meant here.
2. *Manqabat*, India Office MS, f. 435a; unless otherwise noted all citations from the work are from this manuscript.
3. Cf. Teufel, pp. 99, 133, and possibly 135; Teufel does not resolve the problems with this figure's *nisbas*.

portantly, two clearly important figures among the disciples of Hamadānī are frequently cited in the *Manqabat* but are virtually unknown in the *Khulāṣat*. First, Shaykh Muḥammad Ṭāliqānī, cited as a narrator four times, is not mentioned at all by Jaʻfar Badakhshī, although he is named in later sources as a disciple of Hamadānī,[1] and must have been prominent among them, since as Teufel notes,[2] a Muḥammad Ṭāliqānī is buried in Hamadānī's tomb complex at Kulab and is named in his grave inscription as the *mutawallī* of the grave. More remarkably, the *Khulāṣat al-manāqib* contains in only two narratives *possible* references to Khwāja Isḥāq Khuttalānī,[3] whom all later Kubrawī affiliations clearly regard as Hamadānī's principle disciple; as such he is cited as the source of three accounts in the *Manqabat* and three of his disciples are cited for five more, while Jaʻfar Badakhshī's work clearly fails to reflect his real stature within the Kubrawī *silsila*. Here we may note as well that among the disciples of Isḥāq Khuttalānī (who are naturally not mentioned in the *Khulāṣat*), Ḥaydar Badakhshī cites Ibrāhīm Mubārakkhānī, Shaykh Maḥmūd al-Kāmil Shīrāzī, and Shaykh Khalīlullāh Baghlānī; the first two, at least, are known independently from other sources.

The *Khulāṣat al-manāqib*, by contrast, is the work of a figure who played virtually no role in the later organizational life of the Kubrawī or Hamadānī lineages; the work itself is, in fact, somewhat idiosyncratic, and is cast more as a personal memoir of the author's relationship with Hamadānī without pretending to be a complete 'biography.' Extensive sections,[4] indeed, deal more with the author's own spiritual experiences and development than with the career of his Shaykh. Here we should note that although Jaʻfar Badakhshī was himself a direct disciple, he was not in any sense a 'constant companion' of Hamadānī; he did not accompany him, for example to Kashmir, and received the news of Hamadānī's death, which occurred on his way back from Kashmir, in a letter from his brother Qivām al-Dīn Badakhshī. By contrast, the *Manqabat*'s account[5] of Hamadānī's final trip to Kashmir and his death cites the reports of two disciples who did accompany the Shaykh, the same Qivām al-Dīn Badakhshī and Khwāja Isḥāq Khuttalānī.

Moreover, it is important to note that the reliability and/or reputation of the *Manqabat* itself and of many of its author's sources is attested by other independent works. Much of the original factual information (such as names of additional disciples and settings for events) included in the *Manqabat* finds support or confirmation in the *Khulāṣat* itself, as well as in later sources whose authors do not appear to have consulted the *Manqabat* directly, as outlined below. For this reason Ḥaydar Badakhshī's work ought to be regarded as authoritative, by which I mean that it transmits narratives from the recognized disciples of Hamadānī himself (here the *reliability* of the narratives themselves is not the issue); and as such its accounts are

---

1. In the *Jāmiʻ al-salāsil*, on which see below.
2. Teufel, p. 36, citing a Soviet journal article which has not been accessible to me.
3. In the first (Teufel, pp. 135-136) "Shams al-Dīn" and "Isḥāq" are named in an episode set in Khuttalān; Shams al-Dīn Khuttalānī is the source of two narratives in the *Manqabat*. In the second (Teufel, pp. 105-106) Jaʻfar Badakhshī mentions a "Ḥājjī Isḥāq" as his companion during his stay in Khuttalān.
4. Cf. Teufel, pp. 88-92, 94-98, 136-139, etc.
5. Ff. 419a-423a.

often no less trustworthy, if properly understood and interpreted, than the accounts of the *Khulāṣat*.

The *Manqabat*, then, ought to be valued as a source of additional information not preserved in the earlier work, a source complementing, rather than simply distorting or elaborating upon, the text of the *Khulāṣat*. To begin with, as noted, the reliability of many details in the *Manqabat* is supported by the *Khulāṣat* itself. For instance, the names of teachers of Hamadānī (Shaykh Pīr Turkistānī, Shaykh Muḥammad Dihistānī [f. 353a], and Shaykh Khālid Ralsānī [transcription uncertain; f. 356a]) known from the *Khulāṣat* are correctly transmitted, alongside some not mentioned by the earlier work. The *Khulāṣat* also supports Hamadānī's affiliation with Shaykh Muḥammad Azkānī,[1] although the *Manqabat*'s account of their relationship is not given in the earlier work; and similarly, the *Khulāṣat* confirms[2] Hamadānī's presence at a banquet given, apparently in Khuttalān, by a certain "Amīr-i Surkh," which is the setting in the *Manqabat* for Hamadānī's designation of the place for his burial in Kūlāb. At the same time the presence of narratives in the *Manqabat* which conclude with brief 'summarizing' passages found also in the *Khulāṣat* may suggest that Ḥaydar Badakhshī has used original oral or written sources to expand upon the condensed 'abstract' recorded in the earlier work.[3]

The *Manqabat*'s authority is occasionally supported by other early sources on Hamadānī from outside the Kubrawī tradition as well. Among the relatively early works from Teufel's list of those mentioning Hamadānī may be noted Dawlatshāh's *Tadhkirat al-shu'arā* from the end of the 15th century, which names Hamadānī among the eminent Shaykhs of Timur's time and mentions his burial in Khuttalān without citing any source, and from the same period, Jāmī's *Nafaḥāt al-uns*, from which most later accounts of Hamadānī in general biographical or hagiographical works are drawn (e.g. Khwāndamīr, the *Haft iqlīm*, Dārā Shikūh's *Safīnat al-awliyā*). Jāmī's account is important, however, because as Teufel showed,[4] he reproduces one passage on Hamadānī's travels verbatim from the *Manqabat*, without naming his source. Jāmī is notorious for not acknowledging his sources, however (he clearly used the *Khulāṣat al-manāqib* without naming it or its author, for instance) and his evident recourse to Ḥaydar Badakhshī's work not only helps us confirm its date (the *Nafaḥāt* was finished most probably in 883/1478), but testifies to Jāmī's regard for the work as well.

Similarly, Teufel notes[5] that the mid-15th century work of Abū 'Alī Ḥamzah Ādharī, the *Jawāhir al-asrār*, gives Hamadānī's natural genealogy in a form agreeing with that given in the *Manqabat;* this attests, if not to Ādharī's actual citation

1. Teufel, p. 132.
2. Teufel, p. 135.
3. For instance, narrative No. 25 (ff. 385b-390b; the numbers refer to my preliminary numbering of episodes) in the *Manqabat*, relating Hamadānī's confrontation with the unnamed ruler who is clearly Timur, concludes with a statement from Hamadānī on the numerous torments brought upon him by rulers and other officials; a quite similar statement, without the narrative, is found in the *Khulāṣat* (Teufel, pp. 122-123). Likewise, No. 36 (ff. 409b-413a) relates Hamadānī's dealings with another unnamed ruler and ends with a passage on the Shaykh's generosity which echoes a passage in the earlier work (Teufel,p. 102).
4. Teufel pp. 13, 112.
5. Teufel, p. 62, n. 2.

Sayyid ʻAlī Hamadānī Addressing a Prince. From a manuscript of the *Majālis al-ʻushshāq*, dated 959/1552. MS. Ouseley Add. 24, f. 90v (Courtesy of the Bodleian Library, Oxford)

of the *Manqabat,* then at least to the currency of other narrative traditions about Hamadānī, besides those adopted in the *Khulāṣat,* which Ḥaydar Badakhshī was not alone in finding credible. Finally, in the hagiographical *Majālis al-'ushshāq,* ascribed to the Timurid ruler Sulṭān Ḥusayn Bāyqarā but actually written by his courtier Ḥusayn Kāzargāhī at the beginning of the 16th century, a meeting between Hamadānī and Timur is described, thereby again attesting to the tradition of their encounter as affirmed in the *Manqabat* but not in the *Khulāṣat.* While this work's account understandably portrays their relationship as essentially friendly, certain elements in the narrative suggest its common origin in the oral tradition of Hamadānī's followers themselves.[1]

The cumulative effect of these early attestations to the authority of the *Manqabat al-jawāhir* should in itself serve to improve its image and demonstrate the danger of dismissing later transmitters of authoritative narratives. The case is strengthened by the later Kubrawī hagiographical tradition, which, as noted earlier, was unknown to Teufel and has in fact remained unfamiliar to most specialists in the Kubrawiyya.

Of the later hagiographical tradition citing 'Kubrawī' sources (and not simply dependent upon Jāmī) Teufel knew only Nūr al-Dīn Shūstarī's famous *Majālis al-mu'minīn.* This late 16th century work cites the *Khulāṣat al-manāqib* exclusively and makes no mention of the *Manqabat,* which is predictable enough in view of Shūstarī's Nūrbakhshī lineage and overt hostility towards Barzishābādī.

The later works unknown to Teufel include two already accessible works extremely important for understanding Kubrawī history; and a third work of even greater importance has only recently come to light. All three works stem from the Kubrawī successors of Sayyid 'Abdullāh Barzishābādī, and two belong to the Kubrawī hagiographical corpus which includes, apart from them, only two extensive biographies of Ḥusayn Khwarazmī (which, however, contain little material on Hamadānī) and a few brief works on his spiritual descendants.

The better-known of these sources is the *Rawḍāt al-jinān wa jannāt al-janān,* written around 990/1582 by Ḥusayn Karbalā'ī Tabrīzī as a bio-geographical guide to the tombs of the saints buried in Tabrīz. The author's father was a pupil of Sayyid Aḥmad Lāla (d. 912/1507) from Barzishābādī's lineage, and for this reason the work includes extensive biographical material on the Kubrawī Shaykhs from Barzishābādī back to Najm al-Dīn Kubrā. While much of the material is drawn

1. On the *Majālis al-'ushshāq,* cf. Storey, I, *PL,* p. 901; I have used a copy from the Bodleian Library (Cat. No. 1271, Ouseley Add. 24), ff. 90a-91a. Teufel (p. 13) notes this work's account, citing an old lithograph version and ascribing the work to Ḥusayn Bāyqarā; Teufel evidently assumed that the Shaykh's encounter was with a young prince of the Barlas tribe, also mentioned in the narrative, but the text is quite clear that the discussion of Hamadānī's black turban occurred at Timur's court and that the "Great Prince" ("Amīr-i buzurg"=Timur) participated in it. In any event, the discussion echoes a passage in the *Rawḍāt al-jinān,* which I have noted elsewhere ('Eclipse', pp. 57-58), in which Hamadānī's disciple Isḥāq Khuttalānī is the wearer of the black turban; here the encounter is quite hostile, but the core of the narrative is no doubt the same. Without dwelling here on the actual political activities of Hamadānī's successors, I would note that the curious assertion in the *Majālis al-'ushshāq* that Hamadānī was much esteemed among the Barlas and that "even still his followers are numerous in that tribe" may be taken as an indication that the author of the work was well aware of the intense hostility toward Timur among the most important successors of Hamadānī.

from other available sources, Ḥusayn Karbalā'ī's work contains important new material on these Shaykhs ranging from the texts of various *licentia docendi (ijāzāt-nāmas)* to sayings and traditions drawn from now-lost written sources and, evidently, from oral transmission within the Kubrawī order. Less well-known is the *Riyāḍ al-awliyā,* written in the late 16th century by a pupil of Shaykh Muḥammad al-Zāhid al-Jāmī al-Balkhī, himself a direct disciple of Ḥājjī Muḥammad Khabūshānī; it is preserved in a unique manuscript in the library of the Asiatic Society in Calcutta. This work's value for the study of Central Asian Sufism was noted by W. Ivanow in his catalogue description,[1] but it has to my knowledge never been used (outside my article noted earlier) as a source on Kubrawī lineages or on the general history of Sufism in Central Asia. The *Riyāḍ al-awliyā* is particularly valuable for its lists of disciples of each of the chief Kubrawī Shaykhs; it is, for example, the only independent source to name Ḥaydar Badakhshī among the successors of Sayyid 'Abdullāh Barzishābādī.[2]

Both these works evidently draw their information on Hamadānī primarily from Ja'far Badakhshī's work; Ḥusayn Karbalā'ī cites it by name, and does not mention Ḥaydar Badakhshī among Barzishābādī's disciples, while the narratives found in both the *Rawḍāt al-jinān* and the *Riyāḍ al-awliyā* do not appear to include any which are clearly identifiable as having been drawn exclusively from the *Manqabat al-jawāhir*. Nevertheless, these two works name disciples of Hamadānī not mentioned in the *Khulāṣat al-manāqib* but known from Ḥaydar Badakhshī's citations,[3] and the probability that the two later authors did not directly use the *Manqabat* seems to attest independently to the oral transmission of information on Hamadānī's career within the Central Asian Kubrawī lineages stemming from Barzishābādī—oral material, that is, of the type that Ḥaydar Badakhshī must have used.

In particular, Ḥusayn Karbalā'ī's account of the confrontation between Hamadānī and Timur, which I have discussed elsewhere,[4] quite clearly echoes—but does not directly correspond to—one of the unparalleled narratives from the *Manqabat,* related by Qivam al-Dīn Badakhshī, in which Hamadānī is summoned before a ruler hostile to Sufis. The ruler is not named but is clearly Timur, and the narrative involves not only the element of a dog (here in the form of dog slaughtered and prepared in an attempt to induce the Shaykh to eat unlawful food, while in Ḥusayn Karbalā'ī's work the dog is made to symbolize Timur), but the element of Hamadānī's refusal to sit with his back to the *qibla* (which in the *Manqabat* provokes commentary on the ruler's lack of discernment, in Ḥusayn Karbalā'ī's work occasions Hamadānī's comment that facing Timur automatically means turning from the *qibla,* and in later popular legends sets the stage for the miraculous spinning of the palace). In this instance it seems clear that both Ḥaydar Badakhshī and

1. W. Ivanow, *Concise Descriptive Catalogue of the Persian Manuscripts in the Curzon Collection,* Asiatic Society of Bengal (Calcutta 1926), pp. 467-468, No. 704.
2. *Riyaḍ al-awliyā,* MS, f. 123b.
3. *Rawḍāt al-jinān wa jannāt al-janān,* ed. J. Sulṭān al-Qurrā'ī (Tehran, 1344-49/ 1965-70), II, p. 254; *Riyaḍ al-awliyā,* MS., f. 118b.
4. 'Eclipse,' pp. 57-58.

Ḥusayn Karbalā'ī drew upon a common stock of narratives that could be and regularly were adapted for straightforward didactic purposes within the *ṭarīqa*, symbolic and mystical purposes among the closest followers, and for popular edification (with the interests of the Order simultaneously advanced thereby) among the masses; the latter adaptation no doubt serves as the entry point for Sufi oral narratives into folklore. In any event the *lack* of clear textual connection between the two works which echo Hamadānī's meeting with Timur, insofar as it helps confirm the existence of oral traditions outside the literary record, itself provides insight into the use of new or adapted modes of religious discourse by Kubrawī 'partisans' in the 'new' atmosphere of competition among orders at the court and popular levels.

The third work, which like the *Riyāḍ al-awliyā* stems from the Central Asian Kubrawī lineages was not known to me until after the earlier study of the Kubrawiyya was completed. I found an uncataloged copy of the work in the library of Aligarh Muslim University,[1] and subsequently found a notice of an additional copy in Islamabad.[2] The work in question, entitled *Jāmi' al-salāsil,* was written "in the time of Shāh Jahān" by one Majd al-Dīn 'Alī, a grandson of Shaykh Khalīlullāh Badakhshānī, who was a disciple of Shaykh Ḥusayn Khwarazmī. It is an extremely rich work full of untapped material on the Kubrawiyya and other Orders, designed, in the author's words, to present the Sufi Orders *(silsilas)* active "in the regions of Mawarannahr, Badakhshān, and Hindūstān."[3] The *Jāmi' al-salāsil,* like the other two works which discuss Sayyid 'Alī Hamadānī, appears to draw most of its material from Ja'far Badakhshī's work, and also quotes extensively from Hamadānī's own works. More importantly for our purposes, however, its author twice cites Sayyid Muḥammad Ṭāliqānī, a direct disciple of Hamadānī not mentioned in the *Khulāṣat al-manāqib* (but known to Ibn Karbalā') who was one of Ḥaydar Badakhshī's chief sources, for extensive accounts of Hamadānī, and in both cases the citations are from some written source. This reinforces the notion that Ḥaydar Badakhshī had at his disposal not only independent oral tradition handed down among the spiritual descendants of Hamadānī, but written accounts as well, in addition to Ja'far Badakhshī's *Khulāṣat al-manāqib.*

In short, the *Manqabat al-jawāhir* might be characterized as more widely researched than its predecessor, which was based primarily on Ja'far Badakhshī's own recollections. Ḥaydar Badakhshī had access to additional sources, oral and written, which were not available to Ja'far Badakhshī, and which arguably command as much or more authority in comparison to the *Khulāṣat al-manāqib* insofar as they were drawn largely from figures of equal or higher standing among Hamadānī's disciples.This is not to overlook the great likelihood of change and

1. Mawlana Azad Library, Shāh Munīr 'Ālam Collection, Box 3-3 (F) dated Thursday, 6 Sha'bān 1100/26 May 1689, running to 354ff. plus 19ff. of *silsila* charts at the beginning.
2. Aḥmad Munzawī, *Fihrist-i nuskhahā-yi khaṭṭī-i Kitābkhāna-i Ganjbakjsh,* IV (Islamabad: Iran-Pakistan Institute of Persian Studies 1982), pp. 2102-2103, title no. 2493, MS no. 5822 (Inventory No. 1060, comprising 868 pp. preceded by 39 pp. of schematic *silsila* tables; copied by Shaykh Faqīrullāh, dated Sunday, *ghurra-i Muḥarram* [probably the 3rd], 1104/14 September 1692); Munzawī names the author (without discussing his natural or spiritual lineage), cites the beginning and the reason for the work's composition, and gives an overview of the work's disposition.
3. Aligarh MS, f. 2b, cf. f. 68a. I hope to devote a special study to the work at a later time.

adaptation within the oral component of the traditions handed down to the time of Ḥaydar Badakhshī, but it is precisely in such changes and adaptations, and in Ḥaydar Badakhshī's editorial emphasis, that we have an important source on the internal developments on the Kubrawī order, as we will see.

II. The Relationship of the Two Works

With this in mind (i.e. that Ḥaydar Badakhshī used additional reputable sources in compiling his work), it is clear that a simple comparison of parallel narratives in the *Khulāṣat* and *Manqabat* cannot conclusively demonstrate a pattern of baseless elaboration on the part of Ḥaydar Badakhshī. If he had used the *Khulāṣat* as his chief source and simply embroidered the accounts he found there, the reservations of Molé and Teufel might be justified, but in fact, he not only used other sources of considerable authority, but he actually used the *Khulāṣat* quite sparingly. Teufel's assertion[1] that "for the most part," the *Manqabat al-jawāhir* simply repeats the biographical material from the *Khulāṣat al-manāqib,* "often with exaggeration into the legendary," is simply untrue; while such an appraisal may reflect a natural first impression from the later work, a more careful analysis shows quite the opposite.

If we examine the *Manqabat al-jawāhir,* we can identify 49 distinct 'episodes' each introduced by the words, "It is related;" as often as not the stories are anonymous, and it may be implicit in these cases that the narratives are transmitted on the authority of Ḥaydar Badakhshī's Shaykh (in most cases they are clearly not cited from the *Khulāṣat*), but, as noted, the episodes which are explicitly attributed to named transmitters attest to the author's diligence and conscientiousness. Of the 49 narratives in the *Manqabat,* 36 have no parallel in the *Khulāṣat* whatsoever; 11 are paralleled by accounts in the earlier work but show significant differences and/or additions, and only two[2] appear to repeat essentially the same account as in the *Khulāṣat*, but even here Ḥaydar Badakhshī has not merely copied the text of the earlier work verbatim. Curiously, two narratives (one of the unparalleled accounts and one of the elaborated accounts) cite Ja'far Badakhshī as the source of information, suggesting that the author of the *Khulāṣat* did indeed transmit other narratives not included in his book—which, after all, he termed a "summary" *(khulāṣa).*

Of the eleven episodes which are paralleled in the *Khulāṣat* but are clearly augmented or altered, most simply add commentary on elements of doctrine or practice; most of the specific details added in these 'elaborated' narratives are significant only insofar as they suggest that Ḥaydar Badakhshī indeed had access to fuller versions of the original accounts which may have been condensed for the *Khulāṣat al-manāqib*. In one, for instance,[3] Ḥaydar Badakhshī's account simply presents in one episode accounts which appear in two separate passages in the *Khulāṣat*; in another,[4] the *Manqabat* includes doctrinal commentary (on the duties of the *sālik* in 'this path,' i.e. the Kubrawī *ṭarīqa)* following an account known from the *Khulāṣat* about the three things which the Prophet gave to Hamadānī (a tooth-

1. Teufel, p. 10.
2. No. 1, ff. 348b-352a (cf Teufel, pp. 66-67), and No. 12, ff. 364a (cf. Teufel, p. 113).
3. No. 37, ff. 413a-b; cf. Teufel, pp. 99,102.
4. No. 40, ff. 416b-417b; cf. Teufel, pp. 138-139.

pick, a silver spoon for removing earwax, and iron tweezers for removing nasal hair). Similarly, in another case the *Manqabat* inserts Hamadānī's own commentary in the midst of an account of Hamadānī's austerities[1] while others add some minor factual details as well[2] and still others evidence a certain emphasis on elements of practice or on Hamadānī's stature.[3]

Another of the 'altered' or 'elaborated' narratives is the account of Hamadānī's death and burial, which in the *Manqabat* is part of a larger account of a journey to Kashmir;[4] as noted, for the whole account Ḥaydar Badakhshī cites Qivām al-Dīn Badakhshī and Khwāja Isḥāq Khuttalānī, both of whom accompanied Hamadānī to Kashmir, while for the death of Hamadānī, Ja'far Badakhshī's source was a letter from his brother Qivām al-Dīn Badakhshī. The other differences in the accounts are worth noting: the *Manqabat* adds details on Hamadānī's final illness, reports his last words differently (transmitting the tradition that he recited the *bismi'llāh,* whose numerical value is the year of his death, 786), and has him buried in Kūlāb already on 14 Dhū'l-Ḥijjah 786/27 Jan 1385, as against the *Khulāṣat*'s 25 Jumādā I /4 July 1385.[5]

---

1. No. 38, ff. 413b-415a; cf Teufel, p. 100. The account, related by Hamadānī in the course of describing his simple diet of barley bread, notes how once when his lower soul *(nafs)* desired meat he had bought some in the bazaar, but that upon seeing the Prophet in a dream reciting a *ḥadīth* on the *nafs,* he had given the meat to a dog and stayed inside his *khānaqāh* for two full years.
2. I.e. No. 19, ff. 370b-371b; here Ḥaydar Badakhshī cites Ja'far Badakhshī as his source in reporting a discussion with a person from Nīshāpūr, not related in the *Khulāṣat,* in which Hamadānī affirmed that Ja'far Badakhshī's station *(maqām)* was above that of Abū Yazīd [Basṭāmī]; then he cites the *Khulāṣat* specifically for an anecdote (Teufel, pp. 99-100) which he relates, however, with slightly different details (it happens in Damascus according to the *Manqabat,* in Rūm according to the *Khulāṣat),* and after the anecdote adds to the account of the *Khulāṣat* that Hamadānī then returned to Badakhshān, performed four *arba'īn* there, and then renewed his travels, which had continued "until now." In another example, Teufel (p. 124, n. 4) notes the differences between the *Manqabat*'s version (No. 21, ff. 372b-376a) of Hamadānī's encounter with the ruler of Balkh (the *Khulāṣat* does not specify this city) and his heated copper horse and the *Khulāṣat*'s account, but he does not mention the extensive commentary added in the *Manqabat,* avowing that no amount of austerities or prayer or fasting would induce Hamadānī to initiate someone into his *dhikr* if in his heart there remained even a single atom of love for the world and mastery over it; and such a person would be stricken by God, on account of such vain austerities, "from the *daftar* of his friends."
3. For instance, No. 3, ff. 352b-353b, involves an extensively recast version of Hamadānī's recollection of his apprenticeship with Akhī 'Alī Dūstī (cf. Teufel pp. 68, 73-74), in which Dūstī relates that his Shaykh, Simnānī, had foretold Hamadānī's service; characteristically, an element of specific practice is sanctioned in the process, for Simnānī is said to have commissioned Dūsti to instruct Hamadānī in the *dhikr-i chahār ḍarb* (the Khulāṣat [Teufel, p. 81] mentions this mode of *dhikr* without expressly stating that it was handed down from Simnānī). Similarly, the *Manqabat*'s version (no. 4, ff. 353b-356a) of Hamadānī's association with the long-lived Abū Sa'id Ḥabashī (who was already in his eighth century during the Prophet's time) differs considerably in content and structure from the *Khulāṣat*'s version (Teufel, p. 77), most vividly in the vision of the Prophet ascribed to Abū Sa'id in which the birth of Hamadānī, "716 years after my *hijrah*" is foretold. Hamadānī's birth is more commonly dated 714 A.H.
4. No. 42, ff. 419a-423a; cf. Teufel, pp. 125-131.
5. Teufel, p. 130.

Another of these accounts[1] involves Hamadānī's son Muḥammad. Where the *Khulāṣat* relates Shaykh Muḥammad Azkānī's interpretation of one of Hamadānī's dreams as a sign that Hamadānī would have a son, Ḥaydar Badakhshī's account adds the detail that, at the time, Hamadānī was still in 'celibacy' *(tajrīd)* but that he afterwards married at the age of 40 and was blessed with a son. Then he adds the perplexedly ambiguous statement that "The holy Sayyid Qāsim Muḥammad Hamadānī had reached the age of twelve when [during] the turmoil among the kings of Hindūstān, Tīmūr Shāh appeared, and the holy Sayyid was brought before him, as was mentioned previously; and he never again met with his dervishes."[2]

Curiously, the one 'elaborated' narrative used by Teufel to illustrate Ḥaydar Badakhshī's changes in the wording of the *Khulāṣat*'s narratives would seem to attest just as strongly to the later author's critical evaluation of Ja'far Badakhshī's accounts. The episode in question is Hamadānī's meeting, during his youth, with the great Shaykhs and *'ulamā'* gathered together in one place by an unnamed ruler. In the *Khulāṣat*[3] two eminent Shaykhs are explicitly named among the 400 Shaykhs and *'ulamā'* whom Hamadānī met on that occasion: 'Alā' al-Dawla Simmānī and his pupil Quṭb al-Dīn Nīshābūrī. The *Manqabat,*[4] however, cites the figure of 404 saints without giving any names, even though Ḥaydar Badakhshī would certainly not have failed to mention so great a figure as Simnānī—especially in view of his Kubrawī lineage—among those who had blessed Hamadānī, had he considered the *Khulāṣat*'s account reliable; and in fact he provides a clear indication that he did *not* believe that account in another of the 'elaborated' episodes,[5] this describing Hamadānī's relationship with Akhī 'Alī Dūstī. In this narrative, Simnānī, Dūstī's *pīr,* foretells Hamadānī's instruction by Akhī 'Alī, and upon being asked who this Hamadānī is and when he will appear, acknowledges that "I will not see him externally, but you will." It is, of course, entirely possible that Hamadānī (b. 714/1314) met Simnānī (d. 736/1336) as a young man, in view of the former's extensive travels, but in light of Ḥaydar Badakhshī's supposed penchant for the fanciful, such a clear example of greater caution or skepticism on his part than on Ja'far Badakhshī's is worth noting.

THE KUBRAWĪ *TARIQA* IN THE *MANQABAT AL-JAWĀHIR*

The differences between the 'elaborated' narratives in the *Manqabat al-jawāhir* and their parallels (I prefer not to term them 'sources') in the *Khulāṣat*, as well the 39 accounts with no parallel in Ja'far Badakhshī's work, should rightfully constitute

1. No. 39, ff. 415b-416b; cf Teufel, pp. 132-133. The addition at the end of this episode, on Hamadānī's son, is discussed by Teufel, p. 30, n. 1.
2. Sayyid Muḥammad's birth is usually placed in 774/1373, and this would place the encounter with Timur in 786/1384, just prior to Hamadānī's death, which seems unlikely; the mention of "Hindūstān" seems suspicious, and precisely who it was, moreover, who never met with "his dervishes" again is not clear. There is undoubtedly a kernel of information to be derived from this passage, which may have been purposefully kept vague, but the chronologies of Hamadānī's travels, and of his son's birth, are too unclear to allow us to interpret it with any certainty.
3. Teufel, pp. 69-70.
4. No. 7, ff. 360b-361b.
5. No. 3, ff. 352b-353b.

the substantive and 'stylistic' basis for evaluating the *Manqabat* in terms of its relationship to the earlier work and for comparing the two. As I have noted, without knowing the environment in which the *Manqabat* was produced and, therefore, without giving careful attention to this work, Molé and Teufel were convinced that it was merely a later, derivative hagiography marked above all by an implicitly degenerative recourse to the fantastic and miraculous.

It seems more likely, however, in view of what is now known regarding Ḥaydar Badakhshī's place in the Kubrawī *silsila* and the sources of his narratives, that the contrast in tone and content between the two works is not simply the result of Ḥaydar Badakhshī's corruption or distortion of the earlier work, but is rather a consequence of his often clearly selective presentation of Hamadānī's 'biography' in a way that reflects important though little noted transformations in the Kubrawī lineages of his day. If we refrain from simply dismissing the *Manqabat al-jawāhir* out of hand or assuming that its author simply distorted a somehow more legitimate (because earlier) biography of Hamadānī, we may see that the contrasts between the two works can tell us something interesting about what happened in the Kubrawī lineages stemming from Hamadānī in the century following his death.

If we examine those 'elaborated' narratives in the *Manqabat* which add more than factual details or simple commentary, as well as virtually all of the 'unparalleled' accounts, what emerges is a striking pattern, totally absent from Ja'far Badakhshī's work, reflecting internal dynamics in the Kubrawī lineages as well as their responses to external social and political pressures and opportunities.

For the most striking divergence from the spirit and tone of the *Khulāṣat al-manāqib* evident in Ḥaydar Badakhshī's work is the frequent and often less than subtle emphasis on *ṭarīqa*—in particular his own. The existence of the Kubrawiyya as a distinctive and organized Sufi 'path' is both assumed and asserted again and again in the *Manqabat,* and the inescapable conclusion from the accumulated weight of its author's repeated evocations of what we might call '*ṭarīqa*-solidarity' is that by Ḥaydar Badakhshī's time the Central Asian adherents of the Kubrawī lineage stemming from Sayyid 'Alī Hamadānī constituted something they had not constituted less than a century before: a bona fide, self-conscious Sufi order.

The *Khulāṣat al-manāqib* contains virtually no overt discussion of 'the Path' in the sense of an organized 'Order' linked to one *silsila* and distinguished by a particular approach to spiritual life or a characteristic practice; and nowhere does its author pay any particular attention to Hamadānī's lineage beyond his immediate masters and disciples. As for the 'Kubrawiyya' as a Sufi 'Order'—not to mention the 'Hamadāniyya'—it is, quite simply, never spoken of.

Nor are Shaykhs of any Kubrawī lineage singled out in the *Khulāṣat* for any special reverence or attention. Apart from Hamadānī's own Shaykhs, only three 'Kubrawī' figures appear: Najm al-Dīn Kubrā is evidently never mentioned by name, but his writings are frequently cited (often without attribution);[1] Simnānī is portrayed as having met and blessed Hamadānī, and as the Shaykh of two of Hamadānī's teachers (Akhī 'Alī Dūstī and Maḥmūd Mazdaqānī) is prominent in

1. Cf. Teufel, p. 6.

several narratives;[1] and Kubrā's disciple Raḍī al-Dīn 'Alī Lālā (d. 642/1270) is mentioned once,[2] but only insofar as he met the enigmatic figure of Khwāja (or Bābā) Ratan, a long-lived companion of the Prophet, and was thereby suitable for comparison with both Hamadānī (as one who travelled widely and met many Shaykhs) and Ja'far Badakhshī himself (who claims to have met a pupil of Khwāja Ratan in the town of Andkhūd).

In any case, Ja'far Badakhshī does not cite 'Alī Lālā as a Kubrawī Shaykh, and he cites Kubrā's writings in the same way that he cites the doctrinal works of other eminent Sufis; nowhere does he appeal to Kubrā or Simnānī or any earlier Shaykh as the source of a particular doctrinal emphasis or element of spiritual practice that might set a particular 'Order' apart. Ja'far Badakhshī honors the spirit of his own Shaykh, and to a lesser extent the spirits of Hamadānī's teachers; but in the latter case those outside the Kubrawī lineage are no less important *for that reason* than those within it, and the fact that Hamadānī's most influential teacher (Mazdaqānī) belonged to the lineage of Kubrā and Simnānī does not, for Ja'far Badakhshī, carry any special significance. The *Khulāṣat al-manāqib* conveys a clear sense of personal relationship between one master and one disciple, and of the master's relationship with some of his teachers and some of his other disciples; it does *not* convey the sense of a Sufi *Order* properly speaking.

The *Manqabat al-jawāhir,* by contrast, is clearly the work of someone self-consciously promoting the virtues of the Kubrawī order, conceived as such; the work was intended for Kubrawī initiates, and the 'sense' of a strong *ṭarīqa* affiliation is as clear in the Manqabat as it is missing from the *Khulāṣat.* Where Ḥaydar Badakhshī clearly has elaborated or augmented the narratives passed down to him, the most noticeable difference is not the prevalence of the miraculous, but a strong sense of the Kubrawī Order as a distinctive community: simply put, by his time the Kubrawiyya had become a *ṭarīqa.* To begin with the simplest but nonetheless significant example of this ṭarīqa-consciousness, both the author's own additions and the commentary and accounts cited from other narrators are often prefaced by the phrase *'ay rafīq-i ṭarīq'* ('O companion of the Path'), implying what is made explicit elsewhere, namely that this work—unlike the *Khulāṣat*—is specifically addressed to adherents of the Kubrawī *ṭarīqa.* This strong *ṭarīqa*-consciousness is reinforced repeatedly in the *Manqabat* in a variety of direct and indirect ways that are worth considering insofar as they signal the emerging religious, social and political environment to which the new-style *ṭarīqa* responded.

1. Direct Assertion of the Superiority of the Kubrawiyya/ Hamadaniyya

In addition to the various affirmations of the practical advantages of adherence to the Kubrawī Order, as discussed below, the *Manqabat* includes two direct assertions of the Order's superiority. The first appears in the quite telling insertion in the *Manqabat* stressing the particularly Kubrawī affiliation of Hamadānī. The well-known tradition about the great number of Shaykhs (as many as 1400) from

1. Teufel, pp. 73-76.
2. Teufel, p. 93.

whom Hamadānī received *ijāzāt* (for *dhikr*, etc.) may have posed clear problems for an emphasis on training in a single *ṭarīqa;* it is repeated without comment (perhaps none was needed in that pre-*ṭarīqa* atmosphere!) in the *Khulāṣat al-manāqib,* where Hamadānī's links with such a wide variety of Shaykhs implicitly enhance his spiritual stature, but Ḥaydar Badakhshī seems clearly uncomfortable with what may have appeared in his day a rather indiscriminate amassing of Sufi *ijāzāt*. He relates extensive accounts of Hamadānī's relations with several of these Shaykhs, to be sure, for this was clearly part of the Hamadānī tradition he felt obliged to convey, and after citing Ja'far Badakhshī's account of the banquet at which he received, as a boy, *ijāzāt* to be a spiritual director *(irshād) from* 404 saints, adds mention of Hamadānī's extensive journeys through the world (and to the heavens), implicitly suggesting that his multiple links were the consequence of his travels; then (f. 362a), however, he cites a verse by his *ustād* (evidently Barzishābādī is meant here) affirming the superiority of the *silsila-i Hamadānī*' as the wisest of *silsila*s and the closest to the path of God[1] and adds that he [apparently Barzishābādī is meant here] also said, "The best of the *ṭarīqa*s is that of the Kubrawiyya, for it has led most expeditiously to the Path of Truth." *(khayru' l-ṭuruq ṭarīq al-kubrawiyya fa-qad awṣala ta'jīlan ilā ṭarīq al-ḥaqīqa).*

In another unparalleled passage[2] also transmitted by a disciple of Isḥāq Khuttalanī, the Kubrawī Order is portrayed as having a special advantage in the attainment of the Sufi goal of *ma'rifa;* we can also detect hints of the 'competitive edge' provided by this advantage in the developing rivalries over attracting disciples. After relating Hamadānī's response to a question posed by several followers regarding the attainment of gnosis of God, the author concludes,

> Everyone who follows our path will certainly become a knower of God *(khudā-shinās),* for they call this the 'Golden Chain' (*silsilat al-dhahab*). Just as prophethood is completed in the lineage of Ibrāhīm, so sainthood (*walāyat)* and gnosis (*ma'rifat*) are perfected in this *ṭarīq*. Everyone who sets foot upon the Kubrawī path will certainly become a voyager in the way of *ṭarīqat* and *ḥaqīqat*. *B*ut the people of every *ṭarīq* have differences in accordance with their aptitudes; some belong to the party of the righteous *(ṣulaḥā)* some are ascetics (*zuhhād)* and some are gnostics (*'urafā*). And the common people are beasts; what discernment would they have to know whether or not their fodder is edible? So those people should inquire diligently so as to become disciples of someone familiar with the gnosis of God, rather than rely upon something that would bring them to ruin.

Thereupon, the author notes, those present at the gathering observed that although anyone may maintain the fear of God, this does not mean that he is acquainted with Divine gnosis *(ma'rifat)*, to which Hamadānī replied, "nor is it worthy of esteem if they outwardly work miracles." A verse follows implying the uniqueness and distinction of the Kubrawī path: "That high-priced pearl is from another mine / and that singular pearl has a different sign; / the thoughts of this and that are the imaginings of you and me / for the legend of love there is yet a different

1. ba-yaqīn silsila-i hamadānī / az hamma silsilahā purdānī / ' z ānke dar rāh-i khudā waqt-i ṭalab / hast az jumla-i ṭarīq īn aqrab.

2. No. 51, ff. 441b-442b; Srinagar MS ff. 31b-33a.

language."[1]

While criticism of fraudulent or inferior Sufis is a standard feature of doctrinal and hagiographical works alike, the emphasis here on the merits of the Kubrawiyya seems a clear indication that behind this passage lies a very real and practical rivalry between increasingly competitive Sufi orders—a rivalry which was not yet in full flower in Ja'far Badakhshī's time.

2. *The* Manqabat *as a Work Addressed to Kubrawī Disciples*

In an equally explicit context, Ḥaydar Badakhshī twice reinforces the notion of *ṭarīqa*-solidarity as he refers to his purpose in writing his work, first in the introduction[2] when he affirms simply that the work was prepared "so that the followers of this path *(ṭarīq)* and the faithful of this sect *(farīq)* might each day make it their recitation *(wird)* and each night illumine the eye of the heart with this light,"[3] and later as he recounts the particulars of his personal entry into the Kubrawī Order (and offers his own 'apologia' for his work) in an unfortunately damaged part of the accessible manuscript,[4] he begins by citing Hamadānī, "Every traveller *(sālik)* who wishes to set foot on the Journey *(sulūk)* will accept our Path, which is more powerful than other Paths; if he repents before an adept *(wāṣil)* of this Path, he will be worthy of the mystical states, and capable of acquiring the knowledge, of the human and angelic realms, but if it should be with an adherent of another Path, he will not reach that goal."

He compares this to his own situation, for, as he writes, he first belonged to the Shaṭṭārī *ṭarīqa*[5] and rejected the Kubrawī *farīq* on account of its acceptance of *samā'*, which he acknowledges that he "slandered." One day, however, when he was in Barzishābādī's service, the Shaykh cautioned a group of singers not to perform in Mawlānā Ḥaydar's presence, "for he rejects *samā'* and is observant of the law *(mutasharri')*" whereupon Ḥaydar became embarrassed and ashamed, immediately repented, and began a period of seclusion *(khalwat)* following which he received initiation (the *bay'at)* from Barzishābādī. Then, noting that he began collecting the material for his book "so that its readers and hearers will not endeavor

---

1. *ān la'l-i girān-bahā'z kān-i dīgar-ast / w' ān durr-i yagāna-rā nishānī dīgar-ast / andīsha-i īn-ū-ān khayāl-i man wa tu' st / afsāna-i 'ishq-rā zabānī dīgar-ast* (verse appears only in the Srinagar MS).
2. It is missing in the India Office manuscript, but is cited by Teufel, p. 10, from the Tehran Dhahabī *khānaqāh* copy. The first narrative of the India Office copy ends with a statement (ff. 348a-b) on the reason for the work's composition: "The reason for the composition of these 'hidden matters' *(mastūrāt)* was that these wondrous deeds would not be left on the tongues of the common people, where they might be corrupted. For this reason they have been written in detail so that those who related them would not fall into error. Each day as I sat before my Master *(murshid)* it occurred to me that certainly I should collect them.". We may find here a sign of the author's wish to preserve the stories of Hamadānī's deeds and sayings as the specific right and legacy of his *ṭarīqa*, to put the Kubrawī order's stamp on narratives already in popular circulation and therefore in danger of being misconstrued by the masses.
3. *...tā mu'taqidān-i īn ṭarīq wa mukhliṣān-i īn farīq har rūz wird-i khūd sāzand, har shab dīda-i dil az īn nūr bar-afrūzand.*
4. No. 49, ff. 437a-439a.
5. In the India Office manuscript the name of this Order is clearly written and vowelled "Shuttārī" without the emphatic *ṭā*.

to revile this *ṭarīq*," he complains of "the many rejectors of this *ṭarīq*," who are "the bane of the people of that group," and pleads that inasmuch as Nūr al-Dīn Ja'far Badakhshī and Muḥammad Qivām al-Dīn Badakhshī have said things in describing Hamadānī that seemed excessive and unbelievable, "why should what I have said be worthy of deprecation?" A long poem follows, in praise of Hamadānī, in which the author again affirms the benefits of following his Path.

Ḥaydar Badakhshī thus at the same time articulates the growing sense of the Kubrawī Order's difference from other orders as well as its superiority over them in delivering the benefits of Sufi discipline, affirms that his book is intended to benefit adherents of the Kubrawī order and defend it against its detractors, and in the process shows clearly the competitive atmosphere which must have provided the impetus for both the claims of superiority and the apologetic.

3. *Sanction of Kubrawī Doctrinal Affiliation*

Aside from the doctrinal commentary in several of the 'elaborated' episodes noted above, a number of narratives are intended to assert the legitimacy and/or superiority of the doctrinal orientation of Hamadānī and the Kubrawī order (in most cases they also serve to exalt the status of Hamadānī, as noted below). For instance, in one unparalleled episode,[1] Shams al-Dīn Khuttalānī relates that he once was asked to leave the *khānaqāh* while Hamadānī received a group of Sufis, and after an hour heard a loud despairing moan from inside; Hamadānī explained that this was Iblīs lamenting the teaching and instruction *(ta'līm wa talqīn)* imparted by Hamadānī. In another,[2] Muḥammad Ṭāliqānī's account of a series of dreams in which the Prophet confirmed Hamadānī's superiority over Imām Ghazzālī as a *mujtahid,* as well as his elevated stature in general. After this, Ṭāliqānī affirms, "I became a firm believer [in Hamadānī], and wherever I saw one who rejected this *farīq* (i.e. the Kubrawī *ṭarīqa),* I would soften his heart."

In addition, one unparalleled narrative[3] is particularly instructive as a 'defense' of Kubrawī doctrinal and juridical orientation. In a relation ascribed to Ibrāhīm Mubarak-khānī, one of Isḥāq Khuttalānī's followers, Hamadānī recounts that Imām Shāfi'ī had appeared to him in a dream and expressly asked him to adopt the Shāfi'ite *madhhab,* "since no master of a *silsila* is stronger than you." Hamadānī sought and received permission to do so from his ancestor the Prophet, who appeared in the company of all the great companions and *mujtahids*, including Abū Ḥanīfa. Hamadānī received Abū Ḥanīfa's blessing as well, and agreed that he would enjoin worship in accordance with the Ḥanafite *madhhab* but recommend the Shāfi'ite school to "every traveller in this *ṭarīq*" who wished to engage in austerities. Understood against the backdrop of predominantly Ḥanafite Khurāsān and Central Asia, where the Shāfi'ite affiliation of Kubrā amounted to an additional handicap in the emerging rivalry with the Naqshbandiyya, this passage justifies the

1. No. 10, ff. 362b-363a.
2. No. 50, ff. 439a-441b.
3. No. 22, ff. 376a-378a.

Kubrawī tradition of Shāfi'ite affiliation, but at the same time makes allowance for *murīds* more comfortable with Ḥanafite practice in ordinary affairs.

4. *Sanction of Kubrawī Spiritual Practices*

A number of narratives are designed to show the legitimacy and/or superiority of important aspects of spiritual discipline and devotional practice regarded as particularly characteristic of the Kubrawiyya. One,[1] for instance, transmits several sayings of Nūr al-Dīn Isfarā'inī, Simnānī's *pīr* in the Kubrawī lineage, on the practice of austerities, while[2] another concludes with the recommendation that the 'wayfarer' ought to behave in such a way that no one is aware of his piety, harking back to the old *Malāmatī* tradition.

Likewise, the specific methods of interior prayer or *dhikr* practised by Hamadānī's successors are legitimized in several of the accounts of Hamadānī's relationship with his Shaykhs. As noted, the *Manqabat* has 'Alā' al-Dawla Simnānī sanction the *dhikr-i chahār-ḍarb* to be taught to Hamadānī by Akhī 'Alī Dūstī, while in another unparalleled episode,[3] related by Shams al-Dīn Khuttalānī, Hamadānī is instructed in the *dhikr* by five men in splendid garb, wearing crowns, who enter his *ḥujra* with Hamadānī. When after a time Hamadānī came out by himself, he told Shams al-Dīn that the visitors were the Prophet and the four righteous Caliphs *(khulafā-yi rāshidūn)* who had come to recite his *dhikr*. Similar sanction is provided in another unparalleled passage,[4] in which Hamadānī receives in a dream the *bay'at* and instruction in interior prayer from Imām Riḍā while on pilgrimage to the latter's tomb, and upon waking accepts a group of people as his disciples.

More subtly, the practical, day-to-day devotional activities of the order are legitimized through the extensive account[5] of the Prophet's approval of the famous *Awrād-i fatḥīya,* the 'Litanies' assembled by Hamadānī for recitation by his followers. According to this account, while performing the *ḥajj* Hamadānī visited the Prophet's grave and there "requested his permission for the *awrād* which I had collected;" then he saw the Prophet in a dream holding a manuscript containing the *Awrād-i fatḥīya,* whereupon he formally adopted it as his own litany and instructed his disciples to recite it. The *Khulāṣat al-manāqib* mentions the Prophetic origin of Hamadānī's *awrād* in passing, but Ḥaydar Badakhshī's work casts this prophetic sanction in immediate and concrete terms to reinforce the authority of the Hamadānī *Order's* litany.

Perhaps the most telling example of the emphasis on particularly Kubrawī practice appears in discussions of an issue which often came to encapsulate inter-Order rivalries in the age of heightened *ṭarīqa*-consciousness, namely the propriety of *samā'* (musical audition) and *raqṣ* (dance) and of the ecstatic 'trance' *(wajd)*. Aside from a single mention in the *Khulāṣat* of a twice-weekly *samā'* as an important part

---

1. No. 17, ff. 369b-370a; this section is related on the authority of Ja'far Badakhshī and 'Abdullāh Shīrāzī, but is not found in the *Khulāṣat*.
2. No 33, ff. 403a-406a.
3. No 11, ff. 363a-364a.
4. No 20, ff. 371b-372b.
5. No 6, ff. 358a-360a.

of Hamadānī's mystical development[1]—in a narrative which is one of the two adopted with virtually no changes in the *Manqabat*[2]—this issue, which came to dominate the debate in Central Asia over legitimate Sufi practice as the Naqshbandiyya made rejection of the *samā'* and *raqṣ* a cornerstone of its discipline, is entirely absent in Ja'far Badakhshī's work. One unparalleled narrative[3] in the *Manqabat* is devoted to an extensive discussion of the issue by Hamadānī, with a defense of *samā'* and *raqṣ* as permitted and conducive to spiritual development so long as they are undertaken with the permission of the Shaykh. It is the latter's guidance which is central in ensuring the legitimacy and safety of these practices, but Hamadānī will not join those who reject them out of hand.

An even more remarkable discussion of such practices, with explicit connection to the distinction and superiority of the Kubrawiyya as a *ṭarīqa,* is found in another unparalleled episode[4] dealing with issue of *samā'* and *wajd.* This episode is especially noteworthy for its explicit portrayal of the beatific vision as a distinctive legacy of the Kubrawī *ṭarīqa,* expressly obtained by Najm al-Dīn Kubrā as a 'gift' to pass down to the Order of which he is here clearly portrayed as the founder. Ascribed to Shaykh Muḥammad Sarayasanī,[5] this passage relates Hamadānī's response to questions from a group of *'ulamā* on the subject of *samā'* and *wajd.* They ask why it is that "among the 14 *silsilas,*" only one or two allow them, with the *ṭā'ifa-i Kubrawiyya* the most common venue for such activity.

Curiously, Hamadānī here is made to acknowledge that he has forbidden *samā'* in most of his writings, but that in fact the choice in this matter is not left to the individual, for whom it would amount to a tremendous torment. Rather, he approves *samā'* without enjoining it, refusing to condemn those whom it overcomes (noting that "God most High has granted to that group the attainment of His vision in a single gulp"), yet ridiculing those who deny its validity.[6] "And [those of] this division," he continues, "who are followers of this *ṭarīq-i Kubrawiyya,* are Lovers (*'āshiqān*) for whom the business of Love (*'ishq*) is that whenever they hear a pleasing voice, they think it is the voice of their Friend, and whatever good thing may befall them, they ascribe it to the True Beloved," and so on, leading into the discussion of the senselessness of trying to counsel the "Lover" against *samā'* and *wajd.*

Hamadānī is then portrayed as proceeding with a quite illuminating account of the founder of his 'Order,' called here *'Shaykh Walī-tarāsh* [Creator of Saints], known as Najm al-Dīn Kubrā'; we may recall here that Ja'far Badakhshī cites only Kubrā's writings and never portrays him as the founder of an Order. According to

1. Teufel, p. 67; cf. pp. 22, 39.
2. No. 1, 348b-352a.
3. No. 43, ff. 432a-428b; the issue of *samā'* is raised also in one of the 'political' narratives, No. 29, ff. 394a-396a.
4. No. 31, ff. 397a-403a. This section in the India Office MS is broken by two lacunae indicated by missing catchwords (ff. 397b-398a, 398b-399a; an apparent lacuna between ff. 399b-400a suggested by mismatching catchwords and noted by a European hand in fact has no missing text: the catchword was simply not repeated at the top of the following folio); the entire passage is supplied in the Srinagar MS, ff. 33a-40a.
5. In the India Office MS, "Sarāysī"; in the Srinagar MS., "Sarāshī."
6. He compares them to a blind man who cannot know what the sun or moon people look like, and to a man without a sexual organ for whom no amount of explanation can convey its pleasures.

this account, a group of Kubrā's disciples remarked to him that "most of the Sufis of this *ṭarīq* engage in *wajd* and others do not do so," and then asked if this practice was created especially for the first group. Kubrā answered that once as he sat in seclusion with his True Friend, experiencing a mystical state *(ḥāl)* comparable to what the Prophet described in the *ḥadīth* "I have a time with God,"[1] the angels, who were excluded from that intimacy, afterwards told him to choose some special desire that they would grant. After some thought he asked that "everyone who becomes a follower of this *ṭarīq* might be granted the realization of that mystical state" and be blessed in both worlds. He continued, saying that after coming out of that mystical state, he saw the Prophet and asked that he grant the *ḥāl* which he had experienced prior to his *hijra,* whereupon the Prophet also gave him permission *(ijāzāt)* in this matter:

> ...and when I came to myself out of this *ḥāl,* upon whomever I granted initiation I also bestowed that same mystical state, and until the Day of Resurrection, whoever becomes a follower of our *ṭarīq* will also be overcome by that same state, until the very end of the *ṭarīqa.*

Thereupon, Ḥaydar Badakhshī remarks, the leader among those *'ulamā'* who had come to question Hamadānī on this matter was himself overcome by a mystical state and *samā'*, shouting and ripping his cloak. Then all of those present prostrated themselves and, acknowledging their former blindness, became disciples of Hamadānī, remaining so until the end of their lives; "and whoever rejects the mystical states of the dervishes is worse than blind."

Such is the account. It provides a quite unambiguous illustration of a claim that the best spiritual discipline and the supreme mystical attainments are open to those who enter the Kubrawī *ṭarīqa*, simply by virtue of their initiation. And Najm al-Dīn Kubrā, who in the *Khulāṣat* is merely one of many esteemed Sufi writers, becomes here a *ṭarīqa*-founder in a real sense, demonstrating his solicitude for all later adherents of his Order, jealously winning for them the special privilege he himself had been given.

5. Sanction of the Status of Sayyid 'Alī Hamadānī

A common feature of the *Manqabat* is a strong emphasis on the sanctity and power of its subject. As noted earlier, Molé evidently found its laudatory tone excessive and saw in Ḥaydar Badakhshī's work part of the process of Hamadānī's "glorification." To be sure, the *Manqabat* is premised in praise of Hamadānī, and specific instances of asserting the attestation of his high station by the Prophet or by Khiḍr or by eminent theologians or Sufis are quite numerous in the work: he is lauded by Imām Shāfi'i and compared favorably to Imām Ghazzālī, as noted elsewhere, with Khiḍr attesting to Hamadānī's divine gifts[2] and his status as the *quṭb,*[3] while he is

1. See Badī al-Zamān Furūzānfar, *Aḥadīth-i Mathnawī* (Tehran 1334 A.Hsh), no. 100.
2. No. 50, f. 441a.
3. No. 5, f. 356b, in a dream of Shaykh Niẓām al-Dīn Ghūrī Khurāsānī [on Niẓām al-Dīn Yaḥyā Ghūrī, cf. *Rawḍāt al-jinān*, II, pp. 177, 253, 671-2], whom Ja'far Badakhshī (Teufel, p. 71) lists among Hamadānī's Shaykhs.

portrayed as implicitly superior to Ibn 'Arabī in austerities[1] and is the object of a prophecy of Simnānī's[2] and of the Prophet's special care in approving a Shaykh for him.[3] He is likewise praised as an intercessor on the Day of Judgement,[4] and the work is filled with references to Hamadānī's illustrious ancestor, the Prophet,[5] although here we must note that the *Manqabat* offers virtually nothing to those who would like to find 'Shi'ite tendencies' or even particularly pro-'Alid sentiments: when stressing Hamadānī's *Sayyid*-ship the focus is on the Prophet always and never 'Alī (who in fact never appears in any of the Shaykh's dreams or visions, except implicitly when all four *khulafā-yi rāshidūn* appear with the Prophet), and even one of Hamadānī's most famous epithets in later literature *'Alī-i thānī* ('the second 'Alī'), is never mentioned by Ḥaydar Badakhshī.

In any case, in comparison with the likewise laudatory attitude towards Hamadānī in the *Khulāṣat,* there seems to be no notably excessive attention to Hamadānī's person above what might be expected in view of Ḥaydar Badakhshī's greater distance from his subject and in view of the later work's emphasis, as we are suggesting, on Hamadānī's status as a pivotal figure in a genuine *ṭarīqa* and not just as an eminent Shaykh. The latter point is borne out in the work's most enthusiastic encomium, an extensive poem[6] by Ḥaydar Badakhshī which follows his discussion of his own entry into the Kubrawī *ṭarīqa* and of the Order's superiority, as noted above. It honors Hamadānī, promises high attainments to those who become his sincere followers, and repent in his *ṭarīq,* and laments the author's powerlessness to adequately sing his praises, affirming that even the service performed by *khānaqāh* sweeper exceeds his own.

6. Sanction of a Model of Personal Relationship with and Dependence upon Hamadānī

An impressive number of the unparalleled accounts in the *Manqabat* (seven altogether) portray the personal relationship of individual disciples with their Shaykh, Hamadānī, providing models of their submission to the Shaykh's guidance and their participation in the ordinary life of service in the Shaykh's *khānaqāh* as a *ṭarīqa* member. Khwāja Isḥāq Khuttalānī, for example, describes[7] the dream that led him to Hamadānī, the intuitive mutual recognition of master and pupil, a further dream in which the Prophet provides direct approval of Hamadānī, and his early development as a member of the *khānaqāh* community (i.e. he takes the *bay'at,* performs a forty-day period of seclusion, serves as a water-carrier and firewood collector, receives permission for the *khalwat,* etc.). Another narrative,[8] portrays Hamadānī's approval of the charismatic graces *(karāmat)* of his disciple Sayyid Zayn al-

1. No. 37, f. 413b.
2. No. 3, ff. 353a-b.
3. No. 2, f. 352b, confirming the value of serving Shaykh Muḥammad Azkānī Isfarā'inī.
4. No. 46, f. 432b.
5. Cf. No. 50, ff. 439a-441b, where the Prophet promises his direct intercession for Hamadānī, as his descendant, without need of Khiḍr and Ilyās.
6. In No. 49, ff. 438a-439a.
7. No. 16, ff. 368a-369b.
8. No. 30, ff. 396a-397a

'Abidīn, while two concern the often stormy relationship between Hamadānī and his disciple Muḥammad Shāmī: in one, following a report of his Shaykh's dismay at his inattentiveness, Shāmī lauds Hamadānī for the fact that during the 48 years he spent with his *pīr*, the Shaykh never ate unlawful food, however much rulers tried to induce him to do so, and never acted out of anger. The second[1] is even more telling, relating how Shāmī was once beset by a bear while gathering firewood, and, and after crying out an oath by Salmān with no effect, was finally saved by a lion, whereupon he returned and was scolded by Hamadānī for not making the oath in *his* name: "Now if you again run into a lion or a bear or a demon or a boar, swear an oath by me." The Shaykh is thus portrayed as something akin to a protective patron spirit to be appealed to by his *murīds*. A similar protective role is evident as well in several of the narratives in which the disciples in question are political figures (discussed below).

7. Sanction of Communal Affiliation to a Sufi Order

An entirely new element in the master-disciple relationship, and one peculiar to the age of real *ṭarīqa*-organizations, is apparent in two unparalleled episodes which strongly suggest the communal aspects of *ṭarīqa*-affiliation, with entire villages becoming *murīds* of Hamadānī. This phenomenon, which became so pronounced in later Central Asian Sufism, is virtually inconceivable in Sufi terms until the emergence of real *ṭarīqas*. One narrative,[2] ascribed to Qivām al-Dīn Badakhshī, concerns an unnamed man who was directed by the Prophet, in a dream, to Hamadānī as the Shaykh before whom he should perform his repentance. He went to Hamadānī, received the *bay'at* from him, remained several days in his *khānaqāh,* and then returned to his own (unspecified) country; from there he sent word that he had made a donation *(waqf)* of the single *khānī* of gold which he had acquired during his life, in order to receive Hamadānī and his followers and provide a feast for them whenever they would come to his town. Some of Hamadānī's followers were skeptical of this deed's merit, but the Shaykh assured them that good would come of it; and in fact a feast was held, for the entire village and the Shaykh's retinue, as a result of which "Most of the people of that place became disciples in the presence of the holy Sayyid." This account has the ring of a veritable prescription for exactly the kind of communal commitment needed by the Kubrawī order in the new competitive environment of Ḥaydar Badakhshī's time.

Another instance of communal *ṭarīqa*-affiliation is set in 'Alīshāh, a town of Khuttalān, a town whose very conversion to Islam is ascribed to Hamadānī in a separate narrative discussed below. According to this account,[3] Hamadānī once went with a group of his followers to the village of 'Alīshāh where the party was invited to a feast by a prominent man who took pride in his ability to host the Shaykh. After delivering the invitation, however, the man returned home to find that thieves had carried off all that was prepared for the meal; and when Hamadānī and his company

1. No. 35, ff. 409a-409b.
2. No. 46, ff. 432a-433b.
3. No. 15, ff. 366b-368a

arrived at his house, he was nowhere to be found, having fled in shame and embarrassment. All at once the thieves who had stolen his things came to Hamadānī and brought the food which had been intended for the meal. They related that as they arrived home after stealing the man's goods,

> We saw that several Turks had surrounded our houses. We said, "O friends, why have you surrounded our houses and troubled our children? Take whatever it is that you want from us." They said, "What you have just brought here was a gift intended for Sayyid 'Alī Hamadānī; why have you taken it from that poor man's house? It will be better for you if you take it back to his house at once; otherwise we will destroy you."

The thieves begged forgiveness from Hamadānī, which he granted, and after kissing his feet were able to return and regain their homes. The feast was held, the man took the *bay'at,* Hamadānī won fame throughout the town, and "this was the reason for [the people of] 'Alīshāh becoming disciples [of Hamadānī]."

8. Sanction of Hamadānī's Tomb

The pious visitation of the tombs *(mazār)* of Sufi Shaykhs has a long history, of course, but for organized *ṭarīqas* the tombs of the 'founder' or pivotal Shaykhs in the *silsila* became important economic and even 'administrative' centers as well. It is only natural that the *Manqabat,* as an example of hagiography in the service of a *ṭarīqa,* should provide sanction and authority for Hamadānī's *mazār,* and that is indeed the case in one of the unparalleled narratives.[1] While the Shaykh's burial in Khuttalān is noted in the *Khulāṣat,*[2] the later work specifies that during a visit to Kūlāb (using the later name of the town of Khuttalān) Hamadānī saw the Prophet in a dream instructing him to designate a place in the forest near Kūlāb as his future gravesite. In the morning following the dream he led his future followers there ("to the place which is now his holy tomb"), and in response to their inquiries told them that his death (or burial?) would occur after three years and one day and one night. The site was further sanctified by the miraculous gathering of the animals in the vicinity, which frightened Hamadānī's companions until every beast bowed before the Shaykh. On the same occasion Hamadānī enjoined all his followers to make pilgrimage *(ziyārat)* to the spot. In this way the Shaykh's tomb is in effect sanctified by the Prophet, by Hamadānī himself, and by the natural order, being at the same time linked to the *ṭarīqa* through the Shaykh's request for its visitation.

9. Implicit Sanction of Shaykh and Ṭarīqa *by Islamic Proselytization*

In the political and religious climate of late 14th- and early 15th-century Central Asia, with substantial numbers of inhabitants remaining outside Islam, as a legacy both of the influx of non-Muslim Turkic tribes and other population shifts due to the Mongol conquest, and of Mongol rule and its accompanying withdrawal, albeit temporary, of state patronage for Islam even as simply a faith favored over other religions, the work of conversion to Islam was a tremendous source of prestige and

1. No. 41, ff. 417b-419a.
2. Teufel, pp. 129-131.

influence both within the established Muslim community and among the newly converted groups themselves. Whether or not Sufi Shaykhs were primarily responsible for much of the conversion to Islam in this period—and they probably were—they and their followers clearly sought to highlight their role in the spread and solidification of Islam. Accordingly, conversion tales implicitly stress the special sanctity of a Shaykh portrayed as an 'Islamizer,' and with it the place of honor rightfully due to the *ṭarīqa* which he 'founded.' It is worth noting that, as often as not, such conversion tales recount the adoption of Islam on a communal basis, not merely on an individual level; and consequently, there is often a very close bond between the two 'communities' of which a particular Shaykh is regarded as the founder—the *ṭarīqa* which he forms or shapes, and the village, region, or tribe which he 'forms' insofar as he is the bearer of its new Islamic identity.[1]

The *Manqabat* includes several conversion tales, all among the work's unparalleled episodes, in which some wonder performed or occasioned by Sayyid 'Alī Hamadānī leads to a conversion to Islam, as distinct from repentance and entrance into the *ṭarīqa* as discussed above (and below, in the case of political figures). Only one[2] involves the conversion of an individual, who in this case happens to be a *jinn,* who abandoned his unbelief *(kufr)* following Hamadānī's demonstrations of his power. Another, interestingly enough, involves the Islamization of the inhabitants of 'Alīshāh in Khuttalān—a region which, by the way, was heavily settled by Mongol tribes—who are also portrayed in one narrative as having become Hamadānī's disciples, as noted above. In this account,[3] related by Muḥammad Ṭaliqānī, a group of followers accompanied Hamadānī to a place in the forest outside 'Alīshāh, where they spent the night. During the night a great lion appeared and, bowing before the Shaykh, performed repentance, followed by a group of *jinn* in human form who did the same, promising not to harm anyone. "Prior to this no one could pass through those parts," but thanks to Hamadānī's taming of the lions and the *jinn,* the people of the area became Muslims.

Yet another episode[4] presents a standard conversion tale with a 'test' motif, in which Hamadānī, travelling with a group of followers in a country where all the in-

1. As the 'founder' of both a community and a *ṭarīqa*, a Shaykh naturally concerns himself with their future, whence the prevalence of prophecies by such Shaykhs. In Hamadānī's case the *Manqabat* offers one example of such a prophecy (No. 32, f. 403a, Srinagar MS ff. 40a-b) "One day the holy Sayyid was in the *khānaqāh,* with his companions present, and said, 'After twenty years there will be such disorders in this region that no ruler will remain and the people will have no peace, and we will depart from our homeland.' The companions in his noble presence said, 'O noble one, what will be the reason for this?' He said, 'The last of the kings of Gharjistān will come, and will direct his confidence to these people [?]; it will happen such that I will not see my *khānaqāh* again.' The companions said, 'When will it be?' He said, 'At the end of my life.' And indeed it occurred thus, that all the people of the region departed their homeland, and a group of the saints of God were killed in those disorders; this is the word of the great ones [of God, and likewise a wonder of Amīr-i kabīr Mīr Sayyid 'Alī Hamadānī]."
2. No. 14, ff. 366a-366b.
3. No. 44, ff. 428b-430a.
4. No. 13, ff. 364a-366a.

habitants were Christians,[1] held debates with the natives and received their promise to convert if he could resurrect the dead; he did so, raising 70 people at the graveyard, whereupon the entire people converted and also took the *bay'at* to become his disciples.

Hamadānī's most renowned work in conversion is his missionary activity in Kashmir, whose Islamization has been traditionally ascribed to the Shaykh. In light of the strength of the tradition which links Hamadānī to the establishment of Islam in Kashmir, it seems curious that the *Khulāṣat* makes no mention of Kashmir at all; and the absence of this element from the earliest biography of Hamadānī has, in turn, been cited by those who have doubted his historical role in the region's Islamization. Without here entering the debate about the fact and extent of Hamadānī's activity in Kashmir, I would suggest that the absence of any mention of it in Ja'far Badakhshī's work is simply another indication of the 'idiosyncratic' nature of the *Khulāṣat*: Ja'far Badakhshī did not report it because he did not accompany his Shaykh there and therefore had neither direct information nor particular interest concerning it.

For Ja'far Badakhshī, Hamadānī's journey to Kashmir and any indication of conversion work there (on either a royal/regional or individual scale), held no special importance sufficient to merit special discussion in the absence of the author's own recollection. We may note here that even narratives of individual conversion at the hands of the Shaykh are absent in the *Khulāṣat*, where such activity is not yet a vital part of Hamadānī's hagiographical image. For Ḥaydar Badakhshī, however, as well as for later writers, in a time when promoting the role of one's *ṭarīqa* in establishing and upholding a properly Islamic social and political order became a typical feature of hagiographies, Hamadānī's mere presence in Kashmir was in itself reason enough to assert his pivotal role in establishing Islam there. As suggested before, Ja'far Badakhshī intended the *Khulāṣat* to be a record for himself and other immediate followers of Hamadānī, as well as for the general posterity of the Sufi tradition. His work provided a pragmatic discussion of Sufi doctrine and practice and a model of the master-disciple relationship. Ḥaydar Badakhshī, however, wrote for a *ṭarīqa,* and his emphasis upon his Order's role in the 'sacred history' of a region such as Kashmir gives expression to the outlook on history whose formulation and articulation no doubt constituted integral steps in the process of 'creating' that *ṭarīqa*.

Three narratives in the *Manqabat* deal directly with Hamadānī's role in the conversion of Kashmir to Islam. The first is the opening narrative[2] in the India Office

1. The tale may simply represent a not-uncommon transposition of Christians into a conversion account as the chief 'theological' rivals of Muslims; no region or locale is specified, and although the place is referred to as *zamīn-i farang*, it is not certain that European Christians are intended here, since there were still Christian communities remaining even in Central Asia in Hamadānī's lifetime.
2. Ff. 346a-347b. Unfortunately, neither Molé nor Teufel indicates which narrative directly follows the beginning of the *Manqabat* as given in the Tehran Dhahabī manuscript, and it remains unclear whether this is, in fact, the first narrative of the original work. It seems that this is the case, since immediately following this narrative in the India Office copy comes Hamadānī's natural genealogy, and then another brief discussion of the reason for the work's composition, as noted above (n. 76).

copy of the work, and probably formed part of the general introduction of the *Manqabat* to highlight Hamadānī's most notable success. It begins with a curious discussion of the pre-Islamic religion of Kashmir and traces of it which survived "after the appearance of Islam," when "the great Shaykhs came to Kashmir from Iran and Tūrān and destroyed all the idol temples of Brahmanic worship and cast all their libraries into the river."[1] The account continues, noting that in the year 741—no doubt a scribal error for the widely accepted date of 781/1379[2]—there occurred "the arrival of Sayyid 'Alī Hamadānī in Kashmir," where

> in the district (*maḥalla*) of 'Alā' al-Dīn-pūr in the city of Kashmir [i.e. Srinagar], at the place of Mātā Sarasvatī along the banks of the river Bitastā-jī,[3] he had constructed his throne-like *khānaqāh*, which is known in Kashmir as the *dargāh* of Ḥaḍrat-i Shāh-i Hamadān, or the *'Khānaqāh-i mu'allā.'* The people all became Muslims, and every morning and evening performed there their daily duties and obligations of ritual prayer *(namāz)*.

Here the conversion of the people and the facilitation of their observance of the religious duties of Islam is linked with the establishment of this famous *khānaqāh*, whose foundation is in turn ascribed directly to Hamadānī himself.

The second[4] is a more 'normative' conversion tale, related by Qivām al-Dīn Badakhshī and Isḥāq Khuttalānī, who accompanied the Shaykh to Kashmir. It begins with the Prophet's commission, through a dream, to "go to Kashmir and make the people of that place Muslims; for although some there have been ennobled by accepting Islam, they [the rest?] are *mushriks,* worse than *kāfirs*." Hamadānī agreed to go, over the protests of Qivām al-Dīn, who cited the difficulty of the journey and the fact that the people there were all infidels; as the Shaykh described his dream, the Prophet had commanded him to go and make the people there his disciples. They set off and in Qivām al-Dīn's words "as we neared that country we saw that there was no scent of faith or Islam in that land."

Arriving in the city of Kashmir, they saw idol temples everywhere instead of mosques, and went to one idol temple which was the dwelling place of a particular demon whose reputation for demanding a human sacrifice each day had reached them beforehand. Hamadānī told Qivām al-Dīn to sound the call to prayer, and when he did so, an unnamed figure (by whom may be intended the Muslim ruler, implicitly criticized for placing his revenue above the people's conversion) suggested that it would be better simply to take tribute from the unbelievers. At that

1. This passage has the ring of folk tradition. It describes the Barāhima, who practice austerities and seclude themselves in mountain caves, engaging in divine remembrance under fruit-bearing trees near springs, spending day and night in the pursuit of knowledge and worship. Their speciality is the movements of the stars and the wonders of the earth. After the appearance of Islam, the account continues, when their libraries were dumped into the river, most of their books were thrown into the Āchārī (?) pond (perhaps to be connected with the veneration of Shankaracharya in Srinagar) outside the city of Kashmir; the people built a strong wall around it, but "from time to time pages from the books of the Brahmans would appear from the Āchārī pond."
2. As Teufel notes, p. 32, n. 2.
3. Teufel (p. 33) without citing this form of the river's name as given by Ḥaydar Badakhshī, notes the Sanskrit name of the Jhelum as Vitastā (and Greek Hydaspēs).
4. No. 42, ff. 419a-423a; the second half of this narrative (beginning with f. 421a) deals with Hamadānī's death and burial.

-Hamadānī "grew angry, seized him and made him a *murīd;* he made him his servant *(khādim)* in that place, and up to now he is still there" (here Qivām al-Dīn's words are evidently quoted directly).

> After that all the people of that place were ennobled by accepting Islam, and the ruler became a *murīd* as well. And they destroyed that idol temple and erected a *ṣuffah* in its place, on which they performed the prayers, and the people came and became Muslims.

The ruler asked Hamadānī to remain there; he did not accept, but instead set out for his own country. On this journey came his final illness and death, which take up the remainder of the narrative.

The element of the *khānaqāh* is missing here, but the Shaykh's direct responsibility for the discipleship of the ruler and the link between that discipleship and the country's Islamization bespeaks the new emphasis on the *ṭarīqa*. Similar elements appear in the final conversion narrative,[1] focused exclusively on the ruler himself. It is related on the authority of Muḥammad Shāmī, who also accompanied Hamadānī to Kashmir:

> When we arrived in the region of Kashmir, the ruler there had a dream one night in which he saw the sun rise from the south. When morning came, he assembled all his *wazīrs* and asked for the interpretation of that dream but no one was able to make sense out of it. The ruler became distressed, and went before the monk *(rāhib)* of the idol temple where now is built the *khānaqāh* of the holy Sayyid, and asked him. He answered, "A man will come into our realm from the land of Mawarannahr, and will ennoble you with the acceptance of Islam. And he will make me a Muslim as well; although I will dispute it with him a great deal, there will be no avoiding it." When three days had passed, the holy Sayyid's noble arrival in that realm occurred, and upon his arrival the ruler came and became his disciple, composing these lines in praise of the holy Sayyid...

The verse expresses the ruler's gratitude for his conversion at the hands of Hamadānī, as well as his request for the Shaykh's intercession on the Day of Judgement. The author then cites a chronogram *(tārīkh)* composed on Hamadānī's arrival in Kashmir, ascribed to Sultan Quṭb al-Dīn: "When that king came from the kingdom of sainthood/ Kashmir took up the banner of Islam/ They may ask from whom it obtained this ordering/ So I have said, "from that king of guidance."[2]

The historicity of these accounts is not our focus here, although I would note that once the earlier tendency to dismiss the *Manqabat* as even a useful hagiographical source is rejected, its conversion narratives deserve special attention insofar as it is the earliest source to discuss Hamadānī's activity in Kashmir.

10. Sanction of Models of Political Behavior

Fully eleven of the unparalleled narratives found in the *Manqabat al-jawāhir* depict some aspect of Hamadānī's relations with rulers and other figures of secular activity. The very prevalence of such narratives in itself attests to the competitive

1. No. 48, ff. 435a-436a.
2. *Chū āmad ān shah az mulk-i wilāyat / girift kashmīr az islām rāyat / biguftand az kay yāft tartīb-i īn / az ān guftam kay 'z ān shāh-i hidāyat ('z ān shāh-i hidāyat* = 784/1382-83).

atmosphere developing in Khurāsān and Mawarannahr, as court connections became an increasingly important element in the success or failure of *ṭarīqas,* and as successful dealings with rulers became one of the responsibilities of would-be leaders of these Orders; and despite the unfortunate difficulties in interpreting the symbolism and allusions of several of these narratives,[1] it is safe to generalize that Hamadānī's relations with minor or local rulers are portrayed in a stock pattern of the ruler's challenge to the Shaykh, the Shaykh's victory (or dodge), and the ruler's repentance.

In only one case does Hamadānī refuse to accept a ruler's show of repentance; this is the unparalleled narrative[2] involving a ruler who, though unnamed, is none other than Timur,[3] and Ḥaydar Badakhshī's work provides the earliest known version of the narrative of these two figures' meeting—a narrative with an extensive subsequent development, as noted earlier. Timur is portrayed here as an inveterate enemy of the Sufis, whom he slaughters wherever he goes, but he, too, is finally overcome by shame and seeks Hamadānī's goodwill. Hamadānī refuses, however, and despite the ruler's pleas, he tells him simply to "Go and rule." The passage concludes noting that Hamadānī "avoided his company and never again met with him," and then introduces Hamadānī's remarks, repeated in a different context in the *Khulāṣat,*[4] on the countless torments occasioned by unjust rulers, hypocritical scholars, and ignorant judges—which, however, he understood as a divine gift.

The unyielding hostility against the unnamed Timur is no doubt a reflection of the suspicion and eventual assault directed against the Kubrawī circle of Isḥāq Khuttalānī under Timur's son Shāhrukh. With other 'political' narratives in the *Manqabat,* however, what is portrayed is a model for the proper relationship between rulers and not simply Sufi Shaykhs, but *ṭarīqa*-leaders. Several narratives follow the pattern noted above, in which the ruler ends as Hamadānī's disciple. In

1. For instance, No. 9 (ff. 362a-362b) recounts the appearance of a large black snake before Hamadānī's *khānaqāh;* it assumed human form and entered to receive the *bay'at* from the Shaykh; No. 24 (ff. 382b-385b) relates Hamadānī's journey to Ardabīl to announce the word he received from the Prophet at the tomb of Shaykh Junayd Baghdādī, namely that the ruler there was counted among the "people of paradise." The ruler became Hamadānī's *murīd,* took the *bay'at,* gave away all his wealth to the dervishes, and, adopting simple clothing, joined Hamadānī's group; but before they had gone two stages, assassins came and martyred the ruler, and Hamadānī himself washed and buried him. It is possible that some of the 'political' narratives referring to unnamed rulers in general or to unnamed rulers of a particular place (e.g. Balkh or Bukhārā) may in fact represent the transposition of narratives associated with Hamadānī onto figures contemporary with Ḥaydar Badakhshī, as either a prescriptive or congratulatory message to living rulers.
2. No. 25, ff. 385b-390b.
3. The fact that Timur is meant here is supported by the explicit mention later in the *Manqabat* (No. 39, f. 416b) of "Tīmūr Shāh," whose conversation with Hamadānī was "previously mentioned." The gist of the narrative, related on the authority of Qivām al-Dīn Badakhshī, down to its focus on Hamadānī, is as follows: this ruler "was coming from the direction of Hindūstān with a great army," putting to the test all the dervishes at every station; those who managed to answer he set free, but he killed those "who had not reached the rank of *walāyat.*" Therefore many dervishes fled to Arab lands, and many to Kābul and Savād, and when that ruler reached Balkh and killed the ruler there, he sent his men to Bukhārā and Badakhshān and all of Mawarannahr to send all the dervishes there before him, and he had many killed while many fled.
4. Teufel, p. 123.

one unparalleled account[1] an unnamed King of Rūm first tests Hamadānī but following the Shaykh's cure of his vizier seeks instruction from him. In another,[2] an unnamed judge of Bukhārā appeals to Hamadānī when unable to interpret the dream of the ruler he served. Then, jealous of Hamadānī's interpretation and fearful that the ruler will discover his own failure, he tries to poison the Shaykh. He is prevented from doing so when a lion appears and seizes him, and following the Shaykh's intercession to save the judge's life, he prostrates himself, apologizes, swears his allegiance *(bay'at)* and becomes Hamadānī's disciple:

> He abandoned his post, went into seclusion, adopted the course of service in the *khānaqāh* for twenty years, and forgot the things he had read throughout his life. He became a wayfarer on the Path, and wonders appeared to him; and he went nowhere without his holiness' permission, but became one of those accepted at the court of God.

Especially instructive is one unparalleled narrative[3] in which a strong sense of *ṭarīqa,* and of the Kubrawiyya/Hamadāniyya's superiority, is combined with implicit models for the relations between rulers and Shaykhs. Related on the authority of Shaykh Maḥmūd Kāmil Shīrāzī (a *murīd* of Khwāja Isḥāq Khuttalānī), it recounts Hamadānī's dealings with an unnamed ruler of Bukhārā and his servants and centers on the common theme of the rulers's efforts to induce Hamadānī (usually through ignorance, occasionally through intimidation) to eat unlawful food. The frequency of this motif is at first surprising, but in fact the battle over lawful and unlawful food was especially intense in the period of Mongol rule and the issue was commonly evoked, as a reflection of a direct and immediate test of religious commitment, well past the Timurid era. When, following Hamadānī's exposure of the ruse, the Sultan bowed down before the Shaykh and along with 324 persons present at the banquet repented and swore allegiance *(bay'at)* from him, the ruler behaved as a leader of a *ṭarīqa* in Ḥaydar Badakhshī's day would wish him to behave: he had a *khānaqāh* built for Hamadānī, "gave all his goods to the dervishes," and entered his service; and in conclusion the author adds a verse affirming the spiritual attainment assured to every adherent of the *silsila-i Hamadāniyya.*

Another model of a royal disciple devoted to his Shaykh, is provided in an especially instructive episode,[4] recounting the repentance of the ruler of Badakhshān, called in the *Manqabat* Bahrām-shāh al-Ḥūshī (transcription uncertain). According to this unparalleled account, the ruler declared that once he was drinking wine and felt the need to commit some evil act, but was restrained by someone's hand. When he sobered up, he tried in vain to learn which of his advisors had held him back, but later saw Hamadānī in a dream, acknowledging that it was he who had restrained the king and warning him that even though he was a ruler in this kingdom, he would do well to think about his origins and about the Day of Judgement. When he awoke, Bahrām-shāh went to Hamadānī and repented in his presence, and when he sought

1. No. 29, ff. 394a-396a.
2. No. 34, ff. 406a-409a.
3. No. 23, ff. 378a-382b.
4. No. 18, ff. 370a-370b.

to abandon his rule he was dissuaded by the Shaykh. Thereafter he affirmed, "I did all that he commanded, and by his order I received the appellation *Walī*, and I did nothing without his permission." Similar devotion is portrayed in another unparalleled narrative[1] in which Hamadānī rescues one of the leaders of the town of Rūstāq from a premature burial. The man affirmed that he had been among the disciples of Hamadānī but had spent his life in sin without repenting, until the Shaykh rescued him from death. Thereafter, he lived twelve more years occupied with nothing but worship.

Finally, one of the 'elaborated' narratives[2] includes one of the many accounts in the Manqabat of attempts by rulers and/or members of the *ulamā'* to poison Hamadānī; for this one the author cites the *Khulāṣat* and Ibrāhīm Mubārak-khānī.[3] This narrative is of particular interest, however, for in it the *Manqabat* adds a passage stressing the responsibility of religious figures to guide rulers: here the ruler asks the purpose of seeking knowledge *('ilm)* and Hamadānī replies that it is only for gnosis of God *(ma'rifat-i ḥaqq)* and for worship. The *'ulamā'* countered, "This statement is in accordance with the *madhhab-i ṣūfiyya,* but 'Knowledge' *('ilm)* is something else." Hamadānī replied,

> Then say what other thing it is and debate with me; even though you may speak meaningless words among yourselves, you should not say such inappropriate things before rulers, lest they be influenced by what the likes of you blind-hearted [people] say. You should say, [rather], "it is in accordance with the religious Law (*sharī'at*), the Sufi Path (*ṭarīqat*) and Divine Reality (*ḥaqīqat*)."

And the ruler, we are told, was so impressed by his words that he bestowed on him a grant of 4000 *shāhīs*.[4]

CONCLUSION

In discussing these narratives from the *Manqabat al-jawāhir,* my aim has been to show that (1) the work should not be dismissed as a poor imitation of the earlier biography of Hamadānī, and (2) the *Manqabat*'s departures from the earlier biography, in content and in tenor, signal a profound shift in the religious environment in which it was produced, a shift which in turn marks an important new stage in the religious history of Central Asia.

The *Khulāṣat al-manāqib* may be, as most specialists have contended, a more reliable source on the 'life' of Hamadānī, although in this regard we must keep in mind that it is still a hagiographical work intent more upon reflecting the spiritual

---

1. No. 47, ff. 434a-435a.
2. No. 27, ff. 392a-394a; cf. Teufel, p. 122-124. The episode is interrupted in the India Office MS by a *lacuna* [392b-393a] not noted by Teufel; the missing text appears in the Srinagar MS, ff. 23b-25b.
3. It is worth noting that the *Khulāṣat* "summarizes" here, citing Hamadānī's statement that he was often the target of such attempts by rulers and the *'ulamā'*, but that in fact all such attempts were divine gifts; as noted, the same statement is appended in the *Manqabat* to one of the unparalleled episodes (No. 25, ff. 385b-390b), in which a specific example of such attempts is recounted, this one involving an unnamed ruler who is clearly Timur.
4. Another of the 'political' narratives (No. 36, ff. 409b-413a) also ends with the ruler becoming Hamadānī's *murīd* and bestowing money upon him: in this case, 1000 *shāhīs*.

verities represented by the Shaykh than upon recounting the biographical particulars that we may consider important; and we must also remember that with such a purpose its author wrote a rather personal work conveying the Shaykh's impact upon his own spiritual development. In the *Manqabat al-jawāhir,* however, we have a work which, I believe, is not to be disregarded as a source on Hamadānī's life, insofar as it transmits independent traditions about him from sources as close or closer to the Shaykh than the *Khulāṣat*'s author. However that may be, it is clear that the *Manqabat* is less a personal work than one consciously designed to evoke Hamadānī's role in shaping the new style of Sufi life and organization and master-disciple relationship as the Kubrawiyya developed into a bona fide *ṭarīqa.* As such, it reflects the crucial developments of the early 15th century in a way the *Khulāṣat al-manāqib* could not, and has much more to tell us about the emergence of the Kubrawī order as such than the pre-*ṭarīqa* hagiography of Ja'far Badakhshī.

Here, lest it be supposed that the strong emphasis on *ṭarīqa* reflects the over-zealous praise of a new 'convert' to the *silsila,* I would add that the same *ṭarīqa*-consciousness is pronounced in other slightly later Kubrawī works, especially those surrounding Ḥusayn Khwārazmī: it appears in his biographies in a remark about the return of the Kubrawī 'light' to Khwārazm, it appears in his political links when various rulers (e.g. the Uzbek 'Ubaydullāh Khān) write verse for the Shaykh in praise of the Hamadānī order, it appears in his *waqf*-document, noting the endowment's intended purpose of fostering the Kubrawī-Hamadānī order, and it appears quite regularly, especially in the numerous accounts of competition with the Naqshbandīyya, in the newly found *Jāmi' al-salāsil.* From this perspective, the *Manqabat al-jawāhir* is of enormous interest as the first work of a distinctively self-consciously Kubrawī hagiographical tradition.

In short, as a source, the *Manqabat al-jawāhir* adopts some accounts from the *Khulāṣat* almost without change, adopts others with changes, elaborations and/or additions (usually in the form of commentary and doctrinal conclusions), and omits others, while at the same time introducing many accounts not found in the earlier work, some cited from sources not known to the *Khulāṣat* and others cited from figures not mentioned there. And, more significantly, the focus of the new stories, and of the alterations of accounts taken from the earlier work, shows that Ḥaydar Badakhshī's work cannot be considered simply a haphazard compilation aimed at 'miracle-mongering' or at the mere glorification of Hamadānī. Rather, it ought to be recognized as a distinctive new stage in the development of a specifically Kubrawī hagiography, a stage which should tell us that something quite significant has happened between the dates of composition of the two works—essentially the first half of the 15th century. What has happened, I would suggest, is that the Kubrawiyya—or at least one group with a Kubrawī *silsila*—has become a real *ṭarīqa* and has begun to articulate its distinctiveness as an 'Order' as it braces for competition in Central Asia with the newly emerging Naqshbandī rival.

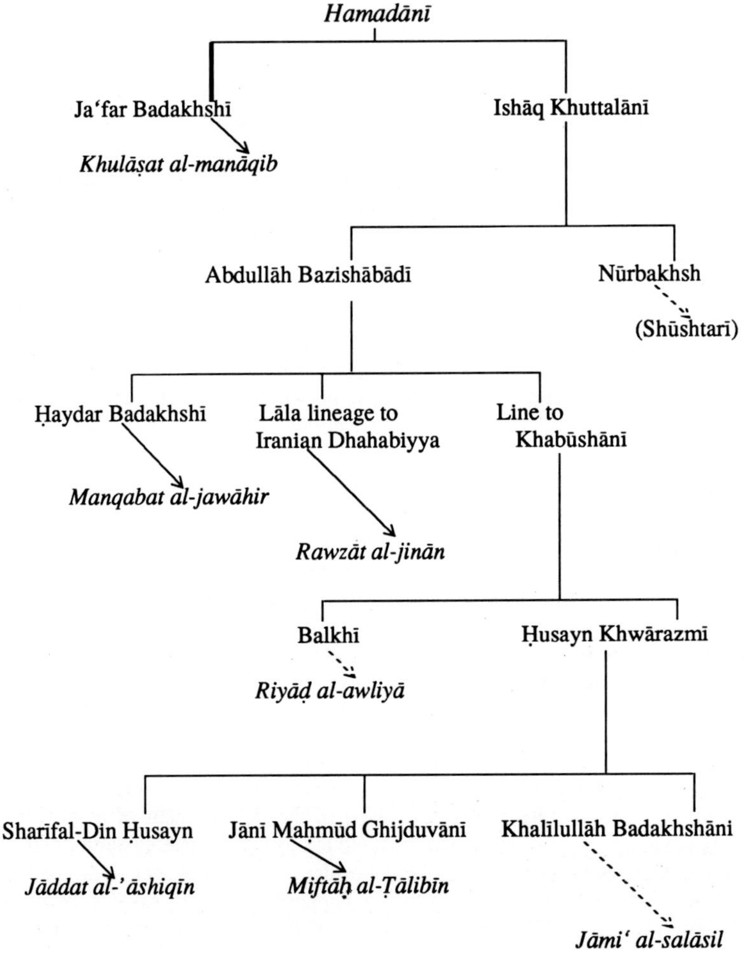
Hamadānī
Ja'far Badakhshī
Khulāṣat al-manāqib
Ishāq Khuttalānī
Abdullāh Bazishābādī
Nūrbakhsh
(Shūshtarī)
Ḥaydar Badakhshī
Manqabat al-jawāhir
Lāla lineage to Iranian Dhahabiyya
Rawzāt al-jinān
Line to Khabūshānī
Balkhī
Riyāḍ al-awliyā
Ḥusayn Khwārazmī
Sharīfal-Din Ḥusayn
Jāddat al-'āshiqīn
Jānī Maḥmūd Ghijduvānī
Miftāḥ al-Ṭālibīn
Khalīlullāh Badakhshāni
Jāmi' al-salāsil

Authority and Miraculous Behavior: Reflections on *Karāmāt* Stories of Khwāja 'Ubaydullāh Aḥrār

Jo-Ann Gross

The purpose of the present study is to explore the meanings of several types of *karāmāt* stories as described in four hagiographies on Khwāja Aḥrār (written within ten years of his death in 1490), spiritual leader of the Naqshbandī Sufi Order in late fifteenth century Central Asia.[1] The selected stories focus on incidents which involve issues of kingship, political authority, economic activity, and moral conduct. It will be shown that such stories contribute to the idealization of the Naqshbandī Shaykh, illustrate the knowledge, piety and miraculous power achieved by and ascribed to Khwāja Aḥrār, and define a system of rules and values for worldly actions. It will be shown, furthermore, that although social historians often avoid utilizing hagiographies because of the blatantly religious motivations of the writers and the tone of their content, sacred biography's religiosity does not necessarily limit its historical and literary worth any more than the political allegiances of some court historians limit theirs.[2]

Islam is a religion which stresses the importance of personal character as exemplified by the lives of prophets and saints. Sufism represents the perfection of Muslim practice and social ethics and the ideal of *adab* in the path toward inner solitude and possible perfection of the soul.[3] Through the examples of stories and sayings, through the worldly actions of individuals, patterns of ethical and moral values are often communicated. This is indeed the case for the hagiographies of Khwāja Aḥrār, the renowned Central Asian Shaykh of the Timurid period.[4] Leader

---

1. The manuscript sources which support this research were acquired through the generous support of the Social Science Research Council; the United States Department of Education, Fulbright-Hays Travel Grant Program; and the International Research and Exchanges Board in 1979-80.

2. Among the examples of the interpretive use of hagiographical sources to understand social history and the role of Sufis are: Devin DeWeese, 'The Eclipse of the Kubraviyah in Central Asia,' *Iranian Studies* 21(1988), pp. 45-83; Simon Digby, 'The Sufi Shaikh as a Source of Authority in Mediæval India,' *Purusartha* 9 (1986), pp. 57-77; R.M. Eaton, *The Sufis of Bijapur 1300-1700* (Princeton: Princeton University Press 1978); W.E. Fusfeld, 'The Shaping of Sufi Leadership in Delhi: The Naqshbandiyya Mujadidiyya, 1750-1920,' (Ph.D. Dissertation, University of Pennsylvania, 1981); J. Gross, 'Multiple Roles and Perceptions of a Sufi Shaikh: Symbolic Statements of Political and Religious Authority,' in *Naqshbandis: Cheminements et situation actuelle d'un ordre mystique musulman*, ed. Marc Gaborieau, Alexandre Popovic, and Thierry Zarcone, (Istanbul/Paris, Éditions Isis, 1990); J. Gross, 'The Economic Status of a Timurid Sufi Shaykh: A Matter of Conflict or Perception?', *Iranian Studies* 21(1988), pp. 84-104; Jürgen Paul, 'Die politische und soziale Bedeutung der Naqšbandiyya in Mittelasien im 15. Jahrhundert,' (Ph.D. Dissertation, University of Hamberg 1989).

3 Notes continued on page 160.

of the Naqshbandī Order in Transoxiana, Khwāja Aḥrār was a prominent religious, political, and economic figure. Based on his extensive *waqf* holdings, Aḥrār played a significant role in the local economy.[1] Based on his hagiographies and contemporary historical chronicles, he was prominent as an advisor to Sultans, and as a mediator in political conflicts of his day.[2] Based on the persistence of popular legends, hagiographical accounts, and extant correspondence between Sufis, Aḥrār was undoubtedly a well-respected and prominent Shaykh within the Naqshbandī Order, and remains venerated to this day.

There are four hagiographical sources available on the life of Khwāja Aḥrār, although there is some repetition in them.[3] The earliest hagiography is the *Majālis-i 'Ubaydullāh Aḥrār,* written by Aḥrār's son-in-law and disciple, 'Abd al-Awwal

3. See the following for introductory sources on the interpretation of *Adab*: F. Gabrieli, 'Adab,' *Encyclopaedia of Islam;* G.E. von Grunebaum, *Medieval Islam* (Chicago, University of Chicago Press 1945), pp. 250-257); Dj. Khaleghi-Motlagh, 'Adab in Iran,' *Encyclopaedia Iranica,* I, pp. 432-439; Ira M. Lapidus, 'Knowledge, Virtue and Action: The Classical Conception of Adab in Islam,' in *Moral Conduct and Authority: The Place of Adab in South Asian Islam,* ed. Barbara Metcalf, (Berkeley, University of California Press 1984), pp. 38-61; Ch. Pellat, 'Adab in Arabic Literature,' *Encyclopaedia Iranica,* pp. 439-444.

Among the Sufi treatises and manuals which explicitly address Sufi *Adab* are: Abū Nasr 'Abdullāh ibn 'Alī al-Sarrāj, *Kitāb al-luma' fi at-taṣawwuf,* ed. R.A. Nicholson (Leiden 1914); Abū Ṭalib Muḥammad ibn 'Alī, *Qut al-qulūb fī mu'āmalāt al-maḥbūb wa waṣf ṭarīq al-murīd ilā maqām at-tawḥīd,* 4 vols. (Cairo 1351/1932); 'Alī b. 'Uthmān al-Hujwīrī, *Kashf al-maḥjūb,* ed. V.A. Zhukovsky (Tehran 1336 A.H.sh.), trans. A. Nicholson (London 1936); Abū Ḥafṣ 'Umar al-Suhrawardī, *'Awārif al-ma'ārif* (Beirut 1966); al-Sulamī, *Kitāb adab al-ṣuḥba wa-ḥusn al-'ushra,* ed. M.J. Kister (Jerusalem 1954) and by the same author, *Jawāmi' ādāb aṣ-ṣūfiyya,* ed. E. Kohlberg (Jerusalem 1976); Abū al-Najīb al-Suhrawardī, *Kitāb Ādāb al-Murīdīn,* abridged trans. M. Milson, *A Sufi Rule for Novices,* (Cambridge: Harvard University Press 1975); and Anṣārī, *Mukhtaṣar fī ādāb aṣ-ṣūfiyya,* ed. Laugier de Beaurecueil, in *Bulletin de l'institut français d'archéologie orientale* 59 (1960), pp. 203-40. For an excellent review of these sources and others, see Böwering, *'The Adab Literature...'*, pp. 62-71.

4. See H. Algar, 'The Naqshbandi Order: A Preliminary Survey of its History and Significance,' *Studia Islamica* 44 (1976), pp. 123-152; 3 studies by Jo-Ann Gross: 'Khoja Ahrar: A Study of the Perceptions of Religious Power and Prestige in the Late Timurid Period,' (Ph.D. Dissertation, New York University 1982), 'The Economic Status of a Timurid Sufi Shaykh: A Matter of Conflict or Perception?' *Iranian Studies* 21 (1988), pp. 84-104, 'Multiple Roles and Perceptions of a Sufi Shaikh: Symbolic Statements of Political and Religious Authority,' in *Naqhsbandis: Cheminements et situation actuelle d'un ordre mystique musulman,* ed. Marc Gaborieau, Alexandre Popovic, and Thierry Zarcone, (Istanbul/Paris: Éditions Isis 1990), pp. 109-122; 2 studies by J. Paul, 'Die politische und soziale Bedeutung der Naqšbandiyya in Mittelasien im 15. Jahrhundert,' (Ph.D. Dissertation, University of Hamberg 1989) and 'Forming a Faction: The Ḥimayāt System of Khwāja Aḥrār,' *International Journal of Middle East Studies,* 23 (1991), pp. 533-48.

1. Chekhovitch, *Samarskites Document XV-XVI Century* (Moscow 1974); Gross, 'The Economic Status...'; M. Rogers, 'Waqfiyyas and Waqf-Registers: New Primary Sources for Islamic Architecture,' *Kunst des Orients* 11(1976/77), pp. 182-96

2. V.V. Barthold, *Four Studies on the History of Central Asia,* trans. V. and T. Minorsky, Vol. II, Ulugh Beg (Leiden, E.J. Brill 1963); Chekhovitch, 'Oborona Samarkanda v 1454 g'., in *Isvestiia AN UzSS,* (1960), pp. 36-44; J. Paul, *op.cit.*; Gross, 'Multiple Roles and Perceptions...'

3. The hagiographical sources referred to in this paper are the *Majālis-i 'Ubaydallāh Ahrār* (India Office DP 8090), by Jalāl al-Dīn 'Abd al-Awwal Nīshāpūrī (also known as Masmū'at); the *Silsilat al-'ārifīn wa tadhkirat al-ṣiddīqīn* by Burhān al-Dīn Samarqandī (Institut Vostokovedeniia, Tashkent #4452/I); the *Manāqib-i Aḥrār* by Mawlānā Shaykh (Institut Vostokovedeniia, Tashkent # 9730); and the *Rashaḥat-i 'ayn al-ḥayat* by Fakhr al-Dīn 'Alī b. al-Ḥusayn al-Wā'iẓ al-Kāshifī (known as al-Ṣafī), ed. by 'Alī Aṣghar Mu'miyan (Tehran 1970).

Nīshāpūrī (d. 905/1500). A second source is the *Silsilat al-'arifīn,* composed by another of Aḥrār's disciples, Burhān al-Dīn Samarqandī (known as Mawlānā Muḥammad Qāḍī). Qāḍī joined Aḥrār in 885/1480 and was with him during the last ten years of Aḥrār's life. The only published source on Aḥrār and the Naqshbandī Order is the *Rashaḥāt-i 'ayn al-ḥayāt,* written by Fakhr al-Dīn 'Alī ibn al-Ḥusayn al-Wā'iẓ al-Kāshifī (known as al-Ṣafī) and completed in 1503-04. The latest of the hagiographical sources is the *Manāqib-i Aḥrār,* composed by another of Aḥrār's disciples, Mawlānā Shaykh. Although there is some dispute regarding Mawlānā Shaykh's authorship of the work, he appears to have collected and copied its contents.

The latter works provide an abundance of information about the disciples, Shaykhs, and activities of the Naqshbandī *ṭarīqa.* In the many descriptions of actions, miracles, and sayings, these sources also relate specific political events in which Aḥrār himself is said to have participated. As sources compiled during the late fifteenth century, a period during which Aḥrār achieved prominence in Central Asia, hagiographies are an important supplement to historical chronicles and documentary sources for understanding Timurid politics and society. For example, the chronicles as well as the hagiographical sources attribute the successful accession to power in 855/1451 of the Timurid Sultan Abū Sa'īd (r. 855/1451–874/1469) to the help and spiritual support of Khwāja Aḥrār.[1] Aḥrār also is described as a mediator in political disputes, a spiritual advisor to the Timurid Sultans Abū Sa'īd in Herat, and Aḥmad and Maḥmūd in Samarqand, a role to be repeated later in Central Asia with the Juybari Shaykhs under the Shaybanids and the Naqshbandīs in Mughal India. The preeminent role of Khwāja Aḥrār is most clearly described by the Timurid historian, Khwāndamīr:

> The greatest in splendor and grandeur as well as the number of followers and assets of all holy men of Turkestan and Transoxiana was Khwāja Naṣīr al-Dīn 'Ubaydullāh. When a young man he had been brought into the *ṭarīqa* by Mawlānā Ya'qūb Charkhī and Mawlānā Niẓām al-Dīn Khāmush. Very soon he began to bring others on to the right path. The noble rulers of Turkestan and Transoxiana, as well as Iraq and Azarbaijan, all believed and paid the utmost respect to him. Abū Sa'īd in particular consulted him on every affair and sometimes went to him on his feet in respect. The children of Abū Sa'īd also followed their father in respecting Aḥrār.[2]

Hagiographical sources inherently highlight the spirituality and piety of the Shaykhs about whom they are written, and thus present an idealized image of the *ṭarīqa* and those Shaykhs and disciples associated with it. The hagiographies of Khwāja Aḥrār appear to focus on several images which represent the ideal model of behavior implicit in the actions of Aḥrār and the ideal model of behavior expected of others, whether rulers or disciples. Consistent with the *Sharī'a*-minded orthodoxy of the Naqshbandiyya, Aḥrār appears as a respected Shaykh who fervently adhered to the *Sharī'a* and had deep feelings of obligation in his defense of justice

1. 'Abd al-Razzāq Samarqandī, *Maṭla' al-sa'dayn,* ed. M. Shafi' (Lahore: 1941-49), Vol. II, pp. 987-988; Mas'ūdi b. Uthmān Kūhistānī, *Tarikh-i Abū al-Khayr Khanī* (Aziatskii Muzei, Tashkent C478), ff. 2316-2396; Kāshifī, *Rashaḥāt-i 'ayn al-ḥayāt,* p. 520.
2. *Ḥabīb al-siyar,* ed. 'Abd al-Ḥusayn Nawā'ī (Tehran 1914), p. 87

Khwāja Aḥrār. From an eighteenth-century Mughal manuscript. British Museum MS. 1974-617-010(2) Courtesy of the Trustees of the British Museum.

and the correct treatment of the Muslim population. The manner in which he acts is one which reflects propriety *(adab)*, good deeds, and ethical conduct.

One of the most pervasive models of *adab* as described in the hagiographical stories concerns Aḥrār's relationship to rulers. Numerous stories attest to Aḥrār's role as an advisor to Sultans, and, in effect, as the upholder of righteous rule. Aḥrār's biographers repeatedly cite him as a model for Sufis serving to uphold justice, not only from within the *ṭarīqa,* but within the circle of the nobles and kings, a model which fully supports the Naqshbandī doctrine of 'solitude in society' *(khalwāt dar anjuman).*[1] These stories also reflect the socio-political climate of late fifteenth-century urban society, since the Naqshbandiyya were very closely aligned with the court elite and intelligentsia in Herat and Samarqand.[2] As Aḥrār is reported to have said, "If we had assumed the position of a Shaykh, no other Shaykh would have had a follower. But we have been assigned a different task, which is to guard the Muslims from oppression, and to this end one must mingle with kings and conquer their souls."[3]

Possibly in response to the expressed disapproval of such mundane involvements by those less politically motivated Sufis, Aḥrār's hagiographers stress the logic of such worldly endeavors. For example, the author of the *Majālis-i 'Ubaydullāh Aḥrār* relates that:

> Imām Anwarid Dabbūsī has written in his book, *Maqṣad al-Aqṣā*, that some people, due to their ignorance, criticize and reject this world and kingship. These are not by any means true. Man by nature needs food and without food, obedience to God's orders and demands is not possible... Without engaging in worldly matters, acquiring these is not possible. Engaging in worldly matters produces ranks among the people, and kingship is only a noble rank among these, and close to the rank of prophethood. And after the latter, no rank is more noble and venerated than the former. Helping the faith and the *umma*, upholding the religion and others, are more effectively done from the rank of kingship than any other one...[4]

Aḥrār clearly saw himself as a preserver of order, justice, and right kingship. This is strongly expressed in the saying attributed to him in the *Majālis-i 'Ubaydullāh Aḥrār:*

> "Times have become very evil. If possible, there is no act better than serving at the court of the kings and rulers [through which] to assist the poor and the oppressed." He [Aḥrār] advised one of the princes that affluence, influence, and social station

1. On the doctrine of *khalwāt dar anjuman,* see Hamid Algar, 'The Naqshbandi Order: A Preliminary Survey of its History and Significance,' *Studia Islamica,* 44 (1976), p. 133.
2. For studies which deal with cultural patronage and socio-economic relationships in Timurid society, see Bert Fragner, 'Social and Economic Affairs,' in *The Cambridge History of Iran,* Vol. 6, *The Timurid and Safavid Periods,* ed. Peter Jackson and Laurence Lockhart (Cambridge University Press 1986), pp. 491-567; Maria Subtelny, 'Socioeconomic Bases of Cultural Patronage Under the Late Timurids,' *International Journal of Middle East Studies* 20 (1988), pp. 479-505; Maria Subteleny, 'A Timurid Educational and Charitable Foundation: The Ikhlāṣiyya Complex of 'Alī Shīr Navā'ī in 15th Century Herat and its Endowment,' *Journal of the American Oriental Society* 1990; J. Gross, 'Symbolic and Economic Capital in the Timurid Period,' in *Fifteenth Century Persian Art and Patronage* (Genoa, forthcoming).
3. *Silsilat al-'arifīn,* f. 163b.
4. *Majālis-i 'Ubaydullāh Aḥrār,* f. 90a-90b.

bear awesome responsibility. [Truly] rich is one who uses his wealth in gaining merit for the hereafter. Every morning when someone arrives at a King's court, his entire endeavor and attention must be focused on warding off oppression and unlawful deeds from fellow Muslims, and prevent from happening what may contravene the *Sharī'a*. He must quickly attach himself to the Prophet and pray and recall that he is carrying the covenant of the prophets with him when he appears before kings, through which he should endeavor to prevent the [royal] crown and throne from being destroyed and laid low [by abuse of it].[1]

Implicit in the many stories of Aḥrār's involvement with rulers is his role as a restraining force, particularly in times of civil strife or conflict. At the point of a military confrontation in Samarqand between the three Timurid princes, Mīrzā 'Umar Shaykh, Sultan Aḥmad, and Sultan Maḥmud, Aḥrār wrote a letter of appeal to Mīrzā Sultan Maḥmūd. As described in the *Ḥabīb al-siyar,* the ultimate conclusion which resulted from Aḥrār's intervention and mediation was one of peace. "Out of respect for him [Aḥrār] these three princes did not engage in war....as long as they lived, they did not fight one another again."[2] Aḥrār's appeal to Sultan Maḥmūd was based on God's disapproval, the sanctity of Samarqand as a holy city, the results that such a conflict would have on the poor, needy, and holy people, and a reminder of the divine consequences of violating peace. For to wage war and inflict suffering on the populace (and by implication, on Aḥrār) would be to wage war and inflict suffering on God.

When Mīrzā Ṣultān Maḥmūd had arrived for combat in the environs of Samarqand a few days before the battle and siege, His Eminence *(Ḥaḍrat Īshān)* blessed be his soul in paradise, wrote and sent a letter in which, after the [usual] greetings, he asserted, "This lowly one along with his company, all born to your service, [would like to bring to your attention] that Samarqand has been called, and thus been also written of, as the protected city of the great [holy] men. To threaten Samarqand is unbefitting of Your Excellency. God Almighty has not allowed such things. The religion of the Prophet Muḥammad, blessed be he and his house, is not approving of this. To brandish the sword in the face of one's own brother is not befitting of Your Excellency. This lowly one in the path of my service and good will towards Your Excellency has fulfilled my duty of service to You by interceding many times. It did not, however, attain your acceptance. By listening to [wrong] people and setting out for this district, and not accepting the services of this lowly one, are all strange matters. While I am rendering You a good service, [those wrong] people further only their own interests. There are many holy people, many people of [divine] peace, and many poor and needy people in Samarqand. To press them [with hardship] any more than this is not appropriate, lest it may injure an [innocent] heart, and offending the hearts of the innocent can bring dire consequences. When the hearts of the believers and the people of divine peace are depressed one must fear. For the sake of God, accept the begging of this lowly one which is solely an unblemished service to Your Excellency, so that with the help of each other [Maḥmūd and Aḥmad], you may do that which satisfies God, the Almighty. Join all and set aright what is in disarray. There are men of God that by sheer favor that He [God] has for them, He considers any threat, any

---

1. *Majalis-i 'Ubaydullāh Aḥrār,* f. 80a-80b.
2. *Habib al-siyar,* p. 109. See other versions of these events described in the *Silsilat al-'ārifīn,* ff. 171b-173b; the *Rashaḥat-i 'ayn al-ḥayāt,* 531-35, and the *Manāqib-i Aḥrār,* ff. 118-119b.

hurting or suffering, brought upon them as being the same as having been waged on Him."[1]

The above mentioned samples are but a select few which are part of a larger pattern of values and ethics exemplified by Aḥrār. Through such models of behavior several ideas are expressed. First, that to be a Sultan is a noble rank, one comparable to prophethood. Second, that the role of the Sufi is to protect the Muslim people, advise Sultans, prevent oppression, and remind kings of their role. And third, that it is not only acceptable, but obligatory for Shaykhs such as Aḥrār to act within the political sphere of rulers. In light of the unusual degree of political involvement of Naqshbandī Shaykhs in urban Khurasan and Transoxiana in the late fifteenth century, such a model confirms the historical role of Naqshbandī Shaykhs as described in the extant chronicles. It also symbolically reaffirms what appears to be a trend dating from the post-Mongol period of the pairing of Sufis and Sultans, particularly among prominent charismatic Naqshbandī Shaykhs.

In contrast to the many stories which describe Aḥrār as the exemplar and enforcer of just, good actions, there are numerous stories which detail the violation of such actions. In such stories, the oppressive actions of rulers, government officials, or associates of Aḥrār's, and the consequences of such actions are described. Such stories are often extreme in their rejection of such behavior. The following is one such story which concerns a certain Arab, Sayyid Aḥmad Sārid, who is said to have been terrorizing several of Aḥrār's employees.

> One day they came to Qarshī when Qarā Aḥmad, an Arab camel-driver, came forth complaining profusely with tears and cries. He told His Eminence [Aḥrār] that Sayyid Aḥmad Sārid, the Arab constable, has been giving him trouble and bothering him. There appeared a great anger in His Eminence, but he did not say anything. When he set out for Samarqand, Sayyid Aḥmad Sārid and Muḥammad 'Alī Kükeltāsh came to the King's highway to escort him into the city. After the usual greetings, they gave accounts of things for a while. During the conversation he [Aḥrār] gradually became inflamed, and turning to Sayyid Aḥmad said,
>
> "Have you terrorized my people and servants and have bothered them? Be sure that I know the method of terror very well. Fear the time that I may approach you in this way."
>
> Then he angrily dismissed them. It came time for prayers. He said his prayers but did not talk to anyone, nor did anyone dare to talk to him until dawn. After a while, Sayyid Aḥmad became ill and his illness became critical. Mīrzā sent several messages by Darvīsh Amīn [to Aḥrār] that [Sayyid Aḥmad says],
>
> "My illness is caused by his anger with me. Your Excellency, oh Mīrzā, out of generosity ask for [the safety of] my life from His Eminence." This message was brought from Mīrzā interceding on [Sayyid's] behalf several times, but he [Aḥrār] did not give it any attention. Instead, addressing [Mīrzā] he replied,
>
> "Truly Mīrzā, Your Excellency has surpassed the limits of importunity. If the affairs of Sayyid Aḥmad was in my hands, of course I would have been magnanimous and forgiven his punishment."
>
> His Eminence continued,
>
> "It is indeed strange that Mīrzā is requesting [for the life of] dead Sayyid Muḥammad from me. I am not Jesus to bring back to life the dead ones. But since

1. *Majālis-i 'Ubaydullāh Aḥrār*, f. 176b-177a.

His Excellency, the Mīrzā, wishes us to come, we shall come."

When they arrived at the gates of the citadel (Ark), a coffin passed them by, the coffin of Sayyid Aḥmad Sārid. At that point they turned back.[1]

That one should not terrorize Aḥrār's employees is not an outlandish request. It is the severity of the punishment for doing so that transcends the norm. The reader sees witnesses Aḥrār power to inflict death, which he does despite the Mīrzā's (possibly Sultan Aḥmad Mīrzā, ruler of Samarqand and Bukhara, and a disciple of Aḥrār's) appeals to him.

The following story, somewhat lighter in tone, again demonstrates Aḥrār's determination to enforce right behavior and punish wrong. In this case his authority is symbolically executed in the form of kingly authority as Aḥrār dons a royal turban. In response to a complaint of oppressive rule, Aḥrār miraculously deposes the ruler and causes him to become ill.

It is related that one day His Eminence arrived in the bazaar of Bukhara. He chanced upon a shop where they made turbans for the royal festival *(nawrūzī)* Suddenly a peculiar manner overcame His Eminence. He removed his turban from his head and placed a royal turban upon his blessed head, adding,

"I have donned the royal garment and wish to rule in the land."

Shaykh Mīrzā approached him, saying,

"The king of Samarqand is said to be an oppressor in the extreme, and the Muslims are hurt by him."

In reply, His Eminence muttered these words, "I depose him."

On the same day an evil befell the king of Samarqand. Soon however, he recovered.[2]

Such stories which concern the ethical boundaries of political authority may reflect the political and economic circumstances of the late Timurid period as much as they provide a moral lesson. Although large-scale landownership by intellectuals, amirs, and religious figures was increasing during the late fifteenth century, the populace was suffering from the imposition of heavy taxes. The balance of power between Turkic military figures and Tajik administrators was not resolved, and Turko-Mongol ideals still were strong, perhaps further reason for Aḥrār's constant reaffirmation of the *Sharī'a*.[3]

However, the political sphere is not the only arena in which Aḥrār is portrayed as performing rather extreme miraculous actions in response to unacceptable behavior. Another pattern of stories found in the hagiographies is that which conveys opposition to Aḥrār himself—whether it be doctrinal disputes, competition for disciples, or mere insult. One such story involves the practice of vocal *dhikr* (silent *dhikr* was the most commonly practiced form at this time and place).

A darvīsh related that Mawlānā Shaykh Muḥammad of Kash was resentful of the Shaykh-born *[Shaykhzāda]* Eliās because he said his religious recitation aloud. Their dispute became acute. A group of Turks from Kash who were disciples of

1. *Manāqib-i Aḥrār*, f. 103b.
2. *Silsilat al-'ārifīn*, f. 53b; also in the *Manāqib-i Aḥrār*, f. 131b.
3. See Beatrice Manz, 'Tamerlane and the Symbolism of Sovereignty,' *Iranian Studies* 21 (1988), pp. 105-122; and Maria Subtelny, 'Centralizing Reform and its Opponents in the Late Timurid Period,' *Iranian Studies* 21(1988), pp. 123-151.

Shaykh Eliās used to molest Mawlānā Shaykh Muḥammad, aiming to discredit him. His Eminence [Aḥrār], in order that no harm come to Mawlānā Shaykh from those Turks, immediately showed favorable inclinations towards Mawlānā. His [Aḥrār's] intentions were not anything beyond this. Shaykh [Muḥammad] was informed about this when the question was put to him,

"Is His Eminence unhappy with you?"

Shaykh [Muḥammad] dispatched a letter to Amir Darwīsh Muḥammad Tarkhān[1] in which he made strange remarks about His Eminence, adding,

"Why are you sitting [so mindlessly] when the faith and the believers are left to the one whose feudal [village landlord-like] buying and selling [commercial dealings] are not in accordance with the *Sharī'a?* Why do you have so much faith in him and pay so much attention to his words?"

Since Amir Darvīsh Muḥammad Tarkhān had strong faith in His Eminence, he could not bear to hide the communication and sent the letter to His Eminence. He [Aḥrar] was angered, and said,

"Oh Shaykh of the beggars, from the day that I appeared, so many Shaykhs and Mawlānās have been trampled under my feet that only God knows the count. What is he implying? That he [Shaykh Eliās] knows the *Sharī'a* and I do not?"

In a short time, cholera afflicted the Shaykh. All his children and kinfolk died, followed by the Shaykh himself.[2]

Although the controversy described above is one concerning the vocal and silent practice of the *dhikr,* several other themes are also present. First is the relationship between Aḥrār and the amir, Darwīsh Muḥammad Tarkhān, who firmly supported Aḥrār against accusations which questioned Aḥrār's rustic background and his religious credentials.[3] Second is a possible undercurrent of Turkic-Tajik conflict, interesting in light of the distinctive *dhikr* practice, although this is difficult to substantiate. More significant to the purpose of this study is the story's resolution. Elias practiced vocal *dhikr,* to which Aḥrār was opposed, but even more damaging, was Shaykh Muḥammad's letter to the amir, which so insulted Aḥrār. The story is resolved through Shaykh Muḥammad's death, while the biographic image of Aḥrār is that of a Shaykh who upholds his position while threatened in the face of accusation and insult. The doctrinal issue of the silent-vocal *dhikr* is secondary to the challenge made to Aḥrār's religious authority and economic role, a challenge which is so dramatically crushed in the story's conclusion.

Aḥrār's worldly activities and his accumulation of wealth also cast doubt on his

---

1. Darwīsh Muḥammad Tarkhān was one of Sultan Aḥmad's amirs. According to Babur, "Of all begs in Sultan Aḥmad Mīrzā's presence, he was the greatest and most honoured. He was an orthodox believer, kindly and dervish-like, and was a constant transcriber of the Koran." *Bāburnāma,*(Memoirs of Bābur) translated from Turki Test of Ẓāhir al-Dīn Muḥammad Bābur Pudshāh Ghazi by A. S. Beveridge (Nwe Dehli 1979 reprint) vol. I, p. 38.
2. *Manāqib-i Aḥrār,* f.105a-105b.
3. Aḥrār's alleged aversion to the conventional Islamic sciences has been alluded to by Soviet scholars (Nabiev, Molchanov, Viatkin) and is also mentioned in the biographies themselves. This interpretation is based on the report that Aḥrār left the *madrasah* in Samarqand to which his uncle had sent him to study in 1436-37 (*Rashaḥat,* p. 404, 412-414). However, his hagiographers demonstrate his knowledge, and refer to his reading of *fiqh* and *tafsīr,* and his discussions of *ḥadīth.* One story from the *Manaqib-i Aḥrār,* f. 129b, also repeated in the *Rashaḥat,* p. 413, is as follows: —Khwāja Faḍl Allāh Shaykh Abū Laythī related, "I do not know the range of the Khwāja's knowledge, but this much I know—that he has studied very little of the conventional sciences. But there are few days that he does not come up with a *Qaḍī*'s verdict."

character. His large following, his extensive economic base, and his political activities most likely created some envy among his fellow Shaykhs, the *'ulamā'*, and perhaps even among the amirs. All four of Aḥrār's hagiographers discuss the pious basis for his acquisition of wealth and power, and provide reports of his philanthropic activities. *Waqf* documents and stories confirm Aḥrār's contribution to the local economy through the endowment of mosques and *khānaqāhs,* through the employment of peasants on his land (private and *waqf*), and through his periodic payments of taxes on behalf of an impoverished population, among other examples.[1]

Despite the philanthropic motivations upon which his economic activities appear to be based according to Aḥrār's hagiographers, there is also evidence that the extent of his economic influence may have challenged the authenticity of Aḥrār's asceticism. However, in light of the Naqshbandī acceptance of worldly activity, the doubt cast on Aḥrār's character is a phenomenon which most likely reflects socio-economic conflicts between individuals in Timurid society rather than any doctrinal conflict. The following saying from the *Manāqib-i Aḥrār* defines the Naqshbandī position regarding the worldly possessions of Shaykhs:

> All investigators of divine Truth unanimously agree that it is important for the teacher to have enough wealth to cover the basic needs of his pupils, since not having such would make the pupils needy of the outside world, while the purpose is to totally severe one's ties with the material world. Some scholars have said that Shaykhs and teachers must be wealthy, and have considered this a necessity for perfection, and since the obedience and respect of the pupils for their teachers would increase. Obedience is a condition for the pupil in the path of total submission.[2]

In contrast to the many sayings and stories which support the economic position of Aḥrār, such as the one quoted above, there are numerous stories which deal with accusations of Aḥrār's worldly activities. Perhaps the most powerful opposition to Aḥrār, certainly the one to which scholars of the Timurid period refer most often, is that of the Shaykh al-Islām of Samarqand, Burhān al-Dīn, who was one of Aḥrār's chief rivals.[3] Stories in the hagiographies concerning their rivalry indicate that Burhān al-Dīn was outspoken in his opposition to Aḥrār, and imply that Aḥrār was prompted to respond forcefully.

It appears that the symbolic punishment of Burhān al-Dīn as described by the hagiographers was in response to his accusations against Aḥrār and his impolite behavior. First, Burhān al-Dīn insulted Aḥrār after the death of the Timurid Sultan Abū Sa'īd in 1469 by implying that Abū Sa'īd's death was Aḥrār's fault. Aḥrār had reportedly advised Abū Sa'īd to proceed with his Turkmen campaign, during which he was killed in 1469. The following story describes Burhān al-Dīn's behavior and

1. O.D. Chekhovitch, *Samarkandskie Dokumenty XV-XVI Century* (Moscow 1974); M. Rogers, 'Waqfiyyas and Waqf-Registers: New Primary Sources for Islamic Architecture,' pp. 182-96; Gross, 'The Economic Status'; A. Urumbaev, *Pisma-Avtografi Abdalrakhmana Dzhami iz Alboma Navoi* (Tashkent 1982); *Manaqib-i Aḥrār*, f. 132, 6b,105b; Rashaḥat-i 'ayn al-ḥayāt, p. 536, 405
2. *Majālis-i 'Ubaydu'llah Aḥrār*, f. 60b-61a.
3. Burhān al-Dīn came from a well established family of Shaykhs in Samarqand. For more on Burhān al-Dīn, see *Rashaḥat*, vol. 2, pp. 610-614.

Aḥrār's reaction to it.

> Haḍrat Īshān related,
>
> "After the news of Abū Sa'īd's death came, Khwāja Mawlānā came out into the road without looking at us and said, *'Salām 'alaykum,'* and made his horse proceed. He did not stop at all. I also learned that Khwāja Mawlānā [Burhān al-Dīn] had come to an agreement with the amirs that they should no longer come here and that they should disobey me."[1]

Burhān al-Dīn also accused Aḥrār of being a gatherer of worldly possessions. In the *Manāqib-i Aḥrār* it is reported by a "darvish who was one of the elders in Khwāja Mawlānā's *Majlis*" that,

> A darwīsh related that in one of Khwāja Mawlānā's audiences, His Eminence's [Aḥrār's] virtueswere highly praised. Khwāja Mawlānā said,
>
> "Set aside your commemoration of this *ja'l* (charlatan), whose entire endeavor is to amass worldly goods."
>
> These words were carried to His Eminence. He said, "He shall die like *ju'l* (excrement)."[2]

According to Mawlānā Shaykh, the author of the *Manāqib,* Burhān al-Dīn became progressively ill, losing his mental capacity and control over his bodily functions. At the end of the story, the reader finds the Shaykh al-Islām in Herat (far from Samarqand),wandering the streets and "talking nonsense," living in the *madrasa* of Amīr Chaqmaq.[3]

> Everyone who came and saw him would remark, "Take this as a miracle of Aḥrār." One day, someone said, "Oh Khwāja, you—the Shaykh al-Islām, who have been the *Ṣāhib-i khaṭ* of Samarqand, by ancestral right, the Shaykh al-Islām, there is no good reason why you, at the end of your life, knowingly and willingly, should live and wander around in other towns with so much disrespect and poverty. How can you interpret this other than as a miracle of Aḥrār?"[4]

Shortly after this, Mawlānā Shaykh reports that Burhān al-Dīn's condition worsened and he died. The story of his opposition to Aḥrār provides an extraordinary example of Aḥrār's miraculous power, and in this case the very telling of it upholds Aḥrār's piety. Independent from the authors' intentions, the incidents provide the

---

1. *Manāqib-i Aḥrār*, f. 122a-122b.
2. *Manāqib-i Aḥrār*, f. 122b. The play on words with *ja'l/ju'l* is extended in the discussion of Burhān al-Dīn in Herat, where he is described as suffering from what appears to be dysentery. In the chronicle sources, there is no mention of Burhān al-Dīn's last days in Herat. Barthold, in commenting on the Shaykh al-Islām's departure from Samarqand, emphasizes his politically weakened position at that time.

   "When 'Abd al-Raqqāq [the author of the *Maṭla'-i sa'dayn]* was writing his work, the Shaykh was still alive, but his arrival in Herat after Abū Sa'īd's death is not mentioned by this historian. In the light of the account given in the *Rashaḥāt*, only one fact can be regarded as authentic, viz. that the failure of Abū Sa'id's enterprise sponsored by the *īshān* provoked resentment against the latter in Samarqand, but that this movement subsided when Abū Sa'id's successor showed that the *ishan* continued to enjoy his unfailing respect and confidence." —V.V. Barthold, *Four Studies on the History of Central Asia*, trans. V. and T. Minorsky, Vol. 2: Ulugh Beg (Leiden, E.J. Brill, 1963), Vol. 2, p. 175
3. *Manāqib-i Aḥrār*, f. 122a.-123a.
4. *Ibid.*, f.123a.

historian with an example of opposition to Aḥrār from a powerful representative of the *'ulamā'* of late fifteenth century Central Asia. Indeed, the incident calls for a more complete investigation of the relations between Sufis and the *'ulamā'* in late fifteenth-century Samarqand to understand the depth of such controversy and competition, a task beyond the confines of this essay.[1]

The stories described above are rooted in the textual environment of hagiography in which Aḥrār is the focus. Through the telling of events and the relaying of stories and sayings, certain qualities of Aḥrār's spiritual and material life are expressed. A spectrum of propriety and impropriety pervades the dramas. The reader sees, for example, that it is more appropriate for the Sufi to partake in worldly affairs in order to benefit Muslim society than to withdraw from society. The reader witnesses the miraculous punishment of those who oppose justice, Islamic law, or Aḥrār. God is the ultimate judge of propriety and impropriety, but in the hagiographical stories Aḥrār appears to be his representative.

Proper conduct describes the moral discipline necessary to attain the ultimate goal of perfection of the soul. Stories which describe such conduct also contribute to the idealization of Aḥrār as a Sufi master *(pīr)*. Stories which illustrate a violation of righteous behavior also define the mystical virtues of Aḥrār, the proof of his good thoughts and deeds, and the miraculous abilities he possessed in setting propriety in balance. They also provide a symbolic image of Aḥrār as an inviolable individual. Behavior such as harassment, insults, and expressions of disbelief violated Aḥrār's social position as well as his saintliness, and warranted severe action. Behavior such as oppression and injustice as practiced by rulers could not be tolerated either. Understood comparatively, the sum of stories such as those described present the reader with a series of idealizations, a pattern of moral and ethical priorities, and a pool of historical data which, taken together with other sources such as chronicles, correspondence, and documents, may provide a deeper understanding of the role of one Central Asian Shaykh within the Persian mystical tradition.

In this brief study it has been shown that hagiographical stories, particularly those concerned with *karāmāt,* provide a rich source for understanding the idealization of Sufi Shaykhs. They also provide a source for understanding the social and economic history of the late Timurid period in Central Asia, a period during which the Naqshandiyya enjoyed prominence in Transoxiana and Khurasan. Surely opposition existed, as it did for any prominent *ṭarīqa* and Shaykh in the Islamic world—whether it focused on the form of practiced *dhikr,* the following of a certain Shaykh, the competition for economic resources, or prestige and influence among political leaders. The question remains, however, as to why a number of Aḥrār's miraculous acts appear to be so excessive, many of which concern either the boundaries of political authority or the worldly activities of Aḥrār. Certainly these examples are not the only types of *karāmāt* mentioned in the hagiographies of Aḥrār. There are others which are more innocuous and in line with those found in many

1. A thorough study of Burhān al-Dīn and his family is being undertaken by this author with the goal of further elucidating this question.

hagiographies in the Islamic world. Perhaps it was a particularly Central Asian development associated with folk Islam, or perhaps a local development in Timurid Central Asia.[1] Only further comparative research can shed light on these questions.

1. There are numerous examples of Turko-Mongolian practices of witchcraft mentioned in the sources for the history of the Mongols. In *The History of the World Conqueror*, for example, Juvaynī mentions the Mongol ruler Güyuk Khān's (r. 1246-48) wife, Fāṭima Khātūn. She is claimed to have bewitched a certain Köten. The structure of the story is strikingly similar to some of the stories concerning Aḥrār. Köten becomes more and more ill, and then eventually dies. – 'Aṭā-Malik Juvaynī, *The History of the World Conqueror*, trans. J.A. Boyle, (Cambridge: Harvard University Press 1958), vol. 2, pp.. 244-247. Her powers were so feared that she was eventually executed. The same story is related by William of Rubrick in *The Mongol Mission: Narratives and Letters of the Franciscan Missionaries in Mongolia and China in the Thirteenth and Fourteenth Centuries* (New York: Sheed and Ward 1955), p. 203. Shamanist and other Turko-Mongolian folk beliefs may have had some influence on the structure and format of such *karāmāt* stories found in these Central Asian hagiographies. I am grateful to Thomas Allsen for his comments and suggestions regarding this issue.

SHĀH NI'MATULLĀH WALĪ

Founder of the Ni'matullāhī Sufi Order

Terry Graham

The powerful Sufi master Shāh Ni'matullāh Walī (731/1330-834/1431), told the mightiest ruler of the day, Tamerlane:

While your domain stretches
from China to Shiraz,
Mine is a realm
which has no frontier.[1]

Born in Aleppo in 731/1331 A.D. of an Arab father (tracing his descent through nineteen generations back to the Prophet) and a Persian mother, Sayyid Nūr al-Dīn Ni'matullāh Kirmānī, better known as Shāh Ni'matullāh Walī, was introduced to Sufism at the age of five, when his dervish father, Mīr 'Abdullāh, took him to a Sufi gathering. The seeds sown at this early age gradually sprouted into a desire to find guidance at the hands of a perfect master. Aleppo was the centre of Ibn 'Arabī's school of the 'Unity of Being' *(waḥdat al-wujūd)*, so that Shāh Ni'matullāh was well-placed to profit from an education that included not only the traditional sciences but an input from the theosophy of Muḥyī al-Din ibn 'Arabī (d. 638/1240 AD), who had settled in Aleppo, where his tomb is a site of visitation to this very day. For further study in the religious sciences he went on to Shiraz, notable at the time as a centre for Shāfi'ite and other Sunni juridical studies. Thereby he entered the homeland of his mother for the first time.[2]

However, there came a point when no amount of book-learning could satisfy the young student's yearning; so, he set out to seek his master. In the course of his wanderings, he served many masters, each providing him help which was to serve him well when he was to encounter the master who was to take him to the highest station. It was in Mecca at the age of twenty-four that he came into contact with the Yemenite master, 'Ārif al-Dīn Abu Muḥammad 'Abdullāh ibn As'ad ibn Asī ibn Sulaymān Nazīl al-Ḥaramayn al-Yāfi'ī (698/1298—768/1367), whose stature was such that he had been given the authority of mastership by no less than six masters, linking him to several chains of initiation,[3] including the Shādhiliyya and the Qādiriyya, in which latter chain he founded the Yāfi'iyya branch, which survives

1. Jean Aubin, *Matériaux pour la biographie de Shāh Ni'matullāh Walī Kirmānī,* (Tehran & Paris, 1983), p. 200.
2. Aubin, *op.cit.*, pp.4 2-3, makes reference to Shāh Ni'matullāh's study in Shiraz.
3. J. Spencer Trimingham, *The Sufi Orders in Islam* (Oxford University Press 1971; rprt. 1973), p. 273.

today in the Yemen.

Apart from his prominence as a Sufi master, Yāfi'ī had an academic reputation of some note, being both a jurist and a collector of Prophetic traditions *(ḥadīth).*[1] He was also a historian whose works were to provide vital sources for the student of Sufism, as well as broader social history, the most notable of these being the *Mir'āt al-jinān wa 'ibād al-yaqẓān.*[2] Shāh Ni'matullāh spent seven years with Yāfi'ī, who brought him to an advanced level of spiritual knowledge and granted him the mandate of mastership. As a Shaykh of Yāfi'ī, he travelled in Egypt, where the hagiographies recount several miracles of him, indicating his possession of a significant spiritual presence by that time.[3] All such accounts are in the context of teaching, where Sufis of lower spiritual station were guided to higher perception through the insight which Shāh Ni'matullāh opened in them.

After residing for a time in Mecca, Shāh Ni'matullāh made his way eastward back to the Iranian cultural world, where he was to spend the rest of his days. After considerable travel, spending time in the northwestern Iranian region of Azerbaijan, he traveled eastward, then north, arriving in the early 1360s in the town of Shahr-i Sabz in the Transoxianan province of Khwārazm (in present-day Uzbekistan), in the heart of the dominions of Tamerlane *(Timūr-i Lang).*[4]

Despite Shāh Ni'matullāh's clear, even emphatic, abjuring of any political involvement and his declared disassociation from any sectarian position, his very success in attracting disciples excited the jealousy of other Islamic figures, who, in turn, roused the suspicions of the administrative authorities of the region. Shāh Ni'matullāh was not alone in innocently falling into the meshes of Timur's clerics and minions. Another prominent Sufi master, Sayyid 'Alī Hamadānī (714/1314—786/1385), the contemporary master in the Kubrawī Order, was likewise subjected to slander and summoned before the ruler.[5]

The conqueror's approach to religion and policy towards Sufis was ambiguous and, as Manz has pointed out, "was above all that of an opportunist; his religion served to further his aims, but almost never to circumscribe his actions....[His] religious practices with their admixture of Turco-Mongolian Shamanistic elements belonged to the Sufi tradition of the marches... Throughout his life [he] showed honour to the Sufi *shaykhs* who belonged to his inner circle."[6] On the other hand, such patronage was a poisoned chalice, for these cosseted masters were, for their

1. Sayyid Nūr al-Dīn Shāh Ni'matullāh Walī-yi Kirmānī), *Kulliyyāt-i Ash'ār-i Shāh Ni'matullāh Walī,* ed., Javad Nurbakhsh (Tehran 1982), p. 19.
2. Victor Danner (trans., annotated & intro), *Ibn 'Aṭā' llāh's Sufi Aphorisms (Kitāb al-ḥikam)* (Leiden: Brill 1973), p. 88, lists this and three other works in published editions.
3. 'Abd al-Razzāq Kirmānī, 'Manāqib-i Ḥaḍrat-i Shāh Ni'matullāh Walī', in Aubin, *op. cit.*, p. 37.
4. Aubin, *op.cit.*, pp. 39 & 283.
5. See Devin DeWeese, 'The Eclipse of the Kubraviyah in Central Asia,' in *Iranian Studies,* vol. XXI, Nos. 1-2, 1988, pp. 57-58, whose account is based on Ḥāfiẓ Ḥusayn Karabalā'ī Tabrīzī, *Rawḍāt al-jinān wa jannāt al-janān,* (Tehran: B.T.N.K., Persian texts series, No. 20, 1965) edited by Ja'far Sulṭān al-Qurrā'ī, pp. 68-69. De Weese notes that "According to the account, Hamadānī's presence in Khuttalān created such a stir that the *sayyid*'s detractors warned Timur of the size of his following, noting that Hamadānī was claiming political authority." (Cf. also De Weese's essay on Hamadānī in this volume. -Ed.)
6. Beatrice Forbes Manz, *The Rise and Rule of Tamerlane* (Cambridge University Press 1989), p. 17.

Portrait of Shāh Ni'matullāh Walī, Museum of Deccan, India.

part, obliged to attest to Timur's "superior spiritual powers" and "to justify his invasion and conquest of Islamic lands."[1]

Hence, he was susceptible to pressure from court Sufis to take policy decisions against those who demurred from sycophancy, and although inclined to exercise clemency in his treatment of independent masters, he was often obliged to take measures against them if the call became too great for him to ignore. This was certainly the case with respect to both the *Sayyids* Shāh Ni'matullāh and 'Alī Hamadānī. It was, in fact, this family connection with the Prophet—being a key focus of respect and devotion for the Shi'ites—which buttressed the claims of the detractors of these two masters at the Timurid court that there was a political dimension to their activity. Whereas not only did neither master have any worldly ambition, but they were both squarely Sunnis by education and formation. They were as remote as they could be from the so-called 'Alid (or 'Alī-supporting) cause of the Shi'ites: Shāh Ni'matullāh was Ḥanafī from the point of view of juridical affiliation, as was appropriate to a man who hailed from Syria, though sympathetic to the Shāfi'īs (also befitting a man who had studied in Shiraz), and Hamadānī was Shāfi'ī as was common for a native of western Iran before the Safavid period.[2] At this juncture a brief comment on the juridical affiliation of Shāh Ni'matullāh is in order.

Jean Aubin, in the introduction to his edition of the Persian hagiographies of Shāh Ni'matullāh, places the master very securely in the Sunnite circles of the city of Shiraz, stressing the importance of the capital of Fars as "the domain of religious [i.e. Sunni Ḥanafī and Shāfi'ī) literature" in the intellectual life of Mongol and Timurid Iran. Aubin urges that further research needs to be undertaken with respect to Shāh Ni'matullāh's theosophical and intellectual background, saying:

> "Dans le cas précis qui nous retient il sera nécessaire, pour comprendre l'originalité de la pensée de Ni'matullah et le retentissement qu'elle a pu avoir, de connaître la vie des madrasas shīrāzīes que lui-même fréquenta dans son adolescence, avant de trouver en Yāfi'ī, à La Mecque, le murshid de ses désirs."[3]

It is hardly necessary to mention that if any city in Iran in Shāh Ni'matullāh's time was associated with Sunnite Islam, it was Shiraz,[4] home of the renowned Shāfi'ite jurist Abu Isḥāq Fīrūzābādī (d. 476/1083), the founding chancellor of the Niẓāmiyya college in Baghdad (established 459/1067), who wrote with equal authority on Ḥanafī jurisprudence, if not setting the stamp on Shiraz's preeminence in both schools, then certainly confirming it for the succeeding centuries, up to the Safavid takeover.

Among Shāh Ni'matullāh's early teachers in the religious and other sciences were many notable Sunni scholars including Rukn al-Dīn Shīrāzī, Shams al-Dīn

1. *Ibid.*
2. On Hamadānī see Marijan Molé, 'Les Kubrawiya entre Sunnisme et Shiisme aux huitième et neuvième siècles de l'Hégire,' in *Revue des Etudes Islamiques* (1961), pp.113-115, who provides a thoroughgoing discussion.
3. *Matériaux pour la biographie de Shāh Ni'matullāh.Walī Kirmānī*, p. 18-19.
4. Annemarie Schimmel notes that "a book written in the late fourteenth century about the venerated tombs of Shiraz, Junayd-i Shīrāzī's *Shadd al-izār*, gives us the impression that the whole of Shiraz consisted exclusively of pious Sunnis." 'The Ornament of Saints: The Religious Situation in Iran in Pre-Safavid Times,' *Iranian Studies*, vol. 7 (1974), p. 105.

Makkī, Sayyid Jalāl al-Dīn Khwārazmī and Qāḍī 'Aḍud al-Dīn 'Uyūn, who is very probably the famous Qāḍī 'Aḍud al-Dīn Ījī (d. 1356).[1] Ījī ('Aḍudī—as he was known familiarly) who held the office of chief *Qāḍī* in Shiraz under Abū Isḥāq Īnjū (d. 1358), the ruler of Fars, and was cited in a eulogy to him[2] was best known for his "*Mawāqif*, a kind of Summa Theologica," which was "the standard work in scholastic theology" during the period.[3] As J. van Ess has noted, "Shi'ite sources... leave no doubt that Ījī always defended the Sunnite cause."[4] Although Ījī was a Shāfi'ite and Shāh Ni'matullāh came from the Ḥanafite domain of Syria, there was a great deal of interchange between followers of the two schools.

Of the theological and juridical authorities cited as teachers of Shāh Ni'matullāh, Khwārazmī (d. unkn), known as *Tāj al-sharī'a* (The Crown of the Religious Law), a distinctively Sunni title, was a notable jurisprudent in Shāfi'ite law, writing the juridical text, *Kifāya fī sharḥ al-hidāya.*[5] As for Rukn al-Dīn Shīrāzī (d. 768/1367), he is the sole figure mentioned among Shāh Ni'matullāh's teachers who was not specifically a juridical or theological authority and therefore, identifiable with a particular school of jurisprudence. This man is, of course, the Sufi and theosopher known affectionately as "Bābā Ruknā Shīrāzī," the author of the *Nuṣūṣ al-khuṣūṣ fī tarjumat al-Fuṣūṣ*, a Persian commentary on Ibn 'Arabī's *Fuṣūṣ al-ḥikam.*[6] He must have had a seminal influence on Shāh Ni'matullāh's proficiency in this school of theosophy.

Shāh Ni'matullāh's close friend in Shiraz, where he was received so warmly by a great throng and feted by the prince, Iskandar, was 'Alī ibn Muḥammad Sayyid Sharīf Jurjānī (d. 816/1413), Sufi theosopher and Ḥanafite jurist.[7] Given the warmth of his reception of Shāh Ni'matullāh in Shiraz as an old friend, there is some suggestion that they might have been fellow students in the city years before, Jurjānī having been eight years the master's junior. In 779/1377 he was given an official teaching post in Shiraz, where he remained—apart from a seventeen-year exile in Samarqand under Timur's reign, from 789/1387 to 807/1404 (during which period he also composed a commentary on Ījī's *Mawāqif*)[8]—until the latter's death, a lion of the city's intellectual milieu.[9]

Apart from Shāh Ni'matullāh's educational background, there is an interesting set of arguments in connection with his relationship with Aḥmad Shāh Bahmanī which may be adduced towards proving the master's Sunni background. It has been maintained by some scholars that Aḥmad Shāh had become a Shi'ite and that this 'Shi'itization' had attracted him to the allegedly 'Shi'ite' Shāh Ni'matullāh. However, this line of approach seems to be based on the casuistry of Shi'ite-oriented

1. See J. Nurbakhsh, *Pīrān-i ṭariqat* (Tehran 1976), p.39
2. See Muḥammad 'Alī Mudarris, *Rayḥānat al-adab* (Tehran 1967), pp. 143-44.
3. Annemarie Schimmel, 'Ḥāfiẓ and his Contemporaries,' *The Cambridge History of Iran*, vol. 6 (Cambridge University Press 1986), p. 929.
4. See s.v.'Adudu'd-Dīn Ījī', *Encyclopaedia Iranica*, vol. 3 (New York 1989), p. 269.
5. 'Alī-Akbar Dihkhudā, *Lughatnāma*, vol. CLXII (Tehran 1962), p. 802.
6. Ed. Rajab-'Alī Maẓlūmī (Tehran 1980).
7. See Dihkhudā, *Lughatnāma*, vol. LXXVIII, p. 323; C. Brockelmann, *EI1*, s.v. 'Jurjānī'
8. Annemarie Schimmel, 'Ḥāfiẓ and his Contemporaries,' p. 930.
9. Cf. Aubin, *op. cit.*, p. 19.

writers who would wish to see these two figures as adherents to their school.

In his study of *Bidar: Its History and Monuments*[1] Yazdani demonstrates, on the contrary, that the epithet *Walī* conferred by Shāh Ni'matullāh on his royal disciple Aḥmad Shāh (later employed by the latter's subjects in reference to their king, and, of course, applied to Shāh Ni'matullāh himself by his followers)–could never have been utilized in a Shi'ite context, arguing that Shi'ites accord saintly status only to their Imāms and do not employ the term *Walī*. Yazdani maintains that all the evidence obtained from the mausoleum of Aḥmad Shāh indicates a Sunni connection for Shāh Ni'matullāh, doubly so, because of his having been a disciple of Yāfi'ī, who even today in his native Yemen is considered to be the founder of an offshoot of the Qādiriyya Order, one with an entirely Sunni pedigree and association. Moreover, besides the Qādirī connection, the official chain of initiation of the Ni'matullāhī Order is featured on the walls of the tomb, leading from Junayd to Yāfi'ī in a line of transmission which had proceeded in an exclusively Sunni context.

Ultimately, the last word should be given to Shāh Ni'matullāh himself. Although he wrote one of the most beautiful odes in the praise of the Shi'ite Imāms, *Walā-yi Murtiḍā*[2] and a magnificent eulogy of *'Alī-yi walī,*[3] the former poem still sung fervently today by Shi'ites, and the latter by Sufis of all stripes and colors, the master's view of Shi'ism was the same as that of his Kubrāwī contemporaries, such as Sayyid 'Alī Hamadānī, who respected the Shi'ite Imāms as *Walī*s in their own right, whereas when it came to an outright statement of affiliation, he provided no more succinct declaration of his Sunnism than the following verse:

Choose the Sunni path,
which is our school;
If you don't, you will stray
you will be in error.[4]

In conclusion, the fact that the immediate spiritual descendents of both Shāh Ni'matullāh and 'Alī Hamadānī turned to the Shi'ite fold is merely a reflection of the flexibility and tolerance with respect to outward forms which they had taught, where social and political circumstances were encountered which compelled conformity to a particular mould for the purpose of protecting the essential method: the pursuit and observance of the *ṭarīqa.*

While the juridical affiliation of these masters was merely a mark of their observance of the *Sharī'a,* the religious law, as the point of departure for the pursuit of the *ṭarīqa,* the spiritual Path, the matter of juridical affiliation carried sectarian weight for someone like Amīr Sayyid Kulāl Bukhārī (d. 773/1371), master of the eponym of the Naqshbandī Order, Bahā' al-Dīn Naqshband (d. 793/1391).[5] A native of the Central Asian region where Shāh Ni'matullāh had newly arrived, Amīr

1. (Oxford 1947), p. 115
2. Sayyid Nūr al-Dīn Shāh Ni'matullāh Walī-yi Kirmānī, *Kulliyyāt-i Shāh Ni'matullāh Walī,* pp. 755-56.
3. *Kulliyyāt-i Shāh,* pp. 758-59
4. *Kulliyyāt-i Shāh,* p. 688.
5. On the Naqshbandī Order, see the essays by Jo-Ann Gross and J.G.J. ter Haar in this volume. -Ed.

The Mausoleum of Shāh Ni'matullāh in Māhān, Iran

Kulāl felt threatened by the newcomer's success in what he, Amīr Kulāl, viewed as the competition to win the hearts and minds of the Turks, Tajiks and Tatars of Turkestan.

As one of several masters of Timur whose affinity for the Sufis led him to 'collect' masters as an avocation, Amīr Kulāl pressured the ruler, as his spiritual protégé, to suppress Shāh Ni'matullāh's activity. Timur's primary religious loyalty, as Manz points out, "belonged almost certainly to the Naqshbandī Sufi Order whose power and influence was already well fixed in Transoxiana,"[1] and what with his politically expedient desire to associate himself with Islamic legitimacy, it was logical for the ruler to prefer affiliation with this order, which gave him the cachet of association with Sunna orthodoxy and Sufism at the same time.

The irony of the situation was that, while Amīr Kulāl alleged to Timur that Shāh Ni'matullāh was carrying the banner for some sort of Shi'ite or 'Alawite uprising, the object of his venom not only harboured no political ambitions, but was even a fellow member of Kulāl's juridical school, the Sunni Ḥanafī! What served to Shāh Ni'matullāh's detriment, however, is that he refused to make a sectarian issue of juridical affiliation, so that his very Sufi detachment[2] from such forms allowed his enemies to allege 'softness' on his part towards whatever shibboleth they had in their minds to attack. It was easy enough for those with sectarian interests at stake to brand popular Sufi masters, like Shāh Ni'matullāh and Hamadāni, as crypto-Shi'ites and, hence, 'heretics', as well as would-be rebels against the state, particularly if they happened to be *sayyids*, as well.

The pressure put on Timur resulted in a difficult situation for the ruler, who desired the harmony and support of all the spiritual figures in his domain, if for no other reason than to have their political influence in converting and pacifying the nomadic tribes of the region. Shāh Ni'matullāh was someone whom he had welcomed with particular warmth. According to the account given in Ṣunullāh

---

1. Manz. *op. cit.*, p. 17.
2. Cf. his *Dīwān* (p. 859) where he abjures any association with sectarianism, declaring:

If they ask me
what is my sect,
O unaware ones,
what sect, indeed!

I have the mirrors
of Shāfi'ī
and Abu Ḥanīfa
standing before me.

All the founders
are good for the Path,
But I have a sect
from my ancestor.

In the science of the prophets
and walīs
I possess the most
attainments.

Ni'matullāhī's hagiographical *Risāla,* when Shāh Ni'matullāh first arrived in Samarqand,[1] Timur sent a messenger to him asking whether he should visit him to pay his respects or should it be the other way round. The master replied, "We should both observe the protocol of the Prophet."[2] Then he interpreted this instruction in the mild tones of spiritual counsel, saying, "Blessed is the ruler who visits and attends to a dervish [or 'pauper,' these being the same word in Persian]. Now what you do is up to you."[3]

When Timur received this reply, he reflected on it, then decided to heed the spiritual admonition implied therein. Thus, he made the move to visit Shāh Ni'matullāh first; then, having observed the protocol of paying his respects to the 'man of religious poverty', he invited the master to the place for a feast of welcome, an occasion which prompted these verses from Shāh Ni'matullāh:

If you would entertain Ni'matullāh
you must spread the festive cloth around the world
But if you build a little cottage to suit his desire
you must enclose the world's seven climes within four walls.[4]

Having been so grandly feted, Shāh Ni'matullāh became so much sought after by the populace of Samarqand, flocking to his doors, that he was forced to seek refuge in the mountains for solitude, where he embarked upon a course of three forty-day retreats *(chilla)* in a cave in the dead of winter with the snow lying deep round about him at a site where there was no human habitation within fifty miles in any direction.[5] The ascetic rigour of these retreats only enhanced his reputation with the Turko-Mongolian nomads who thronged about him in large numbers to be initiated. 'Abd al-Razzāq Kirmānī cites a source maintaining that "in one day ninety thousand persons pledged allegiance. One would seize the master's hand, another the hem of his robe; and in like manner a whole desertful of people pledged allegiance at once. They say that so many people handled his cloak that it was in tatters."[6]

Shāh Ni'matullāh was seen as a protector of the nomads' flocks and herds. When disease and pestilence were warded off, the "Turks, displaying simple faith, came to him, and thereafter no plague afflicted their animals. The next year they returned to the same site and pledged allegiance every one."[7] Thus, Shāh Ni'matullāh had been well-received by Timur, who had given him full licence to go about his work, building a mosque and establishing a *khānaqāh* in Shahr-i Sabz, to which the population of the area were drawn, notably the Turkish-speaking nomadic tribes. The

1. While Shāh Ni'matullāh's sojourn in Transoxiana took place in the course of the 1360's the only relatively precise time-frame which can be deduced is that the events culminating in his expulsion from Transoxiana occurred sometime between 770/1368 and 772/1370–Aubin, *op. cit.*, p. 13.
2. The *ḥadīth* in question is not cited by the biographer.
3. Ṣun'ullāh Ni'matullāhī's account as retold by Mufīd Mustawfī Yazdī in the *Jāma'-yi Mufīdī'*, cited in Aubin, *op. cit.*, p. 164.
4. Ṣunullāh Ni'matullāhī, *op. cit.*, p. 165. The "seven climes" constituted the entire geography of the world as the ancients conceived of it.
5. *Ibid.* & ff.
6. 'Manāqib-i Ḥaḍrat-i Shāh Ni'matullāh Walī', in Aubin, *op.cit.*, p. 122.
7. *Ibid.* The adoption of Islam and Sufism on a communal basis, not merely on the individual level, was characteristic of other Sufi Orders during this period as well. Cf. D. DeWeese's essay in this volume. -Ed.

master's popularity was such that people were flocking in large numbers to be initiated.

Kirmāni goes on to recount that it was Amīr Kulāl, "a master belonging to the lineage of the reverend Bahā' al-Dīn Naqshband," who first sounded the alarm to Timur, balefully warning, "A number of armed persons have sworn allegiance to him. If he lays claim to the kingship, there will be no chance for resistance." Timur's natural response to this dire warning was: "Two kings in a land can only mean trouble."[1]

Thus, Amīr Kulāl, in his powerful position of spiritual advisor to the ruler, represented Shāh Ni'matullāh's activities as political, indeed as a threat to Timur's very dominion, though there was no evidence to prove this. The very fact that, once Timur was compelled to act, he did no more than ask Shāh Ni'matullāh to leave the sensitive Central Asian territory, indicating that he had no personal suspicion of the master's motives and that his action was simply to conciliate the zealots around him, who had masked their self-interest in promoting their narrow brand of sectarian Islam—their spiritual fife, as it were—as the moral principle of safeguarding the political domain of Timur. Bearing no resentment towards Timur, Shāh Ni'matullāh departed from the region, assessing the ruler's limitations in the following verses, implying that his being doctrinaire about the religious law did not make his spirituality any deeper or his policies any more humane!

Ay ki pursī zi ḥāl-i Mīr Timūr / bā tū gūyam ki ḥāl-i ū chūn būd
Gar chi chap būd rāst rah mīraft / rāstī raftanish bi qānūn būd

O you who ask about Timur,
I'll tell you what he was like:
Though deviant, he travelled straight;
In truth, his course was by the Law.[2]

* * *

Pādshāhān-i jahān bisyār dīdastam, walī
Hamchū ān Sulṭān Timur sulṭān-i langī hast nīst.

I've seen many a king in this world, but
There is no sultan as lame as Timurlane.[3]

The first two couplets cited above provide an excellent example of Shāh Ni'matullāh's skillful use of word-play, testimony to his facility as both a poet and a satirist.[4] The words *chap* and *rāst* mean respectively 'left' and 'right' but here they are both given double meanings with *chap* given its other sense of 'deviant' and *rāst* presented as a pun, having the dual sense that its cognate, 'right', has in English. In the last-cited verse the poet's acid pen gives a regal drum-roll of long-syllabic *ān*-s *(pādshāhān, sulṭān, jahān)* to underscore his satire of the monarch, playing on his handicap of being 'lame', which contains the same pair of connota-

1. Ibid.
2. *Kulliyyāt-i Shāh,* p. 853.
3. *Kulliyyāt-i Shāh,* p. 175
4. The tradition of satire in mediæval Persian Sufi poetry is discussed by Hasan Javadi in his *Satire in Persian Literature* (London: Assocated University Press 1988), pp. 71-75.

tions as in English.

The same story is retold, without mention however, of the Naqshbandiyya connection by Ṣunullāh Ni'matullāhī, according to whom Timur's message to Shāh Ni'matullāh was almost apologetic in tone: "Although I have the utmost confidence in you, the corrupt folk around me keep badgering me. It would be best if you were to move to another domain."[1] Shah Ni'matullah acceded to Timur's request but made his position clear in a *ghazal* which suggests that the ruler had sought discipleship with him, but only on his own terms:

Off with you, my prince!
Don't flaunt gold and silver before me!
Stop causing trouble for others;
If you keep on harassing, you too will be harassed!
If you suffer from headaches and hangover,
how can you keep the company of a drunk like me?
My speech is that
of a spirit-expanding Cupbearer;
My breath is that
of a sweet-singing minstrel.
While your domain stretches
from China to Shiraz,
Mine is a realm
which has no frontier.
I serve only
this King of mine;
You go and vaunt
your throne and crown.
Ni'matullāh is the master
of all the rinds,
If you're a disciple,
submit to your master.[2]

Having sent this *ghazal* off to Timur, Ṣunullāh Ni'matullāhī relates that Shāh Ni'matullāh departed from the region, stopping briefly as the home of a friend, Zakariyyā Bāghī. It is said that on the very day when he made this move, Timur fell ill with a host of maladies. Becoming aware that the cause of his indisposition was his breach of the etiquette required by sages and spiritual authorities, he attempted to make amends by humbling himself and taking recourse in the master, begging his forgiveness and seeking his blessing. Timur having made his peace with him, Shāh Ni'matullāh departed.[3]

Leaving Transoxiana around 771/1369, Shah Ni'matullāh stopped at the first major city south of that region, Mashhad, where he went into retreat for forty days.[4] Then he proceeded eastward to Herat, where he spent a year (772/1370 or 773/1371), time enough for him to share in the growing cultural and spiritual life of that city and to marry the granddaughter of Mīr Ḥusaynī Harawī (d. ca. 772/1370), the

1. Aubin, *op. cit.*, p. 167.
2. *Kulliyyāt-i Shāh*, p. 412.
3. Ṣunullāh Ni'matullāhī's account in Aubin, *op. cit.*, p. 167-68.
4. Aubin, *op. cit.*, p. 45.

Sufi Shaykh whose questions, sent to Maḥmūd Shabistarī, prompted the composition of the *Gulshan-i rāz (Rosegarden of Mystery)*, that remarkable summary of Sufi doctrine in poetical form.[1]

From Herat, Shāh Ni'matullāh journeyed southward to the village of Ku-banan, in the mountains near Kerman, where he spent seven years and where his son and successor-to-be, Khalīlullāh, was born in 775/1373. From his centre in Kū-banān he travelled extensively to the communities of the mountains and the plains west of that region, visiting the city of Yazd and such outlying towns and villages as Taft, Bāfq and Abarquh, where he initiated disciples and built *khānaqāhs*.[2]

His following grew so great and there became such a demand from people far and near to visit him that he felt it necessary to move out of his mountain retreat to an area more accessible to the world. He decided on the nearby city of Kerman for a time, then settled ultimately in a village on the highway south of the city, Māhān, which had the advantage of being a small community away from the hurly-burly of urban life, while at the same time being easily reached because of its location on the main route to the Indian Subcontinent. This location was to take on special significance in the last few years of Shāh Ni'matullāh's life, for in 832/1429, as a consequence of the master's far-reaching fame, an appeal came to him from a ruler with a particularly saintly reputation in his own domain, Aḥmad Shāh I of the Bahmanī dynasty, ruling the Deccan in central India. Formerly a disciple of the famous Chishtī master, Gīsūdarāz (d. 825/1422), upon the latter's death, he set about looking for a new master.

Shāh Ni'matullāh's reputation having reached him, he wrote to the master, pleading for him to come to his court. The aging Shāh Ni'matullāh had no inclination for travel but sent a chosen disciple as his emissary, bearing an initiatory *tāj* (traditional Sufi crown) and a letter, addressing him as "the greatest of kings, Shihāb al-Dīn Aḥmad Shāh Walī."[3] Not only was this a signal honor, conferred by a master, but Aḥmad Shāh's piety was such that, having properly earned it, he became the only king in Indian Muslim history to be called a *Walī* by his people, Hindu and Muslim alike.

Upon a second appeal by Aḥmad Shāh, the master sent his grandson, Nūrullāh, to represent him. The warmth of the young man's welcome is indicated by the fact that he was given the hand of the king's daughter in marriage and provided an established place in the city of Bidar at the court of the king who called himself "the meanest of Shāh Ni'matullāh's disciples."[4]

The spiritual importance of Aḥmad Shāh Walī is reflected in the pomp of the *'urs,* the annual commemoration of the death of a Sufi saint, which is observed in his honor to this very day by Muslim and Hindu alike. The ecumenical spirituality and Sufi-like tolerance of this monarch is evinced by the strongly Hindu nature of the ceremony with the blowing of the conch and other features of Hindu ritual,

1. On Shabistarī, see the essay by L. Lewisohn in this volume.
2. Javad Nurbakhsh, *Zindagī wa āthār-i Shāh Ni'matullāh Walī-yi Kirmānī* (Tehran 1959), pp. 34-35; 105.
3. Nurbakhsh, *Zindagī wa āthār-i Shāh,* p. 45.
4. Ibid.

while the presiding figure wears a Sufi *tāj* and cloak for this event, which "is attended by thousands of Hindus and Muslims who consider Aḥmad to be a saint without any distinction whatever."[1]

The way was prepared for a second migration of the Ni'matullāhī family away from religious sectarianism. Where Shāh Ni'matullāh himself had yielded to the narrow-mindedness and self-interest of Timur's Sunni counsellors, his son and successor, Khalīlullāh (d. 859/1455) followed his nephew in exile, bringing the rest of the family to the Bahmanī court, taking refuge from the fanatical Shi'ite dogmatism of the Safavids.

One might well wonder why a man of such power should seem to run away or prepare the way to send his successor away from conflict rather than facing up to it—a man who could guide kings. The reason is that he was essentially a man of peace, following the classical Sufi principle of steering clear of politics, sectarianism or any such divisive activity in the 'world of multiplicity'.[2] As he said of himself in verse:

Throughout my life not an ant
has suffered from me;
This has been my way in the past
and so will ever be.[3]

This verse was composed towards the end of a lifetime which lasted a full century. Shāh Ni'matullāh died on a visit to Kerman in 834/1431.

The master's gentleness and pliancy is shown in his policy of accepting disciples. Where some masters had an elitist approach to Sufism, he would accept all who sincerely sought him out, declaring, "I accept anyone who has been rejected by all the friends of God *(awliyā')*, perfecting him according to his capacity."[4]

An incident during his last journey away from the Māhān-Kerman area in 812/1409 illustrates his tenderness of nature. Invited to Shiraz by the governor of Fars, Iskandar ibn 'Umar Shaykh, a grandson of Timur, Shāh Ni'matullāh was met at the tomb of Sa'dī just outside the city by an enthusiastic multitude. In the welcoming throng was the distinguished philosopher and gnostic, Sayyid Sharīf Jurjānī, who greeted and embraced the master. At that very moment it began to rain, prompting Jurjānī to exclaim with a pun: "God's bounty *(ni'matullāh)* in my arms and God's mercy *(raḥmatullāh)* upon my head!"[5]

Jurjānī's very presence was a mark of the change in era from the harsh intolerance of Timur to the clemency and generous spirit of the tyrant's sons and grandsons. Exiled from Shiraz to Samarqand by Timur, he was permitted to return to the city by his son Shāh Rukh. It was symbolic of the times that the scholar Jurjānī, the

1. H.K. Sherwani, 'Cultural Influences under Aḥmad Shāh Walī Bahmanī', *Islamic Culture* (1944) p. 375
2. On the traditional avoidance of contact by Sufis and *'ulamā'* with rulers in this period, see A.K.S. Lambton, *Continuity and Change in Medieval Persia* (London: I.B. Tauris 1988), pp. 311-314, where the author cites Ghazzālī's *Iḥyā' 'ulūm al-dīn* by way of providing a statement of this principle.
3. Javad Nurbakhsh, *Pīrān-i ṭarīqat*, p. 45.
4. *Ibid.*, p. 47.
5. *Zindagī wa āthār-i Shāh Ni'matullāhWalī-yi Kirmānī*, p. 44.

master Shāh Ni'matullāh, and the ruler Iskandar should all three prostrate together at Shiraz's 'Aṭīq Mosque during the Friday congregational prayers. As Kirmānī recounts the incident:

> On Friday it happened that the Prince, the Master and the Philosopher gathered together for prayer in the royal chamber of the 'Atiq Mosque of Shiraz. The Prince presided. Ḥāfiẓ Rāzī, the Sultan's minister and a student of Sayyid Sharīf, spread his teacher's prayer-carpet to the right of the Sultan. The notables and the populace came to await the Master's arrival. Suddenly he entered the mosque through the doorway of the great bazaar and the crowd fell to kissing his hand and welcoming him, while the Philosopher greeted him from the royal chamber. The crowd pressed in so closely that the Philosopher was nearly trampled underfoot, but the Master seized his hand, pulling him out of the crowd and into the chamber. The Philosopher then picked up his prayer-carpet himself and placed it to the left of the Sultan. Ḥāfiẓ Rāzī wondered at his teacher's gesture, but he replied, "Let it alone. You don't understand the mystical states of the Friends of God *(awliyā)*."[1]

Shāh Rukh's reign provided a period of respite from sectarian strife in Iran, when many groups coexisted in harmony and Sufism, in particular, enjoyed a significant expansion.[2] Shāh Rukh set the standard for both tolerance and cultivation of the arts and sciences by supporting his wife, Gawhar Shād, in her sponsorship of the repair and embellishment of Khurasan's holiest Shi'ite shrine, the tomb of Imām Riḍā, though the couple were Sunnis themselves. Although the ruler was not initiated by Shāh Ni'matullāh, he held him in great respect, giving him free rein in his activities, while his nephew Iskandar was the patron for the construction of a mosque for the master in Shiraz, after having previously, as governor of Yazd, supported the master's projects in that region, including the building of a splendid *khānaqāh* in Taft.[3]

Shāh Ni'matullāh represented the outward contrasts which a man of high station presents to the surface-seeing eye. If he was a humble man who wielded power over kings, he was also a wealthy man who lived in poverty. When he was not engaged in writing his voluminous opus of prose and poetic works, he applied himself to farming, an occupation by which he supported himself during his year in Herat between Transoxiana and Kerman. Despite the vast amount of donations he received from devotees in Māhān, he lived in the utmost simplicity, turning the funds into constructive activity, such as the building and maintenance of *khānaqāhs* and the support of those in need.

Setting an example with his occupation of farming, he encouraged his disciples to take up professions, whereby "the disciples of the Ni'matullāhī Order became actively engaged in social activity, leaving off idleness and indolence. His counsel to the disciples was that the best asceticism and the finest way to purify the heart and refine the *nafs* [the ego or lower soul] was kindness towards others and service to society."[4] In fact, the farmer-master's activity in Herat occasioned a witty exchange with a disciple, who cried out in praise, "O falcon of the Sacred Realm, you are a householder who is tied down *(taqyīd)*, while spiritually aspiring and

---

1. Aubin, *op. cit.*, pp. 86-87.
2. Ehsan Yarshater, *Shi'r-i fārsī dar 'ahd-i Shāh Rukh* (Tehran 1334 A.Hsh.), pp. 42-44.
3. Aubin, *op. cit.*, pp. 105; 48.
4. *Pīrān-i ṭarīqat*, p. 45.

detached from the world *(tafrīd).*" Shāh Ni'matullāhī allegedly replied, "Yes, indeed, if I am a falcon of spiritual state, I have become a teal of the fields."[1] (The term "teal of the field" involves a pun on *marghābī,* one who cultivates *margh,* a rich grass in a *marghāb,* the well-watered ground in which it grows, and *murghābī,* meaning 'duck' or 'teal', as well as referring to an inhabitant of the Murghāb, a region near Herat, watered by the river of that name).

This vocation and service was, of course, in Shāh Ni'matullāh's teaching fundamentally a vital adjunct to the wayfarer's progress on the Path. As he taught in a verse:

Remember God, O friend, abundantly
Engage in inner work while doing the outer.[2]

Kirmānī remarks on Shāh Ni'matullāh's commitment to farming, describing "his total concern for agriculture of various kinds and his periodic activity in this field." Whenever he was properly settled, as he was for a time with his new bride in Herat, "he enjoyed a fruitful yield."[3] Shāh Ni'matullāh's stress on social activity was not merely an ethical or moral injunction. It was part of the master's program of spiritual development, where "the Ni'matullāhī dervish's involvement in social activity caused expansion through Divine favour to overcome contraction in their natures, driving listless and constricted apathy out of the preoccupations of the head and replacing it with the falcon of cheerful commitment, soaring in the firmament of the heart."[4]

Shāh Ni'matullāh not only had a policy of guidance on the social plane, but he was also an authority on the theosophy of Ibn 'Arabī, leaving an extensive body of treatises, 130 of which have recently been collected, edited and published in four volumes by Javad Nurbakhsh.[5] Dr. Nurbakhsh has also brought out the master's weighty Divan of *ghazals, mathnawis,* quatrains and other forms of poetry, as well as having written and published a biography of Shāh Ni'matullāh.[6] The collected treatises include the master's exposition of the principles and practice of Sufism and his disquisitions on the doctrine of the Unity of Being *(waḥdat-i wujūd),* as well as commentaries on Ibn 'Arabī's *Fuṣūṣ.*

The power of Shāh Ni'matullāh's discourse is particularly marked in his use of symbolic metaphor to illustrate his exposition of the doctrine, effectively describing existential reality from the Sufi point of view. He portrays reality variously as the sea, with determined forms as waves and bubbles, to present the illusory nature of multiplicity and the transitoriness of the determined forms of existence, and as a point, with the circle created by the motion of the point representing the phenomenal manifestations of Being. Through some metaphors he expounds the paradox presented by Ibn 'Arabī that the world is a phantom of the imagination, while the

1. Aubin, *op. cit.*, p. 45.
2. *Ibid.*
3. *Ibid..*, p. 45.
4. *Pīrān-i ṭarīqat,* pp. 45-46.
5. *Risālahā-yi Shāh Ni'matullāh Walī-yi Kirmānī,* edited by J. Nurbakhsh (Tehran: Intishārāt-i Khānaqāh-i Ni'matullāhī 1976-78)
6. See p. 174, note 1 and p. 184, note 2 above.

imagination is in itself an aspect of Reality, being one of the five planes, or 'presences,' *(ḥaḍarāt)* of Being.

Shāh Ni'matullāh's relationship with Ibn 'Arabī[1] and his thought puts him in the unique position of being the sole founder of an important classical Sufi *ṭarīqa* who was a conscious expositor of the doctrine of the 'Greatest Teacher' *(al-Shaykh al-akbar)*, although Orders like the Naqshbandiyya and the Shādhiliyya are represented, of course, by commentators appearing in subsequent generations, such as, respectively, Jāmī and Zarrūq.[2] One expression of Shāh Ni'matullāh's position was his paraphrasing of Akbarian doctrine in simple doggerel of a sort that students and disciples could easily use as a mnemonic device. This style pervades, for instance, his *Glossary of Sufi Technical Terms*[3] which is largely an adaptation and Persian translation of the Arabic language *Iṣṭilaḥāt al-ṣūfiyya* by 'Abd al-Razzāq Kāshānī (d. 740/1339),[4] himself a noted interpreter of this school. Shāh Ni'matullāh's expressions of Sufi doctrine are rather second-rate in this treatise from a poetic standpoint, in fact little more than jingles, but they take a more eloquent form in his Divan.

One might say that Shāh Ni'matullāh's original contribution consists in his making of Ibn 'Arabī's enunciated doctrine an applied science. Where Ibn 'Arabī was fundamentally a thinker and a teacher, Shāh Ni'matullāh was first and foremost, a practitioner, a master, concerned with the guidance of disciples on the *ṭarīqa*. Ibn 'Arabī's teachings provided the theoretical background for Shāh Ni'matullāh's programme of training. Although it is quite unfair to characterize the master, as does Trimingham,[5] merely as a "prolific writer of Sufi ephemeras, both prose and poetry," it is true that there is relatively little that is original in Shāh Ni'matullāh's prose treatises, much of it derived from the work of the Akbarian school as represented by his near contemporaries, Kāshānī, who represented the third generation of commentators on the *Fuṣūṣ*, after Qūnyawī and Jandī.[6] Jandī's student Kāshānī, followed by his own pupil, Dāwūd Qayṣārī (d. 751/1350), "wrote what are probably the two most influential commentaries of the tradition," where from Qūnawī on down, in "all these commentators, discussion of *Wujūd* ('Existence') stands at the forefront."[7] Shāh Ni'matullāh's two short treatises, *Wujūd* and *Wujūdiyya,*[8] reflect his direct involvement in this tradition.

Two of the most interesting series of Shāh Ni'matullāh's treatises are those con-

---

1. He directly acknowledges the doctrinal source of his teaching as emanating from Muḥyī al-Din Ibn 'Arabī (d. 638/1240 AD) in an oft-quoted verse:

> *The words of the* Fuṣūṣ *settled in our heart*
> *Like the bezel that is placed in the setting of a ring.*

2. M. Chodkiewicz, 'The Diffusion of Ibn 'Arabī's Doctrine' *Journal of the Muhyiddin Ibn 'Arabi Society*, vol. 9 (1991), p. 51.
3. *Risālahā-yi Shāh Ni'matullāh Walī-yi Kirmānī*, vol. 4, pp. 1-184.
4. Ed. Muḥammad Kamāl Ibrāhim Ja'far (Cairo 1981). Also see the recent English translation of this treatise by Nabil Safwat, *A Glossary of Sufi Technical Terms* (London: Octagon Press 1991)
5. *Op. cit.*, p. 101.
6. See William Chittick, *The Sufi Path of Knowledge* (Albany: SUNY 1989), p. xviii.
7. *Ibid.*
8. *Risālahā-yi Shāh*, vol. 3, pp. 286-97.

cerning the *sharī'a* and the *ṭarīqa*.[1] An example of how he treats the *sharī'a* in symbolic terms which relate practically to the disciple's mode of approach to the Path is his exposition of the rite of Pilgrimage *(ḥajj)*, where he interprets each stage of the ritual as a waystation of the *ṭarīqa*.[2] His precedent for this was, of course, Najm al-Dīn Rāzī's *Mirṣād al-'ibād*,[3] although the important distinction between him and his predecessor lies in his being an active spiritual guide applying the concepts discussed in a practical context, where, in contrast to Rāzī's lyricism, he confines his writing to brief, pithy statements with Koranic and *ḥadīth* references, enhanced by one or two verses providing mnemonic highlights. Thus, the steps of the Path are expounded as staging points where devotional actions may be performed, accompanied by intention framed in the heart, so that the mystic may become purged of certain ego-based characteristics and be ready to advance to the next point.

This dynamic-symbolic approach is applied to the second series of treatises, as well, those relating to the *ṭarīqat*. Of particular interest here is Shāh Ni'matullāh's treatment of love in his treatise, *Maḥabbat-nāma*.[4] Here he has a precedent in the poet-master 'Irāqī's prose treatise, the *Lama'āt*, and in Aḥmad Ghazzālī's *Sawāniḥ*. Shāh Ni'matullāh is sparely expressive in this treatise, and adheres to his practise of giving succinct, to-the-point commentary paired with verses designed for instruction rather than inspiration, such as

Love is, indeed, a divine station
Love is better than kingship in station.

After giving the relevant Koranic references, he proceeds to give a one-line definition of each of the four principle varieties of love *(maḥabbat)* as collated and subsumed by the Akbarian commentators,[5] namely *hawā* (passion), *ḥubb* (love, charity), *'ishq* (love, eros) and *wudd* (love, amity). The important thing is that where Ibn 'Arabī presented these concepts in various places in his *Futūḥāt al-Makkiyya* and his commentators collated and systematized them, Shāh Ni'matullāh has given them a spare pedagogical treatment for disciples to grasp readily for the purposes of inculcation.

As can be seen from the above discussion, Shāh Ni'matullāh has enriched his exposition with paraphrases in Persian verse of Ibn 'Arabī's philosophical expressions. In so doing, he set a standard for successive masters and guides of the Ni'-matullāhī Order, many of whom have been poets of distinction in their own right, presenting the Sufi view in symbolic language, a medium far more conducive to appealing to the heart than intellect-oriented prose. No less than four of Shāh Ni'matullāh's immediate disciples were poets: namely, Darvīsh Muḥammad Ṭabasī (d. unkn.), Shāh Dā'ī (-ilā'llāh) Shirāzī (d. 869/1464-5), Busḥāq Aṭ'ima Shirāzī (d. unkn.) and Ādharī Isfarāyinī (d. 866/1461-2).

1. *Risālahā-yi Shāh*, vol. 1, pp. 1-272.
2. *Risālahā-yi Shāh*, vol. 1, pp. 59-78.
3. Ed. Muḥammad Amīn Riyāḥī (Tehran 1352 A.Hsh), pp. 170-27.
4. *Risālahā-yi Shāh*, vol. 1, pp. 207-15.
5. See Su'ad Ḥakīm's lexicon of Ibn 'Arabī's terminology: *Al-Mu'jam al-ṣūfī* (Beirut 1981), pp. 302-03; and William C. Chittick, 'Ebn 'Arabi as Lover' in *Sufi: A Journal of Sufism*, Issue 9 (1991), pp. 6-9.

The first two were essayists, as well as poets, following in the spirit of their master, their works constituting some of the most inspirational reading for disciples down to the present day. Busḥāq was one of the greatest parodists in the history of Persian literature, devoting much of his work to burlesquing his own master's work. Far from being offended, Shāh Ni'matullāh seems to have been pleased at this display of his disciple's devotion, capped by the comment that while "others talk to God *(Allāh)*, I speak of God's Bounty *(Ni'matullāh)*,[1] providing us with another affectionate pun on the master's name.

Ādharī, like the famous Sanā'ī before him, had been a eulogizer of rulers before he embarked on the Sufi Path. Initiated and trained by Shāh Ni'matullāh, who conferred upon him a diploma with authorization to teach *(ijāza)* and a 'cloak of blessing' *(khirqa-yi tabarruk)*,[2] he became so detached from political association that he even refused a generous subsidy from the very Aḥmad Shāh who was so devoted to his master. Like Ṭabasī and Shāh Dā'ī, he was a distinguished prose writer as well, thus combining like them the two disciplines, as so many of the eminent figures of the Order have done down to the present time, who have carried on Shāh Ni'matullāh's legacy of blending an active professional life with their training of disciples on the Path.

---

1. E.G. Browne, *A Literary History of Persia*, Vol. III (Cambridge University Press1920; rprt 1956), p. 346.
2. Dawlatshāh Samarqandī, *Tadhkirat al-shu'arā*, ed., M. 'Abbāsi (Tehran, n.d.), p. 449.

Sufism and Sa'di, and Sa'di on Sufism

Homa Katouzian

Despite his universally acclaimed eloquence and clarity of expression, Sa'di's opinions, attitude and ideas have been described in different—frequently conflicting—terms. He has been described as a sceptic, a pragmatist, a humanitarian thinker, a moralist, an unethical writer, a religious preacher, and an Islamic mystic, sometimes by the same author and critic. The conflicting views expressed by those who are familiar with Sa'di's own text may be partially explained by the fact that—at least on the face of it—Sa'di's ideas do not always seem to be impeccably consistent. Such apparent or real inconsistencies are familiar from the works of many a great thinker and writer, and are especially understandable in the case of one such as Sa'di who travelled far and wide, and wrote over a long period of time. But there is another reason for the conflict of opinion about Sa'di's moral and intellectual commitments, namely the difficulty to fit his ideas into a major paradigm, conceptual framework or school of thought, or easily locate him in a given category of classical Persian poets. In this essay we shall first discuss Sa'di's relationship with Sufism by examining the views of the major critics of his works, followed by an examination of his views on Sufism and related matters directly from his prose and poetry.

SUFISM AND SA'DI

An earlier Western opinion about the subject has been succinctly expressed in the *Encyclopaedia of Islam*:

> The question whether Sa'di was himself susceptible of mystical feelings is probably to be answered in the negative, as his practical nature made him more inclined towards a moralizing attitude, in which he made mysticism only to serve a higher moral conception of earthly life. In his *Būstān* the lofty mystical sentiments of *Mathnawī* [of Rumi] or the *Manṭiq al-ṭayr* [of 'Aṭṭār] should not be sought for. Sa'di often speaks of the Sufis, but his attitude towards them is always more that of a moralist than a fellow mystic.[1]

Indeed, this may be described as the Western conventional wisdom—albeit with some variations—about Sa'di's rather complex attitude towards, and relationships with Sufism and the Sufis. For example, according to Reuben Levy, Sa'di was "cast in a very different mould from Jalāl al-Dīn Rumi's. His philosophy was much more practical and commonplace, and he was a stranger to metaphysics. He excelled in

1. See the entry on Sa'di by J.H. Kramers in *The Encyclopaedia of Islam.*

producing what are ordinarily called the Christian virtues; humility, charity, gentleness, and the like... But he was no ascetic and he made no attempts to deny to others the earthly delights which doubtless he himself enjoyed."[1] Levy speculates about the probability of Sa'di himself having travelled in the guise of dervishes, and even having been initiated in a Sufi Order, yet he emphasizes that Sa'di "never ventures... to discuss Sufi doctrines with any thoroughness, and for that reason the point of his discourses is more easily and generally comprehensible."[2] Elsewhere, Levy contends that while Rumi was "reflecting on the mysteries of life and on the oneness of the universe, the poet Sa'di was active distilling in verse the mundane experiences accumulated during many years of travel."[3] It is characteristic of the complexity of Sa'di's views about this world and the next that while Levy describes *Būstān* as "an excellent introduction to the whole range of mystic-ethical lore'[4] he goes on to say that "as in the *Gulistān,* expediency is the main lesson taught," and yet he further adds that "the purely ethical spirit is not lacking, and approval is given to a wide and humane toleration."[5]

Yan Rypka's views are also in the same mould, and he goes as far as comparing the *Būstān* with the *Qābusnāma*—a comparison which some may regard as being too far-fetched. He describes Sa'di as being "less interested in abstract mystical speculation than in its application to everyday life, ethics and didactics," but he still maintains that owing to "the practical, sensible way in which it approaches its aims the *Būstān* stands apart from the didactic works of the 6th/12th century and bears a greater affinity to the *Qābusnāma."*[6] Edward Browne does not dwell on the question of Sa'di's relationship with Sufism. He describes him as an "ethical" poet, although he is quick to point out that the ethics in question are not quite the same as those understood in Europe, and makes the typically European remark that "in his works is matter for every taste, the highest and the lowest, the most refined and the most coarse."[7]

Among the more recent critics, Annemarie Schimmel quotes Herder describing Sa'di as "the pleasant teacher of morals," and Joseph von Hammer-Purgstall to the effect that Sa'di's "genius is less alien to the West than that of others, his imagination less overbearing". Schimmel's own comment is that Sa'di's "simple but elegant style, his practical wisdom, his charming anecdotes made him a poet who appealed greatly to the Europeans, especially during the Age of Reason, and has rightly been considered the Persian poet whose works is easiest for Westerners to understand."[8]

1. Reuben Levy, *Persian Literature, An Introduction* (London: Oxford University Press 1923), p. 60.
2. *Ibid,* p. 61.
3. Reuben Levy, *An Introduction to Persian Literature* (New York: Columbia University Press 1969), p. 116.
4. *Ibid.*, p. 117.
5. Ibid.
6. Jan Rypka, *History of Iranian Literature* (Dordrecht Holland: D. Reidel Publishing Company 1968), p. 251.
7. Edward G. Browne, *A Literary History of Persia,* Vol. II (Cambridge University Press 1923), p. 532.
8. Annemarie Schimmel, 'The Genius of Shiraz: Sa'di and Ḥāfeẓ' in Ehsan Yarshater (ed.) *Persian Literature* (New York: The Persian Heritage Foundation 1988), pp.214-215.

Of the leading Iranian critics who have commented on the subject, Badi' al-Zamān Furūzānfar has written about Shihāb al-Dīn (Abū Ḥafṣ 'Umar) Suhrawardī's possible influence on Sa'di's thought. Although not all of the ostensibly autobiographical remarks in Sa'di's works may be taken to be authentic, there is a consensus opinion that he had in fact met this (as opposed to the more famous *Shaykh al-Ishrāq:* Shihāb al-Dīn Yaḥyā ibn Habash ibn Amīrak) Suhrawardī. Furūzānfar mentions five possible influences, two of which are particularly important for our subject. First is the view that as long as a practising mystic is still capable of describing his goal, efforts and experiences, he is still on the Way, for he who reaches the Goal completely breaks and loses contact with the mundane world. This is an important observation which we shall examine further in the following section. The second important influence of Suhrawardī on Sa'di's ideas discussed by Furūzānfar is that "Perfection is in following the *Shari'a,*" or that, in other words, there could be no true mystical experience outside a firm Islamic framework. However, and notwithstanding such possible influences, Furūzānfar argues that it is unlikely that Sa'di had become a follower of Suhrawardī's *ṭarīqa,* if only because their views conflict in many other ways. He goes even further and says that, in general, Sa'di cannot be regarded as a follower of "the Sufi doctrine" because of his closeness to philosophers and men of politics on certain issues, as well as the priority given by him to religious matters in certain respects.[1]

Dhabīḥullāh Ṣafā's opinion is in keeping with that of Furūzānfar. He even emphasizes that Sa'di's education under Abū'l-Faraj ibn Jawzī must have been "in religious sciences, not in Sufism."[2] On the other hand, Rashīd Yāsimī goes as far as claiming that the whole of Sa'di's lyrical poetry — his *ghazaliyyāt*— have an esoteric meaning, and that love for Sa'di is none other than the longing for the eternal Reunion—a view which is very difficult to sustain against much of the evidence.[3] Alī Dashtī's view is almost at the opposite pole. He believes that the view "held by many that [Sa'di] was a gnostic *('arif)* or even a Sufi" is a mistake which is in part due to his relationship with such "religious-minded Sufis" as Suhrawardī, and in part because of his admiration for a couple of great classical Sufis. Another reason which Dashtī gives for "the mistake" is the existence of some mystical poetry among Sa'di's lyrics. But he fails to mention the considerable amount of material on and about Sufism and the Sufis in the *Gulistān* and (especially) the *Būstān*. And he goes on to describe Sa'di as a religious-minded *(mutasharri')* man who would sometimes even sink to lower levels of arid piety.[4]

Finally, Ehsan Yarshater's most recent comment synthesizes the conventional views in a consistent manner, and at an appreciably sophisticated level. Speaking about the *Būstān,* he remarks:

1. See Badi' al-Zamān Furūzānfar, 'Sa'dī wa Suhrawardī' in Ḥabīb Yaghmā'ī, (ed.) *Sa'dī-nāma*, (Tehran: Department of Education 1938).
2. Dhabīḥullāh Ṣafā, *Tarīkh-i adabiyyāt dar Irān,* Vol.III, Part 1 (Tehran University Press 1974), pp. 594-95.
3. See Rashīd Yāsimī, 'Sa'dī wa 'ishq' in *Sa'dī-nāma*.
4. 'Alī Dashtī, *Qalamrū-yi Sa'dī* (Tehran: Kayhan 1959), especially pp. 425-432.

The Poet Humām al-Dīn Tabrīzī Meeting Sa'dī in a Public Bath. From a manuscript of the *Majālis al-'ushshāq*, dated 959/1552. MS. Ouseley Add. 24, f. 83r (Courtesy of the Bodleian Library, Oxford)

Didactic in content, lyrical in tone, anecdotal in composition, this poem is one of the masterpieces of Persian literature. It is probably the best expression of the humanitarian outlook on life and its moral dimensions that evolved in Islamic Persia among enlightened preachers as well as a result of the interaction between religious concepts and Sufi teaching; it embodies an ethical philosophy emphasizing moderation, justice, contentment, humility, detachment, and compassion for the weak and needy. An admirer of the ethics and the tolerant attitude of the venerable Sufis, Sa'di often draws on the lines and sayings of Islamic mystics to illustrate moral virtue. His humanitarianism, however, avoids the pantheistic and ecstatic excesses of some of the extreme Sufis. His approach remains of the application of ethical and devotional principles to common circumstances and problems.[1]

SA'DI ON SUFISM

The three greatest bodies of work produced by Sa'di are the *Būstān, Gulistān* and his books of lyrical poetry (or *ghazaliyyāt)*. Chapter III of the *Būstān* — 'On Love, Intoxication and Delirium', and chapter II of the *Gulistān* 'On the Morals and Manners of Dervishes' almost exclusively concern Islamic mystics and mysticism, although these subjects are occasionally treated elsewhere in the two books as well. Sa'di's lyrical poems may be divided into two groups. A small minority of the *ghazaliyyāt* are didactic in approach and/or broadly mystical in quality, although a *ghazal* quite as mystical in content as those of Rumi is hard to find among Sa'di's extensive lyrical poems. The rest of the *ghazaliyyāt* which make up the bulk of Sa'di's four books of lyrical poetry relate to mundane love—to love of the flesh—and do not allow of any mystic interpretation. For an interpretation of Sa'di's view on, and relationship with, Sufism this fact is of great importance because had Sa'di himself been a pure practising Sufi he would not have been expected to attach so much importance to earthly love, and would not himself have emerged, as he does in many of his moving lyrics, as an ardent lover and admirer of mundane beauty.

It is true, of course, that many classical Persian lyrics contain Sufi symbolism in the guise of mundane love and desire. But it is equally true that many of them are addressed to human beings. In the case of Sa'di's lyrics it would be impossible to discuss the evidence within this limited compass. Yet, the consensus of critical opinion has always held the bulk of Sa'di's lyrics as expressing 'apparent' as opposed to 'real' love. To give but one major example, in his edition of Sa'di's collected works, Furūghī has identified 663 as relating to mundane love *(mughāzala wa mu'āshiqa),* and only a handful as expressing mystic sentiments. His specific selection could be open to argument in certain cases, but the broad classification seems justified on the basis of both form and content.

Chapter two of the *Gulistān* may be thought of as the more empirical counterpart to the much more theoretical treatment of mystical themes in the third chapter of the *Būstān*. The former contains a critical view of Sufi practices which is both positive and negative, praising what may be termed as genuine or pure Sufi practices but rejecting impure morals and behaviour. It contains the shortest, most succinct and most eloquent definition of Islamic — perhaps all — mysticism in the following words:

1. See 'The Development of Persian Literatures' in Eshan Yarshater, (ed.), *Persian Literature*.

> The outward aspect of dervishhood is raiment rent apart and shaven head; its reality is living heart and carnal spirit dead.[1]

However, he goes on to emphasize that, whatever a person's appearance, it is his piety, and devotion, asceticism, etc., that reveals his true mystic commitments, and castigates those who would use mystic beliefs as a pretext for forgetting their religious duties and indulging in frivolous living.

Yet, and despite his own clear definition of the appearance and reality of 'dervishhood' *(darwīshī),* Sa'di is quite broad in his use of the term dervish, and uses it interchangeably and synonymously with *zāhid, 'ābid, pārsā, ṣāliḥ, 'ārif* and *shaykh* to refer to anyone who practices a certain amount of asceticism or pretends to it. The general impression given is that while he has the highest respect for, and attaches the greatest value to the heritage of such venerable and grand Sufis of the past as Bāyazid, Shiblī and Junayd, he is somewhat sceptical about the formalized mysticism of his own times. He writes:

> They asked a Shaykh from Syria about the true meaning of Sufism. He said, "In former days there was a group of men in the world, outwardly distracted, but inwardly collected: now they are a crowd, outwardly collected but inwardly distracted."[2]

There are probably more instances of false or impure mysticism in the *Gulistān* than of the exalted morals and practices of venerable Sufis. An *'ābid* was sent for by a ruler. He took a substance to make him look lean and ascetic, but was killed instantly because it was poisonous.[3] Another *'ābid* was said to eat excessively in the evening and then continue to pray until dawn. An 'enlightened' critic suggested that he would do better to eat less and sleep more.[4] A *zāhid* being guest at the court ate less at lunch, and prayed more at prayer time, than was his habit. When he returned home he asked for food as he was hungry. His son suggested that he should repeat his prayers as well because of his hypocrisy at the court.[5] A ruler told his vizier that he held two classes—the *ulamā'*(theologians) and the *zuhhād* (ascetics)—in great respect. "The philosophical, travelled and experienced vizier" (almost as if it was Sa'di himself) replied that, in that case, he should be kind to both groups by paying the former so they work harder, and not paying the latter so they remain ascetic.[6] Here is one example of Sa'di's comparison of the *ulamā'*with mystics, which has a satirical undertone. Later in the same chapter of *Gulistān* he makes a more serious comparison between the two classes and their callings which — as we shall see later below— is important in understanding his views on the social consequences of mystical and intellectual knowledge.

On the other hand, genuine Sufis and dervishes are held in high esteem, and regarded as being superior, if not to the *'ulamā'* then certainly to the rich and mighty. It is true that in his fictitious debate with the man "in the guise of dervishes but not

---

1. See A.J. Arberry (tr.) *Kings and Beggars, The First Two Chapters of Sa'di's Gulistān* (London: Luzac & Co. 1945), p.104.
2. *Ibid*, p. 88.
3. Muḥammad 'Alī Furūghī, ed., *Kulliyyāt-i Sa'dī* (Tehran: Amir Kabir 1987), p.79.
4. *Ibid*, p. 82.
5. *Ibid*, p. 73.
6. *Ibid*, p. 90.

in their way" *(Gulistān,* chap. VII) Sa'di himself takes the side of the people of means *(tawāngarān)*. But here (and besides the fact that his adversary has been described as not being a true dervish) he has probably thought it wiser to defend the well-to-do in an obviously concocted debate which contains some very scathing remarks about the richer members of the community. Furthermore, he relates *(Gulistān,* chap. II) that

> A certain king regarded with a contemptuous eye a band of dervishes. One of these latter, sensing the fact..... said "O king, in splendor we are less than you in the world here present yet is our life more pleasant; at death we are your equal and better at the Resurrection Sequel."[1]

Still, the *Būstān*'s treatment of Sufis and Sufism is more positive than that of the *Gulistān* which was written a year later. It contains no satirical jibes and almost no empirical examples of the practices of contemporary Sufis which sometimes result in such mocking of their behaviour. Being generally a more theoretical and more intellectual book, the *Būstān*'s chapter III holds some of Sa'di's more profound comments on mystic life and love, the Seeker and the Sought. Elsewhere in the *Būstān* there are some examples of the approach, attitude and conduct of the great classical Sufis, all of which are highly positive and approving in tone. Shiblī is said to have returned an ant to his home after finding it in a sack of wheat which he had carried over a long distance.[2] Bāyazid is quoted to have been thankful for someone pouring a bucket of ash all over him as he was leaving a public bath, because he felt that he deserved (hell) fire and had only received ashes.[3] Junayd is said to have shared his food with a toothless dog while wondering which one of them was in fact better in the sight of God.[4] And alluding to men like Bāyazid, Junayd, etc.—the *abdāl*—he says:

> *In ancient days, so I've heard tell,*
> *Stone would turn to silver in the hands of saints* (abdāl)
>
> *You will not think such words unreasonable:*
> *When you're but content, silver and stone are one!*[5]

Yet, as noted before, it is in chapter 3 of the *Būstān* 'On Love, Intoxication and Delirium' where Sufi ideas are put forward with full force and familiar authenticity:

> *Happy the days of those delirious with care of Him,*
> *Whether they know wounds or yet the salve of Him!*
> *Beggars they, of kingship shy,*
> *Long-suffering in their beggary in hope of Him...*[6]

Man's love of one like himself can be such as to make him forget everything but his beloved, let alone his love of the Eternal Source:

---

1. Arberry, *Kings and Beggars,* pp.103-104.
2. Furūghī, *Kulliyyāt,* the *Būstān*'s chapter 2, p. 264.
3. *Ibid.* (the *Būstān* chapter 4), p. 298.
4. *Ibid.* p. 317.
5. See G.M. Wickens (tr.) *Morals Pointed and Tales Adorned (The Bustan of Sa'di)* (Toronto and Buffalo: University of Toronto Press 1974), pp.172-3.
6. *Ibid.* p. 100.

Since love that's founded upon air
Is such a mischief-rouser, enforcing its behest,
Why they're engulfed beneath Idea's Sea?
In passion for the soulmate's soul, they're careless of their own,
In recollection of the Beloved, careless of the world...[1]

Indeed, almost the whole of this chapter of the *Būstān*—together with the recurring mystical and esoteric concepts and imagery drawn from the symbolism of the Sufi Way: Beauty, Love Seeker, Friend, Truth, Candle and Moth, etc.—may be quoted in evidence both of Sa'di's familiarity with Sufi concepts, categories and ideas, and of his great sympathy for, if not attraction to, them. But he even surpasses himself when he contrasts love with intellect, and concludes that the intellectual approach to knowledge is nothing but "twists and turns":

The way of the intellect is all twists and turns,
But the concern of the gnostics is for God alone!
This can be said to those who recognize realities,
Though adherents of analogy [logic] may carp thereat and say:
"What are the sons of Adam, and the beasts both wild and tame?..."[2]

To say that Sa'di has even surpassed himself in comparing the logic of mysticism as opposed to that of intellectual discovery is not to argue against the evidence, but to observe the fact that Sa'di's general regard for intellectual knowledge is high, and that in some places he regards it as being complementary to, not conflicting with, mystical knowledge. There is one occasion on which Sa'di directly discusses the question of intellect versus love as alternative sources of knowledge, and another, when he contrasts the results of mystic and intellectual knowledge for the community. But before discussing them, it is worth noting that, although the ultimate goal of mystic discovery is, for Sa'di, the highest of all knowledge, he regards many of the mystics themselves as being unworthy of it, and, moreover, he who *is* worthy of it unavailable to bear witness to it:

These pretenders to being His seekers have no news,
For he who heard the news ceased to be heard from.[3]

In other words, many a practising Sufi will not succeed, and the genuine mystics who do, remain unknown, or will not speak of their knowledge;

Lovers are killed by the Beloved,
[But] those who are killed cannot speak.[4]

The five *Majālis* (Lectures or Homilies) are sometimes regarded as not being part of Sa'di's authentic works, though it is not clear on what basis—of either form or content—this view has been formed. Concerning mysticism, at any rate, they contain the same duality of view which regards mystic devotion and religious piety as alternative approaches to the same goal. Thus, in the second Lecture he writes:

1. *Ibid.*, p. 101.
2. *Ibid.*, p. 113.
3. Furūghī, *Kulliyyāt, op.cit.*, p.30.
4. *Ibid.*, p.29.

Know that piety is of two kinds: the piety of the Just *(ṣāliḥān)* and the piety of the gnostics *('ārifān)*. The piety of the Just arises from their concern about the Day of Judgement in the future;.... the piety of the gnostics, from their shame of the Lord of the Two Worlds at present.[1]

However, the mysticism of the *Majālis* tends to increase as it proceeds. God told Muḥammad in the Koran to tell the faithful to explore the world, but scholars have interpreted this to mean the exploration of one's own world, "because if, through the imagination, you wander around the world of your own existence it would be better than if you travel the whole world on foot."[2] When Bāyazid humbly prayed to God for a "drink of reunion"- he heard a voice saying:

Bāyazid, your self is still with you. If you wish to reach us, leave your self at the gate and come inside.[3]

Someone went to Bāyazid and, having listed all the efforts which he had made, wondered when he might reach the Goal. Bāyazid replied:

Here is a stage. The first step is towards people; the second, towards God. Take the first step so as to reach God.[4]

Finally:

Self-knowledge is the ladder for climbing up to the roof of the knowledge of God. How can he who does not know himself gain knowledge of the Sea of Glory.[5] Whenever you get to know yourself you will get to know God. Your self is your key for getting to know Him.[6]

There are, as noted above, doubts about the authenticity of the Lectures, but it is virtually certain that the Essay on Reason and Love *('aql wa 'ishq)* is Sa'di's own. He was asked, in verse, by an admirer to judge which of the two means of gaining knowledge has priority over the other. He replied in prose:

Said the Messenger of God, God's blessing and peace be upon him, the first thing that God Almighty created was the intellect or reason... Therefore [the Questioner's] logic is absolutely sound in bringing reason before love, and regarding it as means of getting closer to God.... [7]

But he goes on to add:

Reason, although superior in so many ways, is not the Way, but the light which shows the Way.... And the use of a light is that, by means of it, they can tell the road from wilderness, good from evil, and enemy from friend. [But] a person with a light would not reach his destination unless he takes to the road.[8]

---

1. *Ibid.*, p. 899.
2. *Ibid.*, p. 902.
3. *Ibid.*, pp. 904-905
4. *Ibid.*, p. 910.
5. *Ibid.*, p. 901.
6. *Ibid.*, p. 913.
7. *Ibid.*, p. 888.
8. *Ibid.*, p. 889.

According to the great Sufis *(Mashāyikh-i mu'tabar)* the seeker will reach a point that is hidden from intellectual knowledge *('ilm)*. This claim would be excessive unless it was also made clear that intellectual knowledge is but a means of reaching the desired goal, not the goal itself. The seeker of the Way *(murīd-i ṭarīqa)* must acquire good morals through intellectual knowledge to enable him to purify his self. Self-purification will lead to isolation from others, and this will result in inner knowledge and the subjugation of his will. The process begins with the continual invocation of God *(dhikr)*, reaches ecstasy, "and the last stage, which knows no end, is called love."[1]

Love, Perfection and Truth are like a great treasure. And just as kings destroy those who know the whereabouts of their treasure, so "the King of the Beginning spills the blood" of those few who acquire real knowledge of Him so that the story of the Treasure will not be retold:

> He who would be given a cup in this feast is first made unconscious, so that the unknown secret of the essence of the Unique Being remains buried.[2]

In sum, although reason is necessary for guiding the Seeker to the right path, most seekers will not succeed because the trial is hard and requires a strong commitment, while those who reach the Goal are lost to humanity because they are then "killed" by the Beloved.

Finally, Sa'di's comparison in the *Gulistān* between the impact and consequences of the roads to knowledge is worth noting: someone went from the *khānaqāh* to the *madrasa*, he says in verse, breaking his pledge to the People of the Way *(ahl-i ṭarīq)*. *I* asked what was the difference between the devotee *('ābid)* and the scholar *('ālim)* which made him choose the latter. He said: "The former is trying to save himself, whereas the latter is trying to save others."[3] In other words, the end result of mystic knowledge is personal and individual, while that of intellectual knowledge is public and social.

CONCLUSION

Sa'di was a graduate of the Niẓāmīyya College of Baghdad, and hence a trained Islamic jurist. Indeed, many if not most of his relatives had been in the same profession:

> *The whole of my clan were Doctors of Religion,*
> *It was the teacher of your love that taught me to write poetry.*[4]

He was a moralist as well as a man of experience who combined his knowledge of theory and practice to produce some of the best didactic literature Persia has known. In addition, he was a man of public affairs who addressed rulers, ministers and public servants on the questions of just government and pious living, and occasionally praised them in verse, though this was normally moderate and was often

1. *Ibid.*
2. *Ibid.*, p. 890.
3. *Ibid.*, p. 93.
4. *Ibid. (Book of Lyrics)*, p. 423.

combined with exhortations for fairness and tolerance. Judging by his lyrical poetry (or *ghazaliyyāt)* he was also a great admirer of youth and lover of beauty who would feel both the happiness of the presence and the sadness of the absence of a human lover. Much of the *Būstān* and *Gulistān* concern the application of broader religious and ethical principles. And excepting the one occasion in *Būstān* cited above, he has a high regard for reason *('aql)* as a means of acquiring knowledge, and describes it as a light without which the path to mystic love *('ishq)* would be hard to discover.

On the other hand, his mystical compositions—especially but not exclusively in the third chapter of the *Būstān*—are outstanding both in their depth and in their degree of attachment to Sufi ideas and doctrines. Indeed, if this one chapter alone of his works had reached the modern reader, he would be unquestionably held as one of the greatest Persian Sufi poets of all times. Apart from that, he holds (both here and elsewhere) in saintly veneration the legacy, memory and legends of the grand old Sufis who were sometimes known as the *mashāyikh* or *abdāl,* and believes that a select few mystics may attain exalted degrees beyond the reach of ordinary mortals, including men of intellect. And yet, he seems to take a critical view of organized Sufi practice of his own time.

The consensus of learned opinion cited in the first section of this essay was that Sa'di could not be described as a practising Sufi himself. On the other hand, the evidence which we have examined from his own text is mixed and somewhat inconclusive. Taken as a whole, it shows him as a man of great familiarity and broader sympathies with Sufism, although he cannot be included in the category of such committed, consistent and all-embracing Sufi poets as Rumi, 'Aṭṭār and 'Irāqī.

Spectrums of Islamic Thought IV

Sa'īd al-Dīn Farghānī on the Implications of Oneness and Manyness

William C. Chittick

INTRODUCTION

If any characteristic is shared by all Islamic ways of thinking, surely this has something to do with *tawḥīd*, the assertion that God is one. The classical texts frequently describe *tawḥīd* as a kind of spiritual or intellectual dynamic that integrates all dispersion into a coherent vision. The grammatical form of the word itself shows that *tawḥīd* involves an active stance taken by a person toward some object. Hence *tawḥīd* does not begin with unity, since that needs to be established. Rather, it begins with the recognition of diversity and difference. The integrated vision that *tawḥīd* implies must be achieved on the basis of a recognized multiplicity. It is in order to provide the means to see beyond this multiplicity that Islamic thought frequently, or characteristically, sets up a series of dichotomies. Already in the Koran we constantly meet with various sets of opposing or contrasting terms, such as this world and the next, the heavens and the earth, the Garden and the Fire, light and darkness, knowledge and ignorance, well-being and corruption, believers and unbelievers.

As the various perspectives of Islamic life and thought took shape over the course of history, different sets of contrasting terms came to be stressed. Heresiologists and historians often mention these sets as marking the specific positions of the schools. One has only to think of such pairings as predestination and free will, eternal and created, or *ta'ṭīl* and *tashbīh*.

When we look at those Muslims who have been called Sufis, we see that their role in Islam has often been understood by placing them on one side of a dichotomy. Thus, for example, we are told that the Sufis take one position, while the jurists and proponents of Kalām take the opposite position. The *Sharī'a* is one thing, while the *Ṭarīqa* is something else. The Sufis look at the inward meaning, while the jurists look at the outward form. The Sufis have an esoteric perspective on things, while the mullas have an exoteric perspective. The Sufis are spiritualizing and non-dogmatic mystics, while the jurists are literal-minded and dogmatic legalists.

But as everyone who has studied the actual texts of the parties in question is well aware, lines are not in fact so clearly drawn. Different authors and schools lay different stresses upon the two sides. A single author may frequently appear to be a Sufi in some of his works, and a jurist or a theologian in other works. Many figures combine the contrasted perspectives in varying degrees. And when we look at the specific works generally recognized as having a Sufi outlook, it is probably fair to say that no two authors take exactly the same doctrinal position. For their part, the

say that no two authors take exactly the same doctrinal position. For their part, the jurists are famed for their internal disputes, as are the theologians. But the dualities and dichotomies are frequently stressed both by the authors themselves and by the mediæval and modern scholars who have studied them. To add to the confusion, many observers have dealt with the differences simply by calling anything that does not fit into the preferred side of the dichotomy by such names as 'heresy,' 'unbelief,' or—to mention one of the favorite contemporary versions of the same attitude—'foreign borrowing.'

Setting up sharp dichotomies between Sufism and *Sharī'a*-minded Islam has certainly made life easier for many historians. But as long as scholars persist in taking one side or the other as 'orthodox' Islam, they will not necessarily provide us with helpful models for understanding what actually has been going on in Islamic history. Of course, dichotomies and divergences do exist and are constantly stressed in many of the original texts. We have to be aware of these dichotomies and take them seriously, but we also have to keep in mind the rhetorical usefulness of stressing differences. When we get down to the task of describing what actually was being said, it may be much more helpful to picture the differing positions in terms of spectrums of differing shades and hues, instead of sharply defined dualities. When one is faced with an issue in Islamic thought, one could then suggest what the two extremes of the spectrum might be, and analyze the various positions in terms of the relative stress placed upon particular points. In any given issue, some authors will fall on the red side of things, some on the violet side, and the vast majority will take up positions in between. On the next issue, the various authors might well take up different colors of the spectrum, not corresponding to their relative place in the previous issue.

This sort of analysis would mean that we can no longer make the sweeping generalizations that many of us have long indulged in without adding numerous qualifications. But by taking this approach, we can help dispel the still current myths about Islam as a sort of monolithic system with little historical and regional variation. Not that it is necessary to go as far as some anthropologists, claiming, in effect, that there has been nothing but a series of local Islams with practically no unifying factors. But we may be able to provide a more accurate picture of the unity *and* diversity of Islamic civilization.

One of the more interesting sets of dichotomies discussed in both the original texts and the secondary literature has to do precisely with those factors that differentiate the Sufis from the jurists and theologians.[1] This is clearly a good example

1. Mark Woodward has shown that the diverse positions of traditional Muslims in Java can be classified on the basis of the respective emphasis that they place on the outward *(ẓāhir)* and inward *(bāṭin)* dimensions of the religion. Only in modern times have certain people considered one dimension valid to the exclusion of the other. Thus we have reformists who see the inward dimension as alien to Islam, and modern, universalizing mystics who see all the specifically Islamic dimensions as outward and extraneous. In both cases, the equilibrium between the two dimensions has been broken. As Woodward puts it, "The balance struck in traditional Javanese Islam is absent, as the complementary axioms are not subordinated but purged from the system." *Islam in Java: Normative Piety and Mysticism in the Sultanate of Yogyakarta* (Tucson: University of Arizona Press 1989), p. 250.

of a spectrum of positions. Before modern times, a certain balance between the outward and inward, or the 'exoteric' and the 'esoteric' was the general rule, though this would not necessarily be obvious if we were to limit ourselves to reading those authors who are critical of positions supposedly taken by their opponents. But in fact Islam has witnessed a constant creative tension between those who stress one side of an issue and those who stress the other. Certainly the discussions frequently degenerate into polemics, but the upshot has been to make available to Muslims a vast range of approaches to the basic teachings of the Koran and the Prophet. The Sufis sometimes cite *ḥadīths* that seem to be alluding to the positive results of this diversity of opinion: "The paths to God are as numerous as human souls." Or again, "The divergence of the *'ulamā'* is a mercy."

One of best known cases of divergent interpretations among Muslim thinkers arose in the wake of Ibn 'Arabī's grand synthesis of Islamic teachings. He was criticized not only by jurists and theologians, but also by a good number of outstanding Sufis, including 'Alā' al-Dawla Simnānī and Gīsū Darāz.[1] The most famous of these Sufis was Shaykh Aḥmad Sirhindī, who attacked Ibn 'Arabī's supposed position by juxtaposing *waḥdat al-shuhūd* with *waḥdat al-wujūd.*[2]

But if anything characterizes the great masters of Sufism, and especially Ibn 'Arabī, it is certainly not that they consider their own position to mark one of the extremes. Quite the contrary, they usually view themselves as taking up an intermediate stance among the conflicting perspectives of Islamic thought and practice. Typically, they recognize the existence and even the validity of deep dichotomies in the way that various issues are approached. Then they attempt to overcome not the dichotomies themselves, but the absoluteness of the dichotomies. They affirm the reality of difference and distinction, but they maintain that a view of things that

1. Some of the most virulent early attacks on Ibn al-'Arabī were carried out by the Hanbalī Sufi Ibn Taymīyya, who claimed that the term *waḥdat al-wujūd* denotes a heretical position equivalent to incarnationism *(ḥulūl)* or unificationism *(ittiḥād). E*lsewhere I have alluded to the way in which Ibn Taymīyya distorts Ibn al-'Arabī's position ('Rumi and *Waḥdat al-Wujūd,*' forthcoming in *The Heritage of Rumi,* ed. Amin Banani and Georges Sabagh [Cambridge: Cambridge University Press). One should keep in mind the fact that, as James Morris has pointed out, Ibn Taymīyya was considered a 'fanatical crackpot' by his contemporaries and has only been taken seriously in relatively recent times. Cf. Morris, 'Situating Islamic Mysticism: Between Written Tradition and Popular Spirituality,' in *Typologies of Mysticism,* ed. R. Herrera, forthcoming, n. 13.
2. Cf. Chittick, 'Rumi and *Waḥdat al-Wujūd.*' One can put the Indian debate into a nutshell by saying that the proponents of *waḥdat al-wujūd* were held to maintain that 'All is He' *(hama ūst.),* while the proponents of *waḥdat al-shuhūd* claimed that the correct position is 'All is from Him' *(hama az ūst)* or 'All is through Him' *(hama bidūst).* In fact, of course, Ibn al-'Arabī takes both positions. 'All is He' corresponds more to the side of God's similarity to the cosmos *(tashbīh),* while 'All is from Him' relates more to the side of His incomparability *(tanzīh). A*nd, according to Ibn al-'Arabī, both of these sides have to be maintained. But in the later tradition, many Muslim authorities tended in one direction or the other, and hence they criticized those who preferred the opposing tendency. The seventeenth [?] century Indian Sufi 'Abd al-Jalīl Ilāhābādī had a clear view of the unbalanced nature of Sirhindī's criticisms. In a treatise in which he recounts a visionary encounter with Ibn al-'Arabī, he says to him, 'O honored Shaykh, some of the recent folk have objected to your persuasion, saying that oneness is in witnessing *(shuhūd),* not in Being *(wujūd).*' As part of his response, Ibn al-'Arabī says, "Everything that they say I have also said in the *Futūḥāt.* All of it are viewpoints that are affirmed in relation to the existence of the cosmos." *Su'āl wa jawāb* (Institute of Islamic Studies, New Delhi, MS. no. 2139), last two pages.

sees interrelationship, complementarity, and polarity corresponds more closely to the Islamic ideal. Through *tawḥīd*, or asserting the underlying unity of the Real, they establish a framework within which all diversity can be situated.

Among the many Sufi authors who provide theoretical frameworks for overcoming dichotomies and integrating dispersed realities is Sa'īd al-Dīn Farghānī (d. 699/1299), an important third-generation member of the school of Ibn 'Arabī. Though at first sight Farghānī's discussion may seem to pertain exclusively to an abstract philosophical level, one soon sees that he provides many helpful correlations among the divergent positions in Islamic thought.

THE SCHOOL OF QŪNAWĪ

As everyone knows, the twelfth and thirteenth centuries witnessed a remarkable flowering of the spiritual and intellectual dimensions of Islam. The fact that both Rumi and Ibn 'Arabī lived during this era is sufficient to establish it as a watershed in Islamic history. Most later expressions of inwardly oriented Islamic teachings can be seen as commentaries on formulations that were made most clearly and explicitly at this time. But because of the towering stature of these two figures, relatively little attention has been paid to some of their outstanding contemporaries and disciples, figures who, if they had lived at any other time and place, would have been looked upon as landmarks in the spiritual and intellectual geography of Islam. Farghānī is a striking example.

Here we need to recall the central importance of the circle of Ibn 'Arabī's stepson, Ṣadr al-Dīn Qūnawī (d. 673/1274), for the development of Sufism in the Persianate world from the thirteenth century onward. In Anatolia, Persia, India, and wherever the theoretical expression of Sufi teachings has had any role to play, Qūnawī and his followers were key intermediaries for the interpretation and diffusion of Ibn 'Arabī's positions. It is highly symbolic that Qūnawī lived and taught not far from Rumi in the city of Konya. Though these two authorities express Sufi teachings in profoundly different ways, they were close friends. In their own works the two provide numerous examples of positions that need to be situated within different colors of the spectrum, but not at the extremes.

Rumi's deep impact on every level of Islamic teaching and practice is well known. But if we look at the intellectual expression of Sufi teachings, Qūnawī has certainly been more influential. Thus, for example, to the extent that Muslim intellectuals have explained the meaning of Rumi's poetry, they have usually been guided by the theoretical framework whose germs are found in the writings of Ibn 'Arabī and whose systematic elaboration goes back to Qūnawī. In effect, Qūnawī played a major role in determining the way in which not only Ibn 'Arabī but also Rumi and the rest of the Persian Sufi poets were read in the eastern Islamic lands.

Qūnawī had a deep impact on Sufis and Muslim thinkers not only though his own writings, but also through the writings of his students and their followers. The most influential commentary on the *Fuṣūṣ al-ḥikam* was composed by Qūnawī's disciple Mu'ayyid al-Dīn Jandī. Jandī in turn was the teacher of 'Abd al-Razzāq Kāshānī, the author of what is probably the best known *Fuṣūṣ* commentary in the Arabic-speaking world. And Kāshānī was the teacher of Dāwūd al-Qayṣarī, whose commentary on the *Fuṣūṣ* is better known than his master's in the Persian-speaking world, though it too is in Arabic.[1]

According to a number of sources, Qūnawī's mother married Ibn 'Arabī after the death of her husband, who had become Ibn 'Arabī's close friend when they met in Mecca in the year 600/1203. Ṣadr al-Dīn was probably born in the year 605/1208-09, so his mother's remarriage would have taken place sometime after that. His native tongue seems to have been Persian. He wrote all his major works in Arabic, but several examples of his Persian prose have also survived. His prose presents striking contrasts with that of Ibn 'Arabī. Qūnawī's writings demonstrate a smoothness, fluency, and coherence that are not usually found in the works of his Shaykh, whose ideas and expression tend to be choppy and broken.

Qūnawī's disciple Jandī is the author of both Arabic and Persian works, though the latter have not been widely read.[2] Probably the best known Persian work to come out of Qūnawī's school was the *Lama'āt* of 'Irāqī, inspired by Qūnawī's lectures on the *Fuṣūṣ*.[3] But in terms of the intellectual development of Ibn 'Arabī's teachings, the most influential Persian work of this circle was certainly Sa'īd al-Dīn Farghānī's commentary on the *Naẓm al-sulūk* or *'Poem of the Way'* of the great Egyptian poet Ibn al-Fāriḍ. And this commentary was itself based squarely on Qūnawī's teachings. Qūnawī tells us that he began reading Ibn al-Fāriḍ's poem with a group of students in the year 643/1245-46 in Egypt and continued to do so in Syriaand Anatolia. Many of his listeners took notes, and afterwards some of them wrote up the results, but the most successful of these recensions was by Farghānī.[4]

Farghānī was not satisfied with this Persian recension of Qūnawī's lectures, at least partly because it could not reach the wide audience that would be interested in the subject matter. He translated it into Arabic and in the process refined and amplified it, such that the Arabic version is about a third again as long as the Persian. Part of the added material is a much longer introduction that sets down the basic principles of Qūnawī's teachings. Jāmī praises this introduction by telling us that "No one else has ever been able to explain the problems of the Science of Reality in such a systematic and orderly manner."[5] The Arabic version of Farghānī"s work is in fact as much a new composition as a translation.[6] Both com-

1. Many of the Persian commentaries on the *Fuṣūṣ* are deeply indebted to Qayṣarī. The first of these, *Nuṣūṣ al-khuṣūṣ fī tarjamat al-fuṣūṣ* (partly edited by R. Maẓlūmī [Tehran: McGill University, Institute of Islamic Studies 1980]), was written by a student of both Kāshānī and Qayṣarī, Rukn al-Dīn Shīrāzī, who died in 769/1367. A second, that by Tāj al-Dīn Ḥusayn Khwārazmī (d. ca 840/1436) is simply a translation of Qayṣarī's work *(Sharḥ-i fuṣūṣ al-ḥikam,* edited by N. Māyil Hirawī, Tehran: Intishārāt-i Mawlā 1364/1985). Many of the passages in Shāh Ni'matullāhī's writings are little more than translations of the works of Qayṣarī and Kāshānī. Jāmī is more original, and also much more widely read, than most. He makes active and conscious use of all the major figures of the school back to Qūnawī, as is clear not only in his *Naqd al-nuṣūṣ* (ed. W. Chittick [Tehran: Imperial Iranian Academy of Philosophy 1977]), but also in his other prose works on Sufism and in some of his *mathnawīs*.
2. Jandī's only Persian work to have been published is *Nafḥat al-rūḥ* (Tehran: Mawlā 1362/1983), edited by N. Māyil Hirawī on the basis of a single MS. from Tehran University, which the editor mistakenly supposes to be unique. Two more, with significant textual differences, are found in Istanbul: Hacı Mahmud Ef. 2447 and Şehid Ali Paşa 1439.
3. Cf. Chittick and P.L.Wilson, *Fakhruddin 'Iraqi: Divine Flashes* (New York: Paulist 1981), pp. 45-46.
4. Notes 4, 5, and 6 continued on page 208.

mentaries are of first importance for the development of metaphysical and philosophical thought among Sufis in the Persianate world, and neither has been studied seriously in modern times.

THE ONE AND THE MANY

In order to suggest something of Farghānī's significance and the approach he takes to Sufi thought, I want to investigate his formulation of two contrasting approaches to reality, approaches that might tentatively be called the way of love and the way of knowledge, or the way of affirming oneness and the way of discerning manyness.

Like Ibn 'Arabī and most Sufis, Farghānī's theoretical teachings center on the names and attributes of God.[1] Perhaps the major theme of his commentary is the question of how the divine names mediate between God and the world. At the same time, he is concerned with many of the other issues related to Ibn 'Arabī's positions. He is one of the first authors to use the expression *waḥdat al-wujūd* or 'Oneness of Being' as a technical term, since this expression is hardly mentioned by Qūnawī, and never employed by Ibn 'Arabī himself.[2] But in Farghānī's formulations, *waḥdat al-wujūd* has a specific meaning that is rarely found among those who support it in later texts, though it is similar to the meaning given to the term by Ibn 'Arabī's opponents. Farghānī sees *waḥdat al-wujūd* as the polar opposite of *kathrat al-*

---

4. Cf. Qūnawī's introduction to Farghānī's *Mashāriq al-darārī*, ed. Sayyid Jalāl al-Dīn Āshtiyānī (Mashhad: Anjuman-i 'Irfān wa Falsafa-yi Islāmī 1398/1978). Jāmī quotes one Shams al-Dīn Īkī, another student of Qūnawī, concerning the circumstances of Farghānī's works: "In the sessions of our Shaykh the possessors and seekers of knowledge used to attend. The shaykh would speak about different sciences. Then he would end the session with one verse from the *'Poem of the Way,'* upon which he would comment in Persian. He expounded marvelous words and God-given meanings, but only the possessors of tasting *(dhawq)* could understand him. Sometimes on another day he would say that a different meaning of the verse had become manifest for him, and he would explain a meaning more wonderful and subtle than before. He often used to say, "One must be a Sufi to learn this poem and to be able to clarify its meanings for others."... Shaykh Sa'īd Farghānī would devote all his attention to understand what our Shaykh said, and then he would record it. He wrote an explanation of the poem first in Persian and then in Arabic. This was all because of the blessing of our Shaykh, Ṣadr al-Dīn." *Nafaḥāt al-uns*, ed. M. Tawḥīdīpūr (Tehran: Sa'dī 1336/1957), p. 542. Farghānī's treatise was to be read widely in the Persian-speaking world. One of the major avenues through which parts of it became disseminated was Shams al-Dīn Maghribī's (d. 810/1408) little treatise, *Jām-i jahān-namā*, which consists mostly of unacknowledged quotations from it. Maghribī's work in turn was the object of several commentaries, especially in India.
5. *Nafaḥāt al-uns*, p. 559.
6. It is interesting to note that even in the Persian-speaking world, the Arabic version of the commentary was extremely influential among those who studied the theoretical dimensions of Sufi teachings. I suspect that in Iran itself, where Arabic was the major language of philosophical and theological speculation, the Arabic version was more widely read than the Persian. In contrast, in India the Persian recension was probably more widely known, especially through the influence of Maghribī's *Jām-i jahān-namā*. Note that the first commentary written in India on Maghribī's work, by Mahā'imī, was in Arabic, not Persian. Later this commentary was translated into Persia.

---

1. Ibn 'Arabī sets down the principle in axiomatic form with his words, "A knowledge of God that is divested of the divine names cannot be relied upon, since it is not knowledge" (*Risāla Lā yu'awwal 'alayh,*' in *Rasā'il Ibn al-'Arabī* [Hyderabad-Deccan: The Dāiratu'l-Ma'arifi'l-Osmania 1948], p. 3). Cf. Chittick, *The Sufi Path of Knowledge* (Albany: SUNY Press 1989), Chapter 2 and *passim*.
2. Cf. Chittick, 'Rumi and *waḥdat al-wujūd*.'

'ilm, the manyness of knowledge. Though God is one in Being *(wujūd),* He is also many in knowledge *('ilm).* This corresponds to the most basic dichotomy in reality. However, at this point I will stop using the term 'dichotomy,' with its suggestion that there is something deep and irremediable about difference, and use the term 'polarity,' since Farghānī's position demands, as we shall see shortly, that there be no absolute distinctions in God or the cosmos. Being and knowledge should not be looked upon as distinct and separate, but as polar and complementary.

At the highest level of Reality, Being and knowledge are identical and no distinction can be drawn between the two. At this level one might speak of an absolute oneness prior to any manyness. This is the level of the unknown Essence *(dhāt)* which cannot be discussed in positive terms. As soon as we conceive of a Reality about which positive statements can be made, we are faced with the distinction between the divine Being and the divine Knowledge.[1] Knowledge—which is identical with consciousness and awareness—belongs to the very Essence of God. The divine Reality, or Being, knows Itself with a knowledge that is identical with Itself, so there is no difference between the knowing subject *('ālim)* and the known object *(ma'lūm).* However, when we speak of knowing, we necessarily set up a subject/object relationship, even if we cannot draw an ontological distinction between the two sides. This perceived relationship in turn makes it possible to distinguish among the divine names. For example, one can say that since God knows His own Reality, He knows all the concomitants and characteristics of His own Reality. Hence He knows Himself as Alive, Knowing, Desiring, Powerful, Speaking, Generous, and Just—these seven names being the 'seven leaders' or the seven fundamental names of God. For Farghānī, one of the most important statements we can make about the Real at this point is that His Being is one while His Knowledge has many objects, even if those objects possess no ontological plurality of any sort.[2] The multiplicity of the objects of knowledge has no effect on the oneness of God's Being. In an analogous way, a human mind is not split up into many minds by the fact that it is aware of many things.

It is extremely important to grasp the nature of the polarity that Farghānī sets up when he speaks of oneness and manyness at this primary level of Reality, since he finds corresponding polarities throughout the created world. Oneness and manyness

---

1. Why these two terms are singled out rather than any others is clear in the context of Islamic thought, especially as developed by Ibn 'Arabī and his followers. First, *wujūd* (Being, existence) was the central concern of Islamic philosophy and one of Ibn 'Arabī's key terms. Knowledge is central because it is the necessary prerequisite for all activity. In Ibn 'Arabī's approach, the discussion has to do with the fact that certain of the divine attributes are broader in scope *(a'amm)* than others, with Being (or mercy, *raḥma;* or life, *ḥayāt)* being the broadest. The argument runs something like this: The cosmos depends upon the Creator *(khāliq)* or the Speaker *(qā'il)* for its existence, while creativity and speech depend upon the divine power *(qudra).* Power in turn is effectuated through desire *(irāda)* while desire depends upon a knowledge *('ilm)* of possibilities. Knowledge in turn presupposes *wujūd,* or the fact that there be a knower. Hence Being and knowledge are the two primary attributes of Reality.
2. Ibn 'Arabī had expressed the same idea in many ways. For example, He calls God the 'One Many' *(al-wāḥid al-kathīr)* and he speaks of the Unity of the (exclusively) One *(aḥadiyyat al-aḥad)* as opposed to the Unity of Manyness *(aḥadiyyat al-kathra)* or of the (inclusively) One *(aḥadiyyat al-wāḥid).* By making these distinctions, he contrasts the One Essence that is beyond nomenclature with the Divinity who is described by all the names.

cannot be distinguished from one another in any absolute way, since both qualities belong to the reality of God. Whether we look at the Real as one or many depends upon our point of view, even if the point of view that considers God's oneness is more fundamental. Hence the universe, inasmuch as it reflects its Origin, can only be understood in terms of relative qualities, and these, since they are relative, change when the point of view changes. There are no absolute dichotomies within the created universe, nor in our formulations and expressions of the nature of things. This means that from the outset, Farghānī gives us a position that not only allows for, but even demands, other, contrasting positions. Every reality demands its polar opposite. Mention of one side implies the other side, much as mention of *yin* implies *yang*.[1]

In order to show that no absolute distinction can be drawn being Being and knowledge, Farghānī states that Being possesses a true oneness *(waḥda ḥaqīqiyya)* and a relative manyness *(kathra nisbiyya)* while knowledge possesses a true manyness and a relative oneness. Hence, both Being and knowledge are one and many, but the quality of oneness predominates in Being, while the quality of manyness predominates in knowledge.

Farghānī describes the true oneness and relative manyness of Being in the following terms:

> Each divine name is nothing but the manifest aspect of Being, which is the Essence Itself, but in respect of Its entification *(ta'ayyun)* and delimitation *(taqayyud)* by a meaning *(ma'nā)* or call it an 'attribute' *(ṣifa)*. For example, 'Living' is a name of the entified, manifest Being, but in respect of its entification and delimitation by a meaning, which is life. Hence, in respect of Being Itself and the entification itself, Being is identical with the Essence, and Its oneness is true. But in respect of the delimitation by that meaning and this meaning's distinction from other meanings... Being is different from what is named. Hence it possesses a relative manyness through those entifications.[2]

In contrast, the divine knowledge possesses true manyness and relative oneness because God knows the divine names and their concomitants, and these many objects of knowledge demand that knowledge be truly differentiated, or else the manyness could not be known for what it is. At the same time, knowledge is a single reality that pertains to the One Being.[3]

When Farghānī turns his attention to discussions more familiar to Muslim philosophers, he elucidates one of the many corollaries of the fact that oneness precedes manyness by explaining the relationship between necessity *(wujūb)* and possibility *(imkān)*. Being in Its oneness possesses the quality of necessity, since It cannot not be. But Being's knowledge pertains to what is possible, since each object of knowledge *(ma'lūm)* correlates with a possible thing *(mumkin)* something that may or may not exist in the cosmos. The multiplicity of the cosmos externalizes the true manyness of the divine knowledge, while the underlying unity of the cosmos—

1. Sachiko Murata has shown that this yin/yang style polarity is normative for much of the Islamic intellectual tradition. Cf. *The Tao of Islam* (Albany: SUNY, forthcoming).
2. *Muntaha' l-madārik* (Cairo: Maktab al-Ṣanāi' 1293/1876), p. 15.
3. *Ibid.*

present most obviously in the fact that each part of it shares in existence—reflects the Oneness of Being. That which is closer to the Oneness of Being possesses a preponderance of properties pertaining to necessity, while that which reflects the Manyness of Knowledge is dominated by possibility.

On the basis of this distinction between necessity and possibility, Farghānī divides the cosmos into three worlds: high, low, and intermediate. Everything that is dominated by the side of oneness and necessity, such as the angels and spirits, pertains to the high world. Everything that is dominated by the side of manyness and possibility, such as inanimate objects, plants, and animals, pertains to the low world. But human beings pertain to the middle realm, where oneness and manyness are balanced.[1] In a parallel way, human beings can be divided into three basic categories depending on the relationship established between the properties of necessity and those of possibility. People in whom necessity predominates are the prophets and friends of God. Those in whom possibility dominates are the unbelievers. And those in whom necessity and possibility are more or less equal are the faithful. So also, each human psyche can be analyzed in terms of three fundamental tendencies: ascending, descending, and in-between. To these is connected the traditional distinction made among the three basic levels of the soul *(nafs):* the soul at peace with God, the soul that commands to evil, and the intermediate, blaming soul.

Other implications of the distinction between oneness and manyness or necessity and possibility become apparent as soon as we look at those divine qualities that have a personal dimension. For example, since the One precedes the many, God's mercy takes precedence over His wrath. The reality of mercy is Being Itself; to exist in the cosmos is to participate in the existentiating mercy known as the 'Breath of the All-merciful.' Wrath is connected in some way to the multiplicity and possibility prefigured in the divine knowledge. When one thing is differentiated from another thing, each of the two things must be lacking in certain qualities that pertain to the unity and all-comprehensiveness of Being. This deficiency in the qualities of Being demands a certain lack of mercy, or a certain domination by properties that pertain not to Being Itself but to nothingness. Hence, any situation that is deficient in existence is related to the divine wrath, though again, there can be nothing absolute about this deficiency.

The relationship between mercy and wrath correlates with that between the two basic categories of divine names that bring the cosmos into existence. These are called the names of mercy and wrath, or beauty *(jamāl)* and majesty *(jalāl)* or bounty *(faḍl)* and justice *('adl)* or gentleness *(luṭf)* and severity *(qahr)*. These pairs of qualities are in turn connected with a large number of polarities or dichotomies. For example, mercy and gentleness are associated with nearness to God and wrath and severity with distance from Him. The people of paradise enter into mercy, while the people of the Fire taste chastisement because, as the Koran puts it, they are distant and 'veiled' from their Lord (83:15).

On the human level, the polarities expressed in the merciful and wrathful names are closely related to the basic distinction that is drawn between spirit and body, or

1. *untaha' l-madārik I*, p. 22.

between the upward and unifying tendency of the soul and its downward and dispersive tendency. The spirit is luminous and relatively close to the oneness of God, while the body is dark and relatively dominated by the properties of manyness and possibility. Hence the spirit correlates with nearness and mercy, while the body correlates with distance and wrath. Again, these are not absolute distinctions, simply a question of predominant attributes.

In short, wherever we can speak of two contrasting names of God—such as Forgiving and Vengeful, Gentle and Severe, Exalting and Abasing—one of the two terms will be more closely connected to the oneness and necessity of Being, and the other to the manyness and possibility of knowledge. At the same time, manyness is found in oneness and oneness in manyness, so the relationships can be reversed in appropriate circumstances. This has all sorts of repercussions on the level of the 'signs' *(āyāt)* of God, or those manifestations of the divine reality that make up the cosmos.[1]

DUALITY IN THE WORLD

In Farghānī's formulation, the typical qualities that pertain to the Oneness of Being are unity, all-comprehensiveness *(jam'iyya)*, realness *(ḥaqqiyya)* freedom from distinction and otherness, and freedom from contamination by what is unreal. But created things are dominated by the manyness that pertains to the divine knowledge. Hence they are characterized by qualities such as multiplicity, dispersion, diversity, strife, otherness, and contamination by the unreal. The true manyness of the things conceals their relative oneness.

Any creature in the universe has two fundamental faces *(wajh)* or aspects *(jiha)* one of which manifests the Oneness of Being and the other the Manyness of Knowledge.[2] The reality of each thing is in fact defined by the relationship set up between these two faces. Without both faces, the thing could not possibly exist. Pure oneness without manyness is an attribute of the Real alone, while pure manyness without oneness could provide no basis for an existent thing.

The first face of each created thing is turned toward the Real Being. This face demands that the thing will manifest properties of oneness such as balance *('adāla)* all-comprehensiveness, luminosity, and realness. On the human level, this face is turned toward and receptive to God's mercy and compassion, the names of gentleness and beauty, which are manifest in the form of truth and guidance.

The second face of each created thing is turned toward the thing itself and everything that is demanded by the thing's own, separate, individual reality. Since this face is veiled from the oneness of the Real, it manifests the opposite qualities: manyness, distance from the Real, darkness, unreality, deviation, and the domination of the veil. On the human level, this second face is connected to rejection of the divine compassion, misguidance, wrath, and the names of severity and majesty.

---

1. I have in mind the significance that is given in Sufi theoretical discussions and Islamic poetry and art in general to such things as night and day, black and white, the veil, and so on. Cf. Annemarie Schimmel's forthcoming book based on her Bampton Lectures delivered in 1990 at Columbia University: *Yūsuf's Fragrant Shirt: Studies in Islamic Symbolism.*
2. *Muntaha'l-madārik II*, p. 214; *Mashāriq al-darārī*, p. 629.

Psychologically speaking, each face has specific effects within the human being. The effect of the face turned toward oneness is submission to God's will *(islām)* and faith in Him, His prophets, and the Last Day. In short, domination by this face becomes manifest as harmony with the names of mercy and the divine guidance. Domination by the second face brings about the opposite qualities, such as immersion in misguidance, which is incarnate in the individual soul and satanic deviation.

On this first level of analysis, the Oneness of Being and the Manyness of Knowledge give rise to a world of tremendous diversity within which two tendencies can be observed among the creatures: The tendency toward oneness, harmony, wholeness, and nearness to God, manifesting the names of gentleness and mercy; and the tendency toward manyness, disequilibrium, dispersion, and distance from God, manifesting the names of severity and wrath.

This analysis may suggest that oneness is good and manyness bad. But of course this is not the implication. On the contrary, both oneness and manyness are present in the Real, since they are polar attributes. Hence both have positive roles to play. The key is always balance and equilibrium between the two.

THE TWO EXTREMES

Farghānī frequently discusses various human dangers inherent in allowing oneself to be dominated either by the face that manifests the Oneness of Being or the face that reflects the Manyness of Knowledge. Each human being has to strive to keep the two faces in equilibrium. If a person fails to do so, certain distortions will prevent the full development of the soul, which is defined by its infinite capacity as an image of the divine Reality. In the process of describing these dangers, Farghānī mentions a number of key concepts that allow us to tie his discussion into the issues mentioned at the beginning of this article.

When the face turned toward the One Being dominates, a person will be attracted toward oneness and move away from manyness. Distinctions and differentiations will play less and less of a role in that person's personality. This movement can become so overwhelming that all manyness will be obliterated from the person's view. And this movement is intimately connected with love. Like all positive qualities, love is first a divine attribute. As such, it is closely allied with the names of beauty and gentleness. The basic characteristic of love is a tendency toward union and the erasing of distinctions. As Farghānī remarks, the reality of love bridges the gap between lover and beloved, seeker and sought. By its very nature, it is unitary *(waḥdānī)* and establishes unity *(muwaḥḥid)*. Through love, those qualities that are shared by the two sides come to dominate. The ultimate result of love is the elimination of everything that keeps lover and beloved apart. Since the Beloved is the One Being, the single Reality of God, love tends toward the lifting of manyness and difference.[1]

1. *Muntaha'l-madārik II*, p. 197; *Mashāriq al-darārī*, p. 606.

As a unifying movement, love can be contrasted with knowledge, which separates, discerns, distinguishes, differentiates, and classifies.[1] Knowledge perceives differences between good and evil, true and false, right and wrong. It provides the basis for all the injunctions of the *Sharī'a*, which are founded on strict definitions and placing things in different categories. Thus human knowledge, like divine knowledge, affirms manyness and establishes its reality. It maintains the difference between God and the servant. To say this, however, is not to deny that there is a mode of visionary knowledge that unveils the underlying Oneness of Being. But in the first evaluation, knowledge differentiates.

Farghānī tells us that every sane person is bound by the laws established by discernment through knowledge. As he puts it, so long as people remain in the present world, they are "captive to the property of the world of wisdom, the manyness of its requirements, and the requirements of the two faces of created realities."[2]

The world of everyday experience pertains to wisdom because the divine wisdom itself has set up the distinctions. Each of the two faces of created reality is determined by the very nature of Uncreated Reality, or by the true Oneness of Being and the true Manyness of Knowledge.[3] As long as people are present in this world, they have to observe the requirements of both faces and maintain the distinction between the tendencies that each face manifests. These distinctions, set up by the divine wisdom itself, demand that there be two basic movements in existence: one toward mercy and union and the other toward wrath and separation. These distinctions are unavoidable, since they define the nature of reality itself. As a result, says Farghānī, people "will be subject to the properties of reward, punishment, calling to account, responsibility, and reckoning in both this world and the next."[4]

The Manyness of Knowledge establishes all the distinctions and differences found in the 'world of wisdom.' It determines the difference between guidance and misguidance and establishes the distinction between mercy and wrath, gentleness and severity. This is all positive and good. But the upshot is that the travelers on the path to God find themselves far from their Beloved, since manyness gives rise to distance and separation.

The Oneness of Being also gives rise to specific effects within the cosmos. It manifests itself in the face that marks the direction of the ascending path, the path back to mercy and gentleness. It brings about the movement of love that erases the distinction between the two sides. Nevertheless, the Oneness of Being cannot be allowed to erase the Manyness of Knowledge completely, any more than the Manyness of Knowledge can be allowed to obliterate the Oneness of Being. Exclusive attention to one side or the other can lead to deviation and disequilibrium. Both need to be kept in balance, just as they are balanced in the Real Himself, who is One in

1. These correlations are of course basic to Islamic thought. It is sufficient merely to look at the 850 instances in which the Koran employs the word *'ilm* and its derivatives to see how these verses stress separation and distinction. In contrast, the word *ḥubb* and its derivatives is employed only about 80 times, but the idea of bringing together and nearness is always present.
2. *Muntaha'l-madārik II*, p. 215.
3. As Ibn al-'Arabī tells us, "the divine name 'Wise' arranges affairs within their levels and places the things within their measures" (*Futūḥāt* II 435.15, quoted in Chittick, *Sufi Path*, p. 174).
4. *Muntaha'l-madārik II*, p. 215.

His Being and many through His names.

In discussing the dangers of too much emphasis on the Oneness of Being, Farghānī turns to certain types of mystical awareness that erase distinctions. In his own words, travelers on the path

> may become joined with the vast expanse of the World of Oneness such that they live in that Presence and gaze upon it, having realized it. They remain forgetful and negligent of created existence, its levels, and all the realities that it contains. They may have no awareness of themselves, their existence, and all the attributes, accidents, and concomitants that are seen to pertain to themselves. They witness and see the One Real Being through the Real Himself, not through themselves or through their own vision.[1]

But this is not necessarily good. For example, this sort of perception is found in *majdhūbs*, those spiritual madmen who have been overcome by the divine attraction. As long as this state remains, it represents imperfection. Such mystical awareness of the Oneness of Being is usually limited in duration. The travelers return to normal consciousness and once again follow the prophetic Sunna and the *Sharī'a*. They put into practice the requirements of knowledge and wisdom. They observe the necessities of the manyness of God's knowledge, which distinguishes between the names of guidance and misguidance. However, some people, having experienced the world of the Oneness of Being, may now consider themselves exempt from the concomitants of the Manyness of Knowledge. They reject the requirements of the 'world of wisdom' and have no concern for good and evil, right and wrong, command and prohibition, or the rulings of the *Sharī'a*. Once the discernment connected with knowledge disappears, so do all the *Sharī'a*'s rulings. In Farghānī's words, such people say,

> In the World of Oneness I saw all things as a single thing. Hence for me there is no more command and prohibition, no more lawful and unlawful, no more distinction among things. For me everything is one, with no difference between lawful and unlawful.[2]

1. *Muntaha' l-madārik* II, p. 215-216.
2. *Muntaha' l-madārik* II, p. 216.

Farghānī then adds that such people are heretics, and their blood can be shed. By saying so he places himself squarely in the mainstream of Sufism, which strives to maintain the balance between the norms of the *Sharī'a* and the *Ṭarīqa.*[1]

In this particular passage Farghānī does not enter into the dangers of placing too much stress upon knowledge. But he does deal with it elsewhere in his works, and in any case it is a well-known theme in Sufi writings. In short, exclusive emphasis upon a knowledge that differentiates and separates leads to a rationalism that is unable to see beyond surface appearances.[2] It results in excessive stress upon the differentiations set up by legalistic and literalistic interpretations of the Koran and the Sunna. Rational thought becomes a veil that maintains difference and prevents the realization of the face turned toward oneness. In speaking of the dangers of this extreme, Farghānī writes,

> The greatest factor bringing about the dispersion that prevents your realization of the reality of all-comprehensiveness is your inclination toward the sciences of philosophy and Kalam.... The veils brought about by these sciences are thicker and denser than all other veils.[3]

CONCLUSION

Finally, let me suggest some of the light that this sort of discussion can throw on current issues in the study of Sufism. First, as implied above, if love and knowledge can be set up as mutually exclusive opposites, this surely has to do with extreme forms in each case. The extreme or exclusive stress upon love overpowers the discernment and distance demanded by God's knowledge of the realities of all things. Correspondingly, extreme or exclusive stress upon the differentiations of knowledge veils the union and nearness demanded by the Oneness of God's Being.

One can find examples of extreme expressions of love in some of the more ecstatic verses of Sufi poetry. If such expressions of unification between God and the creature are taken simply as the vision of one of the two faces of each thing, no objections can be raised. But at different times and places we meet instances where there seems to be an exclusive reliance on the face of oneness, as evidenced by the

---

1. Farghānī's discussion parallels many of Ibn 'Arabī's formulations. As I have shown elsewhere, Ibn 'Arabī frequently talks about the perfected gnostic as one who sees clearly with both eyes. In contrast, other people see with difficulty and usually only with one eye. These two eyes correlate almost exactly with Farghānī's two faces. According to Ibn 'Arabī, one eye sees God's distance and incomparability, the other His nearness and similarity, one light and the other darkness, one permanence and the other transmutation, one manifestation and the other hiddenness, one Unity and the other multiplicity (cf. Chittick, *Sufi Path*, pp. 361-363). These two eyes point to the vision that accompanies Farghānī's two faces: the face turned toward oneness and that turned toward manyness. A parallel discussion is found in the *Iṣṭilāḥāt al-ṣūfiyya* of 'Abd al-Razzāq Kāshānī, where he differentiates between the Possessor of Intellect (who sees multiplicity), the Possessor of the Eye (who sees oneness), and the Possessor of the Intellect and the Eye, the perfect man who sees both multiplicity and oneness at the same time. Cf. *Iṣṭilāḥāt al-ṣūfiyya* (On the margin of Kāshānī, *Sharḥ manāzil al-sā'irīn* [Tehran: Ibrāhīm Lārījānī, 1315/1897-98), under *dhu'l-'aql*, pp. 179-180.
2. Rumi's works are full of criticisms of the unstable 'wooden legs' of the rational thinkers. Usually he contrasts cold rationality with the fire of love, but he speaks often enough about the 'intellect of intellect' for us to realize that he is perfectly at ease with another type of knowledge.
3. *Muntaha'l-madārik II*, p. 159.

harsh criticisms of certain types of Sufism found in the writings of the Sufis themselves. If the Oneness of Being is affirmed and the Manyness of Knowledge denied, then we have an extreme that threatens the balance set up by *tawḥīd.*

Another example of an extreme expression of the Oneness of Being is found in the *shaṭḥiyyāt* or 'ecstatic utterances' attributed to many Sufis. In contrast, the various interpretations offered for these utterances by later authors attempt to re-establish a balance by discerning the right relationships through knowledge. In this same arena one finds the reason for the numerous attacks that were made on *waḥdat al-wujūd,* by Sufis and non-Sufis. When this concept was criticized, it was invariably interpreted as negating the effects of the world of wisdom or the Manyness of Knowledge.

It must always be kept in mind that exclusive attention paid to the manyness of God's knowledge or the plurality of the divine names has a parallel negative outcome. Those who continue to stress manyness and difference end up by establishing absolute distinctions between God and the world *(ta'ṭīl).* They value a knowledge that differentiates and separates above everything that unifies and unites. The result is a cold literalism that kills the spirit of love and compassion. God's wrath and severity take center stage.

One can reformulate this discussion in terms of 'exoteric' and 'esoteric' approaches to Islam. But here the terminology is problematic, since it is difficult to find corresponding terms in the texts.[1] What we see happening is that expressions of Islam tended in two directions, toward expressing oneness and sameness or affirming manyness and difference. In both cases we find extreme examples that delimit the range of a spectrum of positions. Excessive emphasis on unity and oneness led to an antinomian approach to Islam, and, in its extreme forms, to those movements in Sufism known as *bīshar'* in the eastern lands of Islam. Excessive emphasis on the face that manifests the manyness of knowledge led to a literalistic and rationalistic approach to Islam and a denial that 'oneness' of any sort could be established between Lord and servant. The vast majority of Sufis who wrote theoretical works attempted to establish a balance between the two sides—between love and knowledge, Oneness and manyness, mercy and wrath, 'esoteric' and 'exoteric,' or, on another level, between what J. C. Bürgel in this volume calls ecstasy and control.

Among the advantages of Farghānī's approach is the fact that it allows for a description of the actual situation that does not fall into the typical dualities that result when we start employing dichotomous categories like 'exoteric' and 'esoteric,' especially when we impose these categories from the outside. Although at first sight Farghānī's discussion presents itself in the rhetoric of two extremes, the extremes are set up as the two poles of a relationship with the explicit awareness that neither pole can ever be empty of the other side. As a result, the actual situation is presented as a range of positions over a broad spectrum. And it is not difficult to see that the extreme positions hardly ever exist in reality, but rather in the minds of those who set up the ideal situations.

---

1. This set of terms does not seem to help much in clarifying the issue, given the subtlety of the interrelationships between different levels of explanation in the Islamic context. Moreover, one frequently sees these two terms employed as if the Sufis themselves made the same distinctions in exactly the same way and with the same frequency and purpose, which is far from being true. The Sufis employ many sets of terms that allude to a similar or parallel relationship, but each set has its own nuances and needs to be investigated in context.

The *Futūḥāt Makkiyya* and its Commentators: Some Unresolved Enigmas

Michel Chodkiewicz

Translated by Peter Kingsley

Ibn 'Arabī's influence on Persian Sufism, and Persian Sufism's role in transmitting Ibn 'Arabī's thought, are already well-studied phenomena. No doubt the dissemination of the Shaykh al-Akbar's works among authors of Persian culture is even greater than we have so far suspected, and is not confined to the famous writers who for so long have commanded the attention of specialists. My friend William Chittick, during the course of his expedition through Indian libraries, has discovered a considerable number of works which were either completely or virtually unknown: so, for example, the one volume containing a commentary on the *Futūḥāt* which he unearthed in the Andhra Pradesh Library, and for which I hope he will soon publish a detailed analysis of its contents.[1] In a colloquium devoted to Ibn 'Arabī which was held in Sicily last year Hamid Algar announced the existence of several works by masters of the Naqshbandiyya (a *ṭarīqa* that has quite wrongly had a reputation for being hostile to Ibn 'Arabī) which for the most part remain unpublished and are generally ignored in the bibliographies.[2] I am quite convinced that these recent finds are by no means the last, and that many other texts are still waiting to be disinterred—whether in Iran, India or Central Asia. The major role of Persian Sufism in the diffusion of Ibn 'Arabī's teaching is in fact not even confined to the regions I have just mentioned. Paradoxically it is sometimes Persians who have been responsible for introducing him into certain areas of the Arab world: the contemporary Yemenite historian 'Abdullāh al-Habshī has pointed out in a recent book that this was the case in the Yemen. He notes that at Zabīd under the Rasūlid dynasty the majority of members of the Akbarian circle which formed around Shaykh Al-Jabartī, the teacher of 'Abd al-Karīm al-Jīlī, had come from Persia.[3] However, my intention is not so much to describe what there is to be found in this abundant literature as to raise a question about what is not to be found in it – and to attempt to explain this silence.

1. According to W. Chittick the author of this *Sharḥ-i Futūḥāt*, of which he has only found the second volume, is probably Muḥibbullāh Ilāhābādī (d. 1058/1648).
2. In addition to the Naqshbandī texts, Algar also draws attention to other works such as the *Rasā'il Ḥaḍrat-i Sayyid Nūr al-Dīn Shāh Ni'matullāh Walī* (d. 834/1431), which have recently been edited and published by Dr. J. Nurbakhsh (Tehran: Intishārāt-i Khāniqāh-i Ni'matullāhī 1979; 4 vols.) and contain commentaries on some passages from the *Futūḥāt*. See Algar's forthcoming article, 'Reflections of Ibn 'Arabī in Early Naqshbandī Tradition.'
3. 'Abdullāh al-Habshī, *Al-ṣūfiyya wa l-fuqahā fī'l-Yaman* (Sana'a 1976), p. 131.

The *Fuṣūṣ al-Ḥikam* is a comparatively short work and one which, in a very compact form of expression, brings together the great themes of Ibn 'Arabī's metaphysics. As a result it has been the favorite target for the polemics that have violently denounced him and his school from the time of Ibn Taymiyya down to the present day. For symmetrical reasons the *Fuṣūṣ* is the work which has most often been commented on by the direct and indirect disciples of the Shaykh al-Akbar. Very naturally it is also the text which has as a rule benefited the most from the attention of Western specialists. However, I for my part wish to address myself chiefly in the following remarks to the *Futūḥāt Makkiyya.*[1] It will be remembered that the second draft of this *summa* was completed only two years before its author's death: we can therefore assume that it represents his thought in a complete and comprehensive state. We also happen to possess an autograph manuscript (which is the one Osman Yahia is at present using as the basis for his critical edition), and consequently we have a reliable text at our disposal.[2] The importance of the *Futūḥāt* as well as of the *Fuṣūṣ* has never been overlooked in Persian Sufism—a fact proved by an abundance of references. Even though the sheer size of this *opus magnum* is itself enough to discourage anyone attempting to produce an exhaustive commentary, nonetheless it has constantly been used—especially because a reading of it is indispensable for a correct interpretation of the *Fuṣūṣ*. Jandī and Ḥaydar Amulī, plus many other writers, refer to it repeatedly.[3]

Jāmī, the famous fifteenth-century Sufi, also cites the authority of the *Futūḥāt* very often in many of his writings, and one particularly interesting piece of evidence demonstrates the meticulous care he would take to grasp all its subtleties. The author of the *Rashaḥāt-i 'ayn al-ḥayāt* —a famous hagiographical text about the first masters of the Naqshbandiyya—describes an encounter which took place in 874/1469 between Jāmī and Ubaydullāh Aḥrār. Jāmī declared to Aḥrār that in several passages of the *Futūḥāt* he had come up against problems he was unable to resolve, and he outlined one of the most difficult ones. Aḥrār then asked him to close the copy of the *Futūḥāt* he was holding in his hands, and gave him some preliminary explanations; after he had done so he said to him, "Now, let's turn back to the book." When Jāmī reread the problematic passage its meaning became perfectly clear to him.[4]

---

1. All subsequent references to the *Futūḥāt* (= Fut.) are to the Egyptian edition of 1329 A.H., in 4 volumes, or to the reprint, Beirut, Dar Sadir, no date (circ. 1970).
2. That is not the case with the *Fuṣūṣ*. This explains—but does not justify—the hazardous hypotheses entertained by some defenders of Ibn 'Arabī's orthodoxy who are prompted by their ill-inspired zeal to denounce interpolations, which according to them distort its meaning, in the text as it has come down to us. See for example my review of Maḥmūd Ghurab's book, *Sharḥ Fuṣūṣ al-ḥikam* (Damascus 1985), in *Studia Islamica* LXIII, pp.179-182. Needless to say, a new critical edition of the *Fuṣūṣ* based on the manuscripts not taken into account by Afiffi would be extremely desirable.
3. Cf. Jandī, *Sharḥ Fuṣūṣ al-ḥikam,* (Mashad 1982); Haydar Āmūlī, *Naṣṣ al-nuṣūṣ,* ed. H.Corbin and O.Yahia (Tehran-Paris 1975), and *Jāmī' al-asrār* (in H.Corbin and O.Yahya's *La philosophie shi'ite,* Tehran-Paris 1969). In this last work see for example the long quotation from chapter 366 of the *Futūḥāt* on pp. 440f.
4. Fakhr al-Dīn 'Alī ibn Ḥusayn Wā'iz al-Kāshifī, *Rashaḥāt-i 'ayn al-ḥayāt,* ed. 'Alī Aṣghār Mu'-niyān (2 vols., Tehran1970), I, pp. 249-50.

A century later Aḥmad Sirhindī—who is far too often and, as Friedmann has shown, quite unjustly presented as an opponent of Ibn 'Arabī—also refers frequently to the *Futūḥāt* in his *Maktūbāt*.[1] As is well known, the same applies to his contemporary Mullā Sadrā: even though in some of his writings prudence induced him to conceal his borrowings (which are easily identifiable nonetheless), there is no shortage in his works of openly acknowledged references to the *Futūḥāt,* which are sometimes very extensive.[2] And as I have already gone far beyond the mediæval context of this volume, I may as well mention one final example which is altogether contemporary. I am referring to the Ayatollah Khomeyni, whose works (particularly those written in his youth) testify to the fact that he was an assiduous and penetrating reader of Ibn 'Arabī—and particularly of his *Futūḥāt*.[3]

But all these examples will no doubt already be familiar to you, and I am sure each of you would be able to add considerably to this highly arbitrary selection. I will therefore not extend this very brief list any further. The point I wish to make is the following. The innumerable Persian writers (and I hasten to add that the same applies to Arab writers) whose works testify to the fact that they have read and reread the *Futūḥāt,* and who often provide us with extremely perceptive comments on various complex doctrinal themes expounded in the text or on the meaning of passages which require delicate interpretation, *never seem to consider the work as a whole.* The structure of this fundamental book—the number and sequence of its sections *(fuṣūl)* and chapters *(abwāb)* the subtle and extremely rigorous interrelationships between its different parts—appear to be ignored and at the very least are, as far as I know, never explained. Naturally I make no claim to have read all the glosses, paraphrases and commentaries that have been produced by readers of the *Futūḥāt* in over seven centuries; but so far none of the specialists whom I have questioned seems to have discovered a text which invalidates my own observations. Everything suggests that the *Futūḥāt* has always been viewed as an extraordinary cornucopia from which everyone according to his individual inclination draws symbols, technical terms, ideas and expressions without suspecting (or without making us suspect) the coherence of the whole: without looking for the secret of its architecture. Similarly, many of the highly enigmatic pieces of information given by Ibn 'Arabī himself—for example the very surprising lists of spiritual sciences corresponding to each *manzil,* or the precise number of degrees corresponding to each *maqām* —remain unexplained. It must be pointed out that this silence on the part of

1. *Maktūbāt-i Imām-i Rabbānī* (Lucknow 1889). Sirhindī's attention was drawn not only by the doctrinal ideas expounded in the *Futūḥāt* but also by the anecdotes it contains. See for example Letter 58 (in which he criticizes the doctrine of reincarnation, *tanāsukh)* where he mentions the story of Ibn 'Arabī's visionary encounter at the Ka'ba with a man belonging to a humanity prior to our own (cf. Fut., III, pp. 348 and 549). As Y. Friedmann observes (Shaykh Ahmad Sirhindī, Montreal-London 1971, p. 64), the *Mujaddid* "recommends the study of Ibn al-'Arabi's works and considers them indispensable for the proper appreciation of his own spiritual insights."
2. As is the case in *Al-Ḥikmat al-muta'āliyya fī l-asfār al-'aqliyyat al-arba'a*. For further comments on this matter see James W. Morris' introduction to his translation of *Al-ḥikma al-'arshiyya* (*The Wisdom of the Throne,* Princeton 1981), which is a work in which explicit allusions to the *Futūḥāt* —although less frequent—are far from exceptional. Cf. *ibid.*, pp. 178, 234-5, 239-40, etc.
3. This is especially true of the following works by the Ayatollah Khomeynī: *Sharḥ du'ā al-saḥar* (Beirut 1982); *Miṣbāḥ al-hidāya* (Beirut 1983); *Ta'līqāt alā sharḥ Fuṣūṣ al-ḥikam* (Qum 1986).

Islamic writers is repeated by Western scholars in spite of the fact that their studies of Ibn 'Arabī continue to multiply. In both cases, it would seem that the forest is hidden by the trees.

The fact that we find no answer to these questions in poets whose work is strongly influenced by Ibn 'Arabī is not surprising: the literary form they have chosen and the particular nature of their inspiration are not conducive to this kind of analysis. For example, there is the case of Fakhr al-Dīn 'Irāqī. Even though he studied the *Fuṣūṣ* and the *Futūḥāt* with Qūnawī, and admirably crystallizes the 'Divine Flashes' in his verses, he plainly felt no call to translate what he knew and what he felt into painstaking discursive expositions. The same applies to everyone after him who translated Ibn 'Arabī's dazzling message into lyrics—whether in Iran, India or elsewhere.

But, just to confine ourselves to the first generations of disciples, what are we to make of the silence of someone such as Ṣadr al-Dīn Qūnawī—an exceptionally talented disciple of the Shaykh al-Akbar, to whom he in fact bequeathed the manuscript of the final draft of the *Futūḥāt?* How can we avoid being disappointed at finding nothing more than very partial observations in the writings of Jīlī—even though he wrote a *Sharḥ mushkilāt al-Futūḥāt?* In actual fact, in spite of its promising title this short treatise does no more than explain the statements made at the start of chapter 559 of the *Futūḥāt:* the *bāb al-asrār* or 'Chapter of Mysteries.' According to Ibn 'Arabī this chapter contains the quintessence of the *Futūḥāt.* One could therefore expect that in the commentary Jīlī devotes to it he would give some prominence to the secret logic in the composition of a book which he tells us with admiration is "the greatest of books written about this science...and the most distinguished in terms of scope and breadth" *(a'zam al-kutub al-muṣannafa fī hādhā l-'ilm... wa ajalluhā iḥātatan wa was'an)* while elsewhere he specifies that its author "sometimes speaks in clear language and sometimes expresses himself symbolically."[1] But one finds nothing of the kind; the symbols retain their mystery. Obviously it is impossible here to review in turn all the authors from whom one might have hoped for some clarification, or at the very least some enquiries, testifying to a comprehensive approach to Ibn 'Arabī's *summa mystica.* But I believe I am not mistaken in repeating that they avoid the issue I am raising—and indeed that they also refrain from proposing any interpretation at all for a large number of highly abstruse utterances of which I will soon give a few examples. As I mentioned earlier, in this respect the Arab commentators are no more satisfactory than their Persian counterparts: the works of Sha'rānī, of Nābulusī, of 'Abd al-Qādir al-Jazā'irī remain equally silent.

This brings us to the need to pose a fundamental question. If these people—whose perceptiveness as well as their veneration for Ibn 'Arabī are beyond any

1. This comment occurs on the third line of the manuscript of the *Sharḥ mushkilāt al-Futūḥāt* belonging to my private collection. Although the *explicit* specifies that the manuscript contains a commentary on those sections of the *bāb al-asrār* which correspond to the first *eleven* chapters of the *Futūḥāt,* in actual fact it only comments on *ten* of these sections (the last sentence commented on is the one on line 14 of Fut., IV, p. 329). In passing it is worth noting that the Cairo edition of the *Futūḥāt* is clearly faulty where chapter 559 is concerned; in particular, there are a considerable number of anomalies in the numbering of the sections.

Ibn 'Arabī Riding a Black Mule with two Students on Foot. From a manuscript of the *Majālis al-'ushshāq,* dated 959/1552. MS. Ouseley Add. 24, f. 69r (Courtesy of the Bodleian Library, Oxford)

Diagram of the Soul's Progress. From a manuscript of the *Futūḥāt Makkiyya* Arabic MS. Or. 132, f. 417 (Courtesy of the British Library).

doubt—offer no explanation whatever, is this not very simply because there is nothing at all to explain? If the structure of the *Futūḥāt* elicits no comment from them, is this not because it is totally arbitrary and so resists any attempt to justify it? At first sight a glance through the list of contents suggests that the answer is yes: it is extremely difficult to make out any orderly progression or any intelligible connection between the themes that are dealt with one after the other. The same subject is often discussed on several separate occasions in different chapters which are frequently at a considerable distance from each other and each of which seems to ignore the existence of the others. Long passages turn out to consist of the total or partial re-use of material from earlier treatises, which means that their content is necessarily heterogeneous in nature. And furthermore, what we are told by Ibn 'Arabī himself appears to sanction this point of view: "neither this particular book nor any of my other works has been composed in the way that ordinary books are composed, and I do not write them according to the habitual method of authors," he declares.[1] Again, later on he emphasizes that "I have not written one single letter of this book other than under the effect of divine dictation."[2] This frequently repeated assertion as to the inspired nature of his writings tends to suggest that it would be pointless to attempt to discover in them a precise pattern. Ibn 'Arabī lends an additional argument to this hypothesis in the form of a comment on the presentation—which indeed is extremely disconcerting for the reader—of particulars regarding the 'legal statutes' *(aḥkhām)*. He admits that chapter 88, which expounds the principles *(uṣūl)* from which these statutes derive, should logically have preceded rather than followed chapters 68 to 72, which expound their consequences. However, he states, "it was not from my personal choice that I retained this order."[3] And to illustrate this remark he compares the plentiful examples of *non sequitur* in the *Futūḥāt* with the examples to be found in the Surahs of the Koran, where the mutual proximity of successive verses appears to be purely accidental. The statement I have just quoted (and there are many other similar ones in the *Futūḥāt)* encourage one to conclude that a work which has been composed in obedience to such unpredictable inspirations—whether supernatural or not—is bound to be devoid of internal coherence, and that the enigmas it contains are necessarily indecipherable.

I believe it is correct to say that this conclusion is radically false. Paradoxically, the first indication that this must be so is provided by Ibn 'Arabī's analogy between the abrupt breaks in meaning in the text of the Koran and in his own book. In fact, as he explains in another passage, the lack of order in the Holy Book is only apparent: "Here [that is, between consecutive verses which seem unrelated to each other] a relationship of affinity exists, but it is extremely secret."[4] Again: "If you connect each verse with the one preceding it and the one following it, the power of the Divine Word will make you see that the verse in question requires what accompanies it in this way, and only attains its perfection by means of what surrounds it. This is the perspective which belongs to the perfect among spiritual men."[5] In other

1. *Fut.*, I, p. 59.
2. *Fut.*, II, p. 456.
3. *Fut.*, II, p. 163.
4. *Fut.*, III, p. 200.

words this profound unity of the Koran remains unnoticed by the commonality of believers, and even the writers of *tafsīr* are incapable of revealing it to us, but it is perceived by the divinely inspired gnostic, the *'ārif bi-llāh*. This gives us reason to suspect that for Ibn 'Arabī the same essential unity also exists, and somehow or other is detectable, in the *Futūḥāt,* where nothing is to be found "which does not proceed from an in-breathing of the Divine Spirit."[1] The conclusion is all the more unavoidable because he also states that "Everything which we talk about in our gatherings and in our writings proceeds from the Koran and its treasures."[2]

Personally I am convinced that in fact the *Futūḥāt* is neither a disorderly encyclopedia of bookish knowledge nor a heterogeneous collection of passages juxtaposed simply as a result of the caprices of inspiration. Limitations of space in this brief article make it impossible to provide all the necessary answers; but I would like instead to offer a demonstration of this claim insofar as it bears on several important points.[3]

In his critical edition of the *Futūḥāt* which is at present in process of being published, Osman Yahia makes an attempt to find an explanation for the number of chapters contained in its six sections *(fuṣūl).*[4] His comments on the matter probably leave anyone who examines them unsatisfied: according to what he says it would seem that the different numbers were chosen by Ibn 'Arabī because in Islamic tradition they possessed a symbolic value, but without this value having any necessary or intelligible relationship to the nature of the corresponding *fuṣūl*. For example, he observes—as anyone can easily do—that the number of chapters in the *faṣl al-manāzil* (the section on the 'spiritual abodes') is identical to the number of Surahs in the Koran: 114. However, he does not draw any particular conclusion from this observation; the number 114 could somehow or other have been chosen by Ibn 'Arabī for purely aesthetic reasons. As we will see, the truth of the matter is very different. In fact, in this instance as in the case of so many other enigmas, Ibn 'Arabī provides the reader with all the keys he needs. But these keys are deliberately scattered throughout the work, and most often placed in such a way that they remain unnoticed.

Let us look a little more closely at this *faṣl al-manāzil:* the fourth section in the work and one of the most mysterious. It extends from chapter 270 to chapter 383. It is obviously related at least by its title to one of the first chapters of the *Futūḥāt:* chapter 22, which itself is entitled *fī ma'rifat 'ilm manzil al-manāzil. B*ut a priori this chapter 22—which Osman Yahia, plainly disconcerted, calls a *bāb gharīb,* a

5. *Fut.*, IV, p. 137. Cf. also II, p. 548.
1. *Fut.*, III, p. 101.
2. *Fut.*, III, p. 334.
3. I would like to make it clear that the following clarifications, as well as the solutions to this problem which I will eventually provide elsewhere, are very far from being attributable to me alone In the first instance I must reiterate my debt to Michel Vâlsan, who over a period of many years guided me in my discovery of Ibn 'Arabī. My thanks are also due to my learned friend Abdelbaki Meftah: our exchanges of correspondence have on numerous occasions allowed me to clarify and correct my own interpretations. Finally, I am indebted to some among those who today ensure the transmission of the *khirqa akbariyya* for support without which my efforts would have been in vain.
4. See volume III (Cairo 1974), pp. 37-8.

'strange chapter'—poses more problems than it solves. In it we find a list assembling under nineteen principal 'spiritual abodes' *(ummahāt al-manāzil)* a series of secondary *manāzil* which in turn contain a whole series of others. The names given to all these *manāzil* (they are names which we will find reappearing here and there in the *faṣl al-manāzil)* are a puzzle: *manzil al-istikhbār, manzil al-halāk, manzil al-du'ā, manzil al-rumūz* and so on. None of these designations corresponds to the taxonomy used in Sufi literature for distinguishing the different stages of spiritual life (or, for example, to the *manāzil* as listed by Anṣārī in his well-known *Manāzil al-sā'irīn).*

However, when we juxtapose the cryptic remarks scattered throughout chapter 22 on the one hand and throughout the chapters in the fourth *faṣl* on the other, these names suddenly become completely meaningful: each of them corresponds either to a Surah or to a group of surahs. The *manzil al-istikhbār* ('Abode of Interrogation') is the one which groups together the Surahs that begin with an interrogative formula —for example Surah 88 *(Hal atāka ḥadīth al-ghāshiya...).* The *manzil al-ḥamd* ('Abode of Praise'), which is subdivided into five *manāzil,* is made up of the five Suras (1, 2, 18, 34, 35) that begin with the formula *Al-ḥamdu li-Llāh.* The *manzil al-rumūz* ('Abode of Symbols') contains all the surahs which start with the *ḥurūf muqatta'a*— the mysterious individual letters that are also called *nūrāniyya,* 'luminous.' The *manzil al-du'ā* ('Abode of Appeal') is the name applied to all the Surahs starting with the vocative formula *Yā ayyuha...;* the *manzil al-amr* ('Abode of Commandment') brings together the Surahs which begin with a verb in the imperative, such as *qul* ('Speak!').

I will not go on enumerating the rest of these correspondences here, and will leave for a subsequent occasion the task of drawing up an exhaustive list identifying the Koranic references for all these technical terms in chapter 22. But these initial observations are enough to allow us to anticipate the conclusion that each of the 114 chapters in the *faṣl al-manāzil* in fact corresponds to a Surah and—more or less allusively—conveys its esoteric significance. However, it is in vain that one looks for what would seem to be the obvious correspondence between the first of these chapters and the first Surah of the Holy Scripture, between the second chapter and the second Surah, and so on. The relationship one would have expected proves difficult to confirm.

The key to this mystery is actually put in our hands on a number of occasions—and particularly at the beginning of the *faṣl,* in the second verse of the introductory poem which contains the word *urūj:* 'ascent' or 'ascension.' The journey through the spiritual abodes is a journey of ascent which—directly counter to the normal ordering of the Koranic vulgate—leads the *murīd* from the last Surah of the Koran, *Al-nās,* through to the first, *Al-fātiḥa:* 'that which opens,' the Surah in which he receives the ultimate *fatḥ,* the definitive illumination. In other words, it is a question of re-ascending from the furthest point of universal Manifestation (as symbolized by the last word of the Koran: *al-nās,* 'men') back to the divine Principle (as symbolized by the first Surah, *Umm al-kitāb,* 'Mother of the Book,' and more specifically by the point of the *Bā'* in the *basmala*). The apparently inexplicable sequence of the chapters now becomes perfectly coherent, and the correspondence which I have pointed out is demonstrable without any exception whatever in the actual text of each chapter and also often even in their titles. The following few examples will make the matter clear for anyone familiar with the Koran.

The third *manzil* (chapter 272), *manzil tanzīl al-tawḥīd*, very obviously corresponds to the third surah from last: the surah *Al-ikhlāṣ,* the theme of which is divine unity. The fourth (chapter 273), *manzil al-halak,* 'Abode of Perdition,' corresponds to the surah *Al-masad,* which describes the punishment of Abū Lahab. The sixth *manzil* (chapter 275), 'Abode of the Repudiation of Idols,' answers to the sixth surah *su'ūdan* (still working backwards from the end to the beginning) and therefore to the Surah *Al-kāfirūn*. Following the same rule, the nineteenth *manzil* (chapter 288), 'Abode of Recitation,' corresponds to the Surah *Al-alaq,* in which the Prophet is commanded to recite the Revelation transmitted to him by the angel. The forty-ninth (chapter 316), 'Abode of the Divine Pen,' corresponds to the Surah *Al-qalam* —and so on right through to the hundred and fortieth and final *manzil,* the *manzil al-azama al-jāmi'a* ('Abode of Cumulative Immensity') which is the one in which, after arriving at the goal of the initiatic journey, the spiritual wayfarer or *sālik* realizes the secrets of the 'Mother of the Book.' Here again I will refrain from listing every single correspondence. To do so would anyway be superfluous, because anyone in possession of this key will easily be able to complete the brief list I have given.

These cursory remarks are by themselves quite sufficient to confirm that there is nothing at all fortuitous in the arrangement of this *faṣl,* and that—however peculiar the sequence of the subjects which it deals with may appear—this sequence obeys a very precise law. We can, for example, no longer be surprised to see chapter 366, on the *wuzarā al-mahdī* (The Mahdi's Helpers), followed without any apparent justification by the chapter in which Ibn 'Arabī describes his ascension from heaven to heaven until he reaches the threshold of the Divine Presence. In fact according to the schema I outlined above, chapter 366 corresponds to the Surah *Al-kahf,* which is well known for its eschatological nature, while chapter 367 corresponds to the Surah *Al-isrā* which alludes to the celestial Ascension of the Prophet. And one will now understand that the reason why chapter 336 deals with the *mubāya'at al-quṭb,* the 'Pact with the Pole', is because according to the same logic it is echoing the surah *Al-fatḥ,* which refers to the pact between the Companions and the Prophet at Hudaybiyya (Koran XLVIII:10, 18).

We find the solution to other enigmas provided in the same way. I will illustrate this point by referring to chapter 273,[1] which contains some passages that could give the reader the impression either of being the products of a disordered imagination or—on the more favourable hypothesis—of referring to an incommunicable visionary experience. Ibn 'Arabī explains how, guided by the First Intellect, he visited this *manzil* which contains five chambers *(buyūt).* In each of these chambers chests *(khazā'in)* are shut away. Each chest has locks *(aqfāl)* each lock has keys *(mafātiḥ)* and each key has to be turned a specific number of times *(ḥarakāt).* Then the Shaykh al-Akbar describes these chambers together with their contents, one by one: the first chest in the first chamber has three locks, the first of these locks has

1. *Fut.*, pp. 582-6.

three keys, the first of these keys has to be turned four hundred times, and so on. I am sure that more often than not these strange details disarm the reader's curiosity. However, they are easy to interpret once one knows that this *manzil* is the one corresponding to the surah *Al-masad.* The five chambers are this Surah's five verses. The chests are the words in each verse, the number of locks is the number of letters in each of the words, the keys are the graphic signs of which the letters are composed (diacritical points and consonantal *ductus*), and the turnings of the key represent the numerical values of these letters according to the *abjād.* The first chest is therefore the word *tabbat:* it consists of three letters—or three locks. The first of these locks is the *T-ā'*. This is composed of three graphic signs—and therefore three keys—and has a numerical value of 400. Comparable explanations, in which the science of letters *('ilm al-ḥurūf)* plays a major role that is specifically announced in chapter 2 of the *Futūḥāt,* can be given every time one encounters expositions of this type—and regardless of where in the text they occur.[1] Whatever one's views about something which for many people is no more than a gratuitous intellectual game, one is bound to admit that this is a game which is subject to rules.

While still confining ourselves to the *faṣl al-manāzil* in particular, we find the solution to one other riddle at the same time. This is the enigma posed by the tabulations of the spiritual sciences corresponding to every *manzil* which are placed at the end of each of the 114 chapters. These listings group together ideas which are of such a kind that any attempt to discover a rational link between them would be in vain; one's first impression on reading them is of being confronted with a catalogue composed by a writer who has been guided entirely by his own fantasy. Without being in a position here to go into details—that would require juxtaposing a large number of quotations from the Koran against entire pages of the *Futūḥāt*—I will simply point out that each of the sciences referred to is related to the content of either one or several verses in the Surah corresponding to the *manzil* in question. So, once again, we find ourselves faced with statements which in spite of their chaotic appearance derive from the application of a method based on principles that, once explained, prove to be extremely simple.

I will reserve a detailed examination of the structure of the other five sections for another occasion. However, I would like here to raise very briefly the question of the overall architecture of the *Futūḥāt*. The division into six *fuṣūl* is easily explained

1. The *fatā* (the 'mystical youth', according to Corbin's translation) who appears to Ibn 'Arabī in chapter 1 reveals to him the secret of the *imām mubīn* (cf. *Fut.*, IV, p. 367)—in other words the secret of the 'Book that contains all things' (cf. *Fut.*, I, p. 180)—by inviting him to decipher what is inscribed on his own person: as he says at the end of the chapter, "Examine the details of my constitution and the disposition of my form" (*Fut.*, I, p. 48). According to the logic of this graphic symbolism the science of letters (the principles of which are the subject of chapter 2) is the science that makes the 'deciphering' possible and simultaneously explains both the length of the exposition devoted to it and the position it occupies at the start of the *Futūḥāt.* For example, by referring to the science of letters, the *'ilm al-ḥurūf* (the significance of which is conveyed in this way), we can interpret the number of degrees *(darajāt)* corresponding to each of the spiritual categories *(ārifūn, malāmiyya)* and to their subdivisions *(ahl al-uns, ahl al-adāb)* in the series of chapters from 74 to 185 *(faṣl al-mu'āmalāt).* All these numbers—and more generally speaking, all the numbers that appear in the *Futūḥāt*—are obtained by a method of calculation which is perfectly intelligible.

as due to the special significance of the number six in Ibn 'Arabī's teaching. This significance is not simply a result of the fact that six is the number of the days of Creation, as Osman Yahia notes (and also the number of spatial dimensions). For Ibn 'Arabī 6, which is the first perfect number (because 6 = 1/6 + 1/3 + 1/2),[1] is above all else the symbolic number of the Perfect Man *(insān kāmil)*—that is, of the focal point of his entire teaching.[2] This number actually expresses the value according to *abjād* of the letter *waw:* a letter which, although not written, manifests itself in the vocal enunciation of the existentiating *Kun* ('Be!') between the *Kāf* and the *Nūn*, and for this reason is identified by the Shaykh al-Akbar with the 'Reality of Muḥammad' *(ḥaqīqa muḥammadiyya)* which is the 'isthmus' *(barzākh)* between the *Ḥaqq* and the *khalq*, between the Divine Principle and Its Manifestation.[3] This identification is also based on the grammatical function of the *waw,* which in Arabic performs the role of copula and consequently unites what is separated.

But to be more precise, the explanation of the number and sequence of the *fuṣūl* lies in the number and nature of the divine attributes *(ṣifāt)* and modes of relation *(nisab)* upon which the created being depends.[4] Each *faṣl* corresponds to one of these six Names of God. The first *(faṣl al-ma'ārif,* the 'section of knowledges') is plainly related to the first Name, *Al-Alīm,* The Knower. The second *(faṣl al-mu'āmalāt)* dealing with the manners of behaviour by means of which the postulant *(al-murīd,* literally 'he who desires') progresses upon the Path, corresponds to the second of these Divine Names which is, precisely, *Al-Murīd.* Corresponding to the third Divine Name in the series—*Al-Qadīr*, The Omnipotent—is the *faṣl al-aḥwāl,* the section on the spiritual states produced in man by the divine omnipotence without his being able to acquire them through his own strength. The fourth Name is *Al-Qā'il* or *Al-Mutakallim,* 'He who speaks': its relation to the fourth *faṣl,* in which each stage of spiritual realization is identified with one of the Surahs in the Koran, or Divine Word, is equally clear. The next *faṣl* deals with the *munāzalāt,* or 'meetings halfway' between God and creature: meetings in which man converses with God face to face. It corresponds to the fifth Name: *Al-Samī'*, 'He who hears.' Finally, the sixth *faṣl* is the section on the *maqāmāt* or 'stations,' each of which represents a specific mode of contemplation *(mushāhada).* This in turn is related to the sixth Divine Name: *Al-Baṣīr,* 'He who sees.'

It remains to suggest the reason why the *Futūḥāt* consists of five hundred and sixty chapters in all. Here we must bear in mind that this number had been decided on in advance at the very first stages of composition: the summary of the work which is printed between pages 11 and 30 of the Egyptian edition had in fact already been written by the end of the year 599/1203, which is when Ibn 'Arabī started composing the book. Although it is not possible to be absolutely certain, I believe that there are two facts worth noting which are hardly mere coincidences. The first is the

1. *Fut.*, II, p. 469.
2. *Fut.*, *ibid.*
3. *Fut.*, III, p. 283.
4. *Fut.*, II, p. 493. Normally this series of traditional Divine Names — the *asmā al-dhāt* — includes a seventh *(Al-Ḥayy,* 'The Living'). However, Ibn 'Arabī explains that if he speaks of six Names rather than seven this is because *Al-Ḥayy* is the Name which enables the other six to subsist and is therefore in a sense their common principle.

fact that the number five hundred and sixty is also the number of words in the surah *Al-Fatḥ:* it is especially difficult to suppose this is just an accident when on the one hand we remember that before assuming its plural form the title of the work seems to have been *Al-Fatḥ al-Makkī,* and on the other hand we bear in mind the esoteric commentaries on this Surah.[1] The second fact is very simply that the Shaykh al-Akbar was born in the year 560 of the *Hegira.* This date is therefore the point of departure for that extraordinary spiritual 'conquest' from which the *Futūḥāt* would harvest the fruits.

Is it reasonable to believe that none of the individuals whom I mentioned to start with was in a position to provide answers to the various questions I have raised? Or, as an alternative hypothesis, are we to suppose that these questions never occurred to them? Regardless of whether they were Sunnis or Shi'ites, and even if they did happen to dispute his position on specific issues, they all shared a manifest veneration for the Shaykh al-Akbar. Nothing that he wrote was a matter of indifference to them. Each of his works was scrutinized by them with vigilant attention, as we can see from the subtle exegeses of his thought of which their own books provide so many examples. Like Jāmī in the story narrated earlier, they never resigned themselves to not understanding even the most obscure or most ambiguous aspects of Ibn 'Arabī's writings, and they sought a resolution to these enigmas or *mushkilāt* with tireless zeal. To me it is consequently self-evident that the majority, if not all, of them will not have been able either to ignore the problems about which I have spoken or to resign themselves to leaving them unsolved. These possibilities are all the more unlikely because—as I believe I have demonstrated—the solutions are pointed to by a considerable number of clues which they could not have missed.

I am therefore convinced that in this particular case it is a matter of deliberate silence. Very significantly, at the start of his *Naṣṣ al-nuṣūṣ* Ḥaydar Āmulī elaborates in ten pages of preliminaries on the need for secrecy—*kitmān al-asrār al-ilāhiyya an ghayri ahlihā,* 'concealment of the Divine Mysteries from those unworthy of them'—and in justification of this rule he cites verses from the Koran, various *ḥadīth* and a lengthy passage from chapter 31 of the *Futūḥāt.* He also underlines the necessity, for a genuine understanding of Ibn 'Arabī's writings, of a relationship of spiritual affinity *(munāsaba)* with their author, and he points out that such a relationship is exceptional "even among the Poles and their like."

This mandate for discretion—which I have considered it appropriate to infringe here to a small degree—is vigorously stated by Ibn 'Arabī on a number of occasions and also observed by him as well: either because it is a question of knowledge that is dangerous *(muhlika)* and the use of which could lead the imprudent to their perdition,[2] or because the disclosure of certain secrets would enable imposters to claim for themselves improperly a degree of sainthood that is beyond their reach. So—to come back to one of the enigmas which we solved earlier by way of example—after

1. Cf. e.g. *Fut.*, II, p. 60; III, p. 153; IV, p. 50; and Qāshānī, *Ta'wīlāt* (published under the name of Ibn 'Arabī) (Beirut 1968), II, pp. 505-510.
2. Cf. *Fut.*, II, p. 584. Compare also *Fut.*, I, p.190, where Ibn 'Arabī declares that he is deliberately abstaining from communicating certain secrets of the *'ilm al-ḥurūf,* and mentions a little further on that he has taken an oath never to use the powers granted by this science.

speaking of the 'chambers', 'chests', 'locks' and 'keys' of the fifth *manzil* (the one corresponding to the Surah *Al-naṣr)*, he points out that if he keeps silent as to the meaning of these symbolic terms this is to prevent the liar *(al-kādhib)* from laying claim to have come into possession of this science through a personal spiritual realization.[1]

I see no room for doubt that through the course of the ages this same discipline was put into practice by the most eminent of Ibn 'Arabī's interpreters, and that at least in the majority of cases this accounts for the strange lacunas in their commentaries which we noted earlier. Very simply, the silence of the *ahl al-taṣawwuf* in this matter bears out the truth of the law succinctly enunciated almost four centuries earlier than the Shaykh al-Akbar by Dhu'l-Nūn al-Miṣrī: *qulūb al-aḥrār, qubūr al-asrār,* "The hearts of free men are the tombs of secrets"

1. *Fut.*, II, p. 590.

The Sophianic Feminine in the Work of Ibn 'Arabi and Rumi

R. W. J. Austin

In their separate and often very different ways the three great religions which make up what is sometimes called the Abrahamic tradition manifest, despite their radically patriarchal character, interesting strands and undercurrents of feminine imagery and symbolism, this being particularly the case in the exposition and expression of their more esoteric aspects. In Judaism one may note the curious matrilineal transmission of religious identity and the quasi-sacerdotal role of the mother at the Sabbath eve meal. In the case of Catholic and Orthodox Christianity one hardly needs to mention the profoundly pervasive cult of Our Lady, perhaps the most powerful manifestation of non-Judaic, pagan influences in that religious tradition. In Islam, especially in Shi'ite Islam a very interestingly similar and parallel phenomenon is evident in the various forms of the veneration of the Lady Fāṭima; but more of that later.

Apart from such often rather restricted and secondary manifestations, it is, I think well understood that the power, status, image and experience of women, whether as a social, political, religious or spiritual being has always been problematic and not a little threatening to the ruling authorities of the patriarchal religious cultures and societies, whether Abrahamic or otherwise, oscillating as they have tended to do, between the need to strictly control female mate-selection and sexual expression on the one hand, and the lauding and veneration of patriarchally positive and ideal women on the other. Indeed, even in those religious traditions of Indo-European character in which a female spiritual figure is more overtly admitted, the more sensual aspects of the feminine are no less strictly controlled and largely disdained, since all the patriarchal religions are ultimately world-denying and sense-depreciating.

Thus, even for Christians, most of whom believe profoundly in the sanctity of substance and image, there remains a deep hostility to the sensual, and particularly, to the erotic implications and associations of the Feminine. In certain ways this is even more the case with Judaism and Islam in which the notions of the sacred image and body are also banned. Although all such matters formally come under the purview of the Sacred Law in both faiths, the sensual and the sexual have in practice become secularized or—perhaps more accurately—de-sacralised. In Sunni Islam especially, apart from Sufism, this lack of any spiritual sense of the Feminine is most marked. Thus, I think one might say without too much fear of contradiction, that the Feminine, all in all, presents for these traditions a perennial problem and enigma.

Therefore, it is something of a relief and surprise to find the mystical literature of at least two of these religions, especially the mystical poetry, teeming with rich, warm images and metaphors of love and beauty, wine and ecstasy, passions, feelings and lovely female spirituals. How is one to account for this phenomenon? Why this unexpected release of feelings and experiences apparently so out of tune with the exoteric mainstream of religious orthodoxy, which indeed often strongly disapproved and disapproves of such licence.

The answer to these questions lies, I would suggest, in the nature of the mystical experience and its expression. Conveniently, one can speak of two apparently opposite kinds of mystical aspiration: one being the aspiration to merge and unite with the great vital currents and forces of cosmic nature, which R.C. Zaehner has called "nature mysticism," the other aspiring to identity and fusion with purely spiritual realities in a headlong flight from the world of nature.[1] However, transcending or perhaps deeply underlying these two opposing drives, there is an experience of an inexpressible and indescribable wholeness of being, which is common to both aspirations. It is interesting that the two opposing types of mysticism often employ the images and vocabulary of the other which suggests the polarity rather than the simple opposition of the two, since both are motivated by a powerful desire to know, love and ultimately, be united and whole, and both reject the uneasy compromise and *modus vivendi* between heaven and earth which is the experience of the ordinary believer. Thus, for the mystic, however unofficially or perhaps unconsciously, there is a deep-seated aspiration to fundamental human reconciliation, to linking and harmony, to wholeness and *coincidentia*. Above all, the mystic strives to establish a real and binding relationship—whether of love, knowledge or both—between himself and the divine object of his Quest. It is precisely within the context of this relationship-oriented quest that feminine images and symbols seem to play so natural a part, due in large part to that Sophianic nature of the spiritual/divine Feminine, the main theme of this essay, to which I shall return shortly.

Of special importance with regard to the mediating principle of this ardently desired divine-human relationship is that psycho-spiritual medium of which that great interpreter of Islamic esoterism, Henry Corbin, was so devoted and brilliant an exponent: the *'Ālam al-mithāl* or 'intermediary realm of Idea-Images.'[2] It is probably precisely because of this basically unitive nature of the mystical quest that it has, as Rudolf Otto has shown, despite some more exaggerated claims, a greater universal relevance and significance, especially because it has restored in a profound and principal way the place of the Feminine in the scheme of things, both sensual and spiritual.

At this point it is appropriate that I address myself to an examination of the particular term 'Sophianic Feminine' employed in my title, a term first coined, I believe, by Henry Corbin. Its primary meaning, of course, relates to the notion of the Feminine as a manifestation of divine Wisdom or 'Sophia' who makes an early appearance in the Old Testament, both in *Ecclesiastes* and in the *Apocrypha's* book of *Ecclesiasticus* in which she describes her close association with the Most High

1. *Mysticism, Sacred and Profane* (Oxford 1961), Ch. III.
2. *Creative Imagination in the Sufism of Ibn 'Arabi* (London 1969), Ch. IV.

God, dwelling with him for ever.[1] Within Judaism this Sophia or Wisdom-figure develops along very interesting lines, especially in the notion of the *Shekhinah,* as studied by R. Patai in his thought-provoking book on the *Hebrew Goddess.*[2]

Two short quotations from *Ecclesasticus* will suffice to show the two main characteristics which are associated with the Sophianic image wherever she is manifest. Her first, perhaps most important characteristic, is creative and noetic, symbolizing the creative act of the divine Word and the infinite content of divine Knowledge which is its eternal resource. Thus, it is said of her that she is "...the Word which was spoken by the Most High," and that "No man has ever fully known Wisdom; from first to last no one has fathomed her; for her thoughts are vaster than the ocean and her purpose deeper than the great abyss."[3] Her other main characteristic is an overwhelming beauty which commands love and desire. After a long and fine description of herself as being like roses, cypresses and palm trees, she says, "Come to me, you who desire me and eat your fill of my fruit. The memory of me is sweeter than syrup, the possession of me sweeter than honey.'[4] Thus, here in one of the earliest expositions of her symbolic and spiritual presence within patriarchal scripture, she already unites in her image the two main modes of mystical experience and aspiration, namely Love and Gnosis.

What is important to realize concerning this figure is that she is active, creative and enabling. This aspect of her function is clearly present in the root of the word *Sophia* which basically means 'to craft, to design, to be skilful,' which meanings link it very interestingly to a parallel concept and image in Hindu Tantrism, that of the feminine *Shakti,* the root of which is *shak,* 'to make, to do, to empower.' It is precisely the function of the divine *Shakti* to provide the divine Subject/Person with the inspiration for and the content of his creative Self-knowing and revelation, the function of which is clearly illustrated in the above quotations. Thus, in *aeternis* the Sophianic Feminine is the essential instigator or that primordial division of the divine Being into the creative relationship of Subject and Object, of own/Self and other/non-Self, whether in terms of God's discovery of his infinite possibilities in the created Cosmos, or in terms of its discovery of his Selfhood in the Spirit. Thus God must make Himself other in order to relate to Himself, to know Himself, to love Himself, but also to be none other, to be Himself. In this tension of divine self-relationship and non-relationship it is the divine Sophia which is the very trigger and dynamic of that relationship, as also the whole of what can be known and loved as that 'other' required by the experience of relationship.

Thus beauty in this context may be understood as that eternally and fatefully fascinating combination of 'otherness' and 'owness': that 'other' which is mysteriously familiar and akin to one, and that which is one's own but which is also elusively another. It is then that the divine Beauty stirs the divine creative force to will the becoming of the cosmos, and also to stir the cosmos through man to rediscover the divine Selfhood. In other words, the Sophianic Feminine is the mistress

1. *New English Bible* (Oxford 1970), Ch. XXIV.
2. (Avon, 1978).
3. Ch. XXIV, v. 3, vv. 28-29.
4. *Ibid.* vv. 19-20.

who presides over all the possible tensions and harmonies of the principle of relationship itself whether manifest within the divine, human or cosmic contexts, which mystery is very much reflected in Mary's title of *theotokos* or God-bearer, and in the very similar title ascribed by certain traditions to Fāṭima in Islam of *umm abīhā*.

This last observation leads conveniently to my next point, which is that this Sophianic figure is not only a concept, allegory or spiritual image, but, very importantly, more often than not, is manifested in varying degrees and ways in actual human females whose persons and physical forms became, so to speak, carriers and bearers of the spiritual archetype, or as the Irish poet John Montague put it rather more negatively, "bearing the mythic burden."[1]

Two main kinds of Sophianic manifestation may be discerned. The first is of the kind alluded to in speaking of Mary and Fāṭima: the situation in which a profound collective aspiration and a mysterious aptitude and receptivity combine to create a particular manifestation of the archetype with extensive mythical and cultural implications. The second type is the situation in which a particular woman or girl evokes in a man an especially powerful vision of the creative beauty which leaves him and his life changed and which may occasion new creative forces, whether intellectual or physical. In the case of both these types the human bearers of the revelation of Sophianic Beauty and Wisdom certainly have powerful enabling and creative effects. In the case of Mary, one only has to consider the literature, architecture and music she has inspired down the centuries in many lands in Christendom. In Europe, at any rate, perhaps the most influential lady of the second type was the lovely Beatrice who so transformed that towering figure of our culture, Dante Alighieri. The effect of such a Sophianic vision and revelation in the case of Dante has been succinctly and accurately described by William Anderson in his book, *Dante, The Maker:*

> Through his love of her on Earth he formed an indissoluble union of love with her that transcended the incident of her death... he found that the only way to the sight of God was through her as the revelation of his soul... so she, as his illuminated soul represents the search for unity and contains in herself the still causes of history and of creation. Through love of her his love expands to become the love of God... she is in him the gateway to ecstatic joy, the source both of his inspiration and his salvation, the maker of him as a torch of living flame... through her guidance he achieved a total transformation in his emotional and intellectual being.[2]

Some have been tempted to suppose that Beatrice was not really a woman of flesh and blood, but rather some ethereal abstraction of an overheated imagination, some spiritual or intellectual device employed by the poet on his inner quest. Such suppositions completely miss the point of the phenomenon here being explored. The divine transforming alchemy, which is the mission of the Sophianic presence, requires the proper and full relating of the two poles of spirit and flesh, so that the living flesh and form of the lady are transformed by the spirit and the spirit is substantiated by the living flesh. Here, once again, we have a further insight into the meaning of the above-mentioned title of the Virgin's title of 'God-bearer' illustrat-

---

1. *Selected Poems* (Oxford 1982), p.89.
2. (London 1980), p.416.

ing the significance of the usually denigrated flesh and its role in the divine-human equation. As we shall see later, this essential role for the material and the formal in the mystical contemplation of the divine being is something which both Ibn 'Arabī and Rumi lay some stress upon in their writings. In this connection it is interesting to note that all three Abrahamic religions, while wary and disparaging of the flesh and matter from the patriarchal standpoint, nevertheless believe strongly in its redeemability.

Before proceeding to discuss the ways in which our two masters have experienced and expressed the Sophianic Feminine, it might be of interest to explore briefly the way in which it has been, in various guises, manifest in the life and consciousness of Islam from the very beginning, especially in Shi'ite Islam. First of all, Mary, the mother of Jesus, who is such an important figure in Christianity has also a rather special place in the Koran, the scripture of Islam: not only having a chapter named after her and partly devoted to her story, but also being described as having been chosen by God above all other women in the worlds, as being specially devoted to the worship of God and as being—together with her son—a "sign to the worlds."[1] One might also recall that some traditions record that the Prophet Muḥammad commanded the painted image of Mary and Jesus to be spared when he cleared the Ka'ba of idols.[2] Mary is, of course, interestingly associated with the function and symbolism of the *miḥrāb* through her connection with Zakariya[3] and many *miḥrābs* have this verse inscribed upon them.

Another early support for the notion of the special nature of woman in Islam, although later much overlaid by rather more negative and hostile sentiments, is the well-attested love and respect of the Prophet himself for women in general, and for certain women in particular. One thinks, of course, of his devotion to Khadīja and their daughter Fāṭima, the last of whom was to acquire later, especially among Shi'ite Muslims, a status and role very similar to that of Mary in Christendom. She would be called 'the Virgin', 'Mother of her father' and the 'Lady of Sorrows'.[4] Indeed, the development of her cult of veneration not only came to resemble that of Mary but also to have very interesting contacts with it, as Massignon has shown in some very interesting articles.[5] Perhaps the most curious of these contacts is the more recent association of the Marian cult with the name of Fāṭima in the shrine of Our Lady of Fāṭima in Portugal, an association outwardly accidental and fortuitous, but inwardly not without providential significance. Yet another curious example of seemingly coincidental feminine symbolism in early Islam is the entrusting of the newly copied text of the Koran to the keeping of Ḥafṣah, wife of Muḥammad and daughter of the doughty 'Umar, the meaning of her name ('the Keeper') being appropriate to her trust: one is reminded here of the Goddess Hathor whose name means to keep and hold the sacred one.

Of course, later in the history of Sufism, women would play a rather more

---

1. Koran, III: 41, XXI:91.
2. *Life of Muhammad*, trans. A. Guillame (Oxford 1955), p.552.
3. Koran III 36
4. Massignon, L., *Opera Minora* I (Beirut 1963), p. 567ff.
5. *Ibid.*, pp. 550-618.

significant role than they have done traditionally in exoteric Islam: one thinks particularly of the famous Rābi'a al-'Adawiyya. Also, as already mentioned earlier, many Sufi poets have sung the praises of the divine Beauty using images of feminine beauty. One may say therefore, that although the dimension of the Feminine is less overt and more inward in Islam than in Christianity and Judaism, it is by no means lacking. Its earlier manifestations just discussed have, I am sure, provided inspiration and support for the often dramatic enunciation of the experience and vision of the Sophianic Feminine in the Shaykh of Murcia and the Mystical lover of Konya. They, in their turn, undoubtedly inspired and promoted her influence and genius wherever the Sufis gather to express their love of God.

It is now time to consider how the subject of our essay, the Sophianic Feminine, features and functions in the experience and work of two of the greatest exponents of Sufi teaching: Ibn 'Arabī and Jalāl al-Dīn Rumi. Comparison of these two masters of the spiritual path is usually rather difficult, insofar as their mode of expression and exposition could hardly be more different. Ibn 'Arabī, on the one hand, is for the most part a great prose exponent of mystical doctrine, and even in his poetry is mostly devoted to the enunciation of spiritual truths and gnostic insights. Rumi, on the other hand, has bequeathed to the world a huge and chaotic tapestry of mystical love and passion. It is therefore very appropriate that William Chittick has entitled his excellent book on Ibn 'Arabī *The Sufi Path of Knowledge*, and his earlier book on Rumi *The Sufi Path of Love*.[1] It is curious then to note that it is in the writings of the Andalusian master that image of the Sophianic Feminine is most clearly and unambiguously delineated and most directly linked to the mystery of creation and revelation, while in the writings of Rumi, the Feminine as such, is far less specifically and extensively dwelt upon, although her realm of love and ecstasy pervades the experience and expression of Rumi far more fully.

In proceeding to examine our theme in the writings of the Shaykh al-Akbar one is drawn principally to study three aspects of his teaching and experience. Firstly, we must examine the Sophianic implications of the remarkable last chapter of his *Fuṣūṣ al-ḥikam* in which, in the process of offering his interpretation of the celebrated tradition of the Prophet Muḥammad on his love for women, perfume and prayer, Ibn 'Arabī presents us with some truly profound statements on the contemplative and gnostic connotations of the Feminine.[2] Secondly, we must consider that deeply influential meeting at Mecca between the Shaykh and the young lady whose beauty and wisdom were to inspire a fine collection of poems in the classical mode, the *Interpreter of Desires*.[3] It is certainly clear that the Lady Niẓām evoked in Ibn 'Arabī a new and singular awareness and vision of the divine Feminine. Lastly, it is necessary to look at certain aspects of his teachings on the creation of the cosmos and in particular his concept of the *Nafas al-raḥmān* or the 'Breath of the Merciful.'

An examination of the passages in the last chapter of the *Fuṣūṣ al-ḥikam* reveals

1. (Albany: SUNY 1989 & Albany: SUNY 1983).
2. *Ibn Al-'Arabī, the Bezels of Wisdom*, trans. R.J.W. Austin (New York: Paulist Press 1980), pp. 274-278.
3. *Tarjumān Al-Ashwāq: A collection of Mystical odes by Muhyi'ddīn ibn al'Arabī*, trans. R.A. Nicholson, (London 1911).

that the section dealing with the significance and role of the Feminine is divided roughly into four parts.[1] In the first of these, Ibn 'Arabī discusses the way in which God created woman from Adam to form a human polarity in which Adam loves Eve as being made in his image, while Eve loves Adam as deriving her being from him. This polarity, he says, reflects the divine-human polarity in which God loves man whom He has made in His own image, while man loves God as being the source of his own being. He also speaks of the ternary of God-man-woman, thereby illustrating the 'Chain of Love,' so to speak, since, as he says, "Love arises only for that from which one has one's being."[2] Ibn 'Arabī goes on to describe the physical union which man has with woman as "a total annihilation in her," deriving from a desire "which pervades all his parts."[3] It is for this reason, he explains, that God has ordered the major ablution after sexual intercourse so that the purification may match the totality of the consummation and "so that he might one again behold Him (God) in the one in whom he was annihilated, since it is none other than He Whom he sees in her."[4]

He then goes on to show how it can only be in woman that man may truly contemplate the Divine. He argues thus:

> When man contemplates the Real in himself as being that from which woman is created he contemplates God in active mode. If, however, he contemplates God in himself without reference to woman he contemplates the Real in passive mode. In woman he may contemplate God in both passive and active roles.

He reinforces this presentation of woman as a divine icon further by saying,

> Contemplation of the Reality without formal support is not possible, since God, in His Essence, is far beyond all need of the Cosmos. Since, therefore, some form of formal support is necessary, the best and most perfect kind is the contemplation of God in women.[5]

Here he also lays stress as he does elsewhere on the notion of the providential necessity of form and substance as the complementary poles of spirit.

The two final parts of this section, in which Ibn 'Arabī illustrates the highly paradoxical nature of the role and function of the Feminine as an image and symbol of divine realities, are very interesting indeed. In the third part he resorts as he often does, to some ingenious play on the meanings and origins of Arabic verbal roots, associating the word for women, *nisā'*, with the root *nasa* meaning 'delay' or 'postponement.' By these means he seeks to show the subordinate and derivative nature of woman as the "passive creation" brought forth from man, symbolizing, as he says, the relationship of the Universal Nature to God as that on and in which He revealed cosmic forms. Man's love for woman is also related here to her inferior status as a passive being. Here the createdness and passivity of women are stressed, which view is quite in keeping with prevailing legal and social attitudes in Islam.

1. *Bezels*, pp. 274-278.
2. *Ibid.*, p. 274.
3. *Ibid.*, p. 274.
4. *Ibid.*, p. 274.
5. *Ibid.* p. 275.

In the last part, using a similarly curious linguistic device, he seeks to demonstrate that the Feminine is also—in a subtle and pervasive way—superior and prior to man. He deduces this from the fact that, according to the tradition of the Prophet which he is interpreting, the word "three" (enumerating the three things: women, perfume and prayer, which the Prophet loved) is in the feminine form, although one of the things enumerated is masculine, the convention being that the masculine gender usually predominates. Hence he interprets this saying as meaning that the Prophet subtly intended to suggest the governance of the Feminine.[1] Ibn 'Arabī goes on to support this deduction by pointing out that the majority of words associated with origin and creation are feminine such as essence *(dhāt)* cause *('illah)* power *(qudrah)*. Thus, he observes, the masculine noun 'perfume' is placed between the two feminine nouns, 'women' and 'prayer,' just as man finds himself situated between the Divine Essence (a feminine noun) and woman, originating in the first and being the origin of the other.[2]

Therefore, in parts three and four of the last chapter of the *Fuṣūs al-ḥikam* Ibn 'Arabī is alluding to one of the great mysteries of the Sophianic Feminine, namely her primordial creativity and createdness united in the same being, which is the mystery of Mary as Theotokos and of Fāṭima as *umm abīhā*. In any examination of this theme the divine-human paradox is an essential clue to its nature. Thus, in this section of the *Fuṣūṣ,* we see briefly a deep and startling analysis and exposition of various aspects of the Sophianic Feminine, its polar function, its contemplative and visionary function and, perhaps most important of all, its reconciling and linking function as between spirit and matter, God and humankind, man and cosmos.

I think we can be reasonably sure that the meditations of the Shaykh al-Akbar just discussed were inspired in no small part by his encounter, both in form and spirit, with the lovely and spiritually accomplished Lady Niẓām, which encounter I have discussed more fully elsewhere.[3] What is usually missed in dealing with this very important meeting of the master recently arrived from Al-Andalus and the daughter of his new friends at Mecca is the fact that his attraction to her was by no means simply spiritual and intellectual, but also physical and psychic, which is made clear by Ibn 'Arabī himself with the words, "And were it not for those trivial souls who are every ready for scandal and are eager for malice, I would comment here also on the beauties of her body as well as her soul, which was a garden of generosity."[4]

I raise this point in order to reiterate what I said earlier concerning a very important, but often ignored, feature of the Sophianic Feminine, namely the supreme function of hers in translating and transforming realities and images across the great divide of visible and invisible, flesh and spirit. Indeed one might say that it is a great aspiration of the *fedeli d'amore* of whatever culture and tradition—and Ibn 'Arabī and Rumi were certainly of their ilk—to achieve the consummate balance between

1. *Ibid.*, p. 277.
2. *Ibid.*, p. 277.
3. *Journal of the Muhyiddin Ibn 'Arabi Society,* VII (1988), 'The Lady Niẓam - An Image of Love and Knowledge,' pp. 35-48.
4. *Tarjumān*, p. 11.

the two poles of mystical experience. I do not mean to suggest here at all, that Ibn 'Arabī had any form of sexual relationship with Niẓām, but simply that his experience of her and its later effects and fruits in his life and quest would have been very much the poorer and insubstantial without her physical actuality and his attraction to and appreciation of it as explicitly expressed. Of course, the supreme experience of Niẓām is part of a lifelong sense of and sensitivity to the holiness and specialness of the Feminine by the master. It is clear that an early wife in Murcia, Maryam, was a close companion on the Way.[1] In his autobiographical sketches he speaks very highly of at least two women of Andalusia who had a profound spiritual influence upon him. Of one of them, a certain Faṭimāh, he says, "When I met her she was in her nineties... although she was so old and ate so little, I was almost ashamed to look at her face when I sat with her, it was so rosy and soft... She was indeed a mercy to the world."[2]

Turning to Ibn 'Arabī's teachings concerning the origins and processes of creation and becoming we will see that once again he feels and appreciates very much the feminine nature and colour of this great primordial mystery. Before creation, when the divine Reality is entirely Itself to Itself, there is no existence or becoming, only pure being; there is no otherness or number, but only pure unique oneness in an ineffable, unimaginable, undifferentiated wholeness, a merging with which is for many the supreme mystical experience. The Shaykh sees the first glimmering of the creative process expressed in the *Ḥadīth qudsī,* "I was a hidden treasure and longed to be known, so I created the Cosmos." Thus, the first intimation of the process is the longing or love of the Divine One to know Himself, to realise or enjoy Himself in His infinite possibilities. Thus also, the first division emerges from undifferentiated wholeness: that of God, the Subject, the potential Knower, and God, the Known, the Object-of-knowing.

It is interesting that the Arabic word for love *(ḥubb)* is closely connected to the word for seed. This then is the first division within God into 'own' and 'other,' the 'other' being the *sine qua non* of any relationship, whether of Knowledge, Love or anything else. A strong desire then characterizes both parts: the Knower desiring to know, and the Known, the new 'other,' to be known. It is the becoming, the coming into existence of this 'other' which precisely constitutes the creative process. The process itself has two currents, the first being the urge to create the knowable 'other,' the second to re-assert the integrity of the divine Self. This whole dual process is a huge and complex subject to which Ibn 'Arabī devotes many thousands of pages.

Suffice it to say here that he often speaks of the creative process in feminine terms, insofar as the great primordial pressure by the Knower and all the knowable latent essences to be released into existence is described by him as if it were a divine pregnancy or labour, a *karb aẓīm,* while the actual cosmic birth itself is described as being the 'Breath of the Merciful,' *Nafas ar-raḥmān,* a concept which he equates in the chapter of the *Fuṣūṣ* already considered, with the Universal Nature—represented symbolically by woman on earth.[3] With his deep learning in the Arabic

1. *Al-Futūḥāt al-Makkiyyah* (Cairo 1329 A.H.) II, p. 278; III, p. 235.
2. *Sufis of Andalusia,* trans. R.W.J. Austin (London 1971), p. 143.

language and the varied meanings of its vocabulary, there is no doubt but that Ibn 'Arabī was also well-aware of the strong associations of the word *Raḥman* 'Mercy' with the word for womb *Raḥim,* since he understands the word mercy in its divine context as being the same as the very urge to creation itself.

Of course, in the primordial relationship of the divine 'Subject/Own' with the divine 'Object/Other'—without which there is no creative relationship—the divine Object/Other is characterized by Beauty, *Jamāl* which word itself hints strongly at the comprehensiveness and totality of the infinitely knowable Object. In human terms it is precisely this objective totality and beauty which is manifested in woman as that 'other' who is also 'own,' and that 'own' who is elusively 'other;' the 'other' who points the way to 'own-ness', the 'own' who presages 'otherness'. But these are mysteries at which words ultimately fail. It has always been something of a puzzle to me that while greatly occupied in writing vast tomes on the mysteries of creation and re-creation the great mystics nevertheless are always reminding us that their experience is in truth inexpressible.

Ibn 'Arabī then, is undoubtedly one of the major exponents of the vision of the Sophianic Feminine in the world and he has expressed the great divine-human paradoxes and mysteries over which Sophia reigns, far more directly and bravely than most. It is important to realize that his particular contribution to the exposition of these mysteries lies in the fact that his teachings and meditations are based firmly in the contemplation of their manifestation in a human, living bearer of the archetype, as was also importantly the case with Dante, who probably owed not a little to the great Sufi master. In this connection we are also fortunate to have Corbin's profound, if difficult, study of this aspect of Ibn 'Arabī's work.[1]

Now at last to the master dervish of Konya, Jalāl al-Dīn Rumi, known among the Sufis as Mawlānā ('Our Master'). Although this great passionate exponent of love mysticism is, in a certain sense, perhaps more directly a follower of the divine Sophia than Ibn 'Arabī, and although he was responsible for what is perhaps the most unambiguous and succinct statement on the subject of the Sophianic Feminine, in general terms he dealt less with her than the Shaykh al-Akbar. Another apparent problem in this respect is that, apart from God Himself, the supreme beloved object for Rumi was not a woman but a man, namely the enigmatic and little-known Shams al-Dīn Tabrīzī. This apparent problem may be solved in two ways. Firstly, in respect to sanctifying and redeeming love and aspiration, the human gender of the beloved does not really matter, for, in the words of Rumi himself, it is "higher than female and male."[2] That is to say, love is ultimately beyond such distinctions and is ascribed to God in Whom both poles are fused.

Secondly, however, it is the Feminine which has traditionally and perennially been associated with the whole phenomenon of love, passion and beauty, so that one might say that, in the context of our theme, it is the feminine symbol which dominates this sphere. Thus, one might say that while the beloved Shams is acci-

3. *Bezels,* p.277.
1. *Creative Imagination in the Sufism of Ibn 'Arabi* (London 1969).
2. *The Mathnawi of Jalālu'ddīn Rūmī* ed. & trans. R.A. Nicholson, 8 vols (London 1925-40), I, v. 1975.

dentally male, the modality of the experience and the tenor of its expression is essentially associated with the Feminine. It is important to confirm here that for Rumi, as for Ibn 'Arabī, the whole matter of the experience and expression of love and passion is not simply based on theories and intellectual sentiments but also is realized in living forms. In a most interesting passage in his prose work *Fīhī mā fīhi*, Rumi observes that,

> The physical form is of great importance; nothing can be done without the consociation of the form and the essence. However much you may sow a seed stripped of its pod, it will not grow. Sow it with its pod and it will become a great tree. From this point of view the body is fundamental and necessary for the realization of the divine intention.[1]

One might link this very aptly with a verse from his great Mathnawī,

> *No sound of clapping comes from one hand of thine without the other hand.*[2]

Again, the lovely lines:

> *Kings lick the earth whereof the fair are made.*
> *For God hath mingled in the dusty earth*
> *A draught of Beauty from His choicest cup.*
> *'Tis that, fond lover—not these lips of clay—*
> *Thou art kissing with a hundred ecstasies,*
> *Think, then, what must it be when undefiled!*[3]

Yet another aspect of the Sophianic Feminine we have touched on many times in this essay, namely the ineluctable interdependence of polar complementaries—the eternally mutual sympathy of God and man—is summed up by Rumi in his concept of *ham-dāmī*, what Corbin has termed the 'con-spiration' of heaven and earth. He expresses this rather curiously in a couple of lines, "All kings are enslaved to their slaves," and "All loved ones are the prey of their lovers."[4] In a wider context this cosmic cooperation and mutuality is nicely expressed in the words, "When he (the holy one) weeps, heaven begins to weep, and when he moans in supplication the celestial sphere begins to cry 'O Lord.'[5]

The essential oneness which underlies this cosmos of sympathies and interdependencies is well expressed by Rumi in some lines about Mary, when she draws back from the fecundating angel. He says to her, "Thou art taking refuge with God from me: I am in eternity the image of Him Who is the only refuge."[6] Also, "Thou takest refuge from me, and I myself am that refuge."[7] Mary also inspires other lines of his poetry in which he speaks more specifically of the Sophianic Feminine: "The speech of Jesus is derived from the spiritual beauty of Mary, the speech of Adam is a ray of the divine Breath."[8] Here we must remember the strongly creative aspect

1. Cf. *Creative Imagination*, p. 347.
2. *Mathnawī*, III, v. 4397.
3. *Ibid.*, V, v. 372-74. Translated by R.A. Nicholson, *Rumi: Poet and Mystic* (London: George Allen & Unwin 1978) p. 45.
4. *Mathnawī*, I, vv. 1736 & 1739.
5. *Ibid.*, V, v. 491.
6. *Ibid.*, III, vv. 3779.
7. *Ibid.*, III v. 3780.

of the notion of word and speech in the Islamic context. Or again, "By the august influence of Mary's hand the withered bough may acquire the fragrance of musk and freshness and fruit."[1] In the same vein in speaking of the life-giving and restorative powers of divine love he says,

> By love bitter things become sweet, by love pieces of copper become golden. By love dregs become clear, by love pains become healing. By love the dead is made living, by love the king is made a slave. This love moreover is the fruit of gnosis.[2]

Here, as in the first quoted lines from *Ecclesiasticus*, beauty and wisdom, love and knowledge are joined together.

Finally, I come to those lines of the *Mathnawī* which proclaim the Sophianic message perhaps more directly than any other and which certainly compare with Ibn 'Arabī's words in the *Fuṣuṣ* as an exposition of the symbolic mystery which is the theme of this essay. He says in the first book:

> *The Prophet said that woman prevails exceedingly over the wise and intelligent, while ignorant men prevail over women; for in them the fierceness of the animal is immanent.*
> *Love and tenderness are human qualities, anger and lust are animal qualities.*
> *She is a ray of God; she is not that earthly beloved. She is creative: you might say she is not created.*[3]

Indeed, in some beautiful verses preceding these lines, the Persian master would seem to echo Ibn Al-Arabī in presenting us with both faces of the Sophianic Feminine: contrasting the powerful and imperial beauty of her divine and cosmic function with the more passive and apparently dependant human aspect, thus confirming not only the wholeness of the feminine image as a revelation of the divine—pre-eminently apt for holy contemplation—but also that ineluctable polarity and *ham-dāmī* of the male and female as the synthetic and perennial image of the divine Self-love and knowledge. He says:

> *She by whose beauteous face man was enslaved, how will it be when she begins to play the humble slave?*
> *She at whose haughtiness thy heart is trembling, how wilt thou fare when she falls a-weeping before thee?.......*
> *Inasmuch as He created her (woman) that he (Adam) might take comfort in her, how can Adam be parted from Eve?*[4]

I cannot do better here than follow Rumi's words with those of Nicholson's commentary on these same lines:

> Putting aside the veil of form, the poet contemplates in Woman the eternal beauty that is the inspiratrix and the object of all love, and he sees her, in her essential nature, as the medium par excellence by which this increate beauty reveals itself and exerts its creative activity. From this point of view she is the focus of all manifestations and the giver of life and can be identified with the power of their radiations.[5]

---

8. *Ibid.*, VI, v. 4549.
1. *Mathnawī*, IV, v. 3497.
2. *Ibid.*, II, vv. 1529-31.
3. *Ibid.*, I, vv. 2433-37. *Rumi: Poet and Mystic* (London: George Allen & Unwin, 1978) p.44.
4. *Mathnawī*, I, vv. 2421-2422, 2426.

It hardly needs to be said that between them, Ibn 'Arabī and Rumi bequeathed to the Muslim world as a whole—and in particular to the Sufis who followed them—an enormously rich legacy of spiritual vision and insight. Through their disciples and followers this arcane and always suspect and danger-laden image finds fresh echoes and elaborations in that wonderfully fruitful world of Hindu-Muslim mystical and spiritual cohabitation in which Sophia meets and joins with Shakti to radiate both widely and profoundly a rich afterglow of love and inspiration which has provided so much fine Indo-Sufi hymnody up to our own times. An important by-product of this paradoxical re-emergence of the feminine mode in Sufi song and poetry is a greater sensitivity on the part of many of the great Sufi exponents of Divine love to the experience of the world of nature and the senses, albeit refined by spiritual exercises. Thus, through the medium of the 'intermediate world' of spiritual imagination, flesh and spirit are reconciled, a reconciliation often presided over by the shimmering figure of a Lady Niẓām.

5. *Ibid.*, VII, pp. 156.

The Neoplatonic Substrate of Suhrawardi's Philosophy of Illumination: *Falsafa* as *Taṣawwuf*

Ian Richard Netton

As in the case of so many philosophers and thinkers who were mystics, it is clear that the life of Shihāb al-Dīn Abū'l-Futūḥ Yaḥyā ibn Ḥabash ibn Amīrak al-Suhrawardī (548/1153–587/1191), the great *Shaykh al-Ishrāq*, has become enveloped in mystery and myth. This is particularly true of Suhrawardī's strange end. Of this Corbin observed: "Notre jeune shaykh mourut de *façon mystérieuse* dans la citadelle d'Alep."[1] S.H. Nasr noted that "he was either suffocated to death or died of starvation."[2] The mysterious end of the man reflects, emphasizes and in a very real sense, re-creates the mystery of love which is at heart of the man's thought. (This point will be elaborated later.) Of course, we frequently use the word 'myth' in a loose sense to convey an aura of vagueness or mystery or legend.

Yet there is a more scholarly and useful sense of the word 'myth' which might be employed here in any discussion of Suhrawardī. It is true that it is both complex and multivalent: Ruthven cites St. Augustine on the topic of time: "I know very well what it is, provided that nobody asks me; but if I am asked and try to explain, I am baffled;" and Ruthven suggests that Augustine here anticipates "the predicament of anybody who is pressed for a brief and comprehensive definition of myth."[3] He goes on to note that "it was Voltaire's opinion that the study of myths is an occupation for blockheads;"[4] and that, furthermore, "we have no direct experience of myth as such, but only of particular myths: and these, we discover, are obscure in origin, protean in form and ambiguous in meaning."[5] However, it the contention of the author of this paper that 'myth,' properly and specifically defined, and 'myths,' properly and specifically analyzed, may illuminate rather than obscure whatever subject is viewed through the window, or in the context, of its own 'mythic' substrate, and the manifold, multivalent and multi-layered structures of that subject's 'mythic' baggage. As Claude Lévi-Strauss puts it: "From a logical point of view we can understand why images borrowed from experience can be put to use. This is the originality of mythical thinking—to play the part of conceptual thinking."[6] Lévi-Strauss goes on to note: "The really important point is that in all American mythol-

1. Henry Corbin, *Histoire de la Philosophie Islamique* (Paris: Gallimard 1964), vol.I, p. 285.
2. S.H. Nasr, 'Shihāb al-Dīn Suhrawardī Maqtūl' in M.M. Sharif (ed.) *History of Muslim Philosophy* (Wiesbaden: Otto Harrassowitz 1963) vol.I, p. 373.
3. K.K. Ruthven, *Myth, The Critical Idiom*, no. 31 (London: Methuen 1976), p. 1.
4. *Ibid.*, p. 3.
5. *Ibid.*, p. 1.
6. Claude Lévi-Strauss, *Myth and Meaning*, (London: Routledge & Kegan Paul 1978), p. 22.

ogy, and I could say in mythology the world over, we have deities and supernaturals, who play the roles of intermediaries between the powers above and humanity below."[1] This is of vital importance in any analysis of the content of myth; it is also of importance if we choose to define myth, from the point of view of *usage,* as "a narrative vehicle for a primal event, or series of events, which may function as essential dogma, paradigm or key referent in the future development of any culture, religion or philosophy."[2] Or, as Schneidu observes: "Myth either is simply a story, or in Lévi-Strauss's even more reductive view, the story is merely a vehicle through which the repeated themes make themselves heard."[3] Such definitions, of course, imply no value judgement whatsoever as to the objective truth, or otherwise, of the myth: and it is in the light of such definitions that we shall here examine the life and thought of al-Suhrawardī.

The Islamic faith clearly has its 'myth' of martyrdom (and here it must be stressed again that the term does not in any way imply a lack of reality or truth): the myth stretches from the age of the great martyr of Karbalā', Ḥusayn, through Ḥallāj (executed 309/922) and (perhaps) al-Fārābī.[4] up to our own subject Suhrawardī—and, of course, beyond into present. It is an ineluctable reality that the tragic ends of each of these figures enhance, if only unconsciously, the message which they bore during their lifetimes, in the mind of the reader.

Late antiquity, and indeed Islamic philosophy, also had the their 'myth'—in the sense of a vehicle for the framing and conveyance of a message—the myth of Neoplatonism, deliberately designed by its doctrine of emanation to provide a link—however tenuous—between the corporeal known and the Unknowable Divine.[5] Here if anywhere mythology, with deities and supernaturals metamorphosed into intellects which played "the roles of intermediaries between the powers above and humanity below."[6]

Finally mysticism, whether of the Plotinian kind or Islamic *taṣawwuf,* constitutes the mythic frame within which men generally declined to articulate, *intellectually,* his love of the Divine, and frequently chose instead to *feel:* mysticism was thus more a vehicle of pure feeling than pure intellection though this is not by any means to suggest that *taṣawwuf,* for example was totally devoid of intellectual content and nor was ever described in manual or philosophical treatises. Far from it. Mysticism, and the rituals of mysticism, may be described as the 'myth'—indeed, the 'sacrament'—of and for God's divine love. And the essence of the hierarchy of Neoplatonism is itself mystical in impulse: with Plotinus the 'ladder' of emanation becomes a 'ladder' of feeling. "The emanation process itself was compared by Plotinus to the way in which sunlight was continually generated by the sun... each hypostasis was moved or filled by a deep yearning for the principle immediately

---

1. *Ibid.*, p. 22.
2. See my *Allāh Transcendent: Studies in the Structure and Semiotics of Islamic Philosophy, Theology and Cosmology* (London: Routledge 1989), p. 234.
3. Herbert N. Schneidau, *Sacred Discontent: The Bible and Western Tradition* (Baton Rouge: Louisiana State University Press 1976), pp. 272-273 pp. 272-273.
4. See Netton, *Allāh Transcendent*, p. 101.
5. See Netton, *Allāh Transcendent*, pp. 155-117.
6. Claude Lévi-Strauss, *Myth and Meaning*, p. 22.

above it."[1] In such a wise does the 'myth' of Neoplatonism metamorphose the philosophical mechanics of emanation into a mode of love itself. And Islamic Neoplatonism, even of the Ishrāqī model espoused by al-Suhrawardī, as *we shall show,* was no different, with that key motif of philosophical Neoplatonism, *fayḍ* (emanation), becoming a light-filled channel for the movement of *'ishq,* passionate love of and for the Divine.

Firstly, though, to place the above proposition in perspective, we can highlight the basic dynamics of martyrdom at the end of Suhrawardī's life, since these contributed to the *myth* of Suhrawardī, then examine briefly the semiotics of the Koran and, finally, elaborate a few of the many definitions of *falsafa* and *taṣawwuf.* I have noted elsewhere that "al-Suhrawardī is also called 'The Executed' *(al-Maqtūl)* by his detractors and 'The Martyr' *(al-Shahīd)* by his friends" and that "in the second of these designations, which is as common as that of *Shaykh al-Ishrāq,* there may lie an early attempt to endow the mystic with an almost Ḥallājian charisma."[2] Certainly, the two titles, regardless of who applied them, were specifically designed to situate and establish Suhrawardī within a particular context or *myth,* and not simply to differentiate him from two other notable figures who bore the same surname: 'Abd al-Qāhir Abū Najīb al-Suhrawardī (d. 564/1168) and the latter's nephew and pupil Shihāb al-Dīn Abū Ḥafs 'Umar al-Suhrawardī (540/1145—632/1234).[3] Seyyed Hossein Nasr has neatly summarized the grounds of the myth:

> His outspoken manner, his lack of prudence in exposing esoteric doctrines before all kinds of audiences, the keen intelligence which enabled him to overcome all opponents in debate, his mastery in both discursive philosophy and Sufism—all these factors combined to make many enemies for him, especially among some of the doctors of the law *('ulamā').* Finally, they asked for his execution on the grounds of propagating doctrines against the tenets of the faith, and when Malik Ẓāhir [the son of Ṣalāh al-Dīn] refused they petitioned Ṣalāh al-Dīn directly. At a time when Syria had just been recaptured from the Crusaders and the support of the doctors of the law was essential to maintain his authority, Ṣalāh al-Dīn had no choice but to yield to their demand. Pressure was therefore put on Malik Ẓāhir to carry out the wish of the group of religious authorities who opposed the young sage. Suhrawardī was therefore imprisoned and in the year 587/1191 he died, the immediate cause of his death unknown. And so, at the young age of 38, the Master of Illumination met with the same fate as his illustrious Ṣūfī predecessor Ḥallāj, to whom he had been so much attached throughout his youth and whose sayings he quotes so often in his works.[4]

The elementary dynamics of the myth are immediately clear from this succinct account by Professor Nasr: jealousy, and fear of another's trespass on one's own intellectual power combine with religious and political motives in the minds of the custodians of orthodox knowledge and, therefore, religious power, the *'ulamā'*, the latter package such fears in a suitable fashion and confront the holders of secular power and authority with them to ensure that they, the *'ulamā'*, engineer the down-

1. See Netton, *Allāh Transcendent,* p. 62; Plotinus, *Enneads,* V. 1.6; III.8.8; III.8.11.
2. Netton, *Allāh Transcendent,* p. 257.
3. See *ibid.*
4. Seyyed Hossein Nasr, *Three Muslim Sages: Avicenna, Suhrawardī, Ibn'Arabī,* (New York: Caravan Books 1976, repr. of Harvard University Press edn. of 1969), pp. 57-58

Shihāb al-Dīn Yaḥyā Suhrawardī in a Landscape. From a manuscript of the *Majālis al-ʻushshāq*, dated 959/1552. MS. Ouseley Add. 24, f. 51v (Courtesy of the Bodleian Library, Oxford)

The Prison Where Suhrawardī Spent his Last Days in Aleppo, Syria.

fall of one whom they perceive as a profound threat. (The circumstances of Ḥallāj's own overthrow were a similar combination of religion and politics, and that latter's execution was by no means solely the product of that ill-advised and notorious declamation, which has become the most famous of all the *shaṭḥiyāt: Anā 'l-Ḥaqq).*

Semiotics has gained a reputation, sometimes, for being rather more arcane than it actually is. It is true that it should be considered more a methodology than a 'science.' And it is also true that some of its most famous guardians, and practitioners, for example the well-known Italian scholar Umberto Eco, have developed that methodology of semiotics in a highly complex way.[1] But they have also used that same methodology to illustrate the daily phenomena of life in a way which clarifies rather than mystifies. We note, for example, Eco's essay 'A Theory of Expositions' which tries to answer its opening sentence: 'What does Expo' 67—that unsurpassed, quintessential, classic World's fair—mean in today's world?'[2] But it is not just major expositions to which one might attach theories of semiotics. "Everything signifies,"[3] and this is as true of fundamental 'meaning-infused' texts like the Koran as it is of mystico-philosophical works like the *Ḥikmat al-Ishrāq* (Philosophy of Illumination) of al-Suhrawardī. Indeed the Koran be may said to precipitate or actively seek its own semiotic analysis. Not only do we note the dichotomous sense of the Arabic word *āya* (verse of the Koran *and* sign) but it is clear from the most cursory reading that the entire text is "riddled with references to the signs of God."[4] As one Surah puts it:

> We shall show them Our signs in the horizons and in themselves.
> ... *(Sa-nurīhim āyātinā fī' l-āfāq wa fī anfusihim).*[5]

But this Islamic text par excellence is by no means the only one to lend itself readily to semiotic analysis. What, we may ask, are the 'signs' of *falsafa* and *taṣawwuf* in Suhrawardī's magnum opus, the famous *Ḥikmat al-Ishrāq?*[6] Before an identification is made of these, it might be useful to examine briefly what is meant by such words as *falsafa* and *taṣawwuf*. How have such words been defined?

Many definitions exist. *Inter alia, falsafa* has been described as follows:

> The origins of *falsafa* are purely Greek; the activity of the *falāsifa*... begins with Arabic translations of the Greek philosophical texts (whether direct or through a Syriac intermediary). Thus *falsafa* appears first as the continuation of filosofia in

1. See, for example, Eco's *A Theory of Semiotics, Advances in Semiotics* (Bloomington & London: Indiana University Press 1976).
2. Umberto Eco, *Travels in Hyperreality,* (London: Pan Picador 1987), pp. 291-307.
3. The phrase is Roland Barthes': see Jonathan Culler, *Barthes* (London: Fontana Paperbacks, 1983), p.lll; see also *Allāh Transcendent*, pp. 77ff.
4. *Allāh Transcendent*, p. 321.
5. KoranXL1:53; trans. A.J.Arberry, *The Koran Interpreted* (2 vols., London: Allen & Unwin/New York: Macmillan 1971), vol. 2, p. 191.
6. For the Arabic text, see *Kitāb Ḥikmat al-Ishrāq al-Suhrawardī,* in *Oeuvres Philosophiques et Mystiques,* vol. 2, ed. Henry Corbin, Académie Impériale Iranienne de Philosophie, Publication no. 13, Bibliothéque Iranienne, N.S. (Tehran: Académie Impériale Iranienne de Philosophie/Paris: Librairie Adrien-Maisonneuve 1977), pp. 2-260 [referred to hereafter simply as *Ḥikmat al-Ishrāq*].

> Muslim surroundings... [But] though *falsafa* may may be called a continuation of Greek thought there is no perfect continuity.[1]

The warning in the last line is timely and has been stressed in a different form elsewhere by the author of this essay: it does a grave disservice to Islamic philosophy to see it simply as Greek philosophy in Islamic guise, though, of course, no one would, or should, deny the impact of Greek thought.[2] "Islamic philosophy and theology, like every other, grew to some degree according to the intellectual and cultural milieu of which they were a part, or as a considered reaction to that *milieu.*"[3] And part of the Islamic *milieu* was—or became—the cities of Alexandria, Gondeshāpūr, and Ḥarrān.[4] We may, then in the light of these remarks, loosely define *falsafa* here, for our present purposes, as a mode of intellectual inquiry in Islamic thought which at various times placed a primacy on reason, which drew on both the Western *(i.e.* Plato, Aristotle, Plotinus) and the Eastern traditions for its vocabulary and, often, content, but which was much more than a mere syncretism composed of the aforementioned influences. Of course, such a definition is open to argument. elaboration or, indeed, contradiction but what cannot be denied is that one of the 'signs' or basic characteristics of *falsafa* in Islam is the stress on *reason.*

Annemarie Schimmel has provided one of the best introductions to, and definitions of, *taṣawwuf.* While admitting that "to write about Sufism, or Islamic mysticism, is an almost impossible task,"[5] she notes:

> To approach its [Islamic Mysticism's] partial meaning we have to ask ourselves first, what *mysticism* means. That *mysticism* contains something mysterious, not to be reached by ordinary means or by ordinary effort, is understood from the root common to the words *mystic* and *mystery,* the Greek *myein,* 'to close the eyes.'. Mysticism has been called 'the great spiritual current which goes through all religions.' In its widest sense it may be defined as the consciousness of the One Reality—be it called Wisdom, Light, Love, or Nothing.[6]

Two of Professor Schimmel's words here are of particular significance as motifs or 'signs' for our discussion of *taṣawwuf* in a Suhrawardian context: Light and Love. The first will be dealt with later. The latter may be stressed here as an, albeit well-known, indeed clichéd, 'sign' of *taṣawwuf.* As Rābi'a al-'Adawiyya famously articulated it:

> Oh my Lord, if I worship Thee from fear of Hell, burn me in Hell, and if I worship Thee in hope of Paradise, exclude me thence, but if I worship Thee for Thine own sake, then withhold not from me Thine Eternal Beauty.[7]

1. R. Arnaldez, art. 'Falsafa,' *EI* 2, vol. II, p. 769
2. *Allah Transcendent,* esp. pp. 20-21, 128, 264.
3. *Ibid.*, pp. 20-21.
4. *Ibid.*, pp. 7-16.
5. *Mystical Dimensions of Islam* (Chapel Hill: University of North Carolina Press 1975), p.xvii.
6. *Ibid.*, pp.3-4.
7. Trans. by Margaret Smith, *Studies in Early Mysticism in the Near and Middle East* (Amsterdam: Philo Press 1973; repr. from the London: Sheldon Press edn. of 1931), p. 224, from Farīd al-Dīn 'Aṭṭār, *Tadhkirat al-Awliyā,* ed. R. A. Nicholson (London Luzac/Leiden: E.J. Brill 1905), vol. 1, p. 73.

Any semiotic analysis of *taṣawwuf* must, therefore, be infused by the vocabulary of human and divine love. If the stress on reason, to put it succinctly if somewhat simplistically, is a sign or basic characteristic of *falsafa,* then a stress on love is a sign or basic characteristic of *taṣawwuf.* And, just as it may be argued, with some justification, that the basic source and origin in Islamic knowledge, all intellectual inquiry, the use of reason and, by extension, *falsafa* itself, lies in the Koran,[1] so too it may equally well be argued that the primary motors of *falsafa* are Koranic: "God was well-pleased with them, and they were well-pleased with God":[2] so God describes the blessed saints in Paradise; for "He loveth them, and they love Him."[3] This last text is of great significance "as supporting the Sufi doctrine of love *(maḥabba)* and as providing the ultimate authority for the idea of a trinity of Lover, Loved and Love. The conception of a remote, indifferent Potentate of the Universe is wholly overthrown by this picture of the Merciful Allāh ever taking the first step towards man, the elect of His creation, to draw him unto Him by the powerful cords of love."[4] This is not to say that the "remote Potentate" paradigm was absent from Islamic philosophical thought, especially of the Neoplatonic kind. What Arberry stresses here, however, is the motif of *maḥabba,* and this is the one which we shall examine as a key sign of *taṣawwuf* in the *Ḥikmat al-Ishrāq*.

What has been isolated, then, for the sake of simplicity, are two distinct motifs in our argument: the sign of *reason* in *falsafa* and the sign of *love* in *taṣawwuf.* They confronted each other in mediaeval Islam, almost in the manner of the well-known confrontation of revelation and reason,[5] and like the latter the confrontation was not always or necessarily a confrontation of mutual hostility. Certainly, this was not the case with Suhrawardī in whose philosophy, it may be demonstrated, the key technical philosophical terminology of reason acts as a *vehicle* for the 'signs' of *taṣawwuf.*

Suhrawardī's philosophy in his *Ḥikmat al-Ishrāq* and elsewhere fits neatly though partially into the classical paradigm, articulated and outlined above by Arnaldez, of *falsafa* as philosofia.[6] As such it has a number of readily-identifiable recurring strands: Pythagorean, Platonic, Aristotelian and Neoplatonic; to these may be added *inter alia* the Islamic, Zoroastrian, Ishrāqī and Hermetic.[7] And if we are to seek the intention of *Ḥikmat al-Ishrāq,* we could do worse than examine the author's statement on this work—it is significant not only for what it tells us about the motivations of its author but for its reiteration of several of the above-mentioned strands:

1. See Wan Mohd Nor Wan Daud, *The Concept of Knowledge in Islam and its Implications for Education in a Developing Country* (London: Mansell 1989), esp. pp. 36-38.
2. Koran V 119.
3. Koran V 59.
4. A.J. Arberry, *Sufism: An Account of the Mystics of Islam* (London: Allen & Unwin 1950), p. 21
5. For an introduction to this, see A.J. Arberry, *Revelation and Reason in Islam* (London: Allen & Unwin 1957).
6. Hossein Ziai, "Suhrawardi's Philosophy of Illumination" (PhD thesis, University of Harvard 1976) p. 59.
7. See Nasr, *Three Muslim Sages,* p. 59.

> This book of ours is intended for [both] students of mysticism *(al-ta'alluh)*[1] and academic research *(al-baḥth)* It is not for the scholar who has no mystical orientation or ambition. We only propose to discuss this book and its symbols with those who are seriously engaged in the mystic effort or quest. At the very least the reader of this book is expected to have reached the stage at which the Divine Light *(al-Bāriq al-Ilāhī)* has come to him and rooted itself within him... So whoever just wants academic research can follow the path of the peripatetics which is all well and good for academic research on its own. Our talk and discourse about the groundrules of illuminationism *(al-qawā' id al-ishrāqiyya)* cannot be with such a person. Indeed, the basic concern of the illuminationists remains disorganized without [the help of God-given luminous insights *(sawāniḥ nūriyya)*.[2]

There are several points of interest for our discussions in this passage: the very first line forges an immediate link between academic and intuitive knowledge, between *falsafa qua falsafa* in its purely Greek (here Aristotelian) sense (= *al-baḥth)* and the lights of insight associated with *taṣawwuf (-al-ta'alluh)*. The mystical *Ishrāqī* element is clearly elevated above—though ideally linked to—the peripatetic products of contemporary academic research. Suhrawardī does not here denigrate the academic researcher; what he does is establish and exhibit an order of priorities in intellectual thought. The ideal paradigm is perhaps akin to Abū Ḥāmid al-Ghazālī whose life mirrors, in a frequently idealized way, the combination of the academic and the mystic. This passage which we have mind then, constitutes a vehicle of two key motives in Suhrawardian thought: that of reason and that of light. the latter being associated with a more intuitive kind of reason or intellection.

Ziai believes that the *Ḥikmat al-Ishrāq* constitutes Suhrawardian thought in its ultimate form.[3] If we accept this to be the case, then there is an added merit in identifying the particular signs of *falsafa* and *taṣawwuf* in this text since, identified in their final state, they may be used as useful analytical tools for the examination of any earlier work. If we now isolate within *falsafa* some of its *'purely Greek'* elements, and recognize the doctrine of emanation as the key development in later Greek (Plotinian) philosophy, then there are three major semiotic triggers or key words which may be discussed here, as being of vital importance in the *Ḥikmat al-Ishrāq: fayḍ, fayyāḍ,* and *ṣudūr* ('emanation, emanative and procession'). And since it is emanation, one of the key technical terms of later Greek philosophy, which becomes the vehicle of Sufism, and, in particular, the *love* implicit and explicit within that term, we may also examine here some of the key words associated with *taṣawwuf* which appear in the *Ḥikmat;* the most notable are *'ishq, 'āshiq, 'ushshāq, ma'shūq,* and *maḥabba* (*love, lover, lovers, beloved* and *loving-kindness*). It was noted earlier that emanation was a Plotinian device designed to provide a *reasonable, reasoned*—if not wholly, or always completely reasoned or easily comprehensible—link between the Divine and the Human, the pure incorporeal and the sullied corporeal.

---

1. Lit. "self-deification": see Soheil M. Afnan, *A Philosophical Lexicon in Persian and Arabic* (Beirut: Dār al-Mashriq 1969), p. 10.
2. *Ḥikmat al-Ishrāq*, p. 12-13 (my trans.).
3. *Suhrawardi's Philosophy of Illumination*, p. 21.

Emanation is a bridge between these two seemingly antipathical realities. And it is an intellectual device which becomes, as we shall show, a bridge or vehicle of love: in other words, the technical intellectual terminology of philosophy—*fayḍ*, etc.—becomes associated with, indeed, may be said in one real sense to become the vocabulary of *taṣawwuf*, whether the words employed are *maḥabba* or *'ishq*. And, of course, the key Suhrawardian development in all this is that not only do we have a bridge of love, but also a bridge of light, or rather many lights between the diluted reality of earth and the sublime reality of the 'Light-of-lights' *(Nūr al-Anwār)*, God Himself. Suhrawardian emanation, in other words, is inevitably part of a larger theology of light and love. It is in light-infused and light-enriched philosophy of emanated love that find the true uniqueness of al-Suhrawardī, and his *Ishrāqī* philosophy.

Such key words as we have just itemized constitute some of the most easily identifiable 'signs' of the substrate of Neoplatonic doctrine which underlies Suhrawardī's text. Here it is proposed to examine some of the usages or contexts of the words in isolation, then note how they often form certain recurring groups or phrases, centered on the motif or theme of love, and finally survey what I will term Suhrawardī's 'Ladder of Yearning': this is the mythic vehicle in which emanation and love merge and the vocabulary of *falsafa* becomes identical with that of *taṣawwuf*. Let us turn firstly to the technical *philosophical* vocabulary of Neoplatonism: here the key 'sign' or keyword is 'emanation' and it informs and underpins in one form or another the whole of Suhrawardī's text. Its various associated forms in Arabic, whether they be *fayḍ*, *fayyāḍ* or *ṣudūr*, are scattered throughout the *Ḥikmat al-Ishrāq* and appear in a variety of different contexts. Thus we are told that emanation *(al-fayḍ)* is eternal,[1] has many different features[2] and is a characteristic of the Suhrawardian lights in their different kinds.[3] The substrate of emanation is emphasized in such phrases as *al-Nūr fayyāḍ li-dhātihi a*nd similar which also, of course, reinforce the all-important Suhrawardian link between light and emanation.[4] All things derive ultimately by emanation *(ṣudūr)* from the Light of Lights *(Nūr al-anwār)*[5] but the manner of the emanation *(ṣudūr)* of multiplicity from God who is the Light-of-Lights and the One[6] clearly requires some explanation and this is attempted by Suhrawardī.[7]

The other register of Plotinion Neoplatonism which also underpins the *Ḥikmat al-Ishrāq* is also highly visible in the vocabulary of love.[8] In the *Ḥikmat* the principal signs of this are such Arabic words as *'ishq* (passionate love, *érōs)*, *'āshiq* (and its plural *'ushshāq)*, and the less intensive synonym for *'ishq*, which is *maḥabba* (a form which, incidentally, seems to be preferred by Suhrawardī to *ḥubb)*. The word

1. *Ḥikmat al-Ishrāq*, p. 181, see also p. 236.
2. *Ibid.*, p. 178.
3. E.g. see *ibid.*, pp. 141, 218, 236. For further information about the different types of Suhrawardian lights, see Netton. *Allāh Transcendent*, pp. 256-320.
4. See, e.g., *ibid.*, pp. 117, 134, 150, 195, 204.
5. See, e.g., *ibid.*, pp. 131-132.
6. See, e.g., *ibid.*, pp. 131,138.
7. See *ibid.*, pp. 131-35, 138-48.
8. See Plotinus, *Enneads* III 8.7; III 8.8; V.1.6.

'ishq is much associated with the Suhrawardian lights in their various forms and often appears in conjunction with another popular word from the vocabulary of Sufism: *shawq* (longing, yearning),[1] which is clearly intended as a virtual synonym of *'ishq*. The Light-of-Lights is a solitary and self-centered Lover *('āshiq)*, but at the same time is much-loved *(ma'shūq)* by others as well.[2] It is a key motif—almost paradox—of the text that this much-loved Light-of-Lights is wrapped in eternal, 'selfish' contemplation of itself, in an almost Aristotelian[3] isolation; and Suhrawardī's universe of light is filled with loyal lovers *('ushshāq)*[4] who love and yearn perpetually for the light. All these examples, it will be noted, which we have just cited, employ variations on the root *'ashiqa;* however, the text's synonym for *'ishq,* which is *maḥabba,* is even more common, as can be seen below.

The juxtaposition or association of the words *'ishq* and *shawq* has already been noted. If we now examine more closely the *structure* of the text of Suhrawardī's *Ḥikmat al-Ishrāq* it is possible to detect three important themes or intellectual configurations in his thought, in each of which love is a prime component. It is through the articulation of these that we may reach most easily what I propose to call Suhrawardī's "Ladder of Yearning" paradigm[5] where the vocabulary of emanation becomes the vehicle—indeed, is—the vocabulary of love. *Falsafa (fayḍ)* metamorphoses into *taṣawwuf ('ishq, maḥabba)*. The three suggested configurations suggested as important here, from a structural point of view, as forming a primary and constant substrate of the *Ḥikmat* are those of (i) *Love and Light,* (ii) *Love and Emanation,* and (iii) *Love and Dominion or Subjugation (qahr)*. Let us examine each briefly in turn as they appear in a single key statement of Suhrawardī's:

(i) Light *(al-nūr)* (as we have already noted), is characterized as *fayyāḍ li-dhātihi* "emanative in essence," and it has "in its substance" *(fī jawharihi)* love *(maḥabba)* for its origin and dominion *(qahr)* over what is beneath it.[6] Love and light appear in equal measure in such citations.

(ii) The previous statement also stresses the *Emanationist* essence and character of that *Light*.

(iii) Finally this same statement also neatly links the concepts of Love and Dominion, a linkage which reappears on many other pages of the *Ḥikmat al-*

1. See, e.g. *Ḥikmat al-Ishrāq*, pp. 136, 242; see also pp. 134, 185, 223, 224.
2. See *ibid.*, p. 136; see also p. 177.
3. See Aristotle, *Metaphysics*, 8K.12, 7, 1072b.
4. See, e.g., *Ḥikmat al-Ishrāq*, p.227.
5. The term is preferred to Parviz Morewedge's 'Platonic "Ladder of eros"': see his 'Sufism, Neoplatonism, and Zaehner's Theistic Theory of Mysticism' in Parviz Morwedge (ed), *Islamic Philosophy and Mysticism, Studies in Islamic Philosophy and Science* (New York: Caravan Books 1981), p. 231. The terminology of the 'Ladder of Yearning' is consciously modelled here by me on the story of Jacob's ladder in Genesis 28: 10-19 where the ladder, like the classical doctrine of emanation, forms a bridge between earth and heaven. Just as the angels of God ascend and descend Jacob's ladder, so with the doctrine of emanation there is an outpouring from higher to lower, and a yearning from lower to higher. The motif of love in Suhrawardian emanation, 'replaces', as it were,—or better, *supplements* or *clothes*—the angel figure of Jacob's ladder. For in this context, it is interesting to note the identification in Suhrawardī's thought of 'angel' and emanated 'light.' For more on this identification of 'angel' and 'light,' see especially Netton, *Allāh Transcendent*, pp. 256-268.
6. (my italics) *Ḥikmat al-Ishrāq*, pp. 204, see also p. 225.

Ishrāq,[1] and constitutes a basic duality which underpins the entire text.

The present author has pointed out elsewhere—in an Avicennan context, but the statement is equally true of Suhrawardī's thought—that "in one sense emanation *(fayḍ)* and love *('ishq)* may be viewed as two sides of the same channel of cosmic movement: all things come from God by a process of necessary emanation and all things desire to return to God by a process of innate or necessary love."[2] It is this basic concept which informs what I propose to call here the fundamental Suhrawardian paradigm of the *Ḥikmat al-Ishrāq* the 'Ladder of Yearning.' Indeed, if we accept with Ziai that the *Ḥikmat* is the ultimate expression of Suhrawardian thought, we can legitimately hold that this 'Ladder of Yearning' at the heart of the *Ḥikmat* must also mirror in some way the essence of much else that Suhrawardī thought and wrote.

Paul Henry has neatly outlined the basic Plotinian paradigm which prefigures what is found in *Ḥikmat al-Ishrāq,* noting that "in Plotinus... every being is constituted by means of a two-way dynamism which is dialectically simultaneous, the departure from the principle immediately prior and superior and the return to that same principle. As a result any being, whether the universal intellect or the individual soul, while it is not actually identical with its principle—this would be excluded by the law of diminishing causality—nevertheless exists in its self-identity only in the measure in which it is in an immediate relationship of union with and dependence upon its principle. In consequence "the being which knows itself will know also that from which it comes."[3]

In Suhrawardī's *Ḥikmat al-Ishrāq* we find a domination of lower lights by the higher, with the former exhibiting a profound longing for the latter. This constitutes the underlying pattern for the whole order of existence. God is the only One who loves only Himself and has no yearning for anyone or anything else.[4] "The paradigm which is established whereby each inferior light *(nūr sāfi)* loves the higher light *(al-nūr al-'ālī)* to a degree that transcends its own self-love or self-interest extends right up to the top of al-Suhrawardī's ontological hierarchy of lights."[5]

It is in this fashion that philosophy merges into mysticism, *falsafa* becomes *taṣawwuf* and the fundamental technical terms of both such as *fayḍ/ṣudūr* (emanation) and *'ishq/maḥabba* (love) assume a breadth of meaning in which the one may be said to encapsulate or incorporate the other. And, as we have already hinted above,[6] this fundamental relationship and ultimate identification of philosophy and mysticism was already prefigured in the thought of Plotinus himself.[7] It is thus clear that the Suhrawardian paradigm of the 'Ladder of Yearning' upon which the philosopher-mystic has based his text, or rather with which he has infused it,

1. E.g., see pp. 143, 147, 148, 160, 196, 225, 227, 228.
2. Netton, *Allāh Transcendent,* p. 176.
3. Paul Henry, 'Introduction: Plotinus' Place in the History of Thought' in Plotinus, *The Enneads,* trans. by Stephen MacKenna, 2nd rev. edn. (London: Faber & Faber 1956), p. XLVII; Netton, *Allāh Transcendent,* pp. 261-262.
4. See *Ḥikmat al-Ishrāq,* pp. 135-137; Netton, *Allāh Transcendent,* p. 262.
5. Netton, *Allāh Transcendent,* p. 262.
6. See above, nn. 45, 53, 54.
7. See Netton, *Allāh Transcendent,* p. 261.

reflects a more ancient *Plotinian* paradigm. Any attempt therefore, such as that made in this essay, to claim that in Suhrawardian thought *falsafa* and *taṣawwuf* ultimately merge, must acknowledge at least here a Greek antecedent or model. What makes Suhrawardī's thought unique, however, is the way in which he builds upon Plotinus' 'simple' threefold hierarchy and established a much larger emanating hierarchy of lights with Plotinus' One or Good now metamorphosed into the Light-of-Lights *(Nūr al-anwār),* and a complex baroque series of angelic orders of lights beneath that Supreme Light. What he also emphasizes in his thought is the duality of love and dominion inherent in the structure of his emanationist scheme. Emanation *qua* emanation was, clearly known to, and used by, many of his philosophical predecessors such as al-Fārābī and Ibn Sīnā, for example. But in the metaphysics of the first it is difficult to detect much mysticism whether in vocabulary or content; while in that of the second, in whose later thought we can indeed detect a mystical strain, the *stress,* in emanationist theory at least, seems to be more on such themes as 'awareness,' 'contemplation,' 'knowledge' and 'intellection'[1] than 'love' and 'yearning,' though this is not to deny the existence of such latter themes altogether. It is a question of *emphasis* and Suhrawardī, in a particularly vivid way chooses to *emphasize* what we have termed above the 'Ladder of Yearning,' with its 'batteries' of emanated lights.

A final question remains to be answered briefly: to what extent is the philosophical vocabulary of Suhrawardī in the *Ḥikmat al-Ishrāq,* such as we have just surveyed, solely a vehicle for that author's mysticism which is known popularly as 'illuminationism'? There is no doubt that much in the development of Islamic philosophy has changed with Suhrawardī's advent: "the old terminology of *al-'Aql al-Kullī* and *al-Nafs al-Kulliyya* has been supplanted by that of *anwār* in all their complex manifestations and interdependent relationships. Aristotelian concepts of substance have also given way before his light cosmology."[2] Whereas with the thought of his great intellectual predecessor Ibn Sina, it is possible to attempt an assessment in terms of two distinct—if not equal—registers, the Aristotelian and the Neoplatonic, the same approach is much more difficult with Suhrawardian thought; this is because the intimate link which has been demonstrated between some of the technical vocabulary of philosophy, and that of criticism, 'absorbs' and indeed dominates many of the older vocabularies and schools of thought.[3] There is no doubt in all this where Suhrawardī's own inclinations lie. In a highly significant comment in *Ḥikmat al-Ishrāq* he plays down the role of in-depth study by Peripatetics which he believes is by no means indispensable: one can do without much of what they have discussed at length.[4] Anthony K. Tuft summarizes the situation thus: "Suhrawardī... devotes the entire first half of his *Ḥikmat al-Ishrāq* to a skeptical review of logical definition. concluding that it is unable to provide a clear

1. See *ibid.*, pp. 114-117, 163-165.
2. Netton, *Allāh Transcendent* p. 268.
3. Ibid.
4. *Ḥikmat al-Ishrāq*, p. 31. See, also, M.Y. Hairi, 'Suhrawardī's *An Episode and a Trance*. A Philosophical Dialogue in a Mystical Stage', in Morewedge (ed), *Islamic Philosophy and Mysticism*, pp. 177-189, especially the citation of Aristotle's words on p. 187.

picture of reality... Suhrawardī's purpose in this attack on Aristotelian logic is the destruction or revision of the doctrines of physics or metaphysics which, among most contemporary Islamic thinkers, depend directly on this system of logic for their consistency... [Suhrawardī] opens the second section of the *Ḥikmat al-Ishrāq* by noting that light is the one reality so clearly manifest that no definition is needed to clarify it.[1]

Bylebyl, neatly, proposes that Suhrawardī "found himself in the presence of a new set of determining coordinates."[2] I would suggest here that, foremost among such coordinates, is Suhrawardī's own emanationist 'Ladder of Yearning' which is the vehicle, the primal Suhrawardian narrative or myth, whereby light and darkness, God and man, encounter each other and under the impetus of which *falsafa* dissolves almost imperceptibly into *taṣawwuf.* And if voluntary or even involuntary martyrdom, or execution, for one's beliefs may be said to betoken in some way a 'sign' of love for those beliefs (and the Deity within them), then we may say that the 'myth' of Suhrawardī's life and death conforms to a very similar paradigm as that of his thought The 'myth' of Suhrawardī's almost Ḥallājian disregard for—and ultimate 'abdication' of—his own life (voluntarily or involuntarily constitutes as much 'a bridge of love or yearning,' as well as a literary motif, as the intellectual emanationist paradigm of the 'Ladder of Yearning,' which is equally a 'Ladder of Love,' adumbrated above. There is only this major distinction: Suhrawardī's death brings together the Divine and the human *at a moment in time;* Suhrawardian emanation eternally bridges the two worlds of Supreme Light and corporeal darkness.

1. Anthony K. Tuft, 'Symbolism and Speculation in Suhrawardī's The Song of Gabriel's Wing' in Morewedge (ed.), *Islamic Philosophy and Mysticism,* pp. 209-210.
2. Michael Edward Bylebyl, 'The Wisdom of Illumination: A Study of the Prose Stories of Suhrawardi' (PhD thesis, University of Chicago 1976, p. 226)

The Dawning Places of the Lights of Certainty in the Divine Secrets Connected with the Commander of the Faithful by Rajab Bursī (d. 1411)

B.T. Lawson

INTRODUCTION

Not far from the ancient site of Babylon, in the mid-fourteenth century, Rajab Bursī was born in a hamlet situated at the foot of a mountain near the Euphrates called Burs. Shi'ite authors often call him an "extremist/exaggerator" *(ghālī)* because of his uncomprising view of the Prophet and the Imam as eternal principles even though many features of the venerable "extremist tradition" *(ghulūw)* seem to be absent from his work.[1] What is clear is that his work, which pays ceaseless homage to the twelve Imams of *Ithnā-'asharī* Shi'ism, is suffused also with the themes and poetry of many Sufi authors and is heavily influenced by the logocentric ontology of Ibn 'Arabī. This ontology would eventually make itself felt, four hundred years later in, for example, the religio-political program of the Babi movement of mid-nineteenth century Iran whose literature also contains many references to the contents of the book under discussion. Between that time and the time of our author, his work has been quoted, commented upon, and noticed by a variety of different scholars.

Bursī's adoption of the Persianate *takhalluṣ* as a means of signing his poetry appears to be his only literary acknowledgment of specifically Persian culture. His move to Iran seems to have been motivated by an attraction to the probably somewhat less doctrinaire Shi'ite community there rather than an attraction for things Persian. The petty Sufi/Shi'ite dynasty in charge of Khurasān, the Sarbadārids (1337–1381) which included Ṭūs, Bursī's eventual place of refuge, was tolerated by Timur for a while even after his conquest of the area. Rajab Bursī's book is written entirely in Arabic, and none of the other titles ascribed to Bursī indicate Persian works, nor is he known to have written anything in Persian. Nonetheless, his words are often quoted by Persian authors from the Safavid period onward.[2] The book under discussion here was, for example, made the object of large Persian paraphrase and commentary, by order of Shāh Sulaymān Safavī (reg.1666–1694), of over a

1. So Henry Corbin, *Annuaire de la Section des Sciences religieuse de l'École pratique des hautes études,* Paris *[Annuaire]*(1968-69), p.148. For example, there seems to be no excessive interest in the Return of the Hidden Imam *(raj'a)*, his Rising *(qiyāma)*, or his Advent *(ẓuhūr)*. See M.G.S. Hodgson, *"Ghulāt,"* EI². See also the remark by Fritz Meier, 'The Mystic Path,' in *Islam and the Arab World,* edited by Bernard Lewis (New York 1976), p.124.
2. See below, page 269, note 3.

thousand pages, by a scholar from Sabzivār living in Mashhad, al-Ḥasan al-Khaṭīb al-Qāri', dated1090/1680.[1]

The presence, then, of this study in a book of essays devoted to the topic of the legacy of mediæval Persian Sufism might at first strike the reader as somewhat anomalous. It was written by an Arab who seems to have been neither master nor disciple in the traditional Sufi sense; indeed, the main interest of the work is explicitly Twelver Shi'ism. However, the author and his book are both legatee and legator of a species of mystical thought that is not without interest for readers of this volume. This affinity to Persianate thought may be ultimately traceable to the strong influence of Ibn 'Arabī in his work, (together, of course, with his Shi'ism). As is well known, the enthusiasm with which the Great Doctor's thought was received and embellished by Persian authors is a striking fact in the history of Islamic thought.

Rajab Bursī's *Mashāriq al-anwār* has been described as being of the first importance for the study of Shi'ite gnostic metaphysics. Corbin places our author in a distinct stream of thought within Islam extending from Sijistānī (d.ca.360/972), and including such figures as 'Alā' al-Dawla Simnānī (d.736/1336), Ḥaydar Āmulī (d.after 787/1385), Shah Ni'matullāh Walī (d. 834/1431),[2] Rajab 'Alī Tabrīzī (d.1080/1669-70), Qāḍī Sa'īd Qummī (d.1103/1691-1692), Khwājah Muḥammad ibn Maḥmūd Dihdār (10th-11th/16th-17th),[3] and Shaykh Aḥmad al-Aḥsā'ī (d.1241/1826).[4] To this list of kindred thinkers may be added Ibn Abī Jumhūr (d. towards the end of the 15th cent.)[5] and Mullā Muḥsin Fayḍ Kāshānī (d. 1091/1680).[6]

The *Mashāriq* has attracted the attention of a steady stream of scholars from the late fifteenth century to the present, and the majority of these authors have been Persian. Most striking of all, is the continued popularity this book enjoys amongst the generality of contemporary Shi'ites, about which a bit more later. Insofar as the work at hand preserves and transmits mediæval Sufism, the understanding of twentieth century Shi'ism and the heritage it enjoys from mediæval times, may also be deepened through its study.

The cast of thought which characterizes this rich and complex heritage has been briefly summarized by Corbin as reflecting a metaphysics

---

1. This commentary, entitled *Maṭāli' al-asrār*, (Teh. Bib. de l'Univ. Cat.V, p. 1537 has been mentioned by Corbin in a number of places (e.g. *En Islam iranien*, 4 vols. Paris 1971-72 [EII] vol. 4, p. 212) and parts of it translated in *Annuaire* 1968-69 Corbin used this and related texts as part of his courses during the academic years 1968-1970 in Paris.
2. Henry Corbin, *Histoire de la philosophie islamique* (Paris 1986,[Hist.]) p. 63.
3. *Hist.*, p. 461.
4. *EII* 3, p. 318.
5. On whom see Wilferd Madelung, 'Ibn Abî Ǧumhûr al-Ahsâ'îs synthesis of *kalam*, philosophy and Sufism,' in *La Significance du Bas Moyen Age dans le Histoire et la Culture du Monde Musulman*. Actes du 8eme Congres de l'Union Europḗne de Arabisants et Islamisants (Aix-en-Provence 1978), pp. 147-56.
6. On this figure and his mystical temperament see, for example, Etan Kohlberg. 'Some Aspects of Akhbari Thought,' *Eighteenth-Century Renewal and Reform in Islam*, ed. by N. Levtzion & J.Voll (Syracuse: Syracuse University Press 1987), pp.133-160.

not content with identifying real being *(al-wujūd al-ḥaqq)* with absolute being *(wujūd muṭlaq)*, because if this being is absolute, that is to say "freed" of all condition, it presupposes a *muṭliq* that frees it, and this *muṭliq* is being in the real sense, so real that it transcends our category of being.[1]

NAME

Aghā Buzurg Tihrānī lists our author as al-Shaykh Raḍiyadīn Rajab bin Muḥammad bin Rajab al-Ḥāfiẓ al-Bursī al-Ḥillī.[2] Brockelman, following *Dharī'a,* uses this latter name in one entry[3] where he also calls him an extreme Shi'ite. But in two other places Brockelmann lists him as (1) Rajab b. al-Ḥāfiẓ al-Brussawī;[4] and (2) Raḍī al-din Rajab b. Muḥammad b. Rajab al-Ḥāfiẓ al-Birsī al-Ḥillī.[5] al-Ḥurr al-'Āmilī (d.1097/1682) lists his name as Rajab al-Ḥāfiẓ al-Bursī and adds that he was a "scholar, traditionist, poet, writer, and a man of culture."[6] According to one scholar, there is some ground for suspecting that he was neither from Ḥilla nor originally a Shi'ite because the term 'traditionist' *(muḥaddith)* is not a typical designation for a Shi'ite scholar and it is unlikely that the qualification would be given to someone from Ḥilla.[7] The biographer Khwansarī (d.1313/1895-6) refers to him in ornate fashion as the "learned master, the perfect Shaykh and Murshid, the Pole and the divine gnostic."[8] These titles, indicating his position in a Sufi hierarchy need not be taken seriously because we have no knowledge of his social connections. As will be seen however, that he be described in such a way is not due simply to the fulsome rhetoric of a late Qajar source.

Finally, about his *nisba*, al-Bursī, there is some disagreement: it refers to town near Gīlān, or near Turshīz in Khurasān, or the Arab hamlet mentioned above. One opts for the Irāqī town because it was an important area of Shi'ism during this time and, apart from the employment in his poetry of a Persian style *takhalluṣ*, Bursī seems to have written nothing in Persian.[9]

1. *EI1* 3, p.319.
2. *Āghā Buzurg*, Muḥammad Muḥsin al-Tihrānī, *al-Dharī'a ilā taṣānif al-shī'a*. 25 vols. (Tehran and Najaf 1355/1936-1398/1978 [*Dharī'a*]) ii, p. 299.
3. *GAL*, Supp.ii, p. 204 under the category *Der Hadīt.*
4. *GAL*, Supp. p. 660 under the category *Der Mystik.*
5. *GAL*, Supp. iii-2, p. 1266.
6. *Fāḍil*, a *Muḥaddith*, a *Shā'ir*, a *Munsh'ā*, and an *Adīb*. al-Ḥurr al-'Amilī, *Amal al-Āmil*, 2 vols. (Najaf, 1380/1960], vol. 2, pp. 117-118.
7. Kāmil Muṣṭafā al-Shaybī, *al-Fikr al-shī'ī wa al-naza'āt al-ṣūfīya ḥattā maṭla'al-qarn al-thānī 'ashar al-hijrī*. (Baghdad:1966/1386 [*Fikr*]), p. 258.
8. al-Mawlā al-'Ālim wash-Shaykh wal-Murshid al-Kāmil wal-Quṭb al-Wāqif al-Unsī wal-Anis al-'Ārif al-Qudsī Raḍī al-dīn Rajab bin Muḥammad bin Rajab al-ma'rūf bil-Ḥāfiẓ al-Bursī. Muḥammad Bāqir Khwānṣāri, *Rawḍat al-jannāt fī aḥwāl al-'ulamā' wa al-sadāt*. 8 vols. (Tehran 1970-72), vol. 3, pp. 337-345. See also the brief notice in Muḥammad 'Alī Mudarris Tabrīzī Khayabānī, *Rayḥānāt al-adab* (Tehran 1967-70), ii, p.11.
9. *Fikr*, pp. 254-5.

LIFE

Everything we know of his life we owe to the late Safavid biographies, especially the one by 'Abdullāh Afandī al-Jīrānī written between 1107/1695 and 1130/1718.[1] Rajab Bursī was born in the village Burs in 'Irāq, a town famous for its sweet water, situated at the base of a mountain between Ḥilla and Kūfa around the year 743/1342 and died in or after 843/1411. He grew up in Ḥilla and moved *(hajara)* to Khurasan at the age of tweny-six. Of his birth, his teachers, his associates, his students or his death we have no certain knowledge.[2] His tomb, however, is in located in a garden in Ardestan near Isfahan. Bursī fled Ḥilla due to persecution by his fellow Shi'ites because of his 'extreme' beliefs about 'Alī. This is indicated by our author himself in his poetry.[3] It is likely Bursī fled from Ḥilla to Khurasān because of the promise of a freer atmosphere provided by the somewhat heterodox Shi'ite Sarbadārid state there. He withdrew to Ṭūs (present-day Mashhad) to be near the shrine of 'Alī al-Riḍā. Here he remained, presumably occupied with his writing and other spiritual pursuits until his death.[4] Other evidence suggests that his *hijra* did not save him from further persecution.[5] Indeed, one reference to him in an anonymous Sufi work states that he was killed in Ṭūs.[6] The circumstances surrounding such a violent end are so far completely unknown. However, Timurid authority in the region had by this time become more consolidated. It may be that Rajab Bursī's example was thought to be contrary to the Timurīd political agenda. It is also quite possible that rumors of his execution or murder are just that. After all, by this time he had reached a rather advanced age.

Bursī states in an autograph manuscript of one work, possibly the *Mashāriq*, that he finished it 518 years after the birth of the Mahdī, that is in 768/1367, if we accept that in Bursī's view the Mahdī was born in the year 864/250.[7] This means it was completed during the reign of the last Sarbadārid 'Alī Mu'ayyad. Al-Jīrānī states that he wrote another work, the *Mashāriq al-amān*, in 811/1398-9, having seen with his own eyes a copy of this work and others in Māzandarān.

Although Bursī was a contemporary of Ḥaydar Āmulī, the latter seems not to take any notice of him.[8] Apparently, the first to mention him or quote his work was al-Kaf'amī, (d.15th/9th cent.) in his collection of prayers entitled the *Miṣbāḥ*, writ-

---

1. This biographical dictionary has been recently edited and published: 'Abdullah ibn 'Īsā Afandi al-Jīrānī (d.ca.1718) *Riyāḍ al-'ulamā' wa hiyād al-fudalā*. 6 vols. (Qum 1981).
2. *Fikr*, p. 253.
3. E.g. *Mashāriq*, p. 246. The Sarbadārids, existed in the region from 1337/737-1386/788. They were one of a number of dynasties that replaced the Il-Khānids and were eventually conquered by Tīmūr in 782/1380. But the great ruler's Shi'ite sympathies allowed the last Sarbadārid, 'Alī Mu'ayyad, to remain as governor until his death in 788/1386. See Moojan Momen, *Introduction to Shī'ī Islam (*Oxford, 1985), p.93. See also *ibid*., pp. 99-104 for a useful summary of Shi'ism and its increasing appropriation of Sufism in the middle period, 1000-1500.
4. *Fikr*, p. 257.
5. Cited in *Fikr*, p. 256.
6. *Fikr*, p. 255. The work was discovered by 'Abbās Qummī.
7. *Fikr*, p. 258 and notes.
8. I have been unable to confirm whether or not he is mentioned by Ibn Abī Jumhūr (d. at the end of the 15th/9th century). The likely place for such a reference would by his *Kitāb al-Mujlī on* which see the reference to Madelung above.

ten in 1490/895.[1] Muḥsin Fayḍ Kāshānī (d.1091/1680), the influential Sufi Shi'ite of the later Safavid period, mentions Bursī in his *Kalimāt-i maknūna*.[2] Muḥammad Bāqir al-Majlisī (d.1110 or 1111/1699 or 1700), a student of the former, seems to have been the first to revile Bursī's "extremism" *(ghulūw)*, and who because of his great prestige influenced later attitudes towards him, cited Bursī in his *Biḥār al-anwār*.[3]

For a list of Bursī's works we are indebted to al-Sayyid Ni'matullāh al-Jazā'irī (d.1112/1700).[4] Of these twelve titles, only one is printed, namely the *Mashāriq al-anwār*.

MASHĀRIQ AL-ANWĀR

By far the best known of his works is the *Mashāriq al-anwār*. It exists in a number of manuscripts.[5] The first printed edition is that of Bombay dated 1883. In 1959 it was edited anonymously and printed in Beirut. Its popularity is attested by the fact that between that year and 1967 the book went through ten printings. The edition used for this discussion is designated as the tenth printing, but it bears no date.[6] This publication history indicates rather persuasively that the book is important in popular Shi'ite piety. Because, as will be shown, the book teaches a number of gnostic and mystical doctrines it affords a strong insight into the durability of mediæval Sufism's legacy as it continues to be felt in contemporary Shi'ism.

The text as we have it in the printed edition is divided into a three distinct parts: the 'Introduction' (pp. 5-13) which is possibly a separate work of Bursī's entitled *Lawāmī'*(see item # 7 in Appendix) affirming the unity of God and the sanctity of the Imams; the *Mashāriq* proper (pp.14-224); and a *Majmū'a* of his poetry derived from the *Mashāriq* and other sources (pp.225-247).[7] The *Mashāriq al-anwār* proper consists of 204 chapters *(fuṣūl)* introduced with a brief introduction and concluded with a short *khātima*. In both the 'introduction' and the *khātima*, Bursī refers to the persecution he suffered at the hands of those whose belief is corrupt (*tashayyu'fāḥisha*) and specifies the *fuqahā'* as being particularly culpable.

> Know that when I chanted to the envious, those who know nothing of true religion. ...from the Glorious Book...they drove me away. And when I unfolded to them some of the traditions and expounded to them their inner meanings...they became envious of me and slandered me...though I did nothing wrong. Most of what I said had to do with a hidden matter and a mysterious secret. He who is disturbed by such

---

1. *Fikr*, p. 262. Muḥammad b, Ṣāliḥ al-'Āmilī al-Kaf'amī, *al-Misbaḥ*. (Qum 1405/1984). See pp. 176, 183, 316, 363-4.
2. "Fayḍ wrote this during his youth when he was inclined towards *taṣawwuf*." *Fikr*, p. 262. See Mullā Muḥsin al-Fayḍ al-Kāshānī, *Kalimāt-i maknūna min 'ulūm ahl al-ḥikma wal-ma'rifa*. (Tehran 1383/1963), pp.196ff. The title of Bursī's work given by Kāshānī is slightly different: *Mashāriq anwār al-yaqīn fī kashf asrār Amīr al-Mu'minīn*.
3. Vol. 8, pp. 202 (Iran ed. 1302).
4. In his *al-Anwār al-nu'māniya* (written in 1687/1098).
5. See the references to *GAL* and *Dharī'a* above.
6. It is possible that it is older than another edition seen by me dated 1399/1978 printed by the Dār al-Andalus, but this is doubtful. I have been told of an 11th edition dated 1978.
7. *Majmū'a min shi'r al-Shaykh Rajab al-Bursī* (pp.225-247). This is a collection of his poetry from a variety of sources, mainly *Shu'arā' al-Ḥilla; 'Ayān al-shī'a; al-Ghadīr;* and the *Mashāriq* itself.

things has a sickness in his heart while the peaceful heart is gladdened [by such things].

Some thought I was an ignorant one, but they condemn what they understand not... These were the brothers from among the *fuqahā'* ...their minds were obscured by transmitted knowledge... God specializes for his mercy whomever He will and separates him from the envier. "And in their hearts is a sickness which God will increase"[Koran II:10].[1]

An indication of the Sufi nature of this work is also given quite early in the text. In relation to the topic of selflessness as a prerequisite for true knowledge, Rajab Bursī cites the following Tradition.

When God created the soul He called to it with the question "Who am I?" The soul [insolently] responded: "But who am I!?" Then God cast it into the depths of the sea until it came to the Extended Alif[2] *(al-alif al-mabsūṭ)* and it was purified of the depravities of referring to its self and it returned to its proper development. Then God called to it again with the question: "Who am I?" The soul responded this time with: "Thou art the One, the Vanquisher! [Koran XL: 16]." For this reason He said: *"Kill your souls"* [Koran II: 43 & IV:66] because they will never recognize their stations except through vanquishing.[3]

The connection here would seem to be that Rajab Bursī sees his difficulties with his fellow Ḥillīs as a spiritual trial which in the end will be of benefit to him. Thus the allusion to the oft-quoted (in Shi'ite literature) *ḥadith:* "The knowledge of the People of the House is exceedingly difficult *(ṣa'b mustaṣ'ab),* none can bear it except a sent prophet, an angel brought nigh to God or a believer whose heart has been tested for faith."[4]

In the *khātima* he also refers to his *hijra* due to the censure and blame directed against him and cites a tradition from the Prophet extolling the virtues of retreat: "All good is in seclusion *('uzla)*, and good and well-being are found in solitude *(waḥda)*, and there is blessing in abandoning people."[5]

The many chapters of the *Mashāriq* vary greatly in length and subject matter. The first 22 are devoted to an exploration of the numinous content or status of letters of the alphabet which also have numerical value.[6] In any case, it should not be inferred from this that such concerns are absent from the rest of the book. Bursī was, it may be noted, a contemporary of Faḍlullāh Astarābādī (1339-1401), the founder of the Ḥurūfī sect.[7] And it may be also that the work contains a number of cryptic references to the latter, such as the one found at the beginning of the book.[8] As is

1. *Mashāriq*, pp.14-15.
2. This is defined by Bursī elswhere in *Mashāriq*, pp. 20-21; see also Corbin, *Annuaire* 68-69, p. 149.
3. *Mashāriq*, p. 16. 'Alī is also associated with the attribute "vanquisher" *(al-Qahhār)* because of his heroic military prowess at the conquest of Khaybar.
4. *Mashāriq*, p.16; see also *Mashāriq*, pp.197-198.
5. *Mashāriq, p.* 222.
6. It is of some interest that the Persian commentary by Mashhadī, mentioned above, neglects this material.
7. On Faḍlullāh Astarābādī see the article by H. Norris in this volume. Ed.
8. Here he refers to one "who is gladdened by what God has bestowed upon him and opened for him" *[mubtahij bimā faḍalahu Allāh* [sic] *wa faḍḍa lahu]*, *Mashāriq*, p. 15.

well known, however, Bursī would have required no such contemporary validation for his letter and number speculations. By his time, such sciences had been become common coin and practiced by a wide variety authors. Indeed, to the extent that such movements as the Ḥurūfīyya were successful or posed a serious threat to the status quo, it seems reasonable to suppose that the movement spoke a language that struck a responsive cord in the general population.

The chapters are not given topic headings and are designated merely by the word *faṣl*. It is sometimes difficult to know how these chapters were conceived as separate elements. The majority of the material consists of *ḥadīths* and Bursī's commentary on them. These *ḥadīths* are derived from a number of sources, displaying the interest in both Sunni and Shi'ite works common in this period. Thus several are related from Aḥmad Ibn Ḥanbal, Abū Hanīfa, Ibn 'Abbās, and other sources for the Sunni tradition, while numerous traditions are taken from such basic Shi'ite works as the *Kitāb baṣā'ir al-darajāt*.[1]

LOGOS

Beyond the somewhat literalistic conception of Logos implied by a preoccupation with the "science of letters," there is a related theme in the work which expresses the Logos quite independent of the practice of *jafr* or letter speculation. This motif consists in establishing Muḥammad and 'Alī as pre-eternal elements of creation. This doctrine is repeatedly asserted through the *ḥadīths* that Bursī has chosen for his collection, his commentary on these *ḥadīth,* and his poetry. It is also this doctrine, and its implications which have caused Bursī to be condemned not only by his fellow Ḥillīs, but also by such later critics such as Majlisī and Nūrī[2] (notwithstanding that most appear to be impressed by the quality of his poetry).[3]

In this connection, the *Mashāriq* has preserved certain material not found elsewhere in the books of traditions whether Sunni or Shi'ite. Some of this material, according to Corbin, was left out of compilations like the *Nahj al-balāgha* because the implied view of the Imam had certain 'resonances' with Ismaili thought.[4] This hypothesis has recently been confirmed. The Ismaili author, Mu'ayyad Shīrāzī, included the *Khutba al-taṭanīyya* (on which see below) in his *Majālis*.[5] Another typical example, included here, has been described by Corbin as one of those *ḥadīth* most characteristic of Shi'ite gnosis. It is the "recital of a visionary interview between ['Alī's] *lāhūt* (his divine, spiritual, celestial element) and his *nāsūt* (his terrestrial humanity)."[6] It is presented without *isnād:*

---

1. Of Muḥammad al-Ḥasan al-Ṣaffār (d.902).
2. Yaḥyā Nūrī, *Khatamīyat payāmbar-i Islām dar ibṭāl taḥlīlī Bābīgarī, Bahā'īgarī, Qādiyānīgarī.* (Bilingual Fārsī & English edition, Iran 1360 sh./1981), p.20 (English).
3. E.g. Khwānsārī, vol.3, p. 341.
4. *EII* 3, p. 150.
5. I have also been informed that some the material which follows below may be found also in the Gujarati Ginan literature of the Ismailis.
6. *Annuaire* 69-70, p. 234. The commentaries are by: Mīrzā Aḥmad Ardīkānī Shīrāzī (who wrote in 1810 in Shīrāz), Mullā 'Alī ibn Jamshīd Nūrī (1245/1830), Sayyed Kāẓim Rashtī (1259/1843), Ja'far Kashfī (1267/1851), Muḥammad Karīm Khān Kirmānī (1288/1870).

To the First Imām is posed this question: "Have you seen in this world below a certain man?"

The Imām responds to the anonymous questioner: "Yes, I have seen a certain man, and until now I have been asking him questions. I ask him: 'Who are you?'

He answers: "I am clay."

"From where?"

"From clay."

"Towards where?"

"Towards clay."

"And me, who am I?"

"You, you are Abū Turāb (earth dweller)."[1]

"Therefore I am you?"

He shot back, "God forbid, God forbid! This is from *al-dīn* in *al-dīn*. I am I and We are We. I am the Essence of essences and the Essence in the essence of the Essence." Then he said: "[Do you] understand?"

I said, "Yes."

Then he said, "So cling [to this understanding]."

Rajab al-Bursī then comments on this *ḥadīth* to the effect that it represents a conversation between the divine and human worlds *(lāhūt/nāsūt)*.[2] This discussion elucidates the difference between the body *('the temple of man's holiness')* and the soul, or essence of this holiness *(sirr)*:

Thus his statement, "I have seen a certain man, and until now I have been asking him questions," is because the spirit is always attached to the body and considers it the house of its exile... And secondly, that the gnostic *('ārif)* should ever know the difference between the station of dust and the holiness *(sirr)* of the Lord of lords, namely that when he knows himself he knows his Lord. That is, he knows his self, its generated-ness, its poverty, its wretchedness and thus knows of his Lord's might and greatness, and majesty. So his statement: "I am clay" is an allusion to this gnostic, ever in the station of poverty and affirming his generatedness and weakness... And his statement "You are Abū Turāb." alludes to two meanings, one particular and the other general. The first of its meanings is the allusion to Father Educator *(al-āb al-murabbī)*, Guide *(al-murshid)* and the Spirit *(al-rūḥ)* Custodian and Trainer of this body. The second is that Abū Turāb is 'water,' and the meaning is that 'Thou art the father of all existing things and their point of origin and their reality and their true meaning because he is the Most Great Word from which appears the existent things *(mawjūdāt)*, and it is the holy essence *(sirr)* of all engendered things *(al-kā'ināt)*...'

And his statement, "I am the Essence of Essences, and the Essence in the Essences of the Essence" clearly refers to the Hidden Secret *(al-sirr al-maknūn)* on which depends the two phases of "Be thou! and it is." *[kun fayakūn;* Koran II:117] He is

1. A pun that evokes the tradition of 'Alī having been given this nickname by the Prophet. On the name, see Etan Kohlberg, 'Abū Turāb,' *BSOAS* (1978), pp. 347-52.

2. Corbin observes that the later commentators have used all the resources which Shi'ite theosophy and their Neoplatonism have put at their disposal. For example Mīrzā Aḥmad Ardīkānī Shīrāzī petitions the Hermetic idea of the Perfect Man *(insān kāmil)* as Perfect Nature who is the angel of every being and of whom Hermes had his vision. All agree in recognizing the extreme difficulty of this *ḥadīth;* it is certain that this particular one is one of a number of texts which are the most significant for theosophic imamology, those which evoke the problem of the "two natures" posed also in Christology. *Annuaire* 68-9.

the Greatest Name of God *(ism Allāh al-a'ẓam)*[1] and the reality of every engendered thing *(kā'in)*. The essence of every existent belongs to the essence of the Necessary Existent *(wājib al-wujūd)* because it is his holy essence *(sirr)* and his word *(kalima)* and his command/cause *(amr)* and his guardian *(walī)* over all things. ...

Thus through the solution of this riddle the disbelief of the exaggerator *(ghālī)* has been distinguished from the one who speaks properly *(qālī)* [as has] the struggle on the path of the slackard *(tālī)* [been distinguished from the true striving] of the one who has accepted 'Alī as guardian *(mawālī)*. The method of attainment to the Exalted /'Alī of the true knower *('ārif al-'ālī)* has thus been indicated.[2]

'Alī is the connecting mystery *(sirr)* of God in all [things and circumstances], His guardian *(walī)* over all because the [actual] Lord is mightily exalted above what He has existentiated through His purpose *(irāda)* or created through His power *(qudra)* or His will *(mashiyya)*,... to 'Alī all allusions *(ishārāt)* refer by virtue of his statement "There is no difference between them and between Thee except that they are Your servants and Your creation."...

About his statement to him, "Do you understand?" and 'I said, "Yes".' And he said "Cling to this!"—this alludes to the fact that when a man understands that 'Alī is the hidden secret it is incumbent upon him to cling to this so the intellect may accept this apperception.[3]

KHUṬBA AL-TAṬANJĪYA

Another tradition of a similarly gnostic flavour is called *Khutbat al-taṭanjiya*. This *ḥadīth* does not appear in *Nahj al-balāgha*, but is preserved in other Twelver Shi'ite sources.[4] It is related in the 144th chapter of the *Mashāriq* without *isnād* and introduced by Bursī as one of 'Alī's sermons about which one should be particularly careful in interpreting because of its style and content which elevate 'Alī. This is so to such a degree that one could be tempted to class the statements below as ecstatic sayings (*shaṭh*). Bursī says that the sermon contains that which establishes the transcendence of the Creator in a way none can bear.

The Commander of the Faithful delivered this sermon between Kūfa and Medina. He said:

"O People! ...I am hope and that which is hoped for. I preside over the twin gulfs *(Anā wāqif 'ala al-taṭanjayn)*. And my gaze beholds the two wests and the two easts [Cf. Koran LV:17]. I have seen the mercy of God and Paradise clearly through direct [physical] vision. And it is in the seventh sea... and in its swells are the stars and the orbits. And I saw the earth enwrapped as by a garment... I know the wonders of God's creation as no one but God knows them. And I know what was and what will be, and what occurred at the time of the primordial covenant *(al-dharr al-awwal)* *[viz.* the *yawm al-mīthāq;* cf. Koran VII:172] before the First Adam. It has been disclosed to me by my Lord... and this knowledge was hidden from all prophets except the Master of this *Sharī'a* of yours. He taught me his knowledge and I taught him my knowledge. We are the first warning and the warning of the first and the last and

---

1. It is somewhat surprising, given the distinctive approach by our author to the this topic and the other names of God, that there appears to be no need to refer to him (or others like) him in a recent studies of the divine names in Islam.
2. The pun in the Arabic clearly indicates that 'Alī and God may be confused.
3. *Annuaire* 69-70, pp. 233-235; *Mashāriq*, pp. 31-2.
4. See Corbin, *Annuaire* 69-70; *Dharī'a* 7, # 989 where this sermon is identified *as Khutbat al-aqālīm* & *Biḥār* 9, p. 535 and the reference to Ibn Shahrāshūb (d.1192 in Aleppo).

the warning for all times and periods. Through us perishes him who perishes and through us is saved whoever is saved. And you are incapable of what is in us. By him who breaks the seed and drives the winds!... Indeed, the winds and air and birds are made subservient to us. The world below was given me and I shunned it. I am the dome of the world... I know what is above the highest Paradise and what is below the lowest earth and what is in the highest heavens and what is between them and what is under the dust. All this is comprehensive knowledge, not related knowledge. I swear by the Lord of the Mighty Throne! If you desired I could tell you of your forefathers, where they were and what they were and where they are now and what they will be... If I reveal to you what was given in the first eternity and what is of me in the End then you would see mighty wonders and things great.... I am the Master of the first creation before the first Noah. And were I to tell you what transpired between Adam and Noah, the wonders of those arts and the nations destroyed [in that time] then the truth of the statement "evil is what they have done" would be established. I am the Master of the first two Floods [Koran VII:133]. I am the Master of the second two floods [Koran XXIX:14]. I am the Master of the Flood *[sayl al-'aram;* Koran XXXIV:16]. I am the Master of the hidden secrets *(al-asrār al-maknūnāt).* I am the Master of 'Ād and the Gardens. And I am the Master of Thamūd and the Signs. And I am their destroyer. And I am their shaker. And I am their place of return. And I am their destroyer. And I am their director. I am their two gates. I am their leveller. I am their maker to die and I am their maker to live. I am the First, I am the Last, I am the Outward, I am the Inward [Koran LVII:3]. I was with time before time and I was with revolution before revolution. And I was with the Pen before the Pen and I was with the Tablet before the Tablet. And I am the master of the First Pre-eternity. And I am the master of Jabalqa and Jabarsa.... I am the director of the first world when there was no heaven and no earth."

So Ibn Ṣūrīma [?] approached him and said: "Thou art thou, O Commander of the Faithful!" Then 'Alī said: "I am Me, there is no god but God, my Lord and the Lord of all creatures. To Him is the creation and the command, He who directs all things through His wisdom and raises the heavens and the earth through His power... I have commanded Iblīs to prostrate... I raised Idrīs to a high place, I caused Jesus to speak in the cradle. I have divided the world into five... I am that light which appeared on Sinai... I am the Master of the eternal gardens and he who causes the rivers to flow... and I fashioned the climes by the command of the Knower and the Wise. I am that word through which all things are perfected... Indeed the hypocrites who say 'Alī has appointed himself are wrong... 'Alī is a created light and servant of the Provider of sustenance, whoever says other than this, God condemns his deed."[1]

SELF-KNOWLEDGE

Thus far we have concentrated on the so-called gnostic aspects of this work—gnostic because of the repeated emphasis on knowledge—the knowledge of the Imām and recognition of his true dignity. And more importantly, the material is gnostic because of the 'far flung' imagery contained in the traditions—its gnomic, *outré,* and deeply mysterious flavour. But what of 'standard' Sufism? Rajab Bursī does not merit inclusion in a volume on mediæval Persian Sufism simply because of the single pronouncement, in the context of a section on Islamic sects, that "the Sufis are divided into two groups *(firqa)*: the *nūrīyya* and the *khalwīyya."*[2] Nor do the

1. *Mashāriq,* pp. 160-1.
2. *Mashāriq,* p. 205.

passing references to such Sufi heros as Ḥallāj (d. 922),[1] Ibn al-Fāriḍ (d. 1235), and Ibn 'Arabī (d. 1240) suffice to establish our author as a Sufi, although such references have doubtless contributed to his widely attested reputation as a Sufi.[2] Such references *do* point to a certain genuine sympathy with some of the concerns of Sufism. Where Rajab Bursī's Sufism is most clearly in evidence is in those passages which deal with the self, specifically its knowledge and its effacement. Three chapters are specifically dedicated to this theme:

I

The Glorious Lord says in the Gospel: "Know thyself, O man and know thy lord. Thine external is for annihilation *(fanā')* and thine internal is Me."
And the Master of the *Sharī'a* [Muḥammad] said: "The most knowledgeable of you about his Lord is the most knowledgeable about his self."

II

And the Imam of Guidance ['Alī] said: "He who knows his Lord knows his self."
Commentary: The knowledge of the self is that a man knows his beginning and his end, from where he came and to where he is going, and this is based upon true knowledge of 'delimited' existence *(al-wujūd al-muqayyad)*. And this is knowledge of the first effulgence *(al-fayḍ al-awwal)* which overflowed from the Lord of Might. Then Being flowed from it and was made Existence by the command of the Necessary Existent... And this is the single point which is the beginning of the 'engendered things' *(kā'ināt)* and the end of all 'existent things' *(mawjūdāt)* and the Spirit of spirits and light of the apparitional incorporeal beings *(al-ashbāḥ)...*

This is the first number and the secret [that explains the difference between] of the Inclusive Divine Unity and the Transcendent Exclusive Divine Unity *(al-wāḥid* and *al-aḥad.)*[3] And that is because the essence of God is unknowable for man *(bashar)*. So knowledge of Him is through His qualities *(ṣifāt)*. And the single point is a quality *(ṣifa)* of God, and the quality indicates the Qualified, because by its appearance God is known. And it is the flashing of the light *(la' lā' al-nūr)* which shines out *(sha'sha'a)* from the splendour of the Exclusive Unity *(al-aḥadīya)* in the sign *(sīmā')* of the Muḥammadan Presence. To this the following statement alludes: "Whoever knows You, knows you through this sign." This is supported by another saying: "Were it not for us, none would know God. And were it not for God, none would know us." Thus, it is the Light from which dawn all other lights, and the One from which appears all bodies *(ajsād)*, and the mystery from which is generated all mysteries, and the Intellect *('aql)* from which springs all intellects and the Soul from which appears all souls, and the Tablet which contains the hidden secrets and the Throne which spreads throughout heaven and earth, and the Mighty Throne that encompasses all things, and the Eye by which all other eyes see, and the Reality to which all things testify in the beginning, just as they testified in the Exclusive Unity to the Necessary Existent. It is the highest limit of the knowledge of all knowers, the means of access to Muḥammad and 'Alī through the reality of their knowledge, or, through the knowledge of their realities. But this gate is covered by the veil [indicat-

1. *Mashāriq*, p. 27, 177, and 21 respectively.
2. E.g. *Rayḥānāt al-ādab* and *Rawḍat al-jannat* cited above.
3. Briefly, these are two 'modes' of the Divine Oneness: *al-wāḥid* refers to the Oneness that implies also 'within' it the multiplicity of creation, while *al-Aḥad* refers to the utterly unknowable unique, transcendent singleness of God. These ideas are traced to Ibn Arabi. See below.

ed in] "But we give unto you of knowledge only a little." [Koran LXXXV:170] To this alludes the statements of the Imams: that which was given to the Near Angels of the people of Muḥammad was little, so how can the world of man [have more]? And on this topic is the statement: "Our cause is bewilderingly abstruse; none can bear it except a sent prophet and not even an angel brought nigh."[1] He who connects with the rays of their light has known himself because then he has recognized [the difference between] the essence of existence *('ayn al-wujūd)* and the reality of that which is made to exist *(ḥaqīqat al-mawjūd)*, and the absolute single uniqueness of the served Lord *(fardānīyat al-rabb al-ma'būd)*. The knowledge of the self is the knowledge of the reality of 'delimited' existence. This is none other than the Single Point whose exterior is Prophethood and whose interior is Saintship *(walāya)* Thus he who knows *Nubūwwa* and *Walāya* with true knowledge knows his Lord. So he who knows Muḥammad and 'Alī knows his Lord.[2]

This is a particularly good example of the function of the Prophet and the Imam in Bursī's theory of knowledge. It also is a fine example of Bursī's use of the mystical and philosophical language of 'high' Sufism as it had developed by his time. Obviously, the source for such terminology is Ibn 'Arabī. Bursī's contemporary Ḥaydar Āmulī and the later Ibn Abī Jumhūr would, in their distinctive ways, attempt a similar application of the ideas and terminology of the Great Doctor to the intellectual requirements of Shi'ism. These authors in turn helped to prepare the way for the famous Isfahan school of philosophy that flourished during high Safavid times. To continue somewhat with Rajab Bursī's commentary:

III

But, if the pronoun in his word *'nafsihi'* refers to God it means "God himself warns you that they [the Prophet and the Imam] are the spirit of God and His word and the soul of existence and its reality. So in two ways it means "He who knows them knows his Lord." Thus at the time of death he will see with the eye of certainty none but Muḥammad and 'Alī because the Real is too glorious to be seen by the eyes. And the dead one at the time of his death will testify in the Real state and station *(ḥāl* and *maqām)* and see nothing but them at the time of death because he sees with the eye of certainty. Thus Amīr al-Mu'minīn ['Alī] said, "I am the eye of certainty and I am death of the dead." This is indicated in the *Kitāb baṣā'ir al-darajāt*[3] from the Imām Ja'far: "No one in the East or the West dies, whether he loves or hates [Muḥammad and 'Alī], but that he will be brought into the presence of 'Alī and Muḥammad. Then he will be blessed or condemned." This will be at the time of the Trumpet... the soul will be returned to its body. At that time he will see none but Muḥammad and 'Alī because the Living the Self-subsistent, glorified be His name, is not seen by mortal eye, but is seen by the eye of spiritual perception. To this alludes to his statement: "The eyes see him not in the visible realm, but the minds see him through the realities of faith." The meaning is that His existence is testified to because his exterior is invisible and his interior is not hidden.[4]

His discussion of existence, found throughout the work is another good example of Rajab Bursī's reliance on Ibn 'Arabī. His introduction to the *ḥadīth* from 'Alī:

1. Significant variant on the *ḥadīth* mentioned above.
2. M. 188-9.
3. See above.
4. M. 190.

"Have you seen a certain man," is important to notice here:

> If we pursue the subject of the existent beings *(mawjūdāt)*, that they end in a single point which is itself but a quality of the Essence and cause of the existent beings, we may call it by a number of names. It is the Intellect mentioned in the statement: "The first thing God created was the Intellect." And this is the Muḥammadan Presence according to [the Prophet's] statement: "The first thing God created was my light." It is the first of the created existents that came forth from God, exalted be He, without any intermediary. We call it the First Intellect. And inasmuch as created things get the power to think from it, we call it the Active Intellect *(al-'aql al-fa'āl)*. And insomuch as the Intellect emanates to all existent things who in turn perceive the realities of all things by it, we call it the Universal Intellect. So it is absolutely clear that the Muḥammadan Presence is the point of light and the first appearance, the reality of engendered things, the beginning of existent things, and the axis of all circles. Its exterior is a quality of God, and its interior is the hidden dimension of God. It is the Greatest Name outwardly and the form of the rest of the world. Upon it depends whoever disbelieves or believes. Its spirit is a transcript of the Exclusive Unity that abides in the Divine Nature *(lāhūt)*. And its spiritual form is the meaning of the earthly and heavenly kingdoms. And its heart is the treasure house of the life which never dies. This is because God, exalted be He, spoke a word in the beginning which became light. Then he spoke a word which became spirit. And then he caused the light to enter that spirit (or that light to enter that word.) He then made them a veil, which is his word and his light, and his spirit and his veil. And its permeates the world *(sarayān fi' l-'ālam)* as the point permeates all the letters and bodies. This permeation is one in number, as is the permeation of speech with the *ālif* and the permeation of all the names with the Holy Name. The [word] is the beginning of all [things] and the reality of all [things], so that all [things] speak by means of the tongue of spiritual "state" and "station." It testifies to God through his primordial oneness and to Muḥammad and 'Alī of their fatherhood and sovereignty. To this points the statement: "'Alī and I are the fathers of this community." So if they are the fathers of this community it follows that they are the fathers of the rest of the nations, according to the proof from "the specific is over the general and the higher over the lower," not the opposite. If it were not so, there would never be any creation to specify him through "If it were not for thee I would not have created the spheres." So know that the Acts proceed from the Qualities, and the Qualities proceed from the Essence. And the quality which is the Leader of Qualities is in the created things, namely the Muḥammadan Presence.[1]

One of the strongest clues to Bursī's reliance on Ibn 'Arabī is seen above in the word *sarayān* (permeation/suffusion). A comparison with this passage and the passage in the first *faṣṣ* of Ibn 'Arabī's *Fuṣūṣ al-ḥikam* reveals a strong parallelism between Ibn 'Arabī's language and Rajab Bursī's. It is as if the latter were writing while reading Ibn Arabi's book. He does not however make any explicit mention of this.[2] Thus his work acquires the character of a tacit commentary on the *Fuṣūṣ*.

---

1. *Mashāriq*, pp. 30-32. For a more classically-based philosophical discussion see the treatise "That existence is in two parts" *(Mashāriq*, pp. 27-28). This section also contains a commentary on *kuntu khanzān makhfiyān*, a reference to Ḥallāj and Ibn Arabi's terminology.
2. *Fuṣūṣ al-ḥikām*, ed 'Afīfī (Beirut 1400/1980), p. 55

CONCLUSION

The history of Islam provides Muslims with a powerful longing for that rarefied atmosphere of certitude associated with the first community established by the Prophet. One may assume that the basic feature of this cultural nostalgia is that it is directed to a time which was free of the vexing spiritual question of legitimate authority. The *memory* itself of the city of the Prophet, the calling to mind when Muslims enjoyed the unmediated guidance of the Messenger of God is, for example, an unfailing source of authentic religious and spiritual certitude.

Further, the development of Islamic religious thought may also be see as the result of a variety of attempts to maintain this certitude by establishing certain theories of spiritual or religious authority, (distinct, of course, from authoritarianism). Because in Islam certitude is supported by and intimately connected with knowledge *(ʿilm)*, the concern with our quest for certitude underlies the five types of Sufi writing outlined by Prof. Nasr in the introduction to this volume: 1) ethics, 2) doctrine, 3) esoteric sciences, 4) sacred history, 5) depiction of Paradise and the literary creation of a celestial atmosphere. Here the purpose of authority is to free the soul from the perplexities posed to it by reason. The two major divisions within Islam: Sunnism and Shiʿism, present different methods of attaining certainty and 'systematizing' religious authority as a means of freeing the soul through recapturing the vision of that time when Muslims were relatively untroubled by such concerns.

The author/compiler of the text that has been the subject of this essay has achieved a distinctive vision of the nature of this authority and also of the means whereby the believer may have access to it. In so doing, he has drawn upon all the major resources available to the greater Islamic tradition: the Koran, *ḥadīth, Kalām,* Philosophy, and Sufism. The resultant synthesis would appear to be most appealing given the fact that his book went through ten printings in rapid succession during the 1960's in Lebanon. It is eminently representative of the period in Twelver history between the Mongol invasions and the establishment of the Safavids. It preserves a record of the development of this history by reacting against the ways and usages of mainstream Twelver Shiʿism, which may be seen as an attempt to disassociate itself from specific trends in more primitive Shiʿism on the one hand, by rejecting certain religious postures exemplified in some of the material translated below, and identifying more closely with Sunnī Islam by adopting its system of jurisprudence. This phenomenon mirrors a similar development within Sunnī Islam where Sufism may be seen as an attempt to counter the confidence placed in consensus *(ijmāʿ)* as a starting point for recreating the 'celestial atmosphere' of Medina by investing in a more personalistic style of piety.

By the time our author was writing, his home, Ḥilla, had become the centre of Twelver Shiʿism. Ḥilla had been a Shiʿite centre since its establishment by the powerful Shiʿite dynasty, the Mazyadids, in 1101/1690. But it was about a century later that it really came into its own, replacing Aleppo, as the centre of Shiʿite learning. Its fortunes continued to rise in this regard until well after the Mongol invasion. Because the Shiʿite leaders of Ḥilla submitted without reservation to Mongol rule, life in the small city was permitted to continue undisturbed. This augured extremely well for the continued elaboration of a distinctive Shiʿite theology and jurisprudence. Momen states the case most succinctly:

> While Baghdad, the centre of Sunni orthodoxy, had been devastated, Ḥilla, the main centre of Shi'ism, had submitted to the Mongols and was spared. The killing of the 'Abbasid Caliph threw Sunni theology and constitutional theory... into some disorder, while the occulted Imam of the Shi'ites had not been affected.[1]

If Shi'ism is seen in part as a protest movement in reaction to mainstream Sunnī Islam, then the processes set in motion by these historical developments are ironic. Shi'ism was now irreversibly on its way to becoming another orthodoxy. That Bursī's piety shares much with the religious orientation known very generally as Sufism, another 'protest movement,' is confirmed by the fact that our author resorts to the basic terminology and categories of thought of Sufism in attempting to make clear his own chosen 'metho' or vision of authority. Thus a believer is referred to as a gnostic (*'ārif*) who, through his love (*maḥabba*), and knowledge (*ma'rifa*) of the Imāms as the sole bearers of religious authority (*walāya*), both draws nearer to spiritual perfection and to an ever deepening knowledge of his own self, whose superfluous qualities will be shed in the process. The central idea of his vision or system is carried by the word *walāya*. Obviously, I am not suggesting that Rajab Bursī had to go outside the Shi'ite textual tradition for this word. In this instance the coincidence in terminology between Shi'ism and Sufism is not terribly meaningful. The main thrust of this terminology, both in Sufism and in the writings of Bursī, is to establish a personal, intimate link with the 'spirit' of religion. Other terms and motifs, including the considerable influence of Ibn 'Arabī, as will be seen, are more indicative of Sufi influence. But most importantly, Rajab Bursī rejects the position of the *fuqahā'* of Ḥilla as being only partially (if at all) conducive to the kind of certitude his religion demands. Again, this would seem to have a great deal in common with Sufism. In some respects, the difference in attitude between Bursī and his contemporaries may also be compared usefully with the later tensions between the Akhbārīs and the Usulīs, a tension which may be briefly described as one between reason and revelation.[2]

While Rajab Bursī has been condemned by some authors as holding an immoderate belief in the Imams, most who have written about him also speak quite highly of his poetry. It is perhaps the poet in him that speaks in such strong terms. Poets, we are told, perceive reality intensely. It is therefore not surprising that they express themselves with equal intensity. While it would not be a complete mistake to attempt to classify Rajab Bursī's religious doctrine on the basis of his deeply felt experience of his love for the Imams, his book is not doctrine in the strict sense. That his mind was active and searching is clear from the above excerpts. And his recourse to "explanations" of the spiritual laws laid bare throughout the *Mashāriq*, based on Ibn 'Arabī's ideas, appealed to him possibly as much for what they said as for what they left unsaid. In the end, it would be difficult to answer the question: Was Rajab Bursī more in love with the Imāms or the ideas that made this love reasonable?

---

1. Momen, *op. cit.* pp. 91-92.
2. This is however something of an oversimplification. In addition to the article by Kohlberg cited above, see also Juan Cole, "Shi'i Clerics in Iraq, Iran, 1722-1780: The Akhbari-Usuli Conflict Reconsidered," *Iranian Studies*, vol.18, no.1(1985), pp. 3-33.

APPENDIX

Bursī's works as listed in Fikr:

1) *Mashāriq al-anwār (Mashāriq anwār al-yaqīn fī asrār Amīr al-Mu'minīn).* Printed in India in 1303/1885-6 and 1318/1900-1 and in Beirut in 1379/1959-60.
2) *Mashāriq al-amān wa lubāb ḥaqā'iq al-īmān.*
3) *Risāla fī dhikr al-ṣalāt 'alā al-rasūl wa al-ā'imma min munsha'āt nafsihi.*
4) *Ziyāra li-Amīr al-Mu'minīn .*
5) *Lum'a kāshif. (Fi-hā asrār al-asmā' wa al-ṣifāt wa al-ḥurūf wa al-āyāt wa mā yunāsibuhā min al-du'āt wa mā yuqāribuhā min al-kalimāt wa ratabahā 'alā tartīb al-sa'āt wa ta'aqub al-awqāt fī al-layālī wa al-ayām li-ikhtilā al-umūr wa al-aḥkām).*
6) *al-Durr al-thamīn fī dhikr.* 500 Koranic verses indicating the virtues of 'Alī.
7) *Lawāmi'anwār al-tamjīd wa jawāmi'asrār al-tawḥīd.* Possibly appearing at the beginning of the *Mashāriq al-anwār.*
8) *Risāla fī tafsīr ṣūrat al-ikhlāṣ*
9) *Risāla fī kayfīya al-tawḥīd wa al-ṣalāt 'alā al-rasūl wa al-ā'imma 'alayhim al-salām.*
10) *Kitāb fī mawlid al-Nabī wa Fāṭima wa Amīr al-Mu'minīn wa faḍā' luhum 'alay-him al-salām.*
11) Another book on the excellences of 'Alī.
12) *Kitāb al-ālifayn fī waṣf sādat al-kawnayn.* Excerpts of this are reproduced in the *Biḥār al-anwār* (see above).

What is Sufi Music?

V

Jean During

The purpose of this paper is to shed light on a seemingly obvious, but actually obscure, issue in the science of Islamic musicology, namely: is there really a 'Sufi music' in the same way that a distinct genre of Sufi poetry does exist? And if so, is this mystical music different in its specific characteristics from the secular musical genres?

Rather than approaching this question from a purely theoretical and external perspective focusing on the history or theosophical doctrines of Persian music, I will try to concentrate here on its purely musical aspects, examined from various perspectives in order to draw a sort of holographic image. However, insofar as the entire notion of 'Sufi music' as understood in the West, is quite limited and beset with many prejudices, certain distortions first need to be dissipated before our study can begin.[1]

A FEW PREJUDICES

To the Western mind, the notion of Sufi or mystical music automatically conjures up certain features associated with:

—a subtle science of modes and intervals (inherited from Pythagoreanism),
—a science of the sound and vocal techniques (breathing, diaphonic singing, etc.),
—the priority of melody over rhythm and text, or the use of sacred texts and formulas rather than poetry,
—a predilection for singing and wind instruments,
—an individual and intellectual expression rather than a collective and emotional one,
—a slow tempo and hieratic atmosphere.

1. I have dealt with this question in my book *Musique et Mystique dans les Traditions de l'Iran* (Paris: I. F.R.I.: Peeters 1989). For the mystical content of Sufi musical experience *(samā')*, see my *Musique et Extase, l'audition mystique dans la tradition soufie* (Paris: Albin Michel 1988). My recent paper 'L'autre oreille. Le pouvoir mystique de la musique au Moyen-Orient', in *Cahiers des Musique Traditionnelles* (1990, III, 57-78) discusses the general conditions of the power of music. For an introduction to mystical music in the Islamic world, see J. C. Bürgel, *The Feather of Simurgh, The 'Licit Magic' of the Arts in Medieval Islam* (New York 1988), Chap. 4.

However, the present article makes little reference to these writings, while attempting to provide new insight into this question, with musical examples drawn from the living tradition of Sufi music.

Such ideas probably arose through contact with Indian music, and Indian musicians have been careful not to correct them. Another phenomenon which probably contributes to misconceptions which Westerners have of Sufism is that of the so-called 'whirling dervishes,' whose music is typified by the *ney* (reedpipe)—in present-day France the most popular and widespread Sufi instrument.

The *ney*'s preeminent position derives not only from its consecration by Mawlānā Rumi, but also from the fact that it is an archetypal instrument—in fact, among the most archaic and the most traditional, making it even more venerable. Furthermore, its particular sonority and the milieu in which it is usually played tends to evoke a transcendental dimension; the sound of the *ney* is often furnished with a natural or artificial echo which brings to mind immense spaces, providing this fragile instrument with a cosmic dimension, and thus epitomizing the human condition which oscillates between abasement and supreme dignity. More concretely, we may recall that such sonorities remind Westerners of the acoustical space of churches and the sound of the organ.

A MUSICAL EXAMPLE

If mysticism is naturally linked to cosmic space and the harmony of the spheres, this is also the case with the whirling dancers of the Mevlevi Order who, like a celestial machine and the planets, rotate on two axes, orbital and gyratory.

The European observer who listens to the Mevlevi *samā'* can project his personal preconceptions, stemming from his Pythagorean and Christian legacy, onto the performance. It is a liturgy which evokes the melodies and the rotation of the spheres, which elevates the soul and sets the body and its mundane concerns aside, evoking inward reflection, meditation, calm and inner peace in the listener. Each person experiences it in his or her own way, for between listener and musician it is a question of communion rather than communication.

I do not wish to imply that the Mevlevi *samā'* is not true Sufi music; on the contrary, it is, but it should not be considered the sole viable genre of Sufi music. In any case, is there really only one sort of Sufism or one sort of Sufi musical expression? Just as there is a world of difference between Rumi's *ghazals* and Ibn 'Arabī's writings, so do Sufi musical forms vary, reflecting the creative diversity inherent in Islamic mysticism. The truth of this is demonstrated by the fact that at the far extreme of the Mevlevi *samā'* we find another form recently imported to the West which has helped to change popular misconceptions about Sufism, that is to say, Indo-Pakistani *qawwālī* music. To illuminate the essential differences between the Mevlevi and *qawwālī* genres, I have drawn up a comparative table, taking into account various musical levels based on performance, context and musical content. My intention in comparing these two genres is to stress the inherent diversity of Sufi musical forms—a diversity which it is not technically possible, in the confines of the present article, to illustrate more fully.

MEVLEVI MUSIC	*QAWWĀLĪ MUSIC*
limited musical specificity	musical specificity
derived from *samā‘*	fusion of *samā‘* and *dhikr*
entirely composed	partly improvised
collective expression (except in *taqsīm*)	individual and collective expression
fixed text	adaptable text
slow tempo	fast tempo
complex, long and varied rhythms	simple, short, limited rhythms
closed repertoire	open repertoire
continuous, mandala-like structure	succession of separate pieces
traditional instruments	modern instruments
mental *dhikr* (by the participants)	verbal *dhikr* (by the musicians)
prearranged dance of a set type & figure	informal dance
discretion, moderated expression	exaltation, enthusiasm
calm, meditation	extraversion, emotion
communion	communication, interchange
symbolic space and sequences	limited symbolism
ritualization	limited ritualization
closed circuit, State-sponsoring	private sponsoring, offerings and donations
official performances	public performances
classical, learned, elitist	semi-classical, great popular impact

Examining the above chart, one may actually wonder whether a unique genre of 'Sufi music' does exist, for between the two contrasting musical types we find a great number of forms, sometimes closely related, sometimes very remote from each other. We should also take into account some nuances within the above typology: the commercial and popular *qawwālī* music differs from the traditional, Sufi type, especially from the ancient form of Chishtī *samā‘* (*bund samā‘*), the ritual space of which can be as heavily structured as the Mevlevi *samā‘*. Furthermore, the Mevlevi *samā‘* which is performed in modern-day Konya is rather heavy, official and artificial, and on the whole, very different from the private Mevlevi *samā‘* (called *āyin-i jam‘*)[1]

Let us also point out that in the Mevlevi *samā‘*, the celestial melopoeia of the ney serves mainly as opening and conclusion, while the whirling dance performed in six fast beats is, in fact, the climax of the ceremony, even if the latter is reduced to a mere formality in official demonstrations. In any case, the central dance and rhythm of the Mevlevi *samā‘* are much closer in form to the sort of Sufi music typified by the *qawwālī* performance. In point of fact, the *samā‘* performance and *dhikr* gatherings found in many Sufi orders start with a very soft melody and end in excitement, enthusiasm and hand-clapping. It can even happen that the vocal or instrumental melody soars above the *dhikr* which is scanned with force by the dervishes. In some kind of *dhikr* songs, such as those of the *Jarrāhi-Khalwati* Sufi Or-

1. The author is in possession of a short sequence of such a private *samā‘*, recorded in Konya during the night following the great official ceremony, illustrating this point quite vividly.

Sufis in *Samā'*. From a manuscript of Sa'dī's *Būstān* dated 898/1493.
MS. Laud Or. 241, fol. 1b (Courtesy of the Bodleian Library, Oxford)

der from Istanbul, a synthesis of both aspects is achieved.[1]

Qawwālī and Mevlevi forms merely typify two extremes of the musical domain of Sufism. Between them is spread an infinity of nuances and musical expressions. For a better understanding of certain Sufi forms we have to examine the deeper structures, and probe the frontier of what is commonly meant by the word 'music'.

If the 'Sufi character' of Mevlevi compositions and improvisations *(taqsīm)* is less obvious than that of the *qawwālī* genre, it is due to the fact that this musical style is not particular to Sufism or even to mystical expression in general. It is actually found in all Middle Eastern (and particularly, the Turkish) musical traditions. *Qawwālī* music is, on the other hand, an original creation. Above all, as with many Sufi musical forms, it utilizes a specific technique which is both spiritual and, up to a point, 'musical': that is to say, the technique of the *dhikr*.

DHIKR AND MUSIC

If 'pure,' non-measured melody is one pole of the Sufi musical world, its opposite is the sacred word, the *dhikr,* which possesses both rhythm and pulse but lacks melody. The *dhikr* lies at the border between speech and music, and can be considered the Sufi mode of expression *par excellence,* the exclusive domain of Sufism and the Islamic mystical experience. The structure of the *dhikr* is typified by:

1) a repetitive formula;
2) a pulsed or rhythmic articulation;
3) a specific vocal utterance (accentuated breathing, sound produced while-breathing, non-articulated sounds, etc.)

Although some will object that some of these features are also found in much profane music, I would argue that there can be no disagreement about the specifically 'Sufi intent' and therefore, mystical 'content,' of the *dhikr* musical ceremony.[2]

However, before proceeding, I would like to call attention to the existence of a certain 'objective quality' in certain types of Sufi music, which, although imperceptible to the ordinary observer, is quite evident to the experienced and adept practi-

1. Cf. the record published in 1981 in the United States by the dervishes of the Jarrāhi-Khalvati Order performing their *samā'*, entitled, 'Journey to the Lord of Power' (Inner Traditions International Ltd., no. 1001-1002)
2. I have in mind here the Indonesian *kechak,* a ritual originally aimed at inducing trance states and possession, superficially resembling the Sufi *dhikr*. Although in some cultures certain practices may be found which outwardly resemble the *dhikr* ceremony, these practices usually have no sacred significance. Furthermore, within the framework of Islamic culture, the characteristics of the *dhikr* are particular to Sufi practice and to the realization of ecstatic states *(aḥwāl)*. It is quite certain that, within the context of Islamic civilization, any practice similar in form to the *dhikr* ceremony, insofar as it is directed towards analogous spiritual ends, is directly derived from Sufi practice.

   Despite the fact that the exponents of strict academic musicology may object that the characteristics of the *dhikr* do not apply directly to music, i.e., that a *dhikr* is not, properly speaking, musical or artistic (in spite of its obvious majesty and beauty), I think that significant elements derived from the Sufi *dhikr* have impregnated and directly influenced the development of certain Islamic musical forms.

tioner. It is a quality which can be readily detected by connoisseurs, even when listening to alien musical traditions. By way of example, I recall that once, I was listening an Anatolian Sufi minstrel (belonging to the Alawī-Bektāshiyya Order) playing a piece that we could immediately and intuitively identify as a ritual tune. We asked him to listen to a Kurdish melody belonging to the repertoire of the Ahl-i Ḥaqq Sufis, which, in turn he immediately identified as a sacred melody. (These two musical traditions are rather different, but both religious groups have many points in common). It should be emphasized that there was something within the music itself which clearly indicated its objective 'Sufic' quality. Perhaps there was something even more subtle, invisibly connected to the *dhikr* element, about which I shall try to give some account:

The traces of *dhikr* in Sufi music are of two kinds: apparent and hidden, outward and inward. First let us consider the apparent ones: it should be stated that *dhikr* is a multi-faceted phenomenon embodying a plurality of forms ranging from silence to speech, as well as music, properly speaking, which might be itemized as follows:

—The ultimate level is that of a pure mental remembering, without any verbal support.
—This is followed by the silent or mental *dhikr* (called *dhikr-i khafī)* wherein the adept activates, by external or inward movements, an inner energy directed towards specific psychic centres of the body.
—The latter practice can lead to a form of verbal *dhikr (*called *dhikr-i jalī)* per formed collectively or privately.
—In collective performances, the verbal *dhikr* sometimes serves as an ostinato background for a melody,[1]
—which can lead either to the superimposition of the verbal *dhikr* upon a melody
— or to the incorporation of a *dhikr* in a chorus, i.e., a chanted *dhikr*.
—In some cases, a song gradually takes the form of a *dhikr* by reducing its melodic range and by repeating a verbal formula.[2]
—Finally there are melodies devoid of verbal support but whose rhythms suggest to the initiated listener a verbal or silent *dhikr*, communicating the 'objective Sufic quality' mentioned above. In such cases, the structure of both the melody and rhythm are inspired by common *dhikr* formulas.

REPETITION AND *DHIKR*

In such types of music, the most common characteristic is a kind of rhythmic ostinato borrowed from the *dhikr*. Thus, while the dervishes listen to this type of melody, they often start mentally reciting their personal *dhikr,* or any other *dhikr* formula adapted to the rhythm of the melody. This is one of the most natural ways of 'active listening,' even if it is not expressed in an outwardly visible manner.

1. A vivid musical example of this ostinato type of *dhikr* is found in the Naqshbandī *dhikr* from Turkestan, a recording of which is in the author's private collection.
2. A musical example of this type of adaptation of a song to the form of a *dhikr* is found in a *qalandarī* tune from Baluchistan in the author's private collection.

According to this principle, it may be imagined that any melody with an ostinato character is thereby endowed with the quality of the *dhikr* and so should consequently induce a similar inward mystical state. In practice, however, this is incorrect, mainly because repetitive Sufi music is *qualitatively distinct* from other types of repetitive music. Sufi music—all Sufi music—tends towards One End, starting from a given point in order to reach another point, its purpose being to elevate the soul above its ordinary mundanec ondition. The initiated listener alone realizes this movement is occurring by means of messages encoded in the music itself as it undergoes stages of progressive intensification, involving mainly:

—the passage from a slow to a quick tempo, from long motifs to motifs of medium length, on to short ones (featuring, for instance, a succession of differing *dhikr,* beginning in the long *Shahādā* (profession of faith) and culminating in the divine Names, *Ḥayy* or *Ḥaqq*);
—progressive concentration of the melodic space.

Thus, the music achieves what may be termed a mandala in sound and time, at the core of which vibrates the pure energy of the ineffable divine Name, reduced to a breath, a pulsation. But is this mandala form really particular to Sufism?

Actually not; it is found in Uygur music, amongst the North-African Nuba, in Indian *rāga* performances, and, to a lesser extent, in Tājik-Uzbek music, as well as in classical Persian music. In any case, there is nothing more natural and fitted to psychological laws than to begin a performance with a calm and moderate rhythm and to end in an enthusiastic and excited tempo. (Imagine a concert starting with pieces scored in *allegro vivace* and ending with a funeral march!). Furthermore, even if we were to assume the 'mandalic' structure of art-music performances to be precisely inspired by and derived from the rhythms of the Sufi concert, then, concretely speaking, what is the difference between them? Two methodological problems arise at this point:

1) We cannot compare anything with everything. Comparisons must be drawn from within each culture rather than cross-culturally. Rather than seeking out absolute or universal criteria, we should limit ourselves to examining certain common polar principles within different cultures, thus exposing some of the same sacred/profane dichotomies. Although mysticism is universal in its aims, it takes many different forms, even within Islamic culture. In the same way, music as a universal science, is one and universal, but as an art, it takes its precise references from the variegated cultural code which nourishes it.

2) The above principle of relativity leads us back from the absolute to the particular culture, and from the culture to the individual subject himself. Now, without the active participation of the subject who performs or listens to the music, no music is *per se* mystical. Lct us remember that even the most evocative *dhikr* does not work 'automatically'; it is merely a technique employed during *samā'* to activate the intention of the individual and to assist concentration. Separated from the spiritual life, the practice of the *dhikr* cannot cause any 'instantaneous enlightenment,' or lead to a 'state of grace.' Similarly, all music, even though it possess all the desired mystical qualities, will be efficient only by virtue of the intention of the listener and/or performer.

Inversely, the true Sufi may interpret the most mundane of melodies as 'music of the spheres', hearing in it the Divine summons to heed the primordial Covenant of *alastu bi rabbikum* (Koran VII 172); examples of this attitude are innumerable in Sufi literature.

Thus, with these principles in mind, we may present our first general and summary definition of Sufi music:

Sufi music is a music made by, and/or listened to by, Sufis.

As previously pointed out, our Mevlevi reedpipe or *ney* solo differs in no way from a classical *ney* solo; likewise, in a Persian *khānaqāh,* the same poems and the same modes are sung as in a classical concert of traditional Iranian music. The musical ensemble of Moroccan Sufis, under the leadership of their Shaykh, is famous for its fine interpretation of the classical Nuba, but their performance is exactly identical with the type of musical concert found in secular festivals in Fez or Rabat.

However, this proposed union of the sacred and profane genres of music is subject to the following two restrictions:.

1) As suggested above, it is possible that either the classical forms were originally elaborated by the Sufis, or else these forms are in themselves versatile, so that the same tune can be interpreted in both a spiritual and a mundane manner—an axiom which holds true for much of Persian poetry, particularly that of Ḥāfiẓ.
2) It remains that some forms are more suitable than others to spiritual purposes. This is the case in the form of the *dhikr*. However, strictly speaking, we must admit that even the forms outwardly similar to the *dhikr* are not *per se* mystical.

In order to shed more light on this problem, I will attempt to compare two very similar performances, the first secular and the other sacred.

The first is a drum concert featuring the traditional *dāyira bazmī* (lit. a drum for entertainment) which I recorded in Pamir (Tājikistan) following a long day spent in the company of minstrels. Setting their lutes aside, the musicians distributed frame drums *(daf* or *dāyira)* to the folk seated among them; then they started singing and drumming with great vigour. They informed us that this musical form was of extreme antiquity, in fact, the most archaic in their musical tradition, going back to remote times where the sole existing instrument to accompany the human voice was the *daf.* The performance began with rather slow melodies sung by one or two soloists and then repeated by the choir. These gradually increased in tempo, the words sung with great enthusiasm as they chanted, "O beloved, come and bring the wine" *(Ay yār, biyā, may dih!).* There seemed to be some evidence here, apparent from the atmosphere of the gathering, that the wine in question was the fruit of the grape rather than a metaphor for mystical ecstasy, for their kind of music is usually sung during festivals or weddings, and not in the Sufi *khānaqāhs*.

The second performance took place among the Qādirī dervishes of Kurdistan, 2500 km from Pamir, and apparently without any cultural link. Two poems were recited by the dervishes: one, a *ghazal* by Jāmi, beginning, "Again I long for the fields..."(*Bāz havā-yi chamanam āṛazū...*); another, a ballad in which a beloved becomes angry with her lover: "O moon-faced beauty whose rays have set the earth afire, why take offense at me?" *(Ay māh-i 'ālamsūz-i man, az man chirā ranjīda' ī?).*

Both these poems are part of the normal Qādirī repertoire. Here again, the form of the *dāyira bazmī* was found, and is repeated in a similar fashion among the Qādirī of Sanandaj, the melodies of which are different but follow the same principles.

For this performance ten people had gathered in one dervish's house. Although some participants were non-initiates and the meeting was informal, it was the well-known *Khalīfa* Mirzā Ghawthī who was singing and leading the *dhikr*. His intention was clearly to perform a *dhikr,* not to provide the guests with entertainment. The atmosphere became so warm that after a while everybody was overwhelmed and affected by the music. At the end of the singing and drumming, two young men among the non-initiated experienced a state of spiritual elevation, and so decided to commit themselves to the Qādirī path, and being converted, recited the initatic oath of obedience after the *Khalīfa*.

It may be asked what is the difference between these two kinds of performance. Why is the latter performance to be viewed as sacred Sufi music, and the former purely secular? Why does one produce a spiritual effect, and the other not? Setting aside the purely musical aspects of this problem, we may formulate an adequate reply by enumerating the following reasons:

—the intention of the listeners and the musicians in each case was different.

—In the first case, the social context of the gathering inhibited emotional response; in the second case it stimulated it.

—In the first case, the listeners and performers knew nothing about Sufism, being ignorant of any higher anagogic and spiritual significance in the erotic and bacchic imagery of the poetry, and being unacquainted with ecstatic states and consciousness, their attitude evinced merely emotional excitement and *joie de vivre*.

If the above explanation is adequate from a musical standpoint, whence does the essential difference between the two genres arise? Our answer is that the distinction between the two genres, if it does exist, is something which only connoisseurs may comprehend. Suffice it to say that trained ears are able to grasp very fine nuances of meaning which the literal 'letter' of language is unable to express, and thus, inwardly translate or transform secular *materia* into sacred *spiritus*.

However, before leaving this question aside as being ultimately a matter of taste (and here, by taste or *dhawq,* I mean direct perception *[hāl]* or pure intuition), I would like to examine the matter as far as use of verbal concepts *(qawl)* and visual images *(suwar)* can take us.

First of all, generally speaking, cannot we often detect a difference of melodic shape, phrasing and character between a sacred and a secular melody? It is evident, for instance, that the tunes of the secular music of Baluchistan are more extroverted, lighter, and less obsessive, in spite of their repetitiveness, than the 'sacred' *qalandarī*[1] tunes of this province. Although such aesthetic features can be proven only through a detailed analysis, we should not forget, in any case, that in respect to the oral tradition of music, *melodies are not autonomous objects, but come into*

1. See de Bruin chapter 2 this volume.

existence only when realized in performance. For this reason these aesthetic features are completely dependent, more so than in any other repertoire, on the interpretation.

To pursue the matter further, we must leave the level of the outward and probe into the inner subtleties of musical performance, putting musical analysis behind us. And eventually, after passing from the form to the interpretation, from the object to the subject, we return to the question of the *intention* and the way to signify this intention by means of messages that we assume to be encoded within the music. Since a simple phrase can have several meanings or meta-meanings, according to the way it is uttered, several elements must be taken into account: context, proximity of the speaker, status and hierarchical position, culture, length of the pauses, imperceptible and uncontrolled movements, etc. All such features contribute to a large extent to the exchange of information, and the artists are very sensitive to it.

There is also another important decisive factor, which, although imperceptible, is still 'objective,' insofar as it contributes to the effect of the music. This is directly linked to the practice of the *dhikr* as an amplifier and harmonizer of the psychic energy of both listeners and musicians.

Many Sufi melodies, as we have noted above, are marked by the form of the *dhikr*. In some of them, the *dhikr* formula provides the basis for a distinct melody. In others, the melody runs independently, but the listener who is attuned may feel a call to the recite the *dhikr* inwardly. In other cases, there remains only the 'taste' of the *dhikr,* a recollection and an awareness. How does this happen? It is because the musician himself mobilizes all his psychic energy in an attitude of 'remembrance' *(dhikr),* uttering the words and sounds of his song with the same total concentrated consciousness which he invests in his *dhikr*. He is thus investing all his inner energies in the sounds and the words, in turn benefiting from the potential power of the musical forms. This inner energy or force takes shape in the word and the sounds, and is passed on to the listeners who must proceed to decipher the message and 'decode the spiritual lesson' *('ibrat)* hidden in the music

It also may be possible to account for this process in terms of 'energetics,' a science which is part of Western 'New Age' psychology, whose subject is the analysis of certain realities and facts well known and well described by Sufis and mystics of various religious traditions. (Its clearest illustration is supplied by the martial arts of the Far-East). According to the Kurdish Qādirī Sufis, the movement of breathing mobilizes a vital force (probably that which the Chinese call the *qi)* localized at the level of the stomach, which is released either with the vocal utterance or at the very moment the hand touches the instrument (which is in this instance, the Persian tambourine or *daf*). This energy is sent out through the musical sound and reaches the listener, to whom it transmits its effect. I assume that, in turn, it awakens an energy of the same nature in the listener, inducing a change in his state of consciousness. For the Sufi singer or musician, the essential thing in the art of interpretation is the circulation of this energy. There is no doubt that the Sufi minstrel derives his strength and energetic versatility from assiduous practice of the *dhikr,* or through similar forms of meditation.

Here we may well speculate that all traditional music found in various cultures the world over, if correctly transmitted, may have in a similar effect, even without the use of the specific forms described above or explicit reference to a spiritual content. It is true, on a less esoteric level, that all musical masters, whatever tradition they adhere to, follow these same principles more or less intuitively. There appears to be some concrete evidence that a spiritual intent, directed by inspired and enlightened men towards the edification and consciousness-raising of their audience, lies at the origin of most traditional musical forms. The ancient melodies, said Confucius, could have been created only by saints and transmitted by sages.

Given that the form is only secondary to the actual performance, the Sufi sages advise us that the technique of *dhikr,* which involves mastering and directing of inner psycho-spiritual energies, must be given inner illumination by purification of the heart's intent through surrender of the 'imperious self' *(nafs al-ammāra)* and acquisition of noble virtues *(fāḍīlat-i malaki)* if it is not to remain more than an empty and sterile technique. Such is the basic, the essential, condition of 'Sufi music' according to both the Masters of the Path and the Sufi musical masters. The rest lies in the hands of God. Only He provides the musician with talent, inspiration and grace; and only He provides the listener with the grace of the faculty of hearing.

A Kubrawī Manual of Sufism:

The *Fuṣūṣ al-ādāb* of Yaḥyā Bākharzī

Muhammad Isa Waley

I. INTRODUCTION

The subject of this study is the *Awrād al-aḥbāb wa Fuṣūṣ al-ādāb* which was completed in 724/1323-4 by Abū'l-Mafākhir Yaḥyā Bākharzī (d. 736/1335-6). The content, and to some extent the style, of this Persian treatise on Sufi methodology show the influence of several other works. It is distinctive, however, both in the way in which those influences are blended and also in that it reflects in particular the teachings of Sayf al-Dīn Bākharzī of Bukhārā. This Shaykh, who died in 659/1261, belonged to the Kubrawī *Ṭarīqa* or Order and was a major figure in Central Asian Sufism. The *Fūṣūṣ al-ādāb,* the second part of Yaḥyā Bākharzī's treatise, has been published in an excellent edition with an introductory study by Īraj Afshār.[1] This apart, it has received little attention from scholars. The main aim here is to introduce and survey the content of *Fuṣūṣ al-ādāb,* highlighting aspects which seem unusual or of especial interest.

II. THE KUBRAWĪ ORDER: ITS WRITTEN WORKS & DISCIPLINES

Before discussing Bākharzī and his work it is essential to consider briefly its spiritual and historical background. The author of *Awrād al-aḥbāb wa Fuṣūṣ al-ādāb* was the grandson, both physically and by spiritual inheritance, of Shaykh Sayf al-Dīn Bākharzī. Sayf al-Dīn was one of the direct disciples of Shaykh Najm al-Dīn Kubrā of Khwārazm, the eponymous founder of the Kubrawī Order. Among the most notable features of this Order are its discipline and methodology, and its distinctive contributions to the interpretation of the Holy Koran.

The *magnum opus* of Kubrā is an extraordinary work called *Fawā'iḥ al-jamāl wa fawātiḥ al-jalāl.*[2] The *Fawā'iḥ* is a kind of didactic journal of the author's spiritual experiences, written to inform and warn the Sufi seeker about the states, interior events (*waqā'i'*), and stations of the Path, and in particular about the luminous visual and auditory perceptions experienced by the interior organs of perception *(laṭā'if)* during the *khalwa* or retreat. Among the more striking passages in the *Fawā'iḥ* are those in which the Shaykh describes vividly the nature and meaning of some of his visions. The apparent intention is to offer the initiate a diagnostic key

1. *Awrād al-aḥbāb wa Fuṣūṣ al-ādāb, jild-i duwwum: Fuṣūṣ al-ādāb,* ed. Īraj Afshār (Tehran 1345/ 1966) (Hear after referred to in footnotes as *Fuṣūṣ).*
2. Published together with an extensive study by Fritz Meier: *Die Fawā'iḥ al-ǧamāl wa fawātiḥ al-ǧalāl* (Wiesbaden 1957).

to his state as manifested in his experiences. According to the Muslim doctrine of Unity (*tawḥīd*) in its most profound sense, all that befalls us is at once a consequence and a cause of our inner state.[1] Progress depends on understanding how one has reached one's present station in life.

Now, since it is extremely dangerous for the *mutaṣawwif* or Sufi seeker actually to try to have visionary experiences—for sincerity is all-important; the goal of the sincere seeker is not 'to have an experience' but rather to become nothing at all so as to realize God, or the Transcendent Self—it is not conceivable that a spiritual Master like Najm al-Dīn Kubrā should have made such experiences available for his disciples without ensuring their conformity to a 'protective' framework of strict rules of conduct. Accordingly we find that Kubrā wrote a number of smaller treatises dealing with *ādāb* or rules and usages of Sufism. Kubrā set out his fundamental rules of discipline in a treatise called *al-Uṣūl al-'ashara* ('The Ten Principles'). This text also circulated widely beyond the Kubrawī *Ṭarīqa* itself and found several commentators; in this regard the names of 'Abd al-Ghafūr Lārī (writing in Persian) and Ismā'īl Ḥaqqī Burūsawī (in Ottoman Turkish) deserve mention.[2]

Najm al-Dīn's rulebook was based on the 'Eight Principles of Junayd', Shaykh Junayd of Baghdad (d. ca. 297/910) being one of the most renowned Sufis of all. The Eight Rules of Junayd prescribe that the initiate maintain the following, not intermittently but on a continual basis: ritual purity (*wuḍū'*), fasting (*ṣāwm*), silence (*ṣāmt*), seclusion (*khalwa*), and invocation (*dhikr*), using the formula *Lā ilāha illā'Llāh* ('There is no god but God'). In addition, he must concentrate fully upon the Shaykh and be guided by him in all matters; discard all vain thoughts and mental impulses the instant they appear; and submit entirely to the will of God whatever happens. The two additional rules prescribed by Kubrā are to sleep the bare minimum and to observe moderation in breaking the fast.

Najm al-Dīn Kubrā's legacy to the Order which bears his name thus includes, besides many other significant elements which cannot be discussed here,[3] two very distinct and complementary strands: on the one hand strict rules of discipline; on the other, the hermeneutics (*ta'wīl*) of gnostic supra-formal perception. The latter is also closely linked to the distinctive—and extremely significant—approach to the interpretation of the Holy Koran found in the commentary of Najm al-Dīn Kubrā himself and in the commentaries of some other distinguished Kubrawīs,[4] the foremost in this respect being Najm al-Dīn Dāya Rāzī and 'Alā' al-Dawla Simnānī.

Both the rules and the interpretative science associated with Kubrā are much in evidence in the writings of his direct disciples, several of whom were men of great

1. For example: "Whatever calamity may befall you is from what your [own] hands have earned: and He [God] pardons much" (Koran XLII, *al-Shūrā* 30).
2. *al-Uṣūl al-'ashara, tarjuma wa sharḥ-i 'Abd al-Ghafūr Lārī*, ed. Najīb Māyil Harawī (Tehran 1363/1984-5); Ismā'īl Ḥaqqī Burūsawī, *Sharḥ al-Uṣūl al-'ashara* (Istanbul 1256/1841).
3. See further A. Schimmel, *Mystical Dimensions of Islam* (Chapel Hill 1975), pp. 254-58; M. I. Waley, 'Najmo'd-Din Kobrā and the Kubrawiya Order,' *Sufi: A Journal of Sufism*, 2 (Spring 1989), pp. 22-26; and the works cited therein, and 'Najm al-Dīn Kubrā and the Central Asian School of Sufism' in S.H. Nasr (ed.) *Islamic Spirituality: Manifestations*, Vol. 2 (London: SCM Press 1991), pp. 80-104.
4. See H. Corbin, *En Islam iranien*, vol. 3 (Paris 1973), pp. 275-355.

stature in their own right—so much so that Najm al-Dīn Kubrā also acquired the epithet *Walī-tarāsh,* meaning 'Sculptor (or Fashioner) of Saints.' They include Sa'd al-Dīn Ḥammūya, one of the few early Kubrawī masters of Persia, and Majd al-Dīn Baghdādī, author of *Tuḥfat al-barara* and master of Najm al-Dīn Rāzī, whose Koranic *ta'wīl* has just been mentioned and whose *Mirṣād al-'ibād* is a unique didactic work in fine Persian prose dealing in a systematic scheme with the different spiritual types found among mankind; the means of guidance available to them; and their respective origins and destinies.[1]

In Transoxiana one of the leading successors of Kubrā was Sayf al-Dīn Bākharzī. He and Raḍī al-Dīn Lālā Samarqandī are perhaps the most important *khalīfa*s of the Master in terms of their long-term influence. Before discussing Abū'l-Mafākhir Bākharzī and his work, let us consider the life, character and teachings of his grandfather Sayf al-Dīn.

III. SHAYKH SAYF AL-DĪN BĀKHARZĪ: LIFE AND WORK

A summary of the life and work of Sayf al-Dīn Bākharzī is given by Afshār in his introduction to *Fuṣūṣ al-ādāb.*[2] Sayf al-Dīn Sa'īd ibn Muṭahhar ibn Sa'īd Bākharzī was born at Bākharz in the province of Khurasān (today in Afghanistan), in or around 586/1190. He received his early schooling in his native town of Bākharz, whence he proceeded to study *fiqh* (jurisprudence), *qirā'āt* (Koranic recitation) and *tafsīr* of the Holy Koran at the feet of numerous teachers in Nishapur and Herat, Bākharz being situated between those two citadels of Sufism.

Having acquired his grounding in the exoteric sciences Bākharzī took to the road—the circumstances appear to be unknown—and went to Khwārazm where he met and took the hand of the great Najm al-Dīn Kubrā. As part of his training Sayf al-Dīn entered *khalwa* for an *arba'īniyya* (forty-day spiritual retreat) under Kubrā's guidance. His enlightenment of spirit reached the point at which his Master invested him as a qualified Shaykh. Yaḥyā Bākharzī is at pains to mention in his own *isnād* that Sayf al-Dīn received the *khirqa* from Najm al-Dīn's own hand.[3] It is interesting to find that he hyperbolically refers to Kubrā as "Āyat Allāh al-kubrā Abū'l-Jannāb 'Umar," although Najm al-Dīn's name is generally thought to have originated from his college days when his skill in disputation earned him the nickname of *al-Ṭāmmat al-kubrā,* a Koranic phrase (LXXIX 34), meaning "the Greatest Calamity."

At some time before his Master's death, which occurred in 618/1221, Sayf al-Dīn Bākharzī left Khwārazm and settled at Bukhārā, where he established his *khānaqāh* at Fatḥ-Ābād and remained for the rest of his life. He trained a large number of disciples and became one of the most famous and influential Sufis of his time. He died in 659/1261. His *khānaqāh* owned extensive properties and was known for its hospitality; Yaḥyā Bākharzī's text includes a good deal of material on the subject. From his *waqfnāma* it emerges that Yaḥyā also endowed the *mazār* with

1. Najm al-Dīn Dāya Rāzī, *Mirṣād al-'ibād min al-mabda' ilā'l-ma'ād,* ed. Muḥammad Amīn Riyāḥī (Tehran 1352/1973); translated by H. Algar as *The Path of God's Bondsmen* (Delmar 1982).
2. *Fuṣūṣ,* pp. 4-25. There are two main historical sources in Persian.
3. *Fuṣūṣ,* p. 27.

property; later, in 788/1386-7, it was restored and given a garden and new building by Tīmūr.[1] Shaykh Sayf al-Dīn's *baraka* spread far beyond his circle of initiates and he was enormously esteemed by the people of Bukhārā, among whom he was often known as *Shaykh-i 'Ālam,* "Shaykh of the World." Notable men with whom Sayf al-Dīn is said to have associated include, besides Kubrā, Jalāl al-Dīn Rumi (though this is based on two sensational tales in Aflākī and hence inevitably suspect), Naṣīr al-Dīn Ṭūsī, Kamāl al-Dīn Khwārazmī, and (according to the *Rashaḥāt-i 'ayn al-ḥayāt)* Shaykh Ḥasan Bulghārī and Khwāja Gharīb, two prominent Naqshbandīs.[2]

Already it had fallen to a Kubrawī, Shaykh Sa'd al-Dīn Ḥammūya's son Ṣadr al-Dīn Ibrāhīm, to witness the 'conversion' to Islam of Ghāzān Khān, the Mongol Īlkhān of Persia, in 694/1295.[3] One indication of the major role of Bākharzī in 13th-century Transoxiana and Khurasān is the fact that when Berke, the Mongol Khān of the Golden Horde who ruled from 1257 to 1267, embraced Islam he did so in the guiding presence of Shaykh Sayf al-Dīn at the *khānaqāh* of Fatḥ-Ābād.[4] The Kubrawī Sufis, later overshadowed by the Naqshbandīs in this and other respects, then held substantial political influence in addition to their spiritual and moral authority and *baraka.*

The *Shaykh-i 'Ālam* Sayf al-Dīn composed a number of written works. One item that would have been of enormous interest sadly does not appear to have survived. Yaḥyā Bākharzī reports that the Shaykh kept "all his life" a secret diary, which was discovered after Sayf al-Dīn's death. From his account it seems probable that Yaḥyā had seen this document. In it Sayf al-Dīn had recorded all the details of his life: every gift received, every ritual prayer and supplication performed, the dates of his wives' menstruation, every wrong done him by enemies and the envious, and the number of *rak'as* of ritual prayer that he performed at night to expiate them—all those things were written down by Shaykh Sayf al-Dīn in the diary.[5] Sayf al-Dīn Bākharzī is also known to have written the following works:

I. *Sharḥ Asmā' al-ḥusnā [sic].*

This was evidently a commentary upon the Divine Names, a subject upon which many Sufis and others have written; perhaps the best known is Abū Ḥāmid al-Ghazālī's *al-Maqṣad al-asnā fī sharḥ ma'ānī Asmā' Allāh al-ḥusnā.*[6] No other details of this work by Bākharzī have been traced by the writer.

1. See M. Kiyānī, *Tārīkh-i khānaqāh dar Īrān* (Tehran 1369 A.Hsh./1990), pp. 192-95.
2. For Sayf al-Dīn's contacts outside the Kubrawiyya, including Fakhr al-Dīn 'Alī Ṣafī Kāshifī's *Rashaḥāt-i 'ayn al-ḥayāt,* p. 3, see *Fuṣūṣ,* pp. 13-17.
3. See C. Melville, 'Pādshāh-i Islām: The Conversion of Sultan Maḥmūd Ghāzān' in *Pembroke Papers* I (Cambridge 1990), pp. 159-177.
4. See Ibn Khaldūn, *Kitāb al-'Ibar,* vol. 5, p. 534; J. Richard, 'La conversion de Berke et les debuts de l'islamisation de la Horde d'Or,' *Revue des etudes islamiques,* 35 (1967), pp. 173-9; D. DeWeese, The *Kashf al-Hudā* of Kamāl ad-Dīn Ḥusayn Khorezmī (Ph.D. thesis, Bloomington, Ind. 1985), pp. 25-38, 97-101; I. Vásáry, 'History and legend in Berke Khan's conversion to Islam,' in D. Sinor (ed.), *Aspects of Altaic civilization III* (Bloomington, Ind. 1990), pp. 230-252.
5. *Fuṣūṣ al-ādāb,* p. 8.
6. Abū Ḥāmid al-Ghazālī, *al-Maqṣad al-asnā fī sharḥ ma'ānī Asmā' Allāh al-ḥusnā,* ed. F. Shehadi (Beirut 1971).

Sayf al-Dīn Bākharzī on Horseback Preceded by a Prince on Foot. From a manuscript of the *Majālis al-'ushshāq,* dated 959/1552. MS. Ouseley Add. 24, f. 75b (Courtesy of the Bodleian Library, Oxford)

II. *Waqā'i' al-khalwa.*

A treatise in Arabic upon the events and experiences undergone in *khalwa* or retreat. Bākharzī recounts the interpretation of his visions as given him by his Shaykh, Najm al-Dīn Kubrā.[1]

III. *Waṣiyyat al-safar.*

This tract on the rules to be observed by disciples when travelling is named by Yaḥyā Bākharzī as one of the sources of his book. Nothing further seems to be known of it. Meier speculated[2] that it may be a reworking of Majd al-Dīn Baghdādī's *Risālat al-safar.*

IV. *Risāla dar 'ishq.*

A treatise in Persian on the nature of spiritual love. The text is found in an early collection *(majmū'a)* in Tehran University's Central Library.[3]

V. *Rubā'iyyāt* and other poems.

Collections of Sayf al-Dīn's poems exist in various manuscripts. The authenticity of many of the poems is suspect. Though forceful, most of the verses attributed to Bākharzī are not technically accomplished.[4] Very quotable, however, is this one from the *Risāla dar 'ishq*:

> *May God give you Love, that you may know*
> *the heart's burning of mind-dazzled lovers.*

This verse is followed by Sayf al-Dīn's comment in rhymed prose: "It is drunkenness without wine—it is sunkenness without trace!"[5]

IV. LIFE AND WORK OF ABŪ'L-MAFĀKHIR YAḤYĀ BĀKHARZĪ

From the life and works of Shaykh-i 'Ālam Sayf al-Dīn Bākharzī we pass on to his grandson Abū'l-Mafākhir Yaḥyā, the author of *Fuṣūṣ al-ādāb*. In fact rather little is known about him despite the fact that Afshār traced two noteworthy historical

---

1. There is an apparently unique copy in Leiden University Library (ms. no. 2252), but sadly this contains only part of the text; see Kubrā, *Fawā'iḥ al-jamāl*, ed. Meier, p. 42; Brockelmann, GAL S iii, p. 810.
2. F. Meier, *apud* Kubrā, *Fawā'iḥ*, p. 43.
3. This MS. was published by Īraj Afshār in *Majalla-i Dānishkada-yi Adabiyyāt*, 8 (1340/1961-2), no. 4; also by Ḥabīb Yaghmā'ī (Tehran 1343/1964-5). The text was published again by Afshār in *Dū risāla-i 'irfānī dar 'ishq* (Tehran 1359/1980), published as no. 27 in *Farhang-i Īrān-zamīn, Silsila-i mutūn wa taḥqīqāt*. The same volume includes not only the *Savāniḥ* of Aḥmad Ghazālī but also—most important—anecdotes, verses and dicta of Sayf al-Dīn Bākharzī excerpted from Yaḥya Bākharzī's *Awrād al-aḥbāb.*
4. Some of the *rubā'iyyāt* have been published, e.g. in *ZDMG* 57, pp. 345-354. Further bibliographical references are provided by the indefatigable Īraj Afshār in the introduction to his edition of *Fuṣūṣ al-ādāb*, p. 18. There is one manuscript in the British Library, MS. Or. 9348, which however was made as recently as 1904, for Sir Denison Ross.
5. *Risāla dar 'ishq*, ed. Īraj Afshār, p. 97.

sources in which Yaḥyā Bākharzī is mentioned: *Mujmal-i Faṣīḥī* and *Tārīkh-i Mullā-zāda.*[1]

Yaḥyā's father Burhān al-Dīn Aḥmad was the second son of Shaykh Sayf al-Dīn, and received initiation from him first as *murīd* and later as *murshid* in his own right. In response to a request from the Qarākhiṭā'ī noblewoman Tarkān Khātūn of Kerman, a great admirer of Sayf al-Dīn on whose foundation she lavished largesse, Sayf al-Dīn despatched Shaykh Burhān al-Dīn Aḥmad (who was also known by the sobriquet *Shaykh-zāda)* to Kerman. There he settled, founded a well-endowed *khānaqāh,* and attracted a large following. Miraculous deeds *(karāmāt)* of his, such as raising and lowering the *khānaqāh* roof by gesturing with his arms while preaching, are recounted in the *Tadhkirat al-awliyā* by Miḥrābī of Kerman.[2]

Abū'l-Mafākhir Yaḥyā was brought up in Kerman, but owing to the paucity of source material not even an approximate date can be given for his birth. Passages in his treatise show that Yaḥyā at some point travelled extensively, visiting Egypt, Syria, Asia Minor, Iraq, Azerbaijan and Kerman. He was privileged to sit in the company of Sufi Masters in those regions.[3] He received *khirqa*s of initiation from a number of Shaykhs. Details are given by Yaḥyā in the supplement to his initiatic genealogy *(isnād),* of which—with a thoroughness like that of his grandfather Shaykh Sayf al-Dīn—he offers four different versions in the *Fuṣūṣ al-ādāb.*[4]

These initiatic genealogies are: *Isnād al-khirqa,* from the Prophet Muḥammad forwards in time; *Isnād talqīn al-dhikr,* from Shaykh Sayf al-Dīn (who gave the *dhikr* to Yaḥyā when the latter was a boy) and Burhān al-Dīn back to the Prophet; *Ṭarīqa ukhrā fī' l-khirqa,* which acknowledges that at Tabriz in 700/1300-1 Yaḥyā studied part of *al-Maṣābīḥ* (very probably al-Baghawī's *Ḥadīth* compilation *Maṣābīḥ al-Sunna)* with Fakhr al-Dīn 'Umar Mujandarī who also authorized him to teach the *'Awārif al-ma'ārif* of Shaykh 'Umar al-Suhrawardī, whose own initiatic *isnād* is then rehearsed by Bākharzī, back to the Prophet. Lastly, the fourth *isnād* traces Mujandarī's initiatic chain by another line from his teacher Muḥammad ibn Mu'ayyid al-Ḥamawī.

The sources describe Abū'l-Mafākhir Yaḥyā as a gnostic, an expert on *ḥādīth,* and a preacher. In the year 712/1312-13 he moved from Kerman, settling at Bukhārā where he played an important role at the still active and influential *khānaqāh* of Fatḥ-Ābād. Besides the function of teaching which he must have exercised, Yaḥyā is known to have arranged for the daily feeding of the poor at the *khānaqāh.* It was he who offered hospitality to Ibn Baṭṭūṭa on his visit to Bukhārā

---

1. Aḥmad Faṣīḥ Khwāfī, *Mujmal-i Faṣīḥī,* ed. Maḥmūd Farrukh, 3 vols. (Mashad 1339/1960-1-1341/1962-3); see also C.A. Storey, ed. & translated by Iu. Bregel, *Persidskaia literatura,* 1 (Moscow 1972), pp. 355-8. Aḥmad ibn Maḥmūd Mu'īn al-Fuqarā, *Tarīkh-i Mullā-zāda* (or *Kitāb-i Mullā-zāda),* ed. Aḥmad Gulchīn-i Ma'ānī (Tehran 1330/1950-1); also Storey, *op. cit.*, p. 1115. Both works are cited by Afshār in *Fuṣūṣ al-ādāb,* introduction.
2. The chief source on Burhān al-Dīn Aḥmad is Sa'īd Miḥrābī-yi Kirmānī, *Tadhkirat al-awliyā-yi Miḥrābī-yi Kirmānī,* ed. Sayyid Muḥammad Hāshimī and Ḥusayn Kūhī-yi Kirmānī (Tehran 1330/1951-2). For examples of the *karāmāt* of Burhān al-Dīn Aḥmad, see Afshār, ed., *Fuṣūṣ al-ādāb,* introduction, p. 22.
3. See Afshār, ed., *Fuṣūṣ,* introduction, p. 26.
4. For Yaḥya Bākharzī's full *isnāds,* see *Fuṣūṣ,* pp. 27-31.

which must have occurred in or about 735/1334-5.[1] As Mujtabā Mīnuwī pointed out, this shows the incorrectness of the entry in *Kashf al-ẓunūn* which would have Yaḥyā dead as early as 724/1324.[2]

In fact Abū'l-Mafākhir Yaḥyā died in 736/1335-6, in Bukhārā. He was buried immediately to the east of his grandfather. He left behind a family including at least two sons, Burhān al-Dīn Shahīd and Rūḥ al-Dīn Shaykh Dā'ūd, as well as an enduring spiritual and literary legacy.[3]

V. MANUALS ON SUFISM AND SOURCES USED BY YAḤYĀ BĀKHARZĪ.

It is generally thought that by the 7th/13th century, when Yaḥyā Bākharzī flourished, the theoretical basis of Sufism as a discipline had been firmly established and codified. But this is an oversimplification. Essentially, the phenomenon known as *taṣawwuf* or Sufism is and was far from monolithic. The literary evidence alone would suffice to make this abundantly clear. In times and places where Sufism has become solidified beyond a certain point, the freshness and *baraka* of authentic *taṣawwuf* are less in evidence than the forced patterns either of legalistic codification or, on the other hand, of "maraboutisme" or "*īshān*-ism".

The historical period under discussion in the present volume is seen by some scholars within an historical frame of reference as a phase, the second of three, wherein the spontaneous spirituality of earlier "Golden Age" Sufism gave way under various pressures to what J.S. Trimingham characterized as "surrender to a rule".[4] The wonder is that this period of "surrender to a rule" unquestionably witnessed a great flowering of authentic *taṣawwuf,* to which the literary heritage and documented spiritual achievements of the epoch bear ample witness. Thus it appears, from a spiritual perspective, that this apparent heightened legalism was a providential change necessary to maintaining the fruitful equilibrium characteristic of true Islam. To continue bearing good fruit, a tree requires pruning. To whose rule did the Kubrawīs of the 12th to 14th century submit? To the 3rd/9th century ("Golden Age") Rules of Junayd.

At all events, by the early 7th/13th century when Yaḥyā Bākharzī wrote his book a number of treatises on Sufism had become classics and enjoyed extensive repute and influence. They include the *Kitāb al-Luma'*,[5] *Kashf al-Maḥjūb*,[6] *Qūt al-qulūb*,[7]

1. Ibn Baṭṭūṭa, *Riḥla*, vol. 3 (Cairo 1284/1867), pp. 5-6; see also *Safarnāma-yi Ibn Baṭṭūṭa*, translated into Persian by Muḥammad 'Alī Muwaḥḥid (Tehran: 1337 A.H.sh.), p. 373.
2. Cited by Afshār in *Fuṣūṣ*, p. 26; cf. Ḥajjī Khalīfa, *Kashf al-ẓunūn*, vol. 1, p. 150.
3. *Fuṣūṣ al-ādāb*, pp. 18-25.
4. J.S. Trimingham, *The Sufi Orders in Islam* (Oxford 1971), p. 103.
5. Abū Naṣr al-Sarrāj, *Kitāb al-Luma' fī l-taṣawwuf*, ed. R.A. Nicholson (Leiden and London 1914).
6. 'Alī ibn 'Uthmān Hujwīrī, *Kashf al-Maḥjūb*, ed. V. Zhukovskii (Leningrad 1926); *The "Kashfu'l-maḥjub"*, trans. R.A. Nicholson (Leiden and London 1911).
7. Abū Ṭālib al-Makkī, *Qūt al-qulūb fī mu'āmalāt al-Maḥbūb*, 2 vols. (Cairo 1310/1892-3).

al-Qushayrī's *Risāla,*[1] the *Ādāb al-murīdīn* of Abū'l-Najīb al-Suhrawardī[2] and the *'Awārif al-ma'ārif* of 'Umar al-Suhrawardī.[3] The authorship of these works suggests that the written codification of the Sufi Path was largely a phenomenon of the Persianate culture and Iranian Islam, although this may require qualification.[4] There would be value in examining some of these classics, along with related but less-known works such as the *Guzīda*[5] and Quṭb al-Dīn 'Abbādī's *al-Taṣfiya fī aḥwāl al-mutaṣawwifa,*[6] and perhaps some of the didactic poetry, and analyzing their scope and form in order to develop a typology.

Himself a scholar of *Ḥadīth,* Bākharzī stresses that his foremost sources are the Holy Koran and the Traditions of the Prophet. Also to be reckoned as sources are persons quoted in the text. Among the valuable features of Afshār's edition is an index of the 240 or so personal names found in the *Fuṣūṣ.*[7] In a prominent place at the end of his work, Yaḥyā specifically acknowledges the texts on which he drew. These are listed below:[8]

1. The *Qūt al-qulūb* of Abū Ṭālib al-Makkī (d. 386/996).[9]

The plan and the content of Bākharzī's work display close affinities with al-Makkī's book which also influenced Ghazālī's *Iḥyā'*. It is quoted in numerous passages and contexts. Moreover Yaḥyā candidly announces that much of *Awrād al-aḥbāb* is simply a translation of parts of *Qūt al-qulūb.*

2. The *Ādāb al-murīdīn* of Abū'l-Najīb al-Suhrawardī (d. 563/1168).[10]

Shaykh Abū'l-Najīb al-Suhrawardī features in the *silsila* or initiatic chain of the Kubrawiyya, and it is not surprising that he appears in Bākharzī's book. Milson states (incorrectly) in his abridged translation that the *Awrād al-aḥbāb wa Fuṣūṣ al-ādāb* includes an near-complete Persian translation of this work Certainly quotations from Suhrawardī's work abound in the *Fuṣūṣ.*

3. The *'Awārif al-ma'ārif* of Abū Ḥafṣ 'Umar al-Suhrawardī (d. 632/1234).[11]

Abū'l-Najīb's nephew too is highly regarded by Yaḥyā Bākharzī, and there are many similarities of approach and content. Quotations abound, for example in the

1. Abū'l-Qāsim al-Qushayrī, *al-Risālat al-Qushayriyya,* 2 vols. (Cairo 1330/1912).
2. Abū'l-Najīb al-Suhrawardī, *Ādāb al-murīdīn,* ed. M. Milson (Jerusalem 1977); abridged translation by M. Milson: *A Sufi Rule for Novices* (Cambridge, Mass. 1975).
3. 'Umar al-Suhrawardī, *'Awārif al-ma'ārif,* 2nd ed. (Beirut 1983).
4. A conference on "Persian Sufism from its Origin to Rumi" held at The George Washington University in Washington, D.C. in May 1992 is to be devoted to Iranian contributions to the development of early Sufism.
5. Abū Naṣr Ṭāhir Khānaqāhī, *Guzīda dar taṣawwuf,* ed. Īraj Afshār (Tehran 1347/1968).
6. Quṭb al-Dīn Manṣūr 'Abbādī, *al-Taṣfiya fī aḥwāl al-mutaṣawwifa,* ed. Ghulāmḥusayn Yūsufī (Tehran 1347/1968).
7. *Fuṣūṣ,* pp. 359-69.
8. *Fuṣūṣ,* p. 357.
9. See above, note 1.
10. See above, note 3.
11. See above, note 4.

passage on throwing off the cloak during *samāʿ*.[1]

4. *Risālat al-khalwa* and *Risālatayn fī ādāb al-Ṣūfiyya* of Najm al-Dīn Kubrā (d. 618/1221).

The identity of the two treatises on *ādāb* is uncertain. One may well be the Persian *Ādāb al-murīdīn,* in seven sections.[2] The second might be an untitled *Risāla* in Arabic, or another in Persian.[3]

5. *Risāla Waṣiyyat al-safar* of Sayf al-Dīn Bākharzī (d. 659/1261).

This text on the *ādāb* of travelling was mentioned earlier in the discussion of Sayf al-Dīn's writings.

6-8. *Ḥilyat al-abdāl, Amr al-marbūṭ,* and *Kunh mā lā budd minh li-' l-murīd* of Muḥyī al-Dīn Ibn ʿArabī (d. 638/1240).

The *Ḥilyat al-abdāl* was composed in Mecca in 599/1002-3 for two disciples, in order to explain what a person aspiring to the Sufi Path needs to know and to do before meeting a Shaykh.[4]

The *Amr al-marbūṭ* is properly known as *Kitāb al-Amr al-muḥkam al-marbūṭ fī mā yalzam ahl ṭarīq Allāh min al-shurūṭ.* As the title indicates, this is a treatise on the principles and rules of the Sufi Path. It was written by *al-Shaykh al-Akbar* in 602/1205-6.[5]

Kunh mā lā budd minh li' l-murīd, written at Mosul in 601/1204-5, is also known as *Irshād al-ṭālibīn wa tanbīh al-murīdīn wa' l-mustarshidīn.* It concerns ethics and the *ādāb* of the Sufi Path.[6]

9. *Manāzil al-murīdīn* of ʿAbdullāh al-Marjānī.

Unfortunately bibliographical references to this work have yet to be found.

VI. THE *AWRĀD AL-AḤBĀB:* OVERVIEW OF THE CONTENTS.

As already mentioned, Bākharzī's text comprises two parts. The second, *Fuṣūṣ al-ādāb,* has been published in an excellent edition by Īraj Afshār, based on an early manuscript, Nafiz Paşa 355, preserved at the Süleymaniye Library, Istanbul. Afshār

1. *Fuṣūṣ,* p. 212.
2. See F. Meier *apud* Kubrā, *Fawā'iḥ,* ed. p. 51; also *Miscellanea Giuseppe Furlani* (Rome 1957).
3. Text no. 3 in Arabic, in Kubrā's *Fawā'iḥ,* ed. Meier, p. 48; Persian no. 3 in *op. cit.,* p. 51.
4. ʿUthmān Yaḥyā, *Histoire et classification de l'oeuvre d' Ibn ʿArabī,* 2 vols. (Damascus 1964), vol. 1, pp. 291-2.
5. ʿUthmān Yaḥyā *(op. cit.,* vol. 1, pp. 154-6), lists seven alternative titles given to the *Amr al-marbūṭ.*
6. ʿUthmān Yaḥyā, *op. cit.,* vol. 2, pp. 338-9. This work was published at Cairo in 1328/1910 and summarized by M. Asin de Palacios in *El Islam cristianizado* (Madrid 1931), pp. 371-7. The treatise was also translated into English by Tosun Bayrak al-Jerrahi, 'What the Student Needs: Ibn ʿArabi's *Ma La budda Minhu lil-Murid,*' in the *Journal of the Muhiyiddin Ibn ʿArabi Society,* vol. 5 (1986), pp. 29-55.

decided to edit the *Fuṣūṣ* without the *Awrād* for two reasons. He considered the former of greater interest as concerning the theory of the Path, and he deemed himself insufficiently knowledgeable about Sufi practice to deal with the *Awrād al-aḥbāb* which is technical in a more specialized sense. But Īraj Afshār provides an invaluable table of the subjects of each section of *Awrād al-aḥbāb* (pp. 33-34).

The first part of Yaḥyā Bākharzī's work, that is the *Awrād al-aḥbāb,* comprises twenty chapters or *Faṣṣ*. This word, usually rendered in English as "bezel", is familiar to many in connection with *Fuṣūṣ al-ḥikam,* the treatise on the esoteric aspects of the nature of the Prophets by Muḥyī'l-Dīn Ibn 'Arabī.[1] It denotes the part of a signet ring that is shaped to receive a gem. Yaḥyā Bākharzī probably intended simply to suggest that his chapters are the formal structures within which his spiritual meanings are arranged.

The *Awrād* is chiefly concerned with practical matters of worship, some of which are aspects of the Sunna of the Blessed Prophet that were and are widely followed outside Sufi circles. The chapter headings of *Awrād al-aḥbāb* are as follows:

1. Times of the seven *awrād* or litanies recited in daytime.
2. Times of the *awrād* of night time.
3. Obligatory actions *(farḍ)* of disciples, and *nawādir.*
4. Selected formulae of supplication *(ad'iya)* used after the dawn prayer.
5. Invocations *(adhkār)* for after the sunrise *(bāmdād)* prayer.
6. Litanies for daytime
7. Litanies for night time.
8. Knowledge and times of the obligatory prayers.
9. Supplications recommended *(mustaḥabb)* for the supererogatory night prayer on arising from sleep *(tahajjud)*, or at sunrise.
10. Formulae recommended for recitation before sleeping.
11. On dividing the night into portions, part for devotions and part for rest, with a description of those who rise at night and engage in supererogatory prayers.
12. On the glorification and remembrance *(wird)* performed by God's servants during the day and night.
13. On the comportment *(mu'āmala)* of the servant in reciting the Koran; description of those who read it as it should be read.
14. Description of the heedless who do what is disliked when reciting it.
15. Respective merit *(faḍīlat)* of loud or quiet recitation.
16. Friday, its usages *(ādāb)*, and actions desirable on that day. This *faṣṣ* has several interesting sections: e.g. on the duty to render service to people before the time of Friday prayer.
17. Essential practices for disciples: hunger, sobriety, health, seclusion.
18. The spiritual genealogy of the author.
19. The contemplation *(murāqaba)* of those brought nigh to God, and the stations *(maqāmāt)* of those who realize Certainty *(mūqinīn)*.
20. Explanation of the fact that the rational intellect is veiled from God

1. Muḥyī'l-Dīn Ibn 'Arabī, *Fuṣūṣ al-ḥikam,* ed. Abū'l-'Alā' 'Afīfī (Cairo 1946) and R.J.W. Austin's English translation entitled *Bezels of Wisdom* (New York: 1980).

Almighty, being the mirror of this lower world whereas the mirror to the Next World is faith *(īmān)*.

VII. THE *FUṢŪṢ AL-ĀDĀB:* AN OUTLINE OF CONTENTS.

Yaḥyā Bākharzī explains in his text his reasons for writing it.[1] The entire passage is suggestive and eloquent but can only be summarized here. With great modesty (but the formulation is a standard one, not necessarily to be taken literally) the author states his intention thus: because most of the local disciples were ignorant of Arabic it occurred to him that it would be useful to collect material from authoritative Sufi works in the (high, literary) Persian language *(Fārsī)* in order to translate them into *Darī;* the fact that he distinguishes between these two in such terms is itself noteworthy.

The *Fūṣūṣ al-ādāb,* the second part of Yaḥyā Bākharzī's treatise, is much longer than the first. It comprises exactly forty main sections *(Faṣṣ)*, some of which are subdivided into explications *(bayān)* of particular facets of the subject. The author's opening rubric for the *Fuṣūṣ* is in Arabic, as is the rubric of each individual *Faṣṣ*. It provides a serviceable summary:

> Second Part, on the bezels of the usages of Sufis, and their tenets; their way of life, livelihood, apparel, spiritual concert *(samā')*; their companionship with God and with people; rules governing the Shaykh and the disciple and their respective binding duties; rules for servants in their diverse services; the *ḥammām;* rules for travellers whilst journeying and on arrival, rules of the spiritual retreat and the forty-day retreat; the spiritual method of ascetic practises and spiritual struggle and its peculiar qualities. May God be well-pleased with all of them [i.e. true Sufis].[2]

Yaḥyā Bākharzī's systematic and rational personality is evident throughout his work in the style of exposition he uses. As a general rule, the approach is to begin with the general, explaining the basic significance of the topic or issue at hand, and then proceed to the particular. While all this is of course entirely normal, Abū'l-Mafākhir is more methodical than most writers in his didactic expositions. He is also very readable, the prose being admirably crisp and concise. Ample use is made of quotations and anecdotes to illustrate the point and enliven the text. The range of sources drawn on by the writer is broad by the standards of the period. At the same time, he has favourite authorities from whom he often quotes. Foremost is Shaykh Sayf al-Dīn Bākharzī, to whom the *Fuṣūṣ al-ādāb* accords such prominence that in places it seems almost as much a personal tribute to the *Shaykh-i 'Ālam* as a practical guide to Sufism.

The headings of the forty *Faṣṣ* of *Fuṣūṣ al-ādāb* as assigned by the author and tabulated by Afshār may be translated as follows:

---

1. *Fuṣūṣ*, pp. 45-6
2. The heading of *Fuṣūṣ al-ādāb*, in Arabic, reads as follows:
al-Qism al-thānī fī fuṣūṣ ādāb al-ṣūfiyya wa 'aqā'idihim wa akhlāqihim wa mu'āshiratihim wa ma'īshatihim wa libāsihim wa samā'ihim wa ṣuḥbatihim ma' al-Ḥaqq wa'l-khalq wa sharā'iṭ al-shaykh wa'l-murīd wa mā yajib 'alayhimā wa ādāb al-khuddām fī anwā' al-khidamāt wa'l-ḥammām wa ādāb al-musāfir waqt al-safar wa'l-qudūm wa ādāb al-khalwa wa'l-arba'īniyya wa tartīb al-riyāḍa wa'l-mujāhada wa khawāṣṣihā. Riḍwān Allah 'alayhim ajma'īn."

1. Firm belief required in Unity and God's Self-Subsistence.
2. The requirements *(ādāb)* of faith.
3. The superiority of poverty to wealth.
4. The nature of Sufism.
5. Calling the ego to account and guarding against vain thoughts.
6. Norms regarding the *khirqa*, or cloak of initiation; in three parts.
7. Norms regarding details and commandments of the religion; doctrines.
8. The advantages of having rules *(ādāb)*.
9. The ethics of the Sufis.
10. The spiritual stations *(maqāmāt)* of the Sufis.
11. The mystical states *(aḥwāl)* of the Sufis.
12. Differences of approach to the Path *(ikhtilāf al-masālik)*.
13. Manners and usages in disputation *(muḥāwara)*.
14. Ecstatic utterances *(shaṭḥiyyāt)* (those cited are more like paradoxes).
15. Rules, conditions and duties for the Shaykh.
16. Rules, conditions, and duties for disciples in serving Shaykhs.
17. Rules about prayer rug, ewer and ablutions with it, and the staff.
18. Dealings with the heart, and sincerity.
19. Special qualities of the lower soul, and knowledge of them.
20. Rules for keeping company with people of every group *(ṭā'ifa)*.
21. Rules governing the limbs and senses: sections on tongue, hearing, sight, heart, hands, legs.
22. Principles of conviviality *('ishra)* and appointment of a leader *(ta'mīr)* when in company.
23. Discipline, rules and state of servants and similar people.
24. Various kinds of service, and the servants responsible for them.
25. Rules for eating: washing; water-carrier; table-layer; kitchen rules.
26. Rules for the public bath *(ḥammām)* and working in it.
27. Rules for washing clothes.
28. Rules for waiting on guests, and hospitality *(ḍiyāfa)*.
29. Rules for travelling.
30. Rules for arriving back from a journey and entering the *khānaqāh*.
31. Rules for spiritual audition *(samā')*, what is sound and what is unsound. Subsections are: on dancing and tambourine; some usages; more usages of Sufis; throwing off the cloak; repairing torn cloaks; matter of prohibition, licence, or denial the great Sufis are unaffected by *samā'* or ecstasy; on weeping in *samā'*; explanation of technical terms used by minstrels: love,wine, drinking, dregs, goblet, monastery, girdle, Christian, Christian boy, bell, idol, idol temple, tress, face, prayer, *miḥrāb* and *qibla,* mosque, *madrasa* and *khānaqāh;* minaret; Ka'ba; tavern; beauty *(shāhid)*; denial of faith *(kufr)*.
32. Ordinances *(aḥkām)* and rules for Sufis regarding 'spats' or small disputes.
33. Rules and conditions concerning questions and who may ask them.
34. Rules (usages) observed in illness.
35. Rules (usages) observed at the time of death.
36. Rules (usages) observed ain times of tribulation.
37. Rules (usages) governing those granted special indulgences *(murakhkhaṣ)*.

38. Rules, conditions and benefits of the forty-day retreat; in three parts.
39. The self-denial of disciples in eating; the merits of hunger; how gnostics eat.
40. Stories of God's beloved ones; their visions; the sincere *abdāl*.

VIII. THE *FUṢŪṢ AL-ĀDĀB*: SOME FEATURES OF INTEREST

Abū'l-Mafākhir Bākharzī deals with a great many facets of Sufism, both theoretical and practical. Considering its subject and technical nature, it is remarkablly readable and stylishly composed. Professor Afshār has pointed out the fineness of the language used. Many passages display features of stylistic excellence such as the kind of rhythmic cadence which is found in the best classical Persian prose writing. Because the author has acknowledged his main sources and the editor has indexed the names mentioned in the text, it is not difficult to trace the influences behind the work.

Within the compass of the present essay it is of course impossible to do full justice to the contents of Abū'l-Mafākhir Yaḥyā Bākharzī's *Fuṣūṣ al-ādāb*. A number of excerpts in paraphrase or translation may provide some indications of the 'flavor' and prose style of this distinctive Kubrawī Sufi treatise. In this presentation, quotations from the *Fuṣūṣ al-ādāb* are classified under four headings, for convenience: (i) the nature and principles of the Sufi Way; (ii) etiquette and ethics; (iii) service to people and *khānaqāh* organization; (iv) *samā'*, poetry and other sundry aspects of Sufism.

IX. BĀKHARZĪ ON THE PRINCIPLES OF THE SUFI WAY

In his preface to the *Fuṣūṣ al-ādāb,* Yaḥyā Bākharzī explains that since every seeker must understand the nature of that which he seeks, knowledge of the theoretical principles of the Sufi Path is essential for those aspiring to it. Most of its various conventions *(abwāb-i ādāb)* are based upon the Holy Koran or the acts and words of the Prophet and his companions rather than having been originated by the Sufis themselves. It is largely because the latter collected and codified them from diverse sources—here our author specifically mentions the *Ṣafwat al-taṣawwuf* of Abū'l-Faḍl Muḥammad ibn Ṭāhir al-Maqdisī—that they are called "the rules and manners of the Sufis" *(ādāb-i ṣūfiyya).*[1] Bākharzī draws heavily on *aḥadīth* in his treatise, generally translating them into Persian.

The opening *Faṣṣ* is largely devoted to *tawḥīd* or divine Unity, cornerstone of the Muslim articles of faith. It ends, however, with a number of admonitions to the aspiring dervish, three of which may be mentioned here. He must revere *(ta'ẓīm)* anyone who reveres God and His Messenger. He must care for, and have a good opinion of, all mankind, privately praying for all Muslims. He must also be happy to serve the dervishes and tolerate any harshness from them; if a dervish has no other good in him, it is goodness enough that he permit another to do him a service.[2]

What has the *Fuṣūṣ al-ādāb* to say of the *maqāmāt* or stages of the Sufi Path? According to the author, the servant's nearness to his Lord is determined by the

1. *Fuṣūṣ*, text, preface, pp. 1-2.
2. *Fuṣūṣ, 'Aqāyid al-ṣūfiyya fī' l-waḥdāniyya wa' l-qiyāma:* pp. 6-7.

quantity *(miqdār)* of his worship *('ibādat)* of God, be these outward actions or 'the work of the heart.' He supports this assertion with a verse from the Holy Koran (XXXVII 16): "and there is not one of us but has a known station." Abū'l-Mafākhir enumerates fourteen *maqāmāt*, in ascending order: taking heed *(intibāh)*, contrition *(inābat)*, scrupulous fear *(wara')*, devotion *(irādat)*, spiritual poverty *(faqr)*, self-imposed patience *(taṣabbur)*, contentment *(riḍā)*, trust in God *(tawakkul)*, self-examination *(muḥāsaba-i nafs)*, detachment *(zuhd)*, sincerity *(ṣidq)*, patience *(ṣabr)*, and sincerity *(ikhlāṣ)*.[1]

Another key element in the theory of Sufism is that of the transitory mystical states *(aḥwāl*, singular *ḥāl)*. Yaḥyā Bākharzī defines *ḥāl* as "the interaction *(mu'āmala)* of the seeker's heart with God Most High: that is to say, those spiritual meanings *(ma'ānī)* which by virtue of the purity of acts of invocation descend upon his heart and are transformed into a mystical state within him." Bākharzī's relatively brief excursus upon the *aḥwāl* mentions the following, in order: contemplation *(murāqaba)*, nearness *(qurb)*, love *(maḥabbat)*, hope *(rajā)*, fear *(khawf)*, modesty *(ḥayā)*, longing *(shawq)*, intimacy *(uns)*, serenity *(ṭama'nīna)*, certainty *(yaqīn)*, and finally direct vision *(mushāhada)*. The author concludes this section by saying that beyond the state of *mushāhada* come divine inspirations, visions and revelations too sublime to be described in words.[2]

Our author explains in the next *Faṣṣ* that there are diverse types of spiritual personality among those who follow the Path; accordingly, there are diverse approaches or methods of travel *(sulūk-i ṭarīq)*. They are respectively defined as the Ways of worship *('ibādat)*; asceticism *(riyāḍat)*; seclusion *(khalwat wa 'uzlat)*; travel, exile and obscurity *(siyāḥat wa safar wa ghurbat wa gum-nāmī wa bī-nishānī)*; service to mankind *(khidmat)*; striving, enduring terrors and welcoming the spiritual states *(mujāhadat wa taḥammul-i ahwāl wa mubāsharat-i aḥwāl)*; deliberate loss of face and honor before other people (unlike 'Umar al-Suhrawardī, Yaḥyā Bākharzī does not use the obvious term *malāmat)*; impotence and helplessness *('ajz wa shikastagī)*; Teaching and acquisition of knowlegde *(ta'līm....wa ḥifẓ-i 'ulūm)*.

Now, each of these approaches to the Supreme Goal has its peculiar rules *(ādāb)* and conditions *(sharā'iṭ)*. If these are not carefully observed as prescribed by the Shaykhs, Bākharzī warns, the disciple will fail in his endeavor and be left in trouble and turmoil. After citing *aḥadīth* in praise of knowledge, the author concludes with two observations: firstly, knowledge is to action as the spirit is to the body; secondly, it is vital that the seeker's knowledge rule over his reason *('aql)*, not *vice versa*. This serves to make it clear that the author is here speaking above all of *'ilm* in the highest sense: supra-rational knowledge, knowledge of the heart.[3]

---

1. *Fuṣūṣ, Maqāmāt al-ṣūfiyya:* pp. 51-52.
2. *Fuṣūṣ, Aḥwāl al-ṣūfiyya:* pp. 53-54.
3. *Fuṣūṣ, Ikhtilāf al-masālik:* pp. 55-56.

In an interesting chapter devoted to the question of appropriate dress Bākharzī singles out, among those who may be called Sufis by virtue of their having worn garments of wool, the Prophets Adam, Moses, Jesus and Muḥammad.[1] The color of the Sufi's robe or *khirqa* must be in conformity with his inner state. If he wears blue or black, it signifies that he has slain his *nafs* or lower soul; such was the clothing of the Archangel Gabriel when he visited Adam after his expulsion from Paradise. Azure blue is suitable for most people of the Path, showing that they have utterly purged themselves with the soap of contrition. Those who have attained the spiritual world in all respects, attaining every station and tasting of every state, may dress in a robe that is patched *(mulamma')*, hence multicolored. Robes with ornamentation are exclusively for those who bear both outwardly and inwardly the Seal of the Trust (of human viceregency) and whose hearts are the treasuries of divine secrets.[2]

Although Sufis should by definition be 'other-worldly,' circumstances nonetheless often require that they possess *savoir faire*. This point is underlined by a dictum of Sayf al-Dīn Bākharzī, reportedly uttered while preaching at the *minbar:* "These people (Sufis) will not let their enemies get them in a position where they have any dealings with them, friendly or otherwise."[3]

One of Bākharzī's several quotations from Shaykh Muḥyī'l-Dīn Ibn 'Arabī serves as a reminder that it is virtually impossible for the outsider, sympathetic or otherwise, fully to understand Sufism, especially the sayings and actions of saints. Ordinary people do not know what extraordinary people are doing.

"We have seen people who caused their spirituality *(rūḥāniyyat)* to become embodied within their outer appearances *(ṣūrat)*, and then engage that appearance of theirs in some act or other; so that those present have imagined "This is 'So-and-so' performing some action—whilst that [Sufi] himself has passed on to a different place and a different station *(maqām)*."[4]

X. BĀKHARZĪ ON ETIQUETTE AND ETHICS

By entitling his treatise *Fuṣūṣ al-ādāb,* Yaḥyā Bākharzī makes explicit the importance of *ādāb* in the Sufi Path, which in the present context may be translated as "rules and etiquette." His discussion of the topic[5] commences with an interesting exposition of its theoretical basis. Religion *(madhhab)* has an outer and inner aspect. The outer aspect consists of observing courtesy *(ādāb)* in relation to people *(khalq)*; the inner aspect consists in traversing the *(munāzala)* the mystical states and spiritual stations with God. The outer aspect of faith is incomplete without the inner, and courtesy is also indispensable to the seeker on the Path. Bākharzī quotes Sarī Saqaṭī as saying: "Courtesy is the interpreter of Intelligence."

The author proceeds to elaborate further on the subject, in two directions. First, he speaks of the kinds of *adab* shown by the three different classes of human beings:

1. *Fuṣūṣ, al-Libās wa'l-khirqa:* pp. 28-29.
2. *Fuṣūṣ, al-Libās wa'l-khirqa:* p. 30-31.
3. *Fuṣūṣ, Adab al-khādim:* p. 132.
4. *Fuṣūṣ, Ādāb al-mashyakha wa sharā'iṭuhā wa mā yajib 'ala'l-mashāyikh:* p. 88.
5. *Fuṣūṣ, Faḍīlat al-ādāb:* p. 46.

worldly people *(ahl-i dunyā)*, religious people *(ahl-i dīn)*, and the elite *(khuṣūṣ)*. The *adab* of the worldly—corresponding, indeed, to the classical 'humanist' meaning of the term in Arabic—mainly comprises eloquence, rhetoric, knowledge of the branches of learning, traditional tales of kings, and Arabic poetry. To these meanings, religious people generally add the disciplining of the lower soul *(nafs)*, control over the body, improvement of character, observance of the laws of Islam, the forsaking of the carnal appetites and dubious things, and the eager pursuit of good deeds. Finally, the élite add to the above-mentioned virtues those of keeping close watch on the heart and of maintaining an equilibrium between the unconscious and conscious aspects of the psyche in relation to their innermost consciousness *(sirr)*.

The difference between aspirants *(murīdān)* consists in the quantity and quality of their actions. The excellence of those at the intermediate stage *(mutawassiṭān)* is determined by their *adab*. That of gnostics *('ārifān)* is determined by the degree of their aspiration *(himmat)*. Indeed, adds Bākharzī, the worth of any man depends on the quality of his aspiration.[1]

At this point the author moves on from the topic of *adab* to the closely related matter of *akhlāq*, or ethics. He begins by affirming that of all the good qualities that the Sufis may possess, the most important are their good moral characteristics. Bākharzī cites the well-known *ḥadīth* describing as "Koranic" the ethical nature of the Prophet: *Kān akhlāquh al-Qur'ān*. Besides other quotations, he provides a long list of virtues which all initiates must seek to acquire—and more realistically—a far shorter list for ordinary people.[2] The author emphasizes the importance of speaking little and controlling the tongue, as in the following passage:

> Shaykh Ḍiyā' al-Dīn Abū'l-Najīb [Suhrawardī], may God be well-pleased with him, used to advise one of his companions: "Do not address the people of this Path except in the purest of times." This is because the [degree of] light of speech is determined by the light of the heart and the light of hearing too is determined by the heart's light. Unless the heart be illumined there is no benefit in seeing, hearing, or speaking.[3]

Another virtue essential to the Sufi seeker is that of speaking only well of people. The following dictum is cited by Yaḥyā Bākharzī, recounted from Shaykh Abū 'Alī Rūdbārī (who appears in the Kubrawī *silsila)*:

> "To attack *(ḥamla burdan ba-)* a person higher than rank in you is impudence and folly; [to attack] one who is like you is impropriety *(bī-adabī)*; and to attack one who is lesser than you is weakness *('ājizī)*."[4]

For Bākharzī, *ṣuḥbat*, meaning "companionship" or "company," is a technical term which comprises several ascending degrees: acquaintance *(ma'rifat)*, love *(mawaddat)*, familiarity *(ulfat)*, joy in company *('ishrat)*, deep affection *(maḥabbat)*, and finally brotherhood *(ukhuwwat)*. True *ṣuḥbat* is only realized between two people when their inner feelings are harmonized. Among Sufis, the

1. *Fuṣūṣ, Faḍīlat al-ādāb*: p. 47.
2. *Fuṣūṣ, Akhlāq al-ṣūfiyya:* pp. 48-50.
3. *Fuṣūṣ, Ādāb al-qudūm min al-safar wa dukhūl al-khānaqāh:* p. 177.
4. *Fuṣūṣ, Ādābuhum fī'l-'ishra wa'l-ta'mīr fī'l-ṣuḥba:* p. 126.

superiority of the Companions *(ṣaḥāba)* of the Blessed Prophet in respect to knowledge, sagacity, worship, detachment, complete trust in God and contentment *(riḍā)* is ascribed not to any qualities of their own but precisely to the superior quality of their *ṣuḥbat,* this being higher than any other spiritual degree.[1]

In another part of the section dealing with the courtesies of sociability, the author of *Fuṣūṣ al-ādāb* discusses some colloquial expressions—one might almost term them "in-jokes"—employed by certain members of the brotherhood:

> "When dervishes say [of a person] 'The sun rose,' it means that he smiled and became happy; on the other hand, when someone who becomes morose *(turush)* they say 'It has turned cloudy', so that outsiders *(nā-ahlān)* may not understand."

The author goes on to say that more mature and advanced Sufis refrain from using such frivolous expressions.[2]

XI. BĀKHARZĪ ON SERVICE TO PEOPLE AND *KHĀNAQĀH* ORGANIZATION

The following definition of spiritual poverty *(faqr),* found in the *Fuṣūṣ al-ādāb,* is unattributed; hence it is likely that is the source is Yaḥyā Bākharzī himself. The stress upon service to one's fellow man is characteristic:

> The essential condition *(sharṭ)* of poverty is that whoever tells you to do a task you do it and do not refuse it; that you do not tell anyone to do anything; and that you do not regard yourself as superior to or greater than anybody, or seek such a position *(wa ṭālib-i īn ma'nī nabāshī).*"[3]

With regard to the need to render service in a timely manner, Sayf al-Dīn Bākharzī said: "Speed is the perfection of service" *(Kamāl-i khidmat dar ta'jīl ast).*[4]

Humility, good fellowship, hospitality and service to all kinds of people are essentials according to Yaḥyā Bakharzī. Examples were set by the greatest Masters of the Kubrawiyya:

> Najm al-Dīn Kubrā (God's greetings upon him) used to put out a tray, upon which he would collect the clothes of travellers (or guests: *musāfirān*), and would wash them with his own blessed hands. [5]

Another anecdote in the same section concerns the author's grandfather: "Sayf al-Dīn Bākharzī would go to the privy *(mutawaḍḍā)* of the *khānaqāh* at the dead of night. He would clean the privy and with his own hand deal with the clods *(kulūkh)* used by the dervishes for wiping themselves clean."[6]

Service to people on Fridays before the assembly for congregational prayer is enjoined by Abū'l-Mafākhir Bākharzī in the *Awrād al-aḥbāb.* The organization of

---

1. *Fuṣūṣ, Ādābuhum fī'l-'ishra wa'l-ta'mīr fī'l-ṣuḥba:* p. 123.
2. *Fuṣūṣ, Ādābuhum fī'l-'ishra wa'l-ta'mīr fī'l-ṣuḥba:* p. 127.
3. *Fuṣūṣ, Ādābuhum fī'l-'ishra wa'l-ta'mīr fī'l-ṣuḥba:* p. 124.
4. *Fuṣūṣ, Ādāb al-murīdīn wa sharā'iṭuhum:* p. 90.
5. *Fuṣūṣ, Ādāb al-ṣuḥba ma kull ṭā'ifa:* p. 109.
6. *Fuṣūṣ, Ādāb al-ṣuḥba ma kull ṭā'ifa:* p. 109.

the service in the Sufi centre *(khānaqāh)* is prescribed in detail by Yaḥyā Bākharzī, who himself administered the Fatḥ-Ābād centre:

> In a *khānaqāh* or group of Sufis there must be a single person appointed to perform each kind of service, in order that when a dervish requires that service the servant responsible may get up and put that matter to rights. The servant must have ready, complete, and available whatever he knows [to be needed] before the dervish has need of it. In this way, when the time of need comes, the dervish's mind will not be distracted and he will not need to pause or wait, God willing.[1]

The following anecdote about Sayf al-Dīn Bākharzī concerns both the matter of service to the Shaykh, and the possibility of communicating with him wordlessly through concentration of the heart *(tawajjuh)*.

Shaykh Sayf al-Dīn had a page-boy with whom he was displeased only because the page-boy's spiritual gifts were so great that if had he concentrated fully on his Master he would have known by intuition precisely what the latter wanted, without a word being spoken.[2]

Other chapters discuss in some detail the organization of the kitchen and laundry of the *khānaqāh*, and such matters as the serving of food and water to dervishes and guests. The best possible hospitality is due to all visitors and proper etiquette essential.

XII. BĀKHARZĪ ON *SAMĀ'*, POETRY, AND OTHER ASPECTS OF SUFISM

About one-sixth of the *Fuṣūṣ al-ādāb* is devoted to the practice of *samā'*, or spiritual music and dance and related matters. It would be well worthwhile to undertake a separate study of this section of the work; this occasion one can but mention a very few aspects. Yaḥyā Bākharzī stresses the acute danger of *samā'* being practiced by those lacking sufficient experience of awareness, who may unwittingly open the doors to satanic influences on their susceptible souls.[3]

Regarding the practices of the *Shaykh al-'Ālam*, his grandson states that:

> The Shaykh of the World Sayf al-Dīn... did not listen to spiritual music *(samā')* apart from dervishes. He would order the singer to sing poems by Shaykhs of the *Ṭarīqa* and advanced travellers *(sālikān)* on the Way to God. He refused all verse that described ringlets, moles, and cheeks, and would not permit singers to sing it. He said, "These are inward meanings (or realities: *ma'ānī)* which need interpretation *(ta'wīl)* and they are further removed from [easy] understanding. *Samā'* is not the proper place for rational consideration *(tadabbur)* and thought *(tafakkur)*."[4]

The potentially momentous effects of *samā'* are illustrated in an episode involving Sadīd al-Dīn Khwārazmī, a man who had sold his business and all his possessions and come to follow Shaykh Sayf al-Dīn Bākharzī. He served in the kitchen of the *khānaqāh*. One night after finishing his work there and performing

---

1. *Fuṣūṣ, Ādāb anwā' al-khidamāt wa ādāb khuddāmihā:* p. 133.
2. *Fuṣūṣ, Ādāb al-murīdīn wa sharā'iṭuhum wa mā yajib 'alayhim fī khidmat al-Shaykh:* p. 90.
3. *Fuṣūṣ, Ādāb al-samā'*, pp. 191-92.
4. *Fuṣūṣ, Ādāb al-samā'*, pp. 191-2.

the night prayer, he went to join the *samāʿ* of Sayf al-Dīn and his companions. A singer was chanting verses in Arabic and Persian. These are quoted by Yaḥyā Bākharzī, and include the following lines:

Should the herald of Your love come summoning,
I would answer from the confines of my grave.
If they ask on Day of Judgement "Who was slain?"
I alone would call out in response.

Hearing this, Sadīd al-Dīn uttered a cry, fell down, and died. At the funeral prayer the following day, the Shaykh was in a state of tremendous elation, praising and rejoicing at the high spiritual station and gifts of Sadīd al-Dīn.[1]

One section of the *Faṣṣ* on *samāʿ* is concerned with the explanation of poetical symbolism of the physical attributes of the Beloved, etc. The definitions offered by the author are interesting but at times appear slightly narrow. This part of Bākharzī's treatise has been studied and quoted by Dr. Javad Nurbakhsh,[2] one of the few authorities apart from Afshār to have concerned themselves with the *Fuṣūṣ al-ādāb*. Here is one example, a brief explanation of the significance of the word *zulf,* meaning "tress."

> *Zulf:* alludes to *kufr* (denial of faith), veiling, difficulty, ambiguity and anything that makes a man veiled or confused *(maḥjūb)* regarding his own state."[3]

This interpretation by Bākharzī is correct as far as it goes, but neglects another important facet of this symbol: the dazzling complexity of God as He manifests Himself to us through His Attributes—a spectacle that holds the heart in enthralled suspense.

Our author attaches great importance to instructing the disciple always to show endurance and good cheer in times of tribulation. By way of an exemplary story, he tells of how malicious intrigues of the Mongols (*kāfirān*) led to Sayf al-Dīn being arrested whilst performing his prayers, bound, and taken away. The following day he was taken from Bukhārā to the military encampment under guard. As thousands of people accompanied the Shaykh, weeping uncontrollably, the Shaykh joyfully composed a quatrain for the occasion:

You took from me my kith, kin and companions;
You have left me with naught but want and need for company.
This is Your Door, the station of Your favourites!
For what service of mine, Lord, did you do this for me?[4]

Yaḥyā Bākharzī does not disclose precisely how this episode ended; but either sooner or later, the *Shaykh-i ʿĀlam* was set free.

---

1. *Fuṣūṣ, Ādāb al-samāʿ:* pp. 200-201.
2. Javad Nurbakhsh, *Sufi Symbolism,* translated by L. Lewisohn and T. Graham, 5 vols. (London 1984-91).
3. *Fuṣūṣ, Ādāb al-samāʿ:* p. 246; cf. Nurbakhsh, *op. cit.*, vol. 1, p. 78.

XIII. CONCLUSIONS.

Although at this point one expects to have arrived at conclusions, it would be premature to try to offer many here. A conclusive study of Abū 'l-Mafākhir Yaḥyā and his work would need to be based on the whole of it, not on part.

The writer hopes, however, to have shown that a little-known treatise—and there are more where this one came from—can present a useful case study for the development of Sufism in a particular area of the Persian-speaking world. It shows how within a given Sufi brotherhood diverse elements of the heritage of the Holy Prophet and his Family, the Companions and Followers, and the early Shaykhs could be synthesized both creatively and systematically into a method and a textbook like *Awrād al-aḥbāb wa Fiṣūṣ al-ādāb,* designed to provide for the Kubrawī dervishes of Fatḥ-Ābād guidance and nourishment in a form appropriate to the spiritual and material conditions of the time.

Abū 'l-Mafākhir Bākharzī's Sufi treatise also manifests some of the best stylistic traits of the prose literature of Persian Sufism, which although never quite as captivating as the great poetry is at its best quite beautiful. As with so many Sufi writers, his work is informed by a deep appreciation of the power and loveliness of the sung or spoken word.

The present writer hopes to have shown, if this were needed, that Sufis are not necessarily either boringly obsessive nor unfailingly tolerant of human weakness. Neither trait seems to appear in the personality of a man like Shaykh Sayf al-Dīn who, like so many great spiritual Masters, wielded tremendous influence over a wide range of different types of human being.

One of the key themes in the history of Islam is the perpetual contest between the exoteric and esoteric perspectives and their representitives. In the nature of things, there must exist an esoteric or at least an introverted current in the outer disciplines of Islam, just as there must needs exist—as we have seen—a normative, in a sense, exoteric element within the teachings of Sufism. Such are the *ādāb* or rules and usages with which this study has been primarily concerned. It is of interest that Yaḥyā Bākharzī applies this term very broadly: to the articles of faith, for example, as well as to the rules of courtesy between the disciple and other people. The importance of the concept of *ādāb* and its various nuances seems to be underestimated in scholarship on Islamic civilization.

Finally, for the masters of Sufism, *taṣawwuf* is a scientific matter just as *asmā' al-rijāl* or *al-jarḥ wa 'l-ta'dīl* are sciences of religion. It is the science of the human

4. *Fuṣūṣ, Ādāb al-ṣūfiyya waqt al-balā:* p. 270. The passage is a good example both of Yaḥya Bākharzī's rhythmic prose and of Sayf al-Dīn's poetry:
Shaykh al-'Ālam Sayf al-Dīn-i Bākharzī-rā, riḍwān Allāhi 'alayh, jam'ī az kāfirān qaṣd kardand, va dushmanān sa'īhā namūdand, wa īlchī ba Bukhārā āmad, u Shaykh-rā dar namāz giriftand u bar-bastand, vw rūz-i dīgar az shahr bīrūn āwardand u ba-urdū mī-burdand, wa chand hazār ādamī mushāyi'a kardand, wa az sar-i ḥuzn āb az dīda mī-bārīdand, wa Shaykh hamchunān bar-basta dar basṭ u faraḥ būd, īn rubā'ī farmūd ki:

Bī khwīsh u tabār u bī qarīnam kardī
bā fāqa u faqr hamnishīnam kardī
īn martaba-yi muqarrabān dar-i tust
yā Rabb ba chi khidmat īn-chunīnam kardī

Heart. As stated in the Sacred Tradition, the Heart of the True Believer contains God, whom neither Heaven nor Earth can contain.[1]

1. According to an often-cited Sacred *Ḥadīth (Ḥadīth qudsī)* in which God Himself speaks, "Neither My Heavens nor my Earth can contain Me; but the heart of My truly believing servant contains Me."

The Importance of the Spiritual Guide in the Naqshbandi Order

Johan G.J. ter Haar

The question as to what are the distinctive characteristics of the Naqshbandī Order is usually answered in two ways. First of all attention is drawn to the fact that conformity to the Islamic law is of the utmost importance in this fraternity. Strict adherence to the prescripts of the *Shari'a* is a recurring theme in the definitions which many Naqshbandīs have given of their mystical path.[1] Secondly, reference is made to the eleven principles which were introduced into this mystical fraternity during the 13th and 14th centuries AD.[2] The first eight of these principles *(hūsh dar dam, naẓar bar qadam, safar dar waṭan, khalwat dar anjuman, yādkard, bāzgasht, nigāhdāsht and yāddāsht)* are attributed to 'Abd al-Khāliq Ghujduwānī (d. 617-18/ 1220-21), who appears, however, to have attributed the first four to his spiritual guide, Abū Ya'qūb Yūsuf Hamadānī (d. 534/1140).[3] Later, Bahā' al-Dīn Naqshband (d. 791/1389) added three more principles, viz. *wuqūf-i 'adadī, wuqūf-i zamānī* and *wuqūf-i qalbī*.

There are, however, some other features which, in the eyes of the Naqshbandīs themselves, are also highly significant, if not almost equally characteristic, of the mystical path of this fraternity. These features, as far as their origin and their terminology is concerned, belong to the tradition of almost every mystical Order and cannot therefore be regarded as exclusively characteristic of the Naqshbandī path. Nonetheless, they have gained a special popularity with the Nasqhbandī Order or have been adapted to the mystical path of this fraternity and cast in a particular mould, to such an extent that they have become a very important part of the identity of this Order. The way in which the *dhikr* is practised by the Naqshbandīs is a clear example of such a feature.[4] Another example is provided by the prominent role the spiritual guide *(Shaykh, Pīr, Murshid)* plays in this order. The importance of this role is acknowledged in every mystical fraternity, but the Naqshbandīs developed and elaborated this universal theme in their own way. This essay concentrates on

1. For a survey of these definitions see Muḥammad Pārsā, *Qudsiyya: Kalimāt-i Bahā' al-Dīn Naqshband*, ed. by A. Ṭāhirī 'Irāqī (Tehran: Kitābkhāna-i Tahūrī 1975), pp. 51-544.
2. A most detailed description of these principles, based on the most important Naqshbandī sources, is given by Aḥmad Ṭāhirī 'Irāqī in his introduction to Muḥammad Pārsā, *op.cit.*, pp. 50-64.
3. 'Abd al-Khāliq Ghujduwānī, '*Risāla-i Ṣāḥibiyya*,' ed. S. Nafīsī, in *Farhang-i Īrān-zamīn* 1 (1332), p. 91.
4. H. Algar, 'Silent and Vocal *Dhikr* in the Naqshbandī Order' in *Akten des VII Kongresses für Arabistik und Islamwissenschaft*, (Göttingen, 1976), pp.39-47; R. Gramlich, *Die Schiitischen Derwischorden Persiens*, Teil II, (Wiesbaden: Kommissionsverlag Franz Steiner GMBH, 1976), pp.398-401.

two aspects of this development and elaboration. The first is that many a Naqshbandī is reported to have been an *Uwaysī,* that is a mystic who was not (only) initiated by a living, physically present Shaykh, but (also) by the 'spirituality' or 'spiritual presence' *(rūḥāniyyat)* of a deceased Shaykh or even by Khiḍr. The second aspect is the necessity for the novice to establish and maintain strong ties with a Shaykh as an indispensable means for progress on the mystical path. At first sight these two aspects may seem to contradict each other, but in reality they are two complimentary sides of the same coin, since what matters in both cases is the spirit of the spiritual guide and this spirit is apparently not confined to his actual bodily presence.

Before dilating on this subject, I would like to say a few words on the history of the Naqshbandī order. From the point of view of the identity of this brotherhood and the way it developed three separate periods can be distinguished. The first period consists of what Hamid Algar called the prehistory of the Order. It is perhaps more accurate to call it the protohistorical period of the Order. In this period, which began with Abū Bakr and ends with Khwāja Abū 'Alī Fārmadī (d. 478-79/1085-86), the Order had not yet received an identity of its own and the persons who belong to this period and whose names feature in the Naqshbandī pedigree cannot "be regarded as belonging exclusively to the ancestry of the Naqshbandiyya."[1] The second period, the formative phase in the history of the Order, is the phase that gave the Order its identity. To this period belong, first of all, the so-called Masters *(khwājagān),* a group of seven Central Asian Shaykhs, the first of whom was Khwāja Abū Ya'qūb Yūsuf Hamadānī (d. 1140) and the last of whom was Khwāja Amīr Sayyid Kulāl (d. 772/1371). The key figure of this period, however, is, of course, Bahā' al-Dīn Naqshband. The fact that the Order bears his name is an appropriate recognition of the great fame he enjoyed and the lasting influence he exerted.[2] The third period covers the history of the order from Bahā' al-Dīn Naqshband onward. This phase witnessed, among other things, the branching out of the Order into several lines, among whom the Mujaddidiyya, named after Shaykh Aḥmad Sirhindī (d. 1034/1624), the 'renewer of the second millennium' *(mujaddid-i alf-i thānī),* and the Khālidiyya, after Mawlānā Khālid Baghdādī (d. 1243/1827). In accordance with the time-span of the present collection of essays, this article deals primarily with the formative period. Occasionally, for the sake of contrast, reference will be make to the protohistorical and the post-Naqshbandi period as well.

THE *UWAYSĪ* PATH

According to Khwāja Muḥammad Pārsā (d. 822/1420), a disciple of Bahā' al-Dīn Naqshband, many a Naqshbandī Shaykh has walked "the path of the Uwaysīs" *(ṭarīqa-i Uwaysīyān).* The term Uwaysī, so he continues, refers to those "wards" or 'protégé's of God' *(awlīyā'-i allāh)* who 'seemingly' *(dar ẓāhir)* do not need a

1. H. Algar, *op. cit.*, p. 41.
2. A biography of both the Khwājagān and Bahā' al-Dīn Naqshband is given by A. Tahiri 'Irāqī in his introduction to Muḥammad Pārsā, *op. cit.*, pp. 31-49. See also H. Algar, 'The Naqshbandi Order: A Preliminary Survey of its History and Significance' in *Studia Islamica,* XLIV (1976), pp. 131-136.

Khwāja Bahā' al-Dīn Naqshband's Encounter with a Prince Carrying a Green Fur-lined Robe. From a manuscript of the *Majālis al-'ushshāq*, dated 959/1552. MS. Ouseley Add. 24, f. 91v (Courtesy of the Bodleian Library, Oxford)

guide, since the Prophet Muḥammad "cherishes them in the private chamber of his favour, without the mediation of someone else, as he cherished Uways [al-Qaranī]."[1] Only in a very few instances does this definition appear to hold true literally. According to 'Abd al-Raḥman Jāmī, an example of a initiation directly by the prophet Muḥammad is to be found in the case of Jalāl al-Dīn Abū Yazīd Pūrānī (d. 861/1457-58).[2] Shaykh Aḥmad Sirhindī even claimed to have been initiated directly by God. In one of his letters he writes: "Although in the Naqshbandī order my instructor is 'Abd al-Bāqī *[bi' llāh]*, yet the One who has undertaken my instruction is the Everlasting One *(al-bāqī)*.[3] Usually, however, the term *Uwaysī* is taken as referring to an initiation not by a physically present Shaykh, but by the 'spirituality' or 'spiritual presence' ***(rūḥāniyyat)*** of a deceased guide or by Khiḍr.

In the protohistorical period of the Naqshbandī Order there are two instances of an initiation by the 'spiritual presence' of a deceased Shaykh. Abū Yazīd Bisṭāmī (d. 261/875) is said to have been initiated by the spiritual presence of Ja'far al-Ṣādiq (whose date of birth varies, according to the different sources, between 80/699 and 86/705 and who died in 148/765). The second instance is Abū'l-Ḥasan Kharaqānī (352/963–420/1029), who was initiated by Abū Yazīd Bisṭāmī. In these instances the Uwaysī relationship is used to link together two people who cannot have had any actual (physical) contact since the master had died before the birth of the disciple. In the case of the relation between Abū Yazīd Bisṭāmī and Abū'l-Ḥasan Kharaqānī some sources say that the two masters actually did meet, but the generally accepted view is that Bisṭāmī died in 261/875 and therefore cannot have met Abū'l-Ḥasan Kharaqānī, who was born almost a century later.[4]

The question, however, as to why the Uwaysī motive was applied in these two cases, can be answered only very partially and in rather general terms, since the available sources do not provide specific information on this issue. We must assume that those circles in whose midst this idea of spiritual linkage developed, thought it very important that people of widely divergent characters like Ja'far al-Ṣādiq, Abū Yazīd Bisṭāmī and Abū'l-Ḥasan Kharaqānī should all be included in the spiritual ancestry of the Naqshbandīs. Each of them obviously incorporated certain values which were considered to be relevant to the Naqshbandī Order. Since, as has already been mentioned, neither Ja'far al-Ṣādiq nor Abū Yazīd Bisṭāmī nor Abū'l-

---

1. *ān rā haḍrat-i nubūwwat 'alayhi al-salām dar ḥujra-i 'ināyat-i khwud parwarī mīdihad bīwāsiṭa-i ghayr chunānki Uways rā dād.* Muḥammad Pārsā, *op. cit.*, pp. 14-15. Muḥammad Pārsā acknowledges that this definition was first used by Shaykh Farīd al-Dīn 'Aṭṭār. The words *"dar ẓāhir"* are, however, an addition by Muḥammad Pārsā. Cf. Farīd al-Dīn 'Aṭṭār, *Tadhkirat al-Awlīyā'* Part I, ed. by R.A. Nicholson (London: Luzac & Co. / Leiden: E.J. Brill 1907) p. 24. See also A. S. Husaini, 'Uways al-Qaranī and the Uwaysī Sufis' in *The Moslem World* 57 (1967), pp. 103-114.
2. 'Abd al-Raḥmān Jāmī, *Nafaḥāt al-uns,* (Cawnpore, 1885), p.327.
3. Y. Friedman, *Shaykh Ahmad Sirhindī: An Outline of His Thought and a Study of His Image in the Eyes of Posterity* (Montreal and London: McGill-Queen's University Press 1971), p. 28. Another example of a Sufi initiated directly by God is Abū'l-Ḥasan Kharaqānī who declared, at least according to Farīd al-Dīn 'Aṭṭār, that he had no other teacher than God *(op. cit.*, part 2, pp. 23-24). According to other sources, however, Abu'l-Ḥasan Kharaqānī was an Uwaysī in the usual sense of this word (see *infra).*
4. Muḥammad Pārsā, *op. cit.*, 121-12 and *Encyclopaedia Iranica* (London: Routledge & Kegan Paul, 1982-), Vol. 1, s.v. 'Bestami;' Vol. 2, s.v. 'Abu'l-Ḥasan Kharaqānī.'

Ḥasan Kharaqānī belong exclusively to the ancestry of this brotherhood, these values cannot be identified, at least not in Naqshbandī terms.

A somewhat different kind of Uwaysī initiation is to be found in the transitional years between the protohistorical and the formative period of Naqshbandī history, in the link between Abū 'Alī Fārmadī and the first of the Khwājagān, Abū Ya'qūb Yūsuf Hamadānī. 'Abd al-Khāliq Ghujduwānī writes in his *Risāla-i ṣāḥibiyya* that Abū Ya'qūb Yūsuf Hamadānī, after the death of his Shaykh, successfully enlisted the help of the 'spiritual presence' of Abū 'Alī Fārmadī in order to get an answer to questions concerning both Islamic law *(sharī'a)* and the mystical path *(ṭarīqa)*. Abū Ya'qūb Yūsuf Hamadānī passed these answers on to this novices, so he informed his disciple 'Abd al-Khāliq Ghujduwānī.[1] Whether or not the silent *dhikr,* which with 'Abd al-Khāliq Ghujduwānī became standard practice in the Naqshbandī Order, figured in his advice, is not clear since the available sources do not provide consistent information concerning Abū Ya'qūb Yūsuf Hamadānī's stance.[2]

The above-mentioned 'Abd al-Khāliq Ghujduwānī provides the leading example in the Naqshbandī Order of an initiation by Khiḍr. The latter not only taught him the silent *dhikr,* but also stimulated him to join Abū Ya'qūb Yūsuf Hamadānī. The sources differ, however, as to whether Khiḍr instructed 'Abd al-Khāliq Ghujduwānī directly or indirectly. According to the well-known story related in both the *Nafaḥāt al-uns* and the *Rashaḥāt-i 'ayn al-ḥayāt,* 'Abd al-Khāliq Ghujduwānī was told by Khiḍr to recite the *dhikr* silently, whilst submerging himself in water.[3] 'Abd al-Khāliq Ghujduwānī himself, however, is reported to have said that Abū Ya'qūb Yūsuf Hamadānī taught him the silent *dhikr* "by order" *(biwāsita-i sipārish)* of Khiḍr.[4] Although 'Abd al-Khāliq Ghujduwānī thus owed much to Khiḍr, be it directly or indirectly, there is—surprisingly enough—also evidence that suggests a somewhat negative attitude to Khiḍr on the part of Ghujduwānī. The latter is reported to have turned down Khiḍr's request to enjoy his 'society' *(ṣuḥbat)* by remarking: "You drank the water of life and are looking for life, but I entered the world of annihilation and I am looking for annihilation, so how can we possibly associate with one another?" In the same source another curious incident is mentioned. When Khiḍr once, on a day in spring, put on the frock *(khirqa)* that 'Abd al-Khāliq Ghujduwānī had taken off since he was working in his garden, the latter said in a tone of reproach: "It is not proper to take my clothes with the same hand with which you drank the water of life."[5]

From the point of view of spiritual initiation Bahā' al-Dīn Naqshband (718-791/1318-1389) is the true disciple and successor of 'Abd al-Khāliq Ghujduwānī,

---

1. 'Abd al-Khāliq Ghujduwānī, *op. cit.*, p. 7.
2. H. Algar, 'Silent and Vocal *Dhikr* in the Naqshbandi Order' p.42. The advice that Abū Ya'qūb Yūsuf Hamadānī received through the *rūḥāniyyat* of Abū 'Alī Fārmadī might even have included the Naqshbandī principles *hūsh dar dam, nazar bar qadam, safar dar waṭan and khalwat dar anjuman,* since 'Abd al-Khāliq Ghujduwānī attributes them to Abū Ya'qūb Yūsuf Hamadānī, as was already mentioned.
3. 'Abd al-Raḥmān Jāmī, *op. cit.*, p. 242; 'Alī b. al-Ḥusayn al-Kāshifī, *Rashaḥāt-i 'ayn al-ḥayāt,* (Cawnpore 1912), pp.19-20. See also H. Algar, *op. cit.*, p.42.
4. 'Abd al-Khāliq Ghujduwānī, *op. cit.*, p. 79.
5. *'Maqāmāt-i 'Abd al-Khāliq Ghujduwānī'* (ed. S. Nafīsī) in *Farhang-i Irān-zamīn II* (1333), p. 16.

although they never met. This is the classical example in the Naqshbandī brotherhood of a Sufi who takes his first steps on the mystical path in the physical presence of a living Shaykh, but who owes his real initiation to a spiritual guide whom he has never met. The Naqshbandī sources agree that Bahā' al-Dīn Naqshband was introduced to the mystical path of the Khwājagān by Bābā Sammāsī (d. 755/1354), the sixth Khwāja, and subsequently by the latter's successor, Sayyid Amīr Kulāl. The same sources add that he was, however, a novice of Sayyid Amīr Kulāl only "on the outside" *(biḥisb-i ṣūrat),* in the sense that he received his "instruction in the correct manners of traversing the mystical path" *(ta'līm-i ādāb-i ṭarīqat)* from the latter. "In reality" *(biḥisb-i ḥaqīqat),* however, he was an Uwaysī, that is, he received his mystical upbringing from the 'spiritual presence' of 'Abd al-Khāliq Ghujduwānī.[1] What Bahā' al-Dīn Naqshband received by way of this spiritual contact with 'Abd al-Khāliq Ghujduwānī was the order "to act resolutely" *('amal bi'azīmat)* and consequently to practice the silent *dhikr* and abstain from the publicly performed or vocal *dhikr.*[2]

The Uwaysī type of initiation in this case is clearly a determining factor in the development of the identity of the Naqshbandī Order. It explains the introduction of central aspects of this identity. At the same time it accounts for and legitimizes the fact that the introduction of these aspects by way of spiritual contact with a deceased Shaykh involved a certain amount of disloyalty to the actual, living Shaykh. For in order to comply with the instruction of 'Abd al-Khāliq Ghujduwānī concerning the performance of the *dhikr,* Bahā' al-Dīn had to deviate from the custom of Sayyid Amīr Kulāl, who practised the vocal *dhikr.* And therefore, whenever the latter and his followers practised this kind of *dhikr,* Bahā'l-Dīn rose and left their gathering. This behavior greatly upset the disciples of Sayyid Amīr Kulāl, but Bahā'l-Dīn showed no consideration.[3] And when the disciples privately complained to their Shaykh about the behavior of Bahā'l-Dīn, Sayyid Amīr Kulāl after some time publicly reprimanded them by saying that God always looked favorably upon Bahā'l-Dīn and that it was not for human beings to question God's favour. On his deathbed Sayyid Amīr Kulāl is reported to have said, in connection with the same issue, that the deeds of Bahā'l-Dīn Naqshband were inspired by God and based on "divine wisdom" *(ḥikmat-i ilāhī)* and that they had nothing to do with 'human discretion' *(ikhtīyār).*[4] Furthermore, Sayyid Amīr Kulāl acknowledged explicitly that he had been able to guide his novice only to a certain point. On the authority of Bābā Sammāsī he took care of the "upbringing" *(tarbiyyat)* of Bahā'l-Dīn to the best of his ability, but, so he tells Bahā'l-Dīn, "the bird of your aspiration turned out to fly high" *(murgh-i himmat-i shumā buland-parwāz uftāda-ast).*[5] Therefore he gave Bahā'l-Dīn permission to leave and he advised him not to be

---

1. 'Abd al-Raḥmān Jāmī, *op. cit.*, p. 247. Almost exactly the same wording is to be found in 'Alī ibn al-Ḥusayn al-Kāshifī, *op. cit.*, p. 54.
2. The story of Bahā'l-Dīn Naqshband's initiation by 'Abd al-Khāliq Ghujduwānī is analyzed in M. Molé, 'Autour du Daré Mansour: l'apprentissage mystique de Bahā' al-Dīn Naqshband' in *Revue des études islamiques* 27 (1959), pp. 35-66.
3. 'Alī ibn al-Ḥusayn al-Kāshifī, *op. cit.*, p. 54.
4. *Ibidem*, p. 54.
5. *Ibidem*, p. 55.

remiss in his search for the kind of mystical guidance befitting his spiritual aspiration. Thereupon Bahā'l-Dīn spent seven years with 'Ārif Dīg Karanī, a disciple of Sayyid Amīr Kulāl, and subsequently joined Quthum Shaykh and Khalīl Atā, who belonged to the Yasawī line. With the latter he even remained for twelve years.[1]

Bahā'l-Dīn Naqshband is not only the most significant example of the way in which the Uwaysī initiation was applied in the Naqshbandī order. He is also the one who elaborated this idea to a certain extent into a theory, or, to be more precise, who incorporated this idea in his theory of mystical life. According to this theory, the 'spiritual presence' of a deceased Shaykh is a force that can be evoked by a Sufi. Bahā'l-Dīn defines "concentration" *(tawajjuh)* on the 'spiritual presence' of a deceased Shaykh as a "station" *(maqām),* that is to say, a stage on the mystical path which the wayfarer can reach by his own efforts. This station, he explains, is part of that kind of traversing the mystical path which is called 'Progression' *(sulūk)* as opposed to 'Attraction' *(jazba.).* In the latter the Sufi is attracted by or drawn to God, almost passively, but in *sulūk* it is the Sufi who takes the first step and sets out for God. In this condition the wayfarer may be guided by the 'spirits' *(arwāḥ)* of deceased masters, who act as 'mediators' *(wasā'iṭ).* In the condition of *jazba,* on the other hand, there is no mediation.

Bahā'l-Dīn illustrates his theory with two examples. The first is that of Abū'l-Qāsim Gurgānī (d. 469-70/1076-77), who at the beginning of his mystical journey concentrated on the 'spiritual presence' of a master no less than Uways al-Qaranī. He used to recite the latter's name incessantly, as a kind of *dhikr.*[2] Such concentration on the 'spiritual presence' of Uways al-Qaranī brought about for Gurgānī a complete detachment and disengagement from worldly things and the severance of all ties, both the visible and the invisible ones, through which human beings are bound to the material world.[3] The second example is provided by Bahā'l-Dīn himself, who concentrated on the spirituality of Muḥammad ibn 'Alī al-Ḥakīm al-Tirmidhī (d.c. 295/908). The result was a state of "being without any attribute or characteristic feature" *(bīṣifatī).*[4] According to Bahā'l-Dīn Naqshband, this state represents the highest level of mystical experience which the "friends of God" *(awlīyā'-i Allāh)* may reach. God's friends can be characterized, for instance, by 'gnosis' *(ma'rifat)* or 'love' *(maḥabba),* but the highest level is that of being without any of these features.[5] Although this level belongs pre-eminently to the prophet Muḥammad, it can also be attained by God's 'friends.' The latter can attain, to be more precise, a share in this level, as "folk who glean ears from the harvest of his [Muḥammad's] good fortune" *(khwūsa-chīnān-i kharman-i sa'ādat-i ū).*[6] This idea

---

1. *Ibidem,* p. 55
2. Muḥammad Pārsā, *op. cit.*, p. 15 Bahā' al-Dīn quotes Farīd al-Dīn 'Aṭṭār, according to whom Abu'l-Qāsim Gurgānī incessantly used to say Uways! Uways! (*op. cit.*, part 1, p. 23).
3. Muḥammad Pārsā, *op. cit.*, p. 25.
4. Muḥammad Pārsā, *op. cit.*, p. 25.
5. Muḥammad b. 'Alī al-Ḥakīm al-Tirmidhī is reported to have said that a Sufi in whom there is only one feature left, resembles a slave who has to pay his master only one diram to be set free. He will reach his freedom only after he has paid this last diram. See Farīd al-Dīn 'Aṭṭār, *op. cit.*, part 1 p. 97.
6. Muḥammad Pārsā, *op. cit.*, pp.25-26.

of sharing in the mystical achievements of the prophet Muḥammad was to be resumed some two centuries later by Shaykh Aḥmad Sirhindī, who made it the cornerstone of his mystical thought. He was also to mention—in a letter to his own master, Muḥammad Bāqī-bi'llāh (d. 1012/1603)—the "mediation of the spirituality of many a Shaykh *(tawassuṭ-i rūḥāniyyat-i mashāyikh)*."[1]

THE BOND BETWEEN GUIDE AND NOVICE

Concentration on the 'spirituality' of a deceased Shaykh does not, however, render the guidance of a living Shaykh redundant. The one does not exclude the other, rather they complement each other. The important thing is to find a competent guide, which is not always easy. Muḥammad Pārsā explains that previously there were many competent guides, but in recent times their number has fallen sharply, to such an extent that they have become an exceptional phenomenon, "even more precious than red sulphur."[2]

In order to describe the requirements a true Shaykh has to comply with, Naqshbandī sources appear to have a marked preference for the adjectives 'perfect' *(kāmil)* and 'perfecting' *(mukammil, mukmil)*. The true Shaykh is required to have reached the "level of perfection and leading [others] to perfection" *(martaba-i kamāl wa ikmāl [takmīl])*.[3] According to Bahā' al-Dīn Naqshband, those who have reached the end of their mystical journey, that is to say, "those who are perfect" *(kāmilān)* and "have been united [with God]" *(wāṣilān)*, can be divided into two groups. The first group consists of those who have reached the level of perfection, but who are not charged with the duty of leading others to perfection. The reason for this is that they drowned in the "sea of unification" *(baḥr-i jam')* and disappeared completely in the "belly of the fish of annihilation" *(shikam-i māhī-i fanā')*. Since they therefore are not even aware of themselves, how are they supposed to take care of others? The second group is made up of those who are "perfect and perfecting" *(kāmil-i mukammilān)*. They are able to lead other people to perfection since they, after having drowned in the deep sea of unification, were released from the belly of the fish of annihilation and reached the "shore of separation" *(sāḥil-i tafriqa)* and the "arena of subsistence" *(maydān-i baqā')*. They have a share in "prophethood" *(nubūwwat)* as the highest level of mystical experience, whereas members of the first group find themselves on the lower mystical level of "friendship" *(wilāyat)*.[4] Ya'qūb Charkhī (d. 1447), a disciple of Bahā'l-Dīn, depicts the spiritual guide who is not only perfect himself but is also capable of leading others to perfection, as someone who is both "illuminated" *(nūrānī)* and "illuminating" *(nūrbakhsh)*, whereas a Shaykh who is perfect because he has reached the level of

1. Ahmad Sirhindī, *Maktūbāt*, Vol. I, letter no. 16 (Lahore: Nur Company 1964), p. 56.
2. *Bal a'azz min al-kibrīt al-aḥmar*. Muḥammad Pārsā, *op. cit.*, p. 15. Muḥammad Pārsā appears to stress the rarity of this material. In other texts the term 'red sulphur' refers to the Shaykh as "the master of spiritual alchemy (*kibrīt aḥmar, red sulphur*, was the mysteriously working substance in the alchemical process); thus he can transform the base material of the novice's soul into pure gold." A. Schimmel, *Mystical Dimensions of Islam* (Chapel Hill 1975), pp. 236-237.
3. These terms are to be found in e.g. 'Abd al-Khāliq Ghujduwānī, *op. cit.*, p. 99; 'Abd al-Raḥmān Jāmī, *op. cit.*, pp. 280, 282, 291, 294; 'Alī ibn al-Ḥusayn al-Kāshifī, *op. cit.*, pp. 8, 12, 13, 43.
4. Muḥammad Pārsā, *op. cit.*, p. 60.

perfection is *nūrānī* but not *nūrbakhsh*. He distinguishes yet another type of mystical guide, who he calls *kāmil-i muqallid*, that is, the Shaykh who is both perfect and perfecting but who is only capable of leading others to perfection in imitation of a Shaykh who is truly perfect and perfecting.[1]

The task of the spiritual guide *vis-à-vis* his novice in the Naqshbandī Order is quite often, even almost invariably, described as a process of "upbringing" *(tarbiyyat)*. The Shaykh is also in charge of the "instruction" *(ta'līm)*, but the emphasis is on *tarbiyyat*. This reflects the shift in emphasis concerning the task of the Shaykh that can be detected in the history of Sufism in general, a shift from the instructional side of this task to the educational one.[2] Consequently, the relation between a Shaykh and his novice is sometimes depicted as the relation between a father and his son.[3] Ya'qūb Charkhī explicitly states that the *khwājagān* used to consider their novices as their "adopted sons" *(ad'īyā')*. Thus they followed in the footsteps of the Prophet Muḥammad, who adopted Zayd ibn Ḥāritha as his son.[4] An early example of this custom is to be found in the relationship between Abū'l-Qāsim Gurgānī and Abū 'Alī Fārmadī. The latter is reported to have said that Abū'l-Qāsim Gurgānī considered him to be his son.[5] Other examples are 'Abd al-Khāliq Ghujduwānī and Bahā' al-Dīn Naqshband, who are reported to have been adopted as sons by respectively Khiḍr and Bāba Sammāsī.[6]

The spiritual guide is not only like a father to his novice, but he has, rather surprisingly, also something of a mother figure. The task of the Shaykh is sometimes likened to breast-feeding and even to hatching an egg. Sayyid Amīr Kulāl once said to Bahā'l-Dīn Naqshband: "I milked my breast for you."[7] In other instances it is said that thanks to the care of a spiritual guide "the fledgling of the spirituality" *(murgh-i rūḥāniyyat)* of a novice emerges from "the egg of [his] humanity" *(bayḍā-i bashariyyat)*.[8]

The emphasis on the task of the Shaykh, in particular on the educational aspects of this task, manifests itself also in certain customs or techniques based on concentration both on the part of the Shaykh on his novice and on the part of the novice upon his Shaykh. Although these techniques are not applied solely by the Sufis of

1. Ya'qūb Charkhī, *Risāla-i unsiyya*, ed. Muḥammad 'Abu'l-'Alīm, (Delhi: Matba'-i Mujtaba 1924), pp. 18-19.
2. This development is analyzed in F. Meier, 'Ḫurasan und das Ende der klassischen Sufik' in *La Persia nel Medioevo* (Rome 1971), pp. 545-570.
3. Outside the Naqshbandī order the concept is to be found in particular with the Suhrawardī *ṭarīqa*. See R. Gramlich, *op. cit.* Teil II, p. 211.
4. Ya'qūb Charkhī, *op. cit.*, p. 14.
5. 'Abd al-Raḥmān Jāmī, *op. cit.*, p. 237.
6. 'Alī b. al-Ḥusayn al-Kāshifī, *op. cit.*, pp. 19, 42; Muḥammad Pārsā, op. cit., p.9; 'Abd al-Raḥmān Jāmī, *op. cit.*, pp.247. Bahā' al-Dīn Naqshband for his part seems - the source is somewhat ambiguous - to have adopted 'Alā' al-Dīn 'Aṭṭār as his son. See 'Alī b. al-Ḥusayn al-Kāshifī, *op. cit.*, p. 80.
7. *pistān rā barā-yi shumā khūsh kardam.* 'Abd al-Raḥmān Jāmī, *op. cit.*, p. 245.
8. 'Alī b. al-Ḥusayn al-Kāshifī, *op. cit.*, p. 55

the Naqshbandī order, they appear to have gained special popularity with this fraternity. The most important of these techniques are *tawajjuh* and *rābiṭa* or *rabṭ.*[1] For a correct assessment of the role these techniques play in the Naqshbandī order, it is important to realize that they underwent a certain development with regard to both their content and their terminology.

In a Naqshbandī source dating back to the beginning of the 16th century AD, *rābiṭa* means that a novice constantly keeps the "face of the Shaykh" *(ṣūrat-i shaykh)* in his mind, in order to attain not only total submission to the will of the Shaykh, but also a kind of identification with him. The novice loses himself completely in his Shaykh and thus reaches the level of "annihilation in the Shaykh" *(fanā' fi'l-shaykh),* which will ultimately lead him to "annihilation in God" *(fanā' fi' llāh).*[2] Sources from later centuries suggest that successive generations of Naqshbandīs have continued the practice of *rābiṭa* virtually unaltered.[3] The term *tawajjuh,* however, took on a new, or at least a second meaning. According to the above-mentioned Naqshbandī source from the 16th century, it means that a novice pictures the name Allāh as engraved in his heart and continuously puts his mind to it, as a means to be in God's presence.[4] Later the term *tawajjuh* is used to denote concentration on the part of the Shaykh on his novice as a means to transfer the *dhikr* to the latter. The spiritual guide, facing his novice in such a way that their hearts are exactly opposite each other, prays to God that the light of the *dhikr,* which he once received from his own Shaykh, may now go over to his novice. The Shaykh subsequently concentrates on the other so-called "subtle organs" *(laṭā' if)* so that the *dhikr* penetrates the whole being of his novice.[5]

As far as the mystical path of the Khwājagan is concerned, *tawajjuh* and *rābiṭa* do not seem to have played an important role. In the above-mentioned *Risāla-i ṣāḥibiyya* by 'Abd al-Khāliq Ghujduwānī and the *Māqāmāt-i Khwāja 'Abd al-Khāliq Ghujduwānī,* they are not mentioned at all. The same holds true for a treatise on the prerequisites of traversing the mystical path, written by Khwāja 'Alī Ramītanī' (d. 715-16/1315-16 or 721/1321). Bahā'l-Dīn Naqshband, on the other hand, gave the concept of *tawajjuh* on the 'spirituality' of a deceased Shaykh a fairly prominent place in his theory of mystical life, as was already mentioned. He also appears to have been familiar with *tawajjuh* as concentration on the part of a living Shaykh on his novice as well as with *rābiṭa.* We are told that he once applied *tawajjuh* to Burhān al-Dīn, the son of Sayyid Amīr Kulāl. The "effects of that spiritual domination" *(āthār-i an taṣarruf)* were immediately visible, the source adds.[6] According to another story, told by 'Abd al-Raḥmān Jāmī, Bahā'l-Dīn Naqshband

1. *Murāqaba,* which is sometimes looked upon as a separate technique, seems to play a much less important role in the Naqshbandī tradition, at least in the formative period. For *murāqaba* see J. Spenser Trimingham, *The Sufi Orders in Islam,* (Oxford, 1971), pp.211-212; R. Gramlich, *op. cit.,* Teil II, pp.424-428.
2. Jalāl Harawī, 'Risāla-i 'uqdagushāy' in *Farhang-i Īranzāmīn* 6 (1337), pp.288-289, 320.
3. See 19th-century sources such as Shāh Abū Sa'īd, *Hidāyat al-ṭālibīn,* (Karachi, 1385/1965), pp. 28-30; Ra'ūf Aḥmad, *Marātib al-wuṣūl,* (Haydarabad, n.d.), pp. 49-51; Ḍiyā' al-Dīn Aḥmad Kumushkhānalī, *Jāmi' al-uṣūl* (quoted in R. Gramlich, *op. cit.* Teil II, p. 250).
4. Jalāl Harawī, *op. cit.*, pp. 288-89, 320.
5. Shāh Abū Sa'īd, *op. cit.*, pp. 30-32; Ra'ūf Aḥmad, *op. cit.*, pp. 49-51.
6. 'Alī ibn al-Ḥusayn al-Kāshifī, *op. cit.*, p. 44.

once taught the *dhikr* to one of his novices and subsequently left for Mecca. Upon his return he was told that this novice had practised the *dhikr* only a very few times. When Bahā'l-Dīn found out, however, that his novice had seen him in his dreams, he was reassured. In the eyes of Jāmī, this is a clear case of *rābiṭa,* although he does not actually put this term in Bahā'l-Dīn's mouth.[1] In yet another story we are told that Bahā'l-Dīn once advised one of his novices to concentrate on him, that is, to call to mind the face of his Shaykh, and to say: "It is not me, it is the Khwāja."

There are indications to suggest that Khwāja 'Alā' al-Dīn 'Aṭṭār (d. 803/1400), a very prominent disciple of Bahā'l-Dīn Naqshband, made *tawajjuh* on the Shaykh to be an essential part of the Naqshbandī path. Two treatises, written respectively by Ḥasan 'Aṭṭār, the eldest son of 'Alā' al-Dīn, and 'Abdullāh Imāmī Iṣfahānī, one of his disciples, explicitly state that a novice in the Naqshbandī order should first of all call to mind the face of his guide. The second of these treatises specifies that this concentration on the Shaykh is typical of the Naqshbandīs who followed the line of 'Alā' al-Dīn *(ṭā'ifa- i 'Alā'iyya).*[2] The important role of the latter is acknowledged by Bahā'l-Dīn Naqshband, who entrusted the training *(tarbiyyat)* of many of his disciples to 'Alā' al-Dīn.

The techniques of *rābiṭa* and *tawajjuh* as understood by later generations of Naqshbandīs appear to be an elaboration and refinement of the idea of *tawajjuh* put forward by Bahā'l-Dīn Naqshband and his disciple 'Alā' al-Dīn 'Aṭṭār. This elaboration and refinement, however, also involved a kind of mechanization, insomuch as the power of the Shaykh was thought of as operating to a certain extent almost mechanically. Whereas 'Alā' al-Dīn 'Aṭṭār warns that *tawajjuh* on the part of the Shaykh without efforts on the part of the novice soon loses its power, the 19th-century Naqshbandī Shāh Abū Sa'īd (d. 1240-41/1824-25) says that the speed with which a Sufi walks the mystical path depends mainly on the *tawajjuh* of his Shaykh and only to a very small degree on his own talents. He quotes a statement of Muḥammad Ma'ṣūm, son and successor of Shaykh Aḥmad Sirhindī, to the effect that while *dhikr* without *rābiṭa* is fruitless, *rābiṭa* alone is very efficient.[3] On the other hand, one should be careful not to make generalizations on the basis of these few statements. One should always keep in mind that what lies at the bottom of the phenomena touched upon in this article, is the awareness that the decisive factor in the relation between a Shaykh and his novice is the *rūḥāniyyat* of the former, that is a force that is not confined to his bodily presence.

---

1. 'Abd al-Raḥmān Jāmī, *op. cit.*, p. 249.
2. These two treatises are partly quoted in 'Alī b. al-Ḥusayn al-Kāshifī, *op. cit.*, pp. 91-97.
3. Shāh Abū Sa'īd, *op. cit.*, p. 30.

A Sufi Scientist of the Thirteenth Century
The Mystical Ideas and Practices of Quṭb al-Dīn Shīrāzī

John T. Walbridge

LIFE AND RELIGIOUS PRACTICES

Quṭb al-Dīn Shīrāzī (634/1236-710/1311) was a scientist by profession, a student of Nasīr al-Dīn Ṭūsī (d. 672/1273). He wrote extensively on medicine—his first interest—astronomy, mathematics, philosophy, and the 'traditional' sciences. A man of sophistication and culture, he played chess and the *rabāb*, both expertly. He liked wine and good company and had a sense of humor sharp enough to make him enemies in high places. Clearly, he led a full and worldly life.[1]

Quṭb al-Dīn was also a Sufi. His mystical inclinations made themselves felt in various ways. He wrote a commentary on Shihāb al-Dīn Yaḥyā Suhrawardī's[2] *Philosophy of Illumination (Ḥikmat al-ishrāq),* perhaps the most influential work of mystical philosophy in Islam. He wrote about the World of Images *('ālam al-mithāl),* a concept that played an important role in justifying the mystical imagination. His philosophical encyclopædia, *The Pearly Crown,* closes with a discussion of mysticism that is, Quṭb al-Dīn assures us, the most important part of the book. How did Sufism fit into the world-view of such a man?

Quṭb al-Dīn came from a family of Sufis in Shīrāz. His father Ḍiyā' al-Dīn Kāzarūnī, though by profession a physician, had travelled to Baghdad as a young man to study with the renowned Shihāb al-Dīn 'Umar Suhrawardī, the author of the Sufi textbook *'Awārif al-Ma'ārif.* There is a persistent—but unproven—report that Quṭb al-Dīn was a close relative, perhaps a nephew, of the poet Sa'dī (c. 590/1184 to between 691/1292 and 695/1296), who was about the same age as Quṭb al-Dīn's father and who had also studied with Suhrawardī.

When Quṭb al-Dīn was ten, his father invested him with the Sufi frock of blessing (the *khirqa-i tabarruk,* which did not indicate formal discipleship). One of his

1. I have discussed Quṭb al-Dīn's life and works in adequate detail elsewhere. For further information see *The Science of Mystic Lights* (Cambridge, MA: Center for Middle East Studies, Harvard University, forthcoming), particularly chap. 1 where the sources for the biographical information I have given here can be found and App. C, and 'The Political Thought of Quṭb al-Dīn al-Shīrāzī' in Charles Butterworth, ed., *The Political Aspects of Islamic Philosophy,* forthcoming, chap. 9.

2. There are three Suhrawardīs who feature in this essay, two of them unfortunately named Shihāb al-Dīn: Shihāb al-Dīn Yaḥyā, the author of *The Philosophy of Illumination,* was a mystical philosopher executed in Aleppo on Saladin's orders in 587/1191. 'Abdu'l-Qādir Abū Najīb al-Suhrawardī (d. 563/1168) was an influential Sufi teacher in Baghdad and the common spiritual ancestor of both the Suhrawardiyya and Kubrawiyya orders. His nephew, Abū Ḥafṣ 'Umar Suhrawardī (d. 632/1234), was the real founder of the Suhrawardiyya order.

teachers, Shams al-Dīn Kīshī, was a Sufi as well, but Quṭb al-Dīn only mentions him as a teacher of the rational sciences.[1] Quṭb al-Dīn must also have had contact with Najīb al-Dīn 'Alī ibn Buzghush Shīrāzī (d. 678/1281), another disciple of Suhrawardī who had received an *ijāza* from the master, settled in Shīrāz and established a *khānaqāh* where he taught. This man was the leading Sufi in Shīrāz at the time and the representative of the Suhrawardī Order. He would undoubtedly have known Quṭb al-Dīn's father.

Despite his family's association with the Suhrawardiyya, Quṭb al-Dīn actually received his *khirqa* of discipleship from an early representative of the Kubrāwiyya, one Muḥyī'l-Dīn Aḥmad, the son and student of Najm al-Dīn 'Alī ibn Abī'l-Ma'ālī, a student of Najm al-Dīn Kubrā (d. 618/1221).[2] We should remember, however, that Najm al-Dīn Kubrā had been the student of two students of Abū'l-Najib Suhrawardī (Shihāb al-Dīn Suhrawardī's uncle and teacher). Quṭb al-Dīn was thirty at the time and was probably in Marāgha where he was studying with Ṭūsī.

QUṬB AL-DĪN, RŪMI, AND QŪNAWĪ

In about 672/1273 Quṭb al-Dīn came to Konya. Sufis, like other classes of Muslim intellectuals, set great store on meeting prominent teachers. Quṭb al-Dīn surely hastened to meet the two giants of mysticism who lived in that town, Rumi and Ṣadr al-Dīn Qūnawī.

> Quṭb al-Dīn Shīrāzī, at the time when he was in Konya, came to visit Mawlawī [Rumi], but Mawlawī perceived that Quṭb al-Dīn had come to test him, not to acquire blessing. Therefore, he sat silent for a long time, and finally told this story:
>
> Ṣadr-i Jahān, the scholar of Bukhārā, used to leave his *madrasa* every day and go to his garden, passing by the corner of the mosque. Next to that mosque a beggar sat by the side of the road, and every day he would ask Ṣadr-i Jahān for something. That learned man, however, never gave him anything. After a number of years had passed this way, the beggar said to his friends, "I'll lie down here, and you throw a robe over me and pretend I'm dead." The next day the beggar's friends did this. When Ṣadr-i Jahān gave them a few dirhams, the poor man stood up and threw off the robe. When Ṣadr-i Jahān saw that he was not dead, he said to him, "If you hadn't been dead, I wouldn't have given you anything!"

---

1. He is said to have been the disciple of one Shaykh Jibrā'īl in Baghdad. Kamāl al-Din 'Abd al-Razzāq al-Kāshānī, the famous commentator on Ibn 'Arabi, spent some time with him at the recommendation of his own master. See Mudarris Riḍavī, *Aḥwāl wa-āthār-i...Khwāja Naṣīr al-Dīn al-Ṭūsī.* (Tehran University Press 1334 A.H.sh., Intishārāt, no. 282) pp. 106-8.
2. Quṭb al-Dīn Shīrāzī, *Durrat al-tāj li-ghurrat al-Dubāj* [The Pearly Crown for Dubāj's Brow], 'Khātima', Book 4, pt. 2, ch. 2, p.604.32-35.The last section of this work is a book on mysticism in two parts, the second of which is divided into ten chapters. For this essay I have used MS. 4720 of the Majlis Library, Tehran, in which the section on mysticism occupies pp. 596-620. All further references to the *Pearly Crown* in this paper are drawn from the book on mysticism and will be given in the form: "*Crown* 2:3, p.606.20." The numbers represent respectively the part in the book on mysticism, the chapter, and the page and line number in the Majlis MS. This should be clear enough for anyone trying to trace a reference in this or another MS.

By this story Mawlawī was saying to Quṭb al-Dīn, "Until you die, I can say nothing to you. If you want to learn something from me, you must be empty of your pride and fancy." Quṭb al-Dīn rose and never came back to Mawlawī. [1]

Rumi's biographer Aflākī gives a different version, slightly more complimentary to Quṭb al-Dīn but not as funny.[2] Quṭb al-Dīn probably called on Rumi out of curiosity, but the proud young scientist and the old and passionate dervish would not have found common ground. Quṭb al-Dīn would scarcely have been prepared to make the sort of spiritual sacrifice that Rumi would have demanded of him.

A much more significant contact was with Ṣadr al-Dīn Qūnawī (d. 673/1274). Qūnawī was more like Quṭb al-Dīn, a master of the whole field of Islamic learning and the principal custodian of the intellectual heritage of Ibn 'Arabī. He drew hundreds of students to Konya, most of whom studied the exoteric sciences with him. He had carried on a debate by letter with Quṭb al-Dīn's teacher Ṭūsī about philosophy. Quṭb al-Dīn's main activity in Konya was the study of Baghawī's *Sharḥ al-Sunna,* a comprehensive collection of *ḥadīth* popular at the time. Quṭb al-Dīn made his own copy of the book and read it out to Qūnawī for correction. In later years his authority to transmit this book was a source of pride to him. He also says that he learned the practice of continuous recollection of God or *dhikr* from him and lists him among the masters with whom he associated after leaving Shaykh Muḥyī'l-Dīn Aḥmad. However, Quṭb al-Dīn was not a serious student of Qūnawī—he does not seem to have been in Konya long enough, for one thing—and he never cites or quotes Qūnawī by name in his later works.

LATER LIFE

Though Quṭb al-Dīn "always wore Sufi garb,"[3] the presumption must be that his religion through middle age was intellectual and not especially scrupulous. He drank wine "and sat with the scorners." He was a musician. However, in Tabriz in his last years he became very pious, following "the religion of old women." He taught the Koran and *ḥadīth* in mosques, frequently participating in the congrega-

---

1. Muḥyī'l-Dīn Abī'l-Wafā, *al-Jawāhir al-muḍī'a fī ṭabaqāt al-ḥanafīya* (1st ed.; Hyderabad: Nizāmiyya 1332).
2. One day Quṭb al-Dīn Shīrāzī came to call upon Mawlānā and asked, "What is your path?" He replied, "Our path is to die and to deliver our capital to heaven. Until we die, we do not arrive, for as Ṣadr-i Jahān said, 'So long as you do not die, you cannot obtain anything.'" Quṭb al-Dīn said, "Alas! What shall I do?" Mawlānā replied, "Just what I do." Then he began to dance and recite this quatrain

I said, "What shall I do?"
He said, "Just what I do."
I said, "Better than this remedy,
behold what I do."
He turned his face towards me and said,
"O seeker of religion,
ever attend to this,
this which I do."

—Shams al-Dīn al-Aflākī, *Manāqib al-'ārifīn,* Intishārāt-i Anjuman-i Tārīkh-i Turk 3:3 (Ankara: Chāpkhāna-i Anjuman-i Tārīkh-i Turk 1959), p.176.

3. Ibn Ḥajar al-'Asqalanī, *al-Durar al-kāmina fī a'yān al-mi'a al-thāmina* (Hyderabad 1350), p. 76.

tional prayer, and wrote a large Koranic commentary. Several close friends were Sufis, notably the poet Humām al-Dīn Tabrīzī (d. 714/1314), Ṣadr al-Dīn Tabrīzī (known as Ṣadr al-Dīn Faqīh Zāhid whom he mentions as one of the masters with whom he studied after leaving his original master), and Qāḍī Majd al-Dīn Ismā'īl ibn Yaḥyā al-'Umarī al-Shīrāzī (670/1271-2–756/1355), the long-time *Qāḍī al-Quḍāt* of Fārs.[1]

THE MYSTICISM CHAPTER OF THE *PEARLY CROWN* AND ITS AUTHORSHIP

Quṭb al-Dīn's encyclopedia, *The Pearly Crown for Dubāj's Brow (Durrat al-tāj li-ghurrat al-Dubāj),* is one of his two well-known philosophical works, the other being his commentary on Suhrawardī Maqtūl's *Philosophy of Illumination.* It was written in Persian for a certain Amīr Dubāj, a petty ruler in Gīlān, and was completed about 705/1306, a few years before his death. It was written for educated laymen. The heart—and probably the original content—of this large work were six books on philosophy and mathematics. At the suggestion of his patron Quṭb al-Dīn added a *khātima* or appendix consisting of four books discussing religious law, dogmatic theology, practical philosophy (that is, philosophical ethics, economics and politics) and mysticism. The whole book would come to about 2500 printed pages.

The section on mysticism, entitled 'Wayfaring on the Path of the Absolute,' is the last in the book and would amount to about a hundred printed pages. It has two chapters, the first on mystical theology and psychology and the second laying out a rule for mystical life, directed mainly to novices. Like the rest of the book, it is written in a heavily Arabicized Persian, the language of a scholar educated in Arabic. Very often Persian and Arabic words are used interchangeable for the same concepts *(yigānigī* and *waḥdat,* for example). The most clearly 'Persian' feature of the style is the terrifying complexity of the sentences which often descend into a thicket of interlocking subclauses from which no main verb ever emerges. Quṭb al-Dīn, however, did not write this chapter.

There is an unpublished book on Sufi practice, *Manāhij al-'ibād ila' l-ma'ād,* by Sa'd (or Sa'īd) al-Dīn Farghānī (d. 695/1295), a student of Qūnawī who wrote several other works on mysticism.[2] This book has two parts: first, a summary of Muslim law from a Sufi viewpoint, and, second, an account of mystical theology, psychology, and etiquette. Farghānī's work had been written by 686/1287 and so predated Quṭb al-Dīn's work by about twenty years. Though I have not seen the *Manāhij,* the identity of the *Manāhij* with the chapters on *fiqh* and mysticism in the

1. *Crown* 2: 2, p. 605. 27 -29. See *Encyclopædia of Islam,* 2nd ed., s.v. 'Humām al-Din Tabrīzī.' I have found no information on Ṣadr al-Dīn Tabrīzī.
2. This book also exists in Arabic under the title of *Madārij al-i'tiqād,* translated by one Abu'l-Faḍl Muḥammad ibn Idris al-Bidlīsī. Farghānī also wrote a Persian commentary on the *Ṭā'īya* of Ibn al-Fāriḍ called *Mashāriq al-darārī* ed. Sayyid Jamāl al-Dīn Āshtīyānī [Mashhad: Chāpkhāna-i Dānishgāh-i-Firdawsī 1357/1398), which also exists in Arabic under the title *Muntahā al-madārik* (Istanbul, 1293). With exemplary Sufi humility Farghānī seems to have left behind almost no information about his own life apart from the references to his masters found in the *Manāhij.* These are the basis of Jāmi's notice in *Nafaḥāt al-uns* (ed. Mahdī Tawhīdīpūr; (Tehran, 1336 A.H.sh.), pp.559-62. On Farghānī see the study by W.C. Chittick in the present volume.

Pearly Crown can be established by two proofs. First, the section headings of the first and second parts of the *Manāhij* are identical with those in the *Pearly Crown.*[1] Second, Quṭb al- Dīn himself says that the mysticism chapter was written by someone else,[2] and Jāmī in his biography of Farghānī quotes several passages from the *Manāhij* which agree word for word with the corresponding passages of the *Pearly Crown.*

It would be helpful to know something more specific about Farghānī's life. His name indicates that his family was from Farghāna, quite probably refugees from the Mongol incursions of the early thirteenth century. We know that he was a disciple of Shaykh Abū Najīb al-Suhrawardī (d. 563/1168) in Shīrāz and a serious student of Qūnawī in Konya.[3] He must have been Quṭb al-Dīn's age or a few years older. Thus, they most likely knew each other in Shīrāz and probably studied with many of the same teachers there. They would have met again in Konya and possibly in Tabrīz, for Quṭb al-Dīn's friend Humām al-Dīn Tabrīzī (d. 714/1314), was a disciple of Farghānī.

Though their lives were parallel in many respects, they differed in that Farghānī became a Sufi master with an expert knowledge of the theosophy of the school of Ibn 'Arabī and the practice of the early Suhrawardiyya, whereas Quṭb al-Dīn devoted his adult life to the rational and mathematical sciences and to exoteric religious sciences such as law and rhetoric. I thus propose that Quṭb al-Dīn chose to use Farghānī's work because he believed it to be an authoritative presentation of the kind of Sufism of which he himself was an adherent, written by a man he had known and respected, and covering a subject to which he attached great importance but of which he did not himself have expert knowledge. Moreover, its account of *fiqh,* which Quṭb al-Dīn used for another chapter of the *Pearly Crown,* presented Islamic religious law in a mystical way—writing, for example, of the "mysteries *(asrār)*" of the various religious obligations.

The reader should therefore bear in mind that the system of mystical belief and practice summarized below is only that of Quṭb al-Dīn by adoption.

THE *PEARLY CROWN'S* MYSTICAL THEOLOGY[4]

Since mysticism is concerned with the experiential relation of the soul with God, mystical theory must begin with an account of man and God and their relationship, and thus, of creation and cosmology. The solutions to these problems will determine the goal of an individual's personal quest, his expectations, and the character of his mystical exercises. Therefore, Quṭb al-Dīn begins his discussion of mysticism with two premises drawn from metaphysics:

---

1. The outline of the *Manāhij* is found in 'Abd al-Raḥmān ibn Aḥmad Jāmī, *Naqd al-fuṣūṣ,* ed. William C. Chittick (Tehran: Imperial Iranian Academy of Philosophy, 1977), pp. 517-19. I am grateful to Prof. Chittick for pointing this out to me as well as much other advice concerning this paper.
2. *Crown* 2:2, p. 604:17ff.
3. *Crown* 2:2, pp. 604:17ff, 605:22-25.
4. This and the following section on the human soul are based on Crown 1, pp. 596-600.

> It should be understood—may God guide thee on the Straight Path—that God is unique in his Essence, Names and Attributes... Just as true Unity is a concomitant of His holy Essence, Names and Attributes, so duration and eternity are concomitants of the Unity of Existence of his degree... Therefore, the more complete the relation of something to the existence of His Oneness, the more lasting will be its life and permanence.

Likewise, composition and multiplicity are associated with oblivion and corruption. This is, of course, the philosophical commonplace that only the simple is imperishable. Thus the angels, which are one and simple in their existence, are not subject to corruption or annihilation.

Metaphysicians from the days of the Greeks until Kant put an end to such speculations were vexed by the question of how the exalted and simple God of philosophy could be responsible for the multifarious and untidy world of the senses and, conversely, how such a world could have any relation to God—in Neoplatonic terms, the problem of the emanation of the many from the One. To this the philosophers of the monotheistic religions added the question of God's knowledge of particulars—how to explain divine Providence in philosophical terms—for the pagan thinkers led by Aristotle were content to limit God's knowledge to universals, to allow him to know man but not Socrates.

Quṭb al-Dīn begins with the famous *ḥadīth qudsī,* "I was a hidden treasure, but I desired to be known. Therefore, I created the universe that I might be known." He rephrases the second sentence in purely philosophical terms as "The bringing to being of the universe and its inhabitants was concomitant *(lāzim uftād).*" This is a precise formulation which eliminates any hint of volition in the process by explaining creation as a slightly indirect consequence of God's Essence. So the world and its inhabitants come to be, not as a result of the awful and arbitrary divine fiat of the Koranic "Be!" but as an eternal consequence of the divine Essence, which is not, however, really touched by its creatures.

It is existence *(wujūd)* that binds and separates God and His creatures. Existence, Quṭb al-Dīn explains, is a concomitant of Unity; true existence in its fullest sense belongs only to God, for only He is perfectly one. The existence of anything else is only accidental and metaphorical. In other words, existence, which in God is a concomitant of His Unity, occurs outside Him accidentally and metaphorically so that He might be known, while Unity, which is a concomitant of His essence, has its shadow in the unity of the composites. This is "the ray or shadow of the true Unity," established by God in every degree of creation—a doctrine strongly reminiscent of Ibn 'Arabī's description of the dust, itself emanated from the Absolute, upon which the forms are emanated. The existence and form of a thing cannot be conceived of as separate, for existence is a concomitant of the unity expressed by the form.

The world of spirits had priority in creation and manifestation, we are told, since its simplicity gives it the most perfect relation to the Absolute. Thus, the exalted spirits and the Most High Pen were given existence directly and the Preserved Tablet was given existence by means of the Pen. Then, by means of the Pen—the First Intellect—the realities of all things are inscribed on the Tablet in accordance with pre-eternal divine knowledge, each thing receiving an individual spiritual form in accordance with its rank. The Tablet is the master pattern of the world and the storehouse of fate, the intermediary between God in His Unity and the world in its multiplicity, the means whereby particulars may find some relation to the Godhead.

This theory resembles Ibn 'Arabī's doctrine of 'permanent archetypes' *(a'yān thābita)*. Although it is aligned with philosophy against such theories as Kalām atomism—both view God's relation with the world as being most significantly expressed in form and order—differs in its view of this. In Hellenistic and earlier Islamic philosophy larger regularities are important while individuals in their variety are imperfect expressions of the ideal. In this theory, each individual being has its own quintessence which it must work out in its own way.

This cosmology may be compared to the Illuminationist philosophy of Yaḥyā Suhrawardī, to which tradition Quṭb al-Dīn himself adhered. The symbolism of light does not appear here (nor in the philosophical chapters of the *Pearly Crown)*, but this is not essential to Illuminationist theory. The use of the term 'existence' *(wujūd)* is problematic from the Illuminationist point of view, but it can be justified here either as a loose formulation suitable for this kind of text or a legitimate use that does not reify the term improperly. In any case, it is not existence that is the important topic: it is providence and the metaphysical basis of individuality. For these subjects, Illuminationists would find this account quite acceptable. Moreover, this is not technical metaphysics, as we see from the frequent use of terms such as 'Pen' derived from the cosmology of the Koran and the *ḥadīth*. Thus, this account falls somewhere between technical metaphysics—as found, for example, earlier in the *Pearly Crown*—and the visionary recitals of Suhrawardī and Avicenna.

THE HUMAN SOUL

When the human body receives its form, its receptivity is such that it receives a trace of the Universal Soul. This individual soul is manifested in the animal spirit. Like its source, this soul has two aspects: the outer, which is the individual managing soul, and the inner, which is the immaterial spirit. The managing soul is called the 'soul which commands [to evil],' for it tends to be so closely attached to the animal spirit that it takes on blameworthy traits that are, in fact, distortions of plant and animal traits: sloth, anger, greed, etc.

The inner aspect of the human soul is the immaterial spirit *(rūḥ-i mujarrad)*. This is the source of praiseworthy qualities: humility, justice, piety, etc. Since the spirit, in and of itself, is not capable of seeking its Creator, the Universal Soul intervenes before God, who has the First Intellect—the Pen—send a ray of intellect upon the spirit to enable it to worship and attain knowledge. Nevertheless, the spirit, even when infused with intellect, cannot always prevent the soul from being led astray. So attractive and deceptive is the sensible world that all the faculties, including the intellect, may fall under the sway of the commanding soul and be perverted to its purposes. Thus may the soul forget the inevitability of its return to its Creator.

This description of the origin of the soul,[1] its faculties, and its weaknesses is

1. Quṭb al-Dīn may have believed in the preexistence of the soul and reincarnation, though he does not seem to have been eager for this to be widely known. This may be in the background of certain of his explanations. See my *Science of Mystic Lights* (forthcoming), chap.4.

derived from the philosophical tradition, though it is couched in religious terminology. Here it is used to form the basis of a mystical psychology.

Prophecy is the factor which counteracts the human tendency towards spiritual degeneracy. Knowing man's weakness, God in His wisdom sends Prophets with laws couched in inimitable verses so that man might have light to be guided by, and a scale by which "moderation," the image of Divine Unity, might be measured and thereby realized. This moderation so frequently mentioned by Quṭb al-Dīn may be identified with the 'Straight Path' of Islam. By means of the Law man acquires a knowledge of God and His attributes, and glimpses the spirit's true goal. The spirit then rouses the intellect, and the intellect the commanding soul. The soul thus can change its own nature so that it no longer commands to evil. The spirit's awareness of its true goal is called 'inner faith,' whereas the awakening of the soul constitutes its entrance into the circle of Islam, 'submission.' There is a third stage associated with this, beneficence *(iḥsān),* but this comes later in the mystical path.

This has implications for the mystical life. First, prophetic religion will generally be necessary at the beginning to reach the spirit and rouse the soul, probably through appeals to the imagination. Second, the imitation of God, which is the reason for man's creation, is achieved primarily through the ordinances of Divine Laws, for they are the means to establish moderation, the truest copy of Divine Unity. Third, asceticism must be the beginning of the Path, for the animal and material faculties must be subdued. Fourth, asceticism is not the goal of the Path, nor is the knowledge of God and His Attributes that is acquired by obedience to the Law: the true goal is a more perfect knowledge of God acquired by the communion of the human spirit with the Divine Spirit.

For Quṭb al-Dīn, in accordance with normal Sufi theory, the spiritual conditions of the soul were divided into temporary states *(aḥwāl)* and permanent stations *(maqāmāt).* He placed spiritual conditions into two great classes—repentance and asceticism. Each class encompassed a considerable number of possible states in no particular order, but all associated within the larger class.

Thus the seeker in the station of repentance experiences a number of states, in each of which he gradually progresses. When he passes into asceticism, all the states of repentance become stations—permanent conditions of his soul. In addition, each state begins in submission and ends in faith, so that the novice first keeps watch on his soul in obedience to the command of his master and ends doing so out of love of God. This corresponds in each case to the transformation of the soul from 'commanding' to 'blaming' (that is, blaming itself). Each aspect of the human soul requires a similar spiritual journey for its rectification. The only fixed order for the states is that one must master all the states of a given station before going on from repentance to asceticism or beyond.

Quṭb al-Dīn held that the individual has a personality that is not changed on the mystical path, although its manner of expression is.[1] Thus the greedy man does not lose his acquisitiveness, but the greed may be transformed into eagerness to acquire every virtue. Likewise, a proud man becomes zealous in the defense of the Faith,

---

1. His explanation of the punishment of the soul in the afterlife is exactly analogous to this. See my *Science of Mystic Lights,* chap. 4.

and so on. Progress is not automatic, for the soul has much trickery and self-interest, some hidden deep in the heart. Therefore constant attention is required if it is not to degenerate into hypocrisy.

THE MYSTICAL RULE OF THE *PEARLY CROWN*

The second part of Quṭb al-Dīn's treatment of mysticism,[1] entitled 'Dealings with mankind and external manners,' is a Sufi rule laying out standards of conduct for the mystic in his relations with his fellows and with society as a whole. The rule is designed to facilitate the training of the soul characteristic of the first stage of mystical life, but it applies to all mystics—for not only does even a great master retain some trace of human failings, but each mystic must avoid being a test or burden to his fellows.

The basic fact of the Path is known by reason: that the attachment of the soul, the lower self, or *nafs* to the world must be broken for the spirit to realize its goal. But reason can discover only general rules—such as the necessity to accept the authority of a single master—and is thus an insufficient basis for the organization of an actual community, as any Islamic political philosopher would know. Therefore, a law is required, Islamic in the case of Quṭb al-Dīn's readers, that must be scrupulously obeyed. This is why Quṭb al-Dīn normally begins the explanation of a topic with the relevant aspects of mystical psychology and then gives its legal requirements. He thinks that the mystic should try to satisfy the conditions of all four legal schools. Several times he gives a comparative legal analysis of important points.

Moreover, the seeker should not be content with obeying the Law but should go on to satisfy the requirements of justice—the spirit of the Law—and the virtues of generosity connected with each point of Law. Therefore, a merchant mystic must arrange his contracts to be legally valid under all the schools of the Law, must strive to practice his business in such a way as not to do to another what he would not want done to himself—by not overrating his merchandise, for example—and must practice generosity in his trade, by granting better terms to the poor than the rich and by being lenient in payment terms. By this means the Law serves not merely as the basis of ordering the community but becomes a school of virtue and self-control, becoming a most valuable tool on the Sufi Path.

The third basis of Quṭb al-Dīn's rule is the etiquette *(ādāb)* of the Sufi brethren, a set of legally arbitrary rules designed to ensure the smooth functioning of the mystical community and the progress of each seeker. These rules are based on two principles: humbling the lower self and avoiding offense to others. Thus to refrain from licking one's plate at meals and wiping one's hands on bread is both a discipline and a way of avoiding giving offense to others and thereby testing them and disturbing their tranquillity.

Finally, it is worth noting two characteristic themes of the practical parts of Quṭb al-Dīn's mystical theory. The first is the close connection with ordinary life. Although he assumed the *khānaqāh* in the background, his rule seems to be intended in general for those involved in ordinary life. When he discusses work, for example,

1. *Crown* 2:1-10, pp. 600-620.

he is almost exclusively concerned with those who labor for their sustenance, not with those supported by endowments. Likewise, he gives detailed rules for dealings with various classes of non-mystics. Moreover, though the world is distracting, it is not especially evil in itself. Nor is there any great asceticism in his rule but rather complete self-discipline in ordinary things.

On the other hand, his mystical system is characterized by earnestness in all things. Every act in every sphere of life must be weighed for its effect on the life of the spirit. This outlook is utterly different from the simple-hearted joy and delight in Divine mercy which shines through such mystics as Rumi—and different as well from the ecstatic passion of Ḥallāj and Bisṭāmī. Nevertheless, we must bear in mind Quṭb al-Dīn's statement that knowledge of the Law will bring one to the Paradise of Forms and its eternal pleasures, but it is only knowledge of the states of the soul which will bring one the nearness to the Divine Presence that is the inner meaning and the spirit of Paradise. Ultimately, the rules he gives can only lead the seeker to the door of the court of the Desired One.

The Role of the Master (Shaykh)

"The learned are the heirs of the Prophets," said the Prophet. Few Sufis would disagree with Quṭb al-Dīn's explanation that the learned in the Law *(sharī'a)* are only heirs in a lower and external sense: the true heirs are the learned in the mystical sciences of the Path *(ṭarīqa)* and of Reality *(ḥaqīqa)*. The Law concerns the body's intent to return to its origin, the Path relates to the soul's journey towards its goal, while the science of Reality concerns the ultimate point of return. Since the Prophets, however, not only had a perfect relationship with God but also perfectly fulfilled the duties of relationship with men, their heirs must act likewise.

Since the responsibility of the Sufi master towards the novice is very great—for the master accepts total obedience from him and total control over him, as we shall see—his motives must be completely free from selfishness, and he must be truly guided by God. Likewise, he must guide the lives of his novices with firmness, tact and wisdom. The spiritual director's situation is comparable to those learned in the external sciences. The master craftsmen and fathers are also responsible, within the spheres with which they are concerned, for the development of those committed to their care. Thus, both the master of external sciences and the master craftsman must teach their apprentices every aspect of those sciences and arts suiting their capacity and attainment while keeping them from those which are not suitable. The father, while expecting obedience from his child, should not burden him beyond his capacity so as to lead him into disobedience. Similarly, the Sufi master must set the novice to such tasks as will help advance his spiritual condition.

Quṭb al-Dīn's philosophy of education is derived from his conception of the lower soul and the difficulty of the seeker's freeing himself unaided from its bonds. Thus, the duty of the novice is to deliver himself completely into the hands of the master, "like a corpse in the hands of the washer." Not only is the soul strong in its attachments to the world, it is devious. To be freed from its bonds the seeker must submit to discipline and must have an outside observer astute enough to see through hypocrisies of the soul opaque to himself. Thus the seeker needs a mystical master, the Shaykh. The first duty of the seeker is to find a suitable master to whom he may commit himself. The second duty is to submit himself utterly to this master, resigning all initiative to him and seeking continuously not to disturb him. It is a fundamental principle of Quṭb al-Dīn's philosophy of education that the student not only does not know, but does not know what it is that he should learn. Thus the novice is counselled to keep in mind the story of Moses and Khiḍr.[1]

Closely related to this is the etiquette governing the *khirqa* (the Sufi frock), instruction in *dhikr,* and association with masters. The *khirqa* is the patched woolen frock, the symbol of poverty and humility which is the traditional garment of the Sufi. The original significance of the master presenting the novice with his *khirqa* was, of course, to transfer a blessing, just as a king presented an honored servant with a piece of his own clothing to reward him. In Sufism the presentation of the *khirqa* was a rite of passage marking the point at which the master considered his novice to have reached spiritual maturity. By extension the *khirqa* symbolized the Sufi's spiritual parentage, since it was thought possible to trace the chain *(silsila)* of masters back to the beginnings of Islam. The *khirqa* was thus the external symbol of the mystic's claim to partake in the esoteric heritage of Islam. The *khirqa* granted in this sense was called the *'khirqa* of discipleship' and could be received from only one master. Quṭb al-Dīn distinguished it from the *'khirqa* of blessing,' which could be received from many masters.

The inner aspect of this outward symbol was the instruction in *dhikr,* the most important spiritual exercise of the Sufis. This too could only be received from one master, though we may assume from Quṭb al-Dīn's own practice that this prohibition referred specifically to novices, not to advanced Sufis comparing notes on spiritual matters. Only after the death of one's first master or after receiving an *ijāza* from him was it permissible to associate with other masters. This was called "relationship by service and companionship."

At this point something may be said about Quṭb al-Dīn's and Farghānī's *silsila.* Quṭb al-Dīn traced his spiritual genealogy through two intermediaries to Najm al-Dīn Kubrā and traced the latter's lineage through one intermediary to Abu'l-Najīb Suhrawardī. Farghānī's lineage was traced to Shihāb al-Dīn Suhrawardī through his disciple in Shīrāz, Najīb al-Dīn 'Alī ibn Buzghush, and from there once again to Abu'l-Najīb. There is no indication that the followers of a particular master form a school or group. Rather each preserves mystical knowledge and tradition, passed down ultimately from Muḥammad.

Thus, it is quite natural for Quṭb al-Dīn, though a 'Kubrawī,' to use a work written by one of the 'Suhrawardiyya'—terms which he never uses. For Quṭb al-Dīn, at least, the Kubrawiyya and the Suhrawardiyya were not separate movements: each were followers of the same chain of masters, separated only since the time of Abū'l-Najīb Suhrawardī a century and a half earlier. In any case, Quṭb al-Dīn was himself connected to the Suhrawardiyya through his early experiences in Shīrāz. I think that he would have denied that he belonged to a different 'Order' from his father or Farghānī and admitted only that he was the disciple of a different master professing the same mystical tradition.

1. Koran 18: 60-62

Social Relations and Classes

We know from a *ḥadīth qudsī* that God considers love and friendship the best of states. Friendship, in turn, is based on some sort of relationship or homogeneity between the friends. There are, therefore, various classes of friendship based on the strength of the common attitude. Quṭb al-Dīn distinguished three degrees of friendship:

a) Friendship based only on membership in one species. This is the basis of human society in general, and its sign is that seeks only worldly and personal goods.

b) Friendship based on a specific attribute, such as that among those belonging to one city or religion. Its sign is that it seeks otherworldly ends and that each desires for his friend what he desires for himself.

c) Friendship based upon a most specific attribute, such as that which binds Prophets, saints and people of the Sufi Path. Its sign is preferring one friend's welfare over one's own.

The existence of these classes implies that the mystic's dealing with each should be different, in accordance with the principle that "a man is of the religion of his friend." Therefore the mystic, while behaving courteously and correctly towards all, should exercise a certain caution in dealing with those not committed to the Sufi Path. With the third class, however, he should wholeheartedly associate. The hallmark of his dealings should be extreme scrupulousness in preferring others to himself. Accordingly, he should make every effort not to be a burden or test to others. Likewise, the mystic should be respectful to the great, humble with his equals, and kindly and indulgent to servants and inferiors—but in all cases association with handsome youths should be avoided.

This section ends with a curious little coda on the political life of the mystical community: When two people become companions of the above-mentioned third degree, the most intelligent, ascetic, pious, and learned of them must become the leader whom the others follow in all things, for as long as their wishes are not unified in all things by obedience to a common leader, they will be divided. Thus, if something happens, the sincere one will suspect his own soul and strive to dominate it, so that the truth will be manifested. Otherwise, division will result. Should anyone commit an offense, he must humble himself before the master, who will give judgement and impose punishment. No one else may burden or censure the offender. Only in this way will the unity and integrity of the group be maintained. Quṭb al-Dīn was nothing if not authoritarian—for according to his psychology even if a man wishes to improve himself, this is scarcely possible without submission to a (superior) outside authority, capable of imposing discipline and unmasking the hidden deceits of the lower self.

The Mysticism of Work

The physical sustenance needed to preserve the body during the soul's mystical quest may be obtained in any of four ways:

a) by direct reliance on God, appropriate for those who trust in God *(al-mutawakkilīn)* and those who are completely absorbed in spiritual affairs and inner work.

b) By begging for necessities, appropriate for those who want only the bare necessities from the world and those who are unable to work.

c) By the income from charitable endowments, appropriate only for those who are occupied with worship and do not wish to be distracted by the need to think about worldly things.

d) By labor and wages, for the generality of believers high and low. This last is of most general concern.

Legally, labor falls into three classes. The first, government service, should be avoided by the sincere, since government revenues are almost invariably tainted—as indeed are endowments originating from the government. If compelled to serve the government, the sincere must carefully avoid doing injustice. The soldier, especially if he receives the revenues of a fief, must be constantly prepared for military service.[1] In other sorts of labor, the sincere seeker must first satisfy the minimum legal requirements and then go on to practice the virtues and supererogatory acts associated with each: first fulfilling the letter of the Law, then fulfilling the spirit of the Law, that is, its application in a spirit of generosity. Quṭb al-Dīn comments that the best occupations for the sincere mystic are professions such as shopkeeping and tailoring that are of general benefit.

Marriage and Celibacy

Quṭb al-Dīn belonged to the small minority of Muslims who defended celibacy. He points out that the relevant legal texts are confused and contradictory, reflecting divergent circumstances, individuals and time, but he argues that the early Muslims preferred marriage to celibacy for three reasons:

a) The Prophet Muḥammad had spoken against Christian celibacy since it had become excessive, although it was originally justified by the exalted spirituality of Jesus and his followers.

b) The early Muslims lived in a holy age and were protected against the evil consequences of marriage.

c) In those early days it was necessary to have as many Muslim teachers as possible.

By Quṭb al-Dīn's times these factors no longer applied, as certain ascetics and mystics had long realized. In addition, legal sustenance had become so hard to come by that it was unfair to link another's fate to one's own (probably unsuccessful) efforts to obtain licit food and drink. Quṭb al-Dīn, like many Muslims through the centuries had a very low opinion of the spiritual attainments of own his times, a view that does not seem to be completely justified historically.

Nevertheless, for the spiritually advanced, marriage to pious women is allowable, desirable and beneficial, though never for the sake of wealth and beauty. The legitimate reason for marriage is to preserve chastity and seek children for the sake of God. It should never be an excuse for the forbidden. He who marries should try

1. A soldier might receive the revenues of a particular territory in return for maintenance of a specified military force. It may reasonably be supposed that in accordance with the ancient traditions of military contracting that those who received the revenues frequently failed to fulfill the duties associated with them.

to make the wedding correct according to all the Islamic legal schools. He should deal with his wife gently and on her own level, and he should not act so as to draw suspicion on himself and his family. He should scrupulously follow the sunna and observe proper etiquette in sexual relations—keeping a reverent attitude (in this, as in everything else) and showing tender concern for the woman's happiness. He should not, however, allow his family to become a distraction for him.

This chapter is typical of Quṭb al-Dīn's approach to the practical aspects of the mystical life. The mystic must make every effort to follow the Law and observe proper etiquette, thus making every situation an opportunity to acquire virtues and holiness. He should be solicitous in his concern with the well-being and happiness of spiritually ordinary people while not allowing himself to be distracted by them. He may partake of the licit pleasures of the world, but only after progressing to a stage where they no longer really matter to him.

Rules of Travel

According to the legal analysis with which Quṭb al-Dīn begins this chapter, there are three sorts of travel:

a) Obligatory travel, such as *ḥajj, jihād* and response to the invitation of one's parents: travel which is enjoined individually or collectively by the Law.

b) Travel of mourning and virtue, which entails reinforcing *jihād,* visiting the tombs of Prophets and saints and profiting from the hardships of traveling—journeys undertaken to increase piety and virtue.

c) Permissible travel, undertaken for the sake of experience or adventure. This is of no concern to the sincere seekers.[1]

Travel must not be undertaken frivolously and must be with the permission of one's parents and spiritual master. Whatever its other purposes, it should also be used as a tool for the subjugation of the lower soul. Therefore, the traveller should not take advantage of the dispensations allowed to the traveller in the Law. Second, no special efforts should be taken to alleviate the hardships of travel—by riding instead of walking for example—in order to profit from discomfort. Finally, the traveller should make every effort to serve others and to avoid burdening or troubling them. Thus, when the traveller enters a *khānaqāh,* he should not immediately say, "Peace be upon you," lest another happen to be in the midst of ablutions and be forced to choose between replying while not ritually pure or to be rude by failing to respond. Troubles should be met with complete trust in God.

The chapter concludes with a long and very detailed account of a mystic's journey in which all these legal prescriptions, ascetic techniques and items of mystical etiquette are incorporated, so as to give the journey the maximum spiritual benefit.

---

1. These correspond, of course, to three of the five categories of legal behavior in Islamic law: obligatory, desirable, and permissible. The remaining two categories: undesirable and prohibited, are naturally not possibilities for the Sufi.

Musical Audition (Samāʿ)

Quṭb al-Dīn endorses music and dance as spiritual tools.[1] Nevertheless, this is a consequence of his analysis of the soul and its progress. Man has a soul, heart, spirit and intellect. The heart is the boundary between soul and spirit—the inner aspect of soul—and is the locus of faith. Just as the soul uses the exterior aspect of the five senses to perceive the outer nature of objects, the heart uses the inner aspect of the five senses to perceive the inner nature of sensible things.

Though the soul is dominant through the beginning of manhood, and frequently all through life, some are able to escape its dominance and progress in submission and faith. Sometimes, it is something in the world which is the occasion for the soul's perceiving the divine Beauty. This is because the beauty of the thing corresponds to the divine Beauty, for beauty and moderation (*ʿadālat)* in this world reflect the divine Unity. Therefore a beautiful face or scent or sound can lead people to the perception of the divine Beauty and thereby help free them from the bonds of the soul. This, we may remember, is similar to the Prophets' use of inimitable verses to awaken the heedless by appeals to the imagination.

The effect of music, the most common of such spiritual tools, can be enhanced by the addition of appropriate and beautiful words. The effect may be strong enough to result in dancing. Likewise, repetitive circular movements of the body resembling the movements of the heavens can influence the soul and body towards the heavens.

Quṭb al-Dīn gives a fairly strict etiquette of *samāʿ,* although he allows some loosening of ordinary restraint: "Whatever happens in *samāʿ* is of *samāʿ*." The atmosphere must be one of tranquillity, respect and reverence, in appropriate circumstances, and without extraneous activities—not, for example, in times of famine or plague and not in the presence of skeptical bystanders.

As is the case with *dhikr,* the effect of music on the person dominated by the soul may be merely sensual. For this reason certain jurists forbid music, having in mind this class of people. Therefore, their prohibition of music should not be construed as absolutely binding. Indeed, other jurists specifically permit music to those possessing sufficient self-restraint.

QUṬB AL-DĪN AND IBN ʿARABĪ

It is not uncommon to find Quṭb al-Dīn praised as the first to combine the three trends of the Peripatetic Neoplatonism of Avicenna, the Illuminationist philosophy of Yaḥyā Suhrawardī, and the theosophy of Ibn ʿArabī. The evidence for this is biographical and circumstantial: Quṭb al-Dīn studied with the Peripatetics Ṭūsī and Kātibī and wrote a work in the style of the Peripatetic philosophy, the *Pearly Crown.* He also wrote the standard commentary on *The Philosophy of Illumination* of Suhrawardī, studied with Ibn ʿArabī's chief intellectual heir, Ṣadr al-Dīn Qūnawī, and, we may now add, transmitted a book by one of Qunawī's chief disciples. I have argued elsewhere that Quṭb al-Dīn was primarily an advocate of the Illuminationist

1. Though he also wrote about music, which in the medieval curriculum was considered a branch of mathematics. He was, as I mentioned above, an expert player of the *rabāb.*

philosophy of Suhrawardī and that this philosophy is expounded in both his major philosophical works. Though he mentions Ibn 'Arabī in two places, I do not think that Ibn 'Arabī was a significant influence of his thought. It is certainly wrong to say—to pick a typical example: "It was through Quṭb al-Dīn that the rapprochement between the schools of Ibn 'Arabī and Suhrawardī gradually began..."[1]

Nonetheless, Quṭb al-Dīn certainly knew of Ibn 'Arabī. The difficulty is that Quṭb al-Dīn does not actually discuss Ibn 'Arabī. He does quote him, but from the *Futūḥāt:* that huge and diffuse mystical encyclopedia that at least mentions virtually every concept in the Islamic religious tradition. This does not make it easy to pin down Ibn 'Arabī's influence.

First, we know that Quṭb al-Dīn respected Ibn 'Arabī. In *'The Epistle Ascertaining the Reality of the World of Image,'* he introduces a quotation from Ibn 'Arabī with these epithets: "one of the saints, the great and inspired Shaykh Muḥyī'l-Dīn Ibn al-'Arabī."[2] In the Commentary he mentions as evidence for a certain doctrine (that good is predominate in the universe) that it was asserted by Ghazzālī, and that his views were later adopted by "the perfect *(kāmil)* Shaykh Muḥyī'l-Dīn Ibn al-'Arabī in the *Futūḥāt.*"

The doctrine for which Ibn 'Arabī was best known is the 'Unity of Being,' *waḥdat al-wujūd.*[3] The Islamic philosophical tradition understood this as being in direct contradiction to Suhrawardī's teaching of the primacy of quiddity, *aṣālat al-māhiyya.* It is easy to show that Quṭb al-Dīn stood with Suhrawardī on this question, though neither term appears in his writings. The cosmology given in the book on mysticism of the *Pearly Crown* is, however, interesting in this respect. Here the world is seen as manifesting God and His names and attributes. The existence of the world is accidental and metaphorical in relation to the true existence possessed by God alone. Perhaps this is to be read as a milder formulation of Ibn 'Arabī's key insight, that the world is the self-manifestation of God. If this part of the text is Farghānī's, then it ought to reflect Qūnawī's understanding of Ibn 'Arabī. Perhaps then Quṭb al-Dīn thought of Ibn 'Arabī's cosmology as a sort of poetic formulation of the nature of the world as it appears to a mystic—a 'rhetorical' metaphysics appropriate to its context and uses and on a different logical level from the demonstrative metaphysics of such works as the Commentary and the philosophical parts of the *Pearly Crown.* It is thus uncertain how much reliance can be put on this rather poetic text in the absence of supporting evidence in his more prosaic metaphysical texts.

Another possible connection is Quṭb al-Dīn's description of the Preserved Tablet and its role in the creation and preservation of the World and in the fate of individual being a theme much discussed by Ibn 'Arabī. This is strongly reminiscent of Ibn 'Arabī's doctrine of the permanent archetypes *(a'yān thābita).* This, however, is a

1. Seyyed Hossein Nasr, *Three Muslim Sages* (Cambridge: Harvard University Press 1964) p. 154; cf. pp. 118-19.
2. *'ammā al-awliyā' fa... al-Shaykh al-muḥaqqiq al-mukāshif al-mukammal* —Walbridge, *Science of Mystic Light,* Appendix F.
3. See W.C. Chittick, 'Ebno'l-'Arabī's Doctrine of the Oneness of Being,' *Sufi: A Journal of Sufism,* Issue 4, Winter 1989-90, pp. 6-14.

point where Ibn 'Arabī and Suhrawardī are in general agreement against the Peripatetics, both holding that the fates of individuals are determined by the interrelations of the divine emanations. It is not surprising then to find that the one quotation in Quṭb al-Dīn's works from Ibn 'Arabī concerns the World of Image.

THE *PEARLY CROWN*'S SUFISM: CONCLUSIONS & EVALUATION

In this chapter Quṭb al-Dīn—or Farghānī—presents a complete mystical system whose goals and methods are derived naturally from its psychological and metaphysical premises. The question that remains is how this system is to be interpreted in the larger contexts of Quṭb al-Dīn's other works and the intellectual trends of his age. He comments in the chapter on the etiquette of Shaykhs that firm knowledge is based on solid evidence from demonstration, from the Koran, or from sound and open intuition *(kashfī ṣaḥīḥ 'aynī),* a division that precisely corresponds to the distinction we constantly saw in his mystical rule: of reason, the Law, and mystical etiquette.

Although much of the analysis is couched in Koranic terms, the fundamental premises and structure of Quṭb al-Dīn's mystical system are ultimately derived from philosophy. There is also an obvious attempt to use terms which have specifically religious overtones. For example, although terms from the Koran are used, these refer to higher metaphysical objects, not to specifically Islamic cultic or historic concepts. He uses "Pen" to refer to the first intellect, but he avoids the use of terms like "Allāh" or "Sufi," preferring "Absolute" *(Ḥaqq)* and "sincere one." This should probably be understood in the context of the claims of philosophy and certain Sufi schools of thought to represent a transcendent truth which encompasses all religions.

On the other hand, Islamic Law is an integral part of his mystical rule. This, I suspect, is due to two considerations. The first is that prophetic religion is, in the majority of cases, the first step in spiritual progress and is normally the occasion of conversion. The second is that it is necessary for a mystic to pursue the Path through some religious tradition—normally Islam in the case of Quṭb al-Dīn's readers.

Despite the rule's theoretical application to other spiritual traditions, his system was in fact firmly grounded in the Sufi experience of the thirteenth century, the age when Sufism took its mature shape. This was the century of Rumi and Ibn 'Arabī, among many other great names; and it was the time when most of the important Sufi Orders were founded. With the transformation of Sufism into a popular movement, the question of conduct and organization became more central, and a number of mystical rules were composed by some of the leading mystics of the time: the *Ādāb al-murīdīn* of Abu'l-Najīb Suhrawardī, the *'Awārif al-ma'ārif* of his nephew Shihāb al-Dīn Suhrawardī, the *Ādāb al-ṣūfiyya* of Najm al-Dīn Kubrā and the *Mirṣād al 'ibād* of Rāzi, for example. Quṭb al-Dīn could scarcely have failed to know some of these.

The most noteworthy feature of this text is, in fact, that it represents the Sufism of the Orders, not the ecstatic and poetic mysticism of poets such as Rumi nor the theosophy of Ibn 'Arabī—which Farghānī, the real author of the work, knew very well—nor even the Illuminationist philosophical mysticism of Suhrawardī about which Quṭb al-Dīn writes at length elsewhere. Nevertheless, there is no emphasis on differences between the branches of the Sufi tradition. Though the factors that resulted in the establishment of the Orders as distinct and separate institutions exist in this book, there is no indication that these bases of potential division have yet resulted in real division. The close relation of his work to the earlier Sufi manuals cannot be denied: the emphasis on the role of the master, the very practical temper, and the insistence on the need for the novice to be absolutely obedient to his master. An interesting item is the emphasis on the etiquette of the master-craftsman and the apprentice and the parallels between their situation and that of the mystical master and the novice. At this time there were close links and structural parallels between the trade guilds and the emerging Sufi *ṭarīqas*. Quṭb al-Dīn's rule may reflect this.

Though Quṭb al-Dīn may have begun his analysis from philosophical considerations, his ideas on mystical practice were in line with those of the Sufis of his age. The analysis was used to explain and justify actual Sufi practices. He was a rather austere mystic, particularly if we compare him with people like Rumi. He knew, for example, Rumi's style of dance and did not condemn it, but he clearly thought of *samāʿ* mainly in terms of sitting and listening to the singing of mystical poetry. It is also striking how small a role Quṭb al-Dīn gives to love. Insofar as it concerned him, it was confined to the higher mystical stations.

Quṭb al-Dīn moved between reason and religion, between worldly activity and mystical seclusion. He was unwilling to follow some other philosophers in dismissing the religion of ordinary people as naive. At one point he remarks that philosophy is not true wisdom: it is infidelity *(kufr)*. He devoted most of his life to the rational sciences and wrote two large books on philosophy—but wrote a huge traditional commentary on the Koran as a pious exercise. He wore Sufi dress in the courts of kings but never deserted the world for the *khānaqāh*.

This tension is reflected in the form of his work. Quṭb al-Dīn was not a synthesizer. Though he was a master of several varieties of thought and had a good knowledge of many others, he did not pull them together into a grand system. His own philosophical system was that of Suhrawardī. There were also other systems of thought that Quṭb al-Dīn accepted on their own levels: the political philosophy of Fārābī, the dogmatic theology of *Kalām,* and the theosophy of Sufism. These he treated or transmitted in their appropriate places. However, he did not synthesize them into one master system, being rather content to leave them as independent units. Therefore, I think that the ideas expressed in the mysticism chapter of the *Pearly Crown* are to be understood, not as part of Quṭb al-Dīn's philosophical system, but rather as Quṭb al-Dīn's understanding of the authoritative teaching of the Sufis.

A miniature from a Mughal manuscript of the *Nafaḥāt al-uns* by Jāmī, dated 1603, illustrating a story about Najm al-Dīn Kubrā's power of domination over animals. British Library MS. Or. 1362, fol. 263a. (Courtesy of the British Library, London)

"Mysteries of Marriage:" Notes on a Sufi Text

Sachiko Murata

Little seems to be known about the Sufi Shaykh Aḥmad ibn Jalāl al-Din Khwājagī Kāsānī who was born in Kāsān in Farghāna and died in 949/1543. Storey says nothing about his works and tells us simply that one of his disciples wrote his biography with the title *Maqāmāt-i Ḥaḍrat-i Makhdūm A'zam* and that he had son called Khwājā Isḥāq.[1] But Kāsānī is the author of many treatises, all of them apparently in Persian. A collection of twenty-nine of these in 260 folios is found in the Khudābaksh Oriental Public Library in Patna (Persian 2084-2112).Their titles suggest that Kāsānī approched Sufi teachings mainly with spiritual practice in view, and certanily with an eye toward the Persian poetical tradition.[2] A collection in the Institute of Islamic Studies (IIIS) in New Delhi lists twenty two works by Kāsānī in its table of contents but only four are extant.[3]

Among Kāsānī's works is *Wujūdiyya (On Existence),* a title that suggests the approach of Ibn 'Arabī and his followers. However the content reflects liittle awareness of Ibn 'Arabī's teachings. The work deals mainly with existence as problem for the spiritual traveler. The author begins with a well-known saying of one of the early Sufi Shaykhs though he attributes it to the Prophet: "Your existence is a sin to which no other sin can compare." Then he comments:

> O sincere dervish, you should know what existence is. It is of two kinds: True, subsistent, eternal existence and accidental, perishing existence. True existence is the existence of the Real, while accidental and metaphorical existence is the existence of the creatures.
>
> Know, O sincere seeker, that all happiness and good fortune lie in the station of annihilation and nonexistence while all difficulty and unhappiness lie in existence. Why? Because the Prophet immersed and annihilated his own existence, and every-

---

1. *Persian Literature: A Bio-Bibliographical Survey* (London: Luzac 1972), II, p. 973.
2. The titles include the following *Zubdat al-sālikīn, Gul wa nawrūz, Mi'rāj al-'āshiqīn, Murshid al-sālikīn, Wāqi'at al- ḥaqqāniyya, Sawād al-wajh, Ganjnāma, 'Ilmiyya, Ādāb al-sālikīn, Ādāb al ṣiddīqīn, Risāla-yi Bukā' iyya, Tanbīh al-salāṭīn, al-Walad sirr abīh, Nafaḥāt al sālikīn, Risāla-yi dhikr, Sharḥ-i rubā'iyyāt, Bayān-i silsila-yi Khwājagān, Chahār kalima, Silsilat al-ṣiddīqīn, Mir'āt al-ṣafā.*

   An unnamed manuscript in this collection (no. 2096) is called *Wujūdiyya* in other copies found in several Indian libraries (Indian Institute of Islamic Studies, 1002; Aligarh Muslim University. Ahsan 297.7/25, Habib Ganj 21/72; Andhra Pradesh State Oriental Manuscript Library, Sufism 1846; Khudabakhsh 2096).
3. In addition to some of the above, we find *Samā'iyya, Biṭṭīkhiyya, Tanbīh al-'ulamā'*, and *Naṣīḥat al-sālikin.* The two MSS besides Wujūdiyya that are also extant are *Samā'iyya* (1001) and *Ādāb al-sālikin* (1002). Another copy of *Ādāb al-sālikin* is found in Aligarh, Ahsan 297.7/26.

thing that exists, in the ocean of Oneness...

Know that this high station belongs to the Prophet. To the extent that the members of his community follow him, they also share in it... On the outward level, nothing must come into existence [from the traveler] in opposition to the Prophet's *Sharī'a,* and on the inward level nothing must be realized in opposition to his spiritual Path *(ṭarīqa).*

Another surviving manuscript in the IIIs collection (no. 1000) is called *Asrār al-nikāḥ* or *Mysteries of Marriage.* The director of the Institute, S.A. Ali, generously provided me with a copy, and I was able to acquire a second copy from Aligarh Muslim University (Munir Alam 11/1). Though both copies are defective, most of the discussion is clear enough to summarize here. The Aligarh manuscript contains 23 pages of 19 lines; the IIIS manuscript 19 pages of 19 lines.

The primary meaning of the-word *nikāḥ* or "marriage" employed in the title is coitus, though the word is used in Islamic texts to refer to sexual union sanctioned by the *Sharī'a.* Most works that discuss *nikāḥ* pay attention to the rules and regulations concerning correct marriage bonds set down by the *Sharī'a.* By also employing the term *asrār* or "mysteries" in the title-of his work, Kāsānī is pointing to a Sufi approach. He is not concern with issues of the *Sharī'a,* but rather with the significance of marriage for human existence. He does not approach this topic with the sophistication of Ibn 'Arabī and his commentators, but rather with the rhetoric of a preacher speaking to his flock.

The treatise stands in a long tradition of writing about the benefits of marriage and sexual intercourse beginning, of course, with many relevant sayings of the Prophet. Especially influential and widely known were Ghazzālī's discussions in the *Iḥyā' 'ulūm al-dīn* and *Kīmīyā-yi sa'ādat.* Ghazzālī assumes a moralistic and socially-oriented perspective, while Ibn 'Arabī—especially in a well-known passage in the last chapter of the *Fuṣūṣ al ḥikam*—focuses on the mysteries of divine union that become manifest in sexual union. Ibn 'Arabī's discussion, in contrast to Ghazzālī's, seems to have little pratical revelance for any but spiritual masters of the highest rank. Yet, when his remarks in the *Fuṣūṣ* are put into the context of his discussion of the same subject in the *Futūḥāt,* one sees that they throw a good deal of light on his cosmological teachings. Moreover, in his, *Waṣāya* or "counsels" toward the end of the *Futūḥāt,* Ibn 'Arabī draws practical conclusions for all spiritual travelers. By recognizing the divine roots of the feminine dimension of Reality seekers will be able to avoid the danqers of being led astray by passion.[1] .

Kāsānī's perspectlve is much closer to that of Ghazzālī than Ibn 'Arabī, as is to be expected from a Shaykh whose writings are directed toward the practical needs of his own disciples (rather than, as in the case of Ibn 'Arabī, to the intellectual elite of the Islamic community). Kāsānī does show signs of being familiar with Ibn 'Arabī's works, and he quotes from him (apparently the *Futūḥāt)* on one occasion, thereby suggesting that Ibn 'Arabī's discussions, however intellectual and abstruse they might seem to most people, were not without effect on the more practical, day-to-day activities of the Sufi Orders. But Kāsānī is certainly not a follower of Ibn

1. See the detailed discussion of Ibn 'Arabī's views here in Murata, *The Tao of Islam: A Sourcebook on Gender Relationships in Islamic Thought* (Albany: SUNY Press 1992), Chapter 6.

'Arabī in terms of the formulation of Sufi teachings, since his writings, so far as I can judge, are manuals of instruction written in the spoken language of his time for disciples who have little training the Islamic sciences. As such they form good examples of a certain form of Sufi activity of a more 'popular' sort.

Asrār al-nikāḥ also reflects Kāsānī's concrete situation in society. He makes use of the tradition of Sufi teachings on marriage to justify his own practices. He did not write the work primarily as a theoretical exposition in the manner of Ibn 'Arabī, but rather as a practical answer to problems he faced in his own environment. He is clearly reacting to crlticisms that were directed against himself or perhaps some of his close disciples. The issue is not, as in Ibn 'Arabī, why Sufis should love women and how they can avoid the possibility of misguidance that women may represent, but rather why Sufis should not be blamed for loving women, even if that means taking many wives (within the limitations set down by the *Sharī'a).*

Several times in the treatise Kāsānī employs the word *mubālagha* to refer to the practice of taking several wives. Lane's *Arabic-English Lexicon* defines the word as "exceeding the usual, or ordinary, or the just, or proper, bounds, or degree, in a thing," while Steingass's *Persian-English Dicitionary* gives equivalents such as "endeavor, effort, exertion, exaggeration, excess." Perhaps "going to great lengths" suggests the sense of the word in Kāsānī's treatise. Clearly he is defending polygamy, but more than that, he is suggesting why the Sufis are especially entitled and even duty-bound to have several wives

One can easily imagine Kāsānī's contemporaries criticizing him for having more than one wife. After all, Sufis lay claim to a more 'spiritual' orientation than other Muslims, and having several wives and many children does not seem to support such a claim. This would not be the first time that Sufis had been blamed for appreciating the good things of this world. As Tor Andrae remarks concerning an earlier period, "Critics maintained that the Sufis possessed three outstanding qualltles: they enjoyed food, sweet things and women."[1] Here is Kāsānī's stated purpose in writing his text:

> The reason for composing this treatise was that I observed that most people, out of ignorance and lack of true knowledge, criticize and blame the Muslims in the noble affair of running a household *(kadkhudā'ī)*. They lay limitless reproach and blame on anyone who goes to great lengths *(mubālagha)* in this noble affair. Hence I desired to write down a hint of the mysteries of marriage that reached me as result of my kissing the threshold of this elevated group [the Sufis]. Then, after reading this treatise, people will not blame any Muslim, and especialy not this elevated group, thereby throwing themselves into destruction.

Kāsānī's method in his treatise is to marshal all the evidence he can find, from the Koran, the *ḥadīth,* and Sufi writings, to show that marriage is desired and commanded by God and represents one of the highest human ideals; and that, since the Sufis are especially concerned to actualize the fullness of human possibility, they take this high ideal especially seriously. Kāsānī provides sixteen basic arguments with no special order. The text reads as if he is listing the arguments as they occurred to him. Several of them are well known in the earlier literature, but some

1. *In the Garden of Myrtles* (Albany: SUNY Press 1987), p. 49.

(for example numbers 2, 3 and its continuation 16, and 10) are new to me. I summarize them in what follows:

1. In good Sufi style, Kāsānī begins his explanation with God's goal in creating the world: to populate it. God created Adam and Eve and encouraged them to produce offspring with these words: "Marry such women as seem good to you, two, three, four" (Koran IV 3).[1] Kāsānī concludes that God loves marriage. Hence, striving *(ihtimām)* and "going to great lengths" in marriage is even more loved by God. Blaming anyone—especially the Sufis—in this regard approaches unbelief. In proof, the IIIS manuscript adds a 'sound' *ḥadīth* which, not too surprisingly, is not indexed in Wensinck's *Concordance*: "If a man wlth four wives and one thousand slave girls desires to buy another slave girl, and another man blames him than unbelief is feared for the other man."

2. Marriage has been called the "complete, all-comprehensive act of worship" *('ibādat-i tāmma-yi jām'a)* just like the ritual prayer *(ṣalāt)*. That is why most of the pillars *(arkān)* of the ritual prayer are also found in *nikāḥ,* such as standing, recitation of the Koran, bowing, prostrating oneself, and sitting. Each of these movements in the marriage act takes the forms of movements in ritual prayer. In the same way, each angel is busy with one of the pillars of the ritual prayer. Hence it has been said that some are bowing, some are prostrating themselves, and so on.[2]

---

1. Following this Koranic verse, the IIIS manuscript has a long passage on the permissibility of taking more than one wife that is missing in the Aligarh MS. It may have been added in a later version or by a copyist, since it brings about a certain break in the flow of the text. Most of the points it makes are made again later on, except for the following:

   Know, O sincere seeker that a person can follow this command when he can establish equity *(ta'ādul)* among his wives. If he fears that he cannot establish equity, then he should limit himself to a single wife, so that he will follow the ruling of [the rest of] this verse: "If you fear that you will not be equitable, then only one." If he cannot establish equity and he takes another, then he has opposed this verse and thrown himself with his own hand into great destruction. He has made himself worthy of the threat of "Cast not yourselves by your own hands into destruction [Koran II 195]." We seek refuge in God from that.

   Kāsānī then tells us that the husband establishes equity by providing for each wife every sort of livelihood that he provides for the other(s). However, in a passage that is partly illegible in the manuscript, he seems to be saying that a man is excused from equity in sexual relationships if "natural inclination *(mayl-i ṭabī'ī)*" is lacking. Then he turns to a *ḥadīth* to show that the Prophet kept his several wives satisfied such that none felt that he had a greater inclination toward any other. Kāsānī relates the *ḥadīth* in Persian, without providing a source (in the typical manner of this type of non-technical treatise):

   One day they all said to him, "O Messenger of God! Which one of us do you love the most?" The Prophet replied that he would answer on the following day. During the night he visited each of his wives, giving each a ring and making her promise not to tell anyone. The next day, his wives came to him for his answer. He said, "I love the one to whom I gave something, telling her not to tell anyone."
2. Abū Ṭālib Makkī in the *Qūt al-Qulūb* (Cairo: Maṭba'a Muṣṭafā al-Bābī al-Ḥalabī 1961; vol. 2, p. 200) points out that each group of angels performs one pillar of the ritual prayer such as—bowing or standing, while only human beings perform all the pillars. Hence the angels are astonished at human virtuosity. This, of course, is a 'mythic' presentation of the idea that human beings embrace all divine attributes and all realities in the macrocosm, since they are made in God's image. Other creatures, even angels, only embrace some of the realities and divine qualities.

3. Kāsānī next turns to explicating in some detail the *ḥadīth* of the Hidden Treasure and human superiority over all other creatures. This leads him to consider two types of divine effusion *(fayḍ)*: the general, that reaches all creatures in the forms of nurture, and the specific, which reaches only the elect among human beings and consists of moral and spiritual perfections *(kamālāt)*, mystical tastings *(adhwāk)* and other divine gifts. The greatest human beings are the Prophets, then the friends of God *(awliyā')*, then the sincere disciples *(murīdān-i ṣadūq)*. In each era God appoints servants to be the means whereby the specific effusion reaches creation; in the present era, it is the Sufi Shaykhs who play this role. They are rustless mirrors in whom God's majesty and beauty are displayed plainly. For their followers, the means of cleansing the rust from the heart's mirror is the invocation *(dhikr)* of the first *Shahāda*. If the prophets and Shaykhs had no followers there would be no mirrors to recieve their specific effusion. "The more companions, the more effusion, and the more effusion, the greater the perfection." Hence the Prophets and the 'friends of God' have always sought to gain followers. Thus they may "go to great lengths" in *nikāḥ* because the intimacy thereby established allows them to gain followers who otherwise might not benefit from the divine effusion.

4. In an argument reminiscent of Ibn 'Arabī, Kāsānī reflects that the reason the Sufis love marriage may be that the whole is attracted to its parts. Hence Adam is attracted to Eve, who was created from his rib. Adam was able to find no rest in the Garden until Eve was created from himself. Here (as in many other passages) Kāsānī cites Rūmi to demonstrate his point:

> *Since He created Eve*
> *"that Adam might find repose in her"*[1]
> *So how can Adam cut himself off from her?*[2]

> Adam was a drop from the ocean of God's Reality. His root and his life was there, like a fish whose root and life is in water. Whenever the fish is taken from the water, it flops around and cannot find rest until it is put back into the water... Adam had fallen out of the ocean of God's Reality and could not find rest in anything. He was seeking his own reality. Then God disclosed Himself specifically in the locus of manifestation that is Eve. Hence Adam found in her what he had been searching for and he came to rest. From here one comes to understand the greatness of woman. And one allusion is sufficient for the gnostic.

5. Next Kāsānī cites as a model for the attitude of the Sufis the famous *ḥadīth* upon which Ibn 'Arabī bases many of his arguments: "I was made to love three things of this world of yours: women, perfume—and the comfort of my eye is in the ritual prayer."

6. The reason for marrying women may simply be the desire to obey the command of God. (Koran IV 3, quoted above under number 1)

---

1. Koran VII 189.
2. *Mathnāwī-yi ma'nawī*, (ed.) R.A. Nicholson (Gibb Memorial Series, n.s. 4, London 1925-40), *daftar* I: 2426. (These lines are also cited in exposition of the theme of the "Sophianic Feminine" by R.J.W. Austin in his essay in this volume. -Ed.)

7. The reason may be to obey the command of the Prophet (not indexed in Wensinck): "Marry, reproduce, and become many, for I will boast of you over the other communities on the Day of Resurrection—even the miscarriages *(siqṭ)*." The Sufis take it upon themselves to observe all God's commandments very carefully and precisely, so they naturally go to great lengths in this commandment as well.

8. It may be that the goal is the arrival at God and the vision of Him, since this is promised to the Sufis in this world and is achieved through annihilation *(fanā')*. Annihilation has degrees, and the highest degree belongs to Muḥammad and his sincere followers. "Union" or "arrival" *(waṣl, wuṣūl)* means "for the whole to reach *(rasīdan)* the part, or the part to reach the part." Since the Sufis are the locus of manifestation for the Whole, they achieve arrival by reaching a part of the world, for they see God in whatever they see. The things of the world are their own parts, and their reaching the best part of the world is best for them. "And no part of the world is greater, higher, more subtle, and more noble than female human beings." In proof of this point, Kāsānī cites Rūmī's verse:

> *The face, the mole, the eyebrow, the carnelian lips—*
> *God Himself seemed to shine forth from behind a delicate curtain.*[1]

8A. No one who has imbibed the fragrance of the greatness of woman would contemplate her with the eye of contempt. The Sufis (e.g. Ibn 'Arabī) explain that she is the locus of manifestation for both the activity and receptivity of God. Hence the Prophet said (in a *ḥadīth* found in Ibn Mājā and Dārimī), "The best of you is the best to his wife, and I am the best of you to his wife."

9. The Sufis may marry women for the sake of much worship *(kathrat-i 'ibādat)*, since each act performed for the sake of the marriage act is an act of worship. Here Kāsānī cites various accounts, some of which I have seen in Koran commentaries such as Maybudī's *Kashf al-asrār,* enumerating the reward which the believer accrues through holding his wife's hand, kissing her, fondling her, etc. "When he kisses her, it is as if he has kissed the pillar of the Ka'ba." When he makes an ablution after sexual intercourse, a good deed is written for every drop of water. Hence the goal in this is much worship; they marry a great deal for the same reason that they pray a good deal.

9A. Kāsānī next expands on the merits of making one's wife happy, and cites not only holding her hand and kissing her, but also the Prophet's having footraces with 'Ā'isha. The goal in all this is to make the believers happy, since, he tells us, citing another *ḥadīth* not found in the standard sources, "To make the heart of a believer happy is better than all the worship of the jinn and human beings."

10. According to a tradition, after sexual intercourse the sins of both partners are erased. The mystery behind this tradition is that "annihilation" leads to the erasure of self, and "Your existence is a sin to which no other sin can compare." Hence annihilation through sexual intercourse erases self and sins. One makes a major ablution after intercourse in order to purify the outward dimension of the self just

1. *Mathnāwī-yi ma'nawī,* V 960.

as annihilation has purified the inward dimension.

10A. The goal of all acts of obedience and worship is proximity to God, and no act brings this about better than intercourse, which results in annihilation, immersion (*istighrāq*), and dissolution (*iḍmiḥlāl*) in the beloved.

11. Every act of worship has an enjoyment (*ladhdha*), and the greatness of the act depends upon the greatness of the enjoyment. Each enjoyment is a sample (*numūna*) of the enjoyment of paradise. It is obvious that the enjoyment of arrival is greater than the enjoyment of witnessing (*mushāhada*). Here, in order that his words may not be misunderstood, Kāsānī adds that *what he says about high spiritual degrees in sexual union pertains only to the perfect gnostic who is present with God, not to the ignorant and forgetful person who is far from God.*

12. Next Kāsānī turns to a long comparison of this world to cultivated field, in accordance with the saying, "This world is a field under cultivation for the sake of the next world" *(al-dunyā mazra'at al-ākhirā)*. God appointed human beings as the farmers (*dighān*) of this world and taught them every kind of farming. As for animals, God appointed an appropriate female animal for each male animal as the field for cultivation. The ultimate goal in all the pairing (*izdiwāj*) within the world is the existence of human beings. Hence God commanded men to till their fields. At the same time he appointed the human heart as the mirror in which He displays His own beauty.

Cultivation is of two kinds, general and specific. The first is for the common people and the second for the elect. Following the Prophet, the elect perceived that the general cultivation in itself is of no advantage, for as the saying has it, "This world is a carcass, and those who seek it are dogs." Instead, the elect chose the specific cultivation, which pertains to what God ultimately wants from this world. Just as the general cultivation has different kinds, so also does the specific: such as ritual prayer, fasting, invocation (*dhikr*), and so on. But these kinds of cultivation also take place through pairing, just as knowledge (*'ilm*) must be paired with practice (*'amal*). The fruits of this cultivation are states, stations, gnostic sciences, and divine realities.

Each kind of cultivation has an appropriate fruit. The best of all these cultivations is the cultivation of the human being through the marriage act, since this gives rise to the existence of human beings, who are God's goal in creation. That is why prophets such as Solomon paid so much attention to marriage. The more wives a person has for cultivation, the more human beings are produced from the land, and the more felicity is achieved in the next world.

12A. If the prophets and friends of God select some women over others, this is for the same reason that any farmer chooses the best land and does not waste his effort on other land. And if some prophets did not take wives, this has to do with their specific situations and functions. Here Kāsānī quotes in proof a passage (in Persian translation) that he attributes to Ibn 'Arabī: In one of his visions, Ibn 'Arabī met with the prophet John and asked if being single was a more perfect state than marriage. John replied that it was not. If he did not marry, it was because he had been conceived as a result of his father's prayer, not because of any passion on his parents' part, so passion was not part of his makeup.

12B. One should not imagine that Solomon and David were the best of the prophets because they had the most wives, while Muḥammad had only nine wives. The reason here is that Muḥammad's specific effusion (cf. number 3 above) reached all people without exception, whereas the specific effusion of these two prophets reached only their wives, so they married as many as they could. Moreover, Muḥammad's way was brevity *(ikhtiṣār)* in all things. Thus his words are brief, but full of meaning.

13. Next Kāsānī cites an argument also alluded to by Ghazzālī: The Sufis have special states and qualities that sometimes overcome them, and the only thing that gives them ease in these states is women. As the Prophet said, "I have a time with God during which no angel drawn near or prophet sent out embraces me." When such a powerful state overcame the Prophet, at the beginning of the revelation, because of the manifestation of the greatest angels, he addressed Khadīja with the words, "Wrap me, O Khadīja." Later, whenever he felt he was being overcome by such a state he would say, "Speak to me, 'Ā'isha." He wanted to avoid being overcome by these states because he had a message to deliver, and perfection lies in full awareness. The Sufis also have special states, and like the Prophet they seek rest from them through companionship with women.

14. Another reason for much marriage may be the seeking of many pious children, since the Prophet said (in a sound *ḥadīth)*, "When a person dies, works are cut off from him, except in three things: a pious child who prays for him...."

15. Another reason is to prevent the breaking of the genealogical chain of Adam's children.

16. Finally Kāsānī turns to an explanation based on Islamic psychological teachings concerning passion or 'appetite' *(shahwa):* 'Appetite,' he tells us, is of two kinds, praiseworthy and blameworthy. Blameworthy appetite is that which is exercised outside the framework of the *Sharī'a*. Praiseworthy appetite is of two kinds. The first is possessed by all human beings and stems from the fact that God created Adam and Eve to populate the world and He placed appetite within them so that they would produce many children. The second praiseworthy kind of appetite is found only in the prophets and friends of God. It arises from much worship and invocation and is caused by their advances in the infinite steps on the path of nearness to God. The more they polish their hearts through invoking God, the more this kind of appetite increases within them.

16A. 'Appetite' is one of the branches of the expulsive faculty *(quwwa-yi dāfi'a)*. When people consume food, some of it becomes blood and flesh, and some of it is excreted or secreted. Among the latter is sperm, which is the seed of the human being. It is obvious that this is produced from food. Kāsānī quotes Rumi to support this point:

Appetite arises from eating, so eat less, or engage
in the marriage act to escape from evil.
When you eat, that draws you toward the forbidden.
When you have income, you have to have an expenditure
Since you are greedy in eating, seek a woman quickly,
or else the cat will steal away the sheep's tail.[1]

Since the income of the Sufis lies in the infinite divine effusion, their expenditure is also infinite. When a person has a great deal of income and he spends it, why should he be blamed for that? The elect expend part of the divine effusion through the gnostic sciences, realities, and 'tastings' that they pass on to their sincere disciples, while they expend another part—which is that effusion's secretion in the form of sperm—through marriage. "Hence the great appetite of the Sufis derives from the infinite effusions of God." Though Kāsānī's last argument may be one of the least convincing for modern readers, he stands squarely in the tradition of Rumi. One is reminded of the latter's verses.

One person eats and the food becomes filth,
another eats and it becomes the light of God.
One person eats and gives birth to avarice and envy,
another eats and gives birth to the light of the One.[2]

1. *Mathnāwī-yi ma'nawī*, V 1373-4;1366. The "sheep's tail" is considered to be the best part of the sheep; the proverbial expression means that the person has the best thing stolen away.
2. *Mathnāwī-yi ma'nawī*, *I* 272-73.

The Symbolism of Birds and Flight in the Writings of Rūzbihān Baqlī

VI

Carl W. Ernst

The imagery of birds and flight has long been a universal symbol of the ascension of the human soul to a higher reality.[1] From the winged deities of the ancient Near East to the angels of the Bible and the winged souls of Plato's *Phaedrus*, poets and prophets have depicted the power of the wing to lift the soul through flight to paradise. Among non-scriptural peoples, it is especially in the complex of Central Asian and Siberian religious practices called 'shamanistic' that the symbolism of flight is powerfully displayed.[2] In the Islamic tradition, notable early explorations of the symbolism of birds and flight can be found in the writings of philosophers, Sufis, and poets such as Ibn Sīnā (d. 428/1037), al-Ghazzālī (d. 504/1111), Suhrawardī (d. 587/1191), Khāqānī (d. 595/1199), and above all in the great mystical epic of Farīd al-Dīn 'Aṭṭār (d. ca. 617/1220), *Manṭiq al-ṭayr* or *The Language of the Birds*.[3] But if we think in terms of Persian Sufism, one author in particular claims our attention for his extensive use of the symbolism of birds and flight. This is Rūzbihān Baqlī (d. 606/1209), the Sufi master of Shiraz, a prolific and powerful writer of works on Sufism in both Persian and Arabic. Rūzbihān's characteristically poetic style employs the full range of metaphors of birds and flight to express the different modes of mystical experience. Rūzbihān's concentration on the experiential dimension of Sufism makes his work especially valuable for revealing the mystical understanding of literary tropes.[4] Although he frequently strains symbols to the breaking point, his constant clarification of their mystical significations makes him one of the most revealing authors in the Persian Sufi tradition.

---

1. Manabu Waida, 'Birds,' *Encyclopedia of Religion* (New York: Macmillan Publishing Company 1987), 2:224-227; William K. Mahony, 'Flight,' *ibid.*, 5:349-353.
2. Mircea Eliade, *Shamanism, Archaic Techniques of Ecstasy*, trans. Willard R. Trask, Bollingen Series LXXVI (Princeton: Princeton University Press 1974), pp. 477-482. "Magical flight is the expression both of the soul's autonomy and of ecstasy" (*ibid.*, p. 479).
3. For Ibn Sīnā, al-Ghazzālī, and the philosopher Suhrawardī, see Henry Corbin, *Avicenna and the Visionary Recital*, trans. Willard R. Trask, Bollingen Series LXVI (Princeton: Princeton University Press 1960; reprint ed., Dallas, TX: Spring Publications, Inc. 1980), pp. 165-203, and Farīd al-Dīn 'Aṭṭār Nīshābūrī, *Manṭiq al-ṭayr*, ed. Muḥammad Jawād Mashkūr (3rd ed., Tehran: Nāṣir-i Khusraw 1968), Introduction, pp. xxxi-xlii. The poem by Khāqanī called *Manṭiq al-ṭayr* is found in *Dīvān-i Khāqānī-i Shīrwānī* (Tehran: Intishārāt-i Arisṭū 1362), pp. 31-34; trans. Peter L. Wilson and Nasrollah Pourjavady, The *Drunken Universe: An Anthology of Persian Sufi Poetry* (Grand Rapids, MI: Phanes Press 1988), pp. 119-129.
4. Similar analyses could yield useful insights into Rūzbihān's use of other prominent symbols and metaphors, such as desert, ocean, mirror, vision, tongue, bride, veil, light, mine, clothes, and sun.

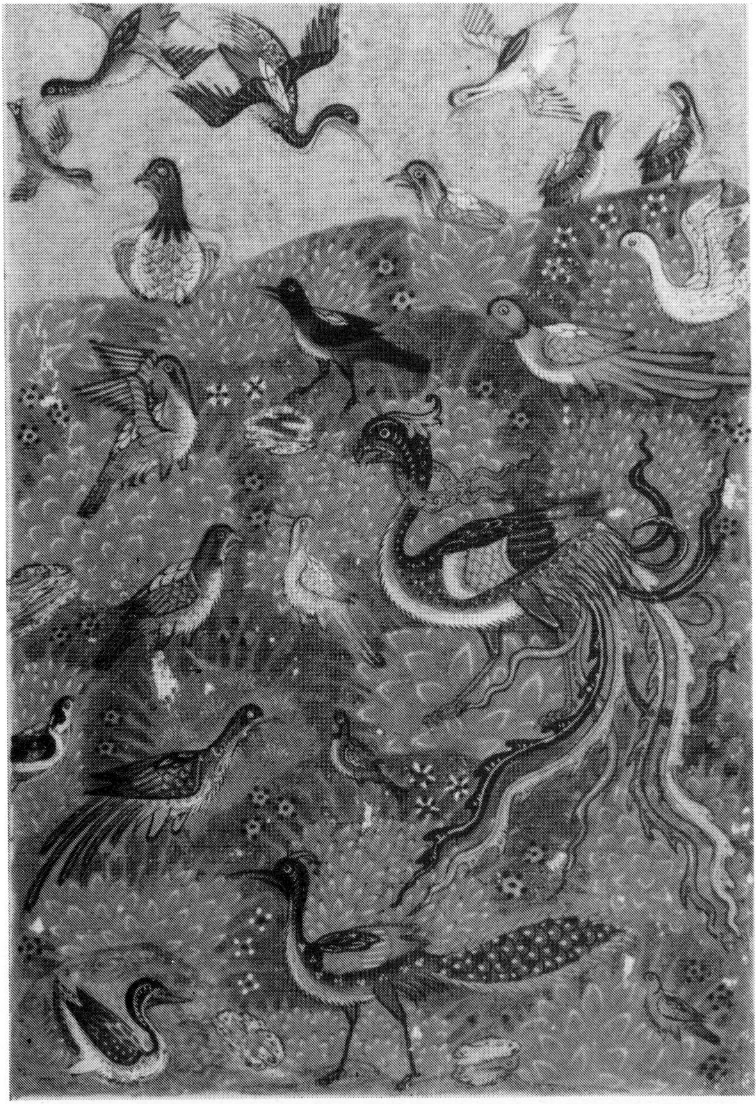

The Conference of Birds. From a manuscript of 'Aṭṭār's *Manṭiq al-ṭayr*, dated 898/1493. MS. Elliott 246, fol. 25v (Courtesy of the Bodleian Library, Oxford)

Rūzbihān lived in Shiraz when it was a small island of prosperity and culture under the rule of the Salghurid atabegs, after the decline of the Seljuks and before the storm of the Mongol conquest.[1] He continued the line of Sufi tradition in Shiraz that went back to Ibn al-Khafīf (d. 372/982) and through him to Baghdadian Sufis such as the martyr al-Ḥallāj (d. 310/922). One may ask, however, from a purely literary point of view, how significant the works of Rūzbihān are for the understanding of later Sufism through the fifteenth century. Direct references to Rūzbihān in later Persian Sufi literature are not terribly common, and they tend to focus on his reputation as a lover of beauty.[2] He is known for his prescription of the three things which the gnostics require of a singer when listening to music *(samā')*: fine fragrances, a beautiful face, and a sweet voice *(rawā'iḥ-i ṭayyiba wa wajh-i ṣabīḥ wa ṣawt-i malīḥ)*. Frequently one also finds mention of the well-known episode in which he forbade a young woman to veil her face, on the grounds that separating beauty and love would be a crime.[3]

Rūzbihān's writings were difficult, however, and there are not many explicit responses to his works by later authors. Some commentaries on his writings do exist, however; an Anatolian Naqshbandī Sufi named 'Abdullāh Ilāhī Sīmābī (d. 896/1491) commented on the *Risālat al-quds (Treatise on the Sacred)*, a work on Sufism addressed to novices,[4] and an anonymous writer also glossed Rūzbihān's treatise on love, the *'Abhar al-'āshiqīn (Jasmine of the Lovers)*.[5] We know that Rūzbihān's works were studied by authors such as Jāmī (d. 897/1492) in fifteenth-century Herat, and that they attracted the interest of the Mughul prince[6] Dārā

1. Cf. C. E. Bosworth, 'The Political and Dynastic History of the Iranian World (A.D. 1000-1217),', in *The Cambridge History of Iran*, vol. 5, *The Saljuq and Mongol Periods*, ed. J. A. Boyle (Cambridge University Press 1968), pp. 172-173.
2. See, e.g., Fakhr al-Dīn 'Irāqī [attr.], *The Song of Lovers*, ed. and trans. A. J. Arberry (Calcutta: Islamic Research Association 1939), pp. 88-90 (text), 57-58 (trans.). See also A.J. Arberry, *Shiraz: Persian City of Saints and Poets* (Norman: University of Oklahoma Press 1960), pp. 86-111, for a brief sketch of Rūzbihān's life and works.
3. Jāmī, *Tuḥfat al-aḥrār* (Lucknow: Tēj Kumār, 1966), pp. 61-62. Jāmī also tells the story in *Nafaḥāt al-uns wa ḥaḍarāt al-quds*, ed. Mahdī Tawḥīdīpūr (Tehran: Kitāb-furūshī-yi Maḥmūdī 1337/1957), p. 256.
4. This commentary, entitled *Manāzil al-qulūb*, is printed in Muḥammad Taqī Danish-puzhuh, ed., *Rūzbihān-nāma*, Silsila-yi Intisharat-i Anjuman-i Athar-i Milli, 60 (Tehran: Chāp-khāna-yi Bahman, 1347/1969), pp. 387-420, from a MS. from Yugoslavia. 2 other MSS. of this text are in Egypt, and another is reported to be in Manisa, Turkey; cf. Abū Muḥammed Rūzbihān al-Bakli al-Şirāzī, *Kitāb Mashrab al-arvāḥ*, ed. Nazif Hoca, İstanbul Üniversitesi Edebiyat Fakültesi Yayinlan, No. 1876 (Istanbul: Edebiyat Fakültesi Matbaası, 1974), Introduction, p. 1. On Ilāhī Sīmābī, who studied in Samarqand, met Jāmī in Herat, and died in Rumelia, see *Rūzbihān-nāma*, pp. 64-66. See also Rūzbihān Baqli Shirazi, *Risālat al-quds wa ghalaṭāt al-sālikīn*, ed. Dr. J. Nurbakhsh (Tehran: Chāp-khāna-yi Firdawsī 1351/1972).
5. Rūzbihān Baqlī Shīrāzī, *'Abhar al-'āshiqīn*, ed. Henry Corbin and Muḥammad Mu'īn, Ganjīna-yi Nivishtahā-yi Īrānī, 8 (Tehran: Anjuman-i Īrān-shināsī-yi Farānsa dar Tehrān 1360/1981), pp. 149-202. These glosses appear to date from the early Safavid period (*ibid.*, Persian Introduction, p. 108).
6. Dārā Shikūh had Rūzbihān's *tafsīr*, *'Arā'is al-bayān*, translated into Persian, and he wrote an abridgement and update of Rūzbihān's commentary on the ecstatic sayings of the early Sufis *(Sharḥ-i shaṭhiyyāt)* under the title *Ḥasanāt al-'ārifīn* (p. 356, n. 2). For the original text, see Rūzbihān Baqlī Shīrāzī, *Sharḥ-i shaṭhiyyāt*, ed. Henry Corbin, Bibliotheque Irānienne 12 (Tehran: Departement d'Irānologie de l'Institut Franco-Iranien 1966).

Shikūh (d. 1069/1659) in the seventeenth century. All these later figures testified to the difficulty of Rūzbihān's style, which at times is admittedly convoluted and obscure. Jāmī remarked that "he has sayings that have poured forth from him in the state of overpowering and ecstasy, which not everyone can understand."[1] Dārā Shikūh found his style "fatiguing."[2] Despite the preservation of Rūzbihān's legacy by his son and grandson in Shiraz, and for all that Louis Massignon has traced the existence of the *ṭarīqa-i Rūzbihāniyya* as far as Timbuktu, it must be admitted that none of his physical or spiritual descendents has been able to reach Rūzbihān's level of mystical attainment or to match him as a stylist in Persian or Arabic.[3] It is not, however, the frequency of references to Rūzbihān that makes him relevant to the study of Persian Sufism; it is, rather, the penetration of his existential insight that makes his writing significant. It is only in recent decades that the rediscovery and publication of his writings has led to a renewed appreciation of his importance for the understanding of Sufism. Muḥammad Mu'īn, the pioneering editor of the *'Abhar al-'āshiqīn,* remarked about this text, that "to understand the works of mystics such as 'Aṭṭār, Rūmī, 'Irāqī, Awḥadī-i Kirmānī, and Ḥāfiẓ, researches on this book are quite necessary."[4] I would enlarge upon this statement and say that the various writings of Rūzbihān Baqlī form a vital resource for understanding the experiential basis of Persian Sufi literature.

Rūzbihān regards the symbol of the bird as multivalent, capable of standing for a wide variety of spirits, persons, and experiences. The importance of this image in Rūzbihān's writings may be gauged by the frequency with which he uses it in the beginnings of his treatises, immediately following the praise of God and the Prophet.[5] When commenting on a phrase used by Ḥallāj, "the fortunate bird," Rūzbihān offered a startling number of possible interpretations:

> The 'fortunate bird'[6] is the hoopoe of Solomon, on whom be peace, or the phoenix of the west, or the royal *humā,* or the bird of success, or the bird of inspiration, or the bird of the spirit, or lucky augury, or the bird of light who circumambulates the

1. Jāmī, *Nafaḥāt,* p. 255.
2. Dārā Shikūh, *Ḥasanāt al-'ārifīn,* ed. Makhdum Rahin (Tehran 1352/1973), p. 3.
3. Louis Massignon, 'La vie et les oeuvres de Ruzbehan Baqli,' in *Opera Minora,* ed. Y. Moubarac (Beirut: Dar al-Maaref 1963), II, 451-465, esp. 455-456 for the *ṭarīqa.* As far as the subject of this paper is concerned, Rūzbihān's descendants have very little to say; there are no references to the symbolism of flight in their biographies of Rūzbihān, and the only mention of birds is an incident in which Rūzbihān detected that a chicken offered to him as food was not lawful *(Rūzbihān-nāma,* pp. 45, 220-221).
4. Mu'īn, Introduction to *'Abhar,* p. 84. In this respect, Mu'īn shared the view of Dr. Qāsim Ghanī, that "from the point of view of the greatness of his mystical station, and from the perspective of ecstasy and spiritual state, Shaykh Rūzbihān is on the level of Shaykh Abū'l-Ḥasan Kharaqānī and Shaykh Abū Sa'īd-i Abū'l-Khayr"; Ghanī also placed Rūzbihān prominently in his list of twenty-eight major Sufi authors. See his *Baḥth dar āthār wa afkār wa aḥwāl-i Ḥāfiẓ,* vol. 2, *Tārīkh-i taṣawwuf dar islām wa taṭawwurāt wa taḥawwulāt-i mukhtalifa-yi ān az ṣadr-i islām ta 'aṣr-i Ḥāfiẓ* (Tehran: Kitābfurūshī Zawwār 1340/1961), p. 395, n. 2; p. 545.
5. Extensive passages with bird imagery are found at the beginning in Rūzbihān's Koran commentary, *'Arā'is al-bayān* (p. 364, n. 2), in his letter to 'Imad al-Dīn Kirmānī (p. 361, n. 6), and in the *Risālat al-quds* (p. 362, n.1), and phrases with bird imagery are frequent in the exordia of other texts as well (e.g., *Sharḥ-i shaṭḥiyyāt,* p. 4, bottom).
6. *Sharḥ-i shaṭḥiyyāt,* p. 365. This passage is a commentary on Ḥallāj's *Riwāya* 21, in which the 'fortunate bird' is one of the symbolic transmitters of a *ḥadīth.*

Rūzbihān Baqlī Preaching in Shiraz. From a manuscript of the *Majālis al-'ushshāq,* dated 959/1552. MS. Ouseley Add. 24, f. 54a (Courtesy of the Bodleian Library, Oxford)

[Muḥammad], blessings of God upon him.

Frequently, also, Rūzbihān speaks of the Prophet Muḥammad using bird symbolism, calling him "the nightingale of the love of pre-eternities, the *Sīmurgh* of the nest of post-eternities."[1] The two birds, the *Sīmurgh* and the nightingale, have sharply differing qualities as symbols of the divine beloved and the human lover (discussed below), but the dynamic role of the Prophet mediates between these two poles. Likewise the Sufi saint Bāyazīd Biṣṭāmī (d. 260/874) is called "the bird of the nest of isolation," alluding to the spiritual state *(ifrād)* with which Bāyazīd is associated.[2] Sufis who have been persecuted and killed are called "the birds of sanctity" who have returned to their nests.[3] In an unedited text on theology, Rūzbihān calls upon the imagery of birds flying in a celestial garden to indicate the role of prophets, angels, and saints: "He manifested the gardens of intimacy and called them 'the enclosure of sanctity,' and in it flew the spirits of the elect, among the prophets, messengers, cherubs, spirituals, gnostics, and unitarians."[4] Somewhat more abstractly, Rūzbihān uses birds and their songs to symbolize particular spiritual experiences that have been revealed by the ecstatic expressions *(shaṭḥiyyāt)* of Sufis such as Bāyazīd and Ḥallāj:

> The bird of isolation sang 'Allāh, Allāh,' the bird of uniting *(tawḥīd)* said, "I am the Real *(anā al-ḥaqq)*" the bird of sanctification said "Glory be to me *(subḥānī)*." When they arose from the New Year's garden of witnessing, they flew with the wings of pre-eternities in the post-eternities of post-eternities. Those birds of divinity brought the secret of divinity to the palace of humanity, and spoke with the soul of divinity in the tongue of humanity.[5]

Similarly, when the divine essence retracts and the soul is cut off from spiritual experience, we are told that "the bird of manifestation has gone to the nest of eternity."[6] Rūzbihān has been followed by his commentator Ilāhī Sīmābī in this tendency to use birds to symbolize spiritual experiences, in this case regarding the primacy of the experience of "opening *(futūḥ)*" as a pre-requisite for receiving "unveilings" of the divine sanctity: "From the atmosphere in which the spirit's *Sīmurgh* [flies], before this, the bird of 'opening' *(futūḥ)* has been seen."[7] In other words, before the spirit can soar like the *Sīmurgh,* it must first take flight with the experience of 'opening.' The anonymous commentator on the *'Abhar al-'āshiqīn* has also seen that Rūzbihān's use of bird imagery is meant to recall spiritual experiences. This can

---

1. *Abhar al-'āshiqīn,* p. 120; cf. also p. 20.
2. *Sharḥ-i shaṭḥiyyāt,* p. 35.
3. *Ibid.,* p. 33.
4. Rūzbihān Baqlī, *Lawāmi' al-tawḥīd,* MS 1460 Ahmet Salis, Topkapı Library, Istanbul, fol. 4b. This fine manuscript, which was not noticed by previous researchers (Mu'īn, Introduction to *Rūzbihān-nāma,* p. 71; Dānish-puzhūh, *Rūzbihān-nāma,* pp. 264-266 [extract], 341, no. 8), seems to be the sole existing complete copy of this work by Rūzbihān. It is an elementary treatise on theology in 35 fols., accompanied by another short text previously not found, *Maslak al-tawḥīd,* in 21 fols. (cf. Mu'īn, p. 71, and *Rūzbihān-nāma,* p. 342, no. 23).
5. *Sharḥ-i shaṭḥiyyāt,* p. 22. On the subject of *shaṭḥiyyāt,* see my *Words of Ecstasy in Sufism* (Albany, N.Y.: State University of New York Press 1985).
6. *Sharḥ-i shaṭḥiyyāt,* p. 187.
7. Sīmābī, *Manāzil al-qulūb,* in *Rūzbihān-nāma,* p. 402 (verse), commenting on the phrase 'unveiling of the sanctity of sanctity' in *Risālat al-quds,* ed. Nurbakhsh p. 44.

that Rūzbihān's use of bird imagery is meant to recall spiritual experiences. This can be seen in a passage in which Rūzbihān speaks of the trapped bird as an image of the soul trapped in the body: "See what bird is in your trap, that the nest of the *Sīmurgh* of the throne cannot bear its grain!" The commentator remarks that "the universal intellect is incapable of comprehending [the soul's] emanation, which is love."[1]

The particular birds most frequently invoked by Rūzbihān are the nightingale and the phoenix-like bird called *Sīmurgh* or *'Anqā*. Unlike Rumi or 'Aṭṭār, Rūzbihān is not too interested in describing other varieties of birds and the qualities they represent.[2] The nightingale, of course, is a staple of Persian poetry, as the figure of the impassioned human lover addressing the unattainable beauty of the divine rose.[3] The *Sīmurgh*, at first a supernatural bird and helper of humanity in ancient Iranian mythology, has become a symbol of the divine in Persian literature.[4] Because Rūzbihān so often stresses the ascension from human attributes to divine ones, he frequently blurs the distinction between the nightingale and the *Sīmurgh*. Thus he urges his reader to ascend to the true home, the heavenly nest:

> Remove the belongings of the *Sīmurgh* from this narrow hut, for the orient of the throne is the nest of your eternal soul. Take the power of Jesus' soul from the heaven of pre-eternity, so that with the birds of angelicity you complete a house for this nightingale of power.[5]

Sometimes he combines the *Sīmurgh* with the *Humā*, the royal bird whose shadow designates a king. "Cast off the shadow of temporality's veil from existence, so that the *Humā* of the Attributes opens the wings of pre-eternity, and the *Sīmurgh* of majesty comes from the orient of eternity."[6] But always the injunction is the same: the soul ascends like a heavenly bird to find its identity, and like the birds in 'Aṭṭār's tale, it finds God as its true self. "When the *Sīmurgh* of the soul flies from the realm of humanity to the world of divinity, the growing soul speaks to itself in the rose-bower of Adam's clay; those seeking the reflection of that shadowing *'Anqā* become the shadow of God."[7] At times the *'Anqā* as the transcendent God becomes overwhelming: "Existence in relation to His might is less than an atom, and all the

1. *'Abhar al-'āshiqīn*, p. 190, commenting on text, p. 62. In a similar fashion, this commentator identifies the "birds of silence" (text, p. 60) as "the people of concentration and meditation" (p. 187).
2. Occasionally Rūzbihān speaks of the peacock (*Sharḥ-i shaṭḥiyyāt*, pp. 226, 236; *'Abhar al-'āshiqīn*, p. 142), the hoopoe (*Sharḥ-i shaṭḥiyyāt*, pp. 365, 370), or the crow (*ibid.*, p. 257; *Rūzbihān-nāma*, p. 322).
3. Annemarie Schimmel, 'Rose und Nachtigall,' *Numen* V (1958), pp. 85-109. For a survey of references to birds in early classical Persian poetry, see C. H. de Fouchecour, *La Description de la nature dans la poésie lyrique persane du XIe siècle: Inventaire et analyse des thèmes* (Paris: Librairie C. Klincksieck 1969), pp. 138-150.
4. Cf. Alessandro Bausani, 'Letteratura Neopersiana,' in *Antonino Pagliaro and Alessandro Bausani, Storia della letteratura persiana* (Milan: Nuova Accademia Editrice, 1960), pp. 290-293; Johann Christoph Bürgel, *The Feather of Sīmurgh: The 'Licit Magic' of the Arts in Medieval Islam* (New York: New York University Press 1988), pp. 5-7.
5. *Sharḥ-i shaṭḥiyyāt*, p. 283.
6. *Ibid.*, p. 143. The 'foolish *Humā*' as image of the human soul appears in *'Abhar al-'āshiqīn*, p. 62, while in a verse by Rūzbihān the *Humā* is the divinity which cannot fit into the nest of the human heart (*Rūzbihān-nāma*, p. 355).
7. *Sharḥ-i shaṭḥiyyāt*, p. 331.

nal wrath."[1] Yet at other times, the soul overwhelmed by the ecstasy of *shaṭḥ* shifts from the self-effacement of the nightingale to the audacity of the hoopoe, who did not hesitate to show off his knowledge before Solomon.

> The lily of beauty reached the stage of the nightingale of perfection. The shadow of the blessed tree of eternity became the illumination of the spring of the nightingales who chant "I am the Real." At the confluence of the sources of pre-eternity the hoopoes of the spirits drank the water of life of "Glory be to me." Thus in the feast of the Solomon of unity, from intoxication they became the sovereigns of existence. With hidden tongue of the human intellect in the sanctified nest beyond canopy and throne, they said "I learned something which you did not."[2]

The plasticity of the nightingale and the *Sīmurgh* in Rūzbihān's imagery is a direct result of the sudden and precipitous outbursts of his spiritual experiences, which he has chronicled in more direct terms in his autobiographical *Kashf al-asrār*.[3] Keeping in mind the freshness of these images in Rūzbihān's hands may help to counter the impression one frequently gets in later Persian poetry, that images such as the nightingale and the rose have been deprived of all life and loveliness at the hands of mediocre poets. Rūzbihān's use of these symbols to indicate the ascensional experiences of the soul can help remind us of what a mystical interpretation of Persian poetry can be.

Rūzbihān makes use of an extended complex of imagery related to birds to express various mystical insights. When combined, these images provide a more comprehensive picture of the celestial habitat of the soul-bird.[4] As we have already seen, the nest of the bird is a symbol of transcendence that reveals that the bird's true home is not earth but heaven. The nest must inevitably be located in a tree that is in the heavenly garden, such as the lotus or *Ṭūbā* tree, as the bird discovers when it finally gains admission: "Since I saw that rose of the rose garden and the dark narcissus, the lotus and the *Ṭūbā* trees are in my garden."[5] But getting to that heavenly garden is not so simple. Because of the rebellious nature of the soul, it must be

1. *Ibid.*, p. 96.
2. *Ibid.*, p. 20, quoting Koran, XXVII 22, the speech of the hoopoe to Solomon (also cited at *ibid.*, p. 370).
3. For this text, see Henry Corbin, *En Islam iranien: Aspects spirituels et philosophiques*, vol. 3, *Les Fidèles d'amour, Shî'isme et soufisme* (Paris: Éditions Gallimard, Bibliothèque des Idees, 1972). Portions of the Arabic text have been published by Paul Nwyia, S.J., 'Waqā'i' al-Shaykh Rūzbihān al-Baqlī al-Shīrāzī muqtaṭafāt' min kitāb *Kashf al-asrār'i wa mukāshafat al-anwār,' Al-Mashriq* LXIV/4-5 (1970), pp. 385-406, and by Nazif Hoca, ed., *Rūzbihān al-Baḳlī ve Kitāb Kaşf al-asrār'ı ile Farsça bāzi şiirleri*, Istanbul Üniversitesi Edebiyat Fakültesi Yayinları, No. 1678 (Istanbul: Edebiyat Fakültesi Matbaası 1971), pp. 103-118. On the basis of the complete text, which was partially edited from 3 MSS. by Henry Corbin, a complete French translation has been promised by Dr. Paul Ballanfat of the Sorbonne.
4. For the motif of the soul-bird in general, see Annemarie Schimmel, As *Through a Veil: Mystical Poetry in Islam* (New York: Columbia University Press 1982), pp. 75-76; id., *The Triumphal Sun: A Study of the Works of Jalāloddin Rumi* (London: Fine Books 1978), pp. 113-124. To the standard stock of images, Rūzbihān does not hesitate to add even the ordinarily disgusting picture of a bird disgorging stones from its crop: "The annotations of those seas belong to the soul-killing birds, who from time to time cast forth the pearl of 'I am the Real' from the shells of their crops" *(Sharḥ-i shaṭḥiyyāt* p. 501).
5. Verse, in *Rūzbihān-nāma*, p. 344. On the motifs of heavenly trees, see Bausani, pp. 286-290.

trapped with bait of grain or sugar. Sometimes it is only the hope of that grain that holds the bird in the trap: "Such a sweet-singing nightingale with so many thousands of songs suddenly fell in the hunter's trap of persecution, and in hope of the grain of seeing the visage of that moon-faced beauty in the thorny rose garden, it remained an attendant at the feast of his pain."[1] Rumi also writes of love trapping the bird of the soul with sugar.[2] This is a reversal of the pessimistic view of the bird's entrapment as a metaphor for the fall of the soul into matter, as Adam fell, also snared by a grain of wheat.[3] In a complex extended passage, Rūzbihān speaks of the entrapment of the bird as the soul's imprisonment in the body, but he optimistically predicts that the soul will free itself and ultimately attain the status of being the hawk on the wrist of the divine hunter:

> Know that when the spirit of humanity was placed in the clay of Adam, and the brides of the spirits were imprisoned in those mines, and the gates of the heart were barred with the obstacles of desires, it was for the sake of testing, so that cage-breaking bird would break out of the prison of temporality with the existence-holding beak, and fly in the atmosphere of divinity, and sit in the gardens of witnessing on the branches of the rose of sufficiency, and with a tongueless tongue tell to the beloved the pain of separation from the face of the beloved. But if it acquires a taste for the reins of desires, it will be imprisoned in the four walls of nature, and will be restrained from flight in the atmosphere of pre-eternity.
>
> Yes, if the secret of longing enters upon him, and he rattles the chain of eternal love, and he brings up that rational spirit from the cage of the body, and makes it fly in the garden of lordship, that hawk *(bāsha)* will wheel about in the existence of angelicity, and overlook the seraglio of might, and will find himself at no other place than the wrist of the hunter of pre-eternity, who catches the birds of the mountains of love with the love-charm of fate.[4]

The soul must take constant effort to practise discipline and avoid bad company, says Rūzbihān: "Start removing yourself from this flock of foolish sparrows, for in the flight of the Western *'Anqā,* your soul will not fly with a broken wing."[5] But the divine mercy will also help to bring the hapless bird out of its imprisonment into the heavenly garden, calling it as God called to Moses on Sinai: "Praise to that lord who brought the bird of felicity from the cage of persecution to the rosebower of purity and trust, with the ringing cry of 'We called him from the right side of the mountain' (Koran, IXX 52), who expelled the crows of nature from the gardens of reality, and who called the nightingale of the most holy spirit with speech."[6] Breaking out of the cage of the body will involve a death, whether physical or spiritual, before the soul can return to its home.[7] But when it does finally return to the garden, Rūzbihān is sure that the bird of the soul will perch on the branches of the rose and sing, recalling and fulfilling the primordial covenant it made by saying yes to

1. *'Abhar al-'āshiqīn,* p. 60.
2. Annemarie Schimmel, *As Through a Veil,* p. 112, with notes 207 and 208.
3. For this theme in Rūmī, see Schimmel, *Triumphal Sun,* pp. 113-114.
4. *Risālat al-quds,* p. 29.
5. *Sharḥ-i shaṭḥiyyāt,* p. 599.
6. Letter to 'Imād al-Dīn Kirmānī, in *Rūzbihān-nāma,* p. 322.
7. Some of the last verses that Rūmī wrote for his friends treated "the soul bird's flight from the cage of the body" (Schimmel, *As Through a Veil* p. 94).

God's question, 'Am I not your lord?' (Koran, VII 171). "Let the rose of beauty grow before those nightingales of everlastingness on the branches of majesty, let the nightingale of 'Am I not [your lord] *(alast)*' speak the secrets of love with those birds of the throne."[1] According to Rūzbihān, the epiphany of God as the red rose is the supreme moment of this reunion.

There are times when Rūzbihān abandons the notion of the bird as symbolic of the soul, taking it instead as a symbol of creation. He is led to do this especially when considering Ḥallāj's exegesis of an enigmatic verse of the Koran addressed to Abraham, "'Take four birds and sacrifice them' [Koran, II 260], for the Real does not fly." Rūzbihān in this way treats the birds as representing the unstable four elements of matter, which must be annihilated and abolished from consciousness, so that the ego can be destroyed and the Real can be revealed:

> If you wish to know our allusion in reality, and to understand knowledge in oneness, and to arrive at that which we described of the annihilation of the creature in the creator, call the four birds of the elements near to you, and with the sword of intoxication, love, and desire, cut them to pieces...Cut the throat of each bird in the court of the spirit]s jealousy, because the elements fly [away] and become unsteady; the knowledge of that does not fly [away]...When you have killed and annihilated the birds of the elements, and torn off from them the wings of spatial dimensions, and loosened yourself from those weights of creation, then no duration, time, place, or witness remains; you reach the world of utter nonexistence, and are astonished in it, so that you do not know who you are...[2]

In a similar vein, Ilāhī Sīmābī on occasion deals with birds as symbols of earthly life, the physicality of which must be transcended:

> Every pigeon flies in a certain way, but this pigeon [flies] in a directionless direction.
> We are not kin to the birds of the air, and our grain is a grainless grain.[3]

So at times the bird-symbolism is used to denote the limitations of physical existence. Most typically, however, Rūzbihān sees the bird as an image of the "rational spirit *(rūḥ-i nāṭiqa),*" the inner essence of humanity, which is forever seeking its divine counterpart even while trapped in the body. "The bird of intimacy, which is the rational spirit, flies in the lesser existence, which is the human body, in conversation with love in the cage of the heart."[4] In a surprising shift of images, Rūzbihān

---

1. *Risālat al-quds*, p. 3. The nightingale singing on the rose branch recurs in *Sharḥ-i shaṭḥiyyāt*, pp. 92, 225, 230, and *'Abhar al-'āshiqīn*, p. 124.
2. *Sharḥ-i shaṭḥiyyāt*, pp. 484-485, commenting on al-Ḥallāj's *Ṭawāsīn* 4.2, which contains the quotation of Koran, II 260. Rūzbihān also offers the interpretation that the four birds are soul, heart, intellect, and spirit, which must be humbled to acknowledge the greatness of God; *ibid.*, pp. 485-486. The symbolism of birds as the four elements recurs in ibid., p. 152. Rūmī identifies the four birds allegorically as representations of different lowly desires; cf. Schimmel, *Triumphal Sun*, p. 113.
3. Ilāhī Sīmābī, *Manāzil al-qulūb*, in *Rūzbihān-nāma*, p. 403 *(mathnawī* verse). This verse is from Rūmī, *Mathnawī-yi ma'nawī*, ed. & trans. R.A. Nicholson, 8 vols. Gibb Memorial Series, n.s. 4 (London 1925-40), Bk. V 351-52.
4. *Abhar al-'āshiqīn*, pp. 70-71. For the use of this characteristic phrase *rūḥ-i nāṭiqa*, which derives from the vocabulary of al-Ḥallāj, see *Risālat al-quds*, p. 29 (quoted above, at n. 39); *Sharḥ-i shaṭḥiyyāt*, pp. 245, 336, 340-341, 363, 408, 414, 603, 632.

stretches the symbol of the soul-bird to the limit, by showing how the soul's wings are consumed by the experiences of nearness and unveiling; the bird has now been transformed into a moth, burning up in the flame of love:

> When the sacred birds of the spirits fly from the rose branches of witnessing temporality, and traverse the atmosphere of the heaven of certainty, their nests are nowhere but in the gardens of nearness. . . . The fire of witnessing reached from the light of unveiling to the wings of their souls. From the wrath of this fire, the wings of their souls are burned, and they remained wingless outside the door of the hidden of the hidden. . . . Since no wing remained, in that station of theirs another wing appeared from pure love. With that wing, like moths, they flew again; round the candle of beauty, on the basin of nearness, the light of their union flamed. When every wing, from spirit in spirit, had burned, they collected the knowledge of realities in the palace of pre-eternity. That knowledge became their wings of love and longing, and they flew in the atmosphere of utter nearness. [1]

The successive destruction of each pair of wings at every level as the soul flies higher conveys the devastating power of this experience of transcendence.

Perhaps the most remarkable guise in which birds appear in Rūzbihān's writings is as personifications of Koranic verses and *ḥadīth* sayings. Many poets relied on the Koran's statement, that "There is nothing that does not glorify him with praise" (XVII 44), to show how all creatures praise God; the beautiful songs of birds were natural examples to use as a metaphor for creation's testimony to the creator (cf. Koran, XXI 79; XXIV 41). Rūzbihān has, in a way, inverted the process of the metaphor. The symbol of the soul-bird had given an externalized form to a psychological reality, the process and experience of transcendence. Now Rūzbihān re-psychologizes the image of the bird, reducing its image content to a minimum and making the symbol as transparent as possible to the underlying experience. Koranic verses, to Rūzbihān, are not mere words, but verbal theophanies, which act as catalysts for the transformation of the listening soul. The power of the Koran to bring about such a transformation is such that certain verses, for Rūzbihān, announce themselves like birds proclaiming the identity of the divine beloved. Thus we find that it is frequently "the bird of 'Am I not [your Lord]'" (cf. Koran VII 171) who reminds us of the primordial covenant by which humanity was sealed to God in pre-eternity.[2] The bird of Koranic theophany does not only speak of the primordial covenant, but also recites the epiphanies to Moses on Mt. Sinai. "Have you not heard from Sinai's tree the *'Anqā*'s cry of 'Truly I am God' (Koran, XXVIII 30)?"[3] The bird's Koranic proclamation of divinity does not concern some distant king, but is a reminder of intimate presence. "If from the suffering of love I heard the call of the birds of the morning of 'God spoke [to Moses]' (IV 164), I would be the partner and companion of the Sinai of 'There is no conspiracy [of three but I am the fourth]' (LVIII 7).'[4] Finally, Rūzbihān puts the prophetic seal on this bird-manifestation of

---

1. *'Abhar al-'āshiqīn*, p. 124; cf. also pp. 48 and 88 for moth imagery.
2. *Sharḥ-i shaṭḥiyyāt*, pp. 225, 230-231, 257 (where God gives the pearl of "Am I not" to the crows of creation), 316; *Risālat al-quds*, p. 3 (quoted above, at n. 43).
3. *Sharḥ-i shaṭḥiyyāt*, p. 318; cf. p. 175: "the birds of manifestation strike the bell of 'Truly I am God' [Koran, XXVIII 30] from the tree of Moses."
4. *Sharḥ-i shaṭḥiyyāt*, p. 229.

scripture, through birds that recall the ascension of the soul, modelled on the Prophet Muḥammad's night journey *(isrā')* to paradise and his confession of his inability to praise the infinity of God.

> Do you not know that knowledge is the wings of nearness, up to the gateway of eternity? Beyond that, one can fly no further with these. . . . Whoever does not come out from the twilight of nature, and does not travel the journey of "Glory to him who brought [his servant] by night" [Koran, XVII 1] in the night of the soul's ascension, does not know the cry of the nightingale of "I cannot count [your] praise" in the garden of the throne.[1]

In this way, Koranic verses become birds that fly like messengers from God and humanity, proclaiming divine lordship. Moreover, not only the Koranic revelation, but also the act of exegesis itself, becomes another bird-flight, in response to the divine word. In a revealing passage located at the very beginning of his massive Koran commentary, the *'Arā'is al-bayān* or *Brides of Explanation,* Rūzbihān describes his approach to scriptural interpretation as one long flight in bird form to the paradisal garden of the Koran.

> When the birds of my mysteries *(asrār)* had finished flying in the states and stations, rising beyond the battlefields of spiritual combat and self-observation, reaching the gardens of unveiling and witnessing, alighting on the branches of the flowers of nearness, and imbibing the wine of union, they became intoxicated by seeing the divine beauty, love-stricken in the lights of divine splendor, and they recovered from [their intoxication] with the station of sanctity by the taste of intimacy. From the dawn of the Unmanifest they seized the blossoms of the subtleties of the Koran and the refinements of the truths of the Criterion. They soared on wings of gnosis, and warbled the best elucidation by means of the melodies of paradise, [intoning] the mysteries *(rumūz)* of God *(al-Ḥaqq)* by means of this tongue, mysteries that He has hidden from the understanding of the people of forms.[2]

The bird of the spirit ascends, then, in response to the call of the bird of revelation.

Flight is a primary metaphor for spiritual experience. Rūzbihān states this boldly in his lexicon of Sufi terminology, when he defines the term "overwhelmings *(ghalabāt)*" as "the flight of the spirit in angelicity."[3] In his commentary on 1001 spiritual stations, he describes flight *(ṭayrān)* as station number 924, and he removes any suggestion of merely physical levitation from the term: "In the station of flight, it is the *khalīfas* who fly with the angels in spirit and body, for they are spirituals, in whom is the likeness of the angels... I have not flown in the air because of my knowledge, but I found that meaning by which they fly in me."[4] Thus he knows the flight of the exalted figures called "successors *(khalīfas)*" not by external

1. *Ibid.*, p. 316. For the well-known *hadith*, "I cannot count your praise," see Annemarie Schimmel, *Mystical Dimensions of Islam* (Chapel Hill: The University of North Carolina Press), pp. 126, 162, 222; Badī' al-Zamān Furūzānfar, *Aḥādith-i Mathnawī,* Intishārāt-i Dānishgāh-i Tehran, 283 (Tehran: Chāp-khāna-yi Dānishgāh 1334/1956), p. 2, no. 3.
2. *'Arā'is al-bayān fī haqā'iq al-Qur'ān* (Calcutta 1883), I, 3, trans. Alan Godlas, 'The Qur'anic Hermeneutics of Rūzbihān al-Baqlī,' Ph.D. dissertation in progress, University of California at Berkeley. I would like to express my thanks to Alan Godlas for bringing this passage to my attention.
3. *Sharḥ-i shaṭhiyyāt,* p. 553.
4. *Mashrab al-arwāḥ,* p. 284.

flight but by perceiving them in the atmosphere of his soul. One begins practicing this kind of flight by meditation, which Rūzbihān describes in a chapter entitled "On the Meditation which is the Wing for the Bird of Intimacy in the Station of Love." In this section, all the metaphors of trapping birds in the desert are used to convey the approach to the beloved through the meditation of love.[1] At its highest, the experience of love brings the lover to a state of utter nearness to the beloved, and then "he may fly like the spirituals of angelicity in the highest of the high with the peacocks of the angels, like Khiḍr, Ilyās, Idrīs and Jesus."[2] Spiritual experience as flight in this way encompasses the highest realms of the angels and prophets.

From the viewpoint of mystical experience, ascension to divinity is the key to the symbolism of birds and flight. Many of Rūzbihān's allusions to flight explicitly invoke the most famous account of mystical ascension in Sufi literature, the ascension of Bāyazīd Bisṭāmī. Rūzbihān himself commented extensively on Bāyazīd's ascension in his *Sharḥ-i shaṭḥiyyāt.*[3] Bāyazīd had described himself as becoming a bird with a body of oneness, and wings of everlastingness, flying in an atmosphere without quality until he reached an eternal tree, of which he ate the fruit; he then realized that all of this vision was a deceit, a trick of his own imagination.[4] Rūzbihān in his commentary amplified on the imagery of wings and flight, introducing, for example, the moth-like burning of the wings of the soul in the flame of divine majesty. The entire sequence of Bāyazīd's vision, if understood as a return of the soul-bird to the heavenly garden, fits very well with Rūzbihān's symbolic picture of the bird's flight to its nest on the branch of the celestial tree, where it will sing to its beloved the song of its pain. In one variation on this theme, Rūzbihān says,

> The pigeon of temporality escaped the beak of the falcon of love. It spread its wings in the atmosphere of identity, near the *Sīmurgh* of the orient of eternity, and it flew at the edge of union. Then, with the tongueless tongue of "I cannot count your praise," it began to tell secrets to the bird of pre-eternity. When it was finished with the hidden secret, it thought that there was no one else but itself.[5]

In the end, the images of birds, wings, and ascensions are only images, figures

---

1. *'Abhar al-'āshiqīn,* p. 106: "When the caravans of intellects pick up the burdens of the spirit's practice, flight in the atmosphere of the heaven of eternity becomes easy. The soul reaches the beloved's place of visitation, the bird of love joins the cage of the bird of intimacy in the station of meditation, and the hunters' trap catches the birds of manifestation in the desert of the heart."
2. *Ibid.*, p. 142.
3. *Sharḥ-i shaṭḥiyyāt,* pp. 80-82. See my *Words of Ecstasy,* Appendix, pp. 167-169, for a translation of this passage. The last sentence of the commentary on p. 169 is to be corrected as follows: "That which he said concerns the eclipse of the Attributes; otherwise, he who is of the Essence—Alas!" For another mystical use of the term "eclipse *(kusūf),*" cf. *Sharḥ-i shaṭḥiyyāt,* p. 92, line 2.
4. It is surprising that R. C. Zaehner's fanciful theory of the Upanishadic origin of this symbolism has once again been revived, even if in a limited form, by Julian Baldick, in *Mystical Islam: An Introduction to Sufism* (London: I. B. Tauris, 1989). The imagery of wings, birds, and trees is abundantly present in the ascension literature of the Near East from ancient times onwards, and it hardly seems necessary or meaningful to suppose that Bāyazīd could only have learned of such an image from Indian sources, which in any case have altogether different structures.
5. *Sharḥ-i shaṭḥiyyāt,* p. 401. For other allusions to Bāyazīd's ascension, cf. ibid., pp. 22, 129, 167, 214; *Risālat al-quds,* pp. 29 (quoted above, at n. 39), 31, *'Abhar al-'āshiqīn,* pp. 3, 124.

through which the soul attempts to comprehend its own nature. Therefore Bāyazīd ultimately denounced them as a deceit.

The fundamental experiences of the soul in tension toward the divine need to find expression, however. Sometimes this can be done verbally, through the abstract technical terms of Sufism, through the ecstatic expressions of the mystics, or through scriptural passages that can act as the locus for the human-divine encounter. But it is also necessary for these experiences to take form, to be refracted in the medium of consciousness and assume the density of symbols taken from the natural world. Then, as Rumi put it, the secret of the beloved can be revealed through stories about others. The poetic imagination uses imagery to express experience. If the poet is successful, the images will continue to function transparently; if the poet is less successful, the images will still work on the level of abstract allegory. But from the point of view of the mystic, the images become false when they solidify to the point of blocking out vision altogether, and take on an importance in themselves. The symbolism of birds and flight always remained, for Rūzbihān, a pliant and dynamic one, in which the lover's nightingale at any moment might be transformed into the beloved's *Sīmurgh*. The alienation of existence was felt as a cage, from which the soul sought escape by flight, at last to find the heavenly garden, or even to perch on the wrist of the celestial hunter. The soul's ascent through self-transcendence was symbolized by the burning or ripping away of its wings, which were ever replaced by new ones. Birds and flight imagery thus formed an extensive complex of images from the natural world, one which was particularly well adapted for the expression of the realities of the soul. Rūzbihān reminds us that the flight of the bird covers the distance between heaven and earth; its arrival on earth and its departure to heaven imitate and embody the journey of the soul from its origin to its end, just as the bird's song can praise God or deliver a scriptural epiphany to humanity. When, therefore, we read Persian poets telling for the thousandth time of the nightingale's song to the rose, or the bird who nests in eternity, we should not be lulled into dullness, anaesthetized by mere repetition. Mystical authors like Rūzbihān can help us recover the experiential power of a symbol even when it becomes threadbare in the hands of lesser writers. Then, perhaps, when we encounter these symbols, we will follow the advice of one of Rūzbihān's followers, and recall that "These are the places of the descent of the *Sīmurgh* of the spirit . . . [and] the ascent of the *'Anqā* of the heart."[1]

---

1. Ilāhī Sīmābī, *Manāzil al-qulūb*, in *Rūzbihān-nāma*, p. 404.

'Abd al-Raḥman Chishtī & the Bhagavadgita: 'Unity of Religion' Theory in Practice

Roderic Vassie

INTRODUCTION

The legendary Shaykh Ṣan'ān of 'Aṭṭār's *Manṭiq al-ṭayr* is exceptional in Sufi literature in turning apostate—albeit temporarily—in his quest for greater fulfillment. This being the case, what does it teach us about the realization, perceived in the writings of so many eminent Sufi masters, of a transcendental unity of religion? Given the extent of the debt owed by Sufi writers to the Koran and Sunna for inspiration when measured against their borrowings from other religious sources, has anything been said by affirming the unity of religions other than that a set of beliefs, rites, laws, etc. recognized as falling within the group 'religions' must, by definition, share some similarities with other members of the same group? To take the question a stage further, have Sufis ever actually taught that all Islam's necessary goals can be achieved by following the religious teachings of one's choice? Is it not rather the case that the interchangeability of religious symbols and ideas in Sufi verse and prose forms part of the art of mystical allegory, of which the Persian-speaking Sufis were consummate masters?

On the basis of 'Abd al-Raḥmān Chishtī's Indo-Persian treatise, *Mir'āt al-ḥaqā'iq* it is clear that in the Mughal empire Sufis conceived of only one tradition as capable of guiding the believer to the *maqṣūd-i bīrang* (sublime goal),'[1] all other ways being to a greater or lesser extent deficient. That tradition was Islam, albeit in its broadest Koranic sense ("He named you 'Muslims' previously and in this book." Koran, XXII 78)

'ABD AL-RAḤMĀN CHISHTĪ

'Abd al-Raḥmān ibn 'Abd al-Rasūl ibn Qāsim ibn Shāh Budh 'Abbāsī 'Alawī Chishtī belonged to the Ṣābirī branch of the Chishtī Order. He inherited the mantle of Shaykh from his brother, Ḥāmid, upon the latter's death in 1623. Initially based in Rudauli, he later moved west to a small village called Dhanīthī on the banks of the Gomti River nearer to Lucknow. In 1683, nearing the age of a hundred, he died and was buried in the building he had himself constructed.

Biographies of the Ṣābirī branch show that he was not only blood relative but also a spiritual descendant of his great-grandfather, Budh. However, in a rare autobiographical passage in his most important work, the hagiographical *Mir'āt al-*

1. British Library MS.. Or.1883, f.259r.

asrār, 'Abd al-Raḥmān Chishtī gives pride of place in his spiritual formation to Ghāzī Miyān (1033), 'Abd al-Qādir Jīlānī (1078-1166), Aḥmad Jām (1142) and Bahā' al-Dīn Naqshaband (1318-1389). A personal servant of Aurangzeb, Muḥammad Bakhtāwar Khān, who died a mere two years later than 'Abd al-Raḥmān, wrote of his contemporary that he was of good manners, praiseworthy character, and that he had on several occasions "attained the presence of the Effulgent."[1]

Living away from the major centres of Islamic learning, as 'Abd al-Raḥmān Chishtī did,—did not mean that he was cut off from the currents of Sufi thought. Apart from showing he possessed the requisite detailed knowledge of the exoteric sciences based on the Koran and Sunna together with a wide repertoire of Persian verse, his works also reveal his familiarity with many of the primary sources of Sufis: the *Fuṣūṣ al-ḥikam* of Ibn 'Arabī, the *Kashf al-maḥjūb* of Hujwīrī, 'Irāqī's *Lama'āt,* the *Fawā'id al-fu'ād* by Amīr Ḥasan Sijzī, the *Fuṣūs al-ādāb* of Najm al-Dīn Kubrā, and so on. In addition he was well-read in Hindu literature, and there is a strong possibility that he understood not just the local dialect of 'Hindawī,' but Sanskrit also.

THE *MIR'ĀT AL-ḤAQĀ'IQ* AS AN ESSAY IN *TAWḤID*

Although there is evidence amongst the Ṣabirī Chishtīs of a relatively open attitude towards contact with Hindu scholars, mystics and learning, 'Abd al-Raḥman specifically mentioned in his introduction that his reason for producing the *Mir'āt al-ḥaqā'iq* was to do for the Bhagavadgita what Shaykh Ṣūfī Qubjahānī had done for the *Yoga Vāsiṣtha* in his *Kashf al-kunūz* (also known as *Awṭār dar ḥall-i asrār).* Little is known about Qubjahānī, though the above-mentioned work is still extant. Dārā Shikūh himself testifies that he was prompted to commission a new version of the *Yoga Vāsiṣtha* following a vision of Rāmacandra in a dream in 1656, warning him of the deficiencies of Qubjahānī's translation.[2]

Before examining 'Abd al-Raḥmān Chishtī's treatment of individual Hindu doctrines at its heart it is useful to determine from the outset his approach to the reading of the Bhagavadgita, since the *Mir'āt al-ḥaqā'iq* is more an interpretation of the Sanskrit text than a translation. This very electic interpretation is packed throughout with what Rieu described as "Islamic notes"[3] being selections from 'Abd al-Raḥmān's store of Koran, *ḥadīth,* and Persian verse quotations (something which Qobjahānī's work lacks).

His introduction, which begins with the Koranic verse, "He is the first and the last, he is the manifest and the hidden,"*(al-Ḥadīd,* XLVII: 3) reads like a résumé of *Waḥdat al-wujūd,* the Sufi doctrine of unity of being or ontological monism, whose

1. See Muḥammad Bakhtawār Khān, *Mir'āt al-'ālam* (London: British Library MS., Add. 7657), f. 449r.
2. See Dārā Shikūh, M. Mahfuz-ul-Haq (ed.), *Majma' al-Baḥrayn = The Merging of the Two Seas* (Calcutta 1929), p. 25.
3. See Charles Rieu, *Catalogue of the Persian Manuscripts in the British Museum* (London: British Museum 1879-83), III, p. 1034b.

formulation is attributed to Ibn 'Arabī.[1] It leads on to a short section in which he states that the Bhagavadgita is the book in which "Krishna explained to Arjuna by analogy the secrets of *tawḥīd.*" The term *tawḥīd,* whose literal meaning is 'unification,' in Islam normally means 'to profess the oneness of God.' However, in the *Mir'āt al-ḥaqā'iq,* it comes to mean the application of the doctrine of *Waḥdat al-wujūd.*

By way of explanation of the phrase *Waḥdat al-wujūd,* 'Abd al-Raḥmān Chishtī quotes a verse ascribed to the father of Muḥammad Gīsū Darāz, Sayyid Rājā (d.731/1330):

> *That Being pure and absolute in every place, age, moment,*
> *In each direction, every alley, every view manifest I saw.*

Elsewhere the word *tawḥīd* is defined as *isqāṭ al-iḍāfāt* (the discarding of adjuncts).[2]

THE *MIR'ĀT AL-ḤAQĀ'IQ* AS A 'CELESTIAL BOOK'

Shedding light on the provenance of Krishna's secret teaching, 'Abd al-Raḥmān Chishtī states that "all Hindu scholars agree that Krishna extracted the secrets of the knowledge of God from the four Vedas." The gloss he provides alongside the term 'Vedas' is *kitāb,* i.e. 'the Book,' used five times in this way within the *Mir'āt al-ḥaqā'iq* proper. Although he nowhere spells it out, his use of the term 'the Book' can only be understood in its Koranic context. ("You who have been given the Book, believe in what we have revealed confirming what is [already] with you."—*al-Nisā'*, IV: 47). The effect of relating the Vedas to the Koran is twofold. Its primary importance is that it lends authority to the Bhagavadgita, by bringing it within the fold of the 'Celestial Books,' and by so doing justifies its translation and study by Muslims. Of secondary importance to this study is the political effect of transforming the Mughal Empire's majority Hindu population into a 'People of the Book.'

That this theory was current in seventeenth-century India is borne out in the introduction by Dārā Shikūh (d. 1070/1659) to the Persian translation he had commissioned of a compilation of fifty Upanishads. Adopting the same forthright manner which led ultimately to his execution for heresy, he refers to the Upanishads as "without doubt the very first Celestial Book, the fountain of reality and the ocean

1. See W. Chittick, 'Ebno'l-'Arabi's Doctrine of the Oneness of Being' in *Sufi: A Journal of Sufism,* Issue 4 (Winter 1989-90), pp. 6-14.
2. Although attributed by 'Abd al-Raḥmān Chishtī (BL MS.Or.1883, f. 262r) to the Prophet *("qāl al-nabī 'alyahi al-salām...")*, it belongs more correctly to the corpus of Sufi tradition stemming from Ḥallāj, who was the first to introduce the doctrine. See L. Massignon, *The Passion of Ḥallāj,* trans. H. Mason (Princeton University Press, 1982), I, p. 126.

of monotheism, being in complete accord with the Glorious Koran on which it is moreover a commentary."[1]

GOD IN THE *MIR'ĀT AL-ḤAQĀ'IQ*

Since the ninth century, if not before, a certain ambivalence had existed in the minds of Hindu commentators as to whether the Bhagavadgita really is a theistic scripture. Rāmānuja, the eleventh-century founder of the Visiṣṭādvaita ('qualified non-dualism') school, was of the view that the main issue of the Bhagavadgita's teaching is *Bhakti Yoga,* being the devoting of all one's thoughts and actions to Krishna as a personal God. His argument is based on the prevalence in the text of such commands to Arjuna as: "Worship me, seek refuge in me, act for my sake, concentrate your thoughts on me, strive to win me." On the other hand Śankarācārya (d. 820), staunch advocate of the Advaita philosophy ('non-dualism,' or 'monism'), saw *Bhakti Yoga* as only the superficial message of the Bhagavadgita, the real one being *Jñāna Yoga,* the struggle to gain knowledge of the 'indefinable, unchangeable, unmanifest, immutable' being, thereby gaining release from *samsāra,* the cycle of death and rebirth.

There is a clear divide between the Krishna of Rāmānuja's commentary who, as an avatar of the God Viṣnu, is himself the goal, and the Krishna of Śankarācārya. For all his divine status Śankarācārya's Krishna depends totally for his existence on the ineffable Brahman and is as much susceptible to *samsāra* as humanity. He is a goal, but only of the faint-hearted, those who lack the necessary strength of purpose to forsake all else in their quest for knowledge of Brahman. 'Abd al-Raḥmān's position regarding Krishna is essentially that of Śankarācārya, his one quibble as a Muslim being that Krishna is neither God nor yet a god but rather a true *muwaḥḥid,* one who understands the secrets of *waḥdat al-wujūd,* and possibly even a prophet.

On account of his approach, 'Abd al-Raḥmān chose to ignore in all but two instances, which will be described later, Krishna's claims to divinity. In this way his introductory statement that *tawḥīd* is at the centre of the Bhagavadgita remains uncompromised. Thus, whenever any reference is made to Krishna's worshipfulness, the *Mir'āt al-ḥaqā'iq* substitutes Brahman for Krishna. The Persian terms used prove 'Abd al-Raḥmān's preference for the Brahman concept of God.

The three main terms used for God by 'Abd al-Raḥmān are: first, *Khudā,* the Persian equivalent of the Arabic *Allāh;* second, *Ḥaqq* meaning 'Truth,' again a perfectly acceptable synonym for God, Koranic in origin though of markedly greater currency among Sufis than amongst their 'lay' brothers; and finally *ān-dhāt,* literally 'That Essence,' found exclusively in Sufi literature, notably in 'Aṭṭār's poetry.

1. See Sayyid Muḥammad Jalāl Nā'īnī (ed.), *Sirr-i akbar* (Tehran 1974), p. 5. Interestingly, this inclusion of the Upanishads amongst the corpus of Celestial books accepted by Muslims can be interpreted in two ways: first that Dārā Shikūh was trying to mask heterodox views behind a screen of orthodox terminology in order to make them more acceptable; and second that he sincerely believed the Upanishads to be as he described them. His unwillingness to recant when accused of heresy by his younger brother Aurangzeb points to the dominance of sincerity over fear of reprisal in the event of discovery. That being the case it would seem logical to infer that the best known practical exponent of the Sufi 'Unity of Religions' theory could only approach the Hindu scriptures insofar as they fitted within the framework of Islam.

Evoking as they do a less personifiable God, the latter two terms are not surprisingly the most used, though as mentioned above there is no attempt on the part of 'Abd al-Raḥmān to use the different nuances each of these two terms possesses to distinguish in any way between Krishna and Brahman in the Bhagavadgita.

A further, delightfully ambiguous term which crops up in the *Mir'āt al-ḥaqā'iq* is *kull,* meaning literally 'All.' Found on three occasions in the text, on none of them does it bear any relation to the Sanskrit. This term is complemented here and there by the appearance of the Persian phrase *hama ū'st* meaning 'He is all,' with all the connotations that it holds for Sufis of a monist bent, and its interpretation is found throughout the treatise in its many verse quotations.

Examination of the choice of epithet used in 'Abd al-Raḥmān's Bhagavadgita helps fill out our picture of his understanding of the divine principle. Paying particular attention to the term *ān-dhāt* (i.e. That Essence), he described it as *bīrang* (colorless, beyond any conceivable attribute). Less common but similar in meaning are: *pāk* (pure), *wāḥīd* (unique), *bī-kayf wa-kam* or *bī-chūn* (unqualitative/unquantitative). All are perfectly compatible with the epithets of Brahman, supreme goal of the Advaitins, but with no clear link between their position in the *Mir'āt al-ḥaqā'iq* and in the Sanskrit text.

THE EXTENT OF KRISHNA'S DIVINITY

The Bhagavadgita places a number of doctrinal obstacles in the way of the exoteric Muslim reader. None appears more insurmountable than the repeated references to Krishna's divinity. For the most part, however, 'Abd al-Raḥmān simply ignored them, substituting a general allusion to God wherever Krishna referred to his own divinity. Unlike Śankarācārya, who could accept with ease the contingent existence of the Hindu pantheon and still argue the rectitude of his non-dualistic philosophy, 'Abd al-Raḥmān as a Muslim was bound by his faith in 'There is no god but God.' To suggest that the worship of ought save God could act either as an alternative or as a first step on the path towards God was anathema ("Those who have taken guardians other than him [say]: 'We only worship them so that they may bring us much closer to God'"—*al-Zumar,* XXXIX 3) Perhaps his intended readers were not familiar enough with the Bhagavadgita to notice the changes 'Abd al-Raḥmān had wrought, but even so they could not have failed to notice had he continued in this vein where these references reach their peak. The theophany mentioned in the eleventh chapter, where Krishna affords Arjuna a vision of his universal form, was surely known to all Muslims of Mughal India. The extent of popular knowledge of this particular passage in the Bhagavadgita is demonstrated by the fact that both 'Abd al-Raḥmān's version and the *Razm-nāma,* Akbar's official Persian paraphrase of the entire Mahabharata, include the same extra-textual device of peering into Krishna's open mouth to explain how Arjuna beheld Krishna's universal form. Clearly, for 'Abd al-Raḥmān to have avoided the issue would have been to cast doubts on the notion that the *Mir'āt al-ḥaqā'iq* was even related to the Bhagavadgita, let alone his claim that it brought into relief the secrets of applied monist theory contained therein. He therefore had no option but to tackle the problem head-on.

Initially the *Mir'āt al-ḥaqā'iq,* like the Bhagavadgita itself, gives Arjuna free rein to describe the scene as he will. Only towards the end are three interpretative quotations from 'Abd al-Raḥmān's stock of Persian Sufi verse interposed. Having set the scene—Krishna revealing his 'original form' to a trembling Arjuna through a brightness surpassing that of several thousand suns wherein the three worlds, Brahman, Siva, the planets and the stars are all contained—the *Mir'āt al-ḥaqā'iq* continues:

> Krishna answered,
> "Arjuna, I annihilate all three worlds. The entire army of the Kauravas, which you saw, I have destroyed. Therefore get up at once and fight, so that I may make you famous."
> As Ḥaḍrat Shaykh Niẓām al-Dīn Awliyā' has said concerning this:
>
> *Where our essence lies, you cannot see a thing.*
> *If we say God [is] there, we are unbelievers.*
>
> Ḥaḍrat Ghawth al-'Ālam says:
>
> *Muḥyī al-Dīn is no more: I am God.*
> *I am God! I am God! I am God!*
>
> Then Arjuna said: "Lord, there is no doubting your power. I have but one last request: since we always ate together and were in the same place, I imagined you, my sincere friend, a [mere] human being. Forgive this failing of mine."
> Regarding this Mawlawī Makhdūm Jīv says:
>
> *My teacher, my disciple; my pain, my remedy:*
> *In all honesty I utter these words: my sun, my God.*
>
> Then Krishna answered:
> "Arjuna, since I love you greatly, for this reason have I shown you my form. No one else has the power to see this form except the person I love greatly; to him I show [this form]. Now look on my old form."
> Arjuna said:
> "Lord, on seeing your old form, my mind is once more at rest."

Here, to all intents and purposes, 'Abd al-Raḥmān Chishtī portrayed the Krishna with whom all India was familiar, whether they believed in it or not. On the surface the Sufi verses appear to justify Krishna's claims: but the message 'Abd al-Raḥmān sought to extract from the Bhagavadgita was not the exoteric one. So, when he quoted 'Abd al-Qādir Jīlānī's verse, "Muḥyī al-Dīn is no more, I am God," the meaning intended by 'Abd al-Raḥmān and understood by his 'close friends' was not that Krishna—or 'Abd al-Qādir Jīlānī for that matter—was God, but rather that they had entered into a mystical union with God where all notion of individuality, of 'me,' 'you' or 'it' was extinguished.

Proof of 'Abd al-Raḥmān's allegorical reading of the Bhagavadgita is found in the quotation cited after the only other passage in the *Mir'āt al-ḥaqā'iq* in which he allowed Krishna's divinity to shine through (IV 60):

> "Arjuna, I am the Creator of the world."
> Hence: 'Fashion yourselves in accordance with the traits of God.'—may He be exalted.

That instant when the sun shines on a mirror,
If that mirror does not say, 'I am the sun,'
—what does it do?

Any divinity which 'Abd al-Raḥmān Chishtī's Krishna possesses must be seen, not as his own, but a reflection of God's. This paradox is driven home by the presumably misquoted verse from the *Dīwān-i Shams-i Tabrīz:*

My teacher, my disciple; my pain, my remedy:
In all honesty I utter these words, my sun, my God.

By recalling this verse which Jalāl al-Dīn Rūmī had addressed to his *pīr* Shams-i Tabrīzī, the *Mir'āt al-ḥaqā'iq* puts the Krishna/Arjuna relationship on a totally new plane, that of the spiritual guide and his disciple, and Arjuna's words, from appearing at best naive at worst blasphemous and heretical to the uninitiated, at once take on an acceptable Sufi sense. No longer was Krishna God in the minds of 'Abd al-Raḥmān's intended readers, in spite of popular Hindu belief to the contrary. Clearly, by thus interpreting the 'secrets' of the Bhagavadgita, 'Abd al-Raḥmān was not aiming to prove that religious plurality should be deemed an expression of the omnipresent Countenance of God ("Wheresoever you turn, there is the Countenance of God."—Koran, *al-Baqara,* II 115) nor yet that all religions had the capacity to convey the faithful at least some way along the road to God. After all, had he wished to take either tack, the option existed to follow more closely Advaita doctrine of devotion to a lesser god for the faint-hearted and for the spiritual athlete knowledge of the Ineffable Reality. Instead he was applying the rule which he attributed in his introduction to the Prophet himself: "Take what purifies and eschew what defiles." Hence, as editor-cum-translator, whatever 'Abd al-Raḥmān left out of the *Mir'āt al-ḥaqā'iq* was deemed worthless and whatever was retained, true.

'Abd al-Raḥmān was well aware that the Hindus believed that Krishna was God, but in his eyes they were wrong to do so, for, in lurching indiscriminately between personal pronouns and divine attributes when referring to himself, Krishna had never intended to be taken for God. But, just as he offered his readers the realization that the Hindus were misguided to raise Krishna to divine status, by the same token his work suggests that Muslims were wrong to reject him outright.

There is, however, a potential flaw in 'Abd al-Raḥmān's exegesis. The fact that he used only Sufi verses to explain his point implies that he could find no quotations from either the Koran or Sunna to support it, and consequently his reading stood doctrinally on very shaky ground. If that is true here the same could not be said of the following.

THE QUESTION OF REINCARNATION

By the year 422/1031 the Hindu doctrine of *samsāra* or 'Reincarnation' had already been singled out in Bīrūnī's *Kitāb taḥqīq mā li'l-Hind* as the single most characteristic element of Indian religion, equivalent in his own words to "monotheism amongst the Muslims, the Sabbath of the Jews and the trinity of the Christians."[1] If one assume that Krishna was as the *Mir'āt al-ḥaqā'iq* portrayed him: an enlightened monist who had reached the very zenith of the Sufi path, or even—by application of Jān-jānān Maẓhar's theory—one of the unnamed prophets of Islam ("We have sent prophets before you, some of whom we have told you about and some of whom we have not."—Koran, *Ghāfir* XL: 78), how then could he have taught an eschatological doctrine so contradictory to that communicated through Islam's final prophet, Muḥammad, regarding birth and death? From 'Abd al-Raḥmān's point of view, was it likely that later generations of Hindus had inserted the *samsāra* doctrine in the Bhagavadgita after having simply made it up, an accusation levelled at other Peoples of the Book, or did it have an Islamic basis, however remote?

The principal text to tackle the reincarnation issue in the Bhagavadgita occurs at II. 26-27, in the middle of a lengthy description of the nature of the self. The *Mir'āt al-ḥaqā' iq,* however contains a translation of the latter stanza only. By contrast with his treatment of Krishna's divine claims, 'Abd al-Raḥmān's commentary on this verse comprises two Koran quotations, one for each half of the verse, and a third from the corpus of authentic *ḥadīth:*

> "Be certain of this too, Arjuna, that whatever comes to be will pass away."
> The word of God: "*Every soul tastes death*"[1]
> "Whatever passes away, Arjuna, will come again to be."
> He—upon whom be peace—has said: "And the resurrection after death..."
> The word of God: "*He brings forth the living from the dead, and he brings forth the dead from the living*."[2]

By application of the 'Take what purifies, eschew what defiles' rule 'Abd al-Raḥmān was able to omit II. 26 of the Bhagavadgita, with its reference to a "cycle of unending births and deaths."[3] So although his translation of verse II. 27 is faithful enough, having effectively isolated it from its context, he was able to read into it the belief, which he as a Muslim held, that the inevitable consequence of death was not reincarnation but resurrection. For 'Abd al-Raḥmān, Hindus are once again presented as having failed to grasp the 'true' (i.e. Islamic) doctrine conveyed by Krishna's words. Once contact was lost with Krishna, the vessel of divine guidance, the best the workings of their own intellects could suggest was that by death and birth reincarnation was meant, which doctrine they expounded by means of interpolation in the text.

THE BHAGAVADGITA AS A MANUAL OF SUFISM

There are three major renderings of the Bhagavadgita in Persian from the Mughal period. The first, in epic verse style, belongs to Fayḍi (d.1004/1595), poet of Akbar's court. This version occasionally remodels the Hindu doctrines of the original into Islamic/Sufi ones, and sometimes it even includes glosses from additional Hindu sources. In general, however, it reads like a watered-down version which, though packed with Hindawī terminology, clearly finds the exigencies of the metre

---

1. See C.E. Sachau (ed.), *Alberuni's India* (London: Trübner 1887), p. 34.
1. *Āl 'Imrān* /III 185; *al-Anbiyā'*, XXI.35; *al-'Akabūt*, XXIX.57.
2. *Yūnus*, X 31.
3. "Even if you believe that the [self] is constantly being born and constantly dying you should not grieve."

more important than faithfulness to the Sanskrit text. In view of this it is tempting regard it in the same light as Fayḍī's *Sawāṭi' al-ilhām,* a Koranic commentary devoid of dotted letters. Produced at a time Akbar's policy of *ṣulḥ-i kull,*[1] Fayḍī's verse rendition should be seen in terms of the diffusion of Hindu scriptures and learning in Persian considered vital to the harmony of the Mughal state.

The second translation is ascribed in some manuscripts to Fayḍī's brother, Abū 'l-Faḍl (d.1011/1602), though it more probable is that, like the Persian translation of the Upanishads mentioned above, it was commissioned by Dārā Shikūh. The work is usually attributed to Dārā Shikūh himself though, given his propensity to make synonyms of the most disparate Hindu and Sufi terms as demonstrated in the *Majma' al-baḥrayn* on the one hand and the absence of this approach to terminology in this version of the Bhagavadgita on the other, his authorship is very much in doubt. This is a faithful translation which, whilst containing about the same number of Hindawī words as Fayḍī's version, on the whole strives to render the Hindu terminology in simple, non-technical Persian.

The third and last version, that of 'Abd al-Raḥmān Chishtī, is different again. Whereas in the introduction to the *Razm-nāma,* the official version of the Mahabharata, Abū'l-Faḍl had stated that the translation was intended to educate the Muslim community concerning the wisdom and traditions on which Hinduism was based, 'Abd al-Raḥmān's express purpose was to confirm to his circle of friends the historical validity of their own beliefs. Hence we find throughout the text that only scant regard is paid to the nuances between the Bhagavadgita's eight *Yogas*. Thus, the *Mir'āt al-ḥaqā'iq* should more properly be seen in terms of a dynamic Sufi reconstruction of the Bhagavadgita where previously distinct ways (or *yogas)* to liberation, each one complete in itself, are transformed into mere stages on a single path, having all but lost the characteristics they originally possessed. The terms *kasb* (achievement), *shughl* (occupation), *tawḥīd* (collectedness, unity), *darwīshī* (asceticism), *taṣawwur* (contemplation), and *'irfān-i kull* (universal knowledge) are scattered here and there. As in the case of Krishna versus Brahman, no attempt is made to link each to a particular Hindu term, though every opportunity to give their use authority by means of judicious 'Islamic notes' is seized.

This sort of treatment could not have been motivated by the same syncretistic urge of which Akbar and his 'Divine Religion' *(Dīn-i ilāhī)* have stood accused. Even after justifying to his circle of friends Krishna's role in the religious quest of India, to 'Abd al-Raḥmān Chishtī there was no question that the Bhagavadgita of the Hindus and by the same token Hinduism itself were manifestations of an underlying mystical unity of religions. The Bhagavadgita was right only insofar as it either was, or could be forced to appear, in accord with the Islamic faith and practice of the Sufis; and it was unequivocally wrong insofar as it diverged from that per-

1. Meaning 'universal peace' or 'reconciling of the whole (society),' the *ṣulḥ-i kull* policy had as its aim the promotion of a heightened level of understanding between Hindus and Muslims as well as other less influential groups within the Mughal Empire. Akbar's belief was that the root cause of religious intolerance was ignorance. Hence a programme of religious and scientific translations was begun. The *Razm-nāma,* an abridgement in Persian of the huge Sanskrit epic which contains the Bhagavadgita and the Mahabharata formed a major part of that programme with numerous manuscript copies, often lavishly illustrated, surviving to this day.

ceived norm. When for example a Hindawī term like *jog* ('yoga') is glossed as *darvīshī,* it is clear that the purpose of the *Mir' āt al-ḥaqā' iq* is not to vindicate Hinduism but rather Sufism, by taking its origins further back in time than ever before.

CONCLUSION

At the beginning of the eighth century A.D. Muḥammad ibn al-Qāsim al-Thaqafi (694-716) led a Muslim army into Sind. Unsure after their victory of how to treat the Hindus of that region, Muḥammad ibn al-Qāsim turned to the *'ulamā'* in his retinue. Though unable to come to a unanimous agreement, it is reported that the majority decision was in favour of the Hindus being treated as a "people of the Book" (Koran, *al-Zumar,* XXXIX 9). However, the long history of Muslim India reveals that this early decision was regarded as anything but binding on subsequent Muslim governors, rulers and invaders.

Perhaps because they lived as members of an albeit powerful minority in the midst of a non-Muslim majority, it is possible to detect within the train of Sufi thought in seventeenth and eighteenth-century India a move to accommodate Hindus, by means of an unwritten convention, within the ambit of the 'People of the Book.' (Indeed one could argue that this is precisely what India's Muslim rulers did when they married Hindu wives.) And yet in so doing their aim was not to call for Muslim toleration of non-Muslim's beliefs but rather to prove that Islam had been preached in every time as well as every place ("And for every nation there is a messenger"—Koran, *Yūnus,* X 47).

Nevertheless, since the beginning of this century the Sufi movement within Islam, whilst—or perhaps because—it has attracted such scholarly interest in non-Muslim countries, has found itself the butt of attacks from a vociferous section of the Muslim intelligentsia. Those who would champion the values of their 'noble predecessors' *(al-salaf al-ṣāliḥ),* whose disposition prompts them to abjure all but the most literal interpretations of the Koran and Sunna, have seen in Sufism "a combination of Manichaean, Gnostic Neo-Platonic, Vedantic and Christian philosophies and speculations."[1] In Egypt the publication of the new critical edition of Ibn al-'Arabi's *al-Futūḥāt al-Makkīya* has brought in its wake its condemnation in books and articles by writers who argue that it is small wonder that Ibn 'Arabi's works provoke such intense interest in orientalist circles, since in them they see their own corrupt Helleno-Judaeo-Christian philosophy reflected.[2]

What works like 'Abd al-Raḥmān Chishtī's *Mir'āt al-ḥaqā'iq* show however is that the Persian-speaking Sufis of Mughal India did not see the similarities and differences between Hindu beliefs and their own in terms of equally valid expressions of humanity's religious quest. Instead, they interpreted any similarities as the last fortuitous vestiges of the pre-Muhammadan prophets' efforts to bring Islam to an Indian people characterized in the main by ingratitude and superstition, of which

1. A. A. Tabari, *The Other Side of Sufism (Faḍā' iḥ al-Ṣūfiyya)* (Kuwait: Revival of Islamic Heritage Society 1988), p. 3.
2. Burhān al-Dīn al-Biqā'i, *Maṣra' al-taṣawwuf, wa Tanbīh al-ghabī ilā takfīr Ibn 'Arabī* (Balbīs [Egypt]: Dār al-Taqwā 1989); also cf. Kamāl Aḥmad 'Awn, *Kitāb al-Futūḥāt al-Makkiyya wa-mā warā' ahu min ayād khafiyya* (Ṭanṭā: Dār al-Bashīr 1989).

traits the manifest differences were evidence. An analogy exists in what the Jesus of the Koran says about the Jews ("They move words from their [correct] places, and of what they were reminded they have ignored a portion." (—*al-Mā'idah,* V 13) When seen in this light, 'Abd al-Raḥmān Chishtī's purpose in writing the *Mir'āt al-ḥaqā'iq* was not to weaken the message of Islam by introducing Muslims to polytheistic practices and ideas—it was an accusation of this nature that led to Dārā Shikūh's execution. Rather his purpose was, on behalf of his select readership, to sift through the manifestations of Hindu polytheism in order to pick out the original Islamic teachings on which he deemed that perceived 'corruption' to be based. Such an analysis is in line with our understanding of at least two influential thinkers of Muslim India, Aḥmad Sirhindī (971/1563-1035/1625) and Jān-jānān Mazhar (1112/1700-1195/1781), both Naqshbandīs, though the latter was also initiated into the Qādirī order.

The Sufi, and in particular the Sufi of the Mughal Empire, is thus acquitted of the 'orthodox' accusation of playing the part of willful purveyor of non-Islamic innovations and heresies. He returns instead to being as his *tadhkiras* show he saw himself: as the beneficiary of a rich spiritual legacy, the source of which he traced back via 'Alī to the Prophet Muḥammad... and beyond.

The Transcendental Unity of Polytheism & Monotheism in the Sufism of Shabistarī

Leonard Lewisohn

I. INTRODUCTION: SHABISTARĪ'S INSPIRATION AND TRADITION

One of the most disturbing phenomena for both non-Muslim and Muslim Iranologists in the study of Persian Sufism is how to interpret the frequent ecstatic sayings of mystics who claimed in their raptures like Rumi to be "neither Muslim, nor Christian, nor Jew, nor Zoroastrian."[1] The present essay thus proposes to examine, by focusing on the writings of Shabistarī, the theological and theosophical foundations the Sufis' unitarian stance on religious diversity. The Sufis' advocacy of the 'unity-of-religions,'[2] constituted a unique ecumenism which had its origins in a visionary consciousness *(kashf-i ḥuḍūrī)* rather than an intellectual inter-faith dialogue *(baḥth-i 'aqlī)* as understood by the modern theologian.[3]

Maḥmūd Shabistarī was born in Tabriz in 687-8/1288-9, where he received his elementary and advanced education. He subsequently became deeply versed in the symbolic terminology and mystical theosophy of Muḥyī al-Dīn Ibn 'Arabī. His erudition and learning in respect to the latter's voluminous writings eventually led him to describe his pursuit of understanding of the "science of religion" as a quest to comprehend Ibn 'Arabī:

> I spent a long part of my life studying the science of divine Unity, traveling through Egypt, Turkey, and Arabia, day after day, night after night. Year in and out, for month on end, like time itself, I trekked through town and country, sometimes burning the midnight oil, sometimes making the moon my bedside lamp.
>
> How vast were the climes I covered and many the scholars of the Sufic Art I met – whose wondrous sayings I loved to collect to make the subject of my own esoteric compositions. In particular, I took pains in the study of the *Futūḥāt al-Makkiyya* and the *Fūṣūṣ al-ḥikam*, neglecting no minute detail in either book. Despite these exertions in scholarship, my heart still felt restless. I was puzzling over this disquiet and anxiety, when a hidden voice seemed to cry out within me, saying: These words are written in the language of the heart; seek their meaning from your heart. Do not fol-

1. See R.A. Nicholson (trans.) *Selected Poems From the Dīvāni Shamsi Tabrīz* (Cambridge University Press, reprinted 1977), p. 125.
2. See Leonard Lewisohn, 'The Unity of Religions' in 'A Critical Edition of the Divan of Maghrebi (With an Introduction into His Life, Literary School, and Mystical Poetry),' Ph.D. Dissertation, at SOAS, University of London, 1988, pp. 177-82. Portions of this essay are adapted from this thesis.
3. Cf. M. Talbi, 'A Community of Communities: the Right to be Different and the Ways of Harmony' in J. Hick and H. Askari (editors), *The Experience of Religious Diversity* (Shaftesbury: Blackmore Press 1985), pp. 81-82 and Karl-Wolfgang Tröger, 'Peace and Islam: In Theory and Practice,' in *Islam and Christian-Muslim Relations*, Vol. 1, No. 1 (1990), pp. 15-16.

low every quest and call; knock not upon every door.

Although the writings of Ibn 'Arabī revived both state and religion, they could not provide my heart any comfort. In fact, the more I pondered upon his good words, there was something profoundly discordant and disturbing about them. When I asked my Master to explain this mysterious condition which overcame me, he commented:

"Ibn 'Arabī's whole intent and effort was to expound in words the mystical vision which he beheld. However, because his pen *(qalam)* lagged behind his footstep *(qadam)* in this exposition, certain slips of the pen (which disconcerted you) occurred. It wasn't that the riot and disturbance came from Ibn 'Arabī himself; it was only an ugly face reflected in the mirror."

My Shaykh and Master, Amīn al-Dīn, could really give you good answers. Bless his pure soul. I have never seen another master of his calibre.[1]

Author of several volumes of mystical poetry, Shabistarī's fame rests mainly on the *Gulshan-i rāz (Garden of Mystery)*,[2] which he composed in the early 14th century in rhyming couplets (the *mathnawī* metre of *baḥr-i hazaj)*[3] amounting to about one thousand distichs. This poem was written in response to twenty-six queries concerning various intricacies of Sufi metaphysics posed to him by another great Sufi of his day: Rukn al-Dīn Amīr Ḥusayni Harawī (d. 718/1318).[4]

The poetic work of Shabistarī shows a genius of metaphysical penetration combined with aphoristic skill in synthesizing intricate dilemmas of Islamic theological and theosophical thought, unequalled by any other mediæval Persian Sufi poet in

1. Shabistarī, *Sa'ādatnāma,* in Ṣ. Muwaḥḥid (ed.) *Majmū'a-i āthār-i Shaykh Maḥmūd Shabistarī* (Tehran: Kitābkhāna-i ṭahūrī 1365 A.Hsh.), vv. 334-343, p. 168. [Henceforth abbreviated as SN.] Concerning Amīn al-Dīn, see M.J. Mashkūr, *Tārīkh-i Tabrīz tā payān-i qarn-i nuhum hijrī* (Tehran 1973), p. 766; Ḥāfiẓ Ḥusayn Karbalā'ī Tabrīzī, *Rawḍāt al-jinān va jannāt al-janān,* ed. Ja'far Sulṭān al-Qurrā'ī, (Tehran 1344 A.Hsh./1965; Persian Texts Series No. 20), Vol. 2, p. 89; 'Azīz Dawlatābādī, *Sukhanvarān-i Azarbaijan* (Tabriz 1357 A.Hsh), Vol. 2, pp. 217-19. Amīn al-Dīn (d. 758/1358) was a well-known Kubrawī Shaykh and disciple of Nūr al-Dīn Isfarāyinī. Elsewhere in the *Sa'ādatnāma* Shabistarī (vv. 1095-1102, p. 212) commends the merits of Abū'l-Najīb Suhrawardī (490/1097-563/1168), and while lamenting the decline of gnostic insight among the Sufi masters of his day, remarks that, "masters of his calibre are few today." Further on (SN vv. 1374-80, pp. 331-32) he praises the psychological acumen *(nafs shinasī)* of the Kubrawī master: Sa'd al-Dīn Ḥamūya. All these allusions demonstrate that Shabistarī's basic mystical affiliation and spiritual persuasion *(silsila, mashrab)* was to the Kubrawī Order, although it should be noted that the Suhrawardī Order which originated in Abū'l-Najīb, and was known as the 'mother-of-the-mystical-lineages' *(umm al-silāsil)* was the source of most of the later influential Orders in Anatolia, Persia, and India (including the Kubrawī Order), which branched off from it (cf. J.S. Trimingham, *The Sufi Orders in Islam,* Oxford University Press 1973, p. 55).
2. The edition of the *Garden of Mystery* used here is that edited by Dr. Javad Nurbakhsh, *Gulshan-i rāz (*Tehran: Intishārāt-i khāniqāh-i Ni'matullāhī 1976); henceforth abbreviated as GR.
3. A metre popular among the Sufi poets. See Finn Theisen's *A Manual of Classical Persian Prosody (*Wiesbaden: Otto Harrassowitz 1982), p. 125.
4. Concerning Harawī's biography, see Muḥammad Lāhījī, *Mafātīḥ al-'ijāz fī sharḥ-i Gulshan-i rāz,* edited by K. Samī'ī (Tehran 1337 A.H. sh.), Introduction, pp. 75-7 (hereafter abbreviated as SGR); Jāmī, *Nafaḥāt al-uns,* edited by M. Tawḥīdīpūr (Tehran 1964), pp. 605-606. Amīr Harawī's grand-daughter married Shāh Ni'matullāh (d. 834/1430) when he visited Herat; subsequently she gave birth in 775/1373 to Shāh Khalīlullāh, who succeeded his father as master of the Ni'matullāhī Order. See J. Nurbakhsh, *Masters of the Path: A History of the Nimatullāhi Sufi Order (*New York: Khaniqahi Nimatullahi Publications 1980), p. 43

brevity of output and profundity of content. For Iranian mystics in the centuries following Shabistarī's death (740/1339),[1] it may be generally said that the *Gulshan-i rāz* represented the culmination *in Persian* of Ibn 'Arabī's teachings. In the words of Henry Corbin, it was, "une sorte de vade-mecum des soufis iraniens."[2] Like Ibn 'Arabī's *Tarjuman al-ashwāq* or 'Irāqī's *Lama'āt,* the *Gulshan-i rāz* was composed in a series of semi-abstract aphoristic flashes of inspiration, the harmony of which is most always only intuitively apprehended.

Yet Shabistarī's poem quickly became popular and by the middle of the sixteenth century, close to thirty commentaries had been written upon it by a number of Persian mystics, both renowned and obscure.[3] The greatest commentator on Shabistarī's *Gulshan-i rāz* was undoubtedly Muḥammad Lāhījī (d. 912/1507). Lāhījī's famous gloss, the *Mafātīḥ al-'ijāz fī sharḥ-i Gulshan-i rāz* evoked this quatrain from his contemporary Jāmī (817/1414–898/1492) who, in the last decade of the fifteenth century, responded to an autograph copy of it sent to him by the author:[4]

Lords of Prayer in their abased neediness
your Poverty in spirit illuminates,
Like springtime's green your thoughts
make glad the Garden of Mystery.
Anyway you may, cast a glance
at my heart's base copper.
So from illusion perhaps
I'll find the road to reality.

Two basic strands of theosophy wind through Lahījī's *Sharḥ-i Gulshan-i rāz*: the lyrical Sufism of Rumi, and ii) the theosophy of Ibn 'Arabī and his followers such as the gnostic poets 'Irāqī and Maghribī.[5] Lāhījī is a visionary theosopher of Shabistarī's own calibre and his exegesis of Shabistarī is steeped in the poetry and theosophy of mediaeval Persian Sufism, being replete with quotations from Shabistarī's other works and ample references to the Divans of Rumi, Maghribī and 'Irāqī, as well as interspersed with the author's personal accounts of dreams, visions and mystical experiences. It is definitely drawn from the same fount of inspiration *(mashrab)* from which Shabistarī's own verse sprung, and thus deserves the fullest attention of all students of Persian Sufism. His commentary is, as Annemarie Schimmel observes, particularly significant to the understanding of the gnostic Ibn 'Arabīan tradition in Persian thought.[6]

1. See J. Nurbakhsh's introduction to GR for a deailed discussion concerning Shabistarī's death-date.
2. Henry Corbin, *Histoire de la philosophie islamique* (Paris: Editions Gallimard 1986), p. 420. Cf. 'Abd al-Ḥusayn Zarrīnkūb, *Justujū-yi dar taṣawwuf-i Irān* (Tehran: Amir Kabir 1978), p. 313.
3. See 'Azīz Dawlatabadī, *Sukhanvarān-i Azarbaijan,* pp. 162-70. A good summary of these commentaries is also provided by H. Corbin, 'Le poème de Mamúd Shabestarī et ses commentateurs'- in *Trilogie Ismaelienne* (Tehran and Paris 1961), pp. 21-23.
4. Cited by M.M. Shırāzī, *Ṭarā'iq al-ḥaqā'iq,* edited by M.J. Maḥjūb (Tehran 1339 A.Hsh.), Vol. 3, p. 130.
5. See Leonard Lewisohn, 'Shabestari's Garden of Mysteries: The Aesthetics and Hermeneutics of Sufi Poetry,' in *Temenos: A Review Devoted to the Arts of the Imagination,* No. 10 (1989), pp. 177-207.
6. Cf. her *Mystical Dimensions of Islam* (Chapel Hill:University of North Carolina 1975), p. 280.

The unique element in Shabistarī's Garden of Mystery is its undoubted quality of ecstatic, selfless—yet extremely learned—inspiration, an inspiration which derives from its sublimity, rather than from Shabistarī's personal genius or muse. It is a poem which seems to be "given rather than made, the utterance rather of the race than of an individual poet,"[1] characteristic of that heaven-sent love-madness *(furor amatoris)* described by Plato in the *Phaedrus,* which inspiration alone qualifies a poet's work for immortality.

The verity of this inspiration seems demonstrated by the fact that he attacks the worship of idols *(but parastī)* with particular vehemence, if not intolerance, in his other great, lengthier yet lesser known, epic metaphysical poem, the *Sa'ādatnāma,*[2] in a spirit quite contrary to that of the *Garden of Mystery. (*In fact the entire first half of the *Sa'ādatnāma* is devoted to the refutation of various so-called "heretical" sects, religions, and deviant philosophers, reviled by Shabistarī in very strong language).[3]

II. LITERARY AND PHILOSOPHICAL SOURCES OF SHABISTARĪ'S ECUMENISM

The present study is confined to exposition of eighteen couplets from the *Gulshan-i rāz (*translated below) which summarize most of the esoteric doctrines which were part and parcel of the Sufis' trans-nomian conception of religion—these doctrines, in fact, may be said to have formed the focal point of an entire school of mediaeval Sufi transcendentalists. Shabistarī's aim in these eighteen couplets was to demonstrate the *unity of devotional intention,* the 'doxological oneness', one might say, of both the polytheist's and monotheist's approach to the Absolute. No doubt he would have endorsed Dārā Shikūh's (1615-1659 A.D.) opinion, expressed two centuries later, that the adepts among the Hindu mystics were the true monotheists or

1. Kathleen Raine, *Defending Ancient Springs* (Suffolk: Golgonoonza Press 1985), p. 23 (referring to Vernon Watkins).
2. As for instance, Shabistarī's disparaging reference in the SN to the Sabeans as polytheists, describing their doctrine as infidelity *(kufr)* and misguidance *(ḍulāl),* and their religion *(madhhab)* as filth (SN vv. 381-93). In this section, it is important to note that while Shabistarī credits Abraham with the honor being the first iconoclast in human history, rejecting the Sabean astro-worship as a form of dualism and irreligion, he concludes his discussion on a more tolerant note, commenting: "The planets' worth in the eyes of God is by no means insignificant, as the verse 'By the Star' (Koran LIII, 1) bears witness. The darkness of the Sabean doctrine, however, derives from ascribing partners *(shirkat)* to (the oneness of) the Divine essence, not from the intellectual perception of (Divine) light in the Divine Signs (of the created world)."
3. These sects and thinkers reviled by Shabistarī include: 1) the Sabeans (SN vv. 381-93); 2) the Nazarene, Nestorian, Jacobite, and Melchite Christian sects (SN vv. 394-97); 3) the philosopher Nasṭūr who flourished during the reign of the Caliph Mā'mūn (SN vv. 397-405); 4) Zoroastrianism and Zoroaster (SN vv. 415-32); 5) Muḥammad Ibn Karrām, founder of the Karrāmiyya sect of anthropomorphists (SN vv. 560-65); 6) The *mutakallim* or scholastic theologians (SN vv. 567-80); 7) Pseudo-Sufis who ignore Kalām and study only the *Fuṣūṣ* of Ibn 'Arabī (SN vv. 599-625); 8) Peripatetic philosophers (Avicenna in particular) who is reproached with negating God's Attributes and denial of the corporeal resurrection (SN vv. 642, 649-63, 674-84); 9) The Ishrāqī Platonic philosophers *(ishrāqiyyān aflāṭūn)*, Suhrawardī Maqtūl in particular (SN vv. 670-73); 10) The metaphysical Ismaili poet Nāṣir Khusraw whom Shabistarī execrates and curses abusively (SN vv. 694-710); 11) The Islamic rationalists *(Mu'tazila)* (SN vv. 714-720, 727-46); 12) Abū al-Ḥasan Maḥmūd 'Umar Zamakhsharī (467-538 A.H., author of *al-Kashshāf*) (SN vv. 735-41).

"unitarians of India" *(muwaḥḥidān-i hind)*; he would also have agreed with the latter's conclusion that there is a difference in the verbal expression of gnosis and theology, but no essential doctrinal distinction between the Hindu adept and the Muslim Sufi.[1] It is this ecumenical quality in Shabistarī's work which makes these eighteen couplets so important for our understanding of the traditional Sufi outlook on polytheism, and the inner meaning of polytheism in the context of the most fundamental tenet of Islamic esotericism—that is to say, the principle of the 'Unity of Being' or 'theomonism' *(waḥdat al-wujūd)*.

Shabistarī's standpoint in regard to religion in both its enlightened *originality* and inspiration represents as much a manifesto of religious freedom for the Muslim mystics of mediaeval Persia as William Blake's thesis that "All Religions are One" served the cause of unitarian Christianity in the Christian West. Yet on the other hand, his originality derives from Sufism's own originality as the quinessential Islamic expression transcending the sectarian distinctions of Sunnism and Shi'ism. The Sufi concept of the Unity of Religions (within the framework of Islamic *tawḥīd)* permitted, for example, integration and toleration of the doctrines of Hindu Vedanta, Jewish Kabbalism, Christian mysticism, and Zen Buddhism—providing a greater possibility of a universal expression than is the case with exoteric Islam.[2]

A brief examination of the religious background of Shabistarī's esoteric teachings is here in order. Although in the *Sa'ādatnāma* Shabistarī directly declares his support for the pure Sufi doctrine of Ḥabīb 'Ajamī (SN vv. 683-84), invoking God's blessings upon the wayfarers on the Sufi Path (SN vv. 29), he also demonstrates his orthodox Sunnism by singling out Abu'l-Ḥasan al-Ash'arī (873-935) for special mention as the thinker "who laid firm the foundation of devotion to God, establish-

---

1. See Daryush Shayegan's masterly study of 'Muḥammad Dārā Shikūh, Bunyāngudhār-i 'irfān-i taṭbīqī,' in *Iran Nameh*, Vol. 8, No. 2 (1990), pp. 197, 198, 200. Shabistarī's visionary ecumenism expounded in these lines certainly influenced Shikūh's bold translation and fearless defence of the Upanishads as one of the celestial books mentioned in the Koran. And since we know that it was Dārā Shikūh's Persian translation of the Upanishads which was used by Anquetil Duperron in his pioneering Latin translation of this Scripture and that it was this text which fell into the hands of Schopenhauer, who believed the discovery and translation of Hindu philosophical texts in his age on par with the discovery and translation of Greek texts in classical antiquity, it is partially true to say that the revival of interest in Oriental religions caused by this Persian-to-Latin translation was, in the long run, due to Shabistarī's ecumenical vision. On Schopenhauer's opinion of Dārā Shikūh, see also B.J. Hasrat, *Dārā Shikūh: Life and Works* (New Dehli: Munshiram Manoharlal Ltd. 1982 revised ed.), p. 257.
2. See Victor Danner, *The Islamic Tradition: An Introduction* (New York: Amity House 1988), Chap. 4. The absurdity of the narrow and "all-invading autocracy" of exotericism (as F. Schoun termed it, 'The Limitations of Exoterism' in *The Transcendent Unity of Religions*; London: TPH 1984), pp. 7-33) which parades as the exclusive orthodoxy, has been noted by I.R. Netton: "The use of such rigid, single, and emotive terms as 'orthodox' and 'unorthodox' produces an erroneous assumption, with its concomitant false historicity, that Islam is fundamentally a monolith. It leads to, or is the product of, a frame of mind which considers that religion is capable of scant variation or development; for its articulation may be categorized on the moral level, arbitrarily, once and for all, as right or wrong, true or false, legal or illegal, authentic or unauthentic. The Islamic faith was, and is, able to embrace a variety of legal schools and legal interpretations, and not only come to terms with but actually adopt the manifestations of a mystical impulse." *Allah Transcendent: Studies in the Structure and Semiotics of Islamic Philosophy, Theology and Cosmology* (London: Routledge 1989), p. 19. Also cf. A. Al-Azmeh, 'Orthodoxy and Ḥanbalite Fideism', in *Arabica* (1989), pp. 254.

Maḥmūd Shabistarī with Disciples. From a manuscript of the *Majālis al-'ushshāq*, dated 959/1552. MS. Ouseley Add. 24, f. 85v (Courtesy of the Bodleian Library, Oxford).

ing the Sunni faith and supporting the catholic community of Islam *(jamā'at).*" (SN vv. 27-28). Of course, Sunnism was also typical of the townspeople of Tabriz during Shabistarī's lifetime as Mustawfī in the *Nuzhat al-qulūb* observed;[1] it also characterized the leaders of the Kubrawī *silsila* as well.[2]

Following Ibn 'Arabī, Shabistarī exhibited extreme disdain for the exoteric clergy; and just as the Greatest Master remarked that "the exoteric scholars *('ulamā' al-rasūm)* in relation to the Folk of Allah [the Sufis] are like the pharaohs in relation to God's messengers. God created no one more onerous and troublesome for the Folk of Allah than these exoteric scholars..."[3]—so Shabistarī derided jurisprudents who "use sixty kilograms of water in making ablutions for prayer;" and attacked the *mullas* whose "flesh and bones are nourished off the morsels gleaned from Princes' tables, being are enthralled to money and possessions." (SN 1541)

The Sufis, according to Shabistarī, are the true "artists" *(hunarmand)*, whose natural foe is the *mullas'* conceit and pride. (SN 1535, 1538, 1557) Like Ibn 'Arabī again, he preaches from his own personal practise and educated experience here. Boasting of his erudition in the science of *fiqh,* he states: "I am well-versed in jurisprudence, having read and composed many books on this science which are acclaimed far and wide, and require no commendation, so I do not say these negative things about the jurisprudents out of ignorance." (SN 1547-48) His vision is thus the very opposite of dogmatism--its inspiration being drawn from a tradition learned in the very exoteric sciences it transcended and disdained. Albeit this dislike for the anti-unitarian dogmatism of the Muslim clergy is not particular to Shabistarī; it is generally characteristic of all the Sufi poets of this period, and particularly all those who composed poetry in the *qalandariyyāt* genre.[4]

If we consider his teachings from the esoteric level of the Spiritual Path *(ṭarīqat)* his writings certainly reflect a general tendency among the Kubrawīs to interpret religion *(madhhab)* as being composed of various gradations of inner 'levels' of belief, as, for instance, espoused by Nasafī in the introduction to the *Kashf al-ḥaqā'iq*.[5] Other sources for this universalistic and esoteric attitude are to be found in the general relativistic attitude towards the nature of religious truth professed by mediaeval Muslim thinkers of various schools,[6] as well as the general "promiscuous religious milieu" and "ambivalence...of the religious sensibility"[7] of fourteenth-century Iran.

---

1. Ḥamdullāh Mustawfī, in describing the townspeople of Tabriz in 1340, relates that "Most of them are Sunnis of the Shāfi'ī *madhhab.*" Cited by Dr. R. 'Aivaḍī (ed.) *Divān-i Humām-i Tabrīzī,* (Tabriz 1970), introduction, p. 40.
2. Cf. H. Algar, 'Some Observations on Religion in Safavid Persia', *Iranian Studies* (1974), p. 288.
3. Cited by W.C. Chittick, *The Sufi Path of Knowledge: Ibn 'Arabī's Metaphysics of the Imagination* (Albany: SUNY 1989), p. 247.
4. See Ehsan Yarshater, *Shi'r-i fārsī dar 'ahd-i Shāh Rukh* (Tehran 1334), p. 172. See section 2 of my 'Overview' to this volume.
5. Edited by Aḥmad Mahdawī Dāmaghānī (Tehran 1965), pp. 7-8.
6. See for instance Nikki Keddie's analysis of this trait of mediaeval Islamic thought in 'Symbol and Sincerity in Islam', *Studia Islamica* XVIII (1963), p. 27-63.
7. B.S. Amoretti, 'Religion in the Timurid and Safavid Periods' in *The Cambridge History of Iran,* (Cambridge University Press, 1986), Vol. 6, p. 617.

The intellectual context of this ambivalent attitude towards religious dogma among Shabistarī's contemporary Kubrawī masters (Isfarāyinī [d. 717/1317], Simnānī [d. 736/1326], and Maghribī [d. 810/1408], in particular) can found in a philosophical tradition followed by Sufis, theologians and philosophers alike, a tradition which emphasizes that knowledge can be attained by one or a combination of three means: (1) revelation derived from Scripture *(wahy)*, (2) reason *('aql)*, and (3) *kashf* (unveiling)—corresponding to the methods pursued respectively by the theologians, philosophers and the Sufis. These apparently divergent perspectives were held by members of the three schools to be "much more complementary than exclusive."[1] Even if Shabistarī's own method, as we have explained in detail elsewhere,[2] is entirely visionary, utilizing the Sufis' *kashf, dhawq* (heart-savour/creative intuition and sapiential 'taste'), and *taḥqīq* (direct experiential verification and realization), the theological background of his method as it appears in the context of previous Islamic philosophy, is based on this unique tripartite structure.

With particular lucidity he illustrates this learned *scientia sacra* underlying his inspiration in the introduction to his philosophical masterpiece, the *Ḥaqq al-yaqīn*, explaining that his discussion in it "is conducted to the point of certainty, and is founded on the Trilogy[3] of: Transmitted Science *(naql)*, Reason or intellectual discussion *('aql)*, and Heart-savour *(dhawq)*. In order to verify any spiritual truth *(ḥaqīqat)* or prove any argument in this composition, two just proofs based on Transmitted Science and Reason are adduced: that is, a clearly convincing proof and a citation from the Koran are submitted to the reader's consideration. After completion of the study of the rational and the transmitted sciences *('ulūm-i 'aqlī u naqlī)*, the method to be followed by the reader is to seek the spiritual capacity *(isti'dād)* to understand this science through ecstatic consciousness borne of heart-savour *(dhawqiyyāt)*."

Also significant for our concern with Shabistarī's ecumenism is the demand made on the reader of the *Ḥaqq al-yaqīn* to "seek freedom from the restrictions of imitative devotion and habit and abandon fanaticism *(ta'aṣṣub)*" – this is the very problem which plagues all religious exotericism and typifies the smug dogmatism of both mediæval and modern Muslim fundamentalism.[4] The reader of the *Ḥaqq al-yaqīn* is also enjoined "to carefully deliberate and ponder upon each subject of discussion," for, as Shabistarī admits, "I have chosen to adopt a very condensed style, using extreme brevity in the choice of expressions. In some cases, the veiling and

---

1. 'Mysticism Versus Philosophy in Earlier Islamic History: The Al-Ṭūsī, Al-Qūnawī Correspondence', in *Religious Studies* 17 (1981), p. 94.
2. 'Shabestari's Garden of Mysteries: the Aesthetics and Hermeneutics of Sufi Poetry', pp. 179-80. It is also reminiscent of the method adopted by Dārā Shikūh in his seminal work of synthesis between Hindu esoteric polytheism and Muslim Sufi monotheism, the *Majma' al-baḥrayn*. "I have composed this piece of research," declared Dārā, "according to my own visionary experience and heart-savour, for my own kin. I am not concerned in it with the common, exoterically oriented people of either religion." From D. Shayegan, article cited, p. 203.
3. On similar three-fold divisions of knowledge among Muslim thinkers, see S.H. Nasr, 'Islamic Education, Philosophy and Science' in *Traditional Islam in the Modern World* (London: KPI 1987), pp. 126-33.
4. Continues on page 387.

hiding of certain ideas in this book is even intentional."[1] The warning issued in this statement, by the way, applies to all the readers and students of Shabistarī's other works, such as the *Garden of Mystery*. In fact, 'concise complexity' may be said to be the fundamental characteristic of Shabistarī's literary style. Therefore, in reading the following eighteen lines we should recall this profound 'tripartite' structure which forms the intellectual substratum of his mystical philosophy.

III. TRANSLATION OF THE TEXT, GR 56-57

Esoteric Idolatry

1 *On Love's Path all idols are signs and emblems*
which theophanically betoken Unity and Love;
the cincture's symbol is your fealty to serve mankind.
2 *Since both faith and infidelity—both piety*
and blasphemy—in Being are always
abiding and residing, thus idolatry
and Unity are both but one essentially.
3 *Since from Being all things are proceeding in*
diversity, so one from this entirety
must ultimately take an idol's shape.
4 *Beheld from Being's range and scope, the idol is*
all Truth. Think deep, oh savant: Falsity
5 *There does not adhere. Since God Almighty*
has fashioned it and he's a perfect architect
so from the Good, all that which emanates—
know it proceeds beatifically.
6 *For Being is* summum bonum, *highest good, everywhere*
you look; the source of bad and woe that's there
Exists elsewhere – in Nullity.
7 *If Muslims knew what idols were, they'd cry*
that faith itself is in idolatry.
8 *And if polytheists could just become aware*
of what the idols are, they'd have no cause to err
9 *in their beliefs. The graven image they*
have seen is but external handiwork and form,
and so by Holy Writ their name is 'infidel.'
10 *No one will call you 'Muslim,' thus, by the word of Law*
if you cannot perceive the Truth concealed therein,
see the God within an idol hid.

---

4. See S.H. Nasr, 'What is Traditional Islam?' in *Traditional Islam in the Modern World* (London: KPI 1987), pp. 18-25. AS A.K.S. Lambton has noted, religious fundamentalism, whether Jewish, Christian, or Islamic, "is an ideology of the book as the all-sufficient guide in every condition and circumstance of life in whatever century or for whatever purpose. It neglects transcendence and open-endedness and avoids the need for a creative re-interpretation of faith. It sees God in the light of its own concepts." 'The Clash of Civilizations: Authority, Legitimacy, and Perfectibility' in (R. M. Burrell, ed.) *Islamic Fundamentalism* (Papers read at a seminar held at the School of Oriental and African Studies, University of London on March 10th, 1988) (London: Royal Asiatic Society 1989), p. 33.

1. In *Majmū'a-i āthār-i Shaykh Maḥmūd Shabistarī*, p. 286 (12-19).

11 Whoever sees unveiled the real infidelity
and face to face perceives the truth-of-heresy
detests all rites, all forms of fake 'Islamic' falsity.
12 All infidelity has Faith inside;
within each idol's heart a soul resides
and every heresy has hymns and litanies
13 and daily, infidelity recites the rosary—
"Verily, all which is, does hymn his praise."[1]
so where's your enmity?
14 In what I say – have I digressed or missed the Way?
Say "'God!' – and leave these fools in vanity and play."[2]
15 Who else but God could gild its face
or give an idol such finesse and grace?
Unless it be his will, who'd be an idol's votary?
16 The Doer, Orator and Agent-actor too –
all these were him. He acted not amiss, he spoke
aright, and was in fact, both well and good.
17 'See One, say One, know One:' this axiom
sums up the root and branches of Imān.
18 The Koran's word attests to this, not me alone
professes it: "No fault exists," the Scripture says
"in the creation of the All-Beneficent."[3]

IV. SHABISTARĪ'S DOCTRINE OF ESOTERIC IDOLATRY

The philosophical doctrine versified by Shabistarī in the above lines reveal that commitment to understanding the truths of other religions is a necessary aspect and practical part of Sufi teachings; his method involves the direct realization and experimental verification *(taḥqīq)* of the trans-formalistic, esoteric origin of divergent religious beliefs. His doctrine *(mashrab* rather than a *madhhab)*, which is discussed below – is both trans-nomian and trans-sectarian; the contraries of Purity vs. Impurity and Faith vs. Infidelity being viewed and resolved as separate theophanies of Divine Being or manifestations of various Divine Qualities. Brilliantly explained by his commentator, Lāhījī, in prose, and by his literary heir, Maghribī, in poetry, this doctrine is based on three sources: i) the poet's own visionary insight into the meaning of several Koranic passages (e.g. III: 191, XLIV: 39, XVII: 23, II: 115, etc.); ii) the daring Antinomian doctrine of 'true infidelity' *(kufr-i ḥaqīqī)* already advanced several centuries earlier by Ḥallāj, 'Ayn al-Quḍāt Hamadānī, and later, Rūzbihān Baqlī; and iii) Ibn 'Arabī's theomonism, an idea which "goes beyond mere metaphor or simile," but is in fact "the ultimate semiosis in Islamic thought"-where "...everything is a sign or a signal of God..." so that "semiotics in the context of his [Ibn 'Arabī's] theology may be simply defined as an identification and classification of the signs of God who is existence *(al-Wujūd)*."[4]

1. Koran XVII 44
2. Koran VI 91.
3. Koran LXVII 3
4. *Allah Transcendent*, p. 303.

Maḥmūd Shabistarī Discoursing. Persian MS. No. Or. 11,837, f. 112b (Courtesy of the British Library)

In the present section an attempt is made to delineate the metaphysical concepts which underlie the Sufis' view of the 'unity-of-religions' as set out by Shabistarī in these lines, and provide a synopsis and analysis of Lāhījī's exegesis on these verses. Although reflections of Shabistarī's views on the subject are found echoed in the verses of all the major Sufi poets of this period: Qāsim-i Anwār, Shāh Ni'matullāh, Maghribī, and Jāmī, his doctrine, more importantly, has direct antecedents in Kubrawī mystical theology, and is particularly reminiscent of the esoteric views of Nasafī (died circa 680/1282), one of the first exponents and interpreters of Ibn 'Arabī's theosophy in the Persian language.[1]

This theory of 'esoteric idolatry'—as I have termed it—expounded by the master in these lines is based both on several articles of Islamic theology and precisely defined principles of traditional Sufi theosophy, the latter expressed in the sophisticated philosophical language of ontology. Any discussion of Shabistarī's doctrine of religious unity would be superficial without consideration of these (actually amounting to over seven) esoteric dimensions.

They are as follows:

1) the Transcendent Unity of God's Creativity;

2) the Relativism of Good and Evil, hence, of Faith and Infidelity;

3) the Cosmic Law of Contraries which Necessitates the Existence of Faith and Infidelity;

4) the Psychological Origin of Infidelity in Egotism;

5) the Theophanic Unity of All Religions based on the Transcendental Unity of Being;

6) the Primordial Philosophical Unity of Intent of All Aspirants; and

7) the True Infidelity that Transcends Exoteric Monotheism's 'Idol of Reason.'

These seven concepts will be discussed below in the order mentioned above.

1. The Transcendent Unity of God's Creativity or Oneness of Divine Action (tawḥīd-i af'ālī).

Not only is this doctrine explicitly stated in the foregoing translation (see verse 17) to support Shabistarī's unitarian outlook on religious diversity, it is also plays an important role in some of the theological formulations in the *Sa'ādatnāma*. One example of Shabistarī's conviction in this principle is his assertion in the latter treatise that anyone who refuses to believe that God creates every single event and act is a complete infidel *(kāfar)*.[2] Originating in al-Ash'arī's scholastic theology, the doctrine was also advocated by Ibn 'Arabī and the Sufi thinkers of his school, such as

1. See Isabelle de Gastines (trans) introduction to Nasafī's *Le Livre de l'Homme Parfait (Kitāb al-Insān al-Kamil)* (Paris 1984), p. 10.
2. SN vv. 1125. See also SN vv. 1170-71, 1126-29.

'Irāqī.[1]

In his commentary on verse seventeen of the above translation, it is clearly expressed by Lāhījī, who writes that the Sufi gnostic

> in every form should behold God's theophany manifest, whether this form be infidelity *(kufr)* or Islam. Verbally one should acknowledge that the only Real and True Being *(mūjūd ḥaqīqī)* is God, the Real *(Ḥaqq)* and thus *everything which is, is Him.* Make it your heart's firm conviction that all which exists, is God, and all else besides is pure nullity and nonexistence.
>
> A further meaning of the couplet, may be expressed as follows: 'See One' in all activity, alluding to the Oneness of Divine Actions *(tawḥīd-i af'ālī);* 'Say One' [alone exists in creation] in quality, indicating the Oneness of Divine Qualities; and 'Know One' [throughout creation alone exists] in essence, referring to the Oneness of the Divine Essence. In short, the principles and derivatives of Faith in God culminate in Divine Unity *(tawḥīd)* and the science of Divine Unity is the root of all religious beliefs and gnostic certitudes. [As 'Aṭṭār says:]
>
> *Be single-faced –*
> *Be unidirectional in duality;*
> *Be single-hearted:*
> *Have but one* qibla, *and face but one way.*
>
> *Anyone who doesn't lose himself*
> *in the Sea of Unity,*
> *Even if a man*
> *never became 'human.'*
>
> *(SGR 647)*

2. The Relativity of Evil

Sustaining the master's vision of the 'Unity of Religions' is the philosophical doctrine of the *Relativity of Evil,* an idea widely advocated by Sufi poets, found, for instance, in both the *Ḥadīqa* of Sanā'ī and the *Mathnawī* of Rumi,[2] as well as in Ibn 'Arabī's works. Elaborating this doctrine in the *Sa'ādatnāma,* while basing himself on a mystical exegesis of certain Koranic passages (e.g. LXVII: 31; XV: 40), Shabistarī explains that insofar as "evil' in respect to its Divine origin is good, thus there is no absolute evil in creation (SN 912), for

> *His infidelity is not infidelity but Faith;*
> *His chastisement is not chastisement but Grace.*[3]

---

1. "The source of all activity is one, but everywhere displays new colors and is called by a different name... – Only if the secret of *God created you and what you do* (Koran XXXVII: 96) were to wink its eye at them, would they ever come to know perforce that all power, all activity is ours only so much as HE is us." – *Fakhruddin 'Iraqi: Divine Flashes* (trans. W.C. Chittick, P.L. Wilson) (London: SPCK 1982), pp. 103-04. See also W.C. Chittick, *The Sufi Path of Knowledge,* p. 208. For a discussion of the role of this doctrine in early Persian Sufism, see M. Abdul Haqq Ansari, 'The Doctrine of One Actor: Junayd's View of *Tawḥīd,' The Muslim World* (1983), pp. 33-56.
2. See *Mathnawī-yi ma'nawī,* edited by R.A. Nicholson, 8 vols., Gibb Memorial Series, n.s. 4 (London 1925-40), Bk I: 1996--99, IV 65-80.
3. SN 911; cf. *Mathnawī -yi ma'nawī,* Bk. I: 1997.

Above and beyond this, the Eternal Divine Will, states Shabistarī, is untainted by the contraries 'good' and 'evil', which belong merely to the realm of mortality, the created sphere (SN 910); they pertain merely to the realm of God's Qualities, not to the Divine Essence (SN 917). Since what is evil and death to one person, is goodness and life to another, thus there can be no absolute evil (SN 917; cf. *Mathnawī-yi ma'nawī,* Bk. IV: 66-69).

Lāhījī's commentary on Shabistarī's sixth verse uses a parable to elucidate this idea of infidelity as a necessary evil, concluding his explanation with a citation from the *Sa'ādatnāma,* thus demonstrating how attentive this eminent exegeist was to the philosophical unity in Shabistarī's thought:

> Existence or Being, wherever it is, and in whatever form it is found, is sheer and absolute Good. If an evil is appears to be manifested in Being, that evil is from elsewhere *(ghayr)*[1] which is [ultimately] nonexistence or nullity *('adam).* According to the Sufi sages and theosophers who verify the truth of things *(muḥaqqiq),* it should be understood that this problem has been resolved in the following fashion: Since Being is sheer good, any 'evil' which appears manifested therein arises from nonexistence.
>
> The following example illustrates this point: Imagine that Zayd slays 'Umar by striking off his head with a sword. This circumstance should considered good insofar as Zayd possesses the ability to take away life. The sharpness of Zayd's sword is also good and from the point of view that the limbs of Umar were receptive to such an act, it is good. The sole evil involved here concerns the concurrent 'privation of life' or 'nonexistence' *('adamiyyat)* required by this act.
>
> Hence, considered from this [ontological] standpoint, 'evil' and 'bad' are but a retrogression to nonexistence, while Existence remains, wherever it is, the *summun bonum.* Viewed from the cosmic perspective of [the innate goodness of] Being and Existence, idolatry cannot therefore be said to be in essence 'evil'. [The Shaykh elucidates this principle in the *Sa'ādatnāma,* vv. 924, 932 as follows]: "Good and Evil: the former is existence and the latter is nonexistence. Put this truth to practice – don't just preach it. Nothing evil ever proceeds from the Omniscient Being; whatever God does is just and right." (SGR 640-41)

3. The Law of Contraries

Supporting the above doctrine is a *Law of Contraries* dictating that evil must exist if only in order to maintain harmony in creation. For this reason Shabistarī asserts that "the pleasures of Paradise derive from Hell; the taste of cake is felt by the sense of hunger; the effect of a healing balm depends upon the existence of a sore" (SN 943-45); ideas which are also part of the Sufi tradition deriving from both Rumi and Ibn 'Arabī.[2] Such contraries complement each other, being proof ultimately, of

1. *Ghayr* literally means, "other, alien, else, without," but it is also used in Persian to render the English prefixes "un-, in-, and non-." As the commentary indicates, the term here implies nonexistence or nullity. For a discussion of the significance of this term in Ibn 'Arabī's lexicon, see W.C. Chittick, *The Sufi Path of Knowledge,* p. 356.
2. *Mathnawī-yi ma'nawī,* Book II: 2535-43.

God's supremacy and mastership, as Rumi says.[1]

Consequently, Shabistarī is quite confident that "a little evil for the sake of a great deal of good, is, in effect, an overwhelming good" (SN 933). Hence the existence of infidelity (cf. SN 925-31) is subsumed under the category of a necessary evil. In the context of his exegesis on Shabistarī's second verse, Lāhījī is quite unequivocal about the necessity for the ordinary Muslim to understand the doctrine of the relativity of evil; commenting on this verse (SGR 639) in exposition of the ontological unity of faith and infidelity, he notes:

> The poet implies that, because blasphemy *(kufr)* and religion *(dīn)* are, with regard to appearances, ideas of contrary natures – nonetheless they are both subsistent through Existence *(hastī)* and Being *(wujūd)*. Since the Absolute Existence is God, bearing witness to Divine Unity and profession of God's Oneness are thus, in source and essence, identical to idolatry. Indeed, it would be associating something with God *(shirk)*, to regard blasphemy *(kufr)* and the idol as other than Divine in respect to their true reality. Holding such an attitude would make you a heretic to true Divine Unity *(tawḥīd-i ḥaqīqī)*. As the verse [Maghribī, Ghazal 11: 6] goes:
>
> *There is no one else but you*
> *whom they adore in the pagoda*
> *Any person who bows down*
> *upon brick, stone, or wood.*

4. The Psychological Origin of Evil

4. The *Psychological Origin of Evil* also demonstrates the ultimate nonexistence of evil. As evil exists only in the eye of the beholder, it is but a product of human finitude, and thus, a self-centered, disharmonious standpoint from which to approach life. Shabistarī states:

> When you see good and evil coming from Him, then everything you perceive will be 'good.' As long as you are possessed by egotism, you are a foe to God. As long as you perceive God's action from your own finite perspective, good will appear to you as evil. No one who is conceited [literally, who 'beholds himself'] can see the good in the world: here ends all debate on this issue. (SN vv. 1170, 1176-79)

Hence, infidelity, seen from the visionary's viewpoint, is Good's alter-ego and God's secret advocate. Maghribī (d. 810/1408), who lived in the same period and geographical vicinity as Shabistarī and whose poetry, as Qāsim Ghanī observed, was the best exposition of Shabistarī's symbolic theory in the history of Persian literature,[2] expresses these ideas in a few verses cited by Lāhījī in his exegesis:

---

1. "Infidelity and Faith bear witness from this point of view to God's sovereign power, both to Him pay homage. If God could do no ugliness, He would be imperfect. For this purpose has He created both the dualist and the pure-hearted monotheist." *Mathnawī-yi ma'nawī*, Bk. II: 2542-43.
2. *Baḥth dar āthār wa afkār wa aḥwāl-i Ḥāfiẓ: Tārīkh-i taṣawwuf dar islām az ṣadr-i islām tā 'aṣr-i Ḥāfiẓ* (Tehran 1977, 3rd edition), vol. 2, p. 563.

What to men is infidelity and sin
For me is Faith and true doctrine.
All the world's gall and bitterness
To my taste seems sweet, delicious.

An eye which sees the Truth
for lies has no sight at all:
For all 'untruth' that is conceived
Or what is perceived as lies, mendacity
Lies in the eyes themselves deceived—
The vantage-point of men without veracity.

For in the briar-patch of pride and envy,
Deceit, hypocrisy, polytheism and jealousy,
The blossom of Unity cannot flourish.[1]

On the other hand, the enlightened gnostic Sufi *('ārif)* who bothers to verify the reality of things *(muḥaqqiq)* "beholding Divine Unity before him, sees the inward light of (Divine) Being everywhere," Shabistarī tells us in the *Garden of Mystery*. (GR 9). Lāhījī, interpreting this line, characterizes this perfect mystic or "realizer *(muḥaqqiq)*" as a "perfect being to whom the reality of things as they truly are is manifest. This ideal reality *(ma'nā)* however, is only fathomed by one who has realized the degree of Divine unveiling *(kashf-i ilahī)* and in sheer clarity of Vision *('aīn al-'ayān,* [literally, through the 'Eye-of-Eyes']) witnesses that God *(Ḥaqq)* is the Reality of everything, perceiving that no other being besides the One Absolute Being exists – the existence of all other entities being something merely superimposed and relative." (SGR 58)

In interpreting Shabistarī's fifth verse in the translation given above, Lāhījī also expounds this doctrine, asserting that "Everything which God Almighty, the Creator of all things, creates is good, and from Good evil never issues. 'Evil' relates purely to us, but vis-à-vis God that same 'evil' is total Good and absolute wisdom."(SGR 640-41)

5. The Theophanic Unity of Religions

5. The doctrine of the *Theophanic Unity of all Religions Based on the Transcendental Unity of Being* is also a fundamental tenet of the *Garden of Mysteries*. In elucidating this idea (verse 16 above) the Shabistarī adopts a purely visionary position, inciting his audience of unitarian Sufis to rend the veil of colors and perceive the 'white radiance of Eternity' through the icons, within the 'idols' of all faiths—to behold the *visio Dei*. The doctrine propounded in verses sixteen and seventeen particularly suits the poet's audience: all seers, all Sufis, all gnostics; and to those unto whom spiritual love is second nature, it is proper that religion be direct Vision, and that Faith be not dogma, but *devoilement* or revelation.

Shabistarī's sixteenth verse also has precise antecedents in contemporary Kubrawī mystical theology (albeit also mainly derived from Ibn 'Arabī) as the following passage from the *Zubdat al-ḥaqā'iq* composed a generation before

1. *Divān-i Maghribī*, in 'A Critical Edition of the...', edited by L. Lewisohn, *Ghazal* 35.

Shabistarī by the Persian Kubrawī Shaykh 'Azīz al-Dīn Nasafī, records:

> There is no more than One Being and that Being is God, besides Whom there is no other being. That would be impossible. This One Being possesses an inner *(bāṭin)* and an outer *(ẓāhir)* aspect, the former consisting of a Single Light, the soul *(jān)* of the world, which shows itself through many diverse orifices: Itself speaking, Itself hearing, Itself receiving and bestowing, Itself professing and denying (the Truth)... All vision, hearing, speaking, possession, and sovereignty are portions of this One Light... Although all the divine Qualities, Actions and Names are composed of this Light, it is still One Entity, remaining a unity unto itself, in regard to which all living beings are merely its appearances *(maẓāhir).*[1]

The theophanic unity of all religious beliefs is the central and fundamental doctrine underlying Shabistarī's theory of religious unity, and even if there are indeed similar expressions of this doctrine found in the *Futūḥat*[2] of Ibn 'Arabī, his versification of this idea is unique in the history of mediæval Persian Sufism in both its appealing ecumenism and sensational directness. The following passages from Lāhījī's commentary (on verses 7, 8,9, 16) emulate the master in attempting to reveal rather than veil this broad-minded and cosmopolitan view of religious diversity:

> If the Muslim who professes Divine Unity *(tawḥīd)* and disavows the idol, were to become aware and conscious of what the idol is in reality, and of Whom it is a manifestation of, and of what Person it is who appears in the idol's form – he would certainly comprehend that the religion of the Truth *(Ḥaqq)* is in idolatry. Since the idol is a theophany *(maẓhar)* of the Absolute Being Who is God *(Ḥaqq)*, therefore *in respect to its essential reality, the idol is God*. Now, seeing as the religion and rite of Muslims is Truth-worship *(Ḥaqq-parastī)* and [as has been explained above] idolatry and Truth-worship are one and the same, therefore *true religion is in idolatry.*
>
> ...Likewise if the polytheists *(mushrik)* who adore idols were to become aware of the idol and its reality, and were to understand that the idol is actually a theophany of God, and that through its form God manifests Himself, and thus he actually prostrates, adores and is devoted to the One Supreme Being – where then in his religion and faith should he have gone astray, and have been in error?
>
> ...If you who make claims to Islam and orthodoxy, perceive naught but the idol's visible form and do not envision God hidden behind the veils of the its determined form—and it is this particular form which is a corporeal receptacle for God's theophany—you properly and legally *(dar shar)* also cannot be called a Muslim! In fact,

1. *Zubdat al-ḥaqā'iq*, ed. Ḥ. Nāṣirī (Tehran: Kitābkhāna Tahūrī 1985), pp. 76-77, 75.
2. W.C. Chittick, one of the most eminent of the modern interpreters of the Doctor Maximus, expounds the sage's ontological unity of religious beliefs as follows: "Each belief represents a subjective limitation of the fabric of existence; the fact that someone holds a belief proves that it coincides in some way or another with the situation of the world, whether or not the believer's mind establishes a real contact with what lies outside of itself, for the believer's mind is itself part of the world. ...This view of belief is based on the doctrine that the cosmos in its indefinite spatial and temporal extensions manifests the whole range of ontological possibilities possessed by Being. Each thing *(shay')* or cntity *('ayn)* is like a ray of color brought into existence by the prism of Infinite Possibility. Through its own specific nature—i.e., its own special limitations that distinguish it from other entities—each entity colors the Invisible Light, thereby making it visible. From one point of view an existent entity manifest the Light of Being by virtue of its very existence; from another point of view it veils or obscures this same Light by means of its own 'color''.–"Belief and Transformation: The Sufi Teachings of Ibn al-'Arabī," *The American Theosophist* 74/5 (1986), p. 186.

you are an infidel *(kāfar)* because you have veiled God's theophany appearing in the idol! (SGR 641-42)

The origin of all religious beliefs is thus seen to be grounded in the Reality of Being, which is itself, ultimately, the Divine Being. Although polytheistic idolatry has one color and monotheism another, both derive from one Light. Each belief is like ray of light which, reflected through the prism of its determined form, transforms the Absolute One Illumination into multicolored ideas—ideas which at once obscure and veil this Light.[1] Discernment of these polychromatic variations of Being's theophanies is a required part of the religious duties of the Sufi (cf. line 10 of the above translation): for the 'soul-color' differs within different individuals; the mystic is thus obliged to recognize the consequent "concordant discord" (Zaehner)[2] of diverse religious beliefs; a concordance which, says Shabistarī, arises from his identification with God's very nature.[3]

As Ibn 'Arabī expresses it, esoteric idolatry or true infidelity is a faith only gnostics can follow. Whereas

> The perfect gnostic recognizes God is every form in which He manifests Himself,... the non-gnostic recognizes Him only in the form of his own belief, denying Him when he manifests Himself in another form *(Futūḥāt* III 132.24)... the People of Allah follow Him whose people they are, so His property flows over them. and his property is lack of limitation, for He possesses all-pervading Being. So his people possess all-pervading vision.[4]

Shabistarī no doubt also drew much inspiration for certain verses cited above from Ibn 'Arabī's view that all love is, ultimately, Love Divine; that beneath every lust lies One transcendent Beloved. Passages such as the following from the *Futūḥāt* seem to have been foremost in Shabistarī's mind when composing couplets twelve and fifteen:

> No one is loved but God, but the name of the created things acts as a veil. In the same way, he who worships a created thing here worships none but God, though he does not know it. He names his object of worship Manāt, al-'Uzza, or al-Lāt. Then when he dies and covering is removed, he knows that he only worshipped God.[5]
>
> ...It is He who in every beloved being is manifested to the gaze of each lover...and none other than He is adored, for it impossible to adore a being without conceiving the Godhead in that being... So it is with love: a being does not truly love anyone other than his Creator.[6]

Such adaptation of Ibn 'Arabī's theosophy to the needs of Persian Sufism is vividly apparent in Lāhījī's commentary as well. Stating that all multiplicity is a manifesta-

---

1. *Ibid.*
2. R.C. Zaehner, *Concordant Discord: the Interdependence of Faiths (*Gifford Lectures on Natural Religion, 1967-69) (Oxford University Press 1970), Chap. 1.
3. "The man of the Path is he, who in every circumstance adapts himself to the diverse [theophanies of the] the divine qualities." SN 1094.
4. *Futūḥāt* III 161.15), trans. W.C. Chittick, in "Belief and Transformation," p. 191
5. *Futūḥāt* IV 260. 28, trans. W.C. Chittick, in *The Sufi Path of Knowledge*, p. 343.
6. *Futūḥāt* II, 326. Cited by H. Corbin, *Creative Imagination in the Sufism of Ibn 'Arabī (*trans. R. Manheim; Bolligen Series XCI, Princeton University Press 1969), p. 146. On this doctrine, cf. I. Netton, *Allah Transcendent*, pp. 285-87.

tion of the Absolute Being, Lāhījī, while commenting on Shabistarī's third verse (SGR 640) and apparently paraphrasing the above passage from the *Futūḥāt,* states, "God is displayed throughout all forms and images. Among these appearances and forms, one assumes the guise of an 'idol'...for 'Wheresoever you turn, there is the face of God.'[Koran II: 115] [As Maghribī says (Ghazal 54: 6,7)]

In the Temple of Somnath
The pagans but adored
Your beauty which shew forth.

From Lat and Manāt
Your loveliness did emanate—
Unto that the infidels
With love fell prostrate.

Lāhījī's commentary on Shabistarī's first verse (SGR 639) is also particularly direct in expressing the theophanic unity of religions:

> To those familiar with inward revelation and presential vision *(ahl-i kashf u shuhūd),* that is to say, to Sufis who have purified their hearts, every aspect and mote of Being acts as a theophanic receptacle *(maẓhar)* and il-lustration *(mujallā)* of that Reality, which is seen to be displayed and revealed throughout all forms. ...Because God *(Ḥaqq)* is revealed in the form of the idol, all the masters, being aware of its (ontological) importance and endowed with a plenitude of virtues, direct their attention towards this idol. In fact, in respect to this ontological principle, all theophanic forms *(maẓhar)* may be termed 'idols', since it is the Divine Beloved *(Maḥbūb-i ḥaqīqī)* which is manifested in their forms, so that all the particles of being are focused upon them. As one poet said:
>
> *Since the beauty of that Exemplar of Beauty*
> *in every atom is exemplified to us*
> *know that I am a Truth-worshipper*
> *even if you see me an idolater.*

5A. The Cosmo-ontological Source of Religious Diversity

As an corollary to this theomonistic unity of religions is what might be termed tentatively as the original *Cosmo-Ontological Source of Religious Diversity.* From this standpoint all religions appear to be only diverse manifestations of archetypal meanings *(ma'ānī)* attired in the vestiture of multiplicity. In this sense, nothing is 'other' than God.

Although a brief allusion to this profound doctrine is provided by Shabistarī in the first two lines of our translation, a detailed and exactingly complicated study of all the metaphysical corollaries of this idea is to found in the introduction to his philosophical treatise, the *Ḥaqq al-yaqīn,*[1] the analysis of which is unfortunately beyond the scope of our present discussion. Maghribī, however, expresses this idea in a relatively simple style in these verses:

---

1. *Majmū'a-yi 'āthār-i Shabistarī,* p. 288-89.

Wherever a man has girt about himself
the cincture of some belief,
her tresses' faith he professes.

Wherever a man of faith does turn
upon the surface of the earth,
the only object of his prayers
is the niche and oratory of her face.

Indeed, it is but she
whom they adore, to whom they pray
the world through,
wherever you see a devotee.[1]

6. The Unity of Devotional Intention

Another fundamental basis of the unity of all religions according to Shabistarī relates to the *Primordial Philosophical Unity which is a Unity of Intention in all Seekers of Truth.* Explaining this concept, Shabistarī follows Ibn 'Arabī's exegesis of the verse: "He governs the affairs of things; He differentiates the signs, that happily you will be certain of the meeting with your Lord." (Koran XIII: 2) This verse is taken by Ibn 'Arabī to mean that the natural government and primordial faith of all nations was based upon "wise laws established by men of intellect as the result of an inspiration from God of which they were unaware."[2]

The doctrine is also enunciated by Shabistarī in the *Ḥaqq al-yaqīn.*[3] (Although it is certainly reminiscent of Blake's universal vision of the world's religions[4]), in Ibn 'Arabī's particular lexicon, this unity of religions resembles a sort of 'innate idea':

> In this way messengers were sent according to the diversity of the eras and the multiplicity of situations. Each declared the truth of the others. None differed whatsoever in the principles in which they were grounded and about which they spoke, even if statutes differed.[5] Revealed laws were sent down, and statutes came to the people. The determining factor was the time and the situation, just as God has declared: "To each We appointed a Law and a Path." [Koran V: 48] So the principles were in agreement with no diversity in anything... The people distinguished between these prophetic ordinances promulgated by God and the wise ordinances established by the sages in accordance with their rational powers. They realized that the prophetic way was more complete and that it came from God. They accepted what they were told about the unseen things and had faith in the messengers.[6]

This is, in essence, what Lāhījī was referring to in stating that "the idol is actually a theophany of God, and that through its form God manifests Himself, and thus the idolater actually prostrates, adores and is devoted to the One Supreme Being." (SGR 642) The metaphysical substratum of this doctrine is based on Ibn 'Arabī's conception of the Divine Names as the abstract 'Forms' or 'Ideas' (in the Platonic sense)[7] which rule all creation, and sponsor the development of all material and in-

1. *Divān-i Maghribī*, ed. L. Lewisohn, *tarjī'band* I, *band* 8: 25-27.
2. *Futuḥāt al-Makkiyya;* trans. W.Chittick, in 'From the Meccan Openings: The Myth of the Origin of Religion and the Law', *The World and I* (3/1; January 1988), p. 661.
3 Note 3 is continued on page 399.

tellectual human progress, as well as on Ibn 'Arabī's interpretation of Koran XVII: 44 ("There is nothing but hymneth his praise"),[1] the very verse quoted by Shabistarī in line thirteen of our translation. In the following extract from his commentary on Shabistarī's thirteenth verse, it is apparent how Lāhījī's exposition of this doctrine leans very heavily on the Akbarian system of Koranic hermeneutics and theory of divine Names:

---

3. Cf. the following passage *(Majmū'a-yi 'āthār-i Shabistarī*, pp. 288-89):

The motion of that which is attracted towards its Attractor occurs only in a direct line which is called 'The Straight Path.' This is the meaning of the verse "Not an animal but He doth grasp it by the forelock." [Koran XI: 56]

A Mystery: The total number of motions and paths (of this attraction) conforms to the infinite uncreated determined prototypes *(ta'ayyunāt)*, and this is the meaning of the verse, "We have appointed for each of you a separate religious law and path." [Koran V: 48]

A Subtle Secret: Nonexistence is the circumference of all the different lines of various paths of existent beings. This surrounding peripheral nonexistence is itself all existence, since the Holy Sacrosanct One—may his stature be exalted—is devoid of all multiplicity, and thus "God surrounds all things."

A Truth: It is imperative that the direction of the line should be turned towards this circumference, so that in whatever direction a being moves, the motion will be turned towards the surrounding circumference. "Unto God belongs the East and the West, and wheresoever ye turn, there is God's countenance. Lo! God is All-Encompassing, All-Knowing." [Koran II: 115]

Conclusion: Due to the alienation and veiling generated by the (state of being of the) archetypal determinations *(ta'ayyun)*, Longing and Love [for the Attractor, that is, God] is aroused. This Longing and Love demand abasement and lowliness [on the lover's part], that is, devoted worship of God, such that "There is none in the heavens and the earth but cometh unto the Beneficent as a slave." [Koran XIX: 93]

Inference: The worship and devotion of a devotee whose individual determined form *(ta'ayyun)* is nonexistent, however it is performed, is expressly destined by an Essence whose own determined form is essentially Existence, for "Thy Lord has decreed that you worship none but Him." [Koran XVII: 23; cf. Ibn 'Arabī's exegesis of this verse in the *Futūḥāt* given in Prof. Chittick's *The Sufi Path of Knowledge*, p. 343] *Therefore all are devotees of God,* for "All are subservient to Him" [Koran II: 116] *no matter who it is who worships him.*

4. Several principles of William Blake's thesis that "All Religions are One" exhibit a remarkable intellectual fraternity with Shabistarī's vision. Thus, his third principle states, "No man can think, write, or speak from his heart, but he must intend the truth. Thus all sects of Philosophy are from the Poetic Genius adapted to the weaknesses of every individual." And his "Principle 7th" reads: "As all men are alike (though infinitely various), so all Religions and, as all similars, have one source." *William Blake: Complete Writings*, ed. G. Keynes, (London: O.U.P. 1972), p. 98.
5. Ibn 'Arabī's appreciation of the universality of prophethood and religious truth derives Koranic verses such as "Every nation has its messenger" (X: 47); "We sent forth among every nation a messenger, saying, 'Serve God, and eschew idols' " (XVI: 36); and "We have sent no messenger save with the tongue of his people." (XIV: 4) W. Chittick, 'From the Meccan Openings', p. 664n.
6. *Ibid.*
7. Cf. W.C. Chittick's interesting comparison on Ibn 'Arabī's theory of the divine Names with the Platonic Ideas in *The Sufi Path of Knowledge*, p. 84.

---

1. Cf. Ibn 'Arabī's statement: "No part of the cosmos ever ceases worshipping God in respect of its own preparedness, so the Real necessarily discloses HImself to it in keeping with its preparedness to receive. For there is 'nothing that does not glorify Him in praise,' for He has gripped it with both of His hands in accordance with what it believes, 'but you do not understand their glorification.' (17:44) If their glorification went back to a single affair, no one would fail to understand the glorification of anyone else. but God has said that the glorification of the things is not understood, so this indicates that everyone glorifies his God in keeping with that of Him which he has in himself and others do not have." – W.C. Chittick, *The Sufi Path of Knowledge*, p. 340.

It should be understood that all living beings manifest the divine form in their secret selves and that God is the Spirit of all things. Now, the form of every human being is constantly occupied in praising and invoking blessings upon its own Spirit which in turn manages and controls this form. The limbs, being merely corporeal, would be deprived of every practical and intellectual virtue, and would lack all motion and understanding were it not for the agency of the Spirit. In any case, it has been established that the divine form of each human being is constantly occupied in praising and invoking blessings upon its own Spirit. By medium of this beatific invocation God operates and controls the forms of the world (human beings constituting one of these forms) which in turn glorify and magnify God.

Based upon this magnification of God *(tanzīh)* on the part of these forms, all types of imperfection (that is, the Contraries within the divine Plenitude) are annulled and distanced from the spiritual realm (which is God). This relationship is also reciprocal, for it is through the theophany and appearance of these forms that the world of the Divine Virtues and Perfections (which is, in turn, but an emanation of those forms) can glorify God. ...In any case, all the entities of living beings glorify and magnify God, although as the Scripture states, "but ye understand not their praise;" since we do not fathom the language they speak, just as Turks cannot speak Hindawi.

With this introduction, we may now understand the logic behind the master's statement that "and daily, infidelity recites the rosary." He means that insofar as infidelity *(kufr)* is an existent entity, it also constantly glorifies God and affirms the divine transcendence and distance *(tanzīh)* from all imperfection standing in opposition to the plenitude of divine virtues. *Infidelity itself is a theophanic exposition* (maẓhar) *of these virtues, and so it also glorifies God.* Since God declares in the Koran, "and there is not a thing but hymneth His praise" (XVII 44)—the interpretation of which is that everything, without exception, engages in the glorification *(tasbīḥ)* and magnification *(tanzīh)* of God—how can anyone object to or be piqued with my statement that "daily, infidelity recites the rosary," for infidelity is, after all, *something*.

It should be understood everything which exists, manifests various 'theophanic forms' *(maẓhar)* of different divine Names. Everything possesses a particular Name which is its Spirit and Reality (it being but the corporeal exemplar of that Name) and by medium of this Name it glorifies and praises God. Now, 'infidelity' is a theophanic manifestation or form of the divine Name "the Misleader" *(al-muḍill)* which divine Name it glorifies and praises. Seen from the standpoint of the unity which all things enjoy by virtue of the indivisibility and the concentration of their mutual attention upon the divine Essence, all the theophanic forms of various divine Names are also in reality glorifying and praising the divine Name "Allah": the Name of the divine Essence. (SGR 645)

So despite its apparently antinomian tinge Shabistarī's doctrine of the unity of devotional intention within all seekers of truth does have a Koranic basis. This is quite obvious in the *Ḥaqq al-yaqīn,* where in the course of "replying to a possible objection" the poet pronounces: "The unbeliever's denial [of Divine Oneness] is merely accidental because this denial can be corrected by a minor indication which enables him to regain his *original innate predisposition* and so once again confess, 'and if your were to ask them, who created the heavens and the earth...they would say: 'God.' [Koran XXIX: 61]"[1]

1. *Majmū'a-yi 'āthār-i Shabistarī*, p. 289.

8. Esoteric Idolatry and the Idol of Reason

8. When a religious belief in a Single Personal God ceases to reflect its Absolute Reality, when the icon ceases to act as a mirror of a higher truth and becomes instead an idol opaque to all spiritual vision, the failure of dogmatic monotheism is most apparent. God at this point, says Shabistarī, becomes an *Idol of Reason,* (recalling Blake's symbol of the deity Urizen, the 'horizon' of human ratiocinative comprehension of God who "self-closed, all repelling" weaved "the spider's web" of the "Net of Religion.")[1] Shabistarī's eleventh verse *(supra)* which takes the esoteric dimension of the doctrine of 'true infidelity' *(kufr-i ḥaqīqī)*[2] to its farthest point, is again indebted to Ibn 'Arabī. He certainly would have endorsed Ibn 'Arabī's universalist view of God as superseding the belief-systems of dogmatic monotheism concocted by the reasons of theologians.[3]

As noted above, Shabistarī's doctrine has direct antecedents in Kubrawī mystical theology, and is particularly reminiscent of Nasafī's esoteric views – in particular, Nasafī's conception of the "Divine Essence," which transcends the false personal god of exoteric monotheism (a mere Idol of Reason), directly parallels Shabistarī's views on the limitations of dogmatic monotheism. According to Nasafī

> Most people worship an imaginary and artificially erected god, for each person has constructed some imaginary form in their minds which they deemed the absolute 'God.' They worship this form as God although it is but an artificial product of their mind. Worse than this however, is the fact that they find fault with others whom they vilify as "idol-worshippers" calling them "heathen" and "pagan votaries of graven images" while these same accusers, the fault-finders are themselves – are hung up in the same idolatry. For their faith is but idolatry. They are unaware of the Lord of Lords, the Absolute Good.
>
> Here we may add that although certainly everything has its own particular 'lord', there is a world of difference between this 'lord' and the Lord of Lords. *Those who*

1. See *Blake: Complete Writings,* 'The First Book of Urizen', Chap.I: 5; XXV: 23 and Blake's poem 'The Human Abstract'
2. Space does not permit here a detailed analysis of genealogy of the idea of 'real infidelity' *(kufr-i ḥaqīqī)* in Sufism. 'Ayn al-Quḍāt Hamadānī (executed 526/1132) classified this concept into four divisions and cites a letter purportedly from Abū Sa'īd ibn Abī'l-Khayr (d.440/1049) to Avicenna (d. 428/1037) asking for enlightenment on the subject of infidelity:

   Shaykh Abū Sa'īd wrote to Shaykh Abū 'Alī (Avicenna), "Guide me to the proof (of God)," and in his answer he wrote, "(It is) entry into real infidelity and departure from metaphorical Islam, and that you do not turn your face towards (anything) except that which beyond the three individualities, so that you become a submitter *(muslim)* and an infidel. For if you are beyond these, you are neither faithful nor infidel, and if you are below these, you are a Muslim idolater. If you are ignorant of all this, then you are worthless, so do not count yourself as a part of the totality of beings." Cited by Carl Ernst, *Words of Ecstasy in Sufism (*Albany: SUNY 1985), pp. 81-82. Shabistarī's reference in verse 11 of the above translation to "Real infidelity" and "metaphorical Islam" is thus traceable to the writings 'Ayn al-Quḍāt and, ultimately, to Ḥallāj.
3. "That which a human being keeps in his mind is only the belief in his heart; that is how much he encompasses of his Lord. So if you practice meditation, recognize upon whom you are meditating and what is escaping you. You will know only your own essence, since the contingent being establishes a relationship only with someone like itself. In this case, that someone will be what you have of Him in yourself, and what you have in yourself is contingent, so it is of the same kind as you. In truth you do not worship anything but what you have erected in yourself. That is why doctrines of God are so diverse... *(Futūḥāt* III 161.15), translated by W.C. Chittick, 'Belief and Transformation', p. 187.

> *attain to the Face* (wajh) *of God but not to the Essence of God are but idolaters, day and night engaged in fighting and disputing with people, fanatically intolerant and opposed to the conduct of anyone who differs from them. Whoever transcends the Face and realizes the Essence, worships God as a unitarian* (muwaḥḥid) *alone, and being freed from idol-worship, makes peace with all mankind and is thus emancipated from opposition to and denunciation of other peoples' ideas;* while he who attains only to the Divine Face remains a polytheist, associating other deities with God *(mushrik)*, even if outwardly he profess himself a devotee of Allāh.[1]

This remarkable passage merits comparison with Shabistarī's commentary in the *Sa'ādatnāma* on Sūrah VI, verse 91 of the Koran ("And they do not assess the power of God with a just measure"), where he states: "Anything which is apprehended by reason and the optical vision, may be judged by reason to be mortal and created. Such a god is but an image concocted from your subjective fantasy, because it is subject to the limitations of your ratiocination and vision. Now, having erected from the fabric of your personal fantasy a deity named 'Allāh'—how long shall you persist in this narcissistic self-worship?" (SN 488-90) Such lines show how conscious Shabistarī was of the perversity of religious views except those acquired through visionary discovery *(kashf)* and heart-savour *(dhawq)*, and for this reason in a verse near the end of the *Garden of Mystery (*GR 61) he incites his audience to overturn the hollow Islamic formalism of exoteric faith, and to become 'liberated' from all forms of religious dogmatism:

> *Detach thyself, be* ḥanifī
> *And from all faiths' fetters free;*
> *So come, like the monk, step up*
> *into religion's abbey.*

Lāhījī commentary on this line is most illuminating and shows the breadth and profundity of the Sufis' attitude towards religious freedom:

> Be detached and free and pure from contamination by the restrictions of religion, imitative devotion, customs, and habit. Be like the true monk and "step up into religion's abbey," which means to come into mosques and other places of worship, girding yourself with the cincture of service, acting as the monk whose very vocation is detachment, being liberated and disengaged from all formal and spiritual interests or obstructions. Do not be inhibited by the fetters of infidelity (*kufr*) and Islam, for whatever is in essence good, and is a cause of human perfection, is of course, praiseworthy. Leave every religion and people to their own rites and observances, since to be bound by mere words and expressions generally employed in other religions – such as 'Idol' *(but)*, 'Cincture' *(zunnār)*, 'Synagogue' *(dayr)*, 'Christian' ... is itself just another type of infidelity *(kufr)*. Professing such conceptual restrictions is contrary to the way and method of the Sufi gnostics. (SGR 689)

The foregoing exposition of the eight basic principles underlying Shabistarī's doctrine of esoteric idolatry – actually a transcendental monotheism based on Love of One Being whose diverse theophanies the different faiths of mankind represent (see disgram on page 403) – I hope has served as an adequate exposition of his visionary ecumenism.

1. *Zubdat al-ḥaqā'īq*, p. 83.

THE MYSTICAL PHILOSOPHY OF ESOTERIC IDOLATRY

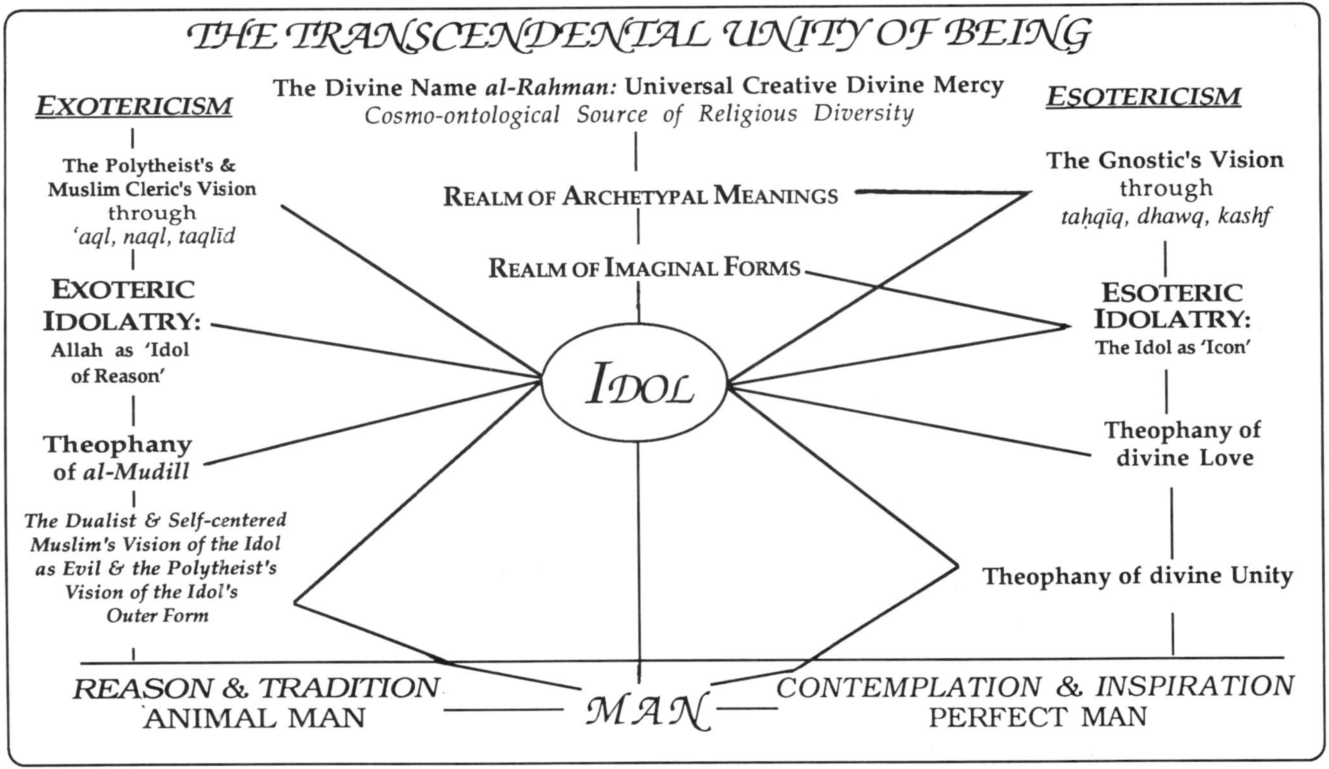
THE TRANSCENDENTAL UNITY OF BEING
The Divine Name al-Rahman: Universal Creative Divine Mercy
Cosmo-ontological Source of Religious Diversity
EXOTERICISM
The Polytheist's & Muslim Cleric's Vision through 'aql, naql, taqlīd
EXOTERIC IDOLATRY: Allah as 'Idol of Reason'
Theophany of al-Mudill
The Dualist & Self-centered Muslim's Vision of the Idol as Evil & the Polytheist's Vision of the Idol's Outer Form
REALM OF ARCHETYPAL MEANINGS
REALM OF IMAGINAL FORMS
IDOL
ESOTERICISM
The Gnostic's Vision through taḥqīq, dhawq, kashf
ESOTERIC IDOLATRY: The Idol as 'Icon'
Theophany of divine Love
Theophany of divine Unity
REASON & TRADITION
ANIMAL MAN
MAN
CONTEMPLATION & INSPIRATION
PERFECT MAN

V. CONCLUSION: THE TRANSCENDENT UNITY OF RELIGIONS

> Every ant which leaves its nest and goes to the desert will see the sun—but not know what it sees. What irony! Everyone perceives Divine Beauty with Certainty's Eye, for in reality nothing exists but Transcendent Unity; they look, they see, but do not comprehend. They take no pleasure in the view, for to enjoy it one must know through the Truth of Certainty what he is seeing, through Whom, and why.
>
> —'Irāqī[1]

In a recent article on the historical origin of Buddhist topi found in early Persian poetry in Khurasān immediately in the early Islamic period, A.S. Melikian-Chirvani, after a careful investigation of the philology and etymology of poetic images related to Buddhism in the Persian classics, demonstrates that all the references to 'beautiful idols' *(but-i zībā),* 'moon-faced idols' *(but-i māhrūy)* were ultimately based on encounters by early Persian poets, such as Fakhr al-Dīn Gurgānī, with Buddhist temples filled with painted and ornamented sculptures of Buddha. Melikian-Chirvani also points out that the Persian term for idol *(but)* is in fact etymologically derived from the word 'Buddha', observing that the intention of poets such as Manūchihrī and 'Unṣurī in hymning the praises of 'the idols of Qandahar' or 'Nūbahār' was in fact, to celebrate the 'Buddha of Qandahar' or 'Nawbahār': "The Persian term *but* (idol) in the poetry of this period was a topos created as an imaginative illustration of the sculptures of Buddha embellished with ornaments and jewels and painted in bright colors to be found in Khurasān, bearing testimony to the familiarity of these poets with Buddhist religious rituals involving the decoration and making of effigies of the Buddha in temples."[2]

It is of great significance that Shabistarī through visionary intuition developed the notion of idols as *theophanies* of Love and Divine Unity; his vision is direct and universal, involving an insight into the archetypal source-meaning *(ma'nā)* of the object analyzed—what he called its "primordial designation" *(waḍ'-i awwal).*[3] He is thus seeking the 'inscape' of words after the fashion of a Gerard Manley Hopkins or a Rainer Maria Rilke, beholding it in its essence by means of poetic imagination (*khiyāl*: the imaginal faculty of the mystics).

The fact that the term *but* is cognate with and derived from the word *Budd,* (Buddha) and originally referred to graven images of Buddha found in northern Khurasān in the tenth century, heightens the sublimity of Shabistarī's views on the unity of religions. Here his intuitive insight into the inner meaning of this term is obviously deeper than the usual employment by Sufi poets of the symbolism of non-Muslim religions as an excuse for a celebration of their mystical esotericism.[4] Shabistarī's vision attests to the timeless origin of the science of comparative religions, and his poetry speaks the language of imagination, the spiritual reality of which is objective no matter how archaic its poetic images and how obscure its phe-

1. *Divine Flashes*, p. 120.
2. 'Bāztābhā-yi adabī āyīn-i Būdda dar Īrān Islāmī', *Iran Nameh,* VIII: 2 (1990), p. 277.
3. See GR 57, line 8.

nomenal forms appear.[1]

Shabistarī's enlightened defence of the worth of other religions is most apparent in his doctrine of the *Law of Contraries* which espouses the relativity of heresy and true faith and dictates the necessity for the existence of other faiths. Faith is truly sincere only when performed in the spirit; the mere rite or form, the letter and the ritual act, are themselves valueless; in fact, says Shabistarī, they constitute a type of secret idolatry insofar as "Any type of devotion which is performed out of habit and by rote is merely food for passion. The only remedy [from hypocrisy] for a person of religious sensibility is to be found in the form of contraries *(ṣūrat-i aḍdād)*. That is to say, it is more virtuous for you to frequent a pagan temple *(dayr)* than to attend a mosque imagining yourself superior to others." (SN 1384-86)[2]

A million 'Muslims' killed each other in the religiously inspired Iran-Iraq war (1979-89), and since the end of the summer (1990) over 1300 Hindus and Muslims have perished in clashes over the storming of the mosque of Ayodhya by Hindu 'holy men.'[3] This vision of esoteric idolatry by Sufi gnostics such as Shabistarī

4. Poetic images involving the praise of idols, Brahams, and Zoroastrians *(gabr)* in Persian literature with the accompanying symbolism of non-Islamic religions, observed A. Bausani, "are simply symbols of something contrasted with official Islam and, in lyrics, also a symbol of a mystical reality deeper than any exoteric religion...Any non-Islamic religion can serve this purpose: true, historical Zoroastrianism has nothing to do with it and it is not necessary to suppose a direct continuation. The constellation of concepts that could be called the *kufr*-motif also included Iranian elements, but it is present also in Arabic literature of that time and is strongly connected with the Malāmatī school of Sufism.' – 'Muḥammad or Darius? The Elements and Basis of Iranian Culture' in S. Vryonis Jr. (ed.) *Islam and Cultural Change in the Middle Ages* (Wiesbaden 1975), p. 53.

1. The English poetess and exponent of the 'arts of the imagination', Kathleen Raine, composed the following lines in an attempt to revision this timeless religious ground of which Shabistarī spoke so eloquently:

   When is an idol an icon? When is an icon an idol? The icon is transparent as a representation of the spiritual reality it depicts; an idol replaces and obscures that reality—something understood by the Jewish religious vision which so rigorously condemned 'idolatry'. But the difference between icon and idol is purely subjective. All is idolatry that takes the outer form to be in itself an object of veneration. But, again, the most tawdry of idols or holy pictures can become transparent vehicles for spiritual meanings when they reflect and transmit a living vision. It is not 'the heathen in his blindness' who is most inclined to worship 'wood and stone', for the poetry of these representations of our inner worlds is very much part of our human heritage from the beginning—the depiction and embodiment of our visions, whether of Kali's black mask or Shiva's lingham, a Katchina of the Hopi people or of the sublime aspect of the Lord Buddha. It was doubtless the Christian missionary in his literal-minded blindness who could not see beyond the 'wood and stone'. The West, which has its own idolatries, has lost, under the influence of the materialism or recent centuries, access to that inner order of which idols may be icons, and in whose absence the most beautiful icons are but idols. – 'Revisioning the Sacred for Our Time', unpublished typescript lent to the author (written in 1988).
2. A reference to the Koran, Sūrah XXXVIII: 76. "Iblis said: I am better than him. Thou created me of fire, whilst him Thou didst create of clay."
3. *The Independent* (London daily newspaper), 28 October 1990, p. 15. The symbolism of the fact that the only refuge for Muslims in New Dehli—many of whom at present have been forced to flee from this conflict—is flocking for safety to the tomb *(dargah)* of the thirteenth-century Sufi mystic Niẓam al-Dīn Awlīyā' (1239-1325), should not be overlooked here. Cf. D. Pinto, S.J. 'The Mystery of the Nizamuddin Dargah: The Accounts of Pilgrims', in Christian W. Troll (ed.), *Muslim Shrines in India* (Oxford University Press 1989), pp. 112-124.

remains the only salvation for the unity of religions in the modern world, whether this be practically applied under the aegis of a politically secular ideology or under a religiously based social democracy. Fanaticism and religious fundamentalism is the way of diversity, strife and hate, but the Sufi path of love as represented by Shabistarī's doctrine of esoteric idolatry points the way to unity, love and service to all mankind, regardless of race, creed or colour.

SELECTED BIBLIOGRAPHY

'Abbādī, Quṭb al-Dīn Manṣūr. *al-Taṣfīya fī aḥwāl al-mutaṣawwifa.* Tehran: 1347/1968.
Abi'l-Wafā', Muḥyī al-Dīn. *al-Jawāhir al-mudi' a fī ṭabaqāt al-ḥanafīya.* Hyderabad:
  Nīzāmiyya, 1332.
Abu-Izzeddin, Nejla. *The Druzes: A New Study of Their History, Faith and Society.* Leiden:
  1984.
Āfāqī, Ṣābir. "Ṣūfīyān-i Kashmīr wa naqsh-i ānān dar nashr-i farhang wa adab-i fārsī."
  Hunar va mardum nos. 112-13. February-March (1972): 66-87
Aflākī, Shams al-Dīn Aḥmad al-. *Manâqib al-'ārifīn.* 2 vols. Ankara: Türk Tarih Kurumu,
  1959-61.
Afnan, Soheil M. *A Philosophical Lexicon in Persian and Arabic.* Beirut: Dār al-Mashriq,
  1969.
Afshār, Īraj, ed. *Dū risāla-i 'irfānī dar 'ishq.* Farhang-i Īrān-zamīn. Silsila-i mutūn wa
  taḥqīqāt. Tehran: 1359/1980.
Afshār, Īrāj. "Khānaqāh-hā-yi Yazd." *Sufī: Faṣlnāma Khānaqāh Ni'matullāhī.* Issue no.
  8 (1369 A.Hsh): 11-15.
Ahmad, Aziz. "The Sufi and the Sultan in Pre-Mughal Muslim India." *Der Islam* (1963).
Ahmad, N. "The Influence of Persian and Persian Culture in India." *Indo-Iranica* vol. 38
  nos. 1-4 (1984).
Al-Azmeh, A. "Orthodoxy and Ḥanbalite Fideism." *Arabica* (1989).
Algar, H. "Some Observations on Religion in Safavid Persia." *Iranian Studies* (1974).
_____. "The Naqshbandi Order: A Preliminary Survey of its History and Significance."
  Studia Islamica XLIV (1976).
_____. "Silent and Vocal Dhikr in the Naqshbandī Order." *Akten des VII Kongresses für
  Arabistik und Islamwissenschaft* Göttingen: 1976.
Āmūlī, Sayyid Ḥaydar. *Kitāb naṣṣ al-nuṣūṣ fī sharḥ fuṣūṣ al-ḥikam.* Ed. H. Corbin and O.
  Yahia. Tehran: Bibliothèque Iranienne, 1975.
Ansari, M. Abdul Haqq. "The Doctrine of One Actor: Junayd's View of *Tawḥīd.*" *Muslim
  World* (1983): 33-56.
Anwār, Qāsim-i. *Kulliyyāt-i Qāsim-i Anwār.* Ed. S. Nafīsī. Tehran: Kitābkhāna Sanā'ī,
  1337 A.Hsh./1958.
Arberry, A.J., trans. *Kings and Beggars, The First Two Chapters of Sa'di's Gulistān.*
  London: Luzac & Co, 1962.
_____. *Sufism: An Account of the Mystics of Islam.* London: Allen & Unwin, 1950.
_____. *Classical Persian Literature.* London: Allen & Unwin,1958.
_____. *Revelation and Reason in Islam.* The Forwood Lectures for 1956 delivered in the
  University of Liverpool. London: Allen & Unwin, 1957.

_____. *Shiraz: Persian City of Saints and Poets.* Norman: University of Oklahoma Press, 1960.

_____., Ed. *The Legacy of Persia.* Oxford University Press, 1963.

_____. *Aspects of Islamic Civilization.* Ann Arbor: University of Michigan Press, 1967/ 3rd ed. 1990 Reprint.

_____. *The Koran Interpreted.* 2 vols. London/New York: Allen & Unwin/Macmillan, 1971.

_____., trans. *The Doctrine of the Sufis* [translation of Kalābādhī's *Kitāb al-ta'arruf]*. Cambridge University Press, 1977.

Arjomand, S A. *The Shadow of God and the Hidden Imām: Religion, Political Order, and Societal Change in Shi'ite Iran from the Beginning to 1890.* University of Chicago Press, 1984.

'Aṭṭār Nīshābūrī, Farīd al-Dīn.. *Tadhkirat al-auliyā'*. Ed. R.A. Nicholson. 2 vols. London/ Leiden: 1905.

Aubin, Jean. *Matériaux pour la biographie de Shāh Ni'matullāh Walī Kermānī.* Reprint. Tehran & Paris: 1983.

Austin, R.J.W. "The Lady Niẓam: An Image of Love and Knowledge." *Journal of the Muhyiddin Ibn 'Arabi Society.* VII (1988): 53-48.

Avery, Peter. "Fitzgerald's Persian Teacher and Ḥāfeẓ." *Sufi: A Journal of Sufism.* Summer 6 (1990).

Awn, Kamāl Aḥmad. *Kitāb al-Futūḥāt al-Makkiyya wa mā warā' ahu min ayād khafiyya.* Ṭanṭā: Dār al-Bashīr, 1989.

Babaie, Susan and Swietochowski, M.L. *Persian Drawings in the Metropolitan Museum of Art.* New York: The Metropolitan Museum of Art, 1989.

Baldick, Julian. *Mystical Islam: An Introduction to Sufism.* London: I. B. Tauris, 1989.

Bamzai, Prithvi Nath Kaul. *A History of Kashmir.* 2nd ed. New Delhi: Metropolitan Book Company, 1973.

Bateson, M.C. J.W. Clinton, J.B.M. Kassarijan, H. Safavi, & M. Soraya. "*'Ṣafā-yi Bāṭin:'* A Study of the Interrelations of a Set of Iranian Ideal Character Types." *Psychological Dimensions of Near Eastern Studies.* Ed. N. Brown & N. Itzkowitz. Princeton: 1977.

Bausani, Alessandro. "Letteratura Neopersiana." *Storia della letteratura persiana.* Ed. Antonino Pagliaro and Alessandro Bausani. Milan: Nuova Accademia Editrice, 1960.

_____. *The Persians: from the earliest days to the twentieth century.* Trans. J. Donne. London: 1971.

_____. "Muhammad or Darius? The Elements and Basis of Iranian Culture." *Islam and Cultural Change in the Middle Ages.* Ed. S. Vryonis Jr. Wiesbaden: Otto Harrassowitz, 1975.

Bayat, Mangol. *Mysticism and Dissent: Socioreligious Thought in Qajar Iran.* Syracuse University Press, 1982.

Bell, J.N. "Avicenna's Treatise on Love and the Nonphilosophical Muslim Tradition." *Der Islam* Bond 63 (1986): pp. 73-89.

Bertels, Y.E. *Taṣawwuf wa adabiyāt-i taṣawwuf.* Translated into Persian by Sīrūs Īzadī. Tehran: Amīr Kabīr, 1976.

Bhagavat-gītā-jī. Trans. Fayḍī ibn Mubārak. Allahabad: 1901.

Binyon, L. *The Poems of Nizami.* London: 1928.

_____. *The Spirit of Man in Asian Art.* Harvard University Press, 1935.

_____. Wilkinson, J.V.S., & Gray, B. *Persian Miniature Painting.* New York: Dover Books, 1971.

Bīrūnī, al-. *Kitāb al-Hind.* Trans. Eduard Sachau as *Albiruni's India: An Account of the Religion, Philosophy, Literature, Geography, Chronology, Astronomy, Customs, Laws and Astrology of India, about AD 1030.* London: Trübner, 1887.

Biqā'ī, Burhān al-Dīn al-. *Maṣra' al-taṣawwuf wa Tanbīh al-ghabī ilā takfīr Ibn 'Arabī.* Balbīs Egypt: Dār al-Taqwā, 1989.

Birge, J. *The Bektashi Order of Dervishes.* London: 1937.

Blake, William. *William Blake: Complete Writings.* London: O.U.P., 1972.

Böwering, G. "'Alī b. Šehab-al-Dīn b. Moḥammad Hamadānī." *Encyclopaedia Iranica.* I [fasc. 8]: 862-864.

Brown, J. *The Darvishes.* Oxford/London: 1927.

Brown, Raymond E. *The Anchor Bible: The Gospel According to John.* New York: Doubleday & Co. Inc, 1966.

Browne, E. G. *A Catalogue of the Persian Manuscripts in the Library of the University of Cambridge.* Cambridge: 1896.

_____. *A Literary History of Persia.* 4 vols. Cambridge University Press, 1920.

_____. *Az Sa'dī tā Jāmī.* Translation with notes by 'Alī Asghar Ḥikmat of vol. 3 of *A Literary History of Persia.* Tehran: 1960.

Bryer, David. "The Origins of the Druze Religion." *Der Islam* (1975-76).

Bukhārā'ī, Aḥmad 'Alī Rajā'ī. *Farhang-i ash'ār-i Ḥāfiẓ.* 2nd ed. Tehran: 1985.

Burrill, Kathleen R F. *The Quatrains of Nesimī: Fourteenth Century Turkic Hurufi, with annotated translations of the Turkic and Persian quatrains from the Hekimoğlu Ali Paşa Ms.* The Hague/Paris: Mouton, 1972.

Bürgel, J.C. "Musicotherapy in the Islamic Middle Ages." *History of Medicine.* New Delhi: 1980. IV:23-28.

_____. *The Feather of Simurgh: The "Licit Magic" of the Arts in Medieval Islam.* New York University Press, 1988.

_____. "The Romance." *Persian Literature.* Ed. E. Yarshater. Columbia Lectures on Iranian Studies III. New York: Persian Heritage Foundation, 1988.

Bākharzī, Abū'l-Mafākhir Yaḥyā. *Awrād al-aḥbāb va Fuṣūṣ al-ādāb, jild-i duvvam: Fuṣūṣ al-ādāb.* Ed. Īraj Afshār. Tehran: 1345A.Hsh./1966.

Cahen, Claude. *Pre-Ottoman Turkey: A General Survey of the Material and Spiritual Culture and History c. 1071-1330.* Trans. J. Jones-Williams. New York: Taplinger, 1968.

The Cambridge History of Iran: The Saljuq and Mongol Periods. vol. 5. Ed. J.A. Boyle. Cambridge University Press, 1968.

The Cambridge History of Iran: The Timurid and Safavid Periods. vol. 6. Ed. P. Jackson and L. Lockhart. Cambridge University Press, 1986.

Casewit, Stephen. "The Mystical Side of the *Muqaddimah:* Ibn Khaldun's View of Sufism." *Islamic Quarterly* vol. 29. no. 3 (1985).

Charkhī, Ya'qūb. *Risāla-i unsiyya.* Delhi: Matba'-i Mujtaba, 1924.

Chishtī, 'Abd al-Raḥman. *Mir'āt al-ḥaqā'iq.* London: British Library MS. Or. 1883.

Chittick, William C. "Ebno'l-'Arabi's Doctrine of the Oneness of Being." *Sufi: A Journal of Sufism* Winter: Issue 4, 1989.

_____. "Mysticism Versus Philosophy in Earlier Islamic History: The Al-Ṭūsī, Al-Qūnawī Corrrespondence." *Religious Studies* 17 (1981): 87-104.

_____. *The Sufi Path of Love: The Spiritual Teachings of Rumi.* Albany: SUNY, 1983.

_____. "From the Meccan Openings: The Myth of the Origin of Religion and the Law." *The World and I* 3.1 (1988).

_____. *The Sufi Path of Knowledge: Ibn al-'Arabī's Metaphysics of Imagination.* Albany: SUNY, 1989.

Cole, Juan. "Shi'i Clerics in Iraq, Iran, 1722-1780: The Akhbari-Usuli Conflict Reconsidered." *Iranian Studies* 18.1 (1985)

_____. *Roots of North Indian Shī'ism in Iran and Iraq: Religion and State in Awadh, 1722-1859*. University of California Press, 1988.

Coomaraswamy, Ananda. *Traditional Art and Symbolism*. vol. 1. Bolligen Series 89. 2 vols. Princeton University Press, 1977.

Corbin, Henry. *Avicenna and the Visionary Recital*. Bollingen Series LXVI. Trans. Willard R. Trask. Princeton: Princeton University Press, 1985.

_____."Le poème de Mamúd Shabestarī et ses commentateurs." *Trilogie Ismaelienne*. Tehran and Paris: 1961.

_____. *Creative Imagination in the Sufism of Ibn 'Arabi*. Trans. R. Manheim. Bollingen Series 99. Princeton: Princeton University Press, 1969.

_____ and O.Yahya (eds.) *"Jāmī' al-asrār:" La philosophie shi'ite*. Tehran-Paris: 1969.

_____. *En Islam iranien (Aspects spirituels et philosophiques)*. 4 vols. Paris: Éditions Gallimard, Bibliothèque des Idees, 1972.

_____. *L'Homme et son ange: initiation et chevalerie spirituelle*. Paris: Fayard, 1983.

_____. *Histoire de la philosophie islamique*. Paris: 1986.

_____., ed. (traduction et notes) *Shihāboddīn Yaḥya Sohravardī: Le Livre de la Sagesse Orientale (Kitāb Ḥikmat al-Ishrāq)*. Paris: Éditions Verdier, 1986.

Culler, Jonathan. *Barthes*. Fontana, Modern Masters. London: Fontana Paperbacks: 1983.

Daftary, Farhad. *The Ismā'īlis: Their History and Doctrines*. Cambridge University Press, 1990.

Dānish-pazhūh, Muḥammad Taqī. *Fihrist-i mīkrūfīlmhā-yi Kitāb-khāna-i markazī-yi Dānishgāh-i Tihrān*. Tehran: 1969.

Danner, Victor, trans. *Ibn 'Atā' illāh's Ṣūfī Aphorisms (Kitāb al-ḥikam)*. Leiden: E.J. Brill, 1973.

_____. *The Islamic Tradition: An Introduction*. New York: Amity House, 1988.

Dashtī, 'Alī. *Qalamrū-yi Sa'dī*. Tehran: Kayhan, 1959.

Daud, Wan Mohd Nor Wan. *The Concept of Knowledge in Islam and its Implications for Education in a Developing Country*. London: Mansell, 1989.

Dawlatābādī, 'Azīz. *Sukhanvarān-i Azarbaijan*. 2 vols. Tabriz: 1357.

Dede, Sakib Mustafa. *Sefîne-yi nefîse-yi Mevleviyân*. Cairo: Matba'a-i Vehbiye, 1283/ 1866-1867.

DeWeese, Devin. "The Eclipse of the Kubravīyah in Central Asia." *Iranian Studies* 21 (1988): 45-83.

Digby, Simon. "The Sufi Shaykh and the Sultan: A Conflict of Claims to Authority in Medieval India" *Iran: Journal of the British Institute of Persian Studies* vol. 28 (1990):

During, Jean. *Musique et Mystique dans les Traditions de l'Iran* (Paris: I.F.R.I.: Peeters, 1989).

_____. *Musique et extase, L'audition mystique dans la tradition soufie*. Paris: Albin Michel, 1988.

Eco, Umberto. *A Theory of Semiotics, Advances in Semiotics*. Bloomington & London: Indiana University Press, 1976.

_____ *Travels in Hyperreality*. London: Pan Picador, 1987.

Eliade, Mircea. *Shamanism, Archaic Techniques of Ecstasy*. Bollingen Series 76. Trans. Willard R. Trask. Princeton: Princeton University Press, 1974.

Ernst, Carl. *Words of Ecstasy in Sufism*. Albany, N.Y: State University of New York Press, 1985.

Ethé, H., ed. *Catalogue of the Persian, Turkish, Hindûstânî and Pushtû Manuscripts in the*

Bodleian Library. Oxford: 1889.

_____. ed. *Catalogue of the Persian Manuscripts in the Library of the India Office*. Oxford: 1903.

Ettinghausen, R. & Ehsan Yarshater, ed. *Highlights of Persian Art*. Colorado: Westview Press, 1979.

Farghānī, Sa'īd al-Dīn. *Mashāriq al-darārī*. Ed. S.J. Āshtiyānī. Mashhad: Chāpkhāna-i Dānishgāh-i-Firdawsī, 1357 A.H.sh./1978.

Faroqhi, Suraiya. "Agricultural Crisis and the Art of Flute-Playing: The Worldly Affairs of the Mevlevî Dervishes." *Turcica* XX (1988)

Fouchecour, C.-H. de. *La Description de la nature dans la poésie lyrique persane du XIe siècle: Inventaire et analyse des thèmes*. Paris: Librairie C. Klincksieck, 1969.

Friedman, Y. *Shaykh Aḥmad Sirhindī: An Outline of His Thought and a Study of His Image in the Eyes of Posterity*. Montreal and London: McGill-Queen's University Press, 1971.

Frye, Richard. *The Golden Age of Persia*. London: Weidenfeld & Nicholson, 1975.

Fuqarā, Aḥmad ibn Maḥmūd Mu'īn al-. *Tarīkh-i Mullā-zāda* (or *Kitāb-i Mullā-zāda*). Tehran: 1330/1960-1.

Furūzānfar, Badī' al-Zamān. *Majmū'ah-i maqālāt wa ash'ār-i Badī' al-Zamān Furūzānfar*. Tehran: Kitābfurūshī Dihkhudā, 1351 A.Hsh./1972.

_____. *Aḥādith-i Mathnawī*. Tehran: Intishārāt-i Dānishgāh-i Tihrān, 1956.

_____. "Sa'dī wa Suhrawardī." *Sa'dī-nāma*. Ed. Ḥabīb Yaghmā'ī. Tehran: Department of Education, 1983.

Gastines, Isabelle de, trans. *Le Livre de l'Homme Parfait (Kitāb al-Insān al-Kamil* by Nasafī). Paris: 1984.

Ghanī, Qāsim. *Baḥth dar āthār wa afkār wa aḥwāl-i Ḥāfiẓ: Tārīkh-i taṣawwuf dar islām wa taṭawwurāt wa taḥawwulāt-i mukhtalifa-i ān az ṣadr-i islām ta 'aṣr-i Ḥāfiẓ*. 2 vols. 3rd. ed. Tehran: Kitābfurūshī Zawwār, 1977.

Ghazzālī, Abū Ḥāmid al-. *al-Maqṣad al-asna fī sharḥ ma'ānī asmā' Allāh al-ḥusna*. Beirut: 1971.

Ghurab, Maḥmūd. *Sharḥ Fuṣūṣ al-ḥikam*. Damascus: 1985.

Gibb, E. J. W. *A History of Ottoman Poetry*. 6 vols. Reprint. London: 1958-63.

Gölpınarlı, Abdülbâki. *Mevlânâ Celâleddîn: hayatı, felsefesi, eserleri, eserlerinden seçmeler*. 3rd ed. Istanbul: Inkılâp, 1959.

_____. *Mevlânâ'dan sonra Mevlevîlik*. Istanbul: Inkılâp ve Aka, 1983.

Gramlich, R. "Die Wunder der Freunde Gottes. Theologien und Erscheinungsformen des islamischen Heiligenwunders." *Freiburger Islamstudien 11*. Wiesbaden: Steiner, 1970.

Grunebaum, G.E. von. *Unity and Variety in Muslim Civilization*. University of Chicago Press, 1955.

_____. *Islam: Essays in the Nature and Growth of a Cultural Tradition*. 2nd ed. London: Routledge & Kegan Paul, 1961.

Habshī, 'Abdullāh al-. *Al-ṣūfiyya wa l-fuqahā' fī l-Yaman*. Sana'a: 1976.

Ḥāfiẓ. *Divān-i Khwāja Shams al-Dīn Muḥammad Ḥāfiẓ*. Ed. Parwīz Nātil Khālarī. 2nd ed. Tehran: 1362 A.Hsh./1982

Hairi, M.Y. "Suhrawardī's *An Episode and a Trance*. A Philosophical Dialogue in a Mystical Stage." *Islamic Philosophy and Mysticism, Studies in Islamic Philosophy and Science*. Ed. Parviz Morewedge. Delmar, New York: Caravan Books, 1981.

Hamadani, Agha Hussain Shah. *The life and works of Sayyid Ali Hamadani (A.D. 1314-1385)*. Islamabad: National Institute of Historical and Cultural Research, 1984.

Hamadānī, 'Ayn al-Quḍāt. *Tamhīdāt*. Ed. Afīf Osseiran. Tehran: 1962.

Hasrat, B.J. *Dārā Shikūh: Life and Works*. New Dehli: Munshiram Manoharlal Ltd., 1982.
Ḥikmat, 'Alī Aṣghar. "Az Hamadān tā Kashmīr." *Yaghmā* IV (1951-52): 337-343
Hodgson, Marshall G. S. *The Venture of Islam: Conscience and History in a World Civilization*. 3 vols. Chicago & London: University of Chicago, 1974, 1977.
Huart, C. *Textes Persans Rèlatifs à la secte des Houroûfîs*. Leyden/London: 1909.
Hujvīrī, 'Alī ibn'Uthmān. *Kashf al-Maḥjūb*. Trans. R.A. Nicholson, Leiden and London 1911.
Husaini, A. S. "Uways al-Qaranī and the Uwaysī Sufis." *The Moslem World* 57 (1967).
Ibn 'Arabī. *Al-Futūhāt Al-Makkiyyah*. Cairo: 1329 A.H.
_____. *Ta'wīlāt*. Beirut: 1968.
_____. *Sufis of Andalusia: The Rūḥ al-quds and Al-Durrrat al-fākhirah*. Trans. R.W.J. Austin. London: Allen & Unwin, 1971.
_____. *Ibn al-'Arabī: The Bezels of Wisdom*. Trans. R.W.J. Austin. London: SPCK, 1980.
_____. *The "Tarjumān Al-Ashwāq": A Collection of Mystical Odes by Muḥyīu'ddīn ibn al-'Arabī*. Ed./trans. R.A. Nicholson. London 1911. Reprint 1978.
Ibn Baṭṭūṭa, *Safanāma-yi Ibn Baṭṭūṭa*. Translated into Persian by Muḥammad 'Alī Muwaḥḥid. Tehran: 1337 A.Hsh.
_____. *Riḥla*. Cairo: 1284/1867.
'Irāqī, Fakhr al-Dīn. *The Song of Lovers*. Trans. A. J. Arberry. Calcutta: Islamic Research Association, 1939.
_____. *Fakhruddin 'Iraqi: Divine Flashes*. Trans. W.C. Chittick and P.L. Wilson. London: SPCK, 1982.
Ivanow, W. *Concise Descriptive Catalogue of the Persian Manuscripts in the Curzon Collection, Asiatic Society of Bengal*. Calcutta: 1962.
_____. *Ismaili Literature*. Tehran: 1963.
Jahāngīrī, Muḥsin. *Muḥyī'l-Dīn ibn 'Arabī: Chihra-yi barjasta-yi 'irfān-i islāmī*. Tehran: 1980.
Jandī, Mu'ayyid al-Dīn. *Sharḥ Fuṣūṣ al-ḥikam*. Ed. J.A. Āshtiyānī. Mashad: 1982.
Joinville, De. *Memoirs of the Crusades* by Villehardouin and De Joinville. Everyman Series. Trans. Sir Frank Marzials. London and New York: 1908.
Jāmī, 'Abd al-Raḥman. *Nafaḥāt al-uns wa ḥaḍarāt al-quds*. Tehran: Kitāb-furūshī-yi Maḥmūdī, 1957.
_____. *Tuḥfat al-aḥrār*. Lucknow: Tēj Kumār, 1966.
_____. *Naqd al-nuṣūṣ fī sharḥ naqsh al-fuṣūṣ*. Ed. W.C. Chittick. Tehran: Imperial Iranian Academy of Philosophy, 1977.
Karbalā'ī, Ḥusayn. *Rawḍāt al-jinān wa jannāt al-janān*. Ed. J. Sulṭān al-Qurrā'ī. 2 vols. Tehran: 1965-70.
Kasravi, Ahmad. *On Islam and Shi'ism*. Trans. Ghanoonparvar, M.R. Costa Mesa, CA: Mazda, 1991.
Keddie, Nikki. "Symbol and Sincerity in Islam." *Studia Islamica* XVIII (1963):
_____. ed. *Scholars, Saints and Sufis, Muslim Religious Institutions in the Middle East Since 1500*. University of California Press, 1972.
Khaldun, Ibn. *Ibn Khaldun, The Muqaddimah*. Trans. F. Rosenthal. New York: 1958.
Khwāfī, Aḥmad Faṣīḥ. *Mujmal-i Faṣīḥī*. Ed. Maḥmūd Farrukh. 3 vols. Mashad: 1339/1960-1–1341/1962-3.
Khwānṣārī, Muḥammad Bāqir. *Rawḍat al-jannāt fī aḥwāl al-'ulamā' wa al-sadāt*. 8 vols. Tehran: 1970-2.
Khān, Muḥammad Riyāḍ. "Khadamāt-i Amīr-i Kabīr Mīr Sayyid 'Alī Hamadānī dar shabh-i qāra-i Pākistān wa Hind (qarn-i hashtum)." *Ma'ārif-i islāmī* 6 (1968)

Khān, Muḥammad Riyāḍ. "*Futuwwatnāma* az Mīr Sayyid 'Alī Hamadānī." *Ma'ārif-i islāmī* 10 &11 (1970): 32-39.

Khānaqāhī, Abū Naṣr Ṭāhir. *Guzīda dar taṣawwuf*. Tehran: 1347/1968.

Khāqānī-yi Shīrvānī. *Dīwān-i Khāqānī-yi Shīrvānī*. Tehran: Intishārāt-i Arisṭū, 1362.

Kirmānī, Sa'īd Miḥrābī-yi. *Tadhkirat al-awliyā'-yi Miḥrābī-yi Kirmānī*. Tehran: 1330/ 1951-2.

Kirmānī, Sayyid Nūr al-Dīn Shāh Ni'matullāhWalī-yi. *Risālahā-yi Shāh Ni'matullāh Walī-yi Kirmānī*. 4 vols. Ed. Javad Nurbakhsh. Tehran: Intishārāt-i Khānaqāh-i Ni'matullāhī, 1976-78.

_____. *Kulliyyāt-i Shāh Ni'matullāh Walī*. Ed. Javad Nurbakhsh. Tehran: 1982.

Kiyānī, Muḥsin. *Tārīkh-i khānaqāh dar Irān*. Tehran: Kitābkhāna Ṭahūrī, 1369 A.H.sh./ 1990.

Klimburg-Salter, D.E. "A Sufi Theme in Persian Painting: the Divan of Sultan Ahmad Galair in the Freer Galery of Art Washington, D.C." *Kunst des Orient* vol. 11. nos. 1-2 (1976-77): 43-84.

Kohlberg, Etan. "Some Aspects of Akhbari Thought." *Eighteenth -Century Renewal and Reform in Islam*. Ed. N. Levtzion & J.Voll. Syracuse: Syracuse University Press, 1987.

Kāshifī, Fakhr al-Dīn 'Alī ibn Ḥusayn Wā'iz al-. *Rashaḥāt-i 'ayn al-ḥayāt*. Ed. 'Alī Aṣghar Mu'miyān. 2 vols. Tehran: 1970.

Kāshānī, Mullā Muḥsin al-Fayḍ al-. *Kalimāt-i maknūna min 'ulūm ahl al-ḥikma wa'l-ma'rifa*. Tehran: 1342 A.Hsh./1963.

Kubrā, Najm al-Dīn. *Die Fawā'iḥ al-ǧamāl wa fawātiḥ al-ǧalāl*. Ed. Fritz Meier. Wiesbaden: 1957.

Lāhījī, Muḥammad. *Mafātīḥ al-i'jāz fī sharḥ-i Gulshan-i rāz*. Ed. Kaywān Samī'ī. Tehran: 1337 A.Hsh./1958.

Lambton, A.K.S. "The Clash of Civilizations: Authority, Legitimacy, & Perfectibility" *Islamic Fundamentalism*. Ed. R.M. Burrell. London: Royal Asiatic Society, 1989.

Landolt, Hermann. *Nuruddin Isfarayini: Le Révélateur des Mystères*. Paris: Verdier, 1986.

Lawrence, Bruce. B. *Notes from a Distant Flute: Sufi Literature in Pre-Mughal India*. Tehran: Imperial Iranian Academy of Philosophy, 1978.

_____. *Defenders of God: The Fundamentalist Revolt Against the Modern Age*. London: I.B. Tauris, 1990.

Lerner, D. *The Passing of Traditional Society: Modernizing the Middle East*. New York Free Press, 1958.

Levy, Reuben. *Persian Literature, An Introduction*. London: Oxford University Press, 1923.

Lewisohn, Leonard. "Shabestari's Garden of Mysteries: The Aesthetics and Hermeneutics of Sufi Poetry." *Temenos: A Review Devoted to the Arts of the Imagination* 10 (1989): 177-207.

_____. "Sharḥ-i ḥāl-i Kamāl Khujandī." *Iran Nameh* (forthcoming 1992)

_____. ed. *Diwān-i Muḥammad Shirīn Maghribī*. Tehran: forthcoming 1993.

Lévi-Strauss, Claude. *Myth and Meaning*. London: Routledge & Kegan Paul, 1978.

Loeffler, R. *Islam in Practice: Religious Beliefs in a Persian Village*. Albany: SUNY, 1988.

Madelung, Wilferd. "Ibn Abî Gumhûr al-Ahsâ'îs synthesis of kalam, philosophy and Sufism." *La Significance du Bas Moyen Age dans le Histoire et la Culture du Monde Musulman*. Aix-en-Provence: Actes du 8eme Congres de l'Union Européne de Arabisants et Islamisants, 1978.

Mahdi, Muhsin. "The Book and the Master as Poles of Cultural Change in Islam." *Islam and Cultural Change in the Middle Ages*. Ed. S. Vyronis Jr.. Wiesbaden: 1975.

Maḥjūb, J. "Futuwwat wa āyīn-i ān." *Sufi: Faṣlnāma Khānaqāh Ni'matullāhī*. no. 11 (1991).

Mahony, William K. "Flight." *Encyclopedia of Religion*. New York: Macmillan Publishing Company, 1987.

Makdisi, George. *The Rise of Humanism in Classical Islam and the Christian West*. Edinburgh: Edinburgh University Press, 1991.

Makkī, Abū Ṭālib al-. *Qūt al-qulūb fī mu' āmalāt al-Maḥbūb*. Cairo: 1310/1892-3.

Mann, Stuart E. *Albanian Literature*. London: 1955.

Martin, F.R. *Miniatures from the Period of Timur in a Ms. of the Poems of Sultan Ahmad Jalair*. Vienna: 1936.

Mashkūr, M.J. *Tārīkh-i Tabrīz tā payān-i qarn-i nuhum hijrī*. Tehran: 1973.

Massignon, L. *Opera Minora I*. Beirut: 1963.

Massignon, Louis. "La vie et les oeuvres de Ruzbehan Baqli." *Opera Minora*. Ed. Y. Moubarac. Beirut: Dar al-Maaref, 1963.

_____. *The Passion of al-Hallāj: Mystic and Martyr of Islam*. Trans. H. Mason. 4 vols. Bolligen Series 98. Princeton: Princeton University Press, 1982.

Maybudī, Abū-l-Faḍl Rashīd al-Dīn al-. *Kashf al-asrār wa 'uddat al-abrār*. 10 vols. Ed. 'Alī Asghar Ḥikmat. Tehran: 1339sh/1960.

Meier, Fritz. "Die Welt der Urbilder bei Ali Hamadani (d. 1385)." *Eranos Jahrbuch* 18 (1950): 115-172.

_____. "Ḫurasan und das Ende der klassischen Sufik." *La Persia nel Medioevo*. Rome: 1971.

_____. "The Mystic Path." *Islam and the Arab World*. Ed. Bernard Lewis. New York: 1976.

Melikian-Chirvani, A.S. "Bāztābhā-yi adābī āyīn-i būdda dar irān islāmī." *Iran Nameh* VIII. 2 (1990): 277.

Melville, Charles, "*Pādishāh-i Islām:* the conversion of Sultan Maḥmūd Ghāzān Khān". *Pembroke Papers (Persian & Islamic Studies in Honour of P.W. Avery)*. Ed. C. Melville. Cambridge: University of Cambridge Centre of Middle Eastern Studies, 1990.

Mélikoff, I. "Un ordre de dervishes colonisateurs: Les Bektachis." *Memorial Omer Lufti Barkan*. Bibliothèque de l'Institut Français d'Études Anatoliennes, XXVIII. Paris: 1980.

Michell, J. "Ibn Taymiyya's *Sharḥ* on the *Futūḥ al-Ghayb* of 'Abd al-Qādir Jīlānī." *Hamdard Islamicus* IV no. 2 (1981):

Milson, M.: s.v. "Sa'dī."

Minorsky, V. *Medieval Iran and its Neighbours*. Variorum Reprints, no. xii. London: 1982.

Molé, Marijan. "La version persane du Traité de dix principes de Najm al-Dîn Kobrâ par 'Alî ibn Shihâb al-Din Hamadânî." *Farhang-i Īrān-zamīn* 6 (1958): 38-66.

_____. "Les Kubrawiya entre sunnisme et shiisme aux huitième et neuvième siècles de l'hégire." *Revue des études islamiques* 29 (1961): 110-124.

_____. "Professions de foi de deux Kubrawis: 'Alī-i Hamadānī et Muḥammad Nūrbakhsh." *Bulletin de l'Institute français de Damas* 17 (1961-62): 133-204

_____. "La Danse exstatique en Islam." *Sources Orientales* 6. Les Danses Sacrées. Paris: Editions du Seuil, 1963.

Momen, Moojan. *Introduction to Shī'ī Islam*. Oxford: 1985.

Morewedge, Parviz. "Ṣūfism, Neoplatonism, and Zaehner's Theistic Theory of Mysticism." *Islamic Philosophy and Mysticism*. Ed. Parviz Morewedge. Delmar, New

York: Caravan Books, 1981.

Morris, James W. *The Wisdom of the Throne: An Introduction to the Philosophy of Mulla Sadra*. Princeton: Princeton University Press,1981.

Mottahedeh, Roy. *The Mantle of the Prophet: Religion and Politics in Iran*. London: 1987.

Mudarris, Muḥammad 'Alī. *Rayḥānat al-adab*. 8 vols. Tehran: 1967.

Munzawī, Aḥmad. *Fihrist-i nuskhahā-yi khaṭṭī-yi fārsī*. 2 vols. Tehran: 1970.

Muḥammad, Riyāḍ. *Aḥvāl wa āthār va ash'ār-i Mīr Sayyid 'Alī Hamadānī, bā shish risāla az way*. Islamabad: Markaz-i taḥqīqāt-i Fārsī-i Īrān va Pākistān, 1985.

Nasafī, 'Azīz al-Dīn. *Zubdat al-ḥaqā'iq*. Ed. Ḥ Nāṣirī. Tehran: Kitābkhāna Tahūrī, 1985.

_____ *Zubdat al-ḥaqā'iq*. Ed. A. Mahdavī Damghanī. Tehran: B.T.N.K., 1965.

Nasr, S.H. "Shihāb al-Dīn Suhrawardī Maqtūl." *A History of Muslim Philosophy*. Ed. M.M. Sharif. vol. 1. Wiesbaden: Otto Harrassowitz, 1963.

_____ *Three Muslim Sages: Avicenna, Suhrawardī, Ibn 'Arabī*. Cambridge: Harvard University Press, 1964.

_____ *Sufi Essays*. London: Allen & Unwin, 1972.

_____ "Rābaṭa-yi bayn-i taṣawwuf va falsafa dar farhang-i Irān." *Iran Nameh* vol. 1. No. 1 (1982): 46-56.

_____ *Traditional Islam in the Modern World*. London: KPI, 1987.

_____ ed. *Islamic Spirituality I: Foundations*. New York: Crossroad, 1987.

_____ ed. *Islamic Spirituality II: Manifestations*. New York: Crossroad, 1991.

_____ *Islamic Art & Spirituality*. Suffolk: Golgonooza Press, 1987.

_____ *Knowledge and the Sacred*. Albany: SUNY, 1989.

Netton. *Allāh Transcendent: Studies in the Structure and Semiotics of Islamic Philosophy, Theology and Cosmology*. London: Routledge, 1989.

Nicholson, R.A. "A Historical Enquiry concerning the Origin and Development of Sufiism, with a list of definitions of the terms *'ṣūfī'* and *'taṣawwuf,'* arranged chronologically." *Journal of the Royal Asiatic Society* Part 1 (1906).

Nicholson, R.A. *Selected Poems From the Dīvāni Shamsi Tabrīz*. Cambridge University Press, 1977 Reprint.

Nurbakhsh, Dr. Javad. *Zindagī wa āthār-i Shāh Ni'matu'llāh Walī-yi Kirmānī*. Tehran: 1957.

_____ *Pīrān-i ṭarīqat*. Tehran: 1980.

_____ *Masters of the Path: A History of the Nimatullahi Sufi Order*. New York: Khaniqahi Nimatullahi Publications, 1980.

_____ *Sufi Symbolism*. Trans. T. Graham, L. Lewisohn, S. Johnston, N. Johnston. 5 vols. London: KNP, 1984–.

_____ *Farhang-i Nūrbakhsh*. 10 vols. London: Khaniqahi Nimatullahi Publications, 1984-91.

Nūrī, Yaḥyā. *Khatamīyat payāmbar-i Islām dar ibṭāl taḥlīlī Bābīgarī, Bahā'īgarī, Qādiyānīgarī*. Tehran: 1360 A.Hsh./1981.

Nwyia S. J., Paul. "Waqā'i' al-Shaykh Rūzbihān al-Baqlī al-Shīrāzī muqtaṭafāt min *Kitāb Kashf al-asrār wa mukāshafat al-anwār*." *Al-Mashriq* LXIV.4/5 (1970): 385-406.

Nygren, Andreas. *Agape and Eros: A Study of the Christian Idea of Love*. Trans. P.S. Watson. London: SPCK, 1982.

Ọcak, A. Yaşar. "Kalenderi Dervishes and Ottoman Administration from the Fourteenth to the Sixteenth Centuries." *Manifestations of Sainthood in Islam*. Ed. C. Ernst and G.M. Smith. forthcoming.

Parmu, R.K. *A History of Muslim Rule in Kashmir, 1320-1819*. Delhi: People's Publishing House, 1969.

Pārsā, Muḥammad. *Qudsiyya: Kalimāt-i Bahā' al-Dīn Naqshband*. Tehran: Kitābkhāna-i

Tahūrī, 1975.

Patai, R. *The Hebrew Goddess*. Avon: 1978.

Pertsch, W. *Verzeichniss der persischen Handschriften der königlichen Bibliothek zu Berlin*. Berlin: 1988.

Pinto S.J., Desiderio. "The Mystery of the Nizamuddin Dargah: The Accounts of Pilgrims." *Muslim Shrines in India*. Ed. Christian W. Troll. Oxford University Press, 1989

Plotinus, *The Enneads*. Trans. Stephen MacKenna. London: Faber & Faber, 1956.

Pourjavady, Nasrollah & Peter L. Wilson.. *The Drunken Universe: An Anthology of Persian Sufi Poetry*. Grand Rapids, MI: Phanes Press, 1988.

Qushayrī, Abū'l-Qāsim al-. *al-Risālat al-Qushayriyya*. 2 vols. Cairo: 1330/1912.

Rafiqi, Abdul Qaiyum. *Sufism in Kashmir from the Fourteenth to the Sixteenth Century*. Varanasi: Bharatiya Publishing House, 1972.

Raine, Kathleen. *Defending Ancient Springs*. Suffolk: Golgonoonza Press, 1985.

Rāzī, Najm al-Dīn Dāya. *The Path of God's Bondsmen*. [The *Mirṣad al-'ibād* translated by H. Algar] Delmar, New York: Caravan Books, 1982.

_____ *Mirṣād al-'ibād min al-mabda' ila 'l-ma'ād*. Ed. Muḥammad Amīn Riyāhī. Tehran: 1352/1973.

Rehder, R.M. "Persian Poets and Modern Critics." *Edebiyat* vol. 2. no. 1 (1977).

Richard, J. "La conversion de Berke et les debuts de l'islamisation de la Horde d'Or." *Revue des études islamiques*. 35 (1967).

Riḍawī, Mudarris. *Aḥwāl wa-āthār-i...Khwāja Naṣīr al-Dīn al-Ṭūsī*. Tehran: Tehran University Press, 1334.

Rieu, Charles. *Catalogue of the Persian Manuscripts in the British Museum*. London: British Museum, 1879-83.

Ritter, H. *Das Meer der Seele. Mensch, Welt und Gott in den Geschichten Farīduddīn 'Aṭṭār*. Leiden: 1978.

Rizvi, S.A.A. *A History of Sufism in India*. 2 vols. Dehli: Mundshiram Manoharlal, 1978.

Ṛumi, Jalāl al-Dīn. *Mathnāwī-yi ma'nawī*. Edited and translated by R.A. Nicholson. 8 vols. Gibb Memorial Series, n.s. 4. London: 1925-40.

_____ *Dīwān-i kabīr yā Kulliyyāt-i Shams*. Ed. Badī' al-Zamān Furūzānfar. 10 vols. Tehran: 1957.

Rūzbihān al-Baqlī al-Shīrāzī. *Rūzbihān-nāma*. Silsila-yi Intisharat-i Anjuman-i Athar-i Milli, 60. Tehran: Chāp-khāna-yi Bahman, 1969.

_____ *Rūzbihān al-Baḳlī ve Kitāb Kaşf al-asrār' ı ile Farsça bāzi şiirleri*. Ed. Nazif Hoca. Istanbul: Edebiyat Fakültesi Matbaası, 1971.

_____ *Risālat al-quds wa ghalaṭāt al-sālikīn*. Ed. Dr. Javad Nurbakhsh. Tehran: Khaniqahi Nimatullahi, 1972.

_____ *Kitāb Mashrab al-arwāḥ*. Ed. Nazif Hoca. İstanbul Üniversitesi Edebiyat Fakültesi Yayinları, No. 1876. Edebiyat Fakültesi Matbaası, 1974.

_____ *'Abhar al-'āshiqīn*. Ed. H. Corbin & M. Mu'īn. Ganjīna-yi Nivishtahā-yi Īrānī, 8. Tehran: Anjuman-i Īrān-shināsī-yi Farānsa dar Tihrān, 1981.

_____ *Arā'is al-bayān fī haqā'iq al-Qur'ān*. 2 vols. Calcutta: 1883.

_____. *Sharḥ-i shaṭḥiyāt (Les paradoxes des soufis)*. Ed. Henry Corbin. Tehran and Paris: 1958.

Rypka, Jan. *History of Iranian Literature*. Dordrecht Holland: D. Reidel Publishing Company, 1968.

Sa'dī. *Morals Pointed and Tales Adorned (The Bustan of Sa'di)*. Trans. G.M Wickens. Toronto and Buffalo: University of Toronto Press, 1974.

_____ *Kulliyyāt-i Sa'dī*. Ed. Muḥammad 'Alī Furūghī. Tehran: Amir Kabir, 1987.

Sa'īd, Shāh Abū. *Hidāyat al-ṭālibīn.* Karachi: 1385/1965.
Ṣafā, Dhabīḥullāh. *Tarīkh-i Adabiyāt dar Irān.* 7 vols. Tehran University Press: 1974.
Samarqandī, Dawlatshāh. *Tadhkirat al-shu'arā'.* Ed. Muḥammad 'Abbāsī. Tehran: Kitābfurūshī Bārānī, 1337 A.Hsh./1958.
Sanā'ī, Abū'l-Majd Majdūd. *Dīwān-i Sanā'ī-yi Ghaznawi.* Ed. Mudarris Raḍawī. Tehran: 1975.
Sarrāf, Murtaḍā, ed. *Āyīn-i javānmardī.* Tehran: 1363 A.Hsh.
_____ ed. *Rasā'il-i javāmardān.* Tehran: French-Iran Institute, 1973.
Sarrāj, Abū Naṣr al-. *Kitāb al-luma' fi' l-taṣawwuf.* Ed. R.A. Nicholson. Gibb Memorial Series, no. 22. Leiden and London: 1914.
Schimmel, Annemarie. *Mystical Dimensions of Islam.* Chapel Hill: University of North Carolina Press, 1975.
_____. *The Triumphal Sun.* London: Fine Books, 1978.
_____. *As Through a Veil: Mystical Poetry in Islam.* New York: Columbia University Press, 1982.
_____. "Rose und Nachtigall." *Numen* V (1985)
_____. "The Genius of Shiraz: Sa'di and Hāfez." *Persian Literature.* Ed. Ehsan Yarshater. New York: The Persian Heritage Foundation, 1988.
Schneidau, Herbert N. *Sacred Discontent: The Bible and Western Tradition.* Baton Rouge: Louisiana State University Press, 1976.
Schoun, F. *The Transcendent Unity of Religions.* London: TPH, 1984.
Shabistarī, Maḥmūd. *Majmū'a-i āthār-i Shaykh Maḥmūd Shabistarī.* Ed. Ṣamad Muwaḥḥid. Tehran: Kitābkhāna-i ṭahūrī, 1365 A.Hsh./1986.
_____. *Gulshan-i rāz.* Ed. Dr. Javad Nurbakhsh. Tehran: Intishārāt-i khāniqāh-i Ni'matullāhī, 1976.
Shāh Dā'ī Shīrāzī. *Kulliyyāt-i Shāh Dā'ī-yi Shīrāzī.* Ed. Maḥmūd Dabīr Sayāqī. Tehran: 1339 A.Hsh./1961.
Shaybī, Kāmil Muṣṭafā al-. *al-Fikr al-shī'ī wa al-naza'āt al-ṣūfiyya ḥattā maṭla' al-qarn al-thānī 'ashar al-hijrī.* Baghdad: 1966/1386.
Shayegan, Daryush. "Muḥammad Dārā Shikūh, Bunyāngudhār-i 'irfān-i taṭbīqī." *Iran Nameh* 8.2 (1990):
Shikūh, Dārā. *Ḥasanāt al-'ārifīn.* Tehran: 1973.
_____. *Majma' al-Baḥrayn.* Calcutta: 1929.
Shīrāzī, M.M. *Ṭarā'iq al-ḥaqā'iq.* Ed. Muḥammad Ja'far Maḥjūb. 3 vols. Tehran: 1339 A.Hsh.
Simnānī, 'Alā' al-Dawla. *Divān-i kāmil-i ash'ār-i fārsī wa 'arabī-yi 'Alā' al-Dawla Simnānī.* Ed. 'Abd al-Rafī' Ḥaqīqat. Tehran: 1985.
Sipahsālār, Farīdūn ibn Aḥmad. Mevlânâ ve Etrafındakiler. [Mevlana and His Circle] Trans. Tahsin Yazıcı. Istanbul: Tercüman, 1977.
Sirhindī, Aḥmad. *Maktūbāt.* Vol. I Lahore: Nur Company, 1964.
_____. *Maktūbāt-i Imām-i Rabbānī.* Lucknow: 1989.
Smith, Margaret. *Studies in Early Mysticism in the Near and Middle East.* London: Sheldon Press, 1931.
Storey. *Persian Literature; A Bio-bibliographical Survey.* 2 vols. London: 1953.
Subtelny, Maria. "Art and Politics in Early 16th Century Central Asia." *Central Asiatic Journal* 27 (1983): 121-48.
Suhrawardī, Shihāb al-Dīn Yaḥyā. *Oeuvres Philosophiques et Mystiques I* (Opera Metaphysica et Mystica I). Ed. Henry Corbin. Tehran/ Paris: Institut Franco-ranien, 1952.
_____. *Oeuvres Philosophiques et Mystiques II* (Opera Metaphysica et Mystica I). Ed. Henry Corbin. 3 vols. Tehran/ Paris: Institut Franco-Iranien, 1970.

_____. *Oeuvres Philosophiques et Mystiques III* (Opera Metaphysica et Mystica III). Ed. Henry Corbin and S.H. Nasr. Tehran/ Paris: Institut Francais de Recherche, 1970.

Suhrawardī, Abū'l-Najīb al-. *Kitāb Ādāb al-murīdīn*. Trans. M. Milson. *A Sufi Rule for Novices*. Cambridge: Harvard University Press,1975.

Suhrawardī, Shihāb al-Dīn 'Umar al-. *'Awārif al-ma' ārif*. 2 ed. Beirut: 1983.

Sulamī, 'Abd al-Raḥman. *La Lucidité implacable (Épître des hommes du blâme) (Risālat al-malāmatiyya)*. Trans. Roger Deladrière. Paris: Arlea, 1991.

Tabari, A. A. *Faḍā' iḥ al-ṣūfiyya* [The Other Side of Sufism]. Kuwait: Revival of Islamic Heritage Society: 1988.

Tabrīzi, Humām-i. *Divān-i Humām-i Tabrīzī*. Ed. Rashīd 'Aywaḍī. Tabrīz: 1970.

Teufel, J.K. *Eine Lebenbeschreibung des Scheichs Alī-i Hamadānī (gestorben 1385): Die Xulāṣat ul-manāqib des Maulānā Nūr ud-Dīn Ca'far-i Badaxšī*. Leiden: E. J. Brill, 1962.

Teufel. "Mu'arrifī-i *Khulāṣat al-manāqib* ta'līf-i Nūr al-Dīn Ja'far Badakhshī dar sharḥ-i aḥwāl-i Sayyid 'Alī Hamadānī az 'urafā-yi Kashmīr." *Oriental College Magazine* 46 and 47 (1971): 175-206

Theisen, Finn. *A Manual of Classical Persian Prosody*. Wiesbaden: Otto Harrassowitz, 1982.

Tiele, C.P., ed. *The Religion of the Iranian Peoples*. Bombay: Parsi Publishing Co., 1912.

Trimingham, J. Spencer. *The Sufi Orders in Islam*. 3rd ed. Oxford University Press, 1973.

Uzluk, Feridun Nâfiz. *Ulu Arif Çelebi' nin Rubâîleri*. Istanbul: Kurtulmuş, 1949.

Vajda, G. "Les lettres et les sons de la langue arabe d'après Abū Ḥātim al-Rāzī." *Arabica* VIII.May (1961): 113-30.

Valad, Sulṭān. *Mathnawī-yi Valadī bi baḥr-i khafīf ma'rūf bi Valadnāma*. Ed. Jalāl Humā'ī. Tehran: Iqbal, 1315.

_____. *Dîvân-ï Türkî-i Sultan Veled*. Istanbul: 1341/1925.

Vásáry, I. "History and legend in Berke Khan's conversion to Islam." *Aspects of Altaic civilization*. Ed. D. Sinor. Bloomington, Ind: 1990.

Vitray-Meyerovitch, Eva de. *Maître et disciple*. [translation of the *Ma'ārif* of Sulṭān Valad] Paris: Sindbad, 1982.

_____. *Rûmî and Sufism*. Trans. Simone Fattal. Sausalito: Post-Apollo, 1987.

Waida, Manabu. "Birds." *Encyclopedia of Religion*. New York: Macmillan Publishing Company, 1987.

Walbridge, John. *The Science of Mystic Lights* (Cambridge, MA: Center for Middle East Studies, Harvard University, Forthcomming.

_____. "The Political Thought of Quṭb al-Dīn al-Shīrāzi." *The Political Aspects of Islamic Philosophy*. Ed. Charles Butterworth. Forthcoming.

Waley, M. I. "Najmo'd-Din Kobrā and the Kubrawiya Order." *Sufi: A Journal of Sufism* Spring.2 (1989): 22-26.

_____. "Najm al-Dīn Kubrā and the Central Asian School of Sufism." *Islamic Spirituality II: Manifestations*. Ed. S.H. Nasr. London: 1991. 2: 80-104.

Wickens, G.M. "The Persian Conception of Artistic Unity in Poetry and its Implications in Other Fields." *BSOAS* vol. 14. part 3 (1952).

_____"An Analysis of Primary and Secondary Significations in the Third Ghazal of Ḥāfiẓ." *BSOAS* vol. 14. part 3 (1952).

_____s.v. "Sa'dī."

Yaḥya, Uthmān. *Histoire et classification de l'oeuvre d'Ibn 'Arabī*. 2 vols. Damascus: 1964.

Yarshater, Ehsan. *Shi'r-i fārsī dar 'ahd-i Shāh Rukh*. Tehran University Press, 1334

A.Hsh./1955.

_____ "Some Common Characteristics of Persian Art and Poetry." *Studia Islamica* XVI (1962):

_____ ed. *Persian Literature*. New York: Persian Heritage Foundation, 1988.

_____ "Communication." *Iranian Studies* vol. 22. no. 1 (1989): p. 63.

Yāsimī, Rashīd. "Sa'dī wa 'Ishq." *Sa'dī-nāma*. Ed. Ḥabīb Yaghmā'ī. Tehran: Department of Education, 1938.

Yazdani. *Bidar: Its History and Monuments*. Oxford: 1947.

Yazıcı, Tahsin. *Ariflerin enkıbeleri*. [Turkish translation of Aflākī's *Manāqib al-'ārifīn*] Istanbul: Hürriyet, 1973.

Zarrīinkūb, A.H. *Farār az madrisa*. Tehran: Amīr Kabīr, 1364 A.Hsh.

_____ "Persian Sufism in its Historical Perspective." *Iranian Studies* vol. 3. nos. 3 &4 (1970)

_____ *Justujū-yi dar taṣawwuf-i Irān*. Tehran: Amir Kabir, 1978.

Index of Places, Names, Technical Terms and Koranic References

PAGE	LINE	INCORRECT	CORRECT
256	note 4	See, e.g., *ibid.*,	See, e.g., *Ḥikmat al-Ishrāq*
257	10	*h*owever,	however,
257	7 from below	"emanative in essence"	("emanative in essence")
257	note 3	*Metaphysics*, 8K. 12,	*Metaphysics*, Bk.12,
258	8	*al-Ishrāq* the	*al-Ishrāq*, the
258	26	*(nūr sāfi)*	*(nūr sāfil)*
258	note 6	See above, nn. 45, 53, 54	See notes 2, 3 above and p. 256, n. 8.
259	5	established	establishes
259	10	was, clearly	was clearly
259	28	Ibn Sina	Ibn Sīnā
259	32	that of criticism,	that of mysticism,
259	last line	definition.	definition,
260	6	clarify it.	clarify it."
260	17	or involuntarily	or involuntarily)
290	20	*(ṣāwm)*,	*(ṣawm)*,
290	21	*(ṣāmt)*	*(ṣamt)*
291	18	native town of Bākharz	native town
295	4	initiation	authorization
296	28	century	century's
297	24	work Certainly	work. Certainly
298	4	the two treatises	these two treatises
298	11	Muḥyī al-Dīn	Muḥyī' l-Dīn
298	19	*li'l-murīd*	*li- 'l-murīd*
300	note 2	*al-Qism*	*"al-Qism*
301	35	matter	matters
301	36	denial the great	denial; the great
302	6	remarkablly	remarkably
303	29	knowlegde	knowledge
304	34	traversing the	traversing
305	22	—and more	and—more
306	9	someone who	someone
306	16	that is the source	that the source
307	28	*Shaykh al-'Ālam*	*Shaykh al-'Ālam*
307	29-30	apart from	except from
308	6	Day of Judgement	Judgement Day
308	6	slain?"	slain
308	7	I alone	by Desire?," I alone
309	25	representitives	representatives
309	note 4, line 5	*vw*	*wa*
343	4	Jalāl al-Din	Jalāl al-Dīn
343	7	*A'zam*	*A'ẓam*
343	16	liittle	little
343	note 2	*al ṣiddīqīn*	*al-ṣiddīqīn*
343	note 2	*al sālikīn*	*al-sālikīn*
344	7	IIIs	IIIS
344	13	the-word	the word
344	18	concern	concerned
344	27	*al ḥikam*	*al-ḥikam*
344	34	Reality seekers	Reality, seekers
344	35	danqers	dangers
345	3	training the	training in the
345	17	*Dicitionary*	*Dictionary*
345	21	wives	wives.
346	11	him than	him, then
346	14	*jām'a*	*jami'a*
346	note 2	prayer such as—	prayer, such as
347	5	*(adhwāk)*	*(adhwāq)*
347	6, 14	Prophets	prophets
347	13	recieve	receive
347	25	*So how can Adam*	*How can Adam*
349	12	to cultivated field	to a cultivated field
349	15	*dighān*	*dihqān*
356	after last line of the text		Add: "throne, or the white cock that is beneath the throne, or…" etc.
359	1	Delete whole line	
359	after last line of the text		Add: "angels of the heaven of power are lowly locusts in the beak of the *'anqā* of his eter- …" etc.
362, 365	no. 4, l. 2/no. 5, l. 2	above, at n. 39);	above, p. 361);

N.B. *All damaged copies of the book (pages missing or out of place) should be sent to the publisher for replacement with perfect copies.*

CORRIGENDA TO LEONARD LEWISOHN (ED.), *THE LEGACY OF MEDIÆVAL PERSIAN SUFISM*

PAGE	LINE	INCORRECT	CORRECT
ii	14	Lecturer in Music University of Strasbourg, Strasbourg, France	Professor, Centre National de la Recherche Scientifique, Paris; Directeur de Recherche, Université de Paris X
7	13	has actually	has actually been
75	note 2	Attār	‘Aṭṭār
76	32	fouttenth	fourteenth
78	note 3	Add to note 3:	The collection was edited by M.R. Shafī‘ī Kadkanī (Tehran 1358 A.Hsh.)
79	24	is mingled	are mingled
79	note 1	*Naturdichtun*	*Naturdichtung*
80	6	*kabab*	*kabāb*
81	39	Even if were be	Even if this were
84	12	*qalandariyyat*	*qalandariyyāt*
86	2	*malamātī*	*malāmatī*
89	10	*Kāshifī al-asrār*	*Kāshif al-asrār*
92	2 from below	*Allāha*	*Allāhu*
93	14	*Jewish Encyclopedia*	*Encyclopaedia Judaica* (Jerusalem 1971-2)
198	8	Love Seeker,	Love, Seeker,
199	10	reunion" - he	reunion," he
199	19	Sea of Glory.[5]	Sea of Glory…[5]
235	26	in *aeternis*	*in aeternis*
235	27	instigator or	instigator of
239	13	he might one again	he might once again
239	33	*nasa*	*nas'a*
247	12	at heart	at the heart
247	24	it the contention	it is the contention
247	25	paper	essay
248	7	Schneidu	Schneidau
248	20	also had the their	also had their
248	24	anywhere mythology	anywhere was a mythology
248	27-28	constitutes	constituted
248	28	men	man
248	31	for example was	for example, was
248	32	and nor was ever	and was never
248	32	treatises.	treatise.
248	note 3	pp. 272-273 pp. 272-273.	pp. 272-273.
248	note 5	pp. 155-117.	pp. 115-17.
249	27, 29	Ṣalāh al-Dīn	Ṣalāḥ al-Dīn
249	35	attached	attracted
249	note 4	pp. 57-58	pp. 57-58.
252	last line	filosofia	philosophia
253	note 1	p. 769	p. 769.
253	note 2	*Allah*	*Allāh*
253	note 7	*al-Awliyā*	*al-Awliyā'*
253	note 7	London Luzac	London: Luzac
254	5	in Islamic knowledge	in Islam of
254	7	of *falsafa* are	of *taṣawwuf* are
254	7 from below	philosofia.	philosophia.
254	note 2	Koran V 119.	Koran V 122.
254	note 3	Koran V 59.	Koran V 57.
254	note 6	p. 59.	p. ix.
255	11	God-given	God-given]
255	15	*(-al-ta'alluh)*	*(=al-ta'alluh)*
255	21	we have mind	we have examined
255	22	motives	motifs
255	22	light.	light,
255	note 2	p. 12-13	pp. 12-13
256	7	lights between	lights, between
256	10	in light-infused	in that light-infused
256	10	light-enriched	*light-enriched*
256	11	that find	that we find
256	5 from below	Plotinion	Plotinian
256	2 from below	*‘ushshāq), and*	*‘ushshāq), ma‘shūq* and